SISSY INSURGENCIES

S

MARLON B. ROSS

Sissy
INSURGENCIES

A Racial Anatomy of Unfit Manliness

DUKE UNIVERSITY PRESS *Durham & London* 2022

© 2022 DUKE UNIVERSITY PRESS
All rights reserved
Cover designed by Matthew Tauch
Text designed by Courtney Leigh Richardson
Typeset in Garamond Premier Pro by Westchester
PublishingSer vices

Library of Congress Cataloging-in-Publication Data
Names: Ross, Marlon Bryan, [date] author.
Title: Sissy insurgencies : a racial anatomy of unfit manliness / Marlon B. Ross.
Description: Durham : Duke University Press, 2022. | Includes bibliographical references and index.
Identifiers: LCCN 2021018499 (print)
LCCN 2021018500 (ebook)
ISBN 9781478015215 (hardcover)
ISBN 9781478017837 (paperback)
ISBN 9781478022459 (ebook)
Subjects: LCSH: Effeminacy—United States—History—20th century. | Sex role—United States—History—20th century. | Gender identity. | Masculinity—United States—History—20th century. | Gender nonconformity—United States—History—20th century. | Male homosexuality—United States—History—20th century. | BISAC: SOCIAL SCIENCE / LGBTQ Studies / Gay Studies | LITERARY CRITICISM / American / African American & Black
Classification: LCC HQ1075.5.U3 R677 2022 (print) | LCC HQ1075.5.U3 (ebook) | DDC 305.3—dc23
LC record available at https://lccn.loc.gov/2021018499
LC ebook record available at https://lccn.loc.gov/2021018500

Cover art: Little Richard poses for an early portrait, c. 1952, Atlanta, Georgia. Photograph by Michael Ochs Archive / Getty Images.

for Ian

CONTENTS

Preamble ix
Sissies Everywhere

1
Can the Sissy Be Insurgent? 1

2
Sissy Housekeeping 51
Cleanliness, Gender Dissonance, and the Spoils of Political Patronage at Washington's Tuskegee

3
Un/fit Manliness 111
Evading Masculine Brutality in James Weldon Johnson's Sissy Narratives

4
Baldwin's Sissy Heroics 165

5
Sissy but Not Gay 233
An Anatomy of the Post–Civil Rights Straight Black Sissy

6
Gay but Not Sissy 283
Race and the Queering of the Professional Athlete

Postscript 343
Whatever Happened or Will Happen to the Sissy-Boy?

Notes 349
Bibliography 403
Index 433

PREAMBLE
Sissies Everywhere

Once we begin to look for them, we see sissies everywhere. Perhaps a liability of a study like this one—composed at a historical juncture when public talk about private gender and sexual propensities is so seemingly frank and yet so titillating and sensationalized—is that the subject, in this case the sissified male, can become unintentionally objectified again. This inquiry is intended to disrupt the encrusted stereotypes of the sissified male, even as it necessarily engages with some familiar tropes that have stigmatized the sissy across the decades. Even in the midst of what appears to be social upheaval—if not societal progress—in regard to the acceptance of gender-nonconforming individuals, the sissy remains stigmatized. The sissy remains the gremlin of the American national imaginary when it comes to the rites and rights of manliness—whether on the battlefield, in the sports arena, in the halls of political power, in the corporate bullpens of business competition, or in the bloodstained streets of revolutionary protest movements. Sissiness haunts every sphere of vaunted masculine empowerment as a cautionary figure of the failure to win, which is assumed to result from a failure of manly drive. American men are still quick to call another man a punk, a wuss, a pussy, a sissy if he loses, especially if he loses in good conscience from overscrupulousness in following the rules.

The actual and fictive black boys and men examined here—Booker T. Washington, George Washington Carver, W. E. B. Du Bois, William Pickens, James Weldon Johnson, Beauford Delaney, Richard Wright, James Baldwin, Amiri Baraka, Eldridge Cleaver, Little Richard, Sylvester James, Emile Griffith, Wilt Chamberlain, Glenn Burke, Dennis Rodman, and many whose names are not quite as famous—have varied complex relations to sissiness, to homosexuality, and to racial leadership. This historical engagement with the racial tenors of nonconforming gender conduct and character—whether through sissy-flirtation or sissy-avoidance or some dialectic between them—finds that sissiness both undergirds and circumscribes endeavors to advance or liberate under conditions entirely uncongenial to the notion of black masculine empowerment. By showing how others have responded to the perception of black men's gender negotiations, we can begin to decipher a cultural and discursive anatomy of the sissy figure across different institutional venues and across different eras of U.S. history. I certainly do not want to fix the sissy into an unchanging gender type, but at the same time, I want to suggest a persistent gender ideology that views the sissy as a danger to proper masculine conduct and character, even if the particular nature of that danger varies with the changing conditions of racial and gender entitlement. The men studied here are exceptional only to the extent that many of them are well-known as leaders within their vocations. The gender tides that they were pressured to navigate have been experienced, if not so publicly, by every black man, to one extent or another. In this sense, we can see our own gender resolutions and insecurities mirrored in their stories. In their lives, perhaps, we can glimpse our own sissy insurgencies and thus better grapple with those insecurities that inhabit, condition, and characterize what it means to live as black boys and men in white male supremacist society.

Too many individuals to name have been inspiring presences for delivering this work, most of whom are cited in the text or notes, but three in particular I have to name here for giving me a kick when I most needed it: Sharon Holland, Robert Reid-Pharr, and Dagmawi Woubshet. A portion of chapter 4 was previously published in *African American Review* 46, no. 4 (Winter 2013): 633–651; and a portion of chapter 5 appeared in the 2017 special issue of *FORECAAST* (*Forum for European Contributions in African American Studies*) titled "Blackness and Sexualities," edited by Michelle M. Wright and Antje Schuhmann. In addition to these journals, I want to thank those institutions where portions of this book first had a hearing, including Cornell University, especially Dagmawi Woubshet; Swarthmore College, especially Anthony Foy; the University of Oklahoma, especially James Zeigler; Brown University, especially Rolland Murray; and the University of Virginia. My research assistants—Dionté Harris, Giuliana Eggleston, and Sarah Winstein-Hibbs—were wonders of efficiency. I want to thank the editors and staff at Duke University Press for looking beyond the flaws of the manuscript to envisage and realize this book. I most want to thank K. Ian Grandison, to whom this book is dedicated, whose intellectual experimentation and commitment to fair play, in all its meanings, continue to surprise, challenge, and inspire me after more than twenty-five years.

I

Can the Sissy Be Insurgent?

> The Negro child learns to annihilate himself, to grow limp, before Mister Charlie and Miss Ann. The middle-class Negro child is trained to be a sissy.
> — CALVIN C. HERNTON, "Dynamite Growing out of Their Skulls"

> No one dares call us sexual niggers, at least not to our faces. But the epithets can be devastating or entertaining. We are faggots and dykes, sissies and bulldaggers. We are funny, sensitive, Miss Thing, friends of Dorothy, or men with "a little sugar in the blood," and we call ourselves what we will.
> — MELVIN DIXON, "I'll Be Somewhere Listening for My Name"

At the culmination of my high school academic career, I was privately instructed by my principal how to perform a manly handshake. It was the day of the annual awards ceremony, in which academic medals would be bestowed on deserving students in a public ritual celebrated in the school's gym. Each time as I trekked up to receive yet another award, my chest swelled with pride and anticipation. Little did I know that my crowning achievement as a high schooler would be dashed immediately after the ceremony by none less than the principal who had so many times shook my right hand in congratulation for a stunning career. Afterward, as the gym emptied and seniors whooped and hollered in recognition that school days were really coming to an end, the principal beckoned me over with his index finger. Expecting yet another pat on the back, instead I got a deflating lesson in manliness. "As you enter the big world," he said in a tone low enough to ensure that only I could hear, "you need to know how to shake hands like a man. You cannot succeed with that limp handshake of yours." He then coached me in the ritual of the manly handshake by having me repeat several times grabbing his hand firmly, aggressively even, practicing one swift unyielding hold, not too long, with an instant, decisive release.

In an environment where my proud black classmates were certain that my rightful place as valedictorian would never be recognized for one of our own kind and where my own father had taken me aside to advise, based on previous experience with my elder siblings, against expecting what I deserved from that school, I could not avoid the suspicion that his coaching had the tincture of racial animus. Whatever his motivation, my reaction was certain as my chest deflated in unmanly embarrassment, and I felt myself shrinking away from him with my proverbial tail between my legs. I felt as though I had been privately called out as that which I had so successfully evaded for my four high school years: a sissy-boy, not quite fit or equipped for, as he put it, the big world that awaited me.

Sissy Good Conduct

> Because I liked reading, writing, and doing creative things, they felt I should be around boys doing boy things. Even though I hung out with the guys in my neighborhood and was actively involved in sports, they still thought it wasn't normal that I sat in my room reading and fantasizing.
> —TERRANCE DEAN, *Hiding in Hip Hop*

Despite having a body exhibiting some noticeable gender dissonance (at least as I perceived myself), I was popular with both teachers and classmates. I was, in fact, a specimen of another telltale sissy formation, what Andrew Tobias, writing under the pen name John Reid, aptly labels "the best little boy in the world," a malady I learned about only years later when I encountered Tobias's novel of that title, which had been published two years before my high school graduation.[1] I was like the protagonist of Tobias's novel, too good to be a normal boy, never in any sort of trouble, got perfect grades, participated dutifully in extracurricular activities, and played football with the avidity that only a South Texas boy can know. Was it my eager participation in school athletics that had shielded me from my own incipient sissiness and made me popular despite my limp handshake? And this, despite the fact that I was also an avid reader, one who especially adored the poetry of lady authors like Emily Dickinson and Edna St. Vincent Millay and who devoured Laura Ingalls Wilder's *Little House* novels as a middle schooler.

Perhaps I instinctively sensed, as Charles I. Nero has so wittily observed, that "reading can make you queer."[2] Thus, I was sure to arm myself with physical prowess on the field to put my classmates off the scent of my adoration for books, poetry, and chummy chats with girls I worked with on yearbook, student council, honor society, and other goody-two-shoes organizations that consumed far too many of my waking hours. When not at some after-hours school event, I could be found invariably at home, still tugging at my mother's skirt, so to speak, and generally being an attentive son to her, if not to my father, alas. My principal intensified any doubt that I had pretty effectively kept subliminal. Having hoped that my feeling of masculine inadequacy was only a matter of my psychological makeup or emotional temperament, both of which could be sublimated, I was alarmed by my principal's schooling me in the manly handshake—by the prospect that it was instead written in or on my body as a physical condition that could not be fully masked, or even worse closeted within my psychology in a way that could not be accessed, much less changed.

As can be found in the testimony of so many other sissy-boys, I knew from my vaguest earliest memories that my person did not comport with the gender expectations on which everyone seemed to agree, and this long before the usual physical awkwardness of puberty, whose arrival only intensified my somatic dissonance. Although this self-narrative may in some ways coincide with those of transgender persons, there are also salient distinctions—most notably no sense of being misgendered in relation to my anatomical sex. I did "boy" things as a kid, and I loved being a boy, getting dirty, climbing trees, playing cowboys and Indians. I had, though, a nagging haunting of discordancy (whether physiological, physical, emotional, or psychic, I could not say), which could expose itself at any unexpected time. My inattentiveness and downright clumsiness around my father, a strict and distant disciplinarian, were as pronounced to him as to me. One day when I was around twelve, he stopped his manual-drive old pickup on a dirt road and told me to get behind the wheel and drive. I was flummoxed. When my younger brother, who seemed naturally expert in all things boyish, took my place behind the wheel, shifted the gears into motion, and maneuvered the old truck like a pro, my father chastised me, saying I needed to model myself on my little brother rather than constantly staring out the window daydreaming. As usual, I tamped down my rage at my dad's unfairness and sought solace in a quiet defiant sullenness that even he could not penetrate. My father had hit home in calling out my propensity for daydreaming, my constant fabrication of a secret life wholly diverging from that circumscribed by my South Texas small-town existence. How could *he* know that daydreaming was a sure symptom of a sissy sensorium, whose undertow I thought, or prayed, was well beneath the surface of my external life? After the truck-driving fiasco, I nurtured furtive daydreams plotting clever scenarios of linguistic assault on my father, an inner life that I knew he was incompetent to control.

One of the speculations I'd like to make here, advancing the work of Nero, is that reading, and especially as compulsive or sophisticated literacy, plays a large role in raising the consciousness of a sissy propensity, if not in the actual making of a sissy. Whereas Nero emphasizes the popular idea that a boy too enraptured by reading will turn queer sexually, I want to consider how reading becomes a safe harbor for the incipient sissy-boy—whether or not as a sign of incipient homosexuality. Reading, we might speculate, provides a harbor in which the sissy-boy can, on one hand, luxuriate silently in his predisposition for sensitive and fantastical daydreaming while, on the other hand, finding himself intimated in storied representations of boys like himself deemed overly sensitive and thus gender dissonant. In his groundbreaking essay "Sissies at the Picnic," Roderick Ferguson makes a similar point about the relations among fantasy, escape, and sissiness, but his fantasy involves a gender and racial cross-identification with the Amazonian powers of the female superhero Wonder Woman:

> It was Wonder Woman that made me want to be a reader. I was determined to discover the history of the Amazons. So I had Mama take me to the regional library, and together we got a library card. Soon thereafter I would walk to the library and check out this large hard-cover book about Greek mythology.... I didn't rest until I had consumed the whole book, learning of ancient mysteries and godlike failures. It was my fascination with books and the things they held inside that marked me as different from the other boys. Soon my brothers and the other boys in my neighborhood noticed that I was spending more time reading indoors than playing baseball and football outside.... My reputation as a sissy became a knot that could not be untied, and I was banished from the world of boys.[3]

In reading, the sissy-boy Rod can experience a heightened racial and gender fluidity not as easily allowed in everyday social interactions under the gender and racial strictures of Jim Crow. At the same time, in Ferguson's account, reading becomes at once a refuge to experiment with his nonconforming gender conduct and also a hindrance to normal boyishness. "As I developed skills as a reader, my abilities to catch an oncoming ball plummeted miserably," he writes.[4] Although this fear of the "oncoming ball" is a characteristic anecdote signaling a sissy propensity, the causal relations among reading, boyish sports, and sissiness remain puzzling. Does the focus on reading dictate a sissy incompetence at sports as a circumstantial result, or was there already something about the physicality or temperament of the boy that lured him into reading as a refuge from sports?

In his study of the racial implications of literacy on perceptions of black masculinity, Vershawn Ashanti Young confesses a similar experience to Ferguson's in rural Georgia, a generation later and in the setting of Southside Chicago: "Literacy habits, like reading novels of a certain kind and speaking what might appear to be standard English, have always made me seem more queer, more white identified, and more middle class than I am. When I fail to meet the class, gender, and racial notions that others ascribe to me, I'm punished."[5] Young's anecdote is helpful insofar as it reminds us forcefully that gender conformity is necessarily experienced through racial identification—a major premise of this book. His self-observation also emphasizes that even though the perception of sissiness is strongly linked with same-gender sexuality in both dominant and marginalized cultures, boys who become straight-identified sexually are occasionally categorized as sissies by others, whether or not they themselves self-identify as such. Like the 1990s mini-trend of straight black sissy memoirists who are the subject of chapter 5, Young experiences disidentification between his heterosexuality and others' perception of his gender queerness. Unlike those memoirists who tend to tap into their childhood sissiness as a resource for racial leadership, Young expresses a profound alienation from blackness resulting from a sense of gender nonconformity. As Young intimates, class status or aspiration cannot be separated from perceptions of sissiness, nor can color, which intersects with assumptions about black men's proper degree of virility, or lack thereof. As Young acknowledges, however, literacy, including timbre and manner of speaking, is but one factor that contributes to the projection of black masculine deficiency. Because literacy and speech habits are clearly acquired skills, a deeper question arises as to what motivates some boys toward an intense desire for literacy while others seem to have an aversion to it, and what other factors shape the perception of a sissy sensorium, along with its self-alienating affect.

Like Young, I intuited from early on that certain kinds of physical bearing could mark one as a sissy, whether too much bodily grace in walking or dancing or too little bodily coordination in running or catching a ball. Similarly, emotional temperament seems to expose a boy to sissy suspicion either when he is too gesturally expressive or when he does not respond with appropriate excitement to boyish pursuits and achievements. How does one figure out that balancing act—how to avoid being too emotional about inappropriate objects or how appropriately to express coolly restrained emotion for deserving objects? Although childhood bookishness tends to be read as a marker of sissiness, it must be emphasized that not all boy readers are sissies and not all sissies are unusually bookish. Nonetheless, there are some relatively fixed coordinates that create a strong suspicion of sissyhood. As we shall see in chapter 6, and as mentioned in Ferguson's essay, the sissy in U.S. culture figures pretty definitively as the antithesis of sportsmanship; perhaps this hinges on the conventional correlation of the domesticated indoors with femininity versus the wild outdoors with masculinity. Boyhood readers become stigmatized as gender nonconforming, especially if they seem not to be able to negotiate the line separating the girlish indoors from the boyish outdoors, for which contact sports serves as an emblem. Perhaps what is at stake in the connection between reading and sissiness is the way in which reading helps to produce a too-good boy, one who is not prone to get into trouble both because his play is curtailed by the domestic space of the house and because his reading itself can proffer imaginary adventures without the real-life risk of outside dangers. Since courting danger helps to define conventional boyishness, reading inadvertently amplifies the sissy-boy's gender deviance.

One of my concerns here is the need to bring "conduct" back into the conversation where social constructs of gender orientation are concerned. Not all good boys are sissies, but many sissies tend to be too-good boys—unless they channel their sissified conduct into a decided swishing behavior, in which case they become flagrantly disruptive to the conventional gender order. Conduct focuses on the ways in which we as subjects form a sense of individual character through habitual behavior in relation to larger social, political, legal, and moral codes. Certainly, performance is an element of conduct, but I find that by emphasizing character and conduct, we get at different dimensions of the ways in which gender is overly assumed to be intrinsic to the self. Perhaps wrongly, conduct tends to be seen as the manifestation of a coherent self, rather than as a series of repeated performances half-consciously acted out for a judging public. When cultural theorists attempted to move beyond identity to account for the repertoire of repeated behaviors that serve to fashion one's relation to social groups, they promoted the concept of performativity, or at times performance, emphasizing the coerced adoption of social roles in the making of individual subjectivity.[6] Somewhere between identity and performance/performativity lies a much less analyzed arena that I label "conduct." I emphasize conduct here because of its intimate connection with ethos, from which the word "ethics" is derived. Ethos is the classical Greek idea of the action that follows from possessing a particular personal nature or character. A person of upright character will conduct themselves accordingly in a correct manner, and such a person will thus possess the authority to persuade others to their side in civic matters. As the study of what constitutes morally appropriate action, ethics derives from ethos as the good life derives from character. While not wanting to jettison the importance of politics, ideology, and collectivity in the understanding of social identity and performance, I want to suggest that how we develop a sense of who we are socially is interwoven with competing and conflicting assessments of how conduct is directed by one's character. The idea that something is "wrong" with a person who does not conform to gender expectations stems from moral—and often moralistic—assumptions, articulated by social injunctions at home, school, house of worship, and other civil institutions, as well as codified in laws, policies, and bureaucratic rules. Just as one's gender identity cannot easily be segregated from one's performance of a sexual orientation, so gender performativity is inextricably bound up with the character that is presumed to govern moral conduct.

Although I want to theorize gender conduct as flowing from assumptions about moral character, I do not want to suggest that conduct is a stable perception of self in relation to other. Indeed, as we shall see, the fungibility of conduct makes it both a fallible gauge of character and a powerful conduit for regulating gender behavior socially, politically, and ideologically. In other words, "conduct" is the unstable barometer through which appropriate gender behavior is judged by the self in interaction with others' perceptions. There are different levels, dimensions, intensities, and tenors of conduct; thus I employ a variety of words to indicate this fungibility in terms of self-perception and others' perception in a particular circumstance at a particular moment, and in terms of the sociohistorical fungibility at work in shaping how men's gender conduct is judged collectively across time. These cognates of conduct—including behavior, habit, practice, comportment, deportment, posture, demeanor, manner, gesture, speech, and gait—suggest the difficulty of pinning down how a male's temperament directs or is directed by his gender orientation. By temperament, I mean the repertoire of emotions, sensations, senses, and rationales that orient a person's relation to himself and others as a gendered actant or objectified subject. Rather than merely a social manifestation of individual character, one's temperament orients and moors a person toward and within a social structure.

The panoply of cognates I employ helps us to consider the fluctuating continuum of conduct. At one end we might place *behavior*, a more stable sense of predictive conduct that applies so broadly and deeply that we use it to describe the biological imperatives of nonhuman animals, as well as the sociological and biological drives of human individuals and communities. *Habit* is less predictive than behavior and usually implies conduct that is largely learned through repetition so iterative that it has become thoughtless or almost automatic, often in response to internal and external pressures. *Practice* is also learned conduct but at a higher level of consciousness and repeated effort—as though there is some challenge or resistance involved in sustaining the conduct as such. Whereas behavior and habit can appear, often falsely, to evacuate moral, political, and ideological considerations, practice brings these back into view—reminding us that part of what makes conduct fungible concerns a person's negotiation of a community's demands, whether highly implicit and assumed or coercive and openly contested.

Whereas all of these cognates operate as a manifestation of individual and collective bodies, the physical embodiment of conduct becomes all the more apparent at the other end of the scale. *Comportment*, for instance, indicates the extent or intensity of the body's conformity to internal and external pressures. Whereas *comportment* emphasizes a person's physiological manifestation of gendered character, as though the conduct flows almost unconsciously from temperament, *deportment* emphasizes a physical action more consciously practiced to achieve a particular end—and thus might be more directly related to a sense of bodily performance in relation to others. *Posture* refers to a person's physical bearing as evidence of gender orientation, while *demeanor* or *manner* refers to how the person faces the social body, literally and figuratively. These dimensions of conduct entail how the body's movement can relay, reliably or falsely, a person's gender conformity, or lack thereof. How one speaks has long been recognized as properly determining one's comfort within one's gender, with a deep and rough voice identified with manhood and a soft and high voice with proper femininity. How one speaks, of course, has long been recognized as exposing one's class, region, and race. As we shall see, one of the signal attributes assigned to the sissy is an improper way of voicing one's gender. This is usually described as a voice that is too proper, too soft, or too histrionic to issue from a male's mouth. *Gesture* captures the notion of how the limbs of the upper body move in a fashion that exposes gender fitness, while *gait* refers to the same dimension of the lower body—the extent to which one's walk conforms to the expectations of one's assigned gender. As Sara Ahmed has theorized, these directional orientations of the person's body are implicated in larger dynamics of cultural identity, such that the sociopolitical structure might be seen to provide guiding coordinates for individual, as well as collective, conduct.[7] Where the judgment of male gender fitness is concerned, all of these modes of conduct are fraught, self-conflicted, and contested—all the more because each holds racial implications.

This theory of conduct will be further elaborated in each chapter. In chapter 2, for instance, we'll consider Booker T. Washington's schoolmarmish "gospel of the toothbrush" as a mode of negotiating acceptable racial leadership by developing over time a reliable gender practice that signals a nonintimidating type of black manliness to white supremacists. The white men with whom Washington negotiates may take his conduct as *behavior*—that is, as conduct that is in biological accordance with the unmanly subservience natural to his race's temperament. Washington's opponents, to the contrary, immediately recognize his conduct as a *practice* that exposes the race to a variety of the ideological pitfalls as they seek to alert the black public to the sociopolitical dangers that might be overlooked by those enamored of Washington's apparent influence among white male rulers.

In turn-of-the-twentieth-century Alabama, Washington's too-good conduct emanates more than the effect of a "good boy"—that is, a "good Negro"; it also inflects his social practice with a tinge of sissiness—a demeanor not so much read onto the body itself as read into his mode of public racial engagement. Although I may be anachronistically stretching the usage of "sissy" here in extending it to Washington's self-humbling conduct in the early Jim Crow Deep South, I believe the suggestiveness of an African American cultural tradition of sissy leadership warrants the speculation. Washington's sissy conduct is not merely a persona put on for an audience of white rulers and black followers. Nonetheless, we should not discount his public dramatization of a sissy persona to diminish the masculine threat represented in acting as "boss of the race." The dilemma for Washington was how to appear to be a "good Negro," totally subservient to the white men with whom he negotiates the fate of the former slaves and to the white ladies under whom he works to achieve an accommodating character. More fundamentally than a practiced performance, however, Washington's gender negotiation develops *conditionally* as a habitual way of constructing a coherent temperament and agency in an everyday conduct necessarily deeply informed and shaped by the peculiar circumstances calling out his complex social, psychic, and emotional response to his slave and postslave upbringing—E. Patrick Johnson's "material way of knowing."[8] In other words, Washington's gender conduct is deeply conditioned by the sociopolitical context of slavery and early Jim Crow, as well as deeply conditioned by the subtle development of a character responsive to the material, institutional, and ideological constraints of that historical context. He becomes how he reliably behaves. And how he consistently behaves proffers a sense of his temperament, the capacities and limits of his unique character in the way he "faces" the world in terms of racial, gender, sexual, and other social structures and formations.

The formative example Washington provides also allows us to frame how available language, geographic scale, and degree of publicness impinge on the valuation of gender conduct—ranging from historically honed gender epithets to fuzzy catchphrases loaded with innuendo, from a highly visible public sphere to the cloistered intimacy of a small community, from a spectacular self-representation aimed at a mass audience to the everyday interactions occurring among a handful of colleagues and acquaintances. For a black man who would seek to head the race, gender conduct is not merely a question of how he comports himself in relation to blacks and whites but also a matter of how "the public," black and white, perceives and receives that comportment through a gender vocabulary both cognizant and inchoate. What Houston A. Baker Jr. says about the critical role of the black "masses" generally in the formation of black leadership is especially apt in considering how gender conduct is arbitrated in and by the mass public in anointing such leadership. "But the black majority and its institutions," Baker continues, "have always provided the only imaginable repository for the formation of a self-interested and politically engaged black public sphere in the United States. Furthermore, the resources of the black majority have enabled both the emergence of effective (self-, or better, community-interested) leadership and radical definitions of black publicness itself."[9] Although Baker is focusing on the black public, the controversial nature of Washington's conduct reminds us how the anointing of such leadership is always a transaction between the demands of the white public sphere and the black masses. To begin our history, Washington serves as a formative case of the conditional or circumstantial sissy, a conduct habitually attuned to others and embedded in the self in response to ideological expectations, historical necessities, and social obligations related to racial status. By political necessity, Washington must broadcast his gender conduct across the national public sphere as proof of worthiness to head the race, and he does so not only through his public speeches, most famously the 1895 Atlanta Exposition address, but also through his very popular books, most famously his 1901 autobiography, *Up from Slavery*.[10] The vernacular tone of his speeches and writings makes his subservient gender conduct a highly accessible spectacle intended to gratify whites while placating black followers. Unfortunately for him, however, the spectacular nature of his gender practice also makes him the sole target of adversaries, whose public attacks on his gender propriety are intended to shame him into a more muscular gender performance. On its grandest scale, gender conduct is shaped by what is legible and illegible on the big stage of popular and mass culture—a dynamic that intensifies as the twentieth century progresses, with the emergence of televisual and digital technologies where the racialized gender conduct of persons seems to be readily accessible for judgment by a cross-racial public, as we shall see especially in chapters 4, 5, and 6.

We know quite a lot about Washington's *public* gender practice because his racial leadership depended wholly on its broad cross-racial visibility in the public sphere, but we know very little about Washington's private gender conduct. This is not unusual for public figures before the advent of mass tell-all narratives (examined in chapters 5 and 6) and mass televisual technologies (examined in chapters 4 and 6). By contrast, there has been very little interest in the public gender conduct of Washington's protégé, George Washington Carver, even though Carver's conduct was characterized ostensibly by highly visible effeminate mannerisms and attire—a sissiness based in the observable physicality of his person. We therefore cap chapter 2 by using Carver as a complement and foil to Washington to consider how contemporaneously a different tenor of gender conduct operates at a local scale in a more privatized context. Carver serves as our formative instance of the "physiological" sissy, one whose conduct seems to offend not on a mass scale but instead within a very parochial setting in which minute bodily details of manner, posture, address, comportment, deportment, gesture, and gait seem to emanate from his material condition as a differently gendered male. To indicate the importance of scale in determining how gender conduct is socially and ideologically fungible, I emphasize the distinction between the mass public nature of Washington's conditional gender practice and the parochial context of Carver's physiological sissiness. That is, we cannot understand the racial implications of sissy conduct without considering its context and scale. Washington's adversaries never charged him with displaying any sign of a nonmasculine affect in his personal presentation. As far as we can tell, he performs heteronormative obligations through conventionally masculine bodily deportment. Ironically, Carver's nonconventional, unmanly demeanor seems to escape public comment exactly because his public engagement was narrowly limited to a scientific, instrumentalist project that was easily consumed as nonpolitical. The very same gender demeanor that was invisible to the mass public, however, became a major cause of controversy within the confines of Tuskegee Institute, where Carver's effeminacy became both a subject of concern for Washington and a target of his academic rivals.

Our engagement with Carver in chapter 2 is thus necessarily speculative and tentative—aimed mainly at nuancing a historically recoverable anatomy of unfit manly conduct at different scales and through a limited vocabulary, from the closely observable body in a tight locale to a broadly observed social practice on an international mass public stage. In considering the limits of the language we use to characterize and categorize gender fitness, this study suggests that the fungible nature of language itself—whether in the discursive domain of the scientific, vernacular, or mass—contributes to the historical and social fungibility of gender conduct. It is generally understood that language available to us today was not current at the turn into the twentieth century, limiting how a person and his public could label any particular apperception of conduct. However, less discussed, there was language available to previous generations in making such distinctions that we no longer use—or even recognize—today. For instance, whether today Carver would identify as a trans person or as nonbinary is difficult to know; at best, we can only speculate on the etymological, biographical, social, political, and racial significance of these material manifestations that seem not to align with the normative engenderment of his time. Washington's and Carver's observers, however, did trade in highly stigmatizing gender epithets that have perhaps lost some of their sting today. As we move deeper into the twentieth century and into the twenty-first, conduct and character will continue to serve as a touchstone for theorizing the sissy exactly because sissy discourse is anchored in the speculative observation of behavior, temperament, posture, manner, and mannerism—all of which carry heavy loads of moral signification, aiding social stigma and abetting social enforcement sometimes through dismissal and mockery (as we shall see with Carver's Tuskegee colleagues), sometimes through innuendo and gossip (as we shall see with Richard Wright's literary reception examined below), and sometimes through psychic/emotional abuse and/or physical violence (as we shall see in the case of figures like James Weldon Johnson's ex-colored man in chapter 3, James Baldwin in chapter 4, Amiri Baraka in chapter 5, and the queer boxer Emile Griffith in chapter 6). Changes in language can serve as an index for how perception and cognition of gender fitness changes along with different sociopolitical movements to effect the democratization of society.

Speculating Richard Wright as Sissy Test Case

As with Young, Ferguson, and Nero, my early reading habits fostered both a racial and a gender cross-identification. It was not until college that I began to find African American texts that seemed to capture facsimiles of my own sissy yearnings. On encountering the young Richard of Richard Wright's *Black Boy* (1945), I instinctively gravitated toward his notion that words could be powerful weapons. When little five-year-old Richard takes his father's figurative words literally, he hangs the kitten that his father has told him to get rid of, responding to his father's ill temper with his own verbal wit, which unfortunately results in the lynching of an innocent kitten. I'm not necessarily suggesting that Richard, the protagonist of Wright's autobiography, is a sissy. Wright is careful to construct the young protagonist in terms that lodge him securely in a naturalized boyishness, in spite of—or perhaps to compensate for—his propensity for reading. We can exploit Wright, though, as an exemplary test case of the challenge presented to anyone attempting to understand the sissy's character and conduct—his physiology, temperament, behavior, role, status, affect, self-identification, and discursive representation—across historical circumstances, geographic climes, and racial formations. Wright's case is helpful to the project of historicizing the notion of sissiness as too-good-boy conduct in terms of the moral and social dilemmas that Jim Crow imposes on masculine performance.

One approach would be to identify particular authors as sissies based on autobiographical, biographical, and fictional accounts. To say the least, this is a tricky matter, and one I'm prone to deploy cautiously by more frequently focusing on an author's textual self-representation and any representation of sissy characters, rather than reductively relying on the question of whether the author himself is a sissy "in real life." Even so, I find that autobiographical modes are an especially rich resource for speculating about racialized formations of gender fitness. Here I am interested less in the formal and thematic (that is, the ostensibly *literary*) applications of the autobiographical subject than in the cultural transactions that necessarily operate between autobiography and social perceptions of self and other as these expose representations and discourses of male gender fitness. As Kenneth Mostern has theorized about the identity politics of autobiography, this genre is deeply institutionalized to represent social identities as though they are solely individualized subjects, but modes of "minority" autobiography tend to spotlight the binds and fissures at work between a represented self and its various publics. "Writing life stories really does engage one in the problematic of presenting an explicitly public identity," Mostern observes, "even when such an identity fails to fully explain the life."[11] Reading racialized self-presentations of these autobiographical subjects as always collectively and publicly constituted through gender conduct, I seek to highlight the situational gender dynamics being negotiated by representing a raced self as a publicly consumable figure. Thus, autobiographies by Washington, Johnson, Baldwin, Baraka, 1990s academic public intellectuals, and openly gay professional sportsmen are understood as inextricably interrelated with mass public perceptions of such subjects as sentiently, cognizantly, and/or willfully gendered—sometimes analyzed as the representation of a public reception within texts, as is the case with Johnson's autobiographies, and at other times analyzed as well in terms of how public discourses shape and are shaped by the intervention of the text, as with the response to Washington's *Up from Slavery*, Baldwin's various autobiographical essays and semiautobiographical fictions, or professional sportsmen's gay disclosure memoirs. I examine the perception, projection, reception, or suspicion of sissiness as it is lodged by others (Washington and Carver in chapter 2, James Baldwin in chapter 4, Amiri Baraka in chapter 5, and openly gay pro athletes in chapter 6), and the response to these accusations, as a marker for the social, ideological, and political uses toward which sissy suspicion is put. In other cases, as with James Weldon Johnson and his character the ex-colored man (chapter 3), gender nonconformity seems the very matter of self-characterization, even if the term "sissy" itself is never used in Johnson's memoir and novel. This requires a degree of speculation about the intentions, affects, and purposes of the representation of particular nonconforming gender characteristics and behaviors. In some cases, however, individuals either express their sissiness (whether implicitly or explicitly) or seem to overly protest it through distancing, denying, and avoiding tactics.

    In all cases, the individual habit of sissy-avoidance, stemming from the hegemony of sissiphobia, abets our understanding of how historical figures have negotiated charges of unfit manliness. Although sissiphobia—the hyperbolic fear of being perceived as, or being too proximate to, a sissy—obviously is closely linked with homophobia, distinguishing between the two helps us to explore the entangled interaction connecting male gender nonconformity with male homosexuality. It is far easier to identify sissiphobia than sissiness, a fact that simultaneously works to the benefit and the detriment of any male accused of being a sissy, for just as sissiness is easily denied because proof is at best speculative, so it is also easily charged due to the predilection to stigmatize the slightest perceived deviation from masculine norms. Because the facile label or insinuation of sissiness also prompts a suspicion of homosexuality, sissiphobia guards against nonnormative gender conduct by linking it so inextricably with sexual conduct that historically has been not only highly stigmatized but also widely illegal as a jailable offense. Unlike homosexual acts and behaviors, there have been no U.S. federal laws or state statutes banning sissiness, so to attack a man as a sissy invites other extralegal modes of social punishment, ranging from ridicule and shaming to physical violence.

We can see how the sissy charge operates by briefly considering how Wright's first biographer, Margaret Walker, deploys it speculatively. Walker provides us a concise dictionary of terms used to designate or indicate suspicion of a sissy nature: "He gave the appearance of an almost effete, slightly effeminate personality. He had a pip squeak voice, small delicate hands and feet, smooth face with very light beard, and rather fastidious ways or mannerisms. He certainly did not exude a strong maleness or masculinity."[12] Although she never uses the word "sissy," a reader has no doubt about the charge, for Walker piles on suspect characteristics—a typical pattern when such a charge is being made—as if to compensate for the claim's speculative nature. Although Walker's firsthand observations should not be facilely affirmed, neither should they be facilely dismissed as gossipy or armchair psychoanalyzing. As a onetime intimate friend and an author in her own right, Walker had powerful skills of observation that could be trained on Wright at close quarters, but she may also have had interested motives.[13] Because there is no proof of evidence, as can be the case with a "practicing" homosexual, judging a sissy disposition is necessarily a speculative, not to say gossipy, enterprise. As both Phillip Brian Harper and Mark Anthony Neal point out in different ways, where others' sexuality is involved, there is always a degree of speculation.[14] Other theorists have pointed out how rumor and gossip have played a crucial role in enabling viable social networks, especially for sexually discreet gay men excluded from dominant gay white institutions and resources even after Stonewall.[15] Gossip about homosexuality, however, is a double force—working as a constructive vehicle for social connectivity among multiply marginalized groups like black queer men but also being exploited as a prohibitive social and state apparatus to discipline, shame, and ruin the lives of anyone suspected of queer sexual behavior. Given that the sissy shadows the homosexual not only as a specter that polices the gender nonconformity supposedly intrinsic to sexual aberration but also as the assumed vestibule of homosexuality in the dominant social imaginary, the proscriptive role of gossip, innuendo, and rumor is all the more salient for disciplining sissy conduct. For one thing, as discussed below, sissiness is liminal and projective, projected onto others or onto the self as existing somewhere between an impossible masculine ideal and an ever-shifting threat of masculine failure. For another thing, "evidence" is necessarily in the eye of the perceiver *and* in the eye of the subject perceived as coded within a particular cultural context at a particular time using language that can be, at best, slippery, and at worst, obfuscating. One man's sense of deficient manly conduct may be another's expression of sensible vulnerability. For this study, rather than frowning on speculation as somehow cognitively and morally culpable, speculation is taken to be an important theoretical enterprise for comprehending the etymological, ideological, historical, social, material, and psychic dynamics of sissification. It is easy to dismiss Walker's observations, as most scholars have done simply by ignoring Walker's implications. Because Wright conducted himself in strict accordance with heterosexual protocols as far as we know, Walker's charges are quickly dismissed. Unless there is a preponderance of evidence suggesting a homosexual liaison, hegemonic heteronormativity, or what Adrienne Rich theorizes as "compulsive heterosexuality," demands the assumption of heterosexuality, especially in the cases of celebrated figures like Wright or Malcolm X.[16] If one is not judged a homosexual, then one is not presumed a sissy. This results in a paradox. While heterosexuality is the overwhelming presumption for everyone, the slightest perceived deviation from masculine conduct causes a rush to sissy accusation, and from such an accusation, the presumption of homosexuality follows precipitously. To speculate on a man's sissiness itself usually serves a stigmatizing social or political purpose beyond the demand to enforce heteronormativity. Sissy-shaming is so common an activity based in both vulgar and subtle assumptions about proper gender conduct that until recently its accusatory stigma has not been systematically articulated, much less systemically challenged. That Walker's speculation enacts a not-so-subtle attack on Wright goes without saying.

Even though Wright's Richard of *Black Boy* could be seen as displaying some telltale signs of sissiness, including the boy's propensity to escape into voracious reading, perhaps more compelling is the way the author insists on naturalizing Richard's boyishness. Wright goes to great pains to ensure that Richard is not perceived as a too-good boy. He is, in fact, something of a rascal, a rebel-in-the-making who boasts and seethes against first a father and then a Jim Crow system that he refuses to allow to unnerve or unman him. In fact, Wright purposely creates a sissy foil, Shorty, to highlight the protagonist's properly gendered courage. Wright exploits this foil to cast his young protagonist as possessing so mannish a native temperament that he cannot help but comport himself in ways that defy emasculating Jim Crow humiliations.

In characterizing Shorty, Wright, like Walker, piles on characteristics that invite suspicion. He spotlights first physical, then phrenological, then psychological, then cultural attributes that we will see referenced repeatedly as markers of a sissy sensorium:

> The most colorful of the Negro boys on the job was Shorty, the round, yellow, fat elevator operator. He had tiny, beady eyes that looked out between rolls of flesh with a hard but humorous stare. He had the complexion of a Chinese, a short forehead, and three chins. Psychologically he was the most amazing specimen of the southern Negro I had ever met. Hardheaded, sensible, a reader of magazines and books, he was proud of his race and indignant about its wrongs. But in the presence of whites he would play the role of a clown of the most debased and degraded type.[17]

Soft, miniaturized physical features first distinguish the "specimen," and his yellowness further softens him. Then the passage turns to phrenology as the narrator assigns to Shorty a foreign look ("the complexion of a Chinese," etc.), an *estrangement* within the familial and familiar that we shall see James Baldwin theorize as the perception of gender queerness. Richard then turns explicitly to Shorty's psychological type ("the southern Negro"), as though the narrator himself is *not* also a "type" of southern Negro. That a budding writer should note another's fascination with reading magazines and books may seem fitting, but mentioning this in the context of the boy's racial passive aggressiveness (proud of his race but a clown in the presence of whites) seems to make the focus on the other's literacy suspect. Wright then proceeds to dramatize Shorty's tendency toward minstrel subservience. When Richard observes Shorty extending his butt so that a white male passenger on the elevator can kick it before plopping a quarter into Shorty's open mouth, Richard is scandalized, feeling "no anger or hatred, only disgust and loathing." When Richard asks Shorty why he would do such a thing, Shorty responds, "'Listen, nigger, . . . my ass is tough and quarters is scarce.'"[18] Wright is here placing Shorty in the position of a black boy so (self-)emasculated that he might be regarded as metaphorically raped by the white master.[19] Consenting, at least ostensibly, to have his anus penetrated by the white man's shoe, Shorty shifts from being the object of Richard's sissy suspicion to becoming a homosexual, at least figuratively. If Shorty will enact this consensual anal penetration *in public*, no telling what he would consent to *in private* for a few more quarters.

Through the white man's kicking Shorty in the ass, Wright implies male anal penetration, and in Shorty's opening his mouth to receive the white man's quarter, Wright furthers the analogy by insinuating symbolic fellatio. Without explicitly calling Shorty out first as a soft sissy and predictably capping with metaphorical implications of faggotry, Wright encourages the reader to speculate beyond mere suspicion. Shorty is not the true subject here. It is Richard's fit manliness that Wright is concerned to shore up. Proof of fit manliness against the castrating horrors of Jim Crow is manifested in Richard's response to Shorty's perversion—a scapegoating of the homo-sissy as a natural race traitor that we will see reprised in some black nationalist writing.[20] Richard's appropriate manly and thus moral reaction of "disgust and loathing" guides our moral response as readers. In the later Chicago section of *Black Boy*, Richard records a similar reaction to a Southside literary group, whereby he observes: "I was encountering for the first time the full-fledged Negro Puritan invert—the emotionally sick."[21] Also in this scenario, Richard links sexual inversion to the kind of racial alienation also discussed by Vershawn Young: "In speech and action they strove to act as un-Negro as possible," Wright observes about the faux-writers in the group.[22] Both Shorty and the Southside faux-literati sharply contrast with Richard's manly directness in the Jim Crow South and in Southside Chicago.

Even as a small child, Richard's native propensity dictates his bold aggression as he prioritizes survival in life-and-death situations. When his mother takes the boy to beg money from his philandering and absent father, Richard not only refuses to go live with his father but also refuses the paltry offer of a nickel—which his mother urges him *not* to take, though the father suggests that she is teaching "him to be a fool." "I wanted to take the nickel, but I did not want to take it from my father," Richard says.[23] Richard's boyish defiance, even in the face of a nickel that the family so desperately needs, indicates how prescient mannishness, when properly disciplined, need not be modeled on his father's failed husbanding and fathering but instead can become the basis of a virile, and thus radically liberating, character and conduct. "I had the feeling that I had had to do with something unclean," Richard remembers. By equating the father's offer with filth, we immediately understand that the boy is making an astute moral judgment not about the father's bodily hygiene but instead about his character and conduct. This passage foreshadows the Shorty incident in which the soft boy trades his mouth and ass for a quarter, whereas the little boy Richard, refusing the nickel, gets distanced from stigmatizing sissy traits like softness, strangeness, passive aggressiveness, minstrel subservience, and race betrayal. Both the father and Shorty figure conduct so abhorrent that it sickens Richard, but each male's conduct resides at opposed ends of a gender scale, with the father's behavior exposing a flaw fully *within* the character of the patriarchal masculine, whereas Shorty's threatens to cast him out of the purview of the masculine altogether. The father is all too much the man, if a morally unfit one. Shorty is hardly a man and is thus morally unfit. Exactly because Richard seems to exhibit qualities—like devotion to reading, poetry, and imaginative flights—that could easily elicit speculation of sissiness, Wright must work harder to distance his autobiographical hero from such suspicion, ironically demanding the presence of other sissies as a foil and thus shielding against the specter of the protagonist's own sissiness. (Walker was probably not the first to charge Wright with sissiness, for a boy like Wright/Richard would be a convenient target for other boys' projections.) The little boy Richard's moral sense of uncleanness in the face of a philandering, incompetent father and husband corresponds to the young man Richard's moral sense of disgust—a natural physiological reaction from the gut—in the face of Shorty's and the Southside inverts' emasculated and emasculating conduct.

Given Wright's use of the sissy foil, and his tendency to feature sissies and fags across his oeuvre, it is not surprising that there has been a persistent, low-key scuffle over how to characterize the author's relation to gender nonconformity. Baldwin infamously attacked Wright in his first published essay, "Everybody's Protest Novel" (reprinted in *Notes of a Native Son*), by reducing his greatest hero, Bigger Thomas, to an Uncle Tom figure, and by placing Wright in an unseemly symbolic sexualized wrestling match with Harriet Beecher Stowe.[24] As Baldwin himself becomes the most articulate literary spokesman on behalf of civil rights, the young turks of Black Power begin to scapegoat him through his sissy reputation, contrasting the soft Baldwin with the hard-bodied Wright. In the most egregious case of over-the-top scapegoating, in an essay significantly titled "Notes *on* a Native Son" (italics added), Eldridge Cleaver accuses Baldwin of wanting to be inseminated by white men in order to have their mulatto babies—a passage voluminously commented on. This charge, though, is capped with Cleaver's defense of Wright as a foil to Baldwin. Vaguely and inaccurately citing Wright's Aggie West passage from *The Long Dream* (discussed in chapter 6) as a case of the "practice by Negro youths of going 'punk-hunting,'"[25] Cleaver claims this as "one of Wright's few comments on the subject of homosexuality."[26] Feeling the need to distance the homosexually obsessed Wright (according to Walker) from homosexuality to make him a hardier foil to Baldwin, Cleaver proceeds to the knockout punch: "I think it can safely be said that the men in Wright's books, albeit shackled with a form of impotence, were strongly heterosexual."[27] Wright's male characters are, then, like Richard's father, all too manly (sexually), if plagued by the social impotence that sometimes occasions a fully masculine appetite and ambition, especially for African American men under Jim Crow. Unlike Cleaver's sissiphobic scapegoating attack on Baldwin, his defense of Wright is rarely commented on, but one cannot grasp the impact of the former without focusing on the gender logistics of the latter.

Cleaver is defensive about "safely" seeing Wright's "men" as "strongly heterosexual" exactly because they are problematically "shackled with a form of impotence."

Cleaver wants to ensure that these characters' "impotence" is not misconstrued as sissiness or faggotry. This is why Cleaver overprotests in making the case for Bigger Thomas's revolutionary virility: "And Bigger Thomas, Wright's greatest creation, was a man in violent, though inept, rebellion against the stifling, murderous, totalitarian white world. There was no trace in Bigger of a Martin Luther King–type self-effacing love for his oppressors. For example, Bigger would have been completely baffled, as most Negroes are today, at Baldwin's advice to his nephew... concerning white people: 'You must accept them *and accept them with love.* For these innocent people have no other hope.' [italics added.]"[28] Raising Bigger to the status of a real person, a practice common among these black nationalist writers, Cleaver allows Wright's "greatest creation" to stand in for the author himself as the properly masculine warrior, however "inept," against white male supremacy. Cleaver's homo-sissiphobic accusation represents a typical scapegoating tactic in the post–civil rights moment among some black nationalists, but this tactic garners its punch from an assertion of an alternative manly code of conduct in black history, here embodied in the fictional Bigger. Like Baraka's attempt to expunge his sissy self by scapegoating nonviolent civil rights leaders (chapter 5), Cleaver is here trying to eviscerate the palpable influence that the homo-sissy Baldwin has had on his own authorial persona, ironically as self-evident in the autobiographical style of *Soul on Ice* itself. Too penetrable, too vulnerable, too soft to engage the enemy at the frontline of the racial war, Baldwin and Shorty are figures for one of the earliest meanings of the term "sissy": unmanly cowardice. Undergirding Cleaver's charge against Baldwin, and Richard's against Shorty, is the disappointment for men whose manly character is ostensibly perverted by the overriding power of white male supremacy. In short, they are insinuated as men sissified by Jim Crow.

Wright's reference to Shorty as a "clown" in the face of whites enlists him in the iconography of the Jim Crow minstrel figure as an improperly gendered black man. From the 1830s to the 1950s, the most popular cultural figuration of black manhood is projected onto minstrel slackness, a sort of physiological softness in demeanor, gesture, and gait that in turn communicates sissy cowardice. Slackness is the visual cue exploited by blackface performers to indicate the essence of black maleness as a lack of masculine nerve. It is the image of the loose-jointed Jim Crow, whose body constitutionally lacks spine, lacks backbone, lacks phallic hardness. Thomas "Daddy" Rice's antebellum blackface performance of the Jim Crow character has often been noted for its mockery of black slave culture and black manhood. Following Michael Rogin, we should go further in considering the sexual implications of blackface minstrelsy.[29] It is not only analogous to gender cross-dressing, as Rogin observes; it is indeed also a mode of *sexual* cross-dressing whereby black manhood is racially mocked by turning the black man, if not into

1.1 A popular etching of Thomas "Daddy" Rice performing "Jump Jim Crow," c. 1835. Courtesy of the Library of Congress.

a woman, then into an effeminate sissy. The one sketch we have of Daddy Rice's performance (figure 1.1) visually communicates in volumes what need not have been verbally articulated for it to have its demeaning gender effect. Right hand on softly feminine oversized hips, left arm lifted with a fey hand gesture, hip jutted out in a posture closely identified with the female African primitive: the drawing captures the gender insult that the words of the song—the only other record of the performance recorded in the annals of history—need not say.[30] Drawing on the legacy of Jim Crow minstrelsy, popular stagings and filming of Negro manhood were often performed to accentuate effeminate physical embodiment: limp wrists, hips flexibly extended, with a skipping gait, or shoulders stooped, head bowed, eyes droopily cast down, feet dragging—the contrary to figurations of fit manliness: the muscled athlete, the alert revolutionary, the upright statesman, or the brave soldier at attention.

Wright's portrait of Shorty draws on African American cultural disgust for the Jim Crow minstrel, which is linked to the Uncle Tom, as a discredited stereotype of unfit black manliness. To desire black manliness—to insist on occupying that gendered, raced identity—is an impenetrable act of bravery so overwhelming in its implications that no white man can possibly imagine the ethical character it requires, much less the quotidian heroic conduct it demands under the Jim Crow regime. No wonder Tomming or playing the clown—playing the Uncle Tom for white men's sadistic pleasure—can be so tempting a mode of economic survival for a soft boy like Shorty. In this case, too-good sissy obedience—which in black nationalist thought is imaged as a desire to be penetrated by the white man—transfigures into too-ready obeisance to white male authority, a habit, if not more endemically a behavior, that guarantees race betrayal. If masculine uprightness strongly implies a moral code that shapes male character predictably toward narrow modes of gender conduct, black men's uprightness becomes intrinsically contested not only by the presumptions of white male supremacy but also by black men's moral judgment of one another, whether privately or by airing dirty laundry. "Goodness" for a black man indexes a relative ethos shaped by the pressures of white supremacy, so much so that in African American vernacular "bad" becomes an epithet signaling a positive style of resistant black manliness, inferring in turn that any black man who is too good deserves to have his manhood called into question.[31] As we shall see, this iconography of the "good Negro" inflects negative reactions to such reforming figures as Booker T. Washington, Martin Luther King Jr., and James Baldwin in particular moments of rising impatience with black male leaders who counsel such strategies as short-term accommodation in exchange for economic profit, long-suffering nonviolence, or taking the moral high ground as an act of transcendent conscience. As the case of Wright's use of gender nonconformity exemplifies, rather than attempting simply to categorize the gender identity of such historical figures and characters, I am more interested here in how the sissy discourse is employed as a writerly strategy to stage or perform a figure's relation to normative masculinity, often in the interest of other ideological and political enterprises. In other words, gender epithets like "sissy" and "faggot" are doing double duty, policing what constitutes proper manliness while also serving particular, often nondemocratic, political, economic, and ideological agendas that keep not only sexual but also gender and racial hierarchies intact, ultimately to the benefit of ruling white men.

Around the same time that I got acquainted with Wright's Richard, I discovered another narrative, James Baldwin's semiautobiographical novel *Go Tell It on the Mountain*, whose too-good protagonist, John Grimes, seemed to harbor a similarly fantastical inner life as a shield against a disciplinarian father. The structure of feeling at work in Baldwin's John Grimes seemed so familiar to me that I shuddered as I read this story of a gentle boy's coming into manhood on the eve of his fourteenth birthday, occasioned by his achieving salvation on the threshing floor of his stepfather's storefront Pentecostal church. To recognize John as my fictive double was to come to terms with my own sissy sensorium, an uncanny epiphany that would forever tinge my criticism on Baldwin with a certain defensive gratitude. Recently, I and other queer theorists have insisted on John Grimes's homosexuality, and appropriately so. Nevertheless, this rush to read John as a homosexual has caused us to overlook how the narrative also functions as a sissy bildungsroman. To speculate on John's emotional and bodily practice, as well as that of Baldwin himself, as that of a sissy, is not intended to evacuate homosexuality as a constitutive component of their sissiness, as I will explain in chapter 4.

If Richard enacts his rivalry with his father through masculine violation, Baldwin's John enacts his rivalry more surreptitiously by outwardly seeming to join his father's church like a good boy. While I theorize this shielding behavior as *sissy passive aggression*—seeming to oversubmit to authority while indirectly undermining it—I do not intend to attach any of the usual negative moral and psychological connotations to this term. Indeed, as we shall see, such passive aggression can, as with Baldwin, enact ideological insurgency against the racial and sexual status quo. We might draw a larger point from this initial contrast between Wright's and Baldwin's deployment of a subtextual sissy discourse in fictions published in the decade after World War II.[32] Although there is no doubt a shared social discourse about the sissy, that discourse is deployed toward different ideological effects and writerly affects even by authors who would seem to share a common racial heritage writing in the same decade. To what extent geography also shapes one's relation to sissiness—Wright from the Deep South writing about the interwar Deep South as an expatriate in France, Baldwin from Harlem writing about interwar Harlem as an expatriate in Switzerland—is also an important factor.

Sissy Liminality

My sense of being a sissy emerged long before any notion of sexual object choice could come into play. Or, more precisely, I early on harbored a sense of some sort of anomalous relation between gender expectations and my own failure to live up to those expectations long before I could even imagine a question of sexual attraction or gender object choice. Sissiness may very well be the vestibule of homosexuality, if not trans identity, for many, but I want strongly to caution against equating these. Unlike homosexuality, which has become increasingly an articulated identity anchored in language, laws, and institutions in a plethora of ways, sissiness remains shadowy, inchoate, disarticulated, noninstitutionalized, even as its speculative existence shores up seemingly more solid racial, gender, and sexual categories. If being too girlish seems a problem, then liking being with boys too much could be just as unsettling. Not knowing "naturally" how much is too much is itself the conundrum. William Blake's maxim "You never know what is enough unless you know what is more than enough" is the converse of the sissy's plight. A manly man like Blake dares to know, or at least conducts himself as knowing, how much is too much by enacting a daring violation across an invisible line. As Blake puts it, "Enough! or Too Much."[33] A sissy-boy seems to come up to that line of Too Much and trembles with uncertainty. Was liking being around girls too much versus liking being around boys the source of my gender discomfiture? This puzzle was further muddled by the fact that different boys at different ages seemed to shift from liking being around boys to liking being around girls enough to like them. Different temporal trajectories certainly help to define the perception of gender nonconformity, as C. Riley Snorton has illustrated in his history of trans identity, observing that the "transitive" character of gender usually projected onto trans persons more aptly applies across all identity formations, including those of sexuality and race.[34] This concept of the transitive nature of sexual and racial identification will be especially helpful in analyzing not only Baldwin's process of learning how to fashion himself as a sissy, mentored by the artist Beauford Delaney, but also James Weldon Johnson's autobiographical and fictional narratives addressing the gender options available to men seeking to wield an air of cosmopolitan urbanity to arm themselves at the height of Jim Crow violence (chapter 3). In the vernacular, the transitive and circumstantial nature of gender is bluntly acknowledged in the rush to suggest, on encountering an improperly gendered person, that time will cure the malady, that perhaps the boy or girl will grow out of it, or that a change of venue (sending the child to fresh air in the countryside or to a military academy) will make the difference. This recognition that gender is conditionally fungible or transitive usually is articulated to reassert heteronormativity, but there is no reason that it cannot work to undermine heteronormative assumptions, as Snorton has shown. Whether a factor of temporality or circumstance, any hint of apparent gender indecisiveness creates alarm because it draws attention to the potential liminality of all gender character and conduct.

Liminality within gender—as much as, if not more than, a line between the genders—is what addled my attempts to be a natural boy, rather than just a good one. For, at the least, I understood that a good boy meant necessarily always risking being too good for proper boyishness. Discursively, however, this gender uncertainty, an anxiety within one's own male body despite taking pleasure in possessing a male anatomy, is routinely articulated as a confusion that causes a boy to cross the line into girlishness. Perhaps it is a failure of language, or of the social imagination, that reads any small lack of masculine competence as necessarily catapulting a boy or man into the feminine—or more precisely an effeminate—sphere. This sissy dilemma seems analogous to the one-drop rule that governed Jim Crow racial identity: the slightest hint of doubt about one's boyishness seems to catapult one into the realm of sissyhood. This feverish binary within the masculine (tough/soft, butch/femme, aggressive/passive, straight/sissy) comes under deep suspicion in this study, as I hope to build on work like that of Eve Kosofsky Sedgwick and Jack Halberstam, who seek to unsettle the line linking a binary gender system (masculine/feminine) to a binary sexuality (gay/straight). In her pivotal essay "How to Bring Your Kids Up Gay: The War on Effeminate Boys," Sedgwick observes that the increasing social acceptance of adult male homosexuality has not automatically benefited "effeminate boys":

> Indeed, the gay movement has never been quick to attend to issues concerning effeminate boys. There is a discreditable reason for this in the marginal or stigmatized position to which even adult men who are effeminate have often been relegated in the movement. A more understandable reason than effeminophobia, however, is the conceptual need of the gay movement to interrupt a long tradition of viewing gender and sexuality as continuous and collapsible categories—a tradition assuming that anyone, male or female, who desires a man must by definition be feminine; and that anyone, male or female, who desires a woman must by the same token be masculine. That one woman, *as a woman*, might desire another; that one man, *as a man*, might desire another: the indispensable need to make these powerful, subversive assertions seemed, perhaps, to require a relative deemphasis of the links between gay adults and gender-nonconforming children. To begin to theorize gender and sexuality as distinct though intimately entangled axes of analysis has been, indeed, a great advance of recent lesbian and gay thought.[35]

Sedgwick's point is borne out by the fact that while homophobia has become a strongly stigmatized behavior in the United States and beyond, there is no commensurate term to capture society's stigma against "effeminate boys"—"effeminophobia" notwithstanding.[36] Sedgwick further points out that "there is a danger . . . that that advance may leave the effeminate boy once more in the position of the haunting abject—this time the haunting abject of gay thought itself."[37] Despite Sedgwick's urging of a queer theory that sees "gender and sexuality as distinct though intimately entangled," and her concern over effeminate boys' becoming the "haunting abject of gay thought itself," very little work has been conducted on the complex relation between the sissy-boy and homosexuality, and on the implications of this relation, in turn, to racial configurations.

One important work that follows up on Sedgwick's theory is Halberstam's *Female Masculinity*, which examines the performance of masculinities among women and analyzes the relation between dominant and subordinate masculinities.

Including some attention to how women of different racial identities perform masculinities, Halberstam also instructively observes that "male and female masculinities are constantly involved in an ever-shifting pattern of influences."[38] He asks whether the question "might be not what female masculinities borrow from male masculinities, but rather what do men borrow from butches."[39] In contesting the line between masculine and feminine by emphasizing the entangled relations among different modes of masculine performance, Halberstam helps us see how even within a sex socially constructed as *one* gender—whether male or female—there is no single manifestation of masculinity, whether performed by women, men, or trans persons. To understand sissy conduct and character as intrinsic to the range of masculinities, pluralizing the masculine, rather than merely as slippage into the feminine, is not intended to underestimate the ideological compulsion to normalize one domineering expression of the masculine as morally ideal and socially upright.

Halberstam's idea that men could learn how to be masculine from butch women is counterintuitive in U.S. discourses of gender and sexuality, but it is a touchstone of my study for understanding how normatively masculine men learn their masculinity from the conduct of sissies as an inverse object lesson. Even though the sissy-boy is most definitely the "haunting abject of gay thought itself," as Sedgwick asserts, he is at the same time a liminal subject whose speculative existence helps to authorize and legitimate a uniform notion of dominant masculinity. As we shall see, sissies serve as a constant reminder of the fragility of the line connecting maleness to conventional masculinity, and they pose a further challenge in that, far from being alien to the dominant masculine, sissies operate on a line defining both the *inner* limit of conventional masculinity and the masculine *alien* (or "abject," to use Sedgwick's term) within the social structure of maleness. Like Halberstam, I want to emphasize that there is a "multiplicity of masculinities" without ignoring the hegemonic impact of the dominant masculine, but I also want to go even further in illustrating the role that race plays in the formation of masculinities as multiple and yet hierarchized in relation to other social categories like race. The tendency of dominant culture to image black men as masculine and yet differently masculinized from middle-class white men helps us to see how the gender conduct of sissies cannot be grasped outside a racial frame. If black men are already one step removed from hegemonic masculinity, when scripted either as subserviently Uncle Tommish or as thuggishly hypermasculine, the black sissy is perceived as further marginalized. I want to suggest here, to the contrary, that just as white middle-class masculinity is unimaginable without its troubled and troubling relationship to black men, so white hegemonic masculinity has been haunted by and constructed on the unstable category of multiply marginalized black sissiness.

The liminality of sissiness exposes not so much a failure *of* masculinity as an inherent failure *in* the masculine as a paradigm that governs the conduct of men and boys. The fear of the sissy among men is the fear that masculinity is not natural *to* or *in* men, that men possess individual and collective vulnerabilities particular to their gender conduct. Not falling prey to sissiness means refusing to hear or feel certain vulnerabilities, and instead to pose as infallibly masculine even at those times when one's maleness feels most in jeopardy. In other words, not all vulnerabilities are unmasculine. The problem for all boys and men, however, concerns how to know which vulnerabilities are acceptable, which ones are not, and under which circumstances. On top of this, a male must instinctively know how to navigate the material gestures of in/vulnerability, usually signaled materially through the body's manner, and such gestural signals may change with time and circumstance. As we will see with the sports disclosure memoirs written at the turn of the twenty-first century (chapter 6), these first out pro athletes must negotiate not only persistent ideas about how a jock is to look and behave but also a changing iconography of how a gay man can look and behave in bodily presentation in the era of the Castro Street Clone as a self-possessed, conventionally gendered macho white man who happens to be "militantly" gay. The line between acceptable and unacceptable vulnerabilities is not historically or culturally stable. Whatever the time or place, those unacceptable vulnerabilities are projected onto the sissy as a contaminating vector of unfit masculinity. As we shall see, even as U.S. gender and sexual norms have changed in response to concerted activism, the sissy has remained a pretty reliable vehicle for marking and measuring upright masculinity in boys and men across the twentieth century and into the twenty-first.

The Sissy Race Card

My teachers, classmates, and team members seemed to embrace me as though I were a normally gendered boy, and I speculate that it was perhaps my decent athleticism that shielded them from my sissiness or, rather, shielded me from their suspicions. There is another possibility, however. In hindsight it is highly likely that in the era of legally forced desegregation, my race veiled my sissiness from others, both black and white, in different ways. I was certainly not the only too-good black boy in my class. There was a gaggle of us, other black middle-class-aspiring middle school boys who performed well academically and athletically. Were any of them also hiding their sissy temperaments behind others' racial assumptions? The further past puberty we got, however, the thinner our numbers became. Sports, bands, partying, girls began to consume more of their time as we progressed through high school, whereas my time was spent increasingly proving something to someone, or overcompensating for something I could not fully comprehend about myself. The further we got past puberty, the more pronounced a "flagrant" sissy's gender anomalousness became, in that sissiness tended increasingly toward what others identified as effeminacy—limp hand gestures, swishing behinds, skipping gaits, girlish giggling, voices that trailed upward in pitch at the end of sentences. Puberty is supposed to deepen the gulf between boy and girl, based in an ideology of bodily consent.[40] Ironically, as homosexuality has become increasingly a legally protected category, the equation of sissiness with homosexuality has been able to offer a sort of shield for gender-anomalous conduct insofar as it provides a social rationale for sissy behavior.

Far too self-conscious of my physical comportment, I guarded mightily against effeminate mannerisms, although it was not always easy to see how I appeared to others, or to know exactly what counted as unboyish in a desegregating school system. In high school, one of my white male classmates, one of my football teammates, casually observed that I carried my books like a girl—hugging them up close to my chest rather than wielding them low at my side. It only took one offhand comment. Though "offhand," so to speak, the comment itself highlights how closely surveilled a boy's demeanor is—not only to a school principal but also to other boys and girls. Because appropriate gender conduct within the masculine is so fugitive, hard to pin down, its informal rules are especially draconian, subject to punishment on the slightest misprision. Carrying my books close to the chest seemed convenient and thus natural—perhaps even visceral—to me, especially given my penchant for toting around so many books at once before the popularity of the backpack. In fact, the boyish way of carrying books, swinging them in the hand at the side as though a weapon in waiting, seems in retrospect to indicate that no boy should carry so many books as to need to hug them at the chest. Once this habit of book-carrying was mentioned to me, however, I recognized how even such a slight gesture harbored the potential for gender shaming. I could easily, if self-consciously, change my book-carrying conduct, but I could not diminish the very self-consciousness that caused my sense of doubt about my masculine fitness. What had been an unconscious habit all of a sudden became a calculated performance that defined my chastened conduct, as I sought to remember the proper book-carrying form. For sure, race clouds the question of how boys and men are perceived socially in regard to masculine conformity, as Neal has so brilliantly articulated through his concept of illegibility. While racial-gender stereotyping projects onto black maleness some attributes as overly legible, it necessarily also projects other attributes as illegible. If black boys are supposed to be cool to the point of overly phallic hardness, what does it mean when a black boy carries his books like a girl, or not enough like a boy? Might this be an effect of inhabiting a different racial culture in a Jim Crow school?

I remember my first college roommate, a white boy from a neighboring town who met me during summer orientation, went through the trouble of finding out my home phone number, and insisted on arranging for us to be roommates. He seemed nice enough, if a tad bit too eager, and after rooming with him for a couple of months, I realized what the problem was. He thought he had found in me an approachable black boy who could make him more cool without his feeling intimidated by my black masculinity. Let's call this expectation the Booker T. syndrome: I was deemed enough of a nonintimidating Negro to serve as his bridge to blackness because I did not seem the rough hypermasculine nigger who haunts and titillates the fantasies of so many whites. One night, when I innocuously walked into the room, my new roommate expressed a sudden delighted admiration for how I walked, and begged me to teach him to "walk black." When I laughingly reported that unfortunately I had miserably failed at conquering that particular skill, he refused to accept the idea, saying that I naturally walked that way and that he could see me dipping and dapping like the college's black basketball players (almost all the black males at my college were basketball players) when I came into the room. Needless to say, I had to abandon him as a roommate. For a white young man who had chosen to room with me *because* of my black maleness, not even my too-good sissy conduct could clue him in, even though it could make me attractive to him as an experimental project to overcome his racial fears and live out his fantasies of cool cross-racial camaraderie.

Although there has been some good scholarship indicating how same-gender sexuality takes on diverse forms across different nationalities and cultures, there has been very little consideration of the implications of cultural difference for sissiness and sissiphobia.[41] I have elsewhere discussed how historically in black literature and popular culture there has been a bifurcation of the sissy into swishing versus respectable figures.[42] In "Sissies at the Picnic" Ferguson observes a similar categorization at work in the black communities of his rural Georgia hometown during the 1970s: "The sissies that I knew ran the gamut of gender styles: some, like Edward, were limp-wristed and sashayed as they walked; others, like my literature instructor, were straight-laced and masculine; still others, like the pianists and choir directors, had a fondness for perms and relaxers."[43] Although Ferguson does tend to equate sissiness fully with homosexuality in his essay, he is one of the few cultural theorists who has helped to articulate the heterogeneous figurations of sissy conduct available within black communities. Clarifying the import of this observation for queer theory more generally, Ferguson explains how the social realities of black sissiness are easily obscured and overlooked within the narratives and theories developed to explain the emergence of modern homosexuality in the West: "There is a history jeopardized by prevalent understandings of queer identities and tired notions about black communities, images discarded by hegemonic formations as trifling and unimportant. Since the hegemonic narrative of modern homosexuality is figured around cosmopolitanism, whiteness, and normative gender practices, that narrative can only approach a discrepant history like mine by suppressing it. I will tell this tale as a way to illuminate the heterogeneous makeup of the black communities that I knew in west-central Georgia, a configuration that confused the precincts of past and present, man and woman, heterosexual and queer."[44] Often reduced to a uniform stereotype in mass media, and pushed under the radar of queer theory, this array of black sissy conduct—from the swishing to the hyperproper—raises a variety of questions concerning the social production, political ideology, and cultural representation of nonconforming genders among men more generally.

Although my interest here is largely centered on African American men's relation to sissy impersonation as conduct and character, it would be irresponsible not to investigate how the sissy appears under the aegis of dominant whiteness as well as under other subordinating racial groups besides blackness. Part of my inquiry here concerns whether sissiness is manifested differently in different racial formations. I am not suggesting that there is no underlying commonality across race in the delineation of a sissy persona, only that such a delineation takes on different forms and consequences due to the peculiar circumstances adhering to the construction of black masculinity under white supremacy. In chapter 4, for instance, I examine the Cold War display of a white sissy like Truman Capote in contrast with Baldwin's sissy insurgency, itself contrasted with the different expressions of sissy conduct of Little Richard in early rock-and-roll and Sylvester James in disco music. In chapter 6, I consider how the pro football player Esera Tuaolo references his Polynesian heritage as a defense against the tendency in the white West to equate homosexuality with sissiness. While Tuaolo uses his "native" marginalized culture to gesture toward a third gender—the *faafafine*—he finds it difficult *not* to transliterate this word as "sissy," thus defeating his own insistence on a cultural distinction that makes a significant gender difference. Here again we run up against the limits of language to enrich, rather than to straitjacket, our perceptions of gender conduct. Nevertheless, Tuaolo communicates powerfully the idea that faafafine is indigenous to Samoan culture, even as he remains entangled in the sissiphobia that he says he learned from the Christian morality unfortunately imposed on his native culture by Euro-American imperialism. White sissies definitely represent a betrayal of the prerogatives granted not only to maleness but also to whiteness. Because white masculinity is the dominant norm for gender identity, white sissies must flaunt their open disregard for the undeniable privilege that white masculinity affords. Because black men are already at least once removed from the dominant norm, to be a sissy is paradoxically both a heightened risk and a cultural resource. As we shall see, across history black men have enacted (both shamelessly and shamefacedly) and also avoided (both affectionately and aggressively) sissy identification. In chapter 5, for instance, we can understand the much-referenced homophobia evident in black cultural nationalist discourse by examining not only these writers' sissiphobia but also their risk of seeing themselves as sissies exactly *because* of their sophisticated literacy. Amiri Baraka represents the perfect case of such, as his early fictional protagonist, Roi, seems modeled on Baldwin's John Grimes, while also enacting a narrative of maturation that ambivalently seeks to pivot the achievement of manhood on sissy-avoidance.[45] In chapter 6, we see how black pro athletes narrate their own sportsmanship through an ambivalent relation to sissiness, at once distancing themselves from sissiness while conspicuously embracing the sissiness in others. Although sissiness is normatively that which is to be avoided at all costs, its presence and influence in African American and American culture are inescapable.

The blossoming field of black masculinity studies has done much to complicate and enrich our understanding of exactly how race intersects with gender, often in confusing and contradictory ways. An especially helpful approach for this study has been Mark Anthony Neal's theorization of "illegible black masculinities."[46] Neal translates the problem of masculine identity formation into a question of legibility without losing the strong sense of what E. Patrick Johnson calls the "material way of knowing." Neal clarifies how we are beset by a multiple bind in accounting for the twists and turns of masculinity's black face when he engages in a project aimed at "rendering 'legible' black male bodies—those bodies that are all too real to us—illegible, while simultaneously rendering so-called illegible black bodies—those black male bodies we can't believe are real—legible."[47] Paradoxically, blackness tends to make masculinity both overly familiar—trapped in unforgiving and deadly stereotypes that have justified lynching castration after emancipation and police murderousness after the second emancipation of civil rights—and at the same time mysteriously alienated from conventional gender norms. Between the raping buck and the Uncle Tom eunuch, black manliness has suffered a pincer motion whereby white dominant culture refuses the in-between, despite centuries of black men who have modeled extraexemplary lives of unparalleled manhood integrity. When black men have, on rare occasion, been represented as sissies, it becomes something of a nigger joke confirming how easily the black raping beast with a superengorged cock can flip into an Uncle Tom eunuch. When posed as a peril for respectable black manliness by African Americans themselves, the black sissy can become a racial embarrassment, much like Du Bois's take on Washington, despite the long history of sissies, whether superciliously respectable or fiercely flagrant, who have achieved an oversized place within the pantheon of black history, from George Washington Carver to James Baldwin, from Little Richard to Dennis Rodman and beyond.

Institutional Sissiness

In addition to speculative inquiry with an emphasis on the material, discursive, ideological expressions of racial conduct and character and on the social and psychic dimensions of liminality, this study also suggests that sissiness is crucial to the institutional operation of hegemonic masculinity. The institutions that regulate access to power depend on the prospect of sissy jeopardy to guard a proper masculinity, but this internal sissy threat may change in subtle ways according to historical and place-specific circumstance, including racial identity. In the same sense that masculinity is sustained through institutions, not merely through the individuals who manifest and perform the masculine, so it could be said that sissification is an institutional phenomenon. Against the discursive practice of conceiving the sissy as an isolated figure whose rarity codifies his abnormality, sissiness historically has been vital to the sustenance of those key institutions—politics, religion, the military and other policing forces, sports, academe, and the family—tasked with governing and protecting white patriarchal masculinity as the source and arbiter of power. The sissy serves as a bugbear scaring men toward proper masculine comportment through sissiphobic mockery, panic, shaming, and violence, but the sissy's present absence is also an odd source of inspiration, demarcating the limits of institutional acceptability even when the sissy lives at the heart of an institution. We can see the institutional function of the sissy at work in a range of venues studied here: from the government's large-scale purging of "soft" men during the Cold War to the intimate acts of sissy shaming portrayed in Baldwin's fictional Temple of the Fire Baptized, the Pentecostal church that his hero John Grimes attends in *Go Tell It on the Mountain*; from the systematic sissy aversion that pro sports like basketball and football inculcate in their athletes to the mockery and dismissal that one of George Washington Carver's black male colleagues used to delegitimize his authority as head of academic agriculture at the Tuskegee Institute. Sometimes institutions seek to police sissiness in draconian ways, such as the Catholic boys' school that expels a postulate on suspicions aroused by his effeminate manner, as narrated in David Kopay's sports disclosure memoir. At other times, the institutional regulation of perceived sissiness can come in the guise of paternalistic encouragement, such as when Emile Griffith's boss, in order to coax him into a boxing career, must discourage his interest in ladies' hats based on the assumption that a black boy with such natural musculature would otherwise be wasting his native potential. The institutional influence of the sissy is not always through negational acts like coaxing, ridicule, dismissal, shaming, or violence, however. As we see with Booker T. Washington's wooing of white industrial patronage, James Weldon Johnson's handling of a career in the U.S. consular service, Truman Capote's exploitation of emerging televisual media, and the 1990s straight black sissy memoirists' use of sissiness to desegregate elite universities, sometimes a sissy demeanor can enable men to maneuver within institutions in which sensitivity, vulnerability, caution, and finesse are tolerated, as long as those characteristics are subordinated to larger masculinist ends. Perhaps the most apt example of institutional sissiness, though, is that of the church sissy, whose particular "soft" talents are highly valued by an institution otherwise doctrinally intolerant of gender deviation. One could even go so far as to say that the church without its circumspect, self-censoring sissies would hardly be church at all.

The sissy is a foundational institutional figure in that the most impactful agencies and organizations of white male power are structured to defend against his influence, much more his presence. The military embodies perhaps that institution whose regulation of hegemonic masculinity has been most uniform and forceful. Indeed, soldiering figures the sissy as its absolute contrary: the soft man, the yellow-bellied coward, the undisciplined soldier who flees the battlefield. The exclusion from and then segregation of African American men in military service in the United States provides an enlightening instance of how racialized sissiness anchors the institutional masculinity of soldiering. From the War for Independence onward, black men have historically been denied combat aptitude as men not quite self-disciplined enough for warfare. Black men have had to prove, again and again with each national war, that they are battle-worthy, and especially that they are worthy of military command. As W. E. B. Du Bois remarks, at the outset of the Civil War both northerners and southerners assumed that slaves would not fight for their own freedom. "Negroes on the whole were considered cowards," he writes, "and inferior beings whose very presence in America was unfortunate."[48] For African American men, and later women and gay men, eager to defeat the long-held assumption that black men would lack the courage to fight on their own behalf for freedom, military service has been one of the central ways to lay claim to those prerogatives of citizenship historically invested in white heterosexual masculinity. Booker T. Washington makes this point when he equates the battlefield valor of black soldiers during the Civil War with fitness for freedom: "The services of the Negro troops performed in the Civil War in fighting for the freedom of their race not only convinced the officers who commanded them and the white soldiers who fought by their side that the Negro race deserved to be free, but it served to convince the great mass of the people in the North that the Negroes were fit for freedom."[49] Because of this intimate link among manliness, citizenship, and brave soldiering, African American leaders were especially upset by Theodore Roosevelt's insinuation in *The Rough Riders* and elsewhere that black troops showed a lack of nerve during the Cuban invasion of the Spanish-American War.[50] As Christopher B. Booker documents, Roosevelt at first praised, privately and publicly, the black troops that fought under him, but "[after] returning to the United States and immersing himself in the realities of political life," he "began to downplay the performance of the black regiments and ultimately challenge their bravery and loyalty"—finding it not only ideologically convenient but also politically necessary.[51] "Yet, while encouraging an aggressive and venturesome masculinity for American whites," Booker writes, "Roosevelt's message for black males was quite the opposite. It was a message heavily influenced by the realpolitik of the era, which dictated that black males be kept at arm's length, even if they formed an important bloc of voters who consistently voted for his Republican Party."[52] In his attack on the manliness of black soldiers, Roosevelt repeats a common notion: that a colored man is not mentally, emotionally capable of comprehending good military discipline without the element of personal loyalty to a white superior.[53]

Because the military, along with sport, is the most prominent institution where masculinity has been tested along explicit racial lines, sissification plays a highly visible role in determining who is fit for service, and even more who is fit for command, based in racial claims of a natural hierarchy of gender within the masculine. For example, in John Richards's essay "Some Experiences with Colored Soldiers," originally published in the *Atlantic Monthly* in August 1919, we find a crystallized articulation of the sissification of the black soldier as a reaffirmation of white men's right to command. As with Roosevelt, this insult to the black soldier focuses on the notion of a loss of nerve on the battlefield. Needless to say, this stereotype merely mimes the one rehearsed by the performance of blackface minstrelsy, the Plantation School of literature, and the zip coon figure in vaudeville so popular across the slave and Jim Crow eras: the idea that the slave's métier is subservient loyalty to the master and his brood, but his weakness is a superstitious fear of haunts and a lack of moral compass. Richards explicitly alludes to the figure of the loyal slave when he tries to explain why it is not sufficient for black soldiers to have solely black officers: "I have said nothing about colored officers, because I have not known them: but this much I think is true: black still turns naturally to white for leadership, just as on the Southern plantation the slave turned questioning eyes to the planter."[54] This is why, for Richards, the colored soldier's only valuable attribute is obedience, absolute happiness in obeying white officers. He paints this scene to punctuate the assertion: "No troops will do well under a slipshod drillmaster, but the colored man will deteriorate and become slack more quickly than the white. He responds immediately, however, to snappy commands and a soldierly appearance."[55] This curtailed sense of the black man's capacity for soldiering is captured graphically in the image of the poorly commanded colored soldier's tendency to "become slack." A soldier at attention is the opposite of "slack"—a physical alertness visually cued as an upright body, spine stiffened, arms stiffly gripping the weapon, head facing forward, eyes eagle-focused ahead, mouth neither grinning nor grimacing. On the battlefield, the metaphor of slackness images a failure of regimentation, discipline, and obedience to command.

We can see how the mélange of slavish stereotypes promoted to insult black soldiering, when they are not focused on the hyperphallic raping predator, congregate around the image of black men's constitutional unfitness for virile manhood. "Given the prevailing racial attitudes of whites in the years before and during the war (and given that slavery had only ceased to exist some fifty years earlier)," Neil A. Wynn writes of World War I, "it is not remarkable that so little change should occur during the war. Even sympathetic whites tended to speak of Afro-Americans in the stereotyped terms of 'uncle,' 'Hottentot,' 'pickaninny' and as 'boys who do not grow up even under shellfire.'"[56] Cowardice is emphasized in these performances of Jim Crow maleness exactly because the coward is taken to be the contrary of proper (white) masculinity. This sissification of black men's military prowess helps to explain why white officers and enlisted men, like Richards himself, have damned with faint praise the achievements of black military men. To acknowledge without reservation the bravery of black soldiers would be to threaten white supremacy as institutionally executed through soldiering as the standard-bearer of masculinity's paramount virtue, courage under fire. There is no more vivid an image of this deliberate sissification of the black male soldier than that provided by veteran Frederick Williams, whose testimony is recorded in William Miles's documentary *Men of Bronze* (1977), on the experience of black military men in World War I. Based on Williams's oral narrative in the film, Phyllis R. Klotman reports: "At home the men had to train ignominiously with broomsticks—they weren't allowed guns; at home and abroad they were met with hostility from their own countrymen and were confined to the role of stevedores (labor troops) until they were finally assigned to the Fourth French Army."[57] The boy or man armed with a broom or mop often signals a sissy disposition, as we'll see in the cases of Booker T. Washington, James Baldwin, and Robert Stepto. The humiliation of black soldiers training with brooms is intended at once to suggest that a black man with a gun would be a threat to whites either because of incompetence or indiscipline while paradoxically also suggesting that he is not man enough for real battle as a real soldier. Even Washington, who eagerly imaged himself in 1901 as wielding a broom to gain entry into Hampton Institute, as we shall see in the next chapter, was upset by the routine typecasting of black soldiers as sissy cowards unfit for duty.

The figure of the brave soldier operates beyond the military institution as a guarantor of the courageous virtue of manhood, and for black masculinity the military soldier has historically been conjoined by black authors and activists to justify the masculine bravado of the race man who "fights" on behalf of civil rights and black liberation. In one of his most famous *Crisis* opinion pieces, "Returning Soldiers" (May 1919), W. E. B. Du Bois urges the soldiers coming back from World War I to "return fighting."

> But by the God of Heaven, we are cowards and jackasses if now that that war is over, we do not marshal every ounce of our brain and brawn to fight a sterner, longer, more unbending battle against the forces of hell in our land.
> We *return*
> We *return fighting*.[58]

Rather than merely a tired metaphor, "fighting" for rights by other than military means—synecdochically referenced as brains and brawn—extends the battlefield to "the fatherland" that oppresses them. Du Bois participates in a long historical discourse equating manly military valor with civil rights activism, exploited by speakers from across the political spectrum, including that of black Civil War veterans, Washington's controversial speech at the Spanish-American War victory parade in Chicago in 1898 (discussed in chapter 2), the *Baltimore Afro-American* newspaper Double-V campaign during World War II, and the Black Power activists of the 1960s (discussed in chapters 4 and 5).[59] According to the logic of this discourse, as so eloquently expressed by Du Bois, to fail to bring the discipline and courage learned as a soldier into the homefront battle is to be no less a coward and a jackass than a soldier who flees the battlefield under fire.

It may not be surprising that the military has historically been a key institution whose very mission is dictated by separating the men from the sissies through a racial logic that projected black men as inordinately sissified in their natural propensity for cowardice, but the same can be said of activism as an institution defined by opposition to the status quo. The struggle over racial justice in the United States has long been analogized to a war, with race leaders imaged as warriors, a logic that reaches an apex during the Black Power era, where Black Panthers modeled themselves on an insurgent military unit, black nationalists evoked imagery of the battlefield, and nonviolent protestors were mocked for refusing to fight like men and for putting women and children on the front lines. In "Dynamite Growing out of Their Skulls," Calvin C. Hernton cryptically captures this metaphor equating racial struggle with warfare and highlights the common idea that the men who advocate nonviolence must be queer: "The philosophy that compels any man to lie down before his enemies when he knows they are going to tread on his flesh—the flesh with which he makes love to his women—seems rather queer to me."[60] Many black nationalists extend the logic that equates the "passive" in "passive resistance" to the passivity of the penetrated faggot—so much so that Martin Luther King Jr. is compelled to defend nonviolence by insisting that it is not passive at all. In direct response to Malcolm X,

King demands that the strategy be more accurately called "nonviolent direct action" rather than "passive resistance," for as long as even the hardiest resistance remains "passive," it is in danger of being perceived as sissified conduct rather than manly valor. King goes further to assert the manliness of "moral force" as an advance over physical violence:

> Acceptance of nonviolent direct action was a proof of a certain sophistication on the part of the Negro masses; for it showed that they dared to break with the old, ingrained concepts of our society. The eye-for-an-eye philosophy, the impulse to defend oneself when attacked, has always been held as the highest measure of American manhood. We are a nation that worships the frontier tradition, and our heroes are those who champion justice through violent retaliation against injustice. It is not simple to adopt the credo that moral force has as much strength and virtue as the capacity to return a physical blow; or that to refrain from hitting back requires more will and bravery than the automatic reflexes of defense.[61]

Against his nonviolent ethos, King goes on to structure the strategy through the lingo of warfare, soldiering, and military rank, trying to turn an increasingly troubling public image of unfit masculinity into one of fitness for nonviolent battle: "To join an army that trains its adherents in the methods of violence, you must be of a certain age. But in Birmingham, some of the most valued foot soldiers were youngsters ranging from elementary pupils to teen-age high school and college students. For acceptance in the armies that maim and kill, one must be physically sound, possessed of straight limbs and accurate vision. But in Birmingham, the lame and the halt and the crippled could and did join up."[62] Against the charge that women and children were replacing men on the frontline, King tries to retain the substance of manly courage and soldierly discipline while arguing for nonviolence as inclusive for people of all ages, genders, and the differently abled. He continues with this entangled analogy for several paragraphs, writing, "In Birmingham, outside of the few generals and lieutenants who necessarily directed and coordinated operations, the regiments of the demonstrators marched in democratic phalanx."[63] King's dilemma and his rhetorical response to it indicate how difficult it is to shift the epistemology of political activism and social revolution away from those dictated by a masculinist ideology. Even though King comported himself with apparent ease as a properly gendered heterosexual, his political and moral stance subjected him to sissy suspicion no less damaging than the attacks on Washington sixty years earlier. As we shall see in chapter 4, Baldwin meets a similar challenge by coyly embracing his homo-sissiness to proffer a more thorough critique of white male supremacy's masculinist mechanics.

The military as a supreme institution of masculine command and the soldier as a supreme exemplar of masculine discipline loom large in the black male quest for masculine respectability. For the military and the militant, the sissy looms as large as a cautionary figure. The difficulty of the conduct of a soldier is that, while being expected to possess the most aggressive masculinity, even to the point of mass killing and daring self-sacrifice, he is also expected to possess characteristics usually projected onto a too-good sissy-boy: obedience, loyalty, fastidiousness in dress and grooming, and guarded intimacy with other men that staves off sexual attraction. The sissy is not just a haunting within the good soldier; he is also a haunting within the institution of military discipline. Rather than devoting a single chapter to the sissy in relation to the military institution, I have thematized this matter across the chapters of this study. Thus, we see African American men respond to assumptions about their soldierly unfitness—whether as exclusion or servility—as a sign of their manhood deficiency across the twentieth century from varying ideological, geographic, and socioeconomic perspectives. We see how Booker T. Washington adapts his hygienic persona in response to his mentor, Samuel Chapman Armstrong, who exploits white military command as a rationale for the kind of servile racial discipline he organizes to control the black students at Hampton Institute. We see James Weldon Johnson narrating his sophisticated negotiation of white military officers in the face of a lynching military mob in his hometown and during civil war when he is in the consular service in Central America. We see how black nationalists attempt to image themselves as armed warriors against the foil of civil rights leaders as cowardly sissies who would rather prostitute themselves to white men's power than man the frontline for black liberation. We see how gay soldiers and professional athletes turn to racial desegregation of the military and sport as a model for their own fight to serve openly on actual battlefields as well as on the metaphorical battlefields of sport.

The enactment of institutional masculinity by sissifying black men to exclude or subordinate them from command in these organizations operates beyond the military establishment in such rigorously guarded venues of power as politics, religion, science, and sport. Ironically, the very attempt to purge the sissy from such institutions causes him to haunt the national imaginings of a manhood crippled by perceptions of effeminacy, weakness, cowardice, and unspecified softness. In some ways, the sissy's institutional effect is all the more powerful in his fleshly absence from the corridors of power because that absence is never an accomplished fact, always a palpable threat to be warned off and fought against. Like a ghost without history or portfolio, the sissy seems to appear mysteriously out of nowhere and out of recorded time.

Sissy Etymologies

The idea of the sissy as a sociopsychological phenomenon is appropriately shrouded in linguistic and historical obscurity. Examining the etymology of the word can get us only so far, but it is at least a place to start. We must keep in mind, however, that in the U.S., gender nonconformity is so entangled with racial assignation that a proper reckoning with the sissy figure can be accounted for only through a concomitant racial analysis. Although etymology cannot deliver to us the material granularity of the sissy experience, it can help us historicize and contextualize the changing semantics of the discourses related to the complex of behaviors and temperaments associated with the phenomena of male gender nonconformity. According to the *Oxford English Dictionary*, the term "sissy" as used in reference to a male is first recorded in 1887, derived from "sis," the shortened form of "sister," and was used to designate an effeminate man.[64] Thinking of the route from "sister" to "sis" to "sissy" reconfirms the gender, rather than sexual, connotation of the word. Like other terms popular during the period—"pansy" immediately comes to mind—it might be revealing that the term emerges in English vernacular at the same time as the development of sexology, which seeks to devise nonjudgmental, scientific terms like "invert" and "homosexual" to describe men who are sexually attracted to men. If "sis" is an endearing diminutive of "sister," was "sissy" originally used among queer men as a form of destigmatizing address, as "girl," "Mary," "Miss Ann," and even "bitch" were used among pre-Stonewall homosexual men, and still among some gay men today? Or was "sis" used by others to stigmatize men who were perceived as incompetently masculine? As we shall see in chapter 3, it is likely that the term "swish," whose provenance emerges in the early decades of the twentieth century, was first used by queer men among themselves, and the same could be true of "sissy."

I want to emphasize again how the extreme gender binary of masculine/feminine in English and other European languages tends to refuse any gray area between male as fully masculine and female as fully feminine. Therefore, to be less than masculine is immediately to be projected as "effeminate." The prefix "ef-" before "feminate" indicates the difference between normative femininity and the nonnormative feminine when exhibited by a person of the wrong (male) sex. Nonetheless, being feminine is not the same as being "effeminate" insofar as the former dictates an appropriate behavior performed by females, whereas the latter indicates discordance between the person's gender conduct and presumed sexual anatomy—whether as biopsychological behavior, naturalized bodily comportment, or social temperament and moral character. The prefix "ef-" means "away from" or "outward," which could indicate the discordance between femininity and its expression in a male; its effect is to intensify the root word it qualifies, such that "effeminacy" is always an exaggerated or panicked form of the feminine exactly because of its expression in or on a person perceived as male. The "ef-" prefix exclaims, heightens, distorts, and alarms both the person whose body or personality exhibits it and the feminine itself as an idealized contrary of not only masculinity but also maleness.

The binary extremism carried by the language, in this case the vernacular, disallows gender intermediation, whereby the "sissy" could be conceived as a conduct, conduit, condition, or identity existing somewhere between masculinity and femininity, if not as an entity or activity within masculinity itself. Because the masculine is the top term in an extreme vertical binary, however—just as white and black coexist in an extreme racial binary—any declension from the masculine necessarily falls into its contrary, a version of the feminine. As Peter Stallybrass and Allon White have explained in relation to the grotesque as a social category, such binary extremism in discourse always reverts as proof to the body itself—in this case the actual person of the sissy serving as the somatic proof of the gender anomaly referenced in the vague term "sissy."[65] Because of the hierarchical nature of extreme binarism, the top term (masculine) is not commensurate with the bottom term (feminine), nor is a declension from masculinity in a man commensurate with a variance from conventional femininity in a woman. For a woman to transgress conventional femininity certainly holds dire dangers, but they are not exactly the same dangers visited upon a male who transgresses hegemonic masculinity. This is why there is no exact corollary of "sissy" to indicate a woman who is incompetently feminine, although "tomboy" perhaps comes closest. "Tomboy" has some positive connotations, though, as it describes a girl who is unusually adventurous, and it also tends to be age-specific, indicating a girl who has not *yet* outgrown her boyishness, whereas "sissy" can be used for a male of any age. In other words, the opprobrium that routinely applies to a sissy-boy only begins to take effect for a boyish girl when she is perceived as having prolonged this behavior beyond tolerance. Even so, "tomboy" applied to a woman does not have the sting of "sissy" applied to a man, for it is a far greater crime for a man to betray his prerogative of manliness than for a woman to aspire to masculinity. Indeed, given that masculinity carries a higher value, it is seen as somewhat understandable, if not acceptable, that a woman would want to abandon femininity to be more like a man.

It is also revealing how such terms of gender transgression are not fully fixed across time and place. An epithet can even migrate from describing a gender-anomalous male to ascribing a gender-anomalous female. For instance, the other common vernacular term for a gender-dissonant female, "butch," was originally used for a tough street boy in the first decade of the twentieth century but by midcentury had come to be applied to the conduct of a masculine woman, especially as paired in a lesbian dyad with a feminine one.[66] In today's gay vernacular, "butch" has migrated back to a descriptor of male conduct, but as it relates to a homosexual dyad between a conventionally masculine man and his "femme" romantic partner. Ironically, terms coined in an earlier era to describe the female invert and her conventionally feminine female partner now are used to reference a similar pairing between two queer men.

Whereas the terms for gender-dissident women are comparatively rare, "sissy" belongs to a continuum of vernacular terms for various degrees and modes of masculine incompetence: pansy, nancy, nance, nelly, fan, flamer, flame, momma's boy, crybaby, namby-pamby, mollycoddle, pantywaist, lightweight, lily liver, softie, girly-boy, poofter, poof, puff, wimp, wuss, pussy, cunt, punk, swisher, swish, fairy, femme, queen, queer, bitch, cocksucker, fag, faggot, homo. Other terms—like being "light in the loafers" or, in black vernacular, having "sugar in the blood"—indicate how such opprobrium tends to spin out into colorful metaphor, as though mere single-term epithets are not enough to gauge the abnormality. These are statements not just about observable bodily comportment or suspect social behavior but also, and more disdainfully, about intrinsic moral character. The plethora of such terms indicates the deep, free-floating level of anxiety—indeed, panic—occasioned by the prospect of failed manliness, whether temporary (as in a moment of cowardice under duress) or seemingly intrinsic or essential (as in a man who cannot achieve or perform masculinity under any circumstance).[67] It is especially instructive how even a term like "punk," which in U.S. slang originally denoted a tough street boy, can be flipped into failed masculinity, as it is used more recently to stigmatize a male who is available to be penetrated, emotionally or physically—a boyish man who, though probably straight, has been forced into a "passive" sexual position with another man.[68] As I emphasize throughout this study, while insecurity, which breeds panic, is cast outside hegemonic masculinity as evidence of a sissy temperament, this constitutes a projection or deflection of an affect that is intrinsic to masculinity itself. To be masculine is to worry about whether one is ever masculine enough, but to shield such worry by projecting it onto the soft other. The sissy, instead, introjects this worry, as discussed above, as a hypersensitive awareness of the fungibility of the line that is supposed to separate virile masculinity from its contrary. The insecurity at the heart of masculinity can unmoor even the most conventional signals of masculine competence, just as the Castro Street Clones of the 1970s took the posture, demeanor, and vestments of working-class manliness and turned them into emblems of a militantly gay masculinity.

There is a correlation between a lack of manliness (penetrability, weakness, timidity, demureness, softness, cowardice), the presumption of effeminateness, and the plausibility of same-gender attraction. As a measure of virility, the sissy is someone who is (too) penetrable emotionally and/or physically and thus occupies the false status of a female (one who is "naturally" penetrated) and by extension a homosexual (one who is unnaturally penetrated). In the face of these correlatives, however, I want to consider how the sissy tiptoes on the line ostensibly separating the failed male from the natural female as well as the line isolating the failed male from the homosexual. Correlations are not here equations but are instead approximations with a difference. A failed male always has the capacity for masculine recuperation (for instance, through an act of courage), because he, after all, possesses the requisite anatomy to claim such virility. It is less certain whether the homosexual similarly has the potential for sexual readjustment, especially after sexual orientation becomes more a matter of physiological etiology and fixed social identity in the decades following the establishment of Freudian psychoanalysis and sexology. Unless he identifies as female or undergoes gender "reassignment" surgery, in which case she is no longer a sissy, the alarm attending the "sissy" epithet derives exactly from the fact that he is a male, one who is not conducting himself as such—not just a gender failure of social categorization but also a categorical moral flaw, if not a heinous sin.[69]

It is exactly in the space of gender differentiation *within* masculinity, the panic that necessarily attends the prerogative of the masculine, that sissy impersonation operates. If the sissy could be firmly ousted from maleness, there would be no reason for panic. Because he is perceived as anatomically male but socially not conforming to the strict idealizations of the masculine, he embodies a deficiency inside maleness and thus within the masculine, a liminal or subliminal boundary marking the masculine as such. The "sissy" epithet encodes gender alarm, then, exactly because, while sissy behavior, temperament, and physicality seem readily legible as failed masculinity, it is impossible to mark that line where a male becomes irretrievably sissified. Applying Mark Anthony Neal's theory of legibility to Rod Ferguson's observation about the diverse expressions of sissy conduct and character among African Americans in the late twentieth-century South, we can understand how a large portion of the panic over sissiness results from the fungibility of the term itself, as well as the fungibility of the kinds of conduct and character represented. Some sissies are so subtle in their behavior and temperament that they can "pass" for straight. Some boys and men can code-switch at the drop of a dime, shifting from a high effeminate manner to a "butch" posture based on a perceived threat or an implied demand for gender conformity in a particular situation. In other words, sissy impersonation is not always self-consistent, a fact that heightens alarm over sissy identity to the point of intensifying the social demand for the sissy to be made legible. That some men can perform conventional masculinity, however, should not be mistaken as merely an act put on for an audience, as we know from gender theories of performativity discussed earlier. Accounting for this fungibility within and across gender is where the theory of performativity is especially helpful. To observe sissy behavior as a kind of gender code-switching emphasizes the extent to which such conduct is a social practice interpolated by an individual subject in constant negotiation with other interested subjects. At the same time, however, for some boys and men sissy behavior seems so ingrained or unavoidable that even in the face of punitive violence, they cannot seem to change their manner. As a complement to performativity as much as a corrective, I deploy the concept of *conduct* here to emphasize that dynamic in which the enactment of sissiness operates somewhere between an habituated gender performance and an inhabited gender identity.

At the slightest hint of an improper gesture, intonation, voice, or affect, a male is immediately labeled and targeted—a zero-toleration policy of sissiphobic enforcement. One could even go so far as to suggest that U.S. culture is *more* comfortable with easily identifiable sissy-boys, who can be verbally mocked and physically violated to ensure their distance from the genuinely masculine, than it is with those boys and men who skirt the line more discreetly, not quite manly enough, a bit too proper, or a bit too gentle. Just as during the Cold War, the government and press saw "soft" menaces everywhere in the corridors of power and fomented policies to purge any male person who raised the slightest suspicion of homosexuality, equated with sissy legibility, so society more generally has taken some comfort in a physical display of presumed sissiness, preferring the obvious threat to the insidiously invisible one.

Likewise, differentiating between the sissy and the homosexual—however subtle, sometimes even indecipherable, as in the panicked reaction of a morally outraged straight man to the appearance of a homo/sissy—occasions a theoretical opening for our inquiry. The man who is physically penetrated by, or desires to penetrate, another male lacks a certain deniability or at least ambiguity—an ambiguity that characterizes the sissy as a male who has failed to be manly enough but has not *yet* crossed the line, as far as we know, into the nonmasculine space reserved for the penetrated homosexual.[70] As will be explored across these chapters, because the sissy is perceived as gender-aberrant, he becomes the vestibule of homosexuality, a liminal site that portends a same-gender sexual orientation and, *in extremis*, a desire to be anally penetrated, even when there is no hard evidence, so to speak, of such conduct. Thus, unlike with the cross-dresser, homosexual, or trans person, sissy conduct becomes primarily a matter of gossip, innuendo, and speculation rather than a matter of law, policy, doctrine, or theology. Also as a result, sissies, unlike homosexuals and trans persons, have not thus far organized an effective, discrete social identity.[71] In the postscript, I ponder this queer possibility in the age of gender fluidity: What would it mean for sissy-boys and sissified men to organize not in a benevolent cause for the softer gender—such as "Gentle Men for Gender Justice"—but instead for the equal rights and social prerogatives of their own soft selves? If there is any doubt that the cause of gender fluidity will be a long, hard battle, the postscript suggests, we need only remember the rise of Donald J. Trump and his blunt celebration of male sexual predation, bullying against those perceived as weak, and white supremacist militias like the Proud Boys. And if we ever doubted that a line still separates white hegemonic masculinity from even the most virile of black manliness, we need only consider how Trump has repeatedly pitted himself against black male professional athletes who support racial justice movements, whether Colin Kaepernick or LeBron James. At least in the embattled gender/racial moment when this book was being written, the fissures between a retrograde white heteronormativity and progressive black manhood could not be more at odds.

The question arises as to how race complicates the sissy's liminality within masculinity and between normative (white) manliness and passive homosexuality. Are there particular connotations to the usage of the term "sissy" among African Americans and other racialized social groups? Just as the vocabulary defining male nonconforming gender changes, at least around the edges, with time and place, so racial and color distinctions transform and migrate. Although white and black sissies are correlatives—cousins under the skin, so to speak—there is a distinction that emerges from the conditions that adhere to black masculinity as a gender formation conceptualized as proximate, if not inimical, to white masculinity as the dominant norm. Black masculinity might be theorized as a subdominant norm, prevailing within blackness however tenuously, but oppressed and marginalized by white male supremacy. We can take this inquiry further by asking whether or how color shapes the person and perceptions of sissiness. Is a light-skinned sissy perceived in the same way as a dark-skinned one? Given the impact of color on the management of black masculinity (by white society as well as through black culture), I would think not. Darker- and lighter-skinned men have different relations to masculinity, exactly because whiteness arbitrates the masculine ideal, and thus the shade of blackness must also predicate different relations to "failed" or liminal manliness. During early Jim Crow, for instance, dark-skinned men were seen as closer to the slave inheritance and thus closer to African savagery. Burdened with the stigma of either African savagery (and thus an aberrantly wild masculinity) or slavish unmanliness (bereft of manly character and of all claims to manhood rights as defined by white institutions), the dark-skinned male betokened the extremes against which white males defined racial and gender supremacy. This is why James Weldon Johnson's faux autobiography of the ex-colored man is so instructive for understanding how "color" colors manliness under Jim Crow. Often the offspring of the slave master, the "mulatto," along with his light-skinned relatives, was given greater proximity to white masculinity, though never allowed unfettered access to it. But skin color in men has been a fluctuating gauge of masculine character. In 1960s black nationalism, dark-skinned men were especially prized, at least symbolically, as preserving an African manhood otherwise diminished and contaminated in lighter-skinned men, whose legacy was defiled by the history of white men's rape of slave women. Lighter-skinned men at the head of the Black Power revolution often expressed self-conscious anxiety about their lack of melanin, and sometimes projected this guilt onto black women for having had intercourse with the slaveholders in the long racial past. As we saw with Wright's depiction of Shorty, there is also an idea that lighter-skinned men are punks—a word with particular resonance in the black vernacular, meaning both "unmasculine" and "cowardly," and that this lack of manliness is constantly threatening to lure them into passive or penetrable homosexuality. In recent lingo spreading in televisual and social media, "pretty boys" has become an expression that is used especially to designate light-skinned men whose preppy grooming and attire counter the popularity of thug fashion under the masculine hardness of hip-hop culture. Pretty boys are not necessarily sissies or gay, but there is an implicit sense that such "boys" are too aesthetically pleasing to be full-fledged manly men, and thus, given the high visibility of gay men in the current political climate, one can never know for sure.

One of the most prominent figures providing a fluctuating template for the interconnection of race, color, and masculine fitness in U.S. culture was constructed by a white northern woman in the 1850s: Uncle Tom, the eponymous character of Harriet Beecher Stowe's blockbuster novel, *Uncle Tom's Cabin*. In Stowe's hands, Uncle Tom exemplifies noble manly conduct through Christian martyrdom. As a dark-skinned slave, his very body contravenes all that is egregious in the white aristocracy of the slaveholding South, and everything that is complicit among northern white men too corrupt or cowardly to root out the un-Christian evil of slavery. For Stowe, Uncle Tom's upright manliness is not surprisingly represented as a Christ-like gentleness, sensitivity, fidelity, simplicity, and self-sacrifice—anchoring values of the domestic sensibility undergirding Stowe's abolitionist ethos.[72] Stowe seeks to transfer the slave's docile servility into a black man's exemplary Christian service. Aware of the strangeness of making a dark-skinned male slave "the hero of our story," she highlights his African features from the outset: "At this table was seated Uncle Tom, Mr. Shelby's best hand, who, as he is to be the hero of our story, we must daguerreotype for our readers. He was a large, broad-chested, powerfully-made man, of a full glossy black, and a face whose truly African features were characterized by an expression of grave and steady good sense, united with much kindliness and benevolence. There was something about his whole air self-respecting and dignified, yet united with a confiding and humble simplicity."[73] Uncle Tom's "glossy" blackness and African phenotype are intrinsic to his manly physicality (large, broad-chested, powerfully made), but it is hard to say whether this big black manliness produces or contrasts with the "soft" moral character he exudes: grave and steady good sense, kindliness, benevolence, self-respect and dignity, and humble simplicity. It is Uncle Tom's Christ-like sensitivity that ultimately seals his fate when he righteously refuses to whip another slave and later when he refuses to reveal to the evil slave master Simon Legree the route that escaped female slaves have taken. If the dark-skinned Uncle Tom could embody the high ground of manly Christian martyrdom in Stowe's Victorian moral system of gentle domestic self-sacrifice, his iconography was bound to shift radically as it migrated into African American culture. Despite Tom's resistance to Simon Legree, he immediately becomes an icon of unmanly race betrayal for African Americans, the worst epithet that can be uttered against a black man by another black person. Even though Booker T. Washington is more frequently aligned with Uncle Tom than not, Addison Gayle Jr. makes use of this black vernacular view of Uncle Tom when explaining the New Negro ushered in by Washington: "The New Negro, therefore, is no Uncle Tom, no cowering, pitying, tenderhearted old slave."[74] What Stowe composes as civilizing Christian virtues of manly self-sacrifice, fidelity, and sensitivity are transposed as unmanly attributes of subservience and cowardice in Gayle's discourse. Although Stowe's daguerreotype for a gentle Christ-like male slave was necessarily a big, glossy-black African man, this did not reflect the social reality of her time, as lighter-skinned men, often mulattoes like Frederick Douglass and Booker T. Washington, were perceived as more civilized, more akin to white manliness, and thus more fit to serve as leaders and intermediaries between black and white.[75] As Riché Richardson points out, in his speeches Malcolm X casts "the Uncle Tom as homosexual," or as bisexual when he depicts the slave "as having a ravenous desire for white women" as part of Malcolm's "strategy for questioning and attacking the manhood and masculinity of the prevailing civil rights leadership."[76] By the 1960s, such civilizing light-skinned leaders are vigorously attacked as Uncle Toms, even when, as in the case of light-skinned Ralph Bunche, the first African American to win the Nobel Peace Prize, he is considered heroic among the white American elite.

As Mark Anthony Neal has noted concerning early twentieth-century movements to provide "'positive' and 'strong' constructions of black masculinity that would directly counter images of the shuffling Sambo or blackface caricatures of black men by white minstrel performers," these caricatures still operate as shorthand epithets used by black men against other black men in an attempt to keep them in line with idealized images of the "strong black man." "Even today," Neal observes, "words like Sambo and minstrel are used by the 'talented tenth' to describe hip-hop."[77] Neal could add "Tom" as perhaps the most aggressive epithet, which, like the others, carries complex connotations of colorism and classism, and also packs insults driven by heterosexism, homophobia, and sissiphobia. By the mid-twentieth century, the Uncle Tom has become so anathema to black manhood aspirations that he becomes the contrary of virile, warring masculinity, often embodied in the historical figure of Nat Turner—so much so that when, in a 1967 Pulitzer Prize–winning novel, William Styron fictionalizes Nat Turner's story as a self-conflicted black man who is having sexual relations with both a white woman and a black man, prominent black writers come to the defense of Turner's manhood in a volume devoted to that cause. When James Baldwin defends Styron on the basis of artistic freedom, he catalyzes the black nationalist suspicion of him as a sissy traitor who prefers intercourse with white men over a united front with his battle-ready black brothers.[78]

Although generally associated with penetrability (weakness, passivity, softness, cowardice), the sissy is *not* always merely weak, soft, passive, or cowardly, a cultural-historical fact that is most prominently articulated in African American discourse and tradition, where sissies are sometimes imaged as street-smart, hard-assed, and knife-crazy. In fact, there is a long history of the *fierce* sissy, one who flaunts his gender anomaly to the point of being a swisher or swish. Less ostentatiously, the black sissy can achieve a certain kind of respectability as a leader of the race, a gender balancing act that hinges on repressive self-restraint, and most tellingly puts some distance between sissy demeanor (too soft, too nurturing, or too sophisticated) and passive homosexual conduct, as most visibly embodied in African American culture through the church sissy. The too-good boy can turn his obedient academic performance and often churchified conduct into professional prowess on behalf of the race, thus flipping a masculine deficit into a racial obligation, making sissy responsibility something to be tentatively admired within the race. There is a lineage of such sissy leaders—Washington, Carver, Johnson, Alain Locke, Langston Hughes, Owen Dodson, James Baldwin, and Bayard Rustin representing different manifestations of this phenomenon, and each indicating how sissiness fluctuates as a measure of virility or its deficiency, as well as a measure of same-sexuality and its absence.

Arenas of Masculine Competence

Each chapter of this study examines a different historical moment and a different aspect of the feud between sissiness and masculinity as a racialized dynamic. Focusing on the most prominent arenas where institutional masculinity is staged for public endorsement of male empowerment—politics, business, science, diplomacy, warfare, religion, activism, academe, and sport—the study demonstrates how in each of these venues the sissy lurks liminally on the edge or subliminally at the heart. Although it could certainly be argued that soft or nonnormative men existed long before the 1880s (mollies, for instance, can be traced back to the eighteenth century in England) when the term "sissy" first gets articulated, I begin this study in this period because of the peculiar situation of black male leadership after emancipation and on the cusp of Jim Crow.[79] As chapter 2 takes Booker T. Washington as a formative case, George Washington Carver as a complement and foil, and their accusers as crucial to understanding their unfit manliness, we find that to understand their quite different sissy dispositions, we must consider the actual material structures they negotiate—from Washington's deployment of business enterprise through industrial education while presenting himself as a happy housekeeper to Carver's tangibly effeminate comportment even as he achieves fame as an agricultural scientist and inventor, vocations usually reserved for the most mannish of men. In anatomizing James Weldon Johnson's gentle manliness in chapter 3, we shift from focusing on an all-black institution to go deeper into official institutions of white patriarchal power in the U.S., exploring the gender and racial politics of Johnson's diplomacy and later his activism as the first African American to lead the nation's premier interracial civil rights organization. Johnson's encounter with the Jim Crow state at home and abroad provides opportunities for examining how he negotiates the white male supremacist military by exploiting the "soft" resources of diplomacy—a deportment that civilizes him in the face of either dismissive insult while serving as consul in Central America or savage violence in his hometown of Jacksonville, Florida. In chapter 4, Baldwin presents the classic case of a homo-sissy, one whose apprenticeship in the black church defines his future career as a prophetic writer and civil rights spokesman on the world stage. Baldwin's transfiguration of church sissiness, though, seems especially conventionally heroic when contextualized through an emerging mass-media age in which hyperblond sissies like Truman Capote and Andy Warhol, on the one hand, and fierce black street swishes like Little Richard and Sylvester, on the other, demand the world's attention as faintly subversive unmanly men infecting the underbelly of a virile Cold War America hysterically fearful of white men's softened temper in an age of sedentary, bureaucratized office work.

When black men enter the arenas of white masculine self-empowerment—Washington in early Jim Crow politics and business; George Washington Carver as an experimental scientist; Johnson in New Negro Renaissance politics, social activism, and diplomacy—they do not necessarily enter as sissified presences, but these prominent cases must make us wonder how black men had to conduct themselves (behavior-wise and morally) over the course of the twentieth century as new technologies of cultural dissemination operated to broadcast gender conduct into the privacy of America's living rooms. Chapter 5 brings us into the arena of avant-garde art and elite higher education, arenas where we perhaps expect sissies to be, but until the post–civil rights era not a place where black men were as leaders of American artistic movements or formerly all-white university faculties until Jim Crow is made ostensibly illegal. Chapter 5 focuses on the transitive and fungible dimensions of gender formation, to borrow from Snorton, to understand how during the modern civil rights era and after, some leading straight black men construct developmental narratives that hinge on a transitive identity as sissy-boys while struggling to maintain their public reputation as heterosexual leaders fully equipped to speak on behalf of the manhood of the race. Amiri Baraka, for example, shifts from an ambivalently sissified persona when he is ensconced as a black token in the bohemian art world of Greenwich Village to a sissiphobic metaphorical warrior when he converts to black nationalism in the mid-1960s. Deeply influenced by Baldwin, he and other black nationalists exert great intellectual energy to pivot from that sissy influence to a virile black nationalism—a pivot that implicates them in the very sissiness they claim to despise. Confronted on the one side with a black ghetto male stereotyped as hypermasculine and on the other side with an emerging black "brother to brother" gay movement and a new white male image of militant gay pride, some black male public intellectuals in the post–civil rights moment negotiate the changing climate of masculine conduct by "coming out" as sissies in memoirs that navigate integrated institutions, academic feminism, cutting-edge gay/lesbian studies, *Cosby Show*–style sensitive patriarchy, and a public image of black maleness caught between affirmative action privilege and a masculinely incompetent black male "underclass." Like black male leaders before them, these men find a resource in sissiness, but explicitly naming it as such, while protecting their heterosexual prerogative by insisting that a sissy need not be a homosexual.

Finally, in chapter 6, we turn to sports as the most captivating arena of masculine self-empowerment, with perhaps the exception of the military, and the gay sports memoir as the most recent instance of how sissiness haunts rough-and-tumble masculinity in the era of gay rights. In fact, often modeled on warfare and the battlefield, the arenas and fields of professional sport embody the most spectacular celebration of manly conduct and character—fixed sites where the nation ritually re-mans itself by showcasing courageous feats of simulated battle usually without war's lethal consequence. Professional sport just might be the last vestige of unembarrassed sissiphobia.[80] Looking at the coming-out narratives of professional athletes in a form I label the sports disclosure memoir, we find the sissy estranged from the masculine norm at the turn into the twenty-first century even as gay men make lumbering strides toward acceptance in America's roughest sports. By concluding with an entrenched preserve of sissiphobia in America's most popular mass sports, the study spotlights again how the charge of unfit conduct even for the toughest of manly men cannot be segregated either from racial identification or from the spectacle of mass consumption and reception.

The sometimes subtle, sometimes blunt racialization that configures sissy signification in U.S. culture can help us decipher the nonconforming dynamics that obtain in masculine conduct and character. Like sissies, black men have historically been relegated to gender nonconformity and nonstandard sexuality. The persistent gender roles that dominant society has foisted onto black manhood have emphasized either masculine overdrive (the buck) or unmanly servitude (Uncle Tom), either hypermuscularity (natural athleticism) or extraordinary resources of seductive expression (in oratory and music). When the black sissy has appeared in dominant mass culture, he is invariably nothing more than a mockery of black men's animal masculinity, an exception that proves the rule, a gender joke whose appearance abets the anxiety and fear that are fueled by black men's overly masculine prowess. Within African American culture, however, sissies are everywhere once we begin to look. The history of racial and sexual oppression has forced black men to take seriously the question of masculine in/competence, perhaps to a point of heightened and deepened self-awareness of the high stakes involved in conforming to white supremacy's conventions of masculine conduct. Sissification is just one way, but a crucial one, that African American men have negotiated the multiple binds of a coercive black masculinity, suppressed in its potential kinship with white male supremacy, beckoning toward alternative tenors of manliness even while trapped by the domains of empowerment that a hard masculinity insistently promises.

2

Sissy Housekeeping

Cleanliness, Gender Dissonance, and the Spoils of
Political Patronage at Washington's Tuskegee

Wash Ferguson [Booker T. Washington's stepfather] was out of work and down-at-heel, as was nearly everyone else in Malden. He could not afford to hire a housekeeper, and his dignity would not allow him to do women's work.
—LOUIS R. HARLAN, *Booker T. Washington: Making of a Black Leader*

My wife and children were incidents of my main life work. I was not neglectful of my family; I furnished a good home. . . . But my main work was out in the world and not at home. That work out there my wife appreciated but was too busy to share because of cooking, marketing, sweeping and cleaning and the endless demands of children.
—W. E. B. DU BOIS, *The Autobiography of W. E. B. Du Bois*

Punking Rivalry in the Contest over Jim Crow Race Leadership

History has not been kind to Booker T. Washington. Although he is a notable figure in U.S. history, he is not generally celebrated as one of the heroes of African American history. Washington's politics of accommodation—temporary public acceptance of Jim Crow separation and discrimination while building up the race through skilled labor and autonomous business enterprise—seems to have lost out to the egalitarian politics of his adversary, W. E. B. Du Bois. Although honored during his own time as the most influential and effective black leader, especially by the white power structure, Washington's accommodationist strategy was and is, at best, controversial. As Christopher B. Booker observes, "The acquiescent accommodationism inculcated by Booker T. Washington marked an era of self-doubt for African American males. This accommodationism peaked during this era, when an all-out assault on the black male's character had been in progress for several decades."[1] Other leading activists of the time—Ida B. Wells-Barnett, William Monroe Trotter, and William Pickens, in addition to Du Bois—could be quite damning in their attacks on Washington and his program, often using language infused with gender insinuations. These adversaries imply that Washington's leadership is somehow less than manly. This is not surprising, given that political leadership at the turn of the twentieth century was so strongly constructed as an attribute of masculine competence—a construction raised to new heights during the "Rough Rider" and "big stick" era of Teddy Roosevelt. Kevin P. Murphy points out that Roosevelt labeled his political opponents "mollycoddles," a term endorsed and explained in the press as "a man who won't take hard knocks, who flinches from the crowd."[2] "By linking their critique of reformers to the stigmatization of the sexual invert," Murphy writes, "party stalwarts discovered a powerful rhetorical weapon with which to oppose reform."[3] Similarly, Alan Trachtenberg explains how "reformers and genteel intellectuals who stood above party battles invited the scorn of the regulars, a scorn couched frequently in images fusing anger at feminizing culture with sexual innuendo, the manly braggadocio of the stalwart: 'political hermaphrodite,' 'miss-Nancys,' 'man-milliners.'" In such disputes, both sides resorted to the distinction between "the realm of the feminine against the realm of the aggressive masculine."[4]

Although Washington and his adversaries were already barred by Jim Crow from what Murphy calls "the rough and manly world of politics,"[5] and although Washington's adversaries never resorted to such ferocious terms as "mollycoddle" or "Miss Nancy," they still had recourse to the gender invective that powerful white men exploited in their jockeying for power. Du Bois's pivotal 1903 book, *Souls of Black Folk*, attacks Washington's leadership amid his own paroxysms of gender anxiety, expressed through proliferating images of aborted manhood, impotent husbanding, and tragic wasting of phallic seed. Articulating his celebrated definition of double consciousness, he writes, "The history of the American Negro is the history of this strife, this longing to attain self-conscious manhood, to merge his double self into a better and truer self." Du Bois laments that in the past "these powers of body and mind have ... been strangely wasted, dispersed, or forgotten."[6] In Du Bois's essay "Mr. Booker T. Washington and Others" (1901), included in *Souls of Black Folk*, he uses the same kind of imagery to issue a direct attack on Washington: "Mr. Washington's counsels of submission overlooked certain elements of true manhood" (39). And again, "Mr. Washington withdraws many of the high demands of Negroes as men and American citizens.... In the history of nearly all other races and peoples the doctrine preached at such crises has been that manly self-respect is worth more than lands and houses, and that a people who voluntarily surrender such respect, or cease striving for it, are not worth civilizing" (43). Washington's strategy would "sap the manhood of any race in the long run" (45), Du Bois quips. As Hazel V. Carby explains, "Beneath the surface" of Du Bois's work, despite his advocacy of sexual equality, there is "a conceptual framework that is gender-specific; not only does it apply exclusively to men, but it encompasses only those men who enact narrowly and rigidly determined codes of masculinity." For Carby, when Du Bois attacks Washington for his "sycophancy and selling out to commercialism," the former figures this gender compromise by making Washington "the metaphorical equivalent of the black mother (or the black female prostitute) who succumbs to the lust of white men." The sting in Du Bois's language derives from the gendered character of his accusations, a sting carried especially in the connotation of the word "sycophancy."[7]

The language of "sycophancy" strongly connotes an inappropriate mode of conduct engaged in specifically by men as men—that is, conduct that is sissifying insofar as it is effeminizing. Du Bois is implying that Washington is behaving like a particular kind of male, one who, rather than deploying his manhood power self-assertively, instead chooses to cling parasitically to another man whose greater political clout he hopes sneakily to wheedle for his own perverse ends. As the *Oxford English Dictionary* reports, quoting from a nineteenth-century English historian of ancient Greece, this label was applied to "a class of men who were universally odious, ... the informers, or sycophants as they were called at Athens." For centuries in Europe, the term constituted one of the most vile epithets that could be tossed at any male who seemed to beggar another man's patriarchal authority presumably because he lacked the capacity to wield his own: "a mean, servile, cringing, or abject flatterer; a parasite, toady, lickspittle."[8] While it has historically been seen as appropriate for women to be flattering and obeisant to a powerful man—indeed, this was considered a female's natural character—for a man to behave in such a way pegged him as perversely unmasculine insofar as he still desired manly power but sought it in a backhanded, subservient manner unbefitting the dignity of a proper man. While a phrase like "sapping manhood" enables Du Bois to sound the alarm concerning the general unmanliness of Washington's behavior, the belittling epithet "sycophant" enables him to classify Washington within a species of degenerate men mocked by more vigorous politicos for centuries. In this sense, Du Bois is punking Washington, to use an anachronistic term that nonetheless captures the nastily gendered nature of the charge. Rather than simply analogizing him to a black mother or prostitute, as Carby observes, Du Bois more insidiously also sizes up the conduct and character of the Wizard—man to man—by judging him to be among the most odious species of man still classifiable, if barely, as a man. As noted in chapter 1, there is no evidence that Washington in any way displayed the physical or physiological attributes of a sissified figure in his comportment, attire, manner, posture, gait, speech, or gesture. His adversaries are not, in this sense, attacking his person per se. They are, instead, attacking his social habit and his ideological practice of embarrassing the ambition of black men in their attempts to achieve all the social, political, and economic attributes of manhood citizenship, as defined by the federal and state constitutions as a male right in contradistinction with women, nonnaturalized resident immigrants, and male youth under the age of twenty-one.

To punctuate this distinction between a sissy social practice and sissy physical embodiment, I'll cap this chapter by briefly examining George Washington Carver, whose case will help us understand the wide berth of sissy conduct, the different valences of the sissy charge, and the scaled racial environs in which such charges can be wielded toward different ends. While the effeminate Carver can be tied to Washington's schoolmarmish apron strings, so to speak, as a scientist dependent on Tuskegee Institute's largesse without being called out publicly for his gender nonconformity, Washington himself was necessarily exposed as a public target, even though he carefully comported himself according to the dictates of the masculine heteronorm. The very publicness of Washington's mission for the race dictated a sissy practice readily visible to whites while simultaneously practicing a patriarchal manliness as an object lesson for blacks.

Ruling white men expected a Washington-like self-humbling that for African American men could seem like rank sycophancy. This seeming contradiction—between Washington's masculine deportment and his adversaries' charge of his unmanliness—is best captured in the most important public performance that launched his international career as head of the race, the Atlanta Exposition Address of 1895. This five-minute speech was deftly calculated to balance a needed subservience to the powerful white men, southern and northern, who were on the stage with him and in the front rows, while also communicating to the segregated black audience his fitness to lead the race as others, especially Frederick Douglass, had done so manfully before him. Describing Washington's training as an orator, which began at Hampton Institute, Marcus H. Boulware distinguishes between the oratorical styles of Washington and Douglass, noting especially how the former saw himself as calculating every detail to sway an audience: "The orator Douglass swayed audiences and himself by the passion of his message. On the other hand, Washington studied every detail and weighed every word, always keeping in mind the final impression he wished to make. In making that impression, he was aware of the importance of personal contact with his audiences. Thus, at the beginning of his speeches, he was somewhat nervous lest he might fail to achieve this visual directness."[9] As Boulware further notes, Washington was aware of how he exploited his initial nervousness in taking the platform to his advantage as a way to ingratiate himself to an audience. Washington's rhetoric is carefully fashioned as dignified oratory without being so elegant as to alarm whites that he might be an uppity Negro. The folksiness of Washington's oratory—a characteristic of everything he publicly spoke or wrote—also communicates that he is not aligned with what Du Bois would only a couple of years later label "the Talented Tenth," with its implications of an educated elite demanding social equality. Instead, Washington's folksy manner of speaking at once identified him as appropriately humble to whites and at the same time approachable and accessible to the mass of formerly enslaved southerners. This vernacular balance was also intended to maneuver the gender predicament implied by his assumption of racial leadership. We can see this gender maneuvering in the most famous image of that most famous speech: "Cast down your buckets."

The homely nature of the image belies its sophistry—indeed, its sycophancy. He splits the image between his black and white audience. He addresses it to the white rulers of the nation second: "Casting down your bucket among my people, helping and encouraging them as you are doing on these grounds and to education of head, hand, and heart, you will find that they will buy your surplus land, make blossom the waste places in your fields, and run your factories. While doing this, you can be sure in the future as in the past, that you and your families will be surrounded by the most patient faithful, law-abiding, and unresentful people that the world has seen."[10] This sycophancy presents itself openly as a bald racial bargain—a kind of political hardball to agree to be softly subservient to white supremacy in order to secure blacks' economic interests. There is, though, an interesting homonym in the figure of blacks "running your factories." To run the factories could mean to be in charge of them as foremen, a charge of middlemanliness that from the earliest Jim Crow was reserved for white working-class men. To run the factories here, the white managers can assume, means only that blacks will be happy to keep their factories running as their hard-working manual (and menial) laborers. He has preceded the above sentences to ensure the latter reading: "Cast down your bucket among these people who have, without strikes and labour wars, tilled your fields, cleared your forests, built your railroads and cities, and brought forth treasures from the bowels of the earth, and helped make possible this magnificent representation of the South" (221). As if that labor were not compelled under the duress of enslavement, Washington pits the formerly enslaved against "those of foreign birth and strange tongue and habits" who are likely to engage in labor unrest for better pay, better hours, cleaner plants, and so on. Although his black audience may very well figure in their heads themselves as foremen managing white men's factories, Washington again assures his white audience that he intends no such thing, as indicated by the sentence that follows the one containing the "run" homonym: "As we have proved our loyalty to you in the past, in nursing your children, watching by the sick-bed of your mothers and fathers, and often following them with tear-dimmed eyes to their graves, so in the future, in our humble way, we shall stand by you with a devotion that no foreigner can approach, ready to lay down our lives, if need be, in defence of yours" (221). The gender genuflection embedded in this sentence is communicated powerfully by the vivid catalogue of effeminate tasks: nursing the young and old, mourning the dead with "tear-dimmed eyes," and standing "humbly" in fatal defense of their white superiors' lives and livelihoods.

Washington smartly addresses his black audience first, preparing them mentally and emotionally for the hard bargain that is to come through the advocacy of a softened black manhood. He urges them, "'Cast down your bucket where you are'—cast it down in making friends in every manly way of the people of all races by whom we are surrounded" (219). As if anticipating the charge of sissy cowardice that will be made against him, Washington includes the phrase "in every manly way" to suggest a certain masculine dignity that his words might otherwise contravene. Indeed, in charging his fellow Negroes, gender unspecified, to cast down their bucket "in agriculture, mechanics, in commerce, in domestic service, and in the professions," he balances professional ambition with domestic servility (219). The subtle gender implications of this distinction between the professions and domestic labor will be explained later in the chapter. The genuflection to domestic subservience is, in fact, the greatest grievance that Du Bois has concerning Washington's accommodation as it relates to education and labor. In the next sentence, Washington again negotiates the gender bind by defining southern opportunity as optimal, suggesting no need to migrate northward: "When it comes to business, pure and simple, it is in the South that the Negro is given a man's chance" (220). What does Washington mean by "in every manly way" and by "a man's chance"? In one sense, these are hackneyed phrases intended to placate the charge of unmanliness that he is already anticipating as a major stumbling block to his sycophantic practice. In another sense, Washington means what he says. He is advocating for what he sees as the essence of a free man's emancipation, gender specificity intended. The *Oxford English Dictionary* indicates the origin of the verb "to emancipate" from Roman law: "To release or set free (a child or wife) from the patria potestas, the power of the pater familias, thus making the person so set free sui juris."[11] For Washington, to perform this act of emancipation means to labor humbly with the hands at the very bottom of the economic ladder on the promise that the accumulation of land and wealth will eventually bring other freedoms to not only an emancipated race but also an emancipated manhood. As he says, "We shall prosper in proportion as we learn to dignify and glorify common labour and put brains and skill into the common occupations of life."[12] The "we" here inscribes the black race, man and woman, into a project that deftly sublimates his gender trickery into a collective action, as though "a man's chance" is the reward for humble, subservient labor, rather than the condition that enables such labor to pay off.

In language fashioned especially to appeal simultaneously, if differently, to the white male rulers and the formerly enslaved masses, Washington from the outset negotiates this gender dilemma—how to be subserviently humble "in every manly way"—by helping his audience to imagine a conduct that can be at once racially humble and manfully dignified. Calculated to appease the cross-racial audience standing before him, the speech is also aimed at mass distribution, which he achieves when it is reprinted in newspapers in both the North and the South and allotted a chapter in his immensely popular autobiography, *Up from Slavery*, published three years after the speech. Understanding that his program will succeed based on how he himself is received as appropriately in his place as a self-humbling black man by whites and yet deemed robustly competent to husband the race's future, Washington exploits the most *commonplace* expressions of masculine propriety ("in every manly way," "a man's chance") ironically to promise a race of men at ease in taking on sissy subservience ("nursing your children," "watching by the sick-beds of your mothers and fathers," "following with tear-dimmed eyes" your dead to their graves)—an imagery whose gender trickery results from the unspecified gender attribution normally made between a woman's "softer" domestic mission and a man's more worldly ambition. This is the racial bargain broadcast across America, as it necessarily bespeaks the gender compromise that Washington's critics will pounce on to eviscerate his leadership.

Speechifying was one of the major ways that black men could gain the attention of the early Jim Crow white power structure without appearing too ambitiously uppity, for whites were comfortable viewing black men as good orators, good talkers, as long as such talk was not aimed at upsetting the color line. Indeed, oratory was seen as suited to the temperament of the race, whose gender temperament was thought to be designed for emotion, fidelity, superstition, and the histrionic—attributes usually identified with women of the dominant race. Such an attitude was glaringly evident in one of the most important tributes made by an influential white man to a black man in the 1890s. William Dean Howells, the most influential critic of his generation, first published his tribute in 1896 in a favorable review of Paul Laurence Dunbar's second volume of poetry, *Majors and Minors*, and republished it in a slightly different version as the introduction to Dunbar's third volume, *Lyrics of Lowly Life*. Repeatedly in that introduction Howells references what he takes to be the different "temperament" of the race, writing "that however gifted his race had proven itself in music, in oratory, in several of the other arts, here was the first instance of an American negro who had evinced innate distinction in literature."[13] Howells continues:

> Yet it appeared to me then, and it appears to me now, that there is a precious difference of temperament between the races which it would be a great pity ever to lose, and that this is best preserved and most charmingly suggested by Mr. Dunbar in those pieces of his where he studies the moods and traits of his race in its own accent of our English.... In nothing is his essentially refined and delicate art so well shown as in these pieces, which, as I ventured to say, describe the range between appetite and emotion, with certain lifts far beyond and above it, which is the range of the race.[14]

Assigning the "range of the race" between "appetite and emotion"—suggesting the softer affects of humor, hankering, tenderness, sentiment, and pathos—necessarily implies what is missing from this range: the more robust dimensions of temperament associated with rationality, valor, gutsiness, ambition, willpower, and the heroic. This view is summed up by the sociologist Robert Park when he calls the Negro "the lady of the races."[15] Even though white allies like Howells and Park were eager to grant black men oratorical mastery, they were, at the same time, still putting black men in a lower, less-than-manly place. Nonetheless, it is important to remember that, as black leaders well understood, public speaking was the main way, besides periodical print, of reaching a broad mass audience in the early decades of the twentieth century. Indeed, notable speeches were routinely printed in mainstream (white) newspapers—a rare opportunity for black leaders to court a cross-racial audience. While black men's speechifying occasions a rare stage for staking a claim to racial leadership, such oratory equally poses racial danger if the orator fails to balance some "manly way" for the black audience while signaling racial sycophancy to the white audience.

Given this common attitude toward Negroes, and particularly the Negro male, Washington understood the difficult gender balancing act required in delivering an acceptable Jim Crow speech aimed at claiming one's authority as a racial spokesman. While the performance of oratory mastery is critical for any Negro who desired leadership of the race in this period, and especially one who desired the endorsement of the white male elite, enacting this gender balance through oratory also presents a danger. How can one speak authoritatively "in every manly way" without sounding uppity? This gender balancing act—at once a proper husband to the race and *not* an uppity Negro claiming his full manly emancipation—was hard to accomplish, even for the Wizard of Tuskegee. Indeed, as Du Bois was careful to point out in the chapter of *Souls of Black Folk* titled "Mr. Booker T. Washington and Others," Washington tripped up badly once in an 1898 speech delivered at the Chicago Peace Jubilee celebrating victory in the Spanish-American War, delivered before an audience that included President McKinley. In his speech "The Better Part," Washington intones: "We can celebrate the era of peace in no more effectual way than by a firm resolve on the part of Northern men and Southern men, black men and white men, that the trenches which we together dug around Santiago, shall be the eternal burial place of all that which separates us in our business and civil relations. Let us be as generous in peace as we have been brave in battle."[16] Washington's first-person plural here is the same strategy that he used in the Atlanta Exposition Speech, but toward a different effect—aggressively attacking, rather than subserviently submitting to, the Jim Crow order. As I indicated in chapter 1, manly victory in warfare was long seen as a venue to assert black men's right to full emancipation. It is in this heady context of being invited to this "Thanksgiving Jubilee" celebrating the nation's imperialist victory that Washington feels emboldened to assert that black men who fought alongside white men in the trenches of Cuba, the same brave soldiers buried in those trenches, should not be treated separately in life. This metaphor of a shared grave directly references and counters his earlier fingers/hand metaphor of the 1895 Atlanta Exposition Speech. In the "Better Part" speech, Washington boldly attacks racial prejudice as "a cancer gnawing at the heart of the Republic, that shall one day prove as dangerous as an attack from an army without or within."[17] The response to this speech was so violent that Washington had to clarify his stance and reaffirm his "separate as the fingers, one as the hand" dictum from the 1895 Address. We can only imagine Washington's oratorical delivery as he seeks to steal this moment to burnish his manly authority before the president and many other dignitaries seated on the dais and an audience solely of white northerners—according to Harlan, "a crowd of 16,000 so tightly packed that he needed a policeman to help make his way into the auditorium"—where the president is seated on the dais behind him.[18] His ready retreat to the Atlanta separatist accommodation was no doubt a signal defeat, and yet one that the Great Accommodator would have anticipated on taking this "man's chance" in the first place. Coming still early in his reign, only three years after the Atlanta Compromise Address, this was not an oratorical misstep that he would make again.

We can gauge Washington's skill as a successful sycophantic orator by contrasting his performance, and the gender conduct that flows with it, with that of the young William Pickens, who learns the hard way when he puts himself forward as a spokesman for the race in his 1903 Yale oratory contest speech, "Misrule in Hayti." The twenty-one-year-old college student from the backwoods of Arkansas makes some dangerous missteps in so clearly aligning himself with Washingtonian accommodation, as vividly recorded in Sheldon Avery's biography *Up from Washington*. To his white audience at Yale, when he advocates for the "'subjugation of the island by America'" as "'an act of kindness,'" he is implicitly agreeing with Washington's rhetoric in *Up from Slavery*, where the temporary enslavement of the American Negro is characterized as a blessing in disguise.[19] Pickens's oratorical ingratiation—not to say, sycophancy—indicates his desire to attract Washington's "stronger hand" in support of his career, especially given that at this point Pickens aspires to become the president of a black college in the Bookerite manner.[20] According to Avery, the Yale address does attract Washington's interest and initial patronage. Pickens's humble attitude toward winning the prize significantly counters his own later account of his aggressive self-confidence in his 1923 autobiography, *Bursting Bonds*, indicating a discursive shift from strategic sycophancy to self-assertive masculinity.[21]

Unfortunately for Pickens, winning the oratory contest brings attention as well from Washington's greatest adversary, William Monroe Trotter, militant editor of the *Boston Guardian*.[22] No doubt such negative attention from Trotter, who lodges an attack on the young student's manhood, helps to reorient Pickens away from a Bookerite strategy of gender self-humbling. Calling Pickens "uncouth and provincial," Trotter suggests that the only reason he is the first Negro to win the coveted prize is his "surrendering his self-respect, sacrificing his pride, emasculating his manhood, and throwing down his race."[23] Washington then attempted to exploit Pickens in a libel suit against Trotter, which must have been a quick and dirty lesson for the young college man in the dangers of accommodationist sycophancy. The gender genuflection that Washington seemed to manage so deftly, Pickens discovered, was much harder than it appeared.

Similarly, by situating black manhood as the subject and object of melancholic wastage, Du Bois risks setting himself up for the kind of charge of "injury" to the race's manhood that Trotter makes against the young Pickens and that Du Bois himself makes against Washington. Even in an age that tolerates—and, indeed, to some extent encourages—lachrymose men much more than our own does, Du Bois's outpouring of lamentation associates the persona of *Souls* more closely with the hysterically grieving mother than with the stolid race husband, despite his attempt to delineate these roles along normative gender lines. That a black male writer of the time could easily pick up on this gender slippage in Du Bois comes from one of Du Bois's own colleagues, Kelly Miller.[24] As a member of the American Negro Academy, a forum in which Du Bois first presents some of the writing that eventually becomes sections of *Souls of Black Folk*, Miller is an important figure in post-Reconstruction political contests.[25] His 1908 book, *Race Adjustment*, leads off with the largely pro-Washington piece "Race Adjustment: Radicals and Conservatives." Implicit in Miller's characterizations of black men who would lead the race is a question of how best to husband the resources of masculinity, cast as a binary between an unbridled, rugged virility (a kind of barbarism) versus a polished, discerning diplomacy (a kind of urbane manliness cultivated by James Weldon Johnson, as discussed in chapter 3). Miller places Trotter at one extreme: "He has thrown away all the restraints of culture, spurned the allurements of refined association, and conducts *The Guardian* with as little regard to literary form and style as if he were a back-woodsman."[26] Miller appeals to a higher plane of manliness than one based in brute physicality. If Miller casts Trotter as the unruly, rude backwoodsman who has wasted his elite talents, he places Washington in the starring role of a man who has husbanded his resources well, despite lacking all of Trotter's elite privileges: "He rises triumphantly on stepping-stones of this dead self to higher things. . . . Washington's equability of temper is most remarkable."[27] What I am calling Washington's gender fluidity Miller labels "equability of temper," a quality needed in an age of emerging Jim Crow. This narrative of Washington's growth clearly charts a development into manhood. Through such laudatory language, Miller is able to meld "power of enlargement" with supple fluidity, a quality that could easily be seen negatively as the political slipperiness of an unctuous lickspittle.

There is no doubt that Miller is rebutting Du Bois's highly influential attack on Washington's manhood in "Of Mr. Booker T. Washington and Others." What is made to be a liability in Du Bois's characterization of Washington's gender positioning is here turned into a supreme performance of manliness. Through his attack on Trotter, Miller is able to warn his friend Du Bois to back away from his flirtations with Trotter. Miller does so by turning Du Bois into an innocent victim of Trotter's machinations: "He wove a subtle net about W. E. B. Du Bois, the brilliant writer and scholar, and gradually weaned him from his erstwhile friendship for Mr. Washington, so as to exploit his prominence and splendid powers in behalf of the hostile forces."[28] Casting Du Bois as the seduced maiden of Trotter's wily machinations, Miller uses language that praises Du Bois while also insinuating a certain immaturity—his being "weaned" from one camp to another—in comparison to Washington's "power of enlargement." In contrast with Washington's "equability of temper," Du Bois's tendency toward "fine frenzy" makes him a moving writer, but an impotent and incompetent race leader. Ironically, Miller turns Du Bois's aggressive bid for manhood rites/rights in *Souls* into a "sad and bitter wail" as he picks up on the elegiac, effusive, lachrymose prose as a benchmark of the author's true nature as a fragile man of frenzied contemplation: "His mind being cast in a weird and fantastic mold, his place is the cloister of the reflective scholar. He lives behind the veil; and whenever he emerges to mingle with the grosser affairs of life we may expect to hear, ever and anon, that sad and bitter wail."[29] Associating Du Bois with the ivory tower and the cloister, Miller, himself an ivory-towered intellectual at Howard University, also puns on one of Du Bois's most famous figures of speech, "the veil," which Du Bois uses to connote the dark side of race oppression experienced in Jim Crow, as well as the torn drape dividing the sacred temple, but which Miller exploits as an effeminizing trope: the veil that chaste, cloistered women wear to protect them from the "grosser affairs of life." Incapable of functioning in the rough-and-tumble world of bare-knuckle politics that Washington has enlarged himself to master, Du Bois's métier consists of a smaller, more delicate sphere of the emotive and the poetic—the very place that Howells views as natural to the tenderer temperament of the Negro.

This contentious debate over Washington's fitness for leadership reveals how gender deportment complicates the framing of political prowess under early Jim Crow. When Trotter's verbal attack on Washington's manhood ultimately leads to the former's use of physical force, Miller's distinction between a brutish and an equitable manliness would seem to carry some weight.[30] We must not overlook the deeper implication of these verbal skirmishes over manhood-sapping. Verbally punking a political opponent necessarily implies a dimension of physical violence if the jeopardy represented by the leader's sapping of manhood is seen as endangering the safety and survival of the race. With lynching rising in the first decades of the twentieth century, Trotter's resort to physical force could well be understood as justified. Sycophancy hardly seems equipped to end white men's lynching violence. In the eyes of Washington's opponents, the prospect of a sissy leader makes the race more vulnerable to harassment and violation.

Although punking a political adversary in the United States has historically been practiced mainly by men against men, as Jackson Katz's *Man Enough?* has documented through a history of the masculinist rhetoric used in U.S. presidential campaigns,[31] the unmanning dynamic of the tactic does not necessarily disappear when a woman enters the fray, especially when the woman is as forceful an activist as Ida B. Wells. In her autobiography, Wells does not pull any punches against the Wizard. She charges Washington with employing sneaky tactics in the interest of sucking up to white northern philanthropists rather than from any genuine principle of black people's intrinsic political strength.[32] According to Wells, Washington's sycophancy accords with his "theory . . . that we ought not to spend our time agitating for our rights; that we had better give attention to trying to be first-class people in a jim crow car than insisting that the jim crow car should be abolished" (264–265). Like Trotter and Du Bois, Wells charges Washington with robbing the race of its "manhood." When the Chicago black literati meet to discuss Du Bois's *Souls* on its publication in 1903, Wells and her husband stand alone in defending Du Bois's argument against the four other members of the book club: "We thought it was up to us to show them the sophistry of the reasoning that any one system of education could fit the needs of an entire race; that to sneer at and discourage higher education would mean to rob the race of leaders which it so badly needed; and that all the industrial education in the world could not take the place of manhood."[33] Although Wells's forceful stance is authentically voiced as her own, her concern for Washington's sapping the race's manhood is also authorized by the way she pictures herself teaming up "almost alone" with her husband. As Patricia A. Schechter observes, Du Bois and Wells had a "shared understanding of 'the race's manhood.'" Schechter captures the gender ambivalence at work in Wells's use of the "manhood" weapon. On the one hand, "the call to manhood summoned the common humanity of all African Americans, much as the concept of the brotherhood of man invoked the ungendered dignity of all members of the human family."[34] On the other hand, manhood cannot be divorced from the prerogatives of a "privileged masculinity." Although a woman could hardly be accused of being a sycophant in the way Du Bois lobs the charge (any more than a woman can be a sissy), a woman's political leadership is just as much in jeopardy of being charged with gender inappropriateness, often through dismissive mockery rather than with the sort of violent alarm we see in these men's punking attacks and counterattacks. Despite the certain backlash to such unfeminine rhetoric and conduct, Jacqueline Goldsby observes that Wells "also sounds pleased by the prospects of violating the gendered expectations for 'race women' activists." In this sense, we could consider Wells an analogous case to the "sissy" Washington, as she, according to Goldsby, "claims the mantle of masculine authority to achieve a level of public visibility otherwise beyond her reach."[35] Schechter points out that Wells's role of "race woman" led many African American men to dismiss her "assertive female behavior" as "tedious and overreaching." Washington himself strikes back, notably in a private letter, charging that Wells is "'fast making herself so ridiculous that every body is getting tired of her.'"[36] Although Washington is careful to avoid entangling himself in these punking tactics in public, he is well aware of the risks they pose to his reputation, as his bid to sue Trotter for libel indicates. As Schechter records, Washington "and his followers ridiculed militants' '"manhood!" hysteria' and argued that economic self-sufficiency and attention to moral duties demonstrated the true 'manhood first' necessary to earn political rights in the future."[37] Evidently, Washington's followers want to emphasize the discordancy between "manhood" and "hysteria," as ostensibly a female malady, by placing "manhood" in quotation marks within the phrase—indicating the alarm that accompanies any deviation from the masculine norm, as I discussed in chapter 1. Thus, Washington's advocates attempt to normalize Washington's own public gender practice by projecting an unmanly hysteria onto his opponents.

That Washington largely resisted engaging publicly in this "'manhood!' hysteria" is not only a measure of his tremendous influence with the white male power structure but also a measure of how self-consciously he distanced himself from the straitjacket of a normative masculinity even as he comported himself respectably as a black patriarch. Refusing to engage in the public skirmish is, in effect, a way of appearing to dismiss the charges against him as beneath his cool (thus, manly) regard. In her study of black leadership, *Charisma*, Erica R. Edwards rightly emphasizes the ways in which black leadership has been historically constructed through and against a charismatic figure or scenario: "I mean to emphasize that charisma participates in a gendered economy of political authority in which the attributes of the ideal leader are the traits American society usually conceives as rightly belonging to men or to normative masculinity: ambition, courage, and above all, divine calling."[38] The punking attacks on Washington indicate the extent to which Edwards's characterization of the masculinist "ideal leader" is certainly at work in the period's "gendered economy of political authority" that Washington is negotiating. At the same time, however, those characteristics of "normative masculinity"—and the implications of dominance, control, ambitiousness, and power associated with them—are systematically withheld from African American men in order to consolidate Jim Crow's separate and unequal ideology. Ultimately, Washington understands that such structural gender normativity is not available to him—at least, if he is to avoid a violent backlash from whites that would eventually oust him from leadership. The "benign" charismatic "terror" that Edwards describes as belonging to normative masculinity cannot be taken for granted by any would-be black male leader at the turn into the twentieth century, as Washington's oratorical legerdemain, dramatic single misstep, and mass public sissy practice most vividly exemplify.

Sissy Housekeeping as Dignified "Menial" Labor

Du Bois's charge of sapping manhood reverberates so deeply partly because it silently rivets on that vivid image of a meticulous male housekeeper that Washington had publicized two years before in his popular autobiography. It is important to emphasize that for Washington's self-narration, and for Du Bois's sissiphobic intervention, the infamous sweeping incident from *Up from Slavery* constitutes *the* pivotal moment that initiates Washington's transition from boyhood to manhood.[39] The black boy wielding a broom anticipates the image of black World War I soldiers being forced to drill with broomsticks, rather than weapons, even though the Hampton classroom seems far afield from the field of battle. When he arrives at Hampton Institute, ragged and unwashed, he is told to sweep the recitation room by the school's white Lady Principal, Miss Mary F. Mackie. Washington communicates the obsessive quality of his sweeping as a transformative virtue that transfigures the mean (or Washington would say "commonplace") menial task into a dignified site of matriculation:

I knew that I could sweep, for Mrs. Ruffner had thoroughly taught me how to do that when I lived with her. I swept the recitation-room three times. Then I got a dusting-cloth and I dusted it four times. All the woodwork around the walls, every bench, table, and desk, I went over four times with my dusting-cloth. Besides, every piece of furniture had been moved and every closet and corner in the room had been thoroughly cleaned. I had the feeling that in a large measure my future depended upon the impression I made upon the teacher in the cleaning of that room.[40]

As we shall see in chapter 4, James Baldwin images the sissiness of John Grimes, the thirteen-year-old protagonist of *Go Tell It on the Mountain,* through the boy's obsessive sweeping and dusting. In composing this passage, Washington is calculating the benefits of such a sissy representation against the liabilities of casting black men's labor as appropriately, and perhaps intrinsically, menial and subservient to a white matron's whim. As we'll discover, however, Washington intends this formative image as transitive, for the autobiography subtly pivots toward the Wizard's own patriarchal authority over his own educational institution, where, ironically, he will foist the same kinds of menial labor onto his female *and male* charges by giving orders to his own black female matrons, who occupy a position correlative to Miss Mackie. Washington makes his bond with Miss Mackie through housekeeping: a habitual way of being in an early Jim Crow environment. Like the idea that only in the South is there "a man's chance," his sweeping the floor establishes the demeanor of ebullient application to menial labor that characterizes his approach to emancipation: "I was one of the happiest souls on earth" (53). To pay for his schooling, Washington accepts from Miss Mackie a position as janitor. He then draws a direct connection between his janitorial work and his physical and emotional proximity to Miss Mackie: "In all my career at Hampton, and ever since I have been out in the world, Miss Mary F. Mackie . . . proved one of my strongest and most helpful friends. Her advice and encouragement were always helpful and strengthening to me in the darkest hour" (53–54). Miss Mackie becomes the "stronger hand" that Pickens theorizes in his "Misrule in Hayti" speech, and as we shall see, it is through his intimacy with this Yankee schoolmarm that Washington becomes the favored protégé of the white man who "made the greatest and most lasting impression upon me"—rising up the gender scale from being a dependent of the Yankee schoolmarm's domestic influence to becoming a sycophant to the great white father's political power.[41]

As Du Bois would have been embarrassingly aware, Washington has pivoted his transition to manhood on an action clearly identified with black women's subordinate status as menial laborers under the supervision of white ladies, rather than more fittingly anchoring it in a conventional masculine rite like going to war or fomenting an insurrection. Du Bois picks up on this when he exploits bellicose men like the enslaved insurgents Denmark Vesey, Gabriel Prosser, and Nat Turner as the standard-bearers of progressive black leadership. Dead-set against the black man as warrior, the black male as housekeeper also has the misfortune of also reattaching the ideal of black male leadership to the icon of the male house slave, whose intimacy with the white master was based in the slave's subservient housekeeping role mediated by the slave mistress. From Du Bois's perspective, the figuration of the housekeeping black man poses an unmanning threat to self-assertive black progress on par with the castrating violence of white lynchers.

Does it seem anachronistic to suggest that Du Bois outmuscles Washington by implying that he is a sissy, in the same way a bully might use the word today to belittle a schoolmate on the playground? Let's return to the word's etymology to sharpen this inquiry. According to the *Oxford English Dictionary*, the epithet "sissy" was already in popular usage by 1887, when the *New Orleans Lantern* uses it to mean "an effeminate person, a coward" in the phrase "Look and walk too much like sissies to do much fightin'."[42] It is not surprising that the label *sissy* is used to make a charge of cowardice on the battlefield, whether in actual warfare or a bar skirmish between two men. The sissy is the contrary of the brave fighter. In 1889 William Dean Howells was already using the adjective "sissyish," and the *Oxford English Dictionary* cites a sentence from 1905 where the more aggressive adjective "sissified" is used but in quotation marks, no doubt to acknowledge it as a neologism. Given Du Bois's claim in his 1968 *Autobiography* that he had "no conception of homosexuality" in 1927, it could be argued that he may have had no conception of sissiness in 1903 when he attacked Washington.[43] The larger and more difficult question is to what extent, if at all, the sissy epithet conjured incipient homosexuality at the turn of the twentieth century, as it certainly does today. Whether Du Bois was familiar with the word or not, whether it connoted homosexual deviance or not, he certainly understood the insult of gender impropriety coded by its usage, and he knew how to enforce the impact of the label's meaning in a more high-minded—one almost wants to say high-handed—manner without slinging the dirty epithet itself at Washington. By recognizing how the "sycophant" (a more established gender epithet in 1903) is a political synonym for "sissy" (a newer epithet), we can understand the gender imputation loaded in Du Bois's charge, and by highlighting the gender embarrassment entailed in Washington's fashioning of a housekeeper demeanor and practice, we can grasp how the turn-of-the-century manhood debate hinges not only on what kind of male leadership is fitting for the race but also on what kind of labor is fitting for leading black men.

If Jacqueline Jones's premise that male captives "actively scorned women's work" and "that slaveholders devised forms of public humiliation that capitalized on men's attempts to avoid these tasks" is in the least bit true, then we could say that, in addition to the familiar threat of black male emasculation through castration, the threat of being sissified through effeminate labor haunts black male subjectivity from the time of enslavement.[44] I have already explained why it is theoretically instructive to hold at bay the collapsing of "sissiness" into homosexuality. Is there also theoretical knowledge to be gained from making a distinction between emasculation as the negating deprivation of male privates to deny masculine privilege and sissification as the denigrating reassignment of males so that they are too intimately attached to women in their presumed anatomy, affect, or labor? While Howells assumes that he is praising Dunbar by saying that the poet had lifted the race's range from mere appetite to somewhere above emotionality, such judgment of a white male poet would hardly be considered praise at all; in fact, it would seem a backhanded insult. Although not as obviously violent, the routine attachment of black men to women's social status represents a violating limit on how high even men of Washington's influence can rise in the gender-determined political and economic spheres. Such a distinction is certainly worth exploring insofar as it foregrounds the ways in which gender disidentification is historically multifariously shaped by a multifaceted political-economic infrastructure (whether slavery, or Jim Crow, or pre–civil rights movement desegregation), which in turn helps to shape an infrastructure of feeling, both as individuated self-expressiveness and as collective cultural expression, like that of autobiography.[45]

Washington, having been a slave himself until the age of nine, would have had firsthand knowledge of this form of male gender humiliation through coerced contact with feminine labor. In *Up from Slavery*, Washington is careful to delineate between masculine and feminine work in lamenting the lethargic effect of slavery on the master's children. "My old master had many boys and girls," he writes, "but not one, so far as I know, ever mastered a single trade or special line of productive industry. The girls were not taught to cook, sew, or to take care of the house. All this was left to the slaves."[46] Washington's mother, according to Louis Harlan, "spent much of her day cooking not only for the master's large family but for the slaves." We can surmise that little Booker would have lightened the burden of his mother's labor by fetching, peeling, stirring, sweeping, or other such chores accessible to a child of six or seven. "As soon as he had grown to sufficient size," Harlan notes, "Booker had the task at mealtimes in the master's house of fanning flies from the table."[47] It is important to remember that the sons of house slaves were often put to use as supplementary domestic labor in the master's house, as was the case with little Booker. Slave boys to the age of puberty were often required to wear dresses indistinguishable from those worn by slave girls, such that by a certain age, the boys' genitalia might be exposed even while they stood to serve at the master's table, as if to accentuate the boy's gender misplacement as consonant with a native, natural, ordained racial order.[48]

There is a crucial difference between helping one's mother in one's own household and being put out to domestic service in another's house or in a public institution—as in Washington's case when he was enslaved or in George Washington Carver's case when he became a launderer under northern Jim Crow. It is the *public* regimen of black male's intimacy with conventionally feminine labor that operates to sissify black men under the slave and Jim Crow regimes. What Sara Ahmed observes about shame, an emotion closely linked with embarrassment, might also be said about the embarrassment that derives from this kind of racial sissification: "The bind of shame is that it is intensified by being seen by others *as* shame." Ahmed then makes out another instructive point about the material effect of shaming: "The very physicality of shame—how it works on and through bodies—means that shame also involves the de-forming and re-forming of bodily and social spaces, as bodies 'turn away' from the others who witness the shame."[49] What happens when this sort of exposure of a person to gender shame does not allow turning away? Does the pubescent slave-boy feel shame in having his privates exposed as he fans his masters at the supper table? Or is the practice of this sort of sissifying servitude for the boy so systematically ingrained that he does not fully recognize the embarrassment intended by the masters' demand? What Jacqueline Jones documents, and Washington's own testimony above indicates, is the extent to which enslaved men did, in fact, register gender trouble in being compelled to perform the menial work usually assigned to women in U.S. society. We can learn a lot about the gender politics of Bookerite accommodationism by analyzing how Washington, as a leader of the race, and Du Bois, as his staunchest critic, handled this gendered sense of racial embarrassment related to the sissification of black men through their compulsory public performance of menial, subservient labor.

The menial place of black men in the Jim Crow economy is intended to embarrass their manhood in the originary sense of *impeding any passage* toward heteronormative privilege and power, but this menial status also has the just-as-important secondary effect of the most familiar meaning of "embarrass": to cause a feeling of self-conscious fluster, stuttering confusion, in this particular case as a disconcerting condition of gender disorientation, like that expressed by Du Bois in articulating the historical wastage of black manhood. The affect of embarrassment and self-embarrassment is a crucial resource for a theoretical understanding of both sissification and racial ideology, for this infrastructure of feeling, so often associated with gender and sexual impropriety, can help to prevent what typically happens when racial and sexual identities are theorized: the reduction to a binary of emasculation versus hypermasculinity where black male identity is involved, or to a binary of shame and affirmative confession where homosexuality is concerned, or to a binary of denial and panic where sissiphobia and homophobia are at stake.

Despite Washington's insistence that he learned his obsessive habit of housekeeping from white Yankee matrons, it is more probable that he inherited his obsessive-compulsive cleanliness at his slave mother's apron strings, or under the tutelage of one of the adult male or female domestics in the master's household. By attributing his housekeeping compulsion to capable, chaste white women's tutelage instead of the "school of slavery" itself, Washington is able to plot black men's menial performance as a progressive rite of manhood rather than as a sissifying encumbrance to it.[50] The larger point here, though, is that Washington's 1901 self-narration as a meticulous housekeeper would not necessarily classify him as a sissy in the eyes of his 1901 *white* readers. For a young white male, such housekeeping tasks would indeed signify and embody an embarrassing male person out of its proper gender place, as we shall see in the case of Samuel Chapman Armstrong when he assigns such domestic tasks to the Negro soldiers under his charge during the Civil War. For a black male of any age, to the contrary, such domestic labor constitutes exactly his proper place under slavery and, as *Up from Slavery* testifies and confirms, under white supremacist Jim Crow rule.

As Sterling D. Spero and Abram L. Harris observe about Jim Crow labor practices, even when black and white men are engaged in similar or the same industrial labor, a distinction is maintained in order to keep black laborers subordinate to white ones, usually as "helpers."[51] The distinction between "skilled" and "unskilled" aids and abets the idea that black men's labor, like women's labor, is supplementary to white men's and thus of lower value. In addition to the economic advantage this gives to industrialists, it also reaffirms the justification for excluding black men from white men's masculine rights and rites. When we add to this that black men under Jim Crow are increasingly excluded from the craft unions, whose jobs help to define the muscularity of working-class white men, black male labor becomes defined as the negation of conventionally masculine labor as well as being defined proactively as closer to supplementary feminine labor.

Washington's humble self-discipline of sweeping and dusting communicated to his contemporary readers, black and white, that so-called menial labor must serve as the foundation for black "self-help" uplift, and because "menial" derives from a French word meaning "pertaining to a household," "belonging to a retinue or train of servants," "servile, low, mean," it is a perfectly fitting index of how sissification operates within the economic machinery of American racial and class politics.[52] In other words, when Du Bois punks Washington as "sapping the manhood of the race," he is declaring intellectual warfare on the long-standing assumption that black boys and men are naturally suited to do the menial work usually assigned to working-class women. If slavery served as a beneficial school for both men and women, as Washington asserts, then it stands to reason that black men's subordination to the status of women's labor in this process was a crucial part of this civilizing and Christianizing education. Perhaps sissification also puts a different spin on the argument between Washington and Du Bois over the role of industrial versus liberal education, which we usually understand solely as a conflict over the role of manual versus intellectual labor. This dichotomy between manual and intellectual tends to suppress the disruptive presence of the *menial*, as both Du Bois's and Washington's camps insist when they speak of a "belief in the dignity of labor," as Du Bois's seventh principle of the Niagara Movement manifesto phrases it.[53] More fundamentally and less analyzed, the repression of the menial as *the* source of contention founders on a gender dispute about the kind of labor appropriate for the training up of black *male* leaders. Du Bois does not doubt that domestic labor—that is, *menial* labor—is appropriate for the mass of black men and women, at least at the race's current stage of economic development. Such labor is not in and of itself undignified, as Washington repeats obsessively in *Up from Slavery* in describing his efforts to enforce his own compulsive housekeeping habits on his Tuskegee students. By sissifying Washington's identity, however, Du Bois implies that domestic service must be seen as a form of gender misplacement for those men responsible for husbanding the race. In his 1940 memoir, *Dusk of Dawn*, Du Bois addresses this issue as a personal dilemma that beset him and his family when he was about to complete high school. "The work open to colored folk was limited," he writes. "There was day labor; there was farming; there was house-service, particularly in hotels; but for a young, educated and ambitious colored man, what were the possibilities?"[54] Day labor, farming, and house service constituted the three categories of manual labor—"unskilled" industrial, agricultural, and domestic service—engaged in by the vast majority of African Americans in the late nineteenth century, regardless of gender. The limited options available to the gender-undifferentiated mass of "colored folk" take on a greater urgency when the job candidate is a young, formally educated colored man coming into his manhood near the Jim Crow nadir.

We have to remember how incredibly unusual it was for a colored youth, even one as extraordinary as Du Bois, to have *never* spent some time in some form of menial service. Actually, very briefly after graduating from Fisk, Du Bois takes a job that easily could be classified as menial and domestic. Notice how Du Bois is quick to distinguish his own role from that of the other young male Fisk graduates:

> After graduation, the members of the Fisk Glee Club went to Lake Minnetonka, a resort in Minnesota, for the summer of 1888, with the idea of working in the dining room and giving concerts. I was to act as their business manager. During college I had developed rather as the executive and planner, the natural secretary of affairs rather than ornamental president and chairman. The only difficulty about the Minnesota excursion was that

> I had never worked in a hotel in my life; I could not wait on table therefore became one of the bus boys. It was so unusual a pageant to watch the dining room that I made no tips and for a long time had difficulty in getting enough to eat, not realizing that in that day servants in great hotels were not systematically fed but foraged for food in devious ways. I saw the Americans, rich and near-rich, at play; it was not inspiring. The servility necessary for the successful waiter I could not or would not learn.[55]

By disidentifying with domestic service both in raising his status to "business manager" and in portraying himself as totally unsuitable to the deviousness and subservience—in other words, sycophancy—required of being a busboy, Du Bois communicates that such labor is beneath him. Black male identity in the early twentieth century was cemented to domestic service, whether in public institutions like the Pullman railcar, the street-corner shoeshine, the hotel dining room, the elevator operator, or the private household. What would normally seem to be an embarrassment, the demotion from waiter to "bus *boy*" (italics added), turns out for Du Bois to be exculpatory, for he succeeds at being so inept at this menial labor that he cannot survive doing it. I suspect that "*would* not learn" is a more accurate turn of phrase than "*could* not learn"—and Du Bois's waffling between the two only amplifies his willfulness versus his ineptness. Despite Du Bois's extraordinary intention of foiling the economic infrastructure of black male Jim Crow identity by refusing and repudiating effeminate domestic service, he cannot, in the end, protect himself from being incorporated into this identity. When he is at Harvard, he makes a point of escorting the prettiest colored girls to the university's official social events, where he is put back in his proper gender place among the menials by a stray white lady: "Naturally we attracted attention and sometimes the shadow of insult as when in one case a lady seemed determined to mistake me for a waiter."[56] This "shadow of insult" stings deep enough for Du Bois to remember and single it out half a century later in composing his memoir. Despite Du Bois's status as a Harvard student and his often-noted air of arrogance, his deportment as a young man ready to conquer the world seems illegible to the random white lady—or, more likely, she *deliberately* mistakes him for the wait staff to put him back in his racial place through an insult that operates through gender embarrassment.

We should not fail to make the palpable connection between the image of menial male domestic labor and sycophancy. Part of what Du Bois experiences as humiliating about the insult at Harvard social events concerns the idea that to be a menial is to be a lickspittle ("the servility necessary for the successful waiter")—as someone who must curry favor subserviently as an Uncle Tom from the whites whom he is serving. When Du Bois aims his "shadow of insult" at Washington, then, the self-portrait of dignified manly labor that Washington promotes in the housekeeping entrance exam devolves into the now-familiar servile, unmanly, and cowardly practice that we associate embarrassingly with the Great Accommodator. Even if Washington could have anticipated Du Bois's sissifying attack, there is not much he could have done to forestall it. The historical, political, and economic circumstances of Jim Crow that Washington hoped to manipulate for the benefit of his race dictated that he image and plot his coming of age through male menial service.

In an attempt to advance beyond Du Bois's decidedly embarrassing understanding of the sissy resonance in Washington's sweeping passage, Houston Baker Jr. uses Mary Douglas and queer theory to argue that Washington's compulsive sweeping "secures access to the Yankee woman's purity" without exposing him to the danger of lynching.[57] According to this interpretation, Washington is ironically both a victim of a racially enforced neurotic impulse beyond his psychic control and simultaneously a sly operator capable of psychologically manipulating superior whites toward his own erotic advantage. Baker's reading renders the Wizard of Tuskegee, whether tragic victim or sexual master, implicitly heroic and, as such, conventionally masculine in his heteronormative drive to possess the untouchable white lady without polluting her with a beastly blackness. This is chivalry through the back door of the white man's house. While appearing to have moved beyond Du Bois's sissifying attack, Baker actually exculpates Washington's gender embarrassment by ironically reinforcing the black leader's heteronormativity. What would most scandalize Washington's readers is not that he might be an effeminate, cowardly sissy or even that he might be a homosexual (only God knows what emasculation will do to a black man's gender identity) but instead that his humble menial labor might cloak a seduction of chaste white womanhood. Of course, Washington's white readers would be eager to accept the idea that even the humblest black servant conceals within himself a rapist of white womanhood. However, this premise is exactly what Washington's self-narration is intended to contravene. Washington takes great pains to desex his narrative—that is, to suppress any hint that there might be any implication of sexual conduct at all—not because he is secretly horny for Yankee white women's flesh (and Baker rests some of his argument on the notion that, contrary to stereotype, the Yankee schoolmarms were young, vivacious, and very pretty indeed). Instead, as I have argued elsewhere, the act of desexing a narrative under Jim Crow is motivated by a desire to refocus the public's attention on the appropriate *political* and *economic* objects and ambitions of racial uplift at a time when white supremacy insisted on scandalizing black men's sexuality by always reducing it to an uncontrollable savage appetite for chaste white ladies.[58] To reduce Washington's sweeping mania to an erotic performance of a racial taboo risks abnegating what is most substantive about his self-narration: the political, ideological, and propagandistic negotiation of Jim Crow disenfranchisement. In the eagerness to flip the script to an erotic interest, we tend to repress the overriding political and economic agenda anchoring the Wizard's sissy impersonation. More to the point for our purposes here, to view Washington's cleaning compulsion as an interracial erotic subtext is to repress again the nonerotic—that is, the *nonnormative gender*— connotation of a sissified affiliation so much at stake in Washington's autobiography, and especially in its reception, then and now.[59]

I think the greater historical and cultural import of Washington's apparent self-sissification lies in how he exploits autobiography to transliterate the lowliness of domestic menial labor into high-minded intellectual discourse. It is easy to miss this ingenious and ingenuous legerdemain. As with the case of his building a classical campus for higher education at Tuskegee while appearing merely to accede to a supplementary industrial education for its students, so he deploys the self-humbling protocols of nineteenth-century autobiography instead to position himself as a legitimate interlocutor in the highest intellectual debates of his time. Picturing himself deep in the mud to help make bricks to build the campus, Washington at the same time raises himself to the status of an international public intellectual, notwithstanding his diatribes against book-learning. The ideas he proffers—many borrowed from Samuel Chapman Armstrong and others—become distinctively his own. The Tuskegee model of industrial education becomes so strongly identified as Washington's original ideas that as these ideas travel abroad, Tuskegee becomes a mecca for those in Asia, Africa, and Central and South America. Both Claude McKay and Marcus Garvey—two important shapers of the Harlem Renaissance—migrate to the United States from Jamaica, like thousands of nameless others—to study Tuskegee's successes and to matriculate at the internationally famed institution. Ironically, from his self-portrait as a sissy housekeeper who justifies the menial labor of African Americans as the basis for their education, Washington steals his intellectual chops as America's leading black educator of his time.

The Fastidious Black Body as Fetish

Washington has to find ways of displaying and disseminating his own habits in words, images, and body gestures that can be appreciated by his "superiors" and easily emulated by his students, disciples, and political dependents. Obsessive cleanliness reminds him that he can be a Negro, the descendant of "slaves" and formerly enslaved himself, without being doomed to the captive condition that has prevented him from properly owning and caring for his own body. Although a punctilious obsession with cleanliness is sometimes affiliated with a sissy sensorium—a man not willing to get his hands dirty—Washington negotiates this fetish for cleanliness so that it communicates both a sign of his racial humbleness and a promise of upward social mobility. While a fear of dirty labor might indicate a sissy demeanor, ironically those men who can avoid such labor in this socioeconomic system (workers later to be dubbed "white" collar as opposed to "blue") are more highly ranked. Indeed, part of what determines the class status of the white men who rule is that they have the means to hire others to do such work for them, whether on their estates or in their factories. In her study *Imperial Leather*, Anne McClintock identifies exactly how a fetish, marking what she calls "a crisis in social meaning," can function in a sociopolitical register beyond Freud's focus on the individuated psyche.[60] Though in a surface sense Washington's fetish object is the smudge of his own body and the utensils and commodities that enable cleaning up (the toothbrush representing the most famous instance and the broom the crucial, most understudied instance), in a more profound sense Washington enacts a fetish ritual without a discrete fetish object. What he is obsessed with is not the token color of his own skin but, rather, pedagogical-propagandistic procedures for finding and showing ways to manage white people's oppressive obsession with skin/color. It is not the totemic power of the broom or toothbrush as objects in themselves that he "worships" (his notion of the "gospel of the toothbrush"), but instead the empowering social practices of hygiene, which can teach racial pride and economic parity to a people negatively stigmatized as belonging to the dirt that defines their labor.[61] By Washington's time, home economics has been clearly articulated as the province of (white) middle-class women, whose professionalization as domestic managers of the household is subordinate to white men's proper political and economic rule in the public sphere.[62] For Washington, home economics serves as a self-conscious process of education appropriate to the male leader of a subordinated race, which, like white women, lacks economic and political authority in the public sphere. It is a haggling relation that he and other black Americans can manage, for it sparks the explosive potential within the impossible imputation connecting black skin to filth, transforming that imputation into evolutionary behavior.[63] While accepting the historical association of black skin with dirt and Negro status with abject (menial) labor in the black soil of the Black Belt, Washington seeks to turn this degradation against itself, just as he turns sycophantic ingratiation into "common" labor at the bottom "in every manly way."

Revising Freud's take on the role of soap as a civilizing agent, Peter Stallybrass and Allon White have pointed out how the value of cleanliness arises out of a need for the rising middle class to segregate itself from the degraded masses in response to the accelerated pace of industrial capitalism and urbanization occurring in nineteenth-century Britain. Those able to afford the aggressively marketed new commodities of manufactured cleaning agents like soap can make a claim for belonging to an upwardly mobile class. Being able to do work that does not get one dirty further separates the professionalizing middle class from increasing numbers of urban industrial workers, not far removed from the soil of agricultural labor.[64]

By the late nineteenth century the American middle class occupies an ambivalent status similar to its British counterpart. As Stuart M. Blumin has documented, the "elusive" American middle class forms its identity through a dualistic attitude toward manual labor, on the one hand celebrating the dignity of work in the Puritan tradition, on the other hand defining upward mobility as a movement away from manual labor and its accompanying grime. At the same time that the (white male) laborer represents genuine manliness, according to Blumin he is frequently characterized in a subhuman fashion: "Sun-darkened skin and dirty and tattered clothes, along with rough hands, mental sluggishness, and even an apelike or otherwise bestial character or carriage were fairly common elements in the depiction of manual workers at mid-century."[65] Blumin's study does not connect this dark, sluggish subhuman figure to the stereotype of African American men that dominates the nineteenth century.[66] It is exactly the image of recently emancipated men that Washington aims to controvert through lessons in bodily hygiene, housecleaning, and the wise management of money and material goods—all characteristics of good housekeeping. "Good" here signifies for Washington not merely the proper conduct of a housekeeper but also self-evident proof of pure moral character. Quite literally, Washington wants to turn the white man's notion of "the good Negro" into a political-economic practice of racial self-help—the dignity of menial labor transformed into the resourcefulness of uplifting entrepreneurship. To maneuver the good Negro from menial subservience to running factories "in every manly way," Washington must pivot this transformation through the image of the too-good sissy-boy, figured autobiographically as himself at the outset of his college matriculation.

Daniel T. Rodgers also points to the contradiction between the work ethic and the injunction "to work one's way as quickly as possible out of manual toil," but further suggests that behind the contempt for industrializing manual labor is another evasion: "Behind all the other terms for the worker who labored at the will and for the profit of another was the oldest, bluntest, and most troubling word of all: 'slave.'" Seeing both slaveholders and the enslaved as morally disfigured by a system that seems to encourage idleness as well as degraded drudgery, many northerners of the nineteenth and early twentieth centuries attempt to depict the slave economy as a "nightmarish inversion of northern work values." "It was necessary to insist," Rodgers writes, "all the more adamantly that the North was different, that it was a land where labor was not only respected but genuinely free."[67] The black mass represents the indignity of labor both as a slave caste, burdened with the drudgery of unfree labor and immobile status, and as a racial group untutored in the Yankee work ethic and thus prone as much to idle lethargy as to unprofitable, static drudgery. Blacks and workers at leisure are represented as naturally lazy, as opposed to the increasing emphasis on white middle-class men so busy with work that they fully deserve leisure time to prevent work illnesses like neurasthenia.[68]

The right to the spoils of capitalist industry is based on a racial ideology of thrifty Yankee know-how and individualism, an ideology also implicit, we shall see, in the conception of America's colonial mission.[69] Because the races are naturally unequal, those unfortunates born into an inferior race would have to enact even greater self-discipline to rise above that race's more polluted condition—hence the obsessive nature of Washington's hygienic fetish ritual. This native pollution of the black body is further intensified in the notion of its different smell—a theory of racial difference that can be traced at least as far back as Thomas Jefferson's 1785 *Notes on the State of Virginia*.[70] The sense of smell is especially revealing insofar as it exposes the ways in which an ethos of gender conduct hinges on the body as a legible vector of judgment. The vector of smell enables us to see the limits on conduct as a racially enabling resource of gender fluidity. As Washington strongly believes, a ritual habit of hygiene can change one's perception of oneself and thus others' perception. The challenge derives from the fact that any person immersed in the kinds of menial labor that Washington extolls—including the labor of cleaning others' domestic spaces—makes it impossible to maintain a pristine body. Rather than a ladder that enables uplift, the practice of committing to dirty labor followed by a rigorous hygiene of cleaning up will instead become a Sisyphean trap. An overly fastidious bodily practice is also implicated in gender suspicion insofar as men who are too attentive to their bodies can be perceived as sissies, such as those who smell too sweet, like the image of perfumed pansies scattered in turn-of-the-century literature. The gender jeopardy of an overly fastidious man is further complicated by the way in which an obsession with hygiene may do little to overcome the racial prejudice that equates blackness with an innate—and thus indelible—stink.

Sometimes racial smell is seen as scientific fact, as is the case with the influential white Chicago sociologist Robert E. Park, Washington's "ghostwriter" beginning in 1905. Following Jefferson a hundred years earlier, Park writes: "At any rate, it seems to be a fact that races and individuals have each a distinctive smell, and this odor becomes, in certain cases, the sensuous basis for racial antipathies."[71] The peculiar stench of black bodies remains both proof and rationale at the most visceral level in the South for the natural segregation of the races, and, as referenced in the study that Charles S. Johnson conducted for the Chicago Commission on Race Relations following the 1919 Chicago race riots, it becomes one of the explanations for the tensions between black migrants and white residents in the urban North.[72] Washington's emphasis on meticulous washing of the black body as the basis for modern uplift, therefore, cannot be separated from the way he and others understand racial disadvantage to operate through these gut-level senses of smell and touch, and in turn these senses cannot be separated from a gender dynamic in which men of the upper classes are protected from the stench of manual labor. Leading white men have their wives, and their wives have their maids, to ensure their cleanliness even beyond the fact that white patriarchs are not required to labor in the fields, mills, mines, and factories that they own and oversee.

Washington has often been read as a self-made black man who mimics and remolds the famous robber barons of the period.[73] I do not so much want to question this characterization as to highlight the kinds of racial, sexual, and gender irregularities that result from Washington's impersonation or "mimicry" of the fabled great (white) man. He moves along an axis from emulation of saintly white Yankee matrons to the emulation of his white male mentor, Samuel Chapman Armstrong, through the triangulated mediation of marriage to middle-class mulatta women of virtually unimpeachable chastity. What Washington fashions is not exactly "feminization," which implies some degree of social coercion, as this has been defined in the scholarship, but *effeminization*, whereby he seems voluntarily to embrace black men's coerced affiliation with women's subordinate status.[74] As we shall see, powerful white men like Samuel Chapman Armstrong, while enacting a rhetoric of "feminization," end up exerting their power over black people, not to mention over others, in conventionally "masculine" ways. While the threat of feminization, especially if it is prolonged or gains priority over a man's development, breeds a fear of emasculation in a man like Armstrong, it also feeds his hunger for an imperialist vocation coded both as manly frontier adventure and as interested patronizing service to a less fortunate race. While Washington "voluntarily" occupies a housekeeping role, and while his fastidious cleaning up of the race still effectuates a distinctively masculine grab for dominance as a racial patriarch, he does not depict himself as developing beyond this housekeeping status to claim an unqualified right to the masculine norm occupied by white supremacy. As can be seen in epigraphs to this chapter, Washington's stepfather and Du Bois both distance themselves from housekeeping even though the line separating men's labor from women's was very much deliberately blurred for African Americans during slavery and after.[75] In aligning his character and conduct with women's menial domesticity that others like his own stepfather and his rival, Du Bois, eschew, Washington puts himself at risk of being charged with unmanning the race while ironically assuming housefatherly leadership of it.

The Wizard's Three Wives

By examining Washington's presentation of his three wives, we can further explore how he manipulates an impossible racial-sexual dilemma into an unprecedented opportunity through sissified conduct. As Tera Hunter has shown, one of the stigmas of the slave past concerns the irregular relationship of the former slaves to marriage—a stigma so powerful that many emancipated couples insisted on undergoing the marriage ceremony again even if they had already done so as slaves.[76] Stigmas of bastardy, bigamy, adultery, and fornication still cling to African Americans in the post-Reconstruction era, despite their increased participation in the legal and religious institution of marriage. In order to assert his worthiness to become the leading black patron, Washington has to overcome this stigma. He does so by overstressing his adherence to routine codes of sexual respectability. He must do so, however, without in any way displaying the modes of sexual aggression, ownership, and control through which nineteenth-century white husbands are supposed to assume their conjugal rights as masters of the household and the nation.[77]

One of the most accessible, deeply coded, and powerful plots available to late Victorian narrative is the conjugal story, tracing first sighting, wooing, courtship, wedding, married life, childbearing, and familial loss of a male protagonist.[78] The assumptions deeply embedded in this plot ritually rehearse and reaffirm the founding values upholding middle-class, heterosexual codes of conduct, and yet in repeating the plot, each narrative also exposes the myriad perils that continuously disturb and occasionally disrupt these normative codes. For instance, in the biography of Washington's mentor, *Samuel Chapman Armstrong: A Biographical Study* (1904), we find a similar use of the conjugal plot but aimed at consolidating the legacy of a great white man. Written by Armstrong's daughter, Edith Armstrong Talbot, according to her understanding of how he wanted his life portrayed, the biography limits attention to the great man's first wife to two spare paragraphs:

> The letters to his mother grew briefer and less frequent from this time, the beginning of his active work at Hampton; but letters to a new correspondent give for a time in equal detail his thoughts and hopes for his work. The recipient of these confidences was Miss Emma Dean Walker, of Stockbridge, Massachusetts, to whom he was married in October, 1869. Hereafter for their married life of nine years the deepest expressions of thought and feeling are to be found in his letters to her.
>
> Emma Walker was a young girl of rare charm of person and character, and brought to her new home at Hampton a spirit of devotion to her

husband's ideals which was of inestimable delight to him. A frail physique prevented active service on her part, and they were constantly separated, both by the needs of the Hampton school for money and by her own wanderings in search of health.[79]

Emma Walker signals Armstrong's coming into his own by representing his separation from the mother and by mirroring his all-consuming commitment to Hampton, a commitment that prevents his attention both to mother and later to wife. The wife's absolute devotion (and implicit sacrifice of her will, ego, and health) to his cause confirms his own life of heroic sacrifice. This pivotal moment is prepared for in the biography through Talbot's construction of Armstrong as both a homesick boy, in need of a good woman's caretaking, and a man of the world, full of innocent, hot-blooded interest in the fair sex. His attention to Emma Walker fixes his desire so that it shall not go astray, and simultaneously it fixes his ambition so that it accrues a proper sphere in which to function. Although we may want to say in loose terms that Armstrong has been "feminized" by Walker, it might be more helpful to suggest that his domestication makes more palpable, though no less forceful, the sway of his desire and ambition in the interest of a larger colonizing project.

Similarly, Washington's single mention of his first wife, Fannie N. Smith, over two paragraphs exploits the conjugal plot to establish the husbandly cleanliness of his conduct and character while at the same time virtually absenting Fannie from the narrative, her role displaced by Washington's intimate subservience to white Yankee schoolmarms. "From the first, my wife earnestly devoted her thoughts and time to the work of the school," he writes, "and was completely one with me in every interest and ambition."[80] Like Armstrong's dutiful biographer, Washington is able to enhance the institutional and racial design of his provident rise to fame by totally subordinating his wife's intention, ability, influence, and symbolic significance to his own. While Washington's narrative does emulate how great white men deploy the conjugal plot, the pattern of his social, moral, political, and bodily identification also swerves in a contrary direction, toward the subordinate "feminine" spaces of his mulatta wives and white female teachers. Claudia Tate picks up on Washington's unusual strategy in speaking of his 1895 Atlanta Exposition Address: "By reconfiguring what is essentially political power as domestic labor, thereby invoking the cultural subordination of woman's sphere, domestic tropes mask political assertiveness in the semblance of conciliation. As a consequence the Address switches discursive codes; it feminizes the rhetoric of political power, transforming politics of state into a female sign of domestic labor—washing laundry and household scrubbing."[81] As he must condition the race's political ambitions through "a female sign of domestic labor," so Washington could not have afforded to showcase the kinds of innocent premarital flirtations that serve as seasoning for Armstrong's filial separation and marital preparation in Talbot's biography. Accordingly, Washington could not have afforded to remain a single man like George Washington Carver even if he had so desired. The race's "stain of bastardy"—to borrow from Du Bois—can be cleaned away only through a race leader who is matrimonially bound. Despite such compensatory conduct, however, Washington is also bound to occupy the liminal position of a too-good Negro whose faithfulness and obedience to, and adoration of, great white fathers sissifies his chastity even as it rectifies the sexual irregularities of his slave inheritance. It is easy to forget that Washington took great risks as the black head of a black college staffed with black faculty at a time when other black higher-education institutions were supervised and staffed by whites. Given that Armstrong had given Washington his blessing as head of Tuskegee, the white male ruling elite's trust in the Wizard was really a reflection of their trust in Armstrong.

In other words, Washington must tread very cautiously in his choice of a spouse if he is to protect the gender balancing act whereby his conduct can be read simultaneously as appropriately subservient by white male rulers and as good husbanding by other African Americans. That Washington is Fannie's teacher and clearly an influence in her attending Hampton might suggest his preparing her as a suitable wife for a man who already at this young age desires a career, unique and yet imitable, in racial husbandry. Washington claims to have meditated constantly on the avenues to success from earliest youth: "I used to try to picture in my imagination the feelings and ambitions of a white boy with absolutely no limit placed upon his aspirations and activities. I used to envy the white boy who had no obstacles placed in the way of his becoming a Congressman, Governor, Bishop, or President by reason of the accident of his birth or race. I used to picture the way that I would act under such circumstances; how I would begin at the bottom and keep rising until I reached the highest round of success."[82] This passage is particularly telling given that Armstrong's daughter points out how he had contemplated running for Congress upon marriage.[83] All the venues of masculine empowerment and entitlement are open to a man like Armstrong. "With few exceptions, the Negro youth must work harder and must perform his tasks even better than a white youth in order to secure recognition," Washington writes.[84] And this means that the slightest miscalculation, even in a decision so personal and intimate as whom to fall in love with, can become the most bungling misstep in the ascent to the highest success. One wonders if he fears a miscalculation in his courtship of Fannie. Harlan discusses the "misunderstanding" that results from Washington's attempt to get his brother, John, and Fannie through Hampton on scholarship: "General Armstrong was willing to take his prize graduate's strongest students on scholarship, but he seemingly harbored a doubt that Booker Washington's brother and sweetheart qualified on their merits."[85] Washington's understanding of merit stresses *visible* signs of worthiness, not intangible, inner attributes.[86] Merit can be hidden "under" the "colour of skin," but must be rewarded when revealed in the material form of success. As K. Ian Grandison has illustrated by analyzing the material landscape of the Tuskegee campus, the Wizard's strategy is based on the fact that visible black success can breed envy and retaliatory violence in white Americans as easily as it can foster goodwill and patronage.[87] Nonetheless, Washington needs to insist in his propaganda that visible signs of black success ameliorate white prejudice in order to establish a framework for fostering such behavior in whites, who lack the intrinsic character of fairness. Fannie's "merit," not as an intrinsic objective in itself but as a visible object of Washington's affection and stabilization, comes into question by what is *not* said about her in *Up from Slavery*. Harlan quotes a letter Washington writes to Hampton friends upon her death, a letter both more touching and more abnegating of his wife's presence than his cryptic dismissal in the autobiography: "'Perhaps the way in which Fanny was able to impress her life upon others most was in her extreme neatness in her housekeeping and general work.... Her heart was set on making her home an object lesson for those about her.'"[88] As Fannie's hygienic virtues seem to mirror those he claims for himself, the minimalist reduction of Fanny's memory to her housekeeping and "general work" befits Washington's propaganda about his own humble contributions as a race leader. Of course, the analogy breaks down as quickly as it is spoken, for Fanny's housekeeping leaves behind no institutional apparatus, no disciples, no political and ideological progeny, no lasting historical impression, no canonical autobiography, no historically preserved buildings, no statuary monuments, no secondary schools named in her honor. Her legacy is like the inscription of her name recorded in the list of Tuskegee officers and teachers upon her marriage, not as a "lady-" or vice principal, teacher, staff member, or even wife, but simply as "Housekeeper."[89]

In the dominant gender ideology of the time, a wife's chastity and good housekeeping are supposed to reflect her husband's competence as worldly provider and protector of the household. The inequality implicit in this act of reflection dictates a wifely conduct that distinguishes her mode of feminine self-sacrifice from a great man's heroic conduct in the world. Washington's portrayal of his second wife, Olivia Davidson, poses a more equal relationship. He clearly marks her as a heroic race patroness, one whose acts of self-sacrifice resemble his own motives and aims, though stemming significantly from a different socio-geographic background.[90] As a race patroness, Davidson is clearly modeled on the Yankee missionary schoolmarms who flood the South in the 1860s and '70s, the ones celebrated in Du Bois's *Souls of Black Folk* and *Black Reconstruction* as the true valiant soldiers of emancipation. Davidson's commitment to the South and unity of purpose with Washington are confirmed by her decision to enter Hampton instead of an elite, classical black college like Fisk or a northern women's college. "Miss Davidson's experience in the South showed her that the people needed something more than book-learning," Washington writes. "She heard of the Hampton system of education, and decided that this was what she wanted in order to prepare herself for better work in the South."[91] Unlike Fanny, who has to be tutored in a one-room school and sneaked through the back door of Hampton through Washington's special pleading, Davidson could have attended any of the best academic institutions admitting women with the blessing (and money) of the First Lady of the United States. Even her choice to enter Hampton is a magnificent sacrifice committing her to an ethos of race integrity. One reason Washington feels compelled to give Davidson a greater presence in the autobiography pivots on her resemblance to these Yankee patronesses, and thus her conduct also emphasizes his own resemblance to these white ladies.

Davidson's resemblance is best captured in Washington's emphasis on her skin color: "Some one suggested to Miss Davidson that, since she was so very light in colour, she might find it more comfortable not to be known as a coloured woman in this school in Massachusetts."[92] By refusing to pass into whiteness, Davidson establishes her credentials even beyond the white female missionaries. Authenticity, like purity, installs its own ideological limits and narrative constraints. Davidson's resemblance to the Yankee missionary proves so crucial to Washington that he, intentionally or accidentally, provides her an erroneous background. According to Harlan, she is born a captive in Virginia, not free in Ohio, as Washington asserts. When Washington states that she attends the "public" schools of Ohio, he seems to imply that she is educated in integrated schools. Harlan indicates that she attends "an excellent private black school" established through "black self-help and a small grant from a white philanthropist." In polishing her halo, Washington omits what must have been the most terrifying experience of her life in Mississippi, where her brother and sister are killed by the Ku Klux Klan (KKK), causing her to leave Mississippi for Memphis.[93] A woman who has braved—and lost family to—the assault of white men in their racial rage looks too much like a woman who might harbor her own racial bitterness. By shaping Davidson to resemble closely the refined self-restraint of Yankee matrons while retaining her racial identity, Washington also protects *his* identity as a nonaggressive, pacified racial husband, his obvious drive toward black self-empowerment not motivated by a need to protect black womanhood out of a sense of rightful self-possession or to assault white womanhood out of racial-sexual retaliation.

Washington must identify with his vice principal and her role in a way unthinkable for Armstrong. More to the point, Davidson is a mirror reflection of

Washington's "effeminate" chastity as a self-sacrificing race matron. Washington resembles the Yankee schoolmarms through her, but Davidson also resembles him through them. We can see his cross-gender identification with Davidson clearly in the insistent "we" that characterizes the roles that both take. Like her, he attends to the nicest details of the grooming and housekeeping habits of Tuskegee's teachers and students. Like him, she travels up and down the country to raise funds from white patrons.

Presentation of his third marriage follows the same pattern, as his third wife, Margaret Murray, synthesizes the first two wives. Like Davidson, she is appointed Lady Principal before their marriage. Like Fannie, the third "Mrs. Washington [is] completely one with me in the work directly connected with the school, relieving me of many burdens and perplexities."[94] In introducing his third wife, Washington also takes several paragraphs to introduce his children, each one a living example of his own social practice of race uplift. It is the only place in the text where Washington alludes to any tension between racial husbandry and domestic husbandry, a tension that Du Bois will turn into a powerful indictment of the hypocrisy of the whole racial system: "The thing in my life which brings me the keenest regret is that my work in connection with public affairs keeps me for so much of the time away from my family, where, of all places in the world, I delight to be. I always envy the individual whose life-work is so laid that he can spend his evenings at home."[95] If Washington can appreciate the absences of domesticity in a far more intense way because such absences are more greatly dictated by his racial situation, it must also be said that he can appreciate the ways in which the grand epic of institution-building and racial patronage depends on the lowly domestic tasks of bodily grooming, housecleaning, and homemaking, tasks normally relegated to lower-class female immigrants and African American women even by the Yankee patronesses he celebrates as the guardians of cleanliness.

Washington as Yankee Schoolmarm

Beyond the strategic import of minimizing the uppityness of black aspiration toward education in an era of white southern reaction, Washington seems to fetishize the scrubbed black body as the sole basis on which all the higher rungs of civilization can be mastered, as we see with his description of his responsibilities at his first teaching job at the Negro secondary school in Malden: "In addition to the usual routine of teaching, I taught the pupils to comb their hair, and to keep their hands and faces clean, as well as their clothing. I gave special attention to teaching them the proper use of the toothbrush and the bath."[96] Even though Washington learns some of these lessons at Armstrong's Hampton, Armstrong himself has not been engaged in teaching such lessons but instead delegates these lowly tasks to others (i.e., the black students under management of white Yankee matrons). In addition to Armstrong's own Puritan background, his stint as a military officer also contributes to his relation to hygiene and housekeeping. According to Tera W. Hunter, white soldiers in the trenches during the Civil War "discovered the arduousness of housework." She quotes a letter to Jefferson Davis from an army veteran requesting domestic help for the camps: "The hardest, and most painful duty of the young Volunteers, is to learn how to Cook, and wash. . . . At home, the young Soldier, has his Food Cooked for him, by his Mother, Sister's or by our Slaves—but not so in the Field of Battle."[97] The white soldier's conflation of "Mother, Sister's" with "our Slaves" indicates the southern white male view of housekeeping as residing in the realm of both the feminine and the enslaved, each in a different way representing domestication, the former as a natural disposition toward nurturance, the latter as a natural or tamed disposition for servility. There is notably no distinction here between male and female slaves, for both genders would have been involved in servile housekeeping, even to the extent, as Hortense Spillers has brilliantly theorized, that chattel enslavement can be seen to suspend many attributes and functions of gender differentiation for the enslaved.[98]

In her biography of Armstrong, Talbot carefully segregates the great white father from the domestic chores he demands from his racial and military inferiors on the battlefield. Exempt from learning the arduous task of housekeeping, he has the added burden, as the commander of one of the first regiments of black troops, of guiding their household order without being contaminated by such work himself. Talbot quotes Armstrong: "Though I am a poor housekeeper, I am a good camp-maker."[99] Though the difference between making camp and keeping house would seem to be insignificant, the implied gender difference between the two—the domestic equated with the feminine indoors, camp with the manly outdoors—is notable, as is the racial difference operating in his attitude toward his black troops. He therefore positions himself as a model for their emulation in matters of social habits: "He also stimulated self-respect among his men by insisting on a high standard of neatness in their camp and individual quarters, himself taking the lead with enthusiasm."[100]

"Taking the lead," however, should not be read too literally, for, unlike for Washington, for Armstrong serving as a model does not mean becoming what Washington precisely calls an "object lesson." Armstrong "insists" on cleanliness and sets an example by having his racial inferiors do the cleaning for him within the domestic space of the tent, as he describes in one of his letters: "I am writing in my own tent. I have a man whose sole business is to keep my tent in good order and my fire a-going, and so zealous is he that on warm days like this he almost roasts me by the great blaze that he makes up. . . . My floor is swept eight or ten times a day, and although I do my best to scatter things around I don't succeed very well.... He has decorated the room with boughs of holly and a cunning bird's nest nestles among the evergreen leaves."[101] Armstrong's right to command is signaled as much by his exclusion from doing the housekeeping as by his insistence on his black soldiers doing it for their own good. Just as his command of the black regiment prepares him for his role as a leading race patron, the domestic idyll set up in the tent reaffirms his status as implicit "head of household" for the other race. As discussed in chapter 1, even though the military is among the most prominent arenas for fashioning manly fitness, white commanders must insist that both the conduct and the character of black soldiers bar them from possessing the most masculine of traits ostensibly bestowed by military service. Armstrong's domestic idyll of "a man" who can do his household chores for him should be directly connected with Washington's intimate relation to Yankee schoolmarms and their naturally hygienic conduct. While Yankee matrons represent the symbolic virtues of sexual and moral cleanliness through their association with physical cleanness, it is black and poor immigrant women who most intimately practice cleaning chores of all types, including bathing the children, washing the clothes, making the beds, and tidying up the houses and yards in the post-Reconstruction South.[102] White upper-class women could seem so clean in their body and attire because they could afford to have black and poor women doing so much of the labor for them, just as Armstrong could afford the fantasy of his tidy household on the battlefield only because he has a black man-servant—a soldier, no less—whose sole duty is to housekeep for him. According to Elizabeth Clark-Lewis, African American women themselves "fought to destroy the vestiges of slavery's denigration and devaluation of their own labor and social status. They felt keenly the burden of the negative stereotypes that they were sexually loose, masculine, dirty, and undignified. To combat the personal stigma of their purported masculinity, women were careful to distinguish their labor from that of men."[103] Cleanliness is thus a double burden for aspiring poor and black women, for they are often responsible not only for the upkeep of their own bodies, children, houses, and yards, but also for those of their employers. It is a double burden for Washington too: he pictures himself learning his role as race leader as much through his apprenticeship with Yankee matrons as through his devotion to Armstrong.

Such ironies would hardly escape Washington's notice, though he would never express them outright. He criticizes the southern aristocracy exactly for the physical and moral laxness that he says result from a slave economy, which teaches them to scorn all forms of "productive industry." "The whole machinery of slavery was so constructed as to cause labour," Washington writes, "as a rule, to be looked upon as a badge of degradation, of inferiority. Hence labour was something that both races on the slave plantation sought to escape."[104] As a foil to the mutual condition of black and white in the South, Washington celebrates free Yankee values of industry (meaning both industrialization and manual labor), thrift (meaning both financial sophistication and humble stewardship of resources), and immaculateness (meaning both physical hygiene and upright conscience). These Yankee values are "free" and freeing, meaning that they have brought about emancipation and that they are accessible without charge to anyone who pursues them diligently. As *Up from Slavery* figures these values in Yankee matrons, however, it also reveals how the Yankee's object lessons, while they must be carefully learned and mimicked, always threaten to make the ambitious black man an object of his own racial subjection. Just as he identifies his institutional and racial leadership ironically with the subordinate domestic role of his wives, so Washington when just a boy has already learned to subordinate himself to the Yankee matrons who serve as his first patronesses. We should not, however, take this subordination to (white) feminine rule at face value. Beyond Washington's infamous genius for sycophantic ingratiation, these passages honoring Yankee white ladies as his substitute mothers (white mammies?) and best teachers suggest his own initiative, autonomy, and racial pride, as well as the more subtle and intimate influence of the black mother's initiative, autonomy, and racial pride.

Viola Ruffner is the first Yankee matron he encounters. Washington's subordination to Mrs. Ruffner as houseboy is simultaneously a step toward intimacy with the white male patron, Mr. Ruffner, the most influential man in the county, the owner of the salt furnace and coal mine. Harlan suggests that as a child Washington learns work as a menial domestic years before, when he is a "houseslave" for the Burroughs family, instead of later when he is earning five dollars a month from Mrs. Ruffner.[105] Washington's comments on Mrs. Ruffner's "style of life" seem purely laudatory, though framed by descriptions of her severity as a boss: "Mrs. Ruffner had a reputation all through the vicinity for being very strict with her servants, and especially with the boys who tried to serve her. Few of them had remained with her more than two or three weeks."[106] Washington holds back the fact that he, too, lasts only a short time before running away, and according to Ruffner, he runs away "half a dozen times."[107]

Harlan's characterization of Viola Ruffner as "a frustrated New England schoolmarm" goes far to explain her relation to the many colored boys she attempts to train in accordance with her strict Yankee values. "I had heard so much about Mrs. Ruffner's severity that I was almost afraid to see her, and trembled when I went into her presence," Washington states, evoking the connotation of a young prophet's encounter with the severe Old Testament God. "I had not lived with her many weeks, however, before I began to understand her."[108] What Washington understands immediately is the need to escape her severe surveillance and the fate of becoming a house-servant, but what he records is a deeper, more prophetic object lesson that honors the chaste severity of her matronage:

> I here repeat what I have said more than once before, that the lessons that I learned in the home of Mrs. Ruffner were as valuable to me as any education I have ever gotten anywhere since. Even to this day I never see bits of paper scattered around a house or in the street that I do not want to pick them up at once. I never see a filthy yard that I do not want to clean it, a paling off of a fence that I do not want to put it on, an unpainted or unwhitewashed house that I do not want to paint or whitewash it, or a button off one's clothes, or a grease-spot on them or on a floor, that I do not want to call attention to. (44)

By internalizing the cleaning compulsion, Washington transforms his object lesson in servitude into a pedagogy. By "internalized" here, I want to suggest not only that obsession with hygiene becomes a psychological compulsion of his personality but also that it becomes the cornerstone of his racial-gender identity through habitual conduct and practiced character. Cleanliness becomes—all at once—a bodily function, a psychological tic, a habitual demeanor, an educational pedagogy, a social practice, a moral aim, and an ideological-political strategy. If black people must do the dirty servile work of society, they should do it with the compulsion that forces the recognition of powerful whites. In the process, they not only gain attention and patronage; they also train themselves to a ruthless self-surveillance in scrutinizing each step toward racial success. Good racial conduct guarantees racial uplift.

In *Up from Slavery* this pattern of subordination to, and emulation of, the Yankee schoolmarm is repeated in relation to Mary F. Mackie, the head teacher at Hampton Institute. Washington can gain access to the great white father, Armstrong, only through this lady, who holds in her hands the decision to admit him or not: "Having been so long without proper food, a bath, and change of clothing, I did not, of course, make a very favourable impression upon her." Reverting to the prophetic lesson he has learned from Ruffner, he snatches the opportunity to clean a room for her as proof of his worthiness: "She was a 'Yankee' woman who knew just where to look for dirt" (51–52). Even when Mackie calls on him to return to Hampton early to help her prepare the facilities for the school year, the intimacy of their laboring side by side, an unattached white lady and a strapping young black man virtually alone on campus—contrary to Baker's ingenious reading—refuses any imputation of a submerged erotic interest: "Miss Mackie was a member of one of the oldest and most cultured families of the North, and yet for two weeks she worked by my side cleaning windows, dusting rooms, putting beds in order, and what not" (72). Keeping the autobiography in its historical context as an object lesson for blacks on how to lift themselves up from slavery and for whites on how they can trust the emancipated blacks as co- or, more precisely, subagents in uplifting the southern economy, Washington says he learns service to the race from these encounters with Mackie, given that "a woman of her education and social standing could take such delight in performing such service, in order to assist in the elevation of an unfortunate race" (72–73).

Alongside this scene of gender instruction operating as racial guidance must be placed an earlier scene where Washington explicitly connects working alongside white women, the imputation of sexual predation, and the absolute trustworthiness of black men: "In order to defend and protect the women and children who were left on the plantations when the white males went to war, the slaves would have laid down their lives.... I do not know how many have noticed it, but I think that it will be found to be true that there are few instances, either in slavery or freedom, in which a member of my race has been known to betray a specific trust" (13). Note here how in contrast with white men's valor on the battlefield, black male slaves enact their subordinated sense of what Washington calls their "place of honour" domestically protecting the white women of the household by being "selected to sleep in the 'big house' during the absence of the [white] males" (13). It is a curious displacement, giving black men a modified manly activity—protecting women in warfare—but one defined by domesticity, subservience, and fidelity to the absent white masters, rather than through derring-do, military prowess, and patriotism to the nation-state on the battlefield. The "specific trust" here is obviously the defense and protection of the white woman's sexual chastity. Given that some master had taken advantage of Washington's own mother in her captive condition, this claim to a "specific trust" in protecting the white master's mistresses and daughters is loaded with a vicious irony, an irony that Washington must erase from view.

Washington's emphasis on the *housekeeping* pedagogy of these Yankee schoolmarms is actually quite ironic, not only inverting the common narrative of their saintly role in educating the freed people but also countering the narrative of their role provided by Frederick Douglass, Washington's predecessor as head of the race. Against Douglass, Washington credits his Yankee matrons not with teaching him book-learning but with training him in housekeeping and bodily grooming. It may be even more imperative for Washington to discriminate his relation with Yankee women from Douglass's, given the controversy that erupted over the elder race leader's marriage to a white woman in 1884.[109] While Washington emphasizes how nonintellectual, domesticated life habits fit his philosophy of practical education, this approach also has the advantage of highlighting his own initiative. He learns the "higher" intellectual pursuits on his own in his spare time, as well as from other blacks in night classes after the "real" work is done. Ironically, then, the attainment of literacy becomes wholly associated with black people's initiative, autonomy, and self-tutoring, despite the autobiography's ingratiating stance toward the virtues of white patronage. "The first thing I ever learned in the way of book knowledge was while working in this salt-furnace," where he teaches himself to decipher the number 18 from repeatedly seeing the "boss of the packers" mark the figure on the barrels allotted to his stepfather.[110] After "inducing" his mother to get him a book, he begins to teach himself the alphabet. He envies a young man from Ohio, the first literate colored person he encounters, who reads the newspaper to the black men and women of Malden. When another literate young colored man from Ohio comes to Malden, the blacks of the town arrange for him to set up school: "As yet no free schools had been started for coloured people in that section" (29).

Mrs. Ruffner and Miss Mackie become inverted mammies as they teach him the bodily and domestic regimen, while Washington's biological mother, despite her illiteracy, takes on the role of the patroness who "procure[s] an old copy of Webster's 'blue-black' spelling-book," though "where she got it I do not know" (27). We also see Washington's mother conspiring with him to get him into night school when the stepfather decides to put him to work in the salt furnace.[111] Harlan verifies the accuracy of Washington's claims about these first efforts at literacy, but the popularity of the mistress–slave boy scene of instruction can be seen from the way such a myth takes root in Washington's former master's family: "A family tradition among the Burroughses is that Laura, or perhaps her sister Ellen, taught Booker to read and write. There was no truth in this."[112] At one point when discussing the trustworthiness of blacks, Washington writes: "I have known of still other cases in which the former slaves have assisted in the education of the descendants of their former owners."[113] Though this inverted hierarchy linking whiteness with the physicality of domestic labor and blackness with the deepest admiration and highest aspiration for intellectual achievement is by no means complete or unconflicted, it is insistently repeated in the autobiography and elsewhere. "This experience of a whole race beginning to go to school for the first time, presents one of the most interesting studies that has ever occurred in connection with the development of any race," he boasts.[114]

The tricksterism at work in Washington's intimacy with the Yankee schoolmarms can be further elaborated through a subtle distinction between *menial* and *manual* labor. Despite his rhetoric otherwise, Washington most likely preferred the *menial* labor of housecleaning indoors under the likes of Miss Mackie to *manual* labor outdoors in the dirty coal and salt mines, as his stepfather had begun to demand. Though coal mining represents the sort of manly manual labor Washington venerated as the cure to the backwardness of the former (male) slaves, it is exactly the desire to leave behind toil in the dirt, the second skin of blackness made by the soot, that leads him to become a house-servant for Mrs. Ruffner.[115] "Work in the coal-mine I always dreaded," he writes. "One reason for this was that any one who worked in a coal-mine was always unclean, at least while at work, and it was a very hard job to get one's skin clean after the day's work was over."[116] This "dread" of the dirt that accompanies the most arduous manual labor, especially coal mining, positions him again as an effeminate man, one lacking the robust muscularity and disregard for the niceties of hygiene required for manly labor at the bottom. His prissy desire for cleanliness ironically makes tidying-up labor inside the home more suitable than masculine labor outside it, even though the menial status of the former effeminizes him in a way that the muscular labor of the latter would not. Even with the case of menial women's labor, however, his iconography as a happy housekeeper nonetheless does not represent the more complicated social reality. We should not confuse his favoring menial domestic labor with a desire to inhabit that status permanently. Despite what he learns about the true industry of laundering from Mrs. Ruffner, he still desires to move beyond laundering as a way to make a living. Similarly, even as he preaches to his wards to "cast down your buckets" where they are, he would never have embarked on laundering as a career choice, as George Washington Carver did as a young man. Washington cannot fully suppress his ambition to rise to a position that dissociates him not only from the dirt of men's manual labor but also from the tidying up of women's menial labor.

These ambivalences and paradoxes also shape the nature of Washington's political leadership. He must promote himself as a sort of racial head but one whose cleanliness and humility approximate more the status of political naif than a double-dealing political boss, placing him in the structural position of the sycophantic reformers scorned by the bare-knuckle, spoils-taking political bosses of the time.[117] Armstrong's Hampton presents an important arena in which Washington is able to learn this balancing act between macho patronage politics and "Miss Nancy" racial caretaking. When Armstrong asks him to take charge of an experiment in managing the education of "wild" reservation Indians at the normal school, Washington handles the racial nitty-gritty of the job as he will later master the minefield of big-time patronage politics. In this scenario, the Indians represent the "spoils" that Washington must manage, and when he does so with finesse, it pays off in Armstrong's recommending the very young man to head the new school to be established at Tuskegee. In his experiment as a "housefather" to Indians, we find the perfect figure for Washington's overall plight as an aspiring race leader. It is one thing to be the father of a race or nation, like George Washington; it is quite another to be a "housefather," which implies a proximity to menial chores, hygiene, and the basics of refining parlor conduct. In taking charge of the Hampton "wild" Indians, however, Washington very cleverly shifts his persona from the handmaiden to Yankee schoolmarms to the housefather for a race whom he can advertise as even lower on the ladder of civilization than the former slaves. To place Washington in charge of disciplining and civilizing "over one hundred wild and for the most part perfectly ignorant Indians" is to test to what extent he himself has disciplined his racial nature into a civilizing object for others' instruction.[118] In other words, it helps to prove that practiced conduct can win out over a restrictive racial nature. The distance black people have traveled from slavery toward civilization, Washington asserts, outpaces the "Indians" in their territorial strongholds, where they once lorded over black slaves. Nowhere is this more apparent than in Washington's series of articles on the progress of his Native American charges, a series he writes for Hampton's propaganda periodical, the *Southern Workman*.[119]

Washington makes the most of each incident as a lesson not only about the progress of the Indians but also, more importantly, about the Negro's already secured place in civilization in comparison to the Indian. In "New Arrivals," he jokes: "Some of the actions of the new boys, before they get initiated into the habits of civilized life, are quite amusing to the old boys, who forget that it has been but a few months since they acted in the same way. Their fun began when one little fellow, who evidently meant to begin his life at Hampton by doing his work well at the table, for that purpose, left his coat in his room."[120] The observation here addresses the question of how the Indians' conduct bespeaks their lower racial status in relation to Negroes. This scandal of the Indian boy's appearing without his coat could almost be a joke on the detailed and meaningless rituals of etiquette in "civilization." It serves instead, however, to demonstrate how Washington's calculated conduct enables his mastery over both civilization and his playful, uncivilized charges: "Things went on in this way for several mornings without improvement, and I had to turn the joke on the old boys by making them take the new boys for roommates and teach them to keep house. Now, the smoothness of their beds and the neatness of their rooms would teach a lesson to some lady housekeepers."[121] This project enables him early on (1880) to construct his "Miss Nancy" housekeeping role. At the same time, he is also constructing the pliability of that role by showing how his mastery of it can be used to jettison him into the contrary role of a leading race patron for others of an inferior race. In effect, the position he occupies in relation to the "wild Indians" is analogous to the position that his mentor, Armstrong, occupies in relation to the primitive former slaves, but transparently without the latter's masculine presumptuousness.

The motivations that lead Armstrong to put Washington in charge of the Indian education experiment at Hampton also cause the federal agency in charge of the colonies to contract with Tuskegee to educate Cubans and Puerto Ricans after the Spanish-American War. Though Washington's experiment with these imperial spoils in the shape of colonial bodies seems to have been less successful than his civilization of the Indians at Hampton, it is the political opportunity and its symbolism that are important.[122] Recognizing that first-class U.S. citizenship is defined by the power to patronize the imperial others who come under your rule as a heightening of that rule, Washington impersonates the position of the colonizer in making room at Tuskegee for the less fortunate Cubans and Puerto Ricans, but in doing so, he is always careful to maintain his reputation as a good, humble housefather.

Sissy Adoration of the Great White Father

If Washington builds his potent racial husbandry on a conduct flexible in its racial and gender practice that enables him to identify across racial and gender lines without disturbing the ironclad dictates of a racially segregated sexuality, then it is because he has also constructed such an identification with the dominant white figure in the autobiography, General Samuel Chapman Armstrong. As father figure, educational mentor, military commander, financial backer, political godfather, and all-around patron for Washington, Armstrong becomes a commanding, godlike presence. While Washington uses hyperbole sparingly in relation to himself and his race, he is overly effusive when speaking of Armstrong. When introducing this "great white father" (to use Harlan's phrase) in *Up from Slavery*, Washington does not spare the hyperbole of absolute adoration:

> I have not spoken of that which made the greatest and most lasting impression upon me, and that was a great man—the noblest, rarest human being that it has ever been my privilege to meet.... I do not hesitate to say that I never met any man who, in my estimation, was the equal of General Armstrong.... I shall always remember that the first time I went into his presence he made the impression upon me of being a perfect man; I was made to feel that there was something about him that was superhuman.... It would be difficult to describe the hold that he had upon the students at Hampton, or the faith they had in him. In fact, he was worshipped by his students.[123]

All of these expressions themselves are formulaic, whether or not they are genuine. They represent the kind of things a (great) man is supposed to utter about the great patriarch who has made his career possible by shaping his conduct and character. Armstrong uses the same language in writing about his mentor, Mark Hopkins, the head of his alma mater, Williams College: "Doctor Hopkins... is a noble man in the highest sense of the word; I never saw his equal; he is essentially a man of power, and combines the highest traits of character."[124] Like the formula of the adoring wife that he borrows from nineteenth-century great-man autobiography, this idol of the great man as mentor subtly reflects back on Washington the greatness he cannot claim outright for himself.

The gender difference between Armstrong as idol for Washington versus Hopkins as idol for Armstrong can be seen in the actual physical distance between Washington and Armstrong as represented in the autobiography. Unlike the side-by-side physical contact that he has with Mrs. Ruffner and Miss Mackie, the contact between Washington and his central white male patron is not physically represented. Armstrong's body remains here disembodied and distant from the physical contact of domestic labor and pedagogy practiced by the Yankee matrons he supervises. That is to say, the great white man's body never becomes a literal object lesson for Washington's emulation. Washington repeatedly uses the word "contact" to describe his relation to Armstrong, but the central anecdote characterizing Armstrong's influence while Washington is at Hampton indicates how cross-racial masculine discipline and discipleship are enacted from a distance and through the difference between the status of the white mentor-patron and that of the black student-ward. This relation can best be described as *homoracial*, in which the black man is excluded from white masculine spheres of power, whereby the black man can never become a rival to the white man.[125] Due to a lack of housing at Hampton, Armstrong "conceived the plan of putting up tents to be used as rooms. As soon as it became known that General Armstrong would be pleased if some of the older male students would live in the tents during the winter, nearly every student in school volunteered to go."[126] As opposed to Washington's own need to portray himself as standing in the mud-pit or taking up an axe in clearing the field for campus construction (much less as teaching students how to brush their teeth and make their beds), Armstrong's example is made through his conceiving of plans and making his wishes known.

That this tent-sleeping anecdote is provided in the context of praising Armstrong's own "Christlike body" seems especially ironic: "More than once, during a cold night, when a stiff gale would be blowing, our tent was lifted bodily, and we would find ourselves in the open air. The General would usually pay a visit to the tents early in the morning, and his earnest, cheerful, encouraging voice would dispel any feeling of despondency."[127] Armstrong relates to his wards as a commander to his troops, no doubt his charge of Hampton patterned after his own command of black troops in the Union army.[128] Just as the general is expected to have better sleeping quarters, no matter how adverse the conditions for his soldiers, so the white missionary patron is not expected to give up all his luxuries in order to prove his commitment and fathering of his black wards—despite the rhetoric of "self-sacrifice." There is something eerie in the way the wind lifts the tent "bodily," exposing the black boys' bodies to the bone-cutting air, while Armstrong appears a ghostly influence, visiting the tent only in the morning. A disembodied voice, Armstrong allows his words to shed their influence on the chilled boys and to inspire in them the will to suffer for their race.

The closest that the two men come to touching in the narrative is the money that moves back and forth between them, and the instruction about money that Armstrong repeatedly gives his black disciple. Money is an appropriate go-between to represent the intimacy of these two men, considering how Washington understands his accommodation to the southern racial backlash. Blacks would be willing to stay on the cold, hard soil of the depleted Black Belt as long as they were given free rein with the money they earned for their sacrifice. Although transcendent adoration sets Armstrong apart in a divine realm, the autobiography reminds us constantly that Washington has impersonated Armstrong in building an institution, reputation, and influence that quickly overtakes Armstrong and his Hampton Institute in the international spotlight. Nonetheless, Washington's peculiar status dictates that his hyperbolic display of worship toward his adopted father not be hedged by the father-son rivalry characteristic of such intimate masculine bonding in the homosocial system that keeps white men in power. His mimicry of his white mentor must always display a difference and deference beyond the apparent distinguishing factor of skin color, a difference seeming to diminish his bid to full manhood rites/rights.

In Homi Bhabha's theory of colonial hybridity, he suggests that the relation between colonizer and colonized always produces not merely a knowing subject and a known object but also, at the same time, a splintering of these identities. The repetition of mimicry, according to Bhabha, returns to the colonizer as a kind of frightening hybridity as he watches the colonized person imperfectly imitate himself.[129] A missionary like Armstrong especially styles himself as a missionary, colonizing expert who necessarily overcomes the expected terror of life among the uncivilized. As McClintock asks in her refinement of Bhabha's theory, "If mimicry always betrays a slippage between identity and difference, doesn't one need to elaborate how colonial mimicry differs from anti-colonial mimicry?"[130] The answer is yes, and we can apply this inquiry to *Up from Slavery* if we read it as an underhanded, if self-conflicted, anticolonial narrative. Furthermore, to make such a distinction one must also elaborate the ways in which the colonizer-patron is also engaged in a *gendering* process of forming a dominating self by reflecting his civilization's image of a man in charge. This process involves the balancing act of becoming attuned to his charges' ways of being while resisting a temptation to become like them. The patron thinks that he has time on his side. He engages in an evolutionary fantasy that bases his identity on control over his wards, as well as on his wards' identification with their potential reform. The patron expects the ward to make mistakes in emulating civilized ways. In other words, the deficiency in his wards' mimicry—their inherent tendency to bungle their lessons—puts the patron-colonizer at ease with his rule.

Armstrong, for instance, waxes confident over the strange amalgamations that result from Negroes and Indians practicing civilized habits. Armstrong puts great stock both in what he labels the inferior race's "imitative faculty,"[131] which he sees as natural to the uncivilized, and in the evolutionary limits of their imitation. Armstrong's confidence increases, as well, with his growing projection of an evolutionary and historical difference between his race and that of his wards. Talbot quotes Armstrong: "'The Indians are grown-up children,' said he. 'We are a thousand years ahead of them in the line of development. Education is not progress, but a means of it.... We forget that knowledge is not power unless it is digested and assimilated. Savages have good memories; they acquire, but do not comprehend; they devour, but do not digest knowledge. They have no conception of mental discipline. A well-balanced mind is attained only after centuries.'"[132] Here again, we see how the structure of white supremacy proffers a man's conduct as evidence of his fitness to rule while simultaneously barring colonized others from being able to habituate such conduct. While not exactly an incapacity of their nature, the inability to progress to such conduct is made an attribute of their lagging racial ancestry. When looking at his disciple, then, Armstrong can remain flattered by his mimicry, for Armstrong is confident that the difference between his student's disciplined conduct and his own is more than skin color, more even than mental capacity. That difference runs in the blood of history, assuring that even the most quick-minded of the lower races, in playing catch-up with the white race, will still lag behind as the white race continues its own evolutionary trajectory "ten generations" ahead.

But what effect does mimicry have on the gendering of the black male ward from an anticolonial perspective? Because mimicry always entails a degree of identification and likewise identification a degree of mimicry, Washington's adoration cannot be seen merely as copying superficially the observable demeanor and gestures of his superiors in order to survive and raise up his race.[133] The mimicry must force a degree of deeper identification, which the ward must comply with despite himself. Despite his sissy adoration of the great white mentor, which implies that Washington can never quite reach the masculine mastery of his white idol, Washington does want to be like Armstrong, if only to possess Armstrong's masculine empowerment. We cannot see Washington's obsession with civilizing cleanliness as merely a ruse, a trickster's game, that Washington puts over on the masters. As Washington identifies his mentors' cleanliness as a source of their superior racial status, he also must begin to identify with the power of that cleanliness—to some unknowable extent—as an intrinsic uplifting resource in itself. The mimicry does, however, help the black disciple to disguise other intentions at work in the process of identifying with the missionary's colonizing reform. Mimicry causes the patron-colonizer arrogantly to overlook the ward's mistakes as natural backwoodsiness and backwardness, as indicated in Talbot's exaggerated sense of her father's influence on his charges: "There was no Negro, however ignorant or dull, who did not at times catch a glimpse of this inspiring vision of his possibilities and, if he remained long under the influence of it, become moved into acceptance of it."[134] It is this sort of racially derived masculine bravura that fosters the colonizer-patron's foolhardy overconfidence, rather than only terror, in confronting the hybridity of the ward. Armstrong would just as likely be prone to underestimate as to fear the rivalrous implications in Washington's rise. Washington, however, could not help but be aware of a shadow masculine rivalry and its many possible outcomes.

Harlan, who views Washington as the consummate big-house servant, largely takes Washington's adoration and emulation as genuine, despite Washington's secret politics opposing Armstrong's teachings. "Like a house servant concealing a part of his personality from his master," Harlan writes, "Washington kept silent about their differences and continued to model his public personality after Armstrong."[135] Despite this public display of untempered adoration, the autobiography mounts toward a finale of subtle inversion between the two men, even as each plays his racial role to a fault. Washington's strategy here borrows from what Houston Baker Jr. has labeled the "mastery of form" or "manipulating the mask" as a kind of minstrelsy that harbors a revolutionary, empowering gesture.[136] As we have seen, the autobiography does not objectify Armstrong's influence as a body on display for the black subject's impersonation, as it does for the black wives', the Yankee matrons', and Washington's own body. Armstrong's "contact" is always disembodied, mental, mediated by physical distance, words, money, and female go-betweens who are held responsible for Washington's housekeeping instructions. This changes, however, toward the end of the autobiography, when Armstrong's body is literally made impotent, paralyzed by a stroke. Washington records as a highlight of his life, and a climax in the autobiography, Armstrong's final visit to Tuskegee. We get an anticipatory glimpse of this disabling of Armstrong first in chapter 3, and then in the final chapter we get a detailed account; thus, the white missionary's disabling embodiment significantly frames the autobiography. As has been theorized recently in disability studies, the racial "handicap" that is ascribed to blackness approximates the status of those whose social identity is constituted through physical and intellectual "disabilities."[137] The gender-deficient sissy son all of a sudden becomes more capable not only as a man but also, by extension, as a specimen of the Negro race. In inverting this scenario, picturing the great white man as disabled next to his sissy black son, Washington compensates for the racial/gender disparity that he has played on throughout the narrative.

Having suffered a stroke, the general is paralyzed and has difficulty speaking. In chapter 3, Washington claims, "It never occurred to me that General Armstrong could fail in anything that he undertook. There is almost no request that he could have made that would not have been complied with." Though the "almost" equivocates tellingly enough, he intends the anecdote that follows to speak for itself: "When he was a guest at my home in Alabama, and was so badly paralyzed that he had to be wheeled about in an invalid's chair, I recall that one of the General's former students had occasion to push his chair up a long, steep hill that taxed his strength to the utmost. When the top of the hill was reached, the former pupil, with a glow of happiness on his face, exclaimed, 'I am so glad that I have been permitted to do something that was real hard for the General before he dies!'"[138] The pathos (almost bathos) of the altruistic scene lies in the disparity between what the general has sacrificed for the black race and what little the former student can offer by way of compensatory gratitude. Yet in the picture of the black disciple pushing the great white father in his invalid condition, we witness the way in which racial gratitude for white patronage cannot suppress the desire for the black disciple to become the enabling hand to the disabled white father.[139] In the final chapter, Washington describes the elaborate welcome the Tuskegee staff and students offer the paralyzed general as they carry him around, care for his every whim, and tend to his every need, as though the great military commander has now become an invalid old lady. Washington's last opportunity to show off the regimental order, spotlessness, and prosperity of Tuskegee also becomes his opportunity to provide for his mentor's physical and psychic needs in the way that a trusted servant nurses his master in illness, or the way a presumptive eldest son indulges the wishes of the elderly patriarch declining toward second infancy, or the way a devoted wife tends to the needs of a weakened beloved husband—with the important exception that Washington is a patriarch in his own household: "[Armstrong] remained a guest in my home for nearly two months, and, although almost wholly without the use of voice or limb, he spent nearly every hour in devising ways and means to help the South." Given that Armstrong could not carry out these "ways and means," Washington's rededicated commitment to the white father's superior command reverberates pity with admiration, indulgence with gratitude: "I said that if a man in his condition was willing to think, work, and act, I should not be wanting in furthering in every possible way the wish of his heart."[140] In the end, Armstrong's body is objectified into a literal object lesson for the black disciple's emulation. "Washington's 'perfect' white man," Maurice Wallace observes, "is a disabled white man—less a model for black masculinity than a reassurance that Washington, in his own socially/politically enforced posture of eunuchism, is not really impotent."[141] By the end, "contact" with Armstrong has become defined through the most tactile intimacies related to physical caretaking, as the black disciple has become the transcending patron, and the white patron's power has been contracted into a paralytic body.

George Washington Carver's Sissy Physiology

Washington's success or failure as a racial patron can never be a settled question, exactly because despite the tangible results of his career, most notably the justly celebrated institution at Tuskegee, what Washington most intimately engaged and achieved is symbolic and intangible in nature, the spectacle of all "races" in the country being forced to imagine, if not believe, that a black man could be a national leader without upsetting the racial and gender hierarchy that placed black men subserviently below whites. Despite Washington's sissy ritual of dirtying up to clean up, of playing the prissy black housefather to black and red charges, he ultimately cannot protect the honor of his manhood from the imputation of a mythic black predatory sexuality. We thus move toward conclusion by reminding ourselves of Washington's heterosexuality to underscore, on the one hand, the distinction between a normative sexual attraction versus an anomalous gender conduct, and, on the other, a crucial distinction between circumstantial and physiological sissiness, where "physiological" here indicates a condition read onto the material body itself. If Washington's socio-moral character and conduct as a housekeeping sissy serve to protect his racial husbandry, ironically his normative sexual orientation in the end places him in jeopardy the moment his (hetero) sexual appetite is exposed to public view.

By briefly contrasting Washington's circumstantial sissy conduct with George Washington Carver's more tangible "physiological" sissiness, we can more clearly see how broad the swath of anomalous manliness was and also how differently encoded sissy dispositions could interact under the racial strictures of early Jim Crow. This distinction between Washington and Carver, furthermore, hinges on the different geographic scales in which their unfit manliness was practiced and scrutinized. While Washington's role as head of the race jettisoned him onto the world stage as a model for black manliness, and made him a target for those who called out his unmanly practice and demeanor, Carver's unmanliness necessarily became the target of sissiphobic suspicion within the everyday parochial confines of the Tuskegee campus, where he lived, worked, and played. Even as Carver was indeed in the national public eye as an experimental scientist and educator, his gender conduct remained closeted in public view. On the one hand, because Carver's effeminate behavior seemed not to be legible in the public roles that he occupied, it did not create the kind of public sissy suspicion that plagued Washington's career.[142] On the other hand, for those who had to work intimately with him, and those who could observe his relations with male colleagues, male students, and Washington himself, Carver's effeminate conduct created the kinds of titillating gossip and scandal that characterize the local in the era before mass televisual and social media.

Washington's dependence on a public display of white approbation makes his reputation especially sensitive to any perceived misstep. In 1911, while on a visit to New York, Washington ends up in a "bad neighborhood" near the Tenderloin late on a Sunday night. When a man from an apartment building where Washington has been ringing a doorbell comes out and begins to beat him, another bystander joins in. Washington is saved by a plainclothes policeman, who arrests him, releasing him only after discovering his identity. The succeeding court trials drag Washington's name through the dirt, even though Washington's first assailant is discovered to have deserted his wife and children, and even though the woman he is living with turns out also to have deserted her legal husband in order to live with the assailant as though they are "man and wife." The bigamous white woman accuses Washington of peeping in a keyhole, looking her directly in the face, and accosting her with the salutation "Hello, sweetheart." Through Washington's well-organized patronage machine, with tentacles reaching all the way to the mayor of New York, he is able to escape an indictment, and his allies muddy further the name of his bigamous assailant, despite the discrepancies in Washington's own story.

On the one hand, it could be argued that Washington's lifetime of obsessive cleanliness keeps him from experiencing the worst public hanging of his reputation, which would have ended the career of any other African American man under similar circumstances, and could have ended in a lynching. On the other hand, Washington's overcompensating sissy circumspection could not protect his reputation from being suspected and attacked for an unproved sexual-racial indiscretion, nor, more significantly, could it protect him from the beating he receives literally at the hands of two obscure, socially taboo white men in a seedy area of New York City. Ironically, as Washington's critics and doubters accept the insinuation of his prurience, they also expose the prurience inherent in the U.S. system of racial surveillance. The system requires ruling white men to be ever vigilant as patrons, peeping through every keyhole for evidence of black men's sexual aggressions and transgressions. Washington's surprise ending, with its entangled erotic lessons of a black man trapped by his own cross-racial ambition and double-dealing racial bigamy on the part of whites, reminds us of how tenuous the balancing act is that requires him to impersonate sissy prudishness and squeamishness in the face of coal-mining labor and corrupt politics. In the final analysis, the bigamous white couple's eagerness to expose the black man's desire as a sexually deviant imposition ends up exposing the perversity of their own racial boundaries and the deviance of their own desire. The episode serves to accede, if not to confirm, the robustness of Washington's heterosexual libido, and it makes us a bit more skeptical about the naturalness of his prissy, fastidious public demeanor—wondering whether it may after all be a trickster's ruse as much as a social practice so habitually enacted as to become behavioral second nature.

There is no evidence that Washington displayed physical characteristics or bodily mannerisms affiliated with sissiness; we thus cannot answer fully how much Washington's person displayed sissy mannerisms, despite conduct that accords so well with a sissy temperament. We know from the recording of a portion of the Atlanta Address that he made for Thomas Edison that he had a rather high tenor speaking voice. Such a voice is often taken as a sign of gender queerness in the dominant culture, as we will see in the case of George Washington Carver. Given that the high tenor, or even the falsetto, possesses a certain value in African American performative culture, we would need far more than a high voice to suggest that Washington's person evinced sissiness.[143] If temperamental, in the sense of a habitual way of interacting with the world based in one's character, Washington's gender nonconformity seems nonetheless conditional, enacted and embedded within his character and conduct in response to a particular cultural-historical situation. If Washington's sissy negotiation can be glimpsed in the charges of unmanliness made against him by his black male and female adversaries, it is also the case that this sissified gender conduct must be understood not only in terms of the larger circumscribing conditions of a Jim Crow regime that denied hegemonic masculinity to black men but also in terms of more local relationships within the Wizard's small community of Tuskegee. In this sense, all sissiness is relational as well as conditional, circumscribed by geography, time, and cultural specificity.

Unlike Washington, Carver presents the classic case of a physiological sissy through his body's mannerisms, posture, comportment, and deportment. A lifelong bachelor, he presents himself in photographs as something of a dandy, one who always wore, like Oscar Wilde, a flower prominently displayed in his lapel. Despite organizing a very popular Bible study class, which students voluntarily attended in the hundreds on top of compulsory chapel attendance, rumors of his homosexuality reverberated locally (that is, around the campus), and some looked suspiciously on the young male students who seemed to form a tight coterie around him. Of course, this is *not* the way his biographers—almost all of whom write for a juvenile audience—choose to script his legacy. There is a resounding silence in most of these works concerning his bachelorhood, his effeminate passions, his comfort with crossdressing (even if for a theatrical performance), his girlish high speaking voice, his "horseplay" with boys, or his over-the-top theatrics when his special status at Tuskegee seemed in jeopardy. In *George Washington Carver: An American Biography*, published in the year of his death (1943), for instance, Rackham Holt—not prone to erase such prominent features as Carver's mincing gait and extremely high, stuttering voice—chooses to attribute such gender anomalies to physiological ailments.[144] Holt provides vital evidence for how whites, for the young Carver resided mostly among whites, perceived the boy and young man. The biographer nonetheless strives to normalize what otherwise was clearly seen as anomalous.

> There were still a few words he could not say without stammering; nevertheless, his voice was as high as a girl's, and once in a small play the young people were to put on he was to have the female lead. When they gave the show in a near-by town, it was decided he should have his picture taken in wig and bustle and leg-o'-mutton sleeves. He fell into his part so completely that not even his enormous hands and feet gave him away, and the lady photographer thought he was of her own sex and chattered away as one girl to another.[145]

Curiously, Carver keeps up this ruse, "until he realized her confidences were such as a boy should not hear, and then he became frightfully embarrassed at the thought of how embarrassed she would be if she discovered how he had fooled her."[146] Rather than a singular instance of cross-dressing, as Holt implies, Carver reprises the female lead as a student at Iowa State (figure 2.1). Even though there is no evidence of his having cross-dressed at Tuskegee, the clothing he chooses nonetheless identifies him more subtly with gender nonconformity.

When Holt emphasizes Carver's unconventional attire, she focuses on the professor's frugality, informality, and tendency to wear "shabby, baggy work clothes most of the time."[147] In formal photographs, however, we can spot not only his famous flower in the lapel but also a certain prissiness of pose beyond the stiff formality so common in Victorian portrait photography. The rather formal photograph of Carver at his easel shown in figure 2.2 portrays him as the renaissance man that he was. A viewer aware of how he gained permission to study in white female art classes, however, might speculate on what the photograph cannot convey: Carver's engagement in cross-racial, sissy pursuits. While Carver at his easel communicates the scientist's more ladylike avocation of painting floral watercolors, the more bureaucratic 1902 group portrait of the Tuskegee Agricultural Staff, with Carver seated in the middle lower row, represents his centrality to one of Tuskegee's most important and famous enterprises (figure 2.3). Perhaps only the flower in his lapel—à la Oscar Wilde—singles him out as not quite fully at

2.1 George Washington Carver cross-dressed for a school play at Iowa State University, c. 1891–1895. Photograph in McMurry, *George Washington Carver*.

home in Tuskegee's utilitarian mission, and instead as a dandy whose comportment does not conform to the conventional manly demeanor of the other men. Thus the flower might be seen as a small emblem of the sissy private conduct known only to the inner life of the institute. Especially in the context of an institution whose principal despised all signs of high cultural luxuriousness as contrary to the school's utilitarian, industrial, chaste, self-humbling mission, Carver's decorative interests and dandy decorum clearly flouted the ethos, if not the ethics, of that mission.[148] As Monica L. Miller has pointed out in *Slaves to Fashion*, "The dandy is a figure who exists in the space between masculine and feminine, homosexual and heterosexual, seeming and being."[149] As Miller observes, because dandies must self-consciously choose this vocation by committing "to a study of the fashions that define them," "the [black] dandy's extravagance or tastefully reserved bodily display signifies well beyond obsessive self-fashioning and play with social hierarchies."[150] In the context of Washington's austere Tuskegee anti-aesthetic, Carver's dandyism seems an eyesore whose very presence flouts and troubles the principal's own Yankee schoolmarmish gender balancing act. To conduct oneself as a dandy in New York or Chicago as a sign of New Negro modernizing sophistication and the right to social capital is one thing. To do so at rural Jim Crow Tuskegee, under the regime of the hyperutilitarian Washington, is altogether another. If not an insurgent conduct, or a subversive one, Carver's effeminate posture and comportment at least gesture toward a stubborn refusal even to attempt to conform to Tuskegee's strict codes of gender conduct. In exposing his own gender compromises to public view, Washington was able through the white patronage he cultivated to create a cloistered sphere wherein the institute's staff, teachers, and students could be free to aspire to the higher education that Jim Crow Alabama had proscribed as taboo for them. Ironically, this cloistered racial sphere at the same time served to protect Carver's effeminate conduct from the larger public, if not from the sissiphobic insults of his insular racial environment.

Repeatedly commenting on Carver's being "set apart from others," Holt is nonetheless eager to minimize the implications of so many seemingly unmanly attributes and unmasculine modes of conduct. As was routine for mid-twentieth-century biographers when confronted with sissiness and potential homosexuality in a respected subject, Holt's narrative assumes a heteronormative perspective against the grain of evidence that she herself presents. The fact of Carver's bachelorhood is a key case in point.[151] Happy to promote the rumor of a vague romantic female interest in the long-distant past over the more rampant rumors of the other Wizard's homosexuality, Holt exploits the conjugal plot to heterosexualize Carver on the flimsiest of evidence. In the singular *critical* biography of Carver, Linda O. McMurry precedes her study by noting "the eccentricities of his personality," perhaps a euphemistic way of alluding to those aspects of Carver's image

2.2 George Washington Carver at his easel. Photograph by Erick Butler, undated. Courtesy of the Tuskegee University Archives, Tuskegee University.

2.3 George Washington Carver (*seated front row, center*) in a group portrait of Tuskegee Agricultural Staff. Photograph by Frances Benjamin Johnston, 1902. Getty Images.

that do not jibe comfortably with the iconography of the leading Negro scientist of the early Jim Crow era. "Had Carver been white," she speculates in a book intent on breaching the myth of the "folk saint," "his choice of careers would probably have been different. If he had placed his personal desires above his sense of responsibility toward his fellow blacks, he most likely would have become either an artist or a botanist engaged in plant breeding or mycological research."[152] There is just a hint here of the tension between Carver's gender identity and his vocation as an agricultural chemist—a contrast between his "artistic" temperament and his highly utilitarian lifework. Unlike other biographers, McMurry does document how Carver appeared "eccentric" to others, as well as his occasional spats with Washington and rival male faculty. Although never resorting to such language, McMurry paints a vivid picture of Carver, boy and man, as the classic case of a physiological sissy. Unlike his older half brother, Jim, who was "tall, robust, and husky" and good at farm labor, Carver was "frail and sickly." McMurry attributes "the high pitch of his voice" that "startled all who met him"

SISSY HOUSEKEEPING · 105

to a childhood illness that affected his larynx, but the high voice accords with other material sissy embodiments that are not so easily attributed to physical ailment. Discounting the rumor that Carver's high voice might be the result of a castration that occurred while he was kidnapped by bushwhackers during the Civil War, McMurry enlists Carver's development of "normal" height and "secondary sexual characteristics" to challenge such rumors.[153] Whatever the etiology, whether attributable to physiology or upbringing, from a very young age Carver's speech, manner, posture, pose, gesture, and gait all bespeak the sissy-boy as a vestibule to potential homosexuality, if not a case of trans personhood undetectable in a period before such an identity had achieved public recognition.

McMurry readily acknowledges Carver's noted "gentleness" as something his peers found queer in a variety of ways. It is with regard to Carver's relationship with his boys, however, that McMurry feels compelled to document the rumors about the other Wizard's suspect sexuality. Carver "administered a mock thrashing by gently scuffling with 'his children,'" she writes. "Such horseplay was not very dignified, and some faculty members regarded the activity with distaste." Carver's "horseplay" with the young male students should be compared with Armstrong's horseplay with the pretty young Yankee maidens whom he recruited as teachers at Hampton. For Armstrong, this behavior is a badge of normative heterosexuality as the founder, patron, and head of an institute for Negroes; for Carver, similar play with boys can only lead to suspicion. "A few even hinted that Carver's relationship with his boys was tainted with homosexuality," McMurry writes.[154] Such dirty linen was aired, of course, only within the confines of the campus. Decades later, in airing such rumors, McMurry is careful to dismiss them rather sheepishly: "His gentleness, religious nature, and appreciation of beauty are traits labeled feminine in Western culture, and the pleasure he took in cooking, sewing, and needlework served to enhance suspicions. Yet the persistent rumors of homosexuality most likely resulted from failure to understand an orientation to life that deviated from the norm" (110). Carver's sissy display must have stood out in the everyday pressures of Tuskegee, such as his flaunting of his interest in needlework (figure 2.4). Given the pressure cooker of a segregated, underfunded new institution thrown into the spotlight of international attention, it is not surprising that there would be jealousies and suspicions about Carver's special treatment as a researcher who sought every way to decrease his teaching load and to devote time to leisurely avocations like the cultivation of flowering plants. His tangible sissiness could only have intensified such animosity. As McMurry observes, part of this would no doubt have stemmed from his relatively high salary, but we also cannot ignore that "his darker color may have also influenced the reactions of some, since most of the faculty and students at Tuskegee were light-skinned mulattoes" (45). Often characterized as an unamalgamated "pure"

African, Carver might have been viewed as socially above his station, which could have both shielded and simultaneously intensified his sissiness. The perception of his difference would have included color, regional origin in Missouri, higher education (holding a PhD from white Iowa State), and feminine interests.

Carver's specialness often put him at odds with Washington, who tried manfully to make his most celebrated professor conform to the principal's dictates, even as he needed to loosen the reins for a faculty member whose fame eventually rivaled Washington's own. Carver saw himself as having made a great personal sacrifice in going to teach agriculture at Tuskegee, rather than following his life's passions of art, music, drama, and horticulture. "At Tuskegee such abilities as breeding delicate flowers and collecting rare fungi are not as highly prized as basic survival skills" (45), McMurry writes. In college, Carver had persisted in his devotion to art, eventually winning the right to enroll in an all-female (and all-white) art class—seemingly having no compunction about his pursuit of a vocation so closely tied with white middle-class femininity.[155] Similarly, as a young man Carver had learned laundering from a series of black women in households where he roomed. He seems boastful when he later admits, "I found employment just as a girl." Setting up a laundry business in Minneapolis in 1880, Carver seems not to have been concerned that he had chosen an enterprise identified strongly

2.4 George Washington Carver crocheting. Photograph by Erick Butler, undated. Courtesy of the Tuskegee University Archives, Tuskegee University.

with black women in the Midwest and South—and a black female industry from which Washington carefully distances his own obsessive cleaning enterprises by excoriating DC laundresses as morally suspect and socially overreaching.[156] What Washington regarded as menial labor that was beneath him, despite his own compulsive housekeeping persona, Carver saw as a feather in his cap—or, more aptly, a flower in his lapel.

It should not be surprising, then, that Carver's career at Tuskegee is marked by incessant skirmishes not only with Washington but also with George R. Bridgeforth, whom Washington hires in 1902 in the hope of a suitable administrator who can compensate for Carver's lack of attention to administrative detail. McMurry helpfully documents the series of peevish memos sent between Carver and Bridgeforth, and from each to Washington. As Washington dared not do, Bridgeforth treats Carver's threats and ultimatums with a derision borne of gender disrespect. Outright accusing his elder colleague of failing to comport himself "like a man," Bridgeforth calls Carver's manhood into question as a way to question his competence to chair the department: "I am here to work as a man and I expect to be treated as such."[157] Such language is rather obviously loaded with the same kind of gender attack that Trotter and Du Bois make against Washington. Whereas these adversaries sound the alarm with belligerent concern, they certainly do not resort to ridicule, given the seriousness of Washington's influence with white rulers. Bridgeforth's mockery of Carver's threats as "in every respect laughable" indicates how the latter's sissy person puts him at a disadvantage in a feud with a colleague who comports himself in a more conventionally masculine way, despite Carver's much greater celebrity as a scientist and teacher.

Despite constant feuding between Washington, the consummate control freak whose patron spoils depended on his mastery of institutional cleanliness, and Carver, the sissy diva who tended to melodramatize any hint of another faculty member's precedence over him, the cloistered privacy of Tuskegee's campus ironically provided a secure place for Carver to live out his palpable sissiness respectably in the heart of Jim Crow. As K. Ian Grandison illustrates in "Negotiated Space," the campus was designed intentionally to present an innocuous, humble, domesticated facade to the public road in order to hide the institution's radical mission of higher education from a hostile white public. Grandison also observes how the boys' residence was situated, along with unsightly industrial enterprises like the sawmill, at the public edge of the campus, providing some degree of defense against occasional threats of violence made by white supremacist groups like the KKK, whereas the women's residence hall was ensconced deep within the campus interior, presumably so that the boys' residences could serve as a fortress to protect the girls.[158] We can only speculate as to why Carver's rooms were oddly located in this feminine interior, rather than more logically in the boys' residence. Heeding his conduct with that tight circle of boys whom Carver called his "children"—a word that, in today's black gay vernacular, means the newest crop of young gay boys—and concerned with rumors of Carver's homosexuality, perhaps Washington thought it wise not to put the fox in the chicks' roost. Or perhaps Carver himself desired to live in the women's residential interior, just as he preferred so many avocations strongly identified with ladyish femininity. In either case, just as bookish learning could be carried on secretly in an interior aimed at the highest level of education while industrial vocations were showcased to the public, so Carver's sissy person and conduct could be secreted within the confines of the campus interior, even as local rumor and speculation could bubble beneath the spectacle of his international acclaim as the race's greatest exemplar of the manly vocations of agriculturalist, scientist, and inventor.[159] Whatever sissy secrets Carver harbored within the relative privacy of the campus, they were kept safe, ironically, by Washington's more public performance of sissy character and conduct aimed at negotiating Jim Crow's relentless violence against any Negro man who dared to conduct himself with the least hint of upfront, virile masculinity.

3

Un/fit Manliness

Evading Masculine Brutality in James Weldon Johnson's Sissy Narratives

> No! stand erect and without fear,
>   And for our foes let this suffice—
> We've bought a rightful sonship here,
>   And we have more than paid the price.
> —JAMES WELDON JOHNSON, "Fifty Years," *Book of American Negro Poetry*

> It is a struggle; for though the black man fights passively, he nevertheless fights; and his passive resistance is more effective at present than active resistance could possibly be. He bears the fury of the storm as does the willow-tree.
> —JAMES WELDON JOHNSON, *Autobiography of an Ex-Coloured Man*

As a "father" of American sociology, and one who grounds sociological theory and practice in explicit racial and implicit gender difference among the races, Robert Park constructs the idea of "the marginal man," epitomized by the mulatto, as an explanation of how men of a socially oppressed racial group eventually adapt to dominant civilization's demands and thus ultimately conform to the (gender) expectations of the dominant group. His idea of the marginal man projects onto the liabilities of African American manhood the benefits of marginality while attempting to retain the contrary benefits of dominant white masculinity, such as confidence in the progressive outcomes of adventuresome aggression, the fraternity of individualism, the marketplace of competition, and the mastery of scientific technique. As discussed in chapter 2 in relation to how Park helps us frame Washington's gender negotiation of oratory, Park's sociological theory poses an especially challenging but productive forum for a writer-activist-diplomat like James Weldon Johnson because Park also theorizes, infamously, the "Negro as the lady of the races." By positioning the Negro in terms of conventionally feminine attributes—oversensitivity, sentiment, poetic expressiveness, felicitous social adaptability—Park makes explicit a dynamic whereby the Negro leader, as long as he is socially marginal, is to the ruling white men what the white woman is to conventional white masculinity: a gender complement and foil, rather than a gender equal. Despite Washington's self-humbling gender antics, whereby he seems to position himself as "the lady of the races," he ultimately seeks to represent himself as a racial patriarch, properly betrothed to a series of wives and properly self-disciplined to (house)father Negro institutions, and to mediate between white male rulers and an uncivilized black folk mass. In a sense, both Washington and his critics, in different ways, are exploring and challenging the equation between race as a gendered phenomenon and what James Weldon Johnson calls "the spirit of self-assertion."[1]

Despite Park's attempt to construct the mulatto man as the archetype of the marginal man through Du Bois's theory of double consciousness, the interest of Jim Crow–era New Negroes in self-conscious modernity tends to disavow such a connection. The presence of a mulatto discourse in Jim Crow writing exists largely as a foil to the dominant ideal of male leadership, for the most fit leader is cast as someone who has, or is struggling to, overcome not only the color line but also color self-consciousness. Especially after the establishment of "separate but equal" as national law after *Plessy v. Ferguson* (1896), the Negro leader can be a true "race man" only when he has resisted a special coalition only with other lighter-skinned men or with white men to instead form an indelible bond with all men of color in defense of the whole race. Even when the eventual goal is assimilation—as it is for many of these writers—the method for getting there could not be through the superiority of lighter over darker skin.[2] As we shall see by examining the work of James Weldon Johnson, a man's skin color has implications not only for how he situates himself as a race leader but also for how he constructs himself in relation to fit manhood. In other words, against white supremacist doctrine, Johnson repeatedly demonstrates how color does not determine gender conduct. At the same time, however, he takes pains to represent how color shapes the perception of manly conduct not only for the male Negro but also for any man who must negotiate the color line, whose gender protocols can easily trip up the most self-assertive race warrior. Answering Park's theory of the marginal man as well as Washington's practice of gender obsequiousness, Johnson asks some rather curious questions concerning the role skin color plays in staging black men's bid for not only race leadership but also, more fundamentally, racial inclusion. What we find in Johnson's narratives of un/fit manliness is a manual for overcoming color self-consciousness, and the sissy cowardice that attends such, in order to rise to the occasion of a sophisticated but self-assertive leadership of the race based in conduct that I label here *gentle manliness*, punning on the class-based genteel ideal of gentlemanliness. The conduct of gentle manliness, as we shall see, entails not only a man's demeanor, manner, dress, gesture, and gait but also his temperament, choice of vocation, and attitude toward racial uplift. What we find in Johnson's own personal history is a man who remarkably avoids the kinds of gender attack leveled against such leaders as Washington, Du Bois, Trotter, and Pickens, despite their divergent gender personas and political strategies. Johnson seems to have husbanded the resources of un/conventional manliness, sometimes appearing assertively manly and at other times sensitively self-humbling, without eliciting the kind of gender rancor that other male race leaders attracted.

The contrast between Washington and Johnson is immensely instructive for understanding the subtle distinction between the former's housekeeping conduct and the latter's gentle manliness, each differently drawing on resources of sissified character to manage quite disparate politico-historical circumstances, which in turn implicate divergent codes of conduct and leadership profiles. As head of Tuskegee, Washington has the benefit of a relatively closed microcosm, where he can act as a racial boss locally while still behaving as the race's head housekeeper in liaison with the white supremacist elite on the world's wide stage. Washington's sycophantic bargain also allows him largely to avoid public wrangling over racially explosive issues like the franchise, lynching, and integration. Although he subtly borrows the authority of his mulatto identity as a racial go-between, he understands that because he is based in the Alabama Black Belt, the characteristic of skin color provides very little, if any, advantage if he, due to some misstep, is perceived as behaving too assertively in assuming any manhood prerogative reserved exclusively for masculinist white supremacy. By contrast, although born only fifteen years after Washington, Johnson (1871–1938) represents the generation born at the hopeful apex of "radical" Reconstruction and coming of age under the horrifying backlash of punitive Jim Crow. Pursuing vocations that constantly place him in the spotlight of cross-racial interactions, Johnson is unable to avoid volatile racial issues, and indeed, as the first African American head of the NAACP, he becomes the leading voice for immediate racial equality, the franchise, desegregation, and the transformative power not only of equitable interracial cooperation but also of intimate physical contact across race.

Even as Johnson is clearly influenced by Washington's sissy demeanor, the younger leader cannot afford the kind of docile character that strongly imbues the Wizard's conduct. Aware of the risks involved in negotiating sissified leadership for a black man, Johnson comments subtly on the difference between unmanly cowardice and "fighting passively." Through the narrator of *Autobiography of an Ex-Coloured Man*, Johnson states, "For though the black man fights passively, he nevertheless fights; and his passive resistance is more effective at present than active resistance could possibly be. He bears the fury of the storm as does the willow-tree" (75). As he directly addresses questions of gender conduct as such, Johnson—unlike Washington, who avoids matters of skin tone—very publicly addresses this matter, exploring in a variety of ways how the material reality of skin color intersects, beneficially and detrimentally, with racial and gender conduct and character. Most instructively, while Washington evades the problem of racial violence through his housekeeper's persona, lynching explodes at the heart of Johnson's public discourse. Exploring a range of Johnson's personal and public writing, Jacqueline Goldsby has persuasively argued that Johnson's firsthand encounter with lynching, while subjecting him to a traumatic silence in its aftermath, ultimately shapes his literary and activist commitment to exposing the horrors of racial violence. She comments on "how frequently lynching occurs [in his oeuvre], almost as if Johnson could not write without depicting or at least mentioning the violence."[3] Keeping in mind Goldsby's insights concerning the myriad ways in which Johnson's character is shaped by posttraumatic stress, how he navigates his many public roles as a gentle man becomes all the more astonishing. Through this polite manly persona, he encourages his cross-racial readers, activist allies, white political patrons, and black supporters to image and imagine the resources and consequences of a gentle manhood for preventing and eliminating the deadly rages of white racial violence, such as the episode of race rioting that he famously dubs "the Red Summer of 1919."

When Johnson anonymously publishes his novel *The Autobiography of an Ex-Coloured Man* in 1912, he broaches many of these issues by asking what role the self-conscious mulatto man might play in bringing the race into urban, cosmopolitan, modern civilization through his experience of being able to move back and forth between the races.[4] It is almost as if Johnson has constructed his nameless protagonist as a fictional hypothesis of Park's marginal mulatto theory, except, as we shall see, the conclusions drawn by Johnson's narratives seem ultimately to defeat Park's theory that the marginal mulatto is the most suitable figure for racial leadership. Among all of the Jim Crow–era race leaders, Johnson is perhaps the one who best embodies the versatility of manly competence, partly because he spans the ideological gamut from Washington's accommodationist version at the turn of the century to the aggressive rebellions against it in the 1910s, from the biracial protest politics of the NAACP to Alain Locke's Renaissance aesthetics of the mid-1920s.[5] While seeming to have some sympathy for the values implicit in each of these ideological camps, Johnson is able, amazingly, to maneuver among them throughout his career without becoming directly embroiled in the kinds of rancorous personal controversies discussed in the previous chapter. Amid his race work, Johnson always keeps his eye on what he calls, in his poem "Fifty Years," "rightful sonship." This means assertively and confidently participating in the American inheritance as a favored son despite ongoing racist humiliations and distractions. To adopt the filial role, as opposed to Washington's pristine housefathering, enables a different negotiation of gender in the assumption of Negro leadership. With a range of interests, skills, and writings as wide as that other "Renaissance man" from the same generation, Du Bois, Johnson establishes credentials as opera librettist and song lyricist, poet, novelist, autobiographer, filmmaker, historian, critic, newspaper editor and columnist, linguist, lawyer, diplomat, political organizer, lobbyist, educational administrator, schoolteacher, professor, socialite, and patron of the Harlem Renaissance. Johnson presents these vocational and ideological shifts as the continuous development of a cosmopolitan gentleman of color in U.S. society. Johnson attaches so deft a fluency to the image of African American manliness that it can come to represent not only the achievement of full manhood "in spite of the handicap" of racism but also the promise of full American citizenship without relinquishing rights to the leadership of a particular racial inheritance.[6] "I will not allow one prejudiced person or one million or one hundred million to blight my life. I will not let prejudice or any of its attendant humiliations and injustices bear me down to spiritual defeat. My inner life is mine, and I shall defend and maintain its integrity against all the powers of hell," he asserts in the only tract that he aims directly at an African American audience.[7] As Joseph T. Skerrett Jr. has argued, there is certainly evidence of Johnson's "anxiety and doubt" stemming from his racial status even in *Along This Way*, but his rhetoric and perhaps his habit was to suppress these doubts and anxieties from his self-portrait, though, as Skerrett suggests, they do come out in his fiction.[8] I want to suggest here that such doubts and anxieties can be read most productively through Johnson's gender self-fashioning in both his own autobiographical subjectivity and that of his fictional autobiographer, the ex-colored man. I also want to suggest that Johnson was drawn to autobiography—oddly in fictive form—exactly because of his interest in manly self-fashioning as a self-conscious act. Whereas Washington's autobiography references gender conduct only in the most folksy secondhand or offhand ways, shrewdly as though he is not conscious of such, Johnson self-consciously spotlights gender dynamics as determinative of courageous or cowardly conduct and character, but not in ways that conform to white masculinist/supremacist norms. In his own autobiography and his fictional one, he insists that self-narration necessarily forces reflection on the fluent complications of apparently inappropriate gender conduct as a resource for racial negotiation—indeed, for racial diplomacy.

Along This Way shapes Johnson's life as a retrospective examination of the Negro's advance from enslavement to the height of the Harlem Renaissance. In this teleology, the emerging decade of the 1930s is seen not as a retreat from biracial uplift that many were beginning to sense but instead as a continuing move upward, so much so that the 1929 stock market crash and its resulting economic effects are referred to in Johnson's autobiography only obliquely. He mentions in passing, for instance, the suicide of his hometown friend, D——:

> I did not see D—— frequently, but our old intimacy was in some measure reestablished.... He had put nearly all he could get together in the then recent Florida real estate boom and the burst of the bubble had hit him hard. One day in the summer of 1930, Grace [Johnson's wife], who was reading the *New York Times*, startled me with the cry that D—— was dead. I snatched the paper, and read that he had risen early, gone into the bathroom and shot himself through the heart. At the hospital, where he died a few hours afterwards, his last words were that he was just tired of life.[9]

"D——," who was capable of passing and had married a white woman, serves as a foil for Johnson's more equanimous mode of color crossings. Like the passing protagonist of *Autobiography of an Ex-Coloured Man*, D——'s life is not necessarily made more fortuitous by his lighter skin color and white wife. Like that of another hometown friend, Dr. T. O. Summers, on whom Johnson bases much of his own cosmopolitan pose, D——'s suicide stresses the inconsistencies of living, in which a man with more apparent claims to an easeful way in life ends up fatally tired of living. Although the 1929 economic crash motivates D——'s suicide, the grief of such national and personal tragedies in no way mars the ebullience of the concluding chapters of *Along This Way*.

Another oblique reference to the Depression in *Along This Way* revolves around the question of whether African Americans might turn in frustration to communism in the coming decade. Johnson's treatment of the notion of violent revolution helps us to grasp how he balances radical racial equality as an endemic U.S. value against the emerging image of the communist agitator as the most robustly masculine, and thus conscientious, embodiment of global radicalism. Considering the prospect of communism's attraction to African Americans, the answer for Johnson is simple: "The race shows practically no inclination to do so, either among the intellectuals or the masses. No group is more in need or more desirous of a social change than the Negro, but in his attitude toward Communism he is displaying common sense." Relying on the gentlemanly value of "common sense" as a larger virtue of African American politics, Johnson sees communism as unacceptable for the race because he judges it to be an unacceptable option for the United States and the New World. Identifying the communist with "sheer idiocy" and "fanaticism" (411), this ideology is characterized with an uncivilized brutality unbefitting a gentle man of common sense.[10]

It is likely that Johnson is here aiming at Du Bois by siding with his own protégé Walter White, whom Johnson had supported to replace himself as head of the NAACP in 1931, and whom Du Bois instinctively distrusted and cast as a timid yes-man in the Washington mold. By the early 1930s, Du Bois has begun to promote a Marxist solution to the woes of blacks during the Depression, along with a strategic segregationism.[11] Whether or not Du Bois is obliquely being attacked, Johnson's construction of his own temper, as much as his politics, disallows him from seeing Marxism as a threat to (or tool of) racial uplift. His battle with the U.S. is one of conscientious objection rather than economic power, for to be antagonistic to the American creed is itself a form of suicide in his eyes. Against Du Bois's increasingly macho vocabulary of Marxist insurgency and black nationalist autonomy in his essays for *The Crisis* in 1933, Johnson in *Along This Way* adheres unswervingly to his gentlemanly character even as the Depression worsens and the New Deal government kowtows to the racist southern Democrats. Like Martin Luther King Jr. after him, Johnson trusts to a moral change: "The only kind of revolution that would have an immediately significant effect on the American Negro's status would be a moral revolution—an upward push given to the level of ethical ideas and practices." Keeping with his ethos of worldliness, however, he immediately universalizes the need for even this sort of "revolution": "And that, probably, is the sole revolution that the whole world stands in need of."[12] Given such free-ranging humanism, it is not surprising that the Depression cannot take a more critical historical role in Johnson's upward narrative, any more than the rise of Jim Crow as an economic system can. At most, it can serve as a somber, submerged operatic backdrop to an ever-enterprising *comédie humaine*.

In fact, Johnson represents 1929 as an apex in his own career, the year in which he receives both a Rosenwald Fellowship, which provides income for a year to allow time for creative writing, and an invitation to represent U.S. interests at the third biennial conference of the American Council of the Institute of Pacific Relations. To be asked to go to Japan as a U.S. citizen—*not* as an African American—and at the same moment to be granted the most prestigious and generous money award for African American cultural achievement seem to encapsulate Johnson's idea that the Renaissance race man can synthesize into a seamless whole politics and art, full U.S. citizenship and full African American identity, Old World sophistication and New World know-how, personal accomplishment and race uplift, social assimilation and social change, manly self-assertion and self-humbling sonship.

Unlike any previous black male autobiographer, Johnson also emphasizes the operation of chance in his life to an unprecedented degree: "I was tempted to question what motives the gods in the guise of Mr. Embree [president of the Rosenwald Fund] and Mr. Carter [secretary of the American Council] might have in bringing me two such boons simultaneously."[13] In an odd way, the unspoken subtext of the ensuing Depression enhances the good fortune that raises Johnson yet another notch just before the economic crash. It would appear that a belief in chance or fortune conflicts with Johnson's emphasis on gentle manliness as a disciplined mode of conduct. Despite the potential self-contradiction here, Johnson pictures gentle manly conduct not only as a disciplined habit and practiced demeanor but also as a matter of the kind of optimistic self-assertive temperament that just happens to be his predicament. As we shall see, however, Johnson takes pains to show us how the blessing of two open-minded, confident parents, the boon of having come of age in a cohesive black neighborhood still harbored by Reconstruction politics—such happenstance contributes to his gentle, open, disarmingly assertive temperament as a grown man. Picturing himself as a favored son consummately of his own time, Johnson nonetheless is also a man out of time—one whose good luck enables him to avoid the worst possible fates that logically should befall a black man with great talents and greater ambitions in a racially rigged world with little room for experiment, error, and ease of movement. Toward the end of the autobiography, he comments explicitly on his good luck: "I have no intention of depreciating my own intelligence and industry, but the farther back I am able to look, the more clearly I discern that such results as I have gained may be, in a fair degree, traced to 'lucky breaks.' If I were giving an exhortation on the subject to young people, I should say, '*Do not trust to luck*, but be, in every way, as fully prepared as possible to measure up to the "lucky breaks" when they come'" (389). As a man who has read the atheistic tracts of Tom Paine and Robert Ingersoll and as someone who has traveled, experienced, and reflected broadly, Johnson can embrace chance more easily than the idea of a "personal God." The only conflict with his father that he tells of concerns the time when he brought Paine's *Age of Reason* into the house: "One day my father summarily commanded me to 'take that book out of the house and never bring it here again.' . . . I was too much astounded by the sudden show of intolerance on my father's part to question the reason for his order. I simply obeyed it" (96–97). In contrast with Wright's oedipal battle with his father over the kitten, Johnson's seemingly Washingtonian response to the authority of his father indicates an almost naturalized ability of knowing when and how to pick a battle. Like most other men of gentle pretensions, Johnson has enough respect for authority not to attack it openly when the odds are low, but enough skepticism of any totalitarian impulse to invent liberating openings where opportunity allows.

Johnson's freethinking agnosticism, however, has more to do with cultivating a moderate, generous, tolerant temperament than with having an intellectual or theological axe to grind or with playing the part of a rebellious son, as he makes clear in the concluding paragraphs of the autobiography: "My glance forward reaches no farther than this world. I admit that through my adult life I have lacked religiosity. But I make no boast of it; understanding, as I do, how essential religion is to many, many people" (413). Repeatedly, Johnson takes "the world," in all of its connotations, as his entitlement: sophistication, skepticism, sociability, generosity, fortuitousness, internationalism, universality, modernity—in a word, *worldliness*. In accordance with Johnson's caution toward "Divine Providence" and destiny, this appeal to "lucky breaks" and "boons" crops up continually in the text as evidence of the ways in which accident and history conspire to produce the Renaissance race man as an even-tempered cosmopolitan gentleman whose backward and forward glance "reaches no farther than this world."

In placing antiblack violence front and center in his narratives, Johnson foregrounds all the more the extraordinary depth of humanizing goodwill required to retain such gentle equilibrium. For Johnson, the sign of manly success amid the horrors of racial injustice entails the ability, when confronted with these moments of racial shock, to respond with the aplomb of generous, freethinking conduct. Although such conduct resonates to some degree with Washington's tempered racial boosterism, it lacks the elder's self-abnegating folksiness, menial subservience, and duplicitous self-humbling. Against Washington, Johnson promotes the idea that a leading race man can be self-assertive without bringing the white man's rage upon his head. Of course, Johnson never has the obligation of managing a cash-strapped Jim Crow institution in the deepest South. His bailiwick finds him in more urbanized areas of the North and South, in high government agencies and biracial civil rights organizations, and in more urbane cultural sites like Tin Pan Alley and Harlem or cultural institutions like Atlanta University, New York University, and Fisk. Like Washington's autobiographical persona, nonetheless, such a temperament contains the risk that the autobiographical narrator will appear effete rather than equanimous, sycophantic rather than sophisticated, mundane rather than worldly, passive and pacified rather than gently and self-assuredly disarming as a man.

An Idyllic Childhood in the Lap of Reconstruction

Johnson advertises his gentlemanly stance as the inheritance of traditions of honorable conduct expected among leading men in any culture but historically, erroneously identified exclusively with the particular heritage of European civilization based in aristocracy and primogeniture. For Johnson, this inheritance is a matter neither of breeding nor of race or nationality, but instead of training, education, experience, circumstance, happenstance, talent, and moral and temperamental character—and, of course, gender conduct and character. Though not an innate inheritance, Johnson's cosmopolitan lineage can be traced to the accident of his birth in a particular time and to particular kinds of worldly parents. Unlike Du Bois, who enlists the entrenchment of his New England bloodline to unwrite the bastardy implied in remote slavery, Johnson characterizes his foreparents as cosmopolitan wanderers whose shiftings between Europe, Africa, the West Indies, and the United States necessarily entangle him in a native claim to all of these places. In self-conscious contrast with Washington's promotion of the parochial Black Belt South as the Negro's natural province, Johnson's gentle manliness lays claim to a transcendent worldliness through which he can judge the small-minded, parochial racial resentments of his white compatriots.

Beginning his narrative with the lineage of his foreparents thus does double duty, staging the background that prepares him for U.S. racial leadership while also staking a claim to the whole world as a native stage for its achievement. By chance, Johnson's parents meet in New York, marry in Nassau, and settle in Jacksonville, Florida. This trajectory is not merely personal or the result of whimsy; it indicates the risk-taking required of those who desire to prosper in the midst of unjust oppression. About his parents' meeting in New York, he writes:

> At school she [Johnson's mother, Helen Louise] also had opportunity to cultivate her considerable talent for music. When she was between eighteen and nineteen she sang at a concert, and James Johnson [his father], who was in the audience, fell in love with the singer.... Within a few months after the concert the Civil War was raging, and my grandmother, listening to the rumors that the colored people in the North would be put in slavery if the South won, became panic-stricken and, taking her daughter with her, boarded a ship and returned to Nassau.
>
> Not long afterwards James Johnson sailed from New York to Nassau. He went to become headwaiter at the Royal Victoria Hotel and to continue his courtship of Helen Louise. (5)

In a tone so different from Washington's, Johnson impersonates gentlemanly worldliness with such finesse that we forget that this is what he's doing. Narrated in the frank but polished syntax of Johnson's prose, the maternal grandmother's panic seems remote—perhaps even a bit exaggerated—next to the romance of her daughter's captivating her future husband at a concert. Packing up and returning to Nassau in response to the Civil War turns out to be fortuitous. Johnson suggests that his father—and thus himself as well—could just as easily have ended up a "British citizen." Instead, James Johnson picks up his family and goes to Florida when "prosperity in Nassau ... collapsed with the close of the Civil War; and the great hurricane of 1866 had blown away its remnants" (6). This penchant for following opportunities wherever they may lead becomes an integrationist theme of the autobiography. Such optimist conduct in the midst of large-scale crises like the Civil War bespeaks how a man's ebullient, assertive temperament can predicate conduct that appears not just second nature but almost thoughtlessly natural. Accordingly, Johnson and his brother, Rosamond, will become vagabond artist-entrepreneurs, following their dreams back and forth across the U.S., to Europe, and to other countries. Johnson's intense, interdependent relations with his parents, friends, wife, strangers, and especially Rosamond also locate him quite differently as a man.[14] In his sociability and worldliness, he desperately needs others. He never experiences anything alone. Unlike the routine representation of manly heroism during the time, such as Teddy Roosevelt's, Johnson narrates how others constantly come to his rescue, and he to theirs. Even Washington in representing the male slaves as subservient to their absent masters during the Civil War images them as potential protectors and rescuers of white femininity. The Wizard's principle of racial self-help insinuates a presumption of a race of men who can rescue themselves into a social practice that self-deprecatingly celebrates the "stronger hand" of white male patronage. In Johnson's narratives this willingness to be rescued by others, although seemingly a feminine quality or, for a man, an effeminate attribute, does not conflict with manly self-sufficiency. How could it, when chance itself is so large an agent of manly achievement?

Happenstance softens the blow of disappointment throughout the narrative, creating a disarmed and disarming function such that Johnson, father and son, can accept circumstances beyond their immediate control without falling prey to resignation, despair, or enervating rage. For instance, at first it appears that Jacksonville is a bad choice for someone with James Johnson's experience of prosperity and future ambitions and with Helen Louise's aesthetic and social sense. At first sight, Jacksonville appeared to his father "so unlike the Richmond of his boyhood or the New York of his youth; even so unlike Nassau, where there was a high standard of English life." Helen Louise was so shocked by the contrast that when she "was ushered into her new home, she broke down and wept." Knowing that the family will prosper, we are left to wonder beforehand whether the good luck of this inauspicious move results from the father's "foresight," or perhaps "he relied on the tip that Northern people and capital were interested in Jacksonville and Florida."[15]

It turns out that Jacksonville provides a world of education for the young boys, or that the family provides a world for them in this small town.

> In the parlor there were two or three dozen books and a cottage organ. When I was seven or eight years old, the organ gave way to a square piano. It was a tinkling old instrument, but a source of rapturous pleasure....

> There was a center marble-top table on which rested a big, illustrated Bible and a couple of photograph albums.... On a small stand was a glass-domed receptacle in which was a stuffed canary perched on a diminutive tree; on this stand there was also kept a stereoscope and an assortment of views photographed in various parts of the world. For my brother and me, in our childhood..., this room was an Aladdin's cave.[16]

This scene contrasts sharply with that depicted by Washington and Du Bois of the rough cabins of black folk of the Black Belt. When Washington, famously, comes across a piano in a former slave's cabin or a French primer in the hands of a Black Belt boy, it infuriates him that his race should try to run before they have learned to crawl. The scene also serves as a counterpoint to Washington's moral opprobrium against slavery as spoiling the masters.

For Johnson, there seems to be no evident conflict between such a soft environment and the harsh reality of racial humiliations. Without boasting, Johnson is delineating a "free" legacy that nonetheless does not shut him off from the vast majority of less fortunate Negroes. Like the stereoscope that gives the Johnson boys a miniature view of the world beyond the house, their neighborhood too is a microcosm of races, nationalities, religions, and classes jostled into one small space. This ease with multiracial settings is projected as preparatory for vital aspects of his many vocations—from negotiating contracts with the big New York music firms when he's a songwriter to negotiating U.S. interests in the midst of civil warfare when he's a diplomat in a foreign country, from dealing with the white NAACP board and lobbying face-to-face U.S. presidents to hosting fashionable parties for New York's social and artistic elite as a Harlem Renaissance patron.

As an NAACP board member, Mary White Ovington in her autobiography associates her affection for the New Negro cause with her family's Irish servants, so Johnson refigures the convention of the black mammy to indicate his ease with whiteness.[17] When his mother takes ill after his birth, a white neighbor who has also just given birth "took me and nursed me at her breast until my mother had recovered sufficiently to give me her own milk." This nursing image to most whites of the time would be more disturbing than Washington's and Du Bois's ministering Yankee matrons. Johnson inverts and at the same time counters one of the few acceptable modes of physical intimacy between black and white, the black mammy nursing the white child. What is shocking to others—no doubt including some African Americans—to Johnson is a natural interracial bond that puts the lie to whites' devotion to their devoted black mammies.

> So it appears that in the land of black mammies I had a white one. Between her and me there existed an affectionate relation through all my childhood....

> I do not intend to boast about a white mammy, for I have perceived bad taste in those Southern white people who are continually boasting about their black mammies.... Of course, many of the white people who boast of having had black mammies are romancing. Naturally, Negroes had black mammies, but black mammies for white people were expensive luxuries, and comparatively few white people had them.[18]

Putting forward his white mammy without succumbing to the bad form of boasting, Johnson lodges a critique of the symbolic role of the black mammy in the racial class system of the South, as he also situates himself on the high ground as a true aristocrat with taste above all those southern whites who cannot help boasting about their mammies. If the black mammy is a sign of social prestige and good breeding, then black people are ironically the natural aristocrats, for all of them truly have had black mammies without the temptation of boasting about the fact. While making of himself an exceptional man tutored for biracial leadership by the unusual experience of having a white mammy, Johnson also binds himself to the black folk, who, though not exceptional in that sense, still share with him that "escutcheon" of natural aristocracy, the black mammy.

While this passage could be compared with Washington's idyllic representation of the good relations between the Negro male slaves and the white mistresses they protect while the white men are away fighting on behalf of the slave system, it honors interracial intimacy with a different tinge. The Negro autobiographer as suckling baby infuses an aura of intimacy, softness, and innocence that is sustained throughout the narrative. The defenseless baby ultimately becomes an accomplished man, if he's lucky, but, as we shall see, no Negro man, however well armed metaphorically or literally, can be fully protected from the brutalities of Jim Crow savagery. We should keep in mind this unusual early image as we later learn about Johnson's near-lynching for appearing to have overly intimate contact with a white-appearing woman in a Jacksonville park. A defenseless baby ready for rescue is hardly the stuff of hard-hitting racial realism that is usually the mode of anti–Jim Crow writing. In Richard Wright's memoir *Black Boy* (1945), for instance, the five-year-old protagonist is whipped nearly to death after he almost burns the house down. While suffering bedridden from the beating, he has a nightmare vision of gigantic white breasts bearing down on him, suffocating him. Although Wright's image might represent one extreme suggesting that there is no milky white innocence for Negro mother or child under Jim Crow, Johnson's other extreme of a beneficent white breast suckling a Negro baby is rare, perhaps even unique in this literature. But the image is a good example of how Johnson prepares his readers for an autobiographical subject whose gender identity is as gentle and disarming as his childhood relationship with his white mammy. Johnson's auspicious beginning in childhood seems to occupy a wholly different universe from Wright's suffocating white breasts, a metaphor for the punishing brutalities awaiting the black boy in a regime that prefigures his babyhood and boyhood as always mannishly predatory, especially in the face of white femininity.

Against the "romancing" that the southern whites engage in as a sort of false nostalgia, the autobiography situates Johnson and Rosamond in an authentically romantic childhood as the preparatory stage for their artistic race work. Books and music play a crucial role.

> I read for myself *Pickwick Papers*, some of the *Waverly Novels*, *Pilgrim's Progress*, the fairy tales of the Brothers Grimm, and took my first dip into poetry through Sir Walter Scott.... These stories left me haunted by the elusiveness of beauty—elusiveness, its very quintessence. Years after, when I read Keats's *Ode to a Nightingale* the thought flashed through my mind that for one whose spirit had not been thus pervaded in childhood it would be impossible even to catch at the tenuous beauty in:
>
> > The same that oft-times hath
> > Charm'd magic casements, opening on the foam
> > Of perilous seas, in faery lands forlorn.[19]

Like so many African Americans trained in the black schools and colleges of the South before World War II, Johnson's sense of the aesthetic resonates especially with the British Romantic poets, and the childhood passages of his autobiography are haunted by a Wordsworthian development from idyllic innocence in nature to the fall into humankind, but his fall is perpetrated by racial self-consciousness, the sin of racial hatreds and exclusions. Before that fall, however, his mother and father tutor him unselfconsciously. His father gives him his first books; his mother reads to him and "was also my first music teacher" (14). Against the image that Frederick Douglass provides of the punishing pain that he experiences when his master forbids the mistress from teaching the slave boy to read, Johnson's mother and father in different ways enable the Negro boy to view the world with absolute confidence but also with openhanded receptivity—a receptivity that hinges on sophisticated literacy in books, music, geography, and the gentle social protocols that make a boy comfortable with conduct deemed sensitive and romantic, guided as much by sensibility as by common sense.

Johnson's portrait of his mother is especially touching, and he seems at no embarrassment or pains to prioritize the lessons he learns from her versus those of his father. Helen Louise crosses color lines because they do not exist for her, given that she is not a product of the U.S. South. When she returns to New York for a visit, she attends a service at St. John's Episcopal Church without giving it a thought: "In the chanting of the service her soprano voice rang out clear and beautiful, and necks were craned to discover the singer. On leaving the church she was politely but definitely informed that the St. John's congregation would prefer to have her worship the Lord elsewhere." She never attends an Episcopal church again, but instead becomes a choir leader in her mother's Ebenezer Methodist Episcopal church, and "racially she continued to be a nonconformist and a rebel" (10). Johnson genders the two sides of his own career between his mother's impractical, artistic nonconformity and his father's practical politics and breadwinning prosperity: "My mother was artistic and more or less impractical and in my father's opinion had absolutely no sense about money" (11). The tension between masculine breadwinning and feminine art does crop up when Johnson has difficulty deciding whether to abandon his principalship in Jacksonville and risk fame and fortune as a songwriter in New York with Rosamond. Valerie Smith comments on this tension evident in the passage in which Johnson describes his decision to leave Jacksonville: "This passage reveals a polarization within Johnson between the impulse toward duty and responsibility on the one hand and toward adventure on the other. The tone displays the fascination with nonconformity that figured in his reflections even near the end of his life."[20] The narrative represents his development as a fluent synthesis of this divide between conformity to masculine duty and the nonconformity of feminine art.

Whatever their failings, both parents make his upbringing a royal experience. His mother "bore more than a slight resemblance to the later portraits of Queen Victoria." Although the father has a "self-acquired" education, he too impresses on the children their entitlements to all the world has to offer.[21] James insists on his sons knowing world history, hearing Shakespeare, and learning Spanish, rather than being trapped in a parochial Americanism. Even his father's work at the hotel provides Johnson with a sense of almost genteel entitlement. The hotel becomes a palace, his father its emperor: "My first definite thought about the hotel was that it belonged to my father." As headwaiter, his father has at his beck and call others who "stand like soldiers at attention." At his father's command, one of the waiters "tucks a napkin under my chin and serves me as though I were a princeling" (16). The father's and son's high regard for the father's position as a hotel waiter must be weighed against Du Bois's outright disdain for the menial domestic labor to which aspiring black men were so often reduced, and Washington's promotion of such labor as uplifting only when accompanied with obsessive hygiene. This ease with royal esteem prepares Johnson for meeting U.S., South American, and Central American presidents, as well as real royalty, like the emperor of Japan.

Just as the Depression is a subtext underlining Johnson's continued rise against the backdrop of economic crisis, suicide, and racial retreat in the final chapters, so in the childhood chapters of *Along This Way*, the politics of Reconstruction serve as a subtext to underline his propitious origins and development as indelibly a child of Reconstruction, revival, and renaissance. There is an unbroken line between his early encounter with odd white people in his neighborhood and his cultivation of white bohemian friends like Carl Van Vechten during the Harlem Renaissance. He gives the example of one of these odd characters in the figure of a white man named Mr. Cole, whom "everybody said . . . was crazy" (21). There is also an unbroken line between his early experience of black music and religion and his mastery and refinement of black folk culture into music like "Lift Ev'ry Voice and Sing," which becomes the Negro national anthem, and religiously inspired poems like those in *God's Trombones*, a text that becomes the most popular poetry for black children to memorize and recite for generations.[22] One of his neighbors, Aunt Venie, elicits as much fear from him as Mr. Cole. Aunt Venie "was said to have fits," but they "were probably the results of religious excesses." Describing Aunt Venie as "the champion of all 'ring shouters,'" Johnson traces the unbroken line between his African past and his New World present and future, connecting his sense of the African American religious revival—with its peculiar music—to the artistic high Renaissance of the 1920s, in which figures like Alain Locke urge a reconnection with Africa as a path to Negro artistic modernity.[23]

Unlike Du Bois's crisis of identity in realizing that he has an obligation to the downtrodden former slaves of the South, Johnson suggests that as a child he suffers from "an unconscious race superiority complex": "All the most interesting things that came under my observation were being done by colored men. They drove the horse and mule teams, they built the houses, they laid the bricks, they painted the buildings and fences, they loaded and unloaded the ships. When I was a child, I did not know that there existed such a thing as a white carpenter or bricklayer or painter or plasterer or tinner."[24] This Reconstruction environment in which black men are strongly identified with manual labor, skilled and unskilled, conjoins with his father's capacity to turn menial labor into a princely inheritance. This foundation provides a sense of masculine entitlement that enables Johnson more confidently than Washington or Du Bois to fuse the menial, the manual, the artistic, and the professional into a self-assertive conduct that seems to draw on manly resources across class lines. Similarly, going to an all-black freedmen's school in his neighborhood, where his mother and their family acquaintances are teachers, provides him with a sense of educational entitlement. This black world of enterprise, skill, and practical knowledge embodies the Bookerite ideal in the flesh, but it is also not without Shakespeare, Keats, piano playing, and other liberal refinements.[25] Furthermore, this experience is not without black authorities of the state.[26] As a result, when President Grant comes to Jacksonville in 1877, the colored people take front and center stage in the ceremonies, and Johnson himself carries out his project of shaking hands with the general who won the Civil War. With such an integral upbringing that makes of his southern town a teeming microcosm, it seems almost unthinkable that Johnson would exhibit a demeanor and comportment that are anything but self-assured. Shaking hands with the president becomes, in short, an expected boon as much befitting his inheritance as enhancing his future gentle manly conduct.

Taking the sting out of manhood development, Johnson destigmatizes what it means to be a black boy in a white man's world, and thus he prepares his reader to see him, as adult male, as fully secure in his soft gentility as he is confident in his manly (I almost wrote "chivalric") jousting on behalf of an oppressed race. As we shall see, Johnson is not unaware that is he flirting dangerously with a portrait of manhood development that could easily be spun as the preparation for a sissy coward in the unrealistic lap of soft luxury. The proof that his childhood, partly by chance, beneficently rears him for sophisticated soft diplomacy in an ugly race war, however, comes with the dissolution of Reconstruction along with childhood, as Jim Crow sprouts up, unexpectedly, like a deadly ambush.

A Gentle Man Facing Jim Crow Violence

This Reconstruction idyll is shattered at the very moment that Johnson leaves Jacksonville for normal school at Atlanta University, and not surprisingly the break into race consciousness, and its peculiar burden for black men, occurs in learning about the Jim Crow car. In the year that Johnson sets out for Atlanta by train with his Cuban friend Ricardo, Florida passes "its law separating the races in railroad cars, and it was just being put into operation; a matter that I, at least, was then ignorant of."[27] Johnson's narration of this Jim Crow encounter should be placed alongside those of so many others, from Homer Plessy, who takes his challenge to the New Orleans law to the Supreme Court in the infamous *Plessy* case, to lone armed encounters dramatized by William Pickens, Ida Wells Barnett, Angelo Herndon, and others.[28] When the conductor tells them to move to the Jim Crow car, Johnson does not understand. Neither does Ricardo, whose English is still poor, and thus in translating the conversation into Spanish for Ricardo, Johnson fortuitously avoids the sort of confrontation we see in other Jim Crow–era narratives: "This was my first impact against race prejudice as a concrete fact. Fifteen years later, an incident similar to the experience with this conductor drove home to me the conclusion that in such situations any kind of Negro will do; provided he is not one who is an American citizen."[29] Although Johnson sees it as a lesson about being a Negro, it is also clearly a lesson about being mulatto, given that the chances of passing for Latino in the parochial South of this period are much greater for those whose skin color is lighter. The impact of this first racial incident also clearly brings home to him the power of language as an access to and beyond "American citizenship." At Atlanta University, he finds that he has "a love of language, and Latin meant more for me than mere class work. It was the same when I came to Greek, and French and German" (73). Directly contradicting Washington's rant against such irrelevant liberal knowledge for a race without economic resources, Johnson is eager to demonstrate how integral his study of language, the classics, and liberal arts at Atlanta University is to his training in gentle manly racial obligation.

One could take this a step further. The young Johnson on his way to college discovers serendipitously, without violent confrontation, how he can manage Jim Crow indignity through a facility with language. Whereas in other Jim Crow narratives, violent retaliation is placed in the forefront of such confrontations, Johnson is able to keep his manhood dignity intact without a gun or a violent rant, two of the strategies represented in the literature. A cowardly retreat does not even seem an option, even though under different circumstances, such as traveling alone, the outcome would surely have been less fortunate. Wright would later suggest that words could be used as weapons against Jim Crow, but in so saying, he was clearly invoking the belligerent power of explosive social realism, not the delicate intonations of a Latinate language falling unknowingly from a liberally reared black man's lips.

The subtext of Jim Crow shapes Johnson's movement toward the classics, university study, sexual desire for women of color, and equanimous manhood. At Atlanta University, Johnson charts his rise to manhood through his first self-conscious appreciation of the greater beauty of colored women. Remembering the catholic range of skin colors observed in the women in the university study hall, he writes: "The bulk of them ran the full gamut of all the shades and nuances of brown, with wavy hair and the liquid velvet eyes so characteristic of women of Negro blood. There was a warmth of beauty in this variety and blend of color and shade that no group of white girls could kindle" (75). Based on the masculine gaze that signals the young boy's aspiration for manhood, this attraction to color not only aestheticizes Negro women; it also posits racial consolidation (attraction for unity in diversity) and gentlemanly cosmopolitanism (catholic tastes) as an aspect of Talented Tenth obligation while masking an uneasy color consciousness that favors neither the lightest nor the darkest of the women. Whereas Washington nurtures an anti-aesthetic as the basis for a housekeeping conduct cathected on hygiene, Johnson promotes the idea that fit black manly conduct must be anchored in the delicate appreciation of the aesthetic, whether the liquid registers of a Latinate language or the effluent colors of Negro womanhood. Ironically in a way not so evident in Washington's self-narration, where the Wizard's wives more equitably mirror his own gender conduct, women in Johnson's memoir are at risk of being objectified as the idealized aims that guide and soften a man's desire—similar to the way women are treated in Samuel Chapman Armstrong's biography, examined in the previous chapter. As we shall see, however, this tendency is contravened in a signal moment of lynching crisis, when Johnson rescues a female companion only to be himself rescued not only by a white military officer but also by the very lady whom he chivalrously escorts to safety.

Like so many others, Johnson first takes up his racial obligation by going into the backwoods to teach, a burden that enriches further his appreciation of and attraction to the aesthetic (and political) potential of the race. He does not present this teaching stint as a threat of emasculation, as Pickens does when he notes how the black male teachers at Talladega are under the thumb of white bosses. Johnson's backwoods experience instead confirms his development into a capable manhood untroubled by the masculine roughness entailed in the racial brutalities of Jim Crow: "In all of my experience there has been no period so brief that has meant so much in my education for life as the three months I spent in the backwoods of Georgia.... Certainly, the field was limited, the men and conditions simple, and the results not particularly vital; nevertheless, taken together they constituted the complex world in microcosm. It was this period that marked the beginning of my psychological change from boyhood to manhood. It was this period which marked also the beginning of my knowledge of my own people as a 'race'" (118–119). Such serendipitous discoveries of the world wherever he happens to be indicates that parochialism may be as much a matter of outlook or demeanor as of actual location. At first it appears that Johnson is going to repeat the sort of allegorization of rural black folk that Du Bois and later Nella Larsen exploit in their narratives of backwoods teaching. In *Souls of Black Folk* Du Bois's memory of his student Josie becomes the personification of a buried, repressed, wasted life of obscure feminine drudgery. Thus, Du Bois transforms his own backwoods teaching stint into the kind of wailing lamentation that we saw Kelly Miller attacking as characteristic of a man not equipped to operate within the bare-knuckle reality of U.S. politics. In Larsen's *Quicksand*, the heroine, as a result of an uncharacteristic moment of conventional feminine vulnerability, likewise sinks into the quicksand of marriage, pregnancy, child-rearing, housewifery, and church matronage. Johnson, too, finds it "impossible to eliminate the element of hopelessness" in observing these common, oppressed people: "The situation in which they were might have seemed hopeless, but they themselves were not without hope" (120). He nonetheless reaffirms his unbreakable connection to the backwoods folk: "I found myself studying them all with a sympathetic objectivity, as though they were something apart; but in an instant's reflection I could realize that they were me, and I was they; that a force stronger than blood made us one" (119). As his upbringing has prepared him to face social difference with an open mind and an open heart, he can observe (objectively) the Black Belt poor with an attitude of sensitive empathy. This attitude predicates a gentle manly conduct that finds common cause with the commonness of the downtrodden masses. Then, in a passage reminiscent of Robert Park, Johnson slightly revises the scene in which he gazes at the diverse colors of women at Atlanta University:

> I saw strong men, capable of sustained labor, hour for hour, day for day, year for year, alongside the men of any race. I saw handsome, deep-bosomed, fertile women. Here, without question, was the basic material for race building. I use the word "handsome" without reservations. To Negroes themselves, before whom "white" ideals have so long been held up, the recognition of the beauty of Negro women is often a remote idea. Being shut up in the backwoods of Georgia forced a comparison upon me, and a realization that there, at least, the Negro woman, with her rich coloring, her gayety, her laughter and song, her alluring, undulating movements—a heritage from the African jungle—was a more beautiful creature than her sallow, songless, lipless, hipless, tired-looking, tired-moving white sister. (121)

He at first leans toward masculinizing the rural women but shifts from calling them "handsome" to noting a "beauty" that surpasses that of white women. Struggling with the division of gender and incipient sexual attraction in his own relation to these rural folk, Johnson again inverts the conventions of beauty as a way of indicating his embrace of the side-by-side muscular labor conducted by black men and women in the hot southern fields. Just as Johnson submerges the ugliness of Jim Crow that he must rise above if he is to remain a child of Reconstruction, so he insists that sharecropping peonage, the most immediate consequence of Jim Crow politics on the rural working masses, cannot submerge forever the mass power that will be the inevitable foundation on which the advance of the race is built. Here we see Johnson mirroring in the backwoods men and women his own soft muscularity, a reciprocal image of mutuality between the potential race leader and his ostensible racial charges. Just as he has banished from his own boyhood any tincture of the masculine brutality that usually occasions a Jim Crow narrative of childhood development, so he has evacuated here the imagery of vicious ignorance and unrelenting brutalization that usually characterizes black leaders' representation of the backwoods Negro under Jim Crow.

In the climactic moment of Jim Crow violence directed against him, Johnson is able to occupy a double position as both a victim of American bigotry and a leading shaper of American destiny in the best tradition of gentle manly conduct, and he is able to do so through his chaste relation to a northern mulatta of high esteem. When this white-appearing female acquaintance from New York comes to Jacksonville to consult with Johnson on an article about the Jacksonville fire that has just occurred, she and Johnson are seen conversing in a park and are mistaken for a cross-racial couple by militiamen who are in town to keep order after the fire. Confronted by dogs and armed militiamen, whom Johnson has already identified as "crackers" from as far away as Savannah, he feels the real potential of his own lynching: "There we stopped. On the other side of the fence death was standing. Death turned and looked at me and I looked at death. In the instant I knew that the lowering of an eyelash meant the end" (167). Rather than trying to escape or trying to explain who he is (which would certainly be foolish), or trying to explain that the woman is indeed "black" (which would be mighty risky), or trying to defend his right to be in the park with whomever he desires as he has experienced in growing up in his hometown (which might be noble but would only antagonize the militia further), Johnson submits absolutely to their authority: "I lose self-control. But a deeper self springs up and takes command; I follow orders" (167). These sentences capture perfectly what it means for a disciplined conduct, borne from a self-assertive upbringing, to step in at a moment of crisis. His loss of self-control goes counter to the equanimous character that has been habituated by a life of gentle, open, self-assured conduct. Maintaining manly dignity in the face of white male savagery requires attention to the most precious detail, like a Romantic painter trying to capture the atmosphere with strokes of a brush: "I knew that the lowering of an eyelash meant the end." This is hardly hyperbole. On one hand, to lower the eyes in the face of white men is a gesture of subordination to a masculine superior. White segregationists insisted that black men lower their heads at the approach of a white man and avert their gaze in the presence of a white woman. Notably, Johnson does *not* conform to effeminating protocol by lowering his gaze. Instead, he steadies his gaze. On the other hand, this calculated refusal to unman himself for the satisfaction of white brutes is wholly practical, rather than some glorified heroic gesture of masculine bravado, of the kind Trotter and Pickens represent so well. His conduct is neither conventionally belligerent and confrontational, the way a real (white) man is expected to behave, nor is it conventionally submissive and cowering, the way a sissy coward would behave and a black man *should* behave when faced with the savagery of white supremacist hate. Johnson's gender conduct defies and befuddles such simple classification.

In the midst of this terror, Johnson includes a tiny detail intended to speak volumes about his unsubmitting stance as a gentle man, or more precisely a gentleman: "I take my companion's parasol from her hand; I raise the loose strand of fence wire and gently pass her through; I follow and step into the group." The "deeper self" that "springs up and takes command" includes both the act of submitting rather than enacting a savage animal instinct for survival and the act of chivalrously tending to his lady's decorative needs (carrying the parasol and handing her through the fence). Our sympathy for his noble manly carriage not only counters any tincture of cowardice; it also damns the militia as brutes and cowards in their inability to catch the nobility of his bearing: "I follow and step into the group. The spell is instantly broken. They surge round me. They seize me. They tear my clothes and bruise my body; all the while calling to their comrades, 'Come on, we've got 'im! Come on, we've got 'im!'" (167).

Just as subtle as the detail of his chivalry defining his true manhood against the crackers' cowardice is the tiny recognition of gentle humanity in another that saves his life.

> And still, I am not terror-stricken, I am carrying out the chief command that has been given me, "Show no sign of fear; if you do you are lost." Among the men rushing to reach me is a slender young man clad in a white uniform. He breaks through the men who have hold of me. We look at each other; and I feel that a quivering message from intelligence to intelligence has been interchanged. He claps his hand on my shoulder and says, "You are my prisoner." I ask him, "What is the charge?" He answers, "Being out here with a white woman." I question once more, "Before whom do I answer this charge?" "Before Major B——, the provost marshal," he replies. At that, I answer nothing beyond "I am your prisoner." (168)

To resist this terror (of the brutish mob, of his own animal instinct), Johnson carries out "the chief command," which comes from his having been socialized for this moment by his parents, by a white mammy, by friends, by the Black Belt backwoods folk, by the community that protects him in his self-knowledge of who he is. Similarly, his upbringing has prepared him instantly to recognize the "slender young man clad in a white uniform" as of higher mettle than the militiamen, all of whom are dressed in khaki. It is not the "looks" alone (the uniform) that alert Johnson to a kindred spirit but the officer's intelligent look (a demeanor that shows in the eyes). The succeeding interchange begins to restore order and some measure of humanity to the mob, as Johnson is luckily able to submit to one who can assure his safety: "As soon as the lieutenant put his hand on me and declared me his prisoner, the howling mob of men became soldiers under discipline." In front of Major B——, Johnson is restored also to himself, as the major "showed astonishment and some embarrassment when he recognized me." It is face to face with the major that he can have his say. In response to the major's apologies, Johnson says, "'You know as well as I do, if I had turned my back once on that crowd or taken a single step in retreat, I'd now be a dead man.'" As

Johnson's biographer writes: "A cosmopolitan self-image enabled him to ward off the potentially crippling psychological effects of his socially marginal position."[30] Interestingly, it is also at this moment that his lady companion takes her stand: "She spoke slowly and deliberately at first; then the words came in torrents. She laid on the Major's head the sins of his father and his fathers' fathers. She charged him that they were the ones responsible for what had happened. As we left, the Major was flushed and flustered" (168–169). We are reminded that she, too, has acted heroically by remaining under control, silent, and poised until the end.

We would be remiss, however, not to grasp the delicate gender dynamic at work in such a passage. While enacting the chivalrous hero, Johnson has actually been rescued by a military man of action, which he is not. He has also been rescued, quite literally, by the heroic composure of his lady companion, whose poise in the face of life-threatening danger equals his own. A black race leader rescued by a white military officer and a white-appearing lady seems hardly the recipe for a manly race leadership. If we look closely, we realize that structurally Johnson is in the position of a damsel in distress—a sensitive, refined, soft-spoken, poetic, gentle man, caught in the grip of a hypermasculine, riotous mob. Even the gesture of taking the parasol from his lady friend highlights his effeminate figuration, a dandy holding a parasol confronted by a mob of crackers. Ironically, it may have been Johnson's gentlemanly appearance—his flawless fashion that would have identified him as an upwardly aspiring dandy—that alerts the militiamen to his presence in the park. As Monica Miller observes in tracing Johnson's adoption of a dandy look, "Johnson figures his growth and increasing worldliness to his exposure to, acquisition of, and analysis of cosmopolitan style."[31] Although such a "dapper" cosmopolitan sartorial appearance could be managed in Manhattan, sporting it in Jim Crow Jacksonville, with a white-appearing lady in tow, puts Johnson at great physical risk. The ambivalence of his chivalric gesture—distinguishing him as a gentleman to his lady but also turning him into a ladylike figure—is only intensified by the manner in which he is rescued by the slender man of military action. In Johnson's framing of the incident, however, this is exactly the point. No amount of masculine posturing could have saved him from the mob. As we shall see, Johnson's own experience with the lynching mob here can be productively contrasted with the sissy cowardice of his fictional character, the ex-colored man. If Johnson is structurally and temperamentally a ladylike sissy in the episode, he is definitely not like the ex-colored man, who flees his black identity in sissified cowardice on witnessing a lynching—even as his passable light skin color could protect him from the lynching mob.

Auspiciously, Johnson discovers, each rescue provides a kindred cosmopolitan "intelligence" to serve as an advancing patron—beginning with his white mammy.

When Johnson is trapped in Jacksonville due to a yellow fever epidemic outbreak that keeps him from Atlanta University, his father provides a remarkable tutor for him, a West Indian cobbler "who spoke English as no professor at the University could speak it."[32] Later, he stumbles on another tutor and a more lasting supporter and "kindred spirit" (99). Dr. T. O. Summers, a noted surgeon, hires him to keep accounts for his medical practice, and the relationship grows into something more: "What was unprecedented for me was that in him I came into close touch with a man of great culture. He was, moreover, a cosmopolite. He had traveled a good part of the world over, through Europe, to North Africa, to Greece and Turkey.... He had wide knowledge of literature, and was himself a poet" (95). Through their "close touch"—which seems so different from Washington's deifying, unequal associations with Armstrong—Johnson and Dr. Summers are able to rise above their Jim Crow environment: "Between the two of us, as individuals, 'race' never showed its head. He neither condescended nor patronized; in fact, he treated me as an intellectual equal" (95). As the ideal race patron—one who constructs himself neither as racially different nor as a patron—Dr. Summers provides the object lesson that Johnson himself enacts when he takes on the role of Harlem Renaissance patron: "He had formed a strong affection for me which he did not hide. I had made him my model of all that a man and a gentleman should be" (98). Another rare portrait in Jim Crow literature, this intimate bond between a white mentor and his black protégé represents the contrary to the savage white mob from which Johnson is rescued.

So unlike the commanding general Armstrong, Dr. Summers has all the attributes of a sissy, sometimes indistinguishable from those of a genteel man of the world. His discreet manliness is constituted through "softer" qualities of culture, verbal dexterity, sophisticated literacy, indiscriminate travel. As we shall see, this portrait of two gentle men attracted by their extraordinary gentleness can sometimes blur over from a potential sissy propensity into homoeroticism—a blurring Johnson flirts with tantalizingly in *Autobiography of an Ex-Coloured Man*. Although laudatory, however, Dr. Summers's gentleness exposes a negative vulnerability in sensitive manliness that risks the sort of fatal self-destructiveness often associated with the suicidal end of sissies and homosexuals in late nineteenth- and early twentieth-century literature. Dr. Summers is almost too good for the brutal realities of the world. His worldliness descends into world weariness and ultimately suicide. If Dr. Summers, through intimate contact, helps to shore up Johnson's claim to a renaissance cosmopolitanism, the white doctor's death by his own hands nonetheless reminds us of the jeopardy that sissy manliness also entails. Apparently, the same gentle conduct that arms Johnson for a savagely violent Jim Crow reality disarms this distinguished, sophisticated doctor, so that ultimately his worldliness incapacitates him for enduring the world itself.

Cosmopolitanism as an Armor against Jim Crow

We might understand the near-lynching that Johnson experiences as a sign that Jacksonville is not to be his home again. As much as the town has fostered a gentle manly conduct that braces him for every obstacle and opportunity the world has to offer, Johnson's demeanor, posture, and attire mark him as a dandy who has outgrown the increasing Jim Crow savagery of his hometown. (That the white savages are from Savannah does ameliorate this judgment to some extent, perhaps.) In the end, Johnson's cosmopolitanism must push him away from Jacksonville. Concerning his excitement on taking a trip to New York with his grandmother when he is twelve, Johnson writes: "It would not have taken a psychologist to understand that I was born to be a New Yorker. In fact, I was partly a New Yorker already.... But being born for a New Yorker means being born, no matter where, with a love for cosmopolitanism; and one either is or is not."[33] After Johnson moves to the city to pursue a songwriting career, his rightful place is confirmed. He, Rosamond, and their friends help to enliven black bohemia, creating a black artist's colony (with many whites welcome) in the literal center of Manhattan. In this environment, Johnson sees himself as able truly to synthesize those competing impulses from his racial, social, and cultural backgrounds. New York becomes the core cosmopolitan space, allowing a harmony of the worlds within the self.[34] Before aestheticist advocates like Alain Locke, Langston Hughes, and Wallace Thurman (all queer men) begin to set the terms for a *cultural*, rather than a political, revolution, Johnson has already embarked on a Negro renaissance aesthetic. To emphasize how Johnson—as opposed to, say, Du Bois—joins forces with these queer aesthetes is to emphasize his comfort with the intimate contact of sissified men, a comfort already prefigured in his affectionately equal bond with Dr. Summers.

Johnson's project is to bring about full citizenship for the Negro by bringing attention to African American art as a shaper of world culture. Similar to his need to master New York, as the country's most worldly city, it is also necessary that he travel farther, not just as a tourist, but more as an authoritative U.S. citizen. As a consul first in Venezuela, then in Nicaragua, Johnson continues the tradition of negotiating U.S. imperial spoils as a way of conditioning and positioning African Americans as mediators between dominant Anglo-Saxon leaders and the leaders of the tropical and subtropical client states and territories of the southern sphere. Booker T. Washington had fulfilled a similar role by advising foreign countries on how to develop industrial schools, by traveling abroad to Europe to view the conditions of the peasants, and by allowing Tuskegee Institute to serve as a civilizing training ground for students from U.S. colonial territories and Indian country. Befitting his cosmopolitan talents and knowledge, Johnson reroutes this mediating strategy. Whereas Washington insisted that he could live and do uplift work only in the Deep South, regardless of how far-flung his name, fame, and educational theories might be spread, Johnson takes the first opportunity to live as an American abroad, and he does so by pursuing a career in one of the most gentlemanly of vocations, the consular service. Ironically, however, Johnson's stint abroad is not what gains him fame among African Americans at home.

Like Washington's tutoring the primitive Native Americans at Hampton, Johnson casts the Spanish-speaking American countries as primitive outposts in which he must negotiate tropical mores: "There have come to the tropics men from a foreign clime who have attempted to put into practice the strenuous life. The effects on them have generally been disastrous. And yet not so disastrous as the effects on those who have yielded too much and become lotus eaters."[35] Attesting again to his equanimous temperament, he is able to sustain his "strenuous" American conduct without intolerantly and futilely attempting to force his own way of life onto the natives. Sounding like Armstrong or, more accurately, like Theodore Roosevelt, Johnson is foremost a robust, pioneer *American* in the wilderness, and it is up to him to enforce U.S. interests to the fullest, which means understanding and adjudicating the habits of the natives without falling so languidly into them that he becomes a lotus eater.[36] His knowledge of the natives pays off in the midst of civil war intrigue in Nicaragua, where his consular post is a port town vital to the interests of the United States and its allies, who have been vanquished from the capital, Managua, by revolutionary forces. Through stalling tactics, he is able to hold the port without bloodshed until a host of U.S. warships comes to the rescue. Ironically, even in the midst of a foreign civil war, Johnson is still in the curious position of the rescued, and his métier is diplomatic stalling, not violently heroic military action itself. Justifying this act of soft intervention, Johnson suggests that the "fundamental policy" is aimed not at a crude economic interest of imperialism but, instead, at the control of the potential trade routes across Central America for the sake of international peace.[37] As contradictory (and flimsy) as this logic may seem—especially in light of his later patronage of Haiti against the U.S. occupation—such sophistries are inevitable when a sophisticated conduct must be buttressed with dominant nationalist interests, whose personal oppression he is struggling against.[38]

As Brian Russell Roberts suggests, Johnson promotes an approach of "strategic indirection" not only as a diplomat abroad but also as a race activist domestically.[39] This strategic indirection, a principle of diplomacy, characterizes Johnson's social (i.e., racial) practice in conducting diplomacy abroad and at home. His race activism, like his diplomacy, is constituted by "fighting passively" rather than the kind of belligerent frontal attack that a blustery brute like William

Monroe Trotter figures as the proper manly conduct of a race warrior. Because strategic indirection substitutes worldly sophistication for the folksy sycophancy of which Washington is accused, Johnson is able to evade the sissiphobic attacks that occasion Washington's gender accommodations. Johnson's tour of duty in these Spanish-speaking countries is not only a process of winning over foreign leaders and commoners to U.S. interests in the region but also a matter of winning over U.S. citizens to acknowledge *his* right to function as a legitimate representative of the U.S. nation-state. Johnson's comfort in the world—his cosmopolitanism—makes both of these tasks a pleasurable challenge. Although Johnson's race is virtually a nonissue among the natives of these countries, not surprisingly it becomes one for some U.S. citizens who come under his jurisdiction during their travel or military service. "I found, too, in Corinto—unlike in Puerto Cabello—that occasionally race prejudice bumped into me," he writes. Because so few U.S. people come through Puerto Cabello, Venezuela, he has no problems; Corinto, Nicaragua, however, is more accessible to the United States and close to the U.S. colony of the Panama Canal, resulting in more contact with his fellow citizens. In describing one such contact with a man from South Carolina, he persists in his ability to stay above injury from such racial prejudice: "I mean to indicate specifically that I did not bump into it. In other words, I was not concerned with its stupid outbursts or with how it bruised its own head."[40] Even the syntax here indicates Johnson's status as passive object of others' racial contentiousness: prejudice bumps into him, rather than the more idiomatic form in which he bumps into it. When he accomplishes a diplomatic feat in negotiations with the leaders of the insurrection in order to buy time for a U.S. naval rescue, he is able to highlight the shared interest of U.S. and American (New World) citizenship: "The ensign who accompanied me to Paso Caballos, a young Southerner, was the only officer on the *Annapolis* with whom my relations were not fully cordial—he himself had pointedly indicated that he did not wish them so. After the parley he came up to me and wrung my hand. He appeared to be proud that we were both Americans."[41] Such moments of consolidated American identity may be brief, but like a poem or song, as they increase in number and quality, they are expected to build a lasting monument of transracial American citizenship. It is Johnson's "strategic indirection," a soft-spoken diplomacy, that makes him successful in such incidents, as he stands firm but pliable amid insurrections, civil war, and U.S. military adventures to ensure its imperial might over the New World hemisphere.

Although Johnson is not a soldier himself, we can see in *Along This Way* how crucial an intimate knowledge of military protocol is for a man who desires to rise in the world. This is the second time that Johnson is rescued by white military officers in the autobiography. Just as in the first incident Johnson's rescue depends as much on his personal familiarity with the officer as his general knowledge of military protocol, note how, in the second incident above, Johnson emphasizes his personal good relations with all except one of the naval officers. As a diplomat overseeing America's imperial interests in a southern sphere in continual political upheaval and civil war, Johnson could not afford to be ignorant of the military or unfamiliar with the commanding officers on whom he depended for the protection of his life, as well as that of his family and diplomatic staff. Although these cameo appearances of white officers are brief, they are pivotal to the narrative's representation of Johnson as a man of the world, one who does metaphorical battle on behalf of the race and the country. The large shadow of the military in the autobiography, nonetheless, indicates how black manliness is riven by a nagging self-doubt. No matter how brave Johnson's conduct in those critical moments in Central America, the long history of white commanders' casting doubt on the mettle of black soldiers haunts Johnson's representation of himself as a man of gentle, self-assertive demeanor.

These pivotal exchanges with white officers expose a man eager, perhaps even anxious, to document his own fitness as a brave warrior against the tendency to sissify black men as unfit soldiers and thus as unfit men, as discussed in chapter 1. As we shall see, *Autobiography of an Ex-Coloured Man* might be seen to document Johnson's own fear of becoming the ex-colored man, not in passing for white but in fleeing the scene of a racial battle. This question of whether the black man has the right stuff, whether as a military commander or a State Department diplomat, arises particularly in relation to America's imperialist ventures around the period when Johnson is pursuing a career in consular service. Despite Johnson's justification of U.S. imperialism in the Caribbean and Central America, he does not make the mistake of the young William Pickens when it comes to the special case of Haiti. Haiti represents that boundary whose crossing can easily jeopardize the balance Johnson has established as a gentle man who is *not* a sissy-coward in the face of white male supremacist violence. In the series of four articles titled "Self-Determining Haiti" that he writes for the *Nation* on his return in 1920, and from which the Haiti section of *Along This Way* is culled, Johnson includes a description of Port-au-Prince that evokes a European city.[42] Ironically, Johnson delegitimates the U.S. occupation based on Haiti's affinity with Europe. Furthermore, in celebrating Haiti's long history of independence, he also implies that the error of the U.S. invasion derives from Haiti's similarity to the U.S. republic. In fact, because of Haiti's "more complete social revolution," its history of national independence is more glorious than that of the United States.[43] This near-utopian view of Haiti wrestles with Johnson's competing, complementing impulses of black autonomy and black assimilation. It shows up as two kinds of cultivated conduct: a more democratic cultivation of the soil for a century and a more cultivated sensibility of Afro-European civilization. Unlike the Mexicans, the Haitians have been able to make of their mestizo culture a monumental New World history. Becoming a liberating patron to Venezuela much in the way that France aided the British colonies, Haiti has transformed its slave and colonial inheritance into the most politically and socially advanced American vision. One way that Johnson relates this advancement is in the idea that there are no peons in Haiti since independence.[44] Beyond political organization, Haiti also demonstrates an advanced state by its cleanliness.[45] Borrowing from Washington's sissy compulsion for cleanliness, Johnson compares Haiti's clean streets and villages with those of the U.S. South and concludes that the United States has little to offer Haiti in taking it on as a client state, much less as a colony. In Haiti he is constantly impressed with the French manners of the social elite: "I called to see ex-President Légitime, a grand old gentleman; indeed, a jet-black Frenchman of the courtly school." Repeatedly mentioning the color of these Haitian intellectuals, statesmen, and artists, he is mesmerized by the combination of "pure black" skin color and French gentility. If his patronage of Haiti's cause in the United States enhances his link to cosmopolitan French civilization, it also paradoxically tightens his identification with African American aesthetics and autonomy.[46]

Despite his pose as a New World gentle man, then, Johnson is not an amalgamationist of either the Charles Chesnutt or the Robert Park type. His progressive stage of culture does not move through the marginal mulatto to modern assimilation, though such a vision is tempting to him. In the final pages of *Along This Way*, he imagines, as Chesnutt had, what it would mean to have perfect amalgamation through interracial breeding to procreate a single American "race": "It seems probable that, instead of developing them independently to the utmost, the Negro will fuse his qualities with those of the other groups in the making of the ultimate American people; and that he will add a tint to America's complexion and put a perceptible permanent wave in America's hair."[47] This is not his ultimate vision, however.[48] Perhaps inspired by his Haitian sojourn to believe more intently in the happy coincidence of a cosmos in which cultures can be mixed without becoming fused, he instead opts for a more autonomous New Negro fate: "If I could have my wish, the Negro would retain his racial identity, with unhampered freedom to develop his own qualities—the best of those qualities American civilization is much in need of as a complement to its other qualities—and finally stand upon a plane with other American citizens."[49] Choosing a mottled cultural complementarity over the monotone of racial fusion is, after all, the most cosmopolitan course, and one in line with Johnson's strategic indirection, his commitment to a gentle, penetrable, soft-spoken temperament over belligerent, invasive hypermasculine penetration of the other.

The Ex-Colored Boy's Gender Double Consciousness

Twenty years before the publication of *Along This Way*, while he was the consul in Corinto, Johnson had anonymously brought out another "autobiography," *The Autobiography of an Ex-Coloured Man*, through a small Boston publishing house. Through the patronage of rich white homosexual Carl Van Vechten, this "autobiography" is republished in 1927 by one of New York's most prestigious houses, Alfred A. Knopf, which was becoming a major player in the Harlem Renaissance. In his 1927 introduction to the "autobiography," Van Vechten is careful to distance the narrative from the man whose signature is now attached to it, considering that the book is confusingly titled an "autobiography": "The Autobiography, of course, in the matter of specific incident, has little enough to do with Mr. Johnson's own life, but it is imbued with his own personality and feeling, his *views* of the subjects discussed, so that to a person who has no previous knowledge of the author's own history, it reads like *real* autobiography. It would be truer, perhaps, to say that it reads like a composite autobiography of the Negro race in the United States in modern times."[50] In discussing the reception of this fictional autobiography within his "real" one, *Along This Way*, Johnson suggests that one of the reasons he feels compelled to write the latter is to forestall the constant confusion of readers who assume that the former represents a narrative of his life.[51] Ironically, as Van Vechten strives to separate the man from the narrative, he ends up binding the two more closely. The book is "imbued with [Johnson's] own personality and feeling, his *views* of the subjects discussed." That the "*real* autobiography" turns out to be a "composite autobiography of the Negro race in the United States in modern times" seems even more puzzling, given the difference between Johnson's "real" autobiography and his fake one. That Van Vechten should see the fake autobiography as the "*real*" one of the Negro in America seems doubly ironic. Scott Herring takes this even further: "The spectacular joke, however, is that *Autobiography*—with its insider-outsider narration making it an influential prototype to [Van Vechten's] *Nigger Heaven*—offers anything but an insightful account of Negro group psychology."[52]

Even if we do not go so far as to dismiss its narration as "mocking" and "sensationalism," *Autobiography* is fundamentally the contrary of *Along This Way*, in that it portrays the life of a man who, because he appears white and grows up in white, parochial New England, is confused about his racial identity.[53] Against the humanist comedy of *Along This Way*, with its celebration of coincident doubleness, *Autobiography* is a Du Boisian wail projecting the tragedy of doubleness and the bastardy of confused racial identity. The ex-colored man fails to achieve a gentle manly conduct that can in turn harmonize the worlds awakening within himself, fails to achieve a temperament that can view the world as the image of an enlarged self. As such, it is a cautionary tale about the dangers of gentle cosmopolitanism, rather than a collective autobiography of the Negro. It is nevertheless true that there are significant similarities between the two autobiographies, especially in some moments in which Johnson almost lifts passages from *Autobiography* to describe scenes of his life in *Along This Way*. The differences, however, are more crucial here. The ex-colored man (though born in Georgia) grows up in a New England environment with a racial experience more similar to Du Bois's than to Johnson's.[54] Whereas the ex-colored man is doomed to be alone and lonely even after he has decided to slip into the white world of respectable marriage and the solid middle class, the Johnson of *Along This Way* is never truly alone. Whereas *Along This Way* is a gratifying experience of personal ambition and racial obligation fulfilled, *Autobiography* plots a series of mournful longings resulting from racial and erotic secrets and denials, or what Valerie Smith calls the ex-colored man's "habitual evasiveness."[55] Although the ex-colored man succeeds in becoming a typical American gentleman in the most superficial sense by passing for white, amassing comforts, and marrying upward, this sort of success cuts him off not only from integrating his African heritage but also from ever satisfying his longing to become a leading uplift patron. Unlike the Johnson of *Along This Way*, who is able to exploit a soft, penetrable manliness to solicit a gentle equanimity capable of resisting Jim Crow savagery, the ex-colored man runs away from his sissy temperament as much as he runs away from his Negro blood. He is doubly alienated, then: first from his rich black inheritance, which in turn alienates him from the potential of a manly alternative to that imposed by white supremacist masculinity.

Autobiography is not only about racial double consciousness, then; it is also about gender double consciousness, about the bending of gender identification in response to a split racial self-consciousness. "From the start," Gayle Wald writes, "the Ex-Colored Man must mediate legally incompatible maternal and paternal racial inheritances—the former permitted and recognized, the latter prohibited and denied, albeit present in the 'zero degree' of the narrator's own flesh."[56] The ex-colored man is in search of his absent white father's inaccessible world of masculine control in the spheres of business, politics, remote obligation, and respectable (missionary) sex. His father is an "absolute blank" to him until he shows up unexpectedly one day when the boy is twelve: "And here he stood before me, just the kind of looking father I had wishfully pictured him to be; but I made no advance toward him; I stood there feeling embarrassed and foolish, not knowing what to say or do." Has the boy wished him to be a "tall, handsome, well-dressed gentleman of perhaps thirty-five"?[57] Or has he wished him to be what remains unspoken, a white man, given that the son has identified his own appearance with his white schoolmates, not his black ones? Only after the son plays Chopin for him does the distance between father and son begin to lessen, as he "stepped across the room, seized me in his arms, and squeezed me to his breast. I am certain that for that moment he was proud to be my father." It is notable that, as a gentleman, the father discovers his paternal pride when the bastard son plays European classical piano (the uber-Romantic Chopin, no less) rather than, say, showing his acumen by throwing a baseball. When the son asks his mother if the father will stay with them, the father replies, "'I've got to go back to New York this afternoon, but I'm coming to see you again'" (35). The father's relation to the son is, at best, remotely obligatory in the moment of parting: "He spoke some words of advice to me about being a good boy and taking care of my mother when I grew up, and added that he was going to send me something nice from New York." The father remains a mystery, however, if not a blank, because the protagonist sees him only once again, years later, by coincidence: "In my mind I ran over the whole list of fathers I had become acquainted with in my reading, but I could not classify him" (36). Due to the father's absence the son grows to be more familiar with the mother's yearning for her lost love than with the man himself: "She loved him; more, she worshipped him, and she died firmly believing that he loved her more than any other woman in the world" (43). This disparity between the father's remote obligation and the mother's visible enactment of eternal devotion can only strengthen the son's identification with the pining victim of jilted love in romance, usually associated with women's subjectivity in romantic fiction. The only objects the son has to remember his father by are a gold piece and "a beautiful, brand-new, upright piano" (39), the gift from New York that the father had obligingly sent him after his sole visit. This splintering double consciousness cannot help but prognosticate a doomed racial character, whose gender conduct will be as self-conflicted as his racial bearings.

The narrator's Du Boisian bastard status gets symbolized in the other memorial, the gold coin. In the hazy but golden memory the ex-colored man has of his early childhood in Georgia, he describes how he comes to possess this paternal keepsake, which his father gives him on the day before the mother and son leave for Connecticut: "I remember how I sat upon his knee and watched him laboriously drill a hole through a ten-dollar gold piece, and then tie the coin around my neck with a string. I have worn that gold piece around my neck the greater part of my life, and still possess it, but more than once I have wished that some other way had been found of attaching it to me besides putting a hole through it."[58] The narrator's desire for the gold piece without the hole in it, of course, points to the fact that he has needed the coin for money in many desperate instances in his life, but the hole has forced him to retain its value as a keepsake rather than as money to be spent. Houston Baker finds another meaning for the keepsake: "The gold piece is not only worthless, but also serves as a symbol of the commercial transactions to which black Americans were prey during the days of American slavery."[59] The father's gesture of giving the boy the gold piece on their separation is intended to represent the promise of the son's share in the father's patrimony, but it is, at best, an empty gesture, not followed up with consistent action. As such, the gold piece becomes, as Baker suggests, more like the legacy of chattel slavery's chain around his neck than the promise of a stake in the father's material and symbolic social assets. Furthermore, the gold piece represents the narrator's relation to white male society's control of the purse strings. In this sense, the pseudo-autobiography seems to be a subtle critique of Washington's attitude toward money as an uplifting agent of exchange between the races. As Marvin P. Garrett has noted, "The narrator's life only serves to belie Washington's position that material success is the key to social and psychological success for the Negro."[60] If Johnson is here castigating Washington's accommodationist program of monetary exchange across the races devoid of physical touch, what would constitute ethical conduct for the ex-colored man? How exactly should such a man learn to behave under unfortunate racial circumstances so contrary to the confident, open, royal upbringing that enables Johnson's gentle manly conduct?

As race shapes gender conduct, gender conduct most assuredly flows from racial character. We see the ex-colored man's moral confusions in the submissive way he responds, like a sycophant, to white patronage. The ex-colored man will be lucky enough to get a wealthy white patron, a father substitute, but he will discover that the millionaire's money has little power to uplift him. Furthermore, the reader discovers that the narrator himself does not understand fully the objectifying, demoralizing aspects of his patronized contact with the millionaire's money. The mother has told him that his father, "a great man, a fine gentleman" himself, "was going to make a great man" of his son and that mother and son had been sent north because the father "intended to give me an education and make a man of me."[61] When the boy is left motherless and without resources, however, the father does not come to the rescue. Unlike the Johnson of *Along This Way*, being rescued like a damsel in distress is *not* an option, exactly because the ex-colored man is always in the process of running away from his gentle temperament in rejecting his racial heritage—not to mention that as someone who identifies as white, to be rescued by another man would seem to diminish his claim to a white supremacist identity. As he rushes toward the powerful straitjacket of normative white masculinity, he also retreats from the pliable gender resources we see Johnson deploying throughout *Along This Way*. Without his patrimony, the only convertible currency that remains from his father's legacy is his visible whiteness. Unfortunately, his whiteness inculcates a longing for the security that the father comes to represent; to the son it is an evanescent security that makes him a fugitive in his father's world.

The maternal, on the other hand, is linked with the boy's emerging Negro identity, with immediacy, romantic yearning, flaunted affection, sentimental excess, economic deprivation, feminine beauty, and the luxurious passion for art, ideals, and causes—gender-fluent attributes that we see celebrated by and in Johnson's narrative persona in *Along This Way*. In a sense, the boy's divided relation to his parents simulates Park's idea of the Negro as "the lady of the races," as the protagonist's gender identification with the mother's status bends him toward a sort of gender deviance from the white father's remote norm. However, the ex-colored man's uneasy existence between these spheres calls into question the legitimacy of their fissure, and thus the effectiveness of the norm itself. Despite its association with immediacy, affection, passion, and excess, the mother's sphere is one of psychological yearning and relative material want. Partly as compensation for his racial deprivation and poverty, partly as silent inculcation of pride for the prestigious origins of his missing white father, the mother raises the ex-colored boy to possess aristocratic pretensions, which in themselves shape the boy's uneasy relation to the dominant expectation of rough, adventuresome boyhood: "My mother dressed me very neatly, and I developed that pride which well-dressed boys generally have. She was careful about my associates, and I myself was quite particular. As I look back now I can see that I was a perfect little aristocrat."[62] In this portrait we cannot help but see the sissy-boy ensconced in his mother's make-believe luxury, obsessed with neatness, cleanliness, and effeminate cultural competence, the portrait of a too-good boy. The protagonist's idea of being a "perfect little aristocrat" seems especially off-key in light of Johnson's portrait of his own boyhood in Jacksonville, where his street becomes a democratic rough-and-ready wide-open world at the same time that his family provides him a natural sense of royal self-esteem. The ex-colored boy's aristocratic bearing derives from a haunting sense of deprivation, denial, and fugitive identity. As a result, the boy's sissy temperament becomes a liability rather than a resource. His too-goodness indexes a needy longing to conform, in contrast with Johnson's own appreciation of eccentricity, gender and otherwise, across the class spectrum.

Because she is being supplied money by the son's father, the mother technically is a kept woman—and of course during the time she would be considered something even more socially and sexually deviant than this, a concubine and fallen woman. However, the father's money provides a semblance of genteel living. Watching his mother read mysterious letters containing money and how she thrusts the letters "into her bosom," the son, too, develops an erotic sense of mystery, romance, and secrecy—but not yet denial, deviance, or shame. It is only after the mother places the boy in a public school, where all races are jumbled together and distinctions of race are made, that the boy's gender fissure manifests itself. It comes, not surprisingly, with the boy's discovery of his "proper" racial assignation, not yet an identity. When some of the white schoolboys call him "nigger" and some of the Negro ones mutter, "We knew he was coloured," he is confused. The only two who stand up for him are "Shiny," the darkest (and smartest) one in the class, and "Red Head," who perhaps identifies with him because of being teased about the color of his hair (and being mentally the slowest). In contrast with Johnson's own appreciation of the gamut of colors that aestheticizes his relation to the women of Atlanta University, the ex-colored man repeatedly experiences color diversity as constraint, coercion, and deprivation. The boy is learning to conduct himself in such a way that he can neither claim the father's inheritance of white supremacist masculine domination over his Negro concubine, nor the mother's sensibility of romantic longing for racial reciprocity and fulfillment.

Being grouped with two extreme colors marked as socially deviant in the class—black skin and red hair—elicits from the narrator "a very strong aversion to being classed with them" and sends the boy into a self-conscious endeavor to see himself as he truly is, to understand how he looks to others.[63]

> I rushed up into my own little room, shut the door, and went quickly to where my looking-glass hung on the wall. For an instant I was afraid to look, but when I did, I looked long and earnestly. I had often heard people say to my mother: "What a pretty boy you have!" I was accustomed to hear remarks about my beauty; but now, for the first time, I became conscious of it and recognized it. I noticed the ivory whiteness of my skin, the beauty of my mouth, the size and liquid darkness of my eyes, and how the long, black lashes that fringed and shaded them produced an effect that was strangely fascinating even to me. I noticed the softness and glossiness of my dark hair that fell in waves over my temples, making my forehead appear whiter than it really was. (17)

Although for Johnson as author adopting the voice of the mulatto boy through the narrator, this passage may constitute a sort of self-conscious fantasy of whiteness, for the child it is an innocent moment of denial, and revealingly that denial takes the form of a displacement from racial dislocation to gender dislocation. Kimberly W. Benston identifies this dislocation with narcissism. "This narcissistic drama . . . effects a destabilizing series of reflections," he writes, "for the scene represents the fracturing of an initial cognition (or consciousness) of blackness into the desired re-cognition of whiteness: the face the hero sees (as hyperbolically 'ivory' as it is homoerotically 'beautiful') is the secret, endangered other of his suddenly activated 'I.'"[64] Benston immediately translates narcissism into homoeroticism, a traditional association with a history that goes back to ancient Greece.[65] Because in patriarchal culture the female is conventionally associated with the object of desire, femininity is often constructed as the female's fascination with (and anxiety over) her own degree of beauty, a fascination frequently figured as the female's obsessive gazing at her own face in a mirror. Johnson exploits this mirror scene of femininity in order to locate the narrator not necessarily as homosexually inclined but rather as gender displaced in dominant culture's hierarchy of subjects and objects of desire. Instead of developing as the masculine subject of desire, his racial dislocation causes him to identify as the effeminate object of others' (whites') more authoritative desire.

As the narrative progresses into his adulthood, the ex-colored man will find himself switching between two contrary sexual-racial positions—a splintering confusion that causes his flighty conduct and cowardly temperament. At first he becomes a "black" man courted by powerful white patrons or imagines being victimized by white brutes in an act of lynching, with its connotations of male genital mutilation. In the end, he becomes a "white" man capable of creating his own object of desire in a hyperwhite woman whom he chooses to court, marry, and mourn. As a boy, he cannot see why he would be called a nigger, but he can see why others would call him pretty and beautiful. The passage accentuates the boy's "pretty," girlish features, to which he clings as a shield against recognizing any Negroid hint lurking in his face. The ironies here are almost too multiple and complex to disentangle. Suffice it to say that his identification with prettiness, so closely allied with a normative aesthetic of beauty that excludes blackness, secures his desire for "fair" or white skin color, but at the same time, paradoxically, it alienates him from a properly gendered boyishness. Boys are often encouraged to seek mannishness as early as possible just to avoid being classified as "pretty," like a girl, exactly because boyhood constitutes a liminal transit in which size, stature, physiognomy, and a high voice can easily make an onlooker confuse the boy for a girl. In other words, the features his schoolmates no doubt read as Negroid when they call him "nigger" are the very same ones that make him appear more "white" to himself. He identifies as a girlish white boy in order to evade becoming Negroid. He runs to his mother and looks into her face with the question "Am I a nigger?": "And then it was that I looked at her critically for the first time. I had thought of her in a childish way only as the most beautiful woman in the world; now I looked at her searching for defects. I could see that her skin was almost brown, that her hair was not so soft as mine, and that she did differ in some way from the other ladies who came to the house; yet, even so, I could see that she was very beautiful, more beautiful than any of them."[66] What he notices is the difference between his "beauty" and hers, but also a difference that separates her more distinctly from other ladies in his experience. When he continues to ask her if he and she are white, she finally responds, "'No, I am not white, but you—your father is one of the greatest men in the country—the best blood of the South is in you." Resisting this shadow that would separate him from his mother and bind him to an unknown father, the boy feels instead "in his heart a fresh chasm of misgiving and fear" (18). In effect, the mother's response enforces a separation between black mother and white son, which in turn implies a separation between unnatural manliness (to be the white son of a black mother cannot be natural) and fit manhood (the properly engendered son of a properly white father).

The boy's gender dislocation goes beyond his unusually "pretty" looks, which are, of course, or *should be* more routinely attached to girls, not boys, at his age (eleven). His behavior as well identifies him as a sissy. This behavior includes the pride he takes in being well-dressed and his particularity about his playmates. The narrator's relation to the more conventionally boyish Shiny and Red Head places him in a girlish position, in some ways like the narrator of *Along This Way*, the protagonist as the object of rescue. The narrator looks up to both Shiny and Red Head (who is fourteen) with the sort of crush that a more delicate boy can sometimes experience in the face of more assertive ones who lend protection rather than bullying. Red Head carries his books on the way home and offers him his "big red agate" to cement their friendship.[67] He develops with Shiny "a sympathetic bond," and Red Head "was the only one who did not so wound me; up to this day I recall with a swelling heart his clumsy efforts to make me understand that nothing could change his love for me." Characteristic of the sissy, as Charles Nero and Rod Ferguson have theorized, he moves further into the seclusion of books and music, growing more reserved and "constantly more and more afraid of laying myself open to some injury to my feelings or my pride" (22–23). Becoming an "'infant prodigy'" on the piano,[68] the boy develops the mannerisms of a great pianist as he explores ways of containing and expressing the self through music, as other avenues of sociability are shut out. He becomes, in effect, a sort of malformed prima donna, prone to histrionics and obsessive concern with how others see him. Even as the boy's behavior is being fixed through a sissy sensorium, his temperament remains fluctuating, not in a positive self-assertive openness like Johnson's urbane worldliness but in a self-negating desperation that precedes an unreliable character.

The intensity of his emotions gets displaced into his piano playing, transforming him at an early age into a cliché of the deeply feeling romantic artist constrained with his peers but at ease with his art.[69] Johnson exploits musical performance to chart the gender shifts in the ex-colored man's racial predicament, from a romanticized childhood innocent of race to the masculine impersonation of aggressive ragtime piano to the abandonment of music altogether in passing as a white patriarch. The movement from playing for his black mother to playing (once) for his white father to playing for black audiences to playing for a white wealthy widow to playing for a white wealthy bachelor to his failed attempt at using music for racial uplift marks his transition from passing to black identification back to passing, and each time his musical ambition reflects his gender and racial confusion.[70] Becoming the private pianist for a white bachelor ensnares the ex-colored man into an unequal romantic exchange bordering on homosexuality, an exchange that makes him a treasured but servile racial dependent, diminishes the virile potential of his ragtime, and returns him to a psychic desire for elite whiteness. His high European life of luxury with the bachelor turns out to be a sissy flight from the realities of blackness even though he is not passing for white. He has, without fully recognizing it, bartered his black manhood for a comfortable existence providing exotic pleasure to another, more powerful man. This sissy idyll is disrupted when he sees his father and half sister at an opera in Paris. How fitting that his disillusionment with his own sissy romance would come in a Parisian opera house. The operatic backdrop cannot help but accentuate the queerness of his situation.[71] The disillusionment in the opera house catapults him toward the novel's climax, when his musical ambitions are dashed in the face of a lynching that causes him to cut his ties not only to music but also to the affective racial capacity that it represents.

The narrator's immersion in art as a sort of salvation indicates a tendency toward decadence, a misappropriation of artistic endeavor away from socially accepted moral ends. (In having the decadent Van Vechten provide an introduction to the book's republication in 1927, Johnson seems to be highlighting the narrative's relation to the decadent tradition of Oscar Wilde.) The obsessive piano playing, like the image of himself as beautiful, shuts him off from the world of boys and thus from the masculine values of physical competition, sporting camaraderie, homosocial jousting, and heroic mastery of others and events. In *Along This Way*, Johnson devotes several pages to his expertise in playing baseball as a boy, even scripting a scene in which he becomes a local hero because of his astonishing capacity to throw a devious curve ball that not even the best sluggers could hit.[72] Johnson associates pitching with the kind of "masculine grace" or "tense power" that accords with his ideal image of self-assertive poise.[73] By contrast, although the mulatto boy learns the grace of virtuoso piano playing, he also develops the kind of temper associated with prima donnas, as mentioned above. His "fits of sentimental hysteria" and "temperamental excesses" shield him from other boys his age, bind him to his mother across the color line in a cathexis of undifferentiated tears, and place him further in the spotlight of self-display.[74]

The ex-colored boy's divided racial identity conjures for him a divided gender temperament that fails in exactly the way Johnson's portrayal of his own gender pliability succeeds. Able to find grace in romantic piano-playing but not in pitching a baseball, the ex-colored boy cannot comprehend, as Johnson himself does, that gender need not be a binarizing straitjacket. Just as the ex-colored boy can imagine race only as a mutually excluding binary between black and white, he can access gender conduct and character only in the extreme, either a sissy tantrum that pushes him toward homosexuality or a normative white supremacist masculinity.

The Ex-Colored Man as Sissy Coward

The ex-colored man develops an unworldly romantic sensibility, which will make him either a "genius" dwelling "in a world of imagination, of dreams and air castles" or something much less noble, a decadent man "unfitted for the practical struggles of life." With the moment of separation from his mother looming, he must make a decision that will bind him either to the immediate, dark maternal or the remote, blank paternal: "My mother told me that my father wanted me to go to Harvard or Yale; she herself had a half desire for me to go to Atlanta University, and even had me write for a catalogue of that school."[75] The mother's "half desire" is significant, for it indicates her own waffling between having her son develop as white and achieve the privileges of the father or consolidate with blackness and struggle with race uplift. The obligations of Atlanta University would be double, requiring the son to aspire within an institution known at the time as the highest seat of Negro learning while also forcing him to accommodate the Negro self. With the mother's death, a decision is no longer required. Going to Atlanta, the ex-colored man sees for the first time large numbers of African Americans with "unkempt appearance, the shambling, slouching gait and loud talk and laughter." The ex-colored man becomes alarmed until he is told that they are lower class, for "these people aroused in me a feeling almost of repulsion."[76] Again, Johnson's response to the backwoods former slaves in *Along This Way* insists on a studied contrast. Where Johnson sees a fundamental strength across gender, men strong in their hard labor and women strong in their handsome fertility, the ex-colored man can see only uncleanness, ignorance, and vulgarity.[77] Although this reaction could be seen as reminiscent of Washington's portrait of his charges at Tuskegee, the ex-colored man lacks not only the Wizard's missionary fervor to clean up the black masses by tempering them with dirty labor but also the Great Accommodator's fluid gender maneuverings to bind himself, at once, to the white male elite and the struggling black bottom.

The ex-colored man's restlessness becomes a travesty of Johnson's own strategic indirection as a worldly roamer. Without the resources to attend Atlanta University, the ex-colored man travels to Johnson's Jacksonville. Rather than being trained in the obligations of Talented Tenth uplift at the university, he gets a crash course in introductory African American folk culture. He becomes, much like Park, an "expert" on black culture, delineating the class structure, strengths, and weaknesses, but such participant-observation gradually turns into racial passing as he begins to identify as a Negro. "Just when I was beginning to look upon Jacksonville as my permanent home and was beginning to plan about marrying the young school-teacher, raising a family, and working in a cigar factory the rest of my life," the factory shuts down and he returns to New York: "All at once a desire like a fever seized me to see the North again."[78] Ironically, this prospect of complacent settlement into a modest African American norm gets disturbed by the accident of the closed factory. The desire that seizes him like a fever raises the question, of course, of whether his settling down into common Negrodom was only a pipe dream all along. Rather than a conduct that allows him to seek opportunity fortuitously wherever he finds himself, as both Johnson and his father had done, the ex-colored man discovers disillusionment at every turn.

In New York, he goes in the opposite direction from a settled ordinary Negro life, becoming an addicted gambler and getting enmeshed in black bohemia. When he is in the boardinghouse in Jacksonville, he is surprised when the African American and Cuban men's animated, loud, aggressive quarrels do not come to a "clash of blows." "I soon learned," he says, "that in all of this clatter of voices and table utensils they were discussing purely ordinary affairs" (68). At first an outsider in this world of rough manly camaraderie, the narrator learns how to adopt the cues of their masculinity in order to fit in. Lacking Johnson's graceful pliability across race and gender, the ex-colored man begins to see himself sinking into risky habits, which he blames on the influence of African American men: "From their example I learned to be careless about money, and for that reason I constantly postponed and finally abandoned returning to Atlanta University" (83). His looseness with money, however, is directly connected with his attempt to prove his manhood among men—manual laborers—who make him feel insecure. This may be another possible place where Johnson is slyly commenting on Washington's equating monetary thrift with casting down your bucket "in every manly way." If a lack of thrift signals for the ex-colored man a certain kind of rough, muscular masculinity that is socially stagnant or even downwardly mobile, it is odd that he would choose to shift from one prodigal conduct to another. In effect, rather than going to Atlanta University, where he could imbibe a Washingtonian approach to monetary uplift, he makes a lateral move to the gaming houses of New York. Whereas the Jacksonville laborers are at least working within the "legitimate" economy, the New York gamblers are participating in a risky and truly violent underground economy. He has ironically shifted downward in the social scale, choosing a stigmatized way of life over a life of laboring production. Like Washington, the ex-colored man flees from dirty manual labor, but unlike the

Wizard, he opts for another mode of conventional, if socially stigmatized, masculinity defined by risk, shiftlessness, violence, and sexual laxness—the contrary of Washingtonian racial husbanding through hygienic housekeeping.

Fleeing in sissy panic from rough working-class muscular masculinity, ironically the ex-colored man lands in another mode of underclass degenerate masculinity but deriving from predatory wits rather than muscular labor. His gambling in New York ironically simply repeats the conduct of monetary improvidence that he had ostensibly rejected among the Jacksonville workers.[79] By gambling recklessly, he seeks to prove to the other men that he has "nerve" (96). The gambling also places him, like his virtuoso piano playing, in the spotlight: "I could feel that I had gained the attention and respect of everybody in the room, every eye was fixed on me, and the widespread question, 'Who is he?' went round" (94–95). Through a catalogue of such flighty conduct, Johnson is able to explore the variety of masculine experience more subtly across nuanced class and racial formations. The gambling demeanor is so different from the risk that Johnson describes his parents and himself taking in *Along This Way*, or the risk that the military men take on the battlefield, for the ex-colored man's masculine risk-taking should not be equated with the former's cosmopolitan, adventuresome ebullience, nor with the latter's mental bravery. As we learn from Johnson's *Along This Way*, there are other ways to secure manly firmness than the violent bravado of a ne'er-do-well or even the violent daring of a soldier on the battlefield. Whether sissy flight or rough-house risk, the ex-colored man is enacting a cowardice that will doom him even when he decides on the most routinely normative behavior of a white middle-class businessman, husband, and father.

Having explored the maternal race in the segregated South, the interracial mix of black bohemia in New York gives him the opportunity to go in search of white patrons as a substitute for the missing father and abandoned patrimony. As Kevin J. Mumford has suggested, the clubs and dancehalls of early twentieth-century Harlem and Bronzeville (Chicago) served as "interzones," places where racial and sexual hierarchies and conventions were apparently flouted while at the same time "the rituals of the interzones recapitulated the ideology of sexual racism that created them."[80] Such locales offer the ex-colored man a perfect sphere for finding a white patron. Though again put in the position of a student learning about the black fast lane, he comes with a more established black social practice. We cannot overlook, however, how his situation seems analogous to that of the whites who visit black bohemia in search of some creative investment for themselves. In addition to the set of whites who merely go slumming, "there was also another set of white people who came frequently; it was made up of variety performers and others who delineated 'darky characters'; they came to get their imitations first-hand from the Negro entertainers they saw there."[81] Unaware of the way in which he, too, is a quick study in racial imitation, he has begun to identify with the darkies imitated rather than the whites who profit on them.

In plotting the ex-colored man's transitoriness, from the southern working men to white patronage, Johnson bifurcates the conduct of such patronage by creating a contrast between a wealthy white woman and a wealthy white man. We are asked to consider whether gender alters the social practice of such patronage. The ex-colored man becomes acquainted with one of the vice district's female habitués, an aristocratic widow: "I found that she was a woman of considerable culture; she had travelled in Europe, spoke French, and played the piano well. She was always dressed elegantly, but in absolute good taste. She always came to the 'Club' in a cab, and was soon joined by a well-set-up, very black young fellow."[82] Cataloguing ostensibly the traits that make a lady of culture—including linguistic fluency—the ex-colored man takes mere etiquette or proprieties for the basis of gentility, rather than an urbanity born of deep thought or a propriety based in catholicity of spirit. Unlike Johnson's own patron, Dr. Summers, the wealthy lady's relation to her colored protégé is one of predatory, satiated mastery. Her companion, of course, is a sweetback, a figure who becomes central to the urban folk novel during the '20s and '30s.[83] Coming as an utter surprise to the ex-colored man, this couple raises the specter of cross-racial sex, but in the contrary arrangement from his impoverished colored mother and his wealthy white father: "I shall never forget how hard it was for me to get over my feelings of surprise, perhaps more than surprise, at seeing her with her black companion; somehow I never exactly enjoyed the sight."[84] This scene of shock in the presence of the black male–white female couple indicates to what extent he, after all, can adapt to his father's world. In eventually passing and marrying an upper-class white woman, in effect he becomes half of such a couple, but because he never sees himself as "black," the shock of seeing himself in such a couple is forestalled.

The ex-colored man does not want to see himself as being in competition with the "very black" companion for the attentions of the white patroness, but it turns out that he is. He tries to ignore her advances, "but the woman was so beautiful that my native gallantry and delicacy would not allow me to repulse her; my finer feelings overcame my judgment" (122). Surely Johnson intends irony here, given that the protagonist's "finer feelings" are directed at the possibility of a tawdry affair with a woman who makes a practice of keeping a gigolo for entertainment: "She was, after all, using me only to excite the jealousy of her companion and revenge herself upon him. It was this surly, black despot who held sway over her deepest emotions" (122–123). In the first of two violent scenes in the novel, Johnson oddly inverts the near-lynching scene from *Along This Way*. While the *Autobiography* protagonist is sitting at her table flirting with the widow, her sweetback comes in and shoots her in the throat.⁸⁵ The ex-colored man follows his animal instinct in running away from the scene of the crime—making a mockery of his own "native gallantry" and "finer feelings." As opposed to Johnson's near-lynching incident, in which his lady companion is colored and is indeed chaste, and in which the relationship too is chaste and is based in a benevolent social cause, the ex-colored man's triangulated affair involves the rivalry of two black men (or one black and one mulatto) over a woman whose chastity is dubious at best.

By offering the prospect of a white wealthy female patron as one option for the protagonist, Johnson highlights the "progress" the narrator has made in his sexual status, from tearful, sissy pianist playing Chopin for an overinvested mother to a freewheeling, ragtime-playing gambler called "the professor." Although he is beginning to establish a habitual way of conducting himself among a segment of the racial group, he "did not become acquainted with a single respectable family," even though he "knew that there were several coloured men worth a hundred or so thousand dollars each, and some families who proudly dated their free ancestry back a half-dozen generations."⁸⁶ In other words, unlike the Johnson of *Along This Way*, who understands that class can be deployed as a resource almost as well as color can, the ex-colored man cannot see his way around such identity categories and therefore cannot reform his behavior toward a less degenerate end. Repeatedly straitjacketing himself in a monochrome identity—whether of race, color, class, or gender—he lacks the imagination needed to fashion a truly worldly and genuinely gentle social practice. According to the Anglo-Saxon norm, which he still harbors within himself, he is still exhibiting excessive behavior. The "delicacy" he experiences as a child has not been totally abandoned, but it is being played to different effect as a man charming enough to gamble at stealing the rich widow away from the "very black" sweetback. Johnson contrasts the sweetback's hypermasculine aggression in using the gun on his lover with the protagonist's unmanly passivity in running away before the scene is played out. The ex-colored man's cowardice directly contrasts with Johnson's own observation about how black men "fight passively."⁸⁷ Given the hint of sadomasochism in the relationship between the white widow and black sweetback, it is clear that the protagonist's first hunch is right; he is no true rival for this "surly, black despot." Not only has the widow failed to become the white patroness that the protagonist surreptitiously desires; he has also failed to perform the rescue role of the natural gentleman.

In his flight from the scene of the crime, the narrator runs into his other wealthy white patron. By shifting the patron cathexis from a white widow to a white bachelor, Johnson highlights the amorphous gender position of the black male client and also the potential homoerotic undertow of the cross-racial, same-gender patronage bond. A further irony is that the maternal sphere of romantic longing that is lacking in the protagonist's macho rivalry for the widow returns in his intense relation to the white bachelor. The mystery begins the moment the protagonist first sees the bachelor: "Among the other white 'slummers' there came into the 'Club' one night a clean-cut, slender, but athletic-looking man, who would have been taken for a youth had it not been for the tinge of grey about his temples. He was clean-shaven and had regular features, and all of his movements bore the indefinable but unmistakable stamp of culture. He spoke to no one, but sat languidly puffing cigarettes and sipping a glass of beer. He was the centre of a great deal of attention; all of the old-timers were wondering who he was."[88] If we were ever dubious of how gentleness, gentility, sissiness, and homosexuality are close cousins in Johnson's worldview, this passage clarifies the interconnections. The bachelor is clearly a gentleman, a gentle man, and, as we later discover, a sissy with salient homosexual tendencies. The protagonist's relation to this mysterious man immediately assumes an erotic tinge through money, queering more explicitly the "contact" that Washington insists is hygienically uplifting in his relation to his white mentor, General Armstrong. In Johnson's fictional memoir, money queers every relation, as it perverts both gender and racial conduct. Again, we should read this as a subtle critique of *Up from Slavery*, where the cross-racial exchange of money is as fetishized as the dirtied/cleaned-up black body. That such attention to monetary exchange is altogether absent from *Along This Way* indicates how Johnson, often linked with a Washingtonian ethos, can distance himself from the Great Accommodator without the kind of sissiphobic rancor that characterizes figures like Du Bois, Trotter, Wells, and Pickens.

As Henry Louis Gates Jr. points out concerning the role of money in the ex-colored man's turn to real estate speculation at the end of the novel: "One of Johnson's most interesting narrative turns here is in associating his protagonist's desire to be white with an almost erotic investment in the project of money-making."[89] Although we do not usually associate monetary exchange with a sissy sensorium, this fictional text can amplify the relationship for us. Washington's insistence that money is the only medium that can save and lift the Negro race is intimately related to his adaptive gender positioning. If it takes playing the prudish schoolmarm to get the attention, applause, and patronage of rich white northern men, then he will sissy it up with the best of them. Playing the sissy can place a male in the objectified role of effeminate passivity, one eager to be the object of racialized patronage and ready to be rescued and thus also potentially ready to be bought—like Wright's Shorty, who is willing to offer up his ass for a quarter.

Actually, this erotic investment in money begins much earlier in the novel than Gates indicates, when the protagonist associates gambling with the general erotic atmosphere of the bohemian "Club." Just as it is possible to gamble on one's manhood in the "Club," so it is a place in which cross-racial sex is explicitly up for barter. In the way the mysterious bachelor pays the protagonist to play the piano and entreats him to come to his apartment, Johnson makes a clear analogy to an erotic—if not sexual—assignation: "When I had finished playing, he called a waiter and by him sent me a five-dollar bill. For about a month after that he was at the 'Club' one or two nights each week, and each time after I had played, he gave me five dollars. One night he sent for me to come to his table; he asked me several questions about myself; then told me that he had an engagement which he wanted me to fill. He gave me a card containing his address and asked me to be there on a certain night."[90]

Like the widow, the bachelor immediately establishes a master-disciple, dominant-submissive relation, one in which the entreated disciple cannot resist or refuse. The sadomasochism that flares to the surface in the triangulated relationship that ends in the widow's murder also becomes apparent in the narrator's relation to the millionaire bachelor, but this time based in a romance of high-minded white patron and undisciplined (native, black) genius. Not only is the protagonist at the bachelor's beck and call; he is also being disciplined by him, disciplined to meet the patron's insatiable need:

> I became accustomed to his manners. He would sometimes sit for three or four hours hearing me play, his eyes almost closed, making scarcely a motion except to light a fresh cigarette, and never commenting one way or another on the music.... The stopping of the music always aroused him enough to tell me to play this or that; and I soon learned that my task was not to be considered finished until he got up from his chair and said: "That will do." The man's powers of endurance in listening often exceeded mine in performing—yet I am not sure that he was always listening. At times I became so oppressed with fatigue and sleepiness that it took almost superhuman effort to keep my fingers going; in fact, I believe I sometimes did so while dozing.[91]

A foil to Johnson's portrayal of his affectionate bond with Dr. Summers, this cross-racial patronage relation is rife with repressed violence, sexual abuse, and racial torture. This nightmare version of his childhood obsession with virtuoso piano playing again seems to distort the idealized portrait of his relation to his mother, as though his sissy childhood has manifested into adult perversion.

Michael G. Cooke has noted the way in which the millionaire's role shifts from father substitute to the "most satisfying... guise of 'mother.'"[92] In this passage, instead of the satisfying mother, we observe the tyrannical master whose wish is the slave's command. Johnson turns the autobiography from the mother's romance to gothic terror, which is sustained in the text until the protagonist is released from blackness through his flight from a lynching. The sadomasochism implied in the previous passage is made explicit as the "good patron" transmogrifies into a fearful "supernatural power": "During such moments this man sitting there so mysteriously silent, almost hid in a cloud of heavy-scented smoke, filled me with a sort of unearthly terror. He seemed to be some grim, mute, but relentless tyrant, possessing over me a supernatural power which he used to drive me on mercilessly to exhaustion."[93] Clearly alluding to Mary Shelley's *Frankenstein* and other such gothic tales of mysterious, uncontrollable creativity, Johnson describes through this character what it feels like to be the sort of total object of the master's gaze (or, in this case, the master's ear). The narrator experiences the terror of gender dislocation as his narrative simulates those of gothic heroines pursued by mysterious, "dark" strangers whose intentions always verge on physical and mental rape. The relationship between the narrator and his patron, Cooke remarks, "takes on a subliminal homosexual character."[94] Although this has the ring of truth to it, it might be helpful to forestall the rush to homosexuality here. Lingering in the liminal space of the sissy, we can begin to see how the terror that the ex-colored man experiences is directly related to his flightiness, his fear of occupying the interstices between socially sanctioned identity categories. Neither quite heterosexual enough nor quite homosexual in act, the ex-colored man's patronage relationship exaggerates the sense in which sissiness is so often affiliated with perversely delayed gratification, and in this narrative the protagonist's queer deferral of sexual intercourse implicates and is implicated in his inability to chart a straight path toward racial identification. A man who flirts with gender indecision insofar as he seems to resist fit manliness but at the same time does not defect fully into sexual inversion as an active homosexual is perceived as no less queer than an outright homosexual. Ironically, sissy cowardice is thought to consist as much in the presumed fretfulness of following through on desire, due to the fear of facing the dreadful social stigma that must accompany such gratification, as it is in releasing all manly discipline to plunge headfirst (no pun intended) into sexual deviancy by being penetrated by another man. The ex-colored man's sissified sexual indecision, however, cannot be fully comprehended outside his insistence on remaining so long in a racial limbo. Contrary to the ways in which Johnson represents himself as easefully navigating across race and gender through a conduct that self-assertively identifies him as a fighting, if passively, race man, the ex-colored man's flittering from one mode of racial behavior to another causes and is caused by his fretful gender indeterminacy. If in today's parlance gender fluidity is seen as progressive, even transgressive, resistance to the suffocating gender binary, Johnson's autobiographical novel reminds us that sometimes what appears to be indeterminacy is actually a fear of the consequences of practiced commitment. Accordingly, when the ex-colored man finally does commit to a race, the white upper-class race, he necessarily also commits to a rigidly conventional patriarchal heterosexuality. That he possesses Negro "blood" in no way alters the conduct of this settled arrangement, for to pass into white maleness predicates an overcompensatory investment not only in the normative conduct of white men but also in the supremacist ideology that constructs whiteness as supremely masculine.

After describing in great detail this terror of a patronage relation that is at once sexually tyrannical and yet sexually deferring, the narrator attempts to diminish its impact: "But these feelings came very rarely; besides, he paid me so liberally I could forget much."[95] As we discover by the end, when he is still unsatisfied despite his financial success as a white man, the narrator believes in the balming effects of money. It is more complicated than this, however. The terms of the contract with the bachelor also indicate a "monogamous" relation, one based in a masculinist paradigm hinging on the same sort of possessive jealousy that destroys the widow and her sweetback: "He told me that he would give me lots of work, his only stipulation being that I should not play any engagements such as I had just filled for him, except by his instructions."[96] The patronage relation also takes on some of the qualities of Johnson's relation to Dr. Summers (who is a likely model given the millionaire's suicide)—an idealized bond of homosocial friendship that belies the economic and racial difference operating to constitute patronage.[97] "There at length grew between us a familiar and warm relationship, and I am sure he had a decided personal liking for me. On my part, I looked upon him at that time as about all a man could wish to be."[98] The irony of this statement—and the significance of "at that time"—is apparent for a reader who knows that this patron is deeply unhappy to the point of suicide and that he cannot lift the narrator above his split self any more than the narrator can satiate the patron's mysterious, unquenchable passion merely by playing the piano for him. When the "millionaire friend" drives up just at the moment that the protagonist has fled the scene of the widow's murder, the patron seems to be rescuing him.[99] As we discover in their ensuing European tour, however, this is not to be the case. Just as the ex-colored man cannot skillfully play the conventional masculine role of one who rescues (when he fails utterly in his attempt to be the whiter gentleman who rescues the millionaire widow from the black brute), he also cannot play the role of one who is rescued when the millionaire bachelor seems to save him only to enslave him in a homoerotic, sadomasochistic affair.

Phillip Harper has pinpointed one way of characterizing the unspoken gender contract between the narrator and his patron: "Between the protagonist's enjoyment of financial support and material luxury and the patron's pleasure in sharing his experience with a less worldly partner, the domesticized relationship that these men experience looks remarkably conjugal and, thus, evidently diverges from standard patterns of heterosexual masculinity."[100] In addition to the conjugal, the personal contract mirrors *and inverts* the sweetbacking relation, with its social stigma intensified by the implied same-sexuality. However, whereas the sweetback usually has a strong masculine identification, the narrator plays a submissive gender role more characteristic of a kept woman or concubine, the converse of the sweetback. In other words, as a gender-deviant black man (whether black buck or black sissy), the ex-colored man arrives at the same status occupied by his mother.

That the protagonist is unknowingly a concubine—an inverted sweetback—is only the beginning of the difficulty. Paris provides the backdrop for the making of a man of the world: "He had taken me from a terrible life in New York and, by giving me the opportunity of travelling and of coming in contact with the people with whom he associated, had made me a polished man of the world."[101] In the narrator's naïveté, Johnson seems to mock his own conviction that a man opened up and enlarged by the world will necessarily develop a sophisticated ability to balance seemingly conflicting racial, gender, sexual, national, and ideological inheritances. Just as the ex-colored narrator mistakes the wealthy white lady's cultured accoutrement for genuine gentility, so he himself fails to understand the difference between a worldly conduct that elevates and a world-weariness that dissipates. The narrator acquires all of the accoutrements of a worldly man, but fails either to grasp his situation or to lift himself above the mentality of an unworthy servant. It is highly ironic that his virtuoso pianism seems to devolve so quickly into the kind of menial domestic servitude and servility that Washington publicly cultivates while privately fleeing and that Du Bois treats with utter contempt when it is expected of self-respecting Talented Tenth black men like himself. The ex-colored man accordingly misreads his "benefactor's" "liberal" interest in him as the achievement of equality. The irony of the phrase "he dressed me, as an equal, not as a servant" must be noted. While still the object of the patron's fashioning, the servant mistakes his object status for equivalence due to the twinning appearance of being dressed like the patron. Although his pay is "far beyond . . . ordinary wages" and his services light, he is no less a hired man—indeed, exactly the sort of menial domestic that Du Bois so dreaded being coerced to perform—and in fact, the debt accrued by this supplement obligates him further to the patron's desire. Feeling that this is the "ideal" life, the narrator is startled when the patron readily admits that he will grow tired of it.[102] Fortunately for the protagonist, the accident of seeing his father at the opera intervenes before the master can tire of the new pleasure of possessing the servant. As Cheryl Clarke has remarked, "The eroticism between Ex-Coloured Man and the benefactor in chapter 8 is displaced onto the piano playing."[103] The patron's displacement of his desire for the narrator onto the narrator's piano performance seems to correlate with the narrator's displacement of his racial and gender dislocation into the music. But just as the patron cannot save the narrator as long as the latter has no sure racial commitment, so, Johnson suggests, the narrator's music cannot uplift the patron, nor the race with which the narrator has temporarily identified. This, we might say, is a case of racial conduct without racial character, a conundrum that must necessarily rob sissy liminality of its potential insurgent resourcefulness and instead trap the ex-colored man in an impossible gender—and thus also racial—dilemma.

Unlike a true man of the world—that is, unlike the Johnson of *Along This Way*—the ex-colored man does not have the equanimity to withstand the violence of being African American, just as he did not have the "nerve" to compete with the "black despot" or to compete with the Germans who have mastered "the new American music" more adeptly than he.[104] On witnessing a lynching—in which a man is burned alive—he experiences "a great wave of humiliation and shame. Shame that I belonged to a race that could be so dealt with."[105] As we find in *Along This Way*, a true cosmopolitan is able to find the world wherever he is, and to find the worlds awaiting within himself. The ex-colored man's humiliation and shame indicate to what extent he cannot be an insurgent sissy who fights passively like Johnson, and thus he cannot conduct himself like a proper Negro man, much less a manly New Negro ready to lead the race toward progressive modernity through a gentle capaciousness. Johnson here is radically revising the dominant notion that the white male embodies supreme manliness. The white man, capable of the greatest brutality, becomes in this logic an extreme case of violently virulent masculinity. The black man becomes, contrarily, one who can adapt manhood into a pliable resource for collective survival in the face of the most awful terror. That the ex-colored man decides to join up with the white brutes instead of siding with oppressed Negro manhood indicates his moral turpitude. As in the case of the widow's murder, he flees, but this time into permanent—or at least perpetual—white masculinity and its superficial comforts and conformities. Eugenia Collier points out about the narrator: "Oddly he feels no shame at being identified with the lynchers."[106] Jacqueline Goldsby further captures the ingeniousness of this episode, given that a requisite "high realism" of the time leads us "to think that the lynching would shock him into declaring allegiance to the cause of civil rights, if not to the Negro race itself."[107] For the ex-colored man, the shock takes him in the opposite direction, thus highlighting the impossible task of realistically depicting such a horrifying event.

For the ex-colored man, the shame lies in being a black man oppressed rather than in reaping the benefits of white masculine oppression. Achieving success in speculative real estate, he becomes, appropriately, a slumlord; marries a woman who is the epitome of whiteness; and settles into domestic regularity, reaching "a grade of society of no small degree of culture."[108] Despite the normal exterior, however, his life is haunted by a "dread" that he cannot shake off.[109] By fleeing into white middle-class male respectability, the ex-colored man lives psychologically on the edge between an inevitable movement into urban civilization and a lingering commitment to his originary cultural identity as a Negro. He embodies, in other words, Park's classic definition of the mulatto marginal man. When he gives up his gender dislocation as an incipient sissy, he gains the social respectability and comforts of being a "straight" man, but he also abandons that part of himself that tied him to bohemian art, risk, a flare for the excessive and sentimental, social change, empathy with the oppressed, and affectionate bonds with the culturally marginal. He is no less confused as a "straight" white man; he is just as lonely and self-doubting, especially when his wife dies giving birth to their second child. Measuring himself against black men like Shiny, who has risen to prominence as a race leader, he finds himself lacking as a man: "Beside them I feel small and selfish. I am an ordinarily successful white man who has made a little money. They are men who are making history and a race."[110] Shiny's superblackness ironically trumps the ex-colored man's "fair" whiteness in the end, and the ex-colored boy's prettiness due to light skin color becomes, pathetically if not tragically, a character deficit that dooms him to the insatiable condition of the millionaire patron whom he has fled. Through the narrator's feeling of manly inadequacy at the core, Johnson is able to invert the usual formula in which the black man is emasculated by his racial identification. Harper reads this closure as the forestalling of normative masculinity as a result of the failure to identify with black manliness. I think there is more irony in this resolution, given that becoming a respectable white man *should*, according to the dominant logic, provide him with the most "healthful" kind of manliness at the heart of normative white masculinity. It is the ex-colored man's "ex" status that has emasculated him, but ironically this emasculation gives him social, economic, and ideological power as a white man. That "ex" could have been a resource that recognizes and exploits gender transitoriness toward a new vision of racial manliness. In the end, instead, that inner stability of a masculine norm is just as elusive for the ex-colored man as his black patrimony or his bid to an interracial reconciliation. His fantasy of the heroism residing in Shiny's position is as much a projection of fixed manliness as his projection of a stable white masculinity before he passes into it. But the die has been cast and he must live with his choice.[111] The best he can do is to write his anonymous memoirs, which reveal the secret that haunts him. Even in penning his autobiography, the protagonist, despite having achieved a mask of white masculine normalcy, is deeply haunted by sissy flight and evasion.

In this sense, Johnson's *Autobiography* simulates the narrative of a sexual unclosing in that he suggests the anxiety of falling into criminal deviance most viscerally captured in the fearful confession of the closeted homosexual. I am not suggesting that Johnson either consciously or subliminally makes the ex-colored man a repressed homosexual. In fact, the narrator's sexual orientation is far from the point; rather, it is his indeterminate gender identity that reveals his racial confusion. Like Chesnutt's character Clara Hohlfelder in the short story "Her Virginia Mammy," the ex-colored man is beholden to the spouse who generously keeps his secret. The marriage bond itself becomes a patronage relation in which the white spouse has a psychological hold over the colored mate. Whereas Chesnutt's Clara is wholly ignorant of this condition, the ex-colored man's self-consciousness creates an inescapable anxiety of being found out *because* the spouse already knows: "I was in constant fear that she would discover in me some shortcoming which she would unconsciously attribute to my blood rather than to a failing of human nature."[112] In the end, the shared knowledge of the narrator's drop of African blood cannot forestall the possibility of an unconscious prejudice any more than the fear that blood will out can be fully overcome by confession. In confessing to us, the narrator is taking a risk that the reader/confidant will take his failure as a result of his blood. By analogizing the narrator's racial confession to a homosexual uncloseting, then, Johnson is able to insinuate how the criminality of the racial secret is exacerbated, rather than diminished, by its revelation. "I think I find a sort of savage and diabolical desire to gather up all the little tragedies of my life, and turn them into a practical joke on society," the narrator writes at the outset of his narrative, forewarning us of the eventual outcome.[113] Although this association of same-gender affection, cross-racial bonds, sissy impersonation, homoeroticism, racial uplift, and the search for African American manhood identity may at first seem to converge peculiarly in Johnson's fiction, this convergence constitutes a major theme in African American literary history, and more largely in U.S. popular and mass culture. In both black and white writing focusing on African American men's outcast status, the longing for a manhood that can withstand the fires of racial oppression gets connected to the social and psychic conditions associated with the erotic longing of the (homo)sexual outcast.

What the ex-colored man cannot learn in full, but what Johnson is able to teach because he has experienced it directly, is that manliness can be as pliable as racial identification, for those with the sissy stamina to occupy liminalities without fainting. What Johnson ultimately teaches us in his sissy narratives is to appreciate the resolve within the gentle man and to know the resources of strength hiding within the most ostensibly downtrodden identities. It is edifying that Johnson relies on the "confessional" narrative mode of autobiography, whether fictional or factual, to explore how a fit manliness based in "fighting passively" can find its resourceful sissy voice, or fail to. Just as fumblingly as the ex-colored man flees from one masculine conduct to another, each time stumbling due to his indecisiveness of racial (and thus ethical) character, Johnson represents himself as skillfully maneuvering across various trying racial situations with a catholic temperament of gender transitivity. As the first word of the title itself indicates, *Along This Way* emphasizes incidental passage, not teleological progress, as the basis of self-narration—providing a narrator who self-reflexively represents an agent who opportunistically responds to circumstances with even-tempered aplomb, rather than with head-on aggression. Chance, circumstance, and a plethora of other factors influence his choice of paths, and he voluntarily invites this influence, rather than viewing it as somehow hampering his manly individualism. Although such strategic indirection counters the dominant notion of masculine vigor, Johnson represents his agency as serendipitously shifting from one vocation to another, from one place to another, from one crisis to another, without ever losing his footing as a self-assertive black man. In Johnson's hands, then, autobiographical narration emphasizes the kind of transitive temporality that C. Riley Snorton discusses as intrinsic to racial and gender subject formation, as discussed in chapter 1.

This sense of a pliable manliness adaptable to a variety of social circumstances shares with Washington a necessarily unconventional gender dynamic insofar as their conduct must deviate from that of ruling white men. However, unlike Washington, whose gender posture is fixated to broadcast to his public a single and singular housefatherly demeanor, received differently by black and white, Johnson deploys autobiography to communicate a more protean gender demeanor— whether ineptly, like the ex-colored man, or dexterously, like himself—that silently schools his public to appreciate what it means for a black man to "fight passively" through "strategic indirection." As Washington's gender conduct assumes and cultivates a reading and oratorical public who can entrust a black man to lead the race—a public posture defined by the folksy, fastidious, sycophantic humbleness represented in the Atlanta Exposition Address—that hyperhygienic demeanor remains very consistent, even though he has two racially specific audiences to gratify. Because Johnson embarks on so many radically different vocations in so many different places around the world across a range of institutional venues— from popular entertainer to civil service, from racial activism to university professoriate—the sense of the publics he addresses is as varied as the fields he masters. On one end, the Central American consular episodes show him cultivating an immediate audience of military men and native leaders; similarly, the Jacksonville near-lynching episode represents an intimate, hostile audience of savagely racist Savannah military men and then a sympathetic and civilized white officer. On the other end, we see Johnson in wholly black environments working with and on behalf of other African Americans. These publics would seem contradictory, as we see him in conversation with individuals and groups up and down the social ladder, from cross-racial Broadway audiences to military commanders, from presidents to Black Belt menial laborers and segregated schoolchildren.

Johnson's ease across these socio-racial divisions, and their ease with him, is captured in his discussion of his ventures into popular culture, where he, on the one hand, achieves a cross-racial audience entertained by trendy Tin Pan Alley songs that sometimes verge on minstrelsy—"some of them very trite, written with an eye on Broadway"[114]—and, on the other, caters to a proud black audience inspired by plain-speaking poetry that synthesizes high intonations with black folk diction in volumes like *God's Trombones*. This capacity to capture divergent audiences in a way the fastidious, schoolmarmish Washington could never risk is vividly pictured in his description of the reception to the song he composed with his brother, Rosamund, "Lift Every Voice and Sing," for a concert celebrating Lincoln's birthday with a mass choir of a hundred children.

> But the schoolchildren of Jacksonville kept singing the song; some of them went off to other schools and kept singing it; some of them became schoolteachers and taught it to their pupils. Within twenty years the song was being sung in schools and churches and on special occasions throughout the South and in some other parts of the country.... The publishers consider it a valuable piece of property; however, in traveling round I have commonly found printed or typewritten copies of the words pasted in the backs of hymnals and the songbooks used in Sunday schools, Y.M.C.A.'s and similar institutions; and I think that is the method by which it gets its widest circulation.[115]

Because Johnson is the cocomposer of the Negro National Anthem, his profile as a race leader achieves a beloved status among the black folk mass—notably through the artistic expression nurtured by his mother—in a way that Washington's sycophantic housefathering is never quite able to sustain across ideological and generational divides. The song embodies Johnson's adept negotiation of high artistic expression with a mass popular reception that is at once sentimental and ennobling. Although not quite so schoolmarmish as Washington's social practice, this act of composition, which Johnson says was cobbled together spontaneously and incidentally, affiliates him securely with the sphere of sensibility, the teacherly, and those institutions that cement public civility to the domestic: schools, churches, YMCAs, and so on.[116] "Nothing that I have done has paid me back so fully in satisfaction as being the part creator of this song," Johnson writes. "I am always thrilled deeply when I hear it sung by Negro children."[117] Johnson sees as his greatest escapade not his warring crusade against lynching as the first black head of the NAACP, nor his strenuous diplomacy on behalf of the nation in a war-torn satellite Central America, nor his intellectual shepherding of New Negro Renaissance patronage, but instead the incidental composition of a sentimental song that inspires him in hearing it sung by the voices of schoolchildren who are in turn inspired by it. This collective reciprocal exchange—notably one that is difficult for even the copyright owners to monetize—of a soft artistic process is the perfect embodiment of Johnson's "fighting passively" through the gentler hand of strategic indirection.

4

Baldwin's Sissy Heroics

> In my childhood, at least until my adolescence, my playmates had called me a sissy.
> —JAMES BALDWIN, "Here Be Dragons"

> The condition that is now called gay was then called queer. The operative word was *faggot*, and later, pussy, but those epithets really had nothing to do with the question of sexual preference: You were being told simply that you had no balls.
> —JAMES BALDWIN, "Here Be Dragons"

James Weldon Johnson probably did not consider himself a sissy. Nevertheless, we can see quite clearly from his representation of his protagonist, the ex-colored man, that he thought deeply and complexly about the gender implications of a man poorly fitted to aspire to the highest achievements of elite culture while fleeing in desperation from the most horrific outrages committed against blackness—a dynamic that well defines the conventional assumptions about the sissy-boy and sissy-man in U.S. culture. While Johnson's fictional protagonist, like Johnson himself, seeks ways to meld an increasingly popular black folk culture (specifically ragtime) with classical techniques as a way to claim leadership within the race, the novel reveals how the failure to achieve this synthesis hinges as much on gender flightiness as on racial indecision—a narrative outcome that highlights even further Johnson's racial-gender adeptness in this regard, as represented in *Along This Way*. We have seen how Washington and Johnson in quite different registers negotiate their need to broadcast their worthiness for racial leadership to diverse publics across intimate, mass oratory, and popular settings. Washington's housefatherly social practice informs and reforms a public sphere defined by the kinds of listening crowds that attended the Atlanta Exposition Address and the kinds of readers who could feel comforted by the homespun assurances of beneficent racial reciprocity in *Up from Slavery*. Likewise, Johnson's gentle manly demeanor cultivates a wide spectrum of public audiences, from the cross-racial popular entertainments of Broadway musicals to the infectiously ennobling sentiments of the Negro National Anthem aimed at segregated black schoolchildren, from the cross-racial members of the NAACP to the high corridors of diplomatic negotiation at the U.S. State Department. In his two autobiographies, Johnson projects an audience at ease with a gender conduct that is at once conventionally self-assertive and unconventionally "passive" in relation to the circumstances, chances, and diverse others who shape his "fighting" agency, from a white suckling mammy and intellectual mentor to a white military commander and brave lady activist of color who can pass for white.

Neither Washington nor Johnson, however, was confronted with the kind of openly sexualized shaming that Baldwin has to negotiate as a sissy who comes of age in the era of televisual mass media. The attacks on Washington's gender impropriety seem limp next to the public shaming that Baldwin suffers, and even these anti-Washington attacks steer clear of the highly personalized hostilities against Baldwin amplified by a mass-media environment that at once enables Baldwin's fame and courts others to cast him in sissiphobic infamy. As we shall see, unlike the popular venues available to Johnson and Washington, venues that are less equipped to expose the private sexual gesticulations of even the most public of men, televisual media create in a racially unspecified, titillated mass audience a sense of sexual legibility about the most private aspects of a public life like Baldwin's. The minute details and signals of bodily conduct—posture, demeanor, speech, gesture, and gait—are amplified for viewers sometimes within the privacy of their own homes. Beyond the literary representations of sissyhood we find in Baldwin's fictional and autobiographical texts, beyond the journalistic representation of his gender conduct in mass-subscription periodicals like *Time* magazine, Baldwin's sissy sensorium is put on public view, and I suggest voluntarily on his part, also risking the sorts of sissiphobic backlash that we see occurring during the heyday of the black nationalist movement.

Using Baldwin as a test case, then, I want to ponder how the emergence of televisual mass media helps to reshape, if not to alter, the perception of sissiness and the weaponry of sissiphobia from the mid-twentieth century onward. I further pursue this inquiry in the following two chapters: chapter 5 focuses on a set of black male public intellectuals who openly, if cautiously, claim a sissified conduct during the era of desegregation through the invention of the straight sissy memoir; and chapter 6 focuses on how the first openly gay professional athletes of the late twentieth and early twenty-first centuries construct a public image of virile athleticism by distancing themselves from the sissy in a new form I term the sports disclosure memoir. Beginning with Baldwin's first protagonist—John Grimes, from his novel *Go Tell It on the Mountain* (1953)—as a semiautobiographical version of the author's own transitory sissiness, this chapter explores how Baldwin fashions a very public sissy demeanor not only through his writing but also through his entanglement with four quite different mass movements implicated in the stigma of the sissy: black Pentecostalism, whose hetero-patriarchal theology ironically embeds an alluring appeal to the precocious sissy-boy; the Red Scare and its attendant panic over "soft" manliness; the nonviolent civil rights movement's demand for muscular leadership to compensate for its emphasis on "passive" nonviolence and turn-the-other-cheek love; and black nationalism's scapegoating of the homo-sissy as an emblem for the emasculating ineptness of civil rights leadership.

Although it may seem an unlikely pairing, it is instructive to compare the gender formation of Johnson's ex-colored man with that of Baldwin's first protagonist, John Grimes. Like the ex-colored man, John grows up in a household where, although the father is very much present, it is a presence as deficient as the ex-colored man's white father's absence. Like the ex-colored man, John is intimately bound to his mother's secret that she has fathered a bastard child, a bastard condition that seems to intensify the sense of the boy's growing sissy estrangement. As we have seen, one's gender formation cannot be solely a private affair, especially for black persons and peculiarly for those men who seek or find themselves positioned as a head of the race. As the ex-colored man tries to exploit the sissy resources of his pianistic talent to cultivate an intermediating role between elite white culture and the black folk mass, so John discovers a sissy resource in his aptitude for literacy when he is praised in first grade by the white-appearing female principal, whose praise shifts the boy's sense of readerliness from a private fantasy life to a capacity for public communication and applause. Whereas the ex-colored man must go in search of a fit gender orientation that can anchor a sense of racial belonging, John is ensconced in a racial environment that is potentially, if anything, too settled to accommodate his gender disorientation.

Unlike the ex-colored man, who has, at best, a doubting and suspect relation to black communities and institutions, John is raised in a black home and embedded in a black church, both fostering a sense of deep racial belonging even as it sows a dread of deep alienation stemming from the (self-)perception of his suspect gender conduct. As we will see, as a boy Baldwin himself finds a temporary home in a church pastored by a powerful black woman, whose tutelage provides a space for him to navigate the seemingly orthodox gender strictures of Pentecostal doctrine. Baldwin does not incorporate this experience into his semiautobiographical novel; nonetheless, we will see how John's place within his father's church is as much advantaged by the church's own contradictory gender practices as he is alienated by the church's apparent patriarchal orthodoxy. Of course, John's racial ambivalence is not further troubled by racial ambiguity that derives from being able to pass as white. It is doubtful that John would choose a settled heteronormative life as a pater familias, for even putting aside John's sissiness, his racial identification precludes the kind of settled, established patriarchal passing on which the ex-colored man regretfully resolves. Unlike the ex-colored man, who is reared in a racially indeterminate setting that intensifies his sense of gender limbo, John grows up, on the one hand, in a setting dominated by a Pentecostal churchiness that pressures his good-boy behavior as a sublimated church sissy, and, on the other hand, tempted by self-conflicting twin impulses beyond the purview of the church: a racially mixed school system that rewards a more secularized good-boy conduct in a wholly different register from Pentecostalism and a racially mixed avenue that arouses a kind of sociosexual gratification that, on the surface, could satiate the boy's queer desires while affirming his penchant for sissy conduct. Baldwin ends his novel not with the poignant racial-sexual self-doubt of the ex-colored man but instead with John's tentative hope in the dawn of his salvation on the threshold between his father's oppressive household and the avenue's alluring deliverance from the church's sexual strictures. Johnson's *Autobiography* accordingly concludes with the ex-colored man's haunting regret at never being able to find a public voice to assume leadership of a race that could use his talents much more than elite white society could. Baldwin's novel ends, instead, by anticipating John's capacity for an intermediating role on the threshold between the private home and the public street, and between the church's promise of private salvation versus its messianic demand for a publicly exposed life to attract a mass following from the street.

According to W. J. Weatherby, the original manuscript version of *Go Tell It* ended with the young hero coming out with the bold statement "I want a man." In getting the novel published, Baldwin agreed to revise the ending, including perhaps axing the coming-out disclosure.[1] This original ending would have dramatically changed the characterization of the protagonist and thus the tenor of the novel, shifting it from a homosexual coming-out narrative to its current form as a sissy bildungsroman. From his first novel to his last, Baldwin explores a range of conducts associated with queer maleness, from the budding church sissy-boy John Grimes to Arthur Montana, the fully matured homo-sissy gospel singer of his last novel, *Just above My Head* (1979). Like Baldwin himself, these characters portray variations on the church sissy, a boy whose moral and social relation to the world is deeply shaped by the commitment to a religious community—especially as defined by Pentecostalism—that judges same-gender desire, but not necessarily sissiness itself, to be a mortal sin. As we shall see, in fact, the Pentecostal church ironically nurtures sissy character and conduct—including individual and institutional caretaking, circumspect social decorum, restrained physical comportment, respect and admiration of womanly capacity, humility of spirit, cultivation of artistic sensibility, too-proper allocation in speech and writing, and a deep appreciation of proselytizing ministry as consistent with the adaptive exploitation of mass social media—while at the same time doctrinally forbidding the inflection toward homosexuality that is usually assumed to accompany a sissy sensorium. As we shall see, the denomination in which Baldwin is reared, and in which John Grimes is indoctrinated, is anchored in a paradoxical ethos that pairs, on the one hand, an intimate, insular setting in which congregants' most private habits are openly scrutinized by the saints during worship with, on the other hand, a commitment to a publicly exposed life that obligates the saved to engage the mass public sphere as an opportunity for proselytizing. As I suggest further below, this paradox helps to explain Baldwin's peculiar relation to public exposure, whereby he is uncannily open to having his private experience scrutinized by a judging public while also being cannily adept at exploiting mass media to communicate a proselytizing message on behalf of racial, sexual, and other kinds of social justice. Courting such opportune social conditions, Baldwin places his sissy comportment, and the bodily display it signals, before the altar of a titillating mass public with a propensity for sissiphobic judgment while exploiting such media to justify and affirm a sissy deportment that is self-consciously defiant.

As with all gender social practice and embodiment, the church sissy thrives in a codependent correlation with other manifestations of gender and sexual nonconformity. While homosexual desire and conduct haunt and harass the church sissy in a variety of complex ways, the jeopardy of homosexuality in the cultural circumstances of Baldwin's youth in Harlem is itself most saliently embodied in the notion of the street swish, a boy or man who has escaped the doctrinal repressions of the church, the familial pressures of the household, and the ideological strictures of dominant masculinity and sexuality to forge an identity as a swishing homosexual. Think of the swish as a church sissy delivered from religious and social dogma and set loose on the street to enact his desire without familiar constraints. The American colloquialism "swish" seems to have entered the language in the 1930s, according to the *Dictionary of American Slang*, which records its meaning as "showing the traits of an effeminate male homosexual."[2] Although the *Routledge Dictionary of American Slang* records the earliest known published usage as 1941, both dictionaries document sources of this usage indicating that it was an insider term prominent among homosexuals themselves. The *Routledge* entry cites an especially interesting source from the March 1960 *Mattachine Review*, the periodical of one of the earliest gay rights organizations: "I have always made fun of the swishing, screaming, flaunting queens and you have always laughed with me."[3] As the quotation confirms, the swish was a figure of fun even within the gay community itself—what Eve Sedgwick refers to so aptly as "the haunting abject of gay thought itself."[4]

As Clarence Major documents through field research for *Juba to Jive*, the term seems to be at peak usage as black vernacular from the 1960s to the 1990s.[5] In the black vernacular, the "street" and the "swish" are coidentified as they become shorthand for this open and ubiquitous display of gender nonconformity in an urbanized setting. For postwar urban America, the street, as Baldwin and others figure it, is the most public space of contested opportunity and danger, not only for the swishing homosexual but for any person who inhabits the U.S. ghettos in these decades.[6] The idea of the swish no doubt has a longer history than the term itself, but the emergence of the term can be understood as reshaping the figure of male gender nonconformity in tandem with cultural shifts in gender expectations. In previous decades, such men may have been labeled "pansies." The term "femme" is often used today among gay black men to refer to effeminate versus masculine gay men. In recent decades, as Vershawn Ashanti Young explores, the term "faggot" has become predominant among working-class heterosexual black men, who often use the term to indicate any deviation from a strict script of urban masculine blackness untainted by white middle-class pretensions and ways of interacting, including aspirations to formal education, nonvernacular speech, and any bodily posture, bearing, or gesture rendered suspect by its perceived intimacy with the white establishment.[7]

I speculate here that the term "swish" emphasizes not merely an erroneous gender makeup, as "pansy," "femme," and the current black vernacular usage of "faggot" also signal, but also a concern with the brash *public* display of such bodily conduct. "Swish"—"flaunt[ing] the body," as Major aptly phrases it—refers to the way a male carries his body, with an unsubtle swaying in the hips that appears to mimic a "loose" woman's way of walking, as opposed to the highly scripted dip and bounce cultivated by working-class African American urban men in the ghettos around World War II.[8] The focus on the open display of gender misprision, and thus sexual nonconformity, indexes perhaps a historical moment in which queer men are more highly visible not only "on the street" but also in mass media, demanding their rights through protests like the Stonewall Rebellion and political organizations modeled on the NAACP and the Student Non-violent Coordinating Committee (SNCC). In other words, it may be that the term "swish" indicates a heightened social consciousness of the claim to occupy public space being made by queer men in this televisual era—a consciousness particularly raised among black urban men as openly gay men, both black and white, begin more militantly to occupy "the street" in areas within or bordering the black ghettos after World War II. At the same time that queer men become more visible on the ground in urban spaces symbolically owned by African Americans, they also become more visible in the mass national imaginary. By focusing on Baldwin's fictional and autobiographical representation of the church sissy and its foils, the street swish and mass-media swish, we can begin to comprehend Baldwin's career as a sissy spokesman—a televisual sissy—for the civil rights movement.[9] Thus, in charting Baldwin's rise from a church sissy-boy to an acclaimed homo-sissy artist and activist whose verbal intelligence and artistic sensitivity earn him a position as *the* most articulate spokesman on behalf of nonviolent civil rights, and in correlating this autobiographical narrative (often fragmented across various essays) in relation to his repeated portraiture of homo-sissies in his fiction, we can arrive at what I'm calling Baldwin's sissy heroics.

Sissy Liminality: Straddling between the Home, the Church, and the Street

Agreeing to eliminate the homosexual declaration in *Go Tell It*, Baldwin nonetheless composes a sensitive portrayal of the social, familial, spiritual, and psychological struggle of a sissy-boy, a bastard son within his own patriarchal household. The published version concludes with John about to cross the threshold of his parents' house as the sun rises after a long night of the soul in which the boy has achieved his salvation, aided by Elisha, an older boy already sanctified, in the Pentecostal church where John's father is an associate pastor. Thematically, the novel structures John's sissiness as just such a threshold—that is, a *liminal* and *subliminal* condition—in which he is repeatedly depicted straddling the line between the home, a privately closed space of socio-moral constriction under the aegis of a disciplinarian father, and the street, a tempting place of unknown and unpredictable sexual opportunities and dangers. Although the patriarchal church is intimately aligned with the home, it is an institution at odds with itself in that, on the one hand, it prescribes a private feeling of salvation that is publicly proclaimed in the insular public space of the congregation, and, on the other hand, it demands a public life exposed to the sinful street with an obligation to exploit every available mode of communication to proselytize the masses. What we discover especially as we move toward narrative closure is that the line separating home from street runs through the heart of the church itself, making that line quite blurry and messy, and thus porous and unpredictably penetrable. Thus, although the sissy-boy seeks safety and belonging in the church, and the church encourages his overt inclusion as a sign of its saving graces, the street and the church, as structurally proximate, offer commensurate anxieties, temptations, and fulfillments.

At the outset of his autobiographical essay *The Fire Next Time* (1963), Baldwin describes his own experience of Pentecostal conversion, which occurred the summer he turned fourteen and is clearly the basis for John's story: "What I saw around me that summer in Harlem was what I had always seen; nothing had changed. But now, without any warning, the whores and pimps and racketeers on the Avenue had become a personal menace. It had not before occurred to me that I could become one of them, but now I realized that we had been produced by the same circumstances. Many of my comrades were clearly headed for the Avenue, and my father said that I was headed that way, too."[10] Both in this essay and in *Go Tell It*, the preacher-father represents the punitive guardian who seeks to judge, control, castigate, and purge any perceived deviation from patriarchal Christian dogma, the doctrine of the church serving as the basis for appropriate gender conduct in the household. The coincidence of Baldwin's father's mysterious hostility to his eldest son—which has a biographical explanation in Baldwin's bastard status—serves Baldwin's narrative agenda of exposing the violent endangerment posed by patriarchal ambitions, which necessarily menace everyone in the household, including the father himself, but especially the budding sissy-boy. Because John has not issued from his (step)father Gabriel's "blood," the boy cannot, in the logic of patriarchal primogeniture, empower Gabriel's line through procreation. That John is so sissified further complicates Gabriel's desire for a powerful patrilineage as a sign of God's grace and blessing on him as a proper patriarch. Not only is there doubt that a sissy has the will to procreate, but there is also the suspicion that any fruit from a queer tree would itself be contaminating rather than sanctified. John's sissiness may even provide Gabriel some sense of relief insofar as this diminishes the chance of John producing a bastard line in competition with Gabriel's legitimate blood, Roy, whose dangerous adventures into the street threaten a fatal end similar to that of Gabriel's firstborn, Royal.

Recognizing both the real jeopardy posed by the street and a different danger within the father's household, the young Baldwin flees into the church for safety—a *storefront* church notably abutting the street.[11] Drawing again from Baldwin's life, the novel's narrative occurs on the eve of John's fourteenth birthday to emphasize the pivotal moment of puberty. During prepubescent childhood, the household can serve as an uneasy harbor to the sissy-boy, as he can for a time take refuge under his mother's apron. As Trudier Harris explains, John "is often identified with things that are traditionally considered more feminine.... John is also presented, in contrast to Gabriel the factory worker, as fragile, quiet, studious, and sensitive to pursuits of the mind."[12] Although John's "feminine" character necessarily attaches him to his mother, Elizabeth, while estranging him further from his father, this triangulation bubbles beneath the surface—largely due to Elizabeth's own self-subordination to Gabriel—until the onset of puberty. With puberty, when even sissies must man up or be penalized for their waywardness, the mother can no longer protect the sissy son through the excuse of his tender age. The household, all along the father's fiat, becomes a place of heightened jeopardy. When John's stepfather prognosticates the son's attraction to the street, he is prophesying a danger in order to issue a stern warning: if the sissy-boy does not man up, he will end up hurled into the street, if not by his own perverse volition, then by his father's punishing hand.

The church, of which the household seeks to be an extension, poses a similar jeopardy, but one that offers a way out through the very Christological doctrine of salvation—patriarchal in substance and structure but maternal in practice and affect—that harasses the gender-nonconforming boy. Too often the black church is read simply as patriarchal. Although this is generally the case doctrinally, in form, practice, tone, it is far from the case. Recent scholarship has begun to acknowledge the gender and sexual complexities within the black church, resulting not only from the influential role of women and queer men but also from the curious ways in which a patriarchal doctrine is offset by the image of a self-sacrificing, long-suffering, gentle, celibate Christ as a model for good Christian conduct. In his ethnographic study, for example, Stephen C. Finley investigates why heterosexual men are so often scarce in the black church. They "associated worship of the divine-male with being feminine and therefore had problems with it because they connected it with women and with the homoerotic," he writes.[13] Further, he suggests that heterosexual men may feel uncomfortable with the passionate, expressive form of black worship: "Regarding acts of worship, this group believed that women were more expressive than men. It was interesting that they also equated worship, especially ecstatic forms, with the feminine. Likewise, a respondent, not un-typically, made it clear that he understood expressive forms of worship as something that women do."[14] In the Pentecostal church of Baldwin's youth, women were especially influential not only in the ecstatic mode of worship but also in holding authoritative offices as founders and pastors of congregations, contrary to most other Christian denominations. It is notable that the young Baldwin receives salvation not in his father's church but in a neighboring church founded and pastored by a woman, Rosa Artimas Horn, popularly known as Mother Horn. Clarence E. Hardy III explains that Mother Horn's Harlem ministry "gained popularity and sparked a lively rivalry with Father Divine, who then tried to run her out of town," and he describes her thus: "She stands out as a woman preacher in the 1930s and 1940s who proudly proclaimed her right to preach despite the male naysayers of her day."[15] Her tutelage is significant in that it indicates how the little sissy-boy transitions to a full-fledged church sissy through the ordination of a woman, a "Mother," shifting his refuge from beneath his mother's apron to beneath the pastor mother's robes. Even though Baldwin soon leaves Mother Horn's church for another, smaller one, where he becomes a teenage preacher, the impact of Mother Horn had to be indelible, as evident in his portrait of her in *Fire Next Time*.

Drawing on the work of Wallace D. Best, Ashon Crawley has brilliantly theorized how a Pentecostal female preacher necessarily conducts herself according to the gender assumptions and expectations set by the congregation's masculinist bias or what he calls "the cultural genitals of the pulpit": "As a historically male site, the pulpit forces people to judge preachers as to how male and, as such, masculine they are. Masculinity becomes the standard by which preachers' performances are intelligible. . . . Using men and masculinity as the standard trope, women preaching become deviant bodies trying to access this meaning and share in the pulpit's power."[16] While I fully agree with Crawley's theory, I also think that, at the same time, the very presence of a female in the Pentecostal pulpit alters, if not disrupts, the masculinist cultural script even as it seeks to inhabit the pulpit's proscribed gender structure. Given that, from the outset, women were able to carve out an influential role as preachers in Pentecostalism, their negotiation of the pulpit is also enhanced by this historical presence.[17] Crawley's detailed gender anatomy of one Pentecostal female preacher's sermon—analyzing performance of voice, gesture, and stride—leads us to wonder about the gender legibility of a sissy presence like the young Baldwin's in the pulpit. Crawley observes how Pentecostal sermons often reference queer persons—especially queer men—as a way to discipline the sexual conduct of the congregants insofar as "sexually deviant bodies serve as a repository containing those unthinkable, unfathomable elements that allow the controlled sexual self to materialize." When a female preacher urges the church to "put on Jesus" as a warning against "ambiguities—of their bodies, their sexualities and from communities that accept this behavior," to what extent is this bodily ambiguity of the female preacher's occupying a properly masculine pulpit staged, as much as it is occluded?[18] As Crawley suggests, that a woman *can* so effectively perform a masculine oratorial script indicates the extent to which gender performance is itself fungible. If we extend Crawley's analysis beyond an actual performance enacted behind the pulpit to a persistent inhabiting of one's temperament and body as social practice and individual conduct, we can more explicitly consider the ways in which material ways of knowing and being gendered operate in everyday experience, and its discursive representations.

As a sissy-boy in the pulpit, did the young Baldwin emulate Mother Horn, his preacher father, or both? Did the congregation respond to his voice, gestures, and stride by assimilating him into masculinity, or did they respond to him similarly to how they might have accommodated a woman in the pulpit, by projecting authoritative masculinity onto a person otherwise ambiguously gendered? Although we cannot know how congregants responded to the young Baldwin's sissy manner, we can certainly speculate based on Baldwin's own autobiographical representation of his experiences in the church, on his fictional representations in characters like John Grimes and Arthur Montana, and on how Baldwin was received in the national pulpit of civil rights activism, with its similar expectations and assumptions of gender-normative masculine conduct as the framework for enacting authoritative leadership. As so many scholars have observed, Baldwin's oratorical style was deeply influenced by his experience in the Pentecostal church. I would suggest, more precisely, that his oratorical conduct was deeply influenced by his experience as a sissy-boy in that church, and that his sissiness, far from being merely a disadvantage, was also a resource for navigating the kind of verbal and rhetorical literateness required in black preaching and later in the spotlight of mass media, as well as for mediating good conduct as a basis for such authority.

As discussed in chapter 1, queer gender and sexual conducts historically reside within every hegemonic institution, in different ways shaping the gender ideology of such institutions both as limit points of cautionary exclusion and also as inflection points erupting as secrecy, rumor, suspicion, and scandal at the heart of these institutions. In the early 1900s, the emerging Pentecostal movement had an ambivalent relationship to the mass media of the day, as it courted the street masses and media attention as a tenet of evangelical ministry but also found itself plagued by sensationalist mass-media coverage that portrayed the church and its leaders as hysterically frenzied, sexually aberrant, and racially tainted. James R. Goff Jr.'s history of the early Pentecostal church documents how Charles H. Parham, a founder, costumed the congregants to draw the attention of contemporaneous mass media:

> The Houston campaign also enjoyed the publicity provided by Parham's energetic band of workers. Early in 1905 Parham had purchased a set of fifteen Palestinian robes depicting the lifestyle of the social classes of Bible times.... Realizing their public appeal, Parham often wore one of the robes in the pulpit. During the daylight street meetings in Houston, he organized impromptu fashion shows by parading his workers in the Palestinian splendor. He also borrowed from Frank Sandford the stratagem of using large, colorful flags and banners. Bearing inscriptions of "unity" and "victory," the Pentecostal robe-clad army marched down the street proclaiming a revolution of apostolic Christianity. The purpose of such displays was twofold: to publicize the nightly meetings and to evangelize Houston's lost.[19]

This tendency toward street flamboyance at once fulfills the new church's desire for attention and undercuts, from the viewpoint of the establishment media and religious denominations, the authenticity and authority of the church's religious expression. This appeal to the exotic and histrionic seemed, indeed, in line with the church's tendency to flout society's and rival denominations' racial and gender decorum. The conduct of the early church did not conform to mainline Protestantism in that it involved women and African Americans as some of its most prominent preachers and missionaries; held ongoing revivals that showcased blacks rubbing shoulders with whites, including white women, during worship; and drew heavily on spiritual practices of ecstatic dance, glossolalia (speaking in tongues) and xenoglossa (speaking actual "foreign" languages not known by the speaker), and communal shouting adapted from native West African religion.[20] Focusing its missions especially on the urban poor in cities like Houston and Los Angeles, and drawing its theology from the idea of Christ's ministry in the lowliest public places to prostitutes, lepers, and the meek who shall inherit the earth, the church also embraced the city street as an optimal place to evangelize, suspending the division between the house of worship versus the sinful street upheld by more respectable denominations. The extensive use of "storefront" buildings as houses of worship exemplifies this liminal relationship between "church" and "street"—an affiliation that fosters, according to Arthur E. Paris, "the conventional view of storefront churches as exotic, esoteric religious expressions inferior to the mainline denominations" and "the tendency to label all the groups that occupied storefronts 'sects and cults.'"[21] Mother Horn and Father Divine, the two most prominent Pentecostal preachers in Harlem during Baldwin's youth, both exploited similar strategies first attempted by Parham and his followers. When Mother Horn arrives in Harlem, in fact, she has in tow a young white woman whom she has healed and "adopted"—a familial arrangement that would appear queer not only in the context of 1930s Protestantism but also in the eyes of dominant secular society.[22]

Beyond the church's "African" practices and racially mixed services, the "queerness" of Pentecostalism appears also as sexual "aberration." The highly tactile, physical nature of the services—the laying on of hands, the dancing, the wrestling on the floor—rendered the church suspect, and practices like Parham's wearing of colorful Palestinian robes in the pulpit could only be further cause for suspicion and rumor. The sporadic sexual scandals plaguing the institution from the outset have also imaged it as queer in theology, religious practice, and sociality. In the first such scandal, founder Parham was arrested in San Antonio for sodomy, a felony under Texas law at the time. Even before his arrest, rumor and suspicion spread among congregants that Parham was involved in homosexual liaisons. His arrest in 1907 was widely reported in the media, intensifying the association between the sect and queerness. About this scandal, Goff writes: "The lack of a clear acquittal in San Antonio along with rumors of Parham's impropriety over the past six months combined to create the public impression of guilt. Few allegations were more damaging and publicly reprehensible in 1907 than homosexuality. Parham could never quite free himself from the millstone. The articles printed in the religious press were far more detailed than those in the San Antonio papers. They were less reliable and undoubtedly were more guilty of rumor and innuendo."[23] Here again, we can see the role of innuendo in queering individuals and institutions who are perceived as not conforming to gender and sexual norms. Innuendo fuels rumor, and rumor in turn fuels scandal, and scandal in turn fuels social stigma and sometimes, depending on the nature of the scandal, legal action. Ironically, the high profile of Pentecostals in a scandalizing mass media in the early decades of the twentieth century, while it queered the social and religious practices of the church, also kept the sect in the public eye and garnered curiosity seekers, some of whom became congregants. That queer sexuality was at the heart of the Pentecostal and Spiritualist movements was hard to deny, given how some of its most popular leaders were hardly shy about their nonnormative gender and sexual character. In discussing the key role of Clarence Cobbs's radio ministry in 1930s Chicago, Davarian L. Baldwin writes: "Even before his radio program, Spiritualist pastor Cobbs and his First Church of Deliverance were both celebrated and berated because of his sacred world flamboyance, open association with politicians and policy gamblers, and quite public expressions of a gay male sexual charisma."[24]

Innuendo and scandal certainly also followed both Father Divine and Mother Horn during the 1930s in Harlem. Father Divine, for instance, was sued, arrested, and imprisoned various times—arrests that were often linked to both his unusual teachings about gender and racial integration (ranging from a belief in a lack of gender distinction early on to his later advocacy of gender segregation and celibacy) and his use of the public sphere for mass gatherings, which led to charges of unlawful assembly and disturbing the peace.[25] Given the teenage Baldwin's local fame as a preacher in the Pentecostal church, even beyond any personal temperamental affect that might have alerted onlookers on the street, his association with the denomination would have enhanced the aura of sexual suspicion for many denizens on the streets of Harlem.

Although little Jimmy's tutelage as a sissy leader within the church is chaperoned by a female pastor, there is a sense in which the too-good boy is already predisposed to find a hedged safety in a church that is already presided over by church matrons, to whom the most powerful male pastor must answer, as well as by a theology that emphasizes a gentle, vulnerable, sacrificial, too-good Christ, despite a rigidly patriarchal church structure. Even as Baldwin's attachment to the

Pentecostal faith as a boy resulted directly from the fact that it was his father's church, the church's suspect queerness may have contributed to its allure for a gender-nonconforming boy—a queerness that Baldwin images through the church's curious interrelation with the sinful street. When Baldwin describes in *Fire Next Time* how one of his friends takes him one Saturday to Pastor Horn's church, he emphasizes her greeting: "My friend was about to introduce me when she looked at me and smiled and said, 'Whose little boy are you?'" Noting that this is the exact same phrase used by "pimps and racketeers on the Avenue when they suggested, both humorously and intensely, that I 'hang out' with them," the young Baldwin is already aware of the structural parallel linking the church to the street.[26] To become a member in this female pastor's church defies the father's ministerial authority and further protects the sissy son as he constructs his vocation as a child preacher—that is, as a church sissy.

The churchiness of the sissy-boy highlights his liminality—a suspect threshold status between masculine and feminine, between straight and queer, always in the act of intensified deferral and becoming in accord with C. Riley Snorton's theory of the transitive nature of gender identification discussed in chapter 1. The church represents for the church sissy, then, not a final resolution of the crisis but instead a temporizing, tentative reprieve. Jeffrey Q. McCune Jr. captures the church sissy's ironic relation to the church's heteronormative structure and theology when he writes, "The gay Christian soloist or congregant usually does not identify with such claims. In fact, he disidentifies with the preacher's polemics."[27] I would push McCune's insight to suggest that, even when the church sissy silences himself, his bodily presence *as sissy* at the heart of the church's ministries palpably queers the institution, its doctrine, and practice. The church sissy represents not only a danger but also an opportunity for the church. For Baldwin, this danger, the boy finds, lurks also within himself, as a perpetual risk that demands perpetual and purposive self-discipling of the body's potential to yield to the temptation of homo-swishing: "Everything inflamed me, and that was bad enough, but I myself had also become a source of fire and temptation."[28] The church sissy's spiritual discipline, ironically, becomes the best sign of his salvation and religious vocation, for the greater the tempting sin, the greater the discipline required to keep it at bay. Paradoxically, a church sissy's best shield—the sensitive intelligence that nurtures the verbal acumen that enables his rise as a child preacher—fails him at the point of articulating the exact danger that plagues him externally and internally. In "The Devil Finds Work" (1976), Baldwin characterizes the occasion of this verbal faltering in the sissy-boy's attempt to name that which results in the perception of him as a "strange" child: "For, I was not only considered by my father to be ugly. I was considered by everyone to be 'strange,' including my poor mother, who didn't, however, beat me for it. Well, if I was 'strange'—and I knew that I must be, otherwise people would not have treated me so strangely, and I would not have been so miserable—perhaps I could find a way to use my strangeness. A 'strange' child, anyway, dimly and fearfully apprehends that the years are not likely to make him less strange."[29] This deep sense of estrangement—amplified by the insistent iteration of the word "strange"—is so palpable and yet so inexplicable to the boy. "Strange" here both exposes and masks Baldwin's self-reference as a gender-queer boy. Others' perception of his strangeness further estranges him within his own household and neighborhood, providing him nonetheless with a claim to specialness—"I could find a way to use my strangeness"—that motivates and justifies a destiny pushing him at first into the church and inevitably beyond the church/home and onto the world stage. The very gifts that single him out as "strange"—his sissy sensorium—also predestine him to a caretaking role on a grand scale.

Rather than shielding him from the street, ironically the young Baldwin's local fame as a preacher makes him even more delectable as a target. "And the fact that I was 'the young Brother Baldwin' increased my value with those same pimps and racketeers who had helped to stampede me into the church in the first place," Baldwin explains in *The Fire Next Time*.[30] These street predators are incentivized further by the boy's evident church sissiness. Terrified that he is so easily "inflamed" and that this can be so easily read on the street (in his manner, in his posture, in his affect?) as being vulnerable to seduction, the young Baldwin then discovers that rather than a haven from such inflaming desire, the church itself poses its own dangers: "It was my good luck—perhaps—that I found myself in the church racket instead of some other, and surrendered to a spiritual seduction long before I came to any carnal knowledge."[31] In reducing the church to a "racket" and his being proselytized to "seduction," he forces us to doubt the line that is supposed to separate the saved from the depraved, the church from the street, the church sissy from the street swish. In some ways it is the church, with its hypocrisies and repressions, that embodies the real jeopardy: "It is not too much to say that whoever wishes to become a truly moral human being . . . must first divorce himself from the prohibitions, crimes, and hypocrisies of the Christian church."[32] As we shall see, however, just as Baldwin cannot leave his sissy self behind in gaining salvation, because that intense desire to be saved is motivated in large part by his sissy estrangement, so he cannot leave the church behind even as he hurls himself into the expansive street we call the world.

We might comprehend Baldwin's notion of "the street," which aligns with an African American urban idiom that emerges with the Great Migration, as a microcosm of a larger dynamic embodied in how white male supremacy polices African American persons in public spaces, especially in the most urbanized environments. Major's entry on "the street" is especially instructive: "Metaphor for the unsafe world beyond the home. Before the forties, many black city dwellers (recently from the South) referred to 'the street' as a 'road,' a habit left over from the rural South, but after the forties the word 'street' itself became common and was immediately identified with violence, underworld or criminal activity, immorality and unethical practices."[33] What Major's definition omits, however, is how the African American idiom of the street also represents the opportunity that accompanies risk—not only from underground economic enterprise but also from legitimate street vendors like "Pig Foot" Mary, who sells down-home treats to pedestrians in Harlem.[34] In black urban centers the street also becomes a public commons, an embodied and mobile public sphere, where the likes of Garveyites, Black Muslims, communists, and Pentecostal ministers hawk their ideas and where an individual can by chance or by design encounter another individual with a similar social, political, or sexual interest. Every black person is potentially exposed on the street, but persons exhibiting sissified—or, even more so, swish—comportment are at once endangered by sissiphobia and homophobia and by the prerogatives of white male violation and also aroused by the diversity of potential anonymous contacts with sympathetic others. For Baldwin, in fact, "the street" becomes shorthand for a network of gender-oriented coercions and violations, opportunities and liaisons, operating through the random anonymity of urban public spaces.

In one of his last published essays, "Here Be Dragons," originally published in *Playboy* in January 1985, Baldwin composes a clear-eyed critique that anticipates the insights developed decades later in queer theory, critical race theory, and masculinity studies. He traces the history of masculinist violence—from slavery through Jim Crow to World War II, from the Cold War era through civil rights to the gay rights movement—as a vehicle for the administration of racial and sexual oppression: "The American *ideal*, then, of sexuality appears to be rooted in the American ideal of masculinity. This ideal has created cowboys and Indians, good guys and bad guys, punks and studs, tough guys and softies, butch and faggot, black and white."[35] Directly following this series of familiar binaries, Baldwin issues a stinging indictment of the whole racial-gender-sexual patriarchal system (for which there is no adequate single word) that burdened him with estrangement as a child within his own home and chased him through the streets of Greenwich Village as a young man: "It is an ideal so paralytically infantile that it is virtually forbidden—an unpatriotic act—that the American boy evolve into the complexity of manhood."[36] This link between patriotism and masculine violence is not merely a parenthetical aside. Baldwin calls out the historical dynamic that justifies racialized sexual violation through a patriotic demand to protect the nation-state—a dynamic intensified and publicized during the Cold War through various congressional hearings, high-profile arrests of homosexuals and communists, and purging of the homosexual/communist figure in Hollywood film and other media.

In "Here Be Dragons" Baldwin abandons some of the sly evasions and equivocations that characterize earlier autobiographical narratives, naming that which as a boy he says faltered on his lips: "It wasn't only that I didn't wish to seem or sound like a woman, for it was this detail that most harshly first struck my eye and ear. I am sure that I was afraid that I already seemed and sounded too much like a woman. In my childhood, at least until my adolescence, my playmates had called me a sissy. It seemed to me that many of the people I met were making fun of women, and I didn't see why."[37] In *Go Tell It* Baldwin had decades earlier complexly connected seeming and sounding like a woman to a sissy's sensitive perspective on reality related to formal schooling and literacy—Nero's idea that reading will make you queer, as well as Vershawn Young's observation that in particular African American settings, the term "faggot" is equated with an overinvestment in white men's institutions. In his father's eyes, John is "ugly," but given that John favors his mother, we might wonder whether what the father sees is his wife's features and demeanor improperly molded onto a boy's face. It may also be that this paternal appraisal is connected more with John's size, "always the smallest boy in his class," and studiousness as signs of a sissy sensorium.

When John is five, his white-appearing principal provides him a different perspective on "his individual existence," telling him that he "is a very bright boy." In such passages, the school becomes a curious alternative to the home/church as a public site that can nurture his sissy intelligence without the kind of punishing scrutiny practiced in the home/church or the dangerous violations prominent on the street. Expecting to be selected for punishment in line with his stepfather's habit, he is startled instead to be selected for praise for his lettering, which the principal has spied on the blackboard:

> That moment gave him, from that time on, if not a weapon at least a shield; he apprehended totally, without belief or understanding, that he had in himself a power that other people lacked; that he could use this to save himself, to raise himself; and that, perhaps, with this power he might one day win that love which he so longed for.... His father's arm, rising and falling, might make him cry, and that voice might cause him to tremble; yet his father could never be entirely the victor, for John cherished something that his father could not reach. It was his hatred and his intelligence that he cherished, the one feeding the other.[38]

This self-awareness of literacy as "if not a weapon at least a shield" comes early and comes with intensified awareness, "since he was noticed by an eye altogether alien and impersonal." Indeed, the alienness of that eye derives in large part not only from the official authority outside the father's purview of household and church but more pointedly also from the authoritative eyewitness of a female's phallic whiteness embodied in the principal's look, "a woman with white hair and an iron face."[39] Like Pastor Horn, a female occupying a man's authoritative and sanctified position, the principal's queering of the gender (and racial) binary seems to reflect the sissy's own liminal condition as a sensitive, overly literate boy. Against his father's insistence "that all white people were wicked, and that God was going to bring them low," John prefers his mother's attitude expressed when a white teacher brings him a remedy for his cold: "His mother had said that God would bless that woman."[40] These early episodes indicate how John begins to prefigure himself as an intermediary between whiteness and blackness, as well as between masculine and feminine, a mediating transitivity that his father rejects outright, given that the father cannot achieve in the white world the authority and control that he seems to wield at home and church. The prefiguration of John's liminal intermediacy also directly hinges on his strangeness, his sissy liminality, pushing him out of his father's house and church in search of "that love which he so longed for."

We might label this early premonition of literacy as a "shield," a sort of defensive aggression, or passive aggression, as discussed in chapters 1 and 3. While giving the appearance of filial obeisance to authority, the sissy often uses smart language to challenge and undermine the very authority that seems to obligate his too-good-boy submission, like Wright's Richard in lynching the kitten. In *God Hates Fags*, Michael Cobb observes how John borrows the linguistic and rhetorical resources of his father's church: "The queer's use of the heterosexually dominant language, however, does not signal that the queer has assimilated the norms of the black church, nor is it even an example of the appropriation of a white religious language for black use. But rather John uses the closest language of authority at hand—the language of state power that drenched his black church."[41] Because Cobb's reading misses the ways in which the black church, especially the Pentecostal church, is already queered in relation to "state power," he perhaps underplays the extent to which John's recourse to religious language indicates the sissy-boy's ambivalent relation to an already ambivalent authority, on the one hand desiring to submit himself to it obediently, while on the other coveting mastery of it in order to bend it to his own queer will and desire. The black church sissy is at once a chosen vehicle of the church's authority and intensely estranged from it, but the black church itself lacks the effectiveness and fullness of patriarchal authority accorded to white male-controlled institutions, as indicated by the insecure gender-racial position of John's father, a man who is threatened by the presence in his own household of a white female schoolteacher, who possesses state-sanctioned authority over him. The black church is at once a welcoming and estranging space for the nurturing of a church sissy because it is itself a queer space: it is pastored by patriarchs who visibly lack patriarchal authority in white society and who answer to matrons whose un/official authority rivals their own—a condition intensified by the peculiar performance of Pentecostal worship, as investigated by sociologist Stephen Finley and others. It is an estranging place for the sissy-boy to the extent that the church seeks to prohibit sexual and gender nonconformity in accord with dominant ideology, but welcoming to the extent that it encourages the productive roles of too-good boys as often the most articulate, gifted male leaders within the church. Conventionally gendered rough boys prefer the street to the church, as is the case with John's half brother, Roy; his stepbrother, Royal; and his stepfather, Gabriel.[42] A conventionally masculine man like Gabriel finds himself striving to remold and master a matronly institution inspirited by a delicate, self-sacrificing, celibate Christ into an institution that can fulfill his procreative desire for a powerful patriarchal lineage. This is the paradox of a patriarchal institution that self-conflictingly embeds the sissy as a supporting agent necessary to, yet alienated from, its doctrine, structure, and mass messaging.

In the same passive-aggressive manner, John has an ambivalent relation to the masculinist uses of the body and tongue as weapons so crucial to the black vernacular. Although Baldwin fuses the vernacular, religious language, and highly literate secular knowledge as an author, he does not tend to adapt the more directly belligerent forms, such as the Dirty Dozens, that would be familiar to him from the Harlem streets. In his semifictional autobiography *Black Boy* (1945), Wright famously charts his way out of Jim Crow by learning how to use "words as weapons." By shifting the image from a "weapon" to a "shield" in *Go Tell It*, Baldwin has already begun to rethink Wright's formulation of the proper manly response to a Jim Crow violence so overwhelming that literal weapons alone could not hope to defeat it.[43] Whereas Wright, like the black nationalist poets after him, turns words into symbolic weapons more powerful than guns, Baldwin shifts the symbolic register from aggression to self-defense—"a shield"—in accordance with the sissy's nascent talents.

In "Here Be Dragons" we see how the sissy-boy's defensive literacy evolves as he puts his sense of estrangement to use through the concept of "androgyny." Baldwin exploits "androgyny," which might be defined as a way the self can straddle society's line between masculine and feminine, to disrupt the ideological, psychic, and bodily violence perpetrated by white patriarchy through the enforcement of this binary. "But we are all androgynous," he writes, "not only because we are all born of a woman impregnated by the seed of a man but because each of us, helplessly and forever, contains the other—male in female, female in male, white in black and black in white."[44] This iconoclastic explosion of racial/gender/sexual binarism extends to an interrogation of the white gay hegemony emerging at the time of this essay. That Baldwin was aware of what theorists now call homonormativity can be seen in a response he gives to a question Richard Goldstein asks him in a 1984 interview, "Do black gay people have the same sense of being separate as white gay people?":

> I think white gay people feel cheated because they were born in principle, into a society in which they were supposed to be safe. The anomaly of their sexuality puts them in danger, unexpectedly. Their reaction seems to me in direct proportion to the sense of feeling cheated of the advantages which accrue to white people in a white society. . . . Now that may sound very harsh, but the gay world as such is no more prepared to accept black people than anywhere else in society. It's a very hermetically sealed world with very unattractive features, including racism.[45]

This observation undergirds Baldwin's portrayal of the white protagonist, David, of his second novel, *Giovanni's Room* (1956), a "straight" man who flees from his homosexual desire for the dark lover Giovanni by escaping into the safety of American middle-class white privilege. It helps to explain Baldwin's own deep suspicion of the "gay" epithet as encapsulating a psychosocial yearning for the safety of heteronormative whiteness.

In tracing the consciousness of his own gender evolution in "Here Be Dragons," Baldwin shifts from the appellation "sissy" on the streets of Harlem as a boy to the more violent epithet "faggot" on the streets of Greenwich Village as a young man. The added venom in "faggot" arises as much from Baldwin's racial assignation as from the perception of his "strange" gender conduct. The combination of black and queer is not additive but instead catalytically explosive. As discussed in chapter 1, the slightest hint of nonconforming gender conduct can be taken as the exposure of a swishing faggot who needs a beating. That line between violent homophobe and faggot victim, however, cannot be sustained in everyday practice. Baldwin's sissy circumspection—his desire not to be like a woman and his uncertainty about what makes him appear sissified to others—cannot prevent him from being read as a homo-swish on the street, and accordingly the fag-basher cannot be prevented from crossing the line from bashing the faggot to desiring to penetrate (or be penetrated by) him.

Baldwin experiences this repeatedly as one of the rare black men in Greenwich Village, which ironically will become one of the pivotal sites where the modern resistance to the heteronorm will be forged by a group of black and Hispanic drag queens. In the early 1940s, however, his black sissiness exposes him to the random violence of men desperate to prove their straight whiteness: "On every street corner, I was called a faggot." The same racialized difference that makes the black sissy a target in segregated downtown New York also makes him a desirable exotic object to the "straight" white attacker. As much as this zigzag between violence and desire terrifies the young Baldwin, it also induces a deep well of sympathy and yearning. Fearing becoming a "candidate for gang rape," he nonetheless cannot help being "moved by their loneliness, their halting, nearly speechless need." What strikes us again about Baldwin's self-portrait of his evolving homosissy consciousness is that even as he acquires the social labels to name particular gender and sexual identities, he insists on the failure adequately to capture the actual bodily, psychic, libidinal, and social dynamics motivating such conduct and character. As the white fag-basher's/sissy lover's need is "nearly speechless," so the essayist's linguistic virtuosity is insufficient to capture the catalytic explosion created by the collision of race, gender, and sexuality. Baldwin emphasizes the extraverbal dynamics exactly because the social labels are so viciously iterative, reductive, repressive, and oppressing. He has no choice but to use labels like "sissy," "faggot," "black," and "white," so he persistently wants to call attention not just to their inadequacy but also to the extensive net of violent acts—acts that paradoxically also harbor a desire for passionate touching—that they unavoidably perpetrate collectively and individually on our hearts, minds, and bodies. "The bafflement and the pain this caused in me remain beyond description," he writes.[46]

"Here Be Dragons" is also edifying because it recounts how Baldwin entered into an erotic relationship with a white stranger from the Harlem streets during the years when he was a teenage preacher. The thirty-eight-year-old racketeer "fell in love with" the sixteen-year-old preacher: "I sometimes wonder what on earth his friends could have been thinking, confronted with stingy-brimmed, mustachioed, razor-toting Poppa and skinny, popeyed Me when he walked me (rarely) into shady joints."[47] Whether the Poppa presented the sissy-boy as his nephew or not, the friends surely would have known the tea. As Herb Boyd reminds us, the Harlem of this period contained "a diversity of ethnic groups competing for jobs, housing, and self-respect."[48] A white man escorting around a black sissy-boy would not be so unusual uptown, and the ease with which this relationship is conducted indicates a different dimension to the sexual danger that awaits a black boy on the street, a danger exacerbated by the disparity between a white boy's worth, even as a sissy, versus that of a black boy's. One wonders whether the Poppa would dare display an underaged white boy downtown in so public a manner: "But I knew that he was showing me off and wanted his friends to be happy for him—which, indeed, if the way they treated me can be taken as a barometer, they were."[49] We are compelled to correlate the kind of refuge that the young Baldwin discovers in this affair of the street with the refuge that the "strange" boy earlier sought in his own household through his mother's protection and that the sainted church sissy sought through the auspices of a woman pastor. Baldwin has moved from the woman pastor's robes to the street Poppa's physical arms. "I showed him all my poetry," Baldwin writes, "because I had no one else in Harlem to show it to."[50] We can only ponder how the Spanish-Irish racketeer would have responded to this soft sissy intelligence—perhaps with the same pride with which he paraded Baldwin around for his friends—but, no doubt, the sissy-boy intuitively knew that the Poppa would be impressed with his prodigious literacy, finding it erotically quaint rather than alarmingly queer. We cannot help but notice how in the process of his shifting allegiances, the manchild continually evades the stepfather's grasp to secure safe harbor where his sissy talents can glow in incubation, if not shine outright. Inflamed and inflaming, the church sissy finds in the relationship with the predatory white Poppa, ironically, an intimate space where he can hone his sissy eloquence. It is exactly because the street is anathema to the patriarchal strictures of church, home, and school that the sissy-boy may find a certain kind of freedom in flirting with the street, always at risk of being shifted toward an unsanctified swishing demeanor.

This same dilemma of the home/church/school in combat with the street is rendered fictively in *Go Tell It* as the protagonist, having been saved, continues to doubt that he is truly safe, both from the enticing street and from the street that exists within him. In the novel, the sexual risk is subtly amplified by John's sissy portfolio and the prospect of homosexual desire that it seems to portend. The question posed by the novel's ambiguous closure is not so much whether the church can save him from his gender nonconformity, for it clearly cannot and has no incentive to try, but whether in occupying the role of a church sissy, he can prevent, or at least preempt, the drive to become a street swish. As long as the boy remains a churchified sissy, he will cling, however ambivalently, to the church as a refuge, and the congregation will embrace this clinging loyalty as a sign of grace—all the more so, the more suspiciously sissified the boy. His sissified clinging becomes a manifestation of the saving grace that the church offers. To seek continued refuge in the church is to hold at bay the potential swishing homosexual portended, expected, or suspected within sissy personhood. Freshly saved, John is nonetheless still struggling with this unforgiving opposition between the sanctified home/church and the sinful street. Rather than resolution, the closure offers a temporary reprieve in the hope of the new personhood promised by the grace of a sacrificially celibate Christ, in this case embodied in John's mentor, Elisha. Is the change he sees on the avenue merely a mirage, or can it be lasting? John remembers leaving "his father's house" to attend the church service through a storm: "Now the storm was over. And the avenue, like any landscape that has endured a storm, lay changed under Heaven, exhausted and clean, and new."[51] The storm, of course, represents the inner turmoil that he suffered on the threshing floor, a spiritual upheaval so great that its convulsions manifest physically as a wrestling match between him and Elisha. But it also symbolizes how the saved soul necessarily remains exposed to the storms that await on the street. "Though conversion is a stratagem used for safety," E. L. Kornegay Jr. writes, "it resists pragmatic resolution to the messiness of black life."[52] We could add also, to the messiness of a *queer* black life, especially one within the church. In his explication of John's conversion, Cobb picks up on the violence of the conversion experience itself as part of Baldwin's critique of the repressiveness of the church. "Yet through such conversion," Cobb writes, "John finds safety in a use of religious rhetoric that is not therapeutic as much as it is strategic."[53] Even in this silent heavenly state, the street is beckoning John as he envisions the awakened avenue: "Men would be standing on corners again, watching him pass, girls would be sitting on stoops again, mocking his walk. Grandmothers would stare out of windows, saying: 'That sure is a sorry little boy.'"[54]

As we shall see, that walk designated as mockable in the 1953 novel will by the time of *No Name in the Street* (1972) become a more overt resource for the mature Baldwin's sissy insurgency. In *Go Tell It*, however, that sissy walk, corralling the body's fear of swishing, marks the recently saved boy as in perpetual danger. As Elisha warns him about the devil's many faces, John begins to waver, wishing that Elisha could always be a "protecting arm."[55] As much as Elisha tries to forewarn John, John struggles, with no appropriate language, to forewarn Elisha about his own misgivings. Elisha responds by kissing John on the forehead, "a holy kiss," and the very next moment, "the sun had come full awake.... It fell over Elisha like a golden robe, and struck John's forehead, where Elisha had kissed him, like a seal ineffaceable forever."[56] This correspondence between the natural event, the sun's rising, and the human action, the unsolicited kiss, runs counter to the disjointedness of John's inner experience, in which his salvation seems so unsettled and unsettling. In a sense that heartfelt kiss, which seals the loving bond between them, is misplaced, for what John desires is a touch more sensual, a kiss on the lips. What Elisha intends we can only speculate, for a kiss between boys, no matter how religiously chaste, marks their Christ-like celibacy as outside the normal purview of masculine conduct. Like the failure of language to capture the risk that even the most sanctified yearning cannot evacuate, so the kiss embodies—and as quickly dissipates—that palpable desire of the boys to find total fulfillment in each other's touch, a fulfillment that both implores and mocks satiation. As Phillip Brian Harper has theorized, the kiss has historically figured and manifested the bounds and bonds of heteronormativity, the perfect resolution to the heterosexual coupling plot.[57] In the U.S. context, therefore, when two males kiss in public, it threatens to upend all sense of gender decorum, throwing gender suspicion onto them. Although it occurs on the public street, Elisha's kiss is intended to resonate with the holiness of the church as evidence of John's effective salvation. Nonetheless, for John, and for us as readers, that kiss cannot be divorced from its setting on the avenue, and from John's doubts about what salvation portends and whether he can sustain its doctrinal demands. Rather than a homosexual confession, the best that John can muster is a request for Elisha's continued prayer: "John, staring at Elisha, struggled to tell him something more—struggled to say—all that could never be said." We are left, then, with a hopeful foreboding as John crosses the threshold of his stepfather's house, as the newly minted church sissy provides the novel's final words: "'I'm ready,' John said, 'I'm coming. I'm on my way.'"[58]

The declarative affirmation of John's final words notwithstanding, the closure is pregnant with ambiguity and ambivalence. What exactly John is ready for—a life committed to the church as a sanctified sissy, a life dictated by the temptations of the street, or some unforeseen path—we cannot say. How appropriate that the novel should end with such in/transitivity. Indeed, because the church sissy necessarily straddles that line between the sainted chorus and the swishing street, his unknown future cannot help but be as liminal as his estranging past. The church/home-versus-street opposition that structures the closure operates more subtly and subliminally than any declaration of homosexual desire, yet there remains a strong implication of an unarticulated desire that cannot be contained within the strictures of the church/home, the school (even with its incentives toward articulate literacy), the street, or the vexed relations among them. When describing the water that courses through the gutters of the sleeping street, Baldwin caps a catalogue of debris with a used condom as a sign of sexual desire that cannot be denied or shut off. Even as the trashed condom signifies the intended blockage of procreative heterosexuality, it also signifies any sexual act that is taboo because it is not sanctioned by heteronormative marriage rites of the home/church. Even "loose" desire mediated by the street, enacted in the dark alleys between the church and the home, is not fully liberated from social strictures. The street has its own rules, by which desire, queer or "straight," seeking its natural fulfillment, will necessarily endure blockages that court the feverish disappointments of satiated pleasure. We have no idea what little "Brother Baldwin" did sexually with the street-hustling Poppa, but we can be assured that however more gratifying to the flesh than Elisha's chaste forehead kiss, the touch between the church sissy and the Poppa could never solicit the salvific potential of a touch at once fully chaste and fully fleshly, one perpetually climaxed and consummated by a "joy unspeakable," "a seal ineffaceable forever."[59] Against the radiant imagery of the rising sun "full awake" like "a golden robe" enfolding and binding two gentle boys together, the actual site of the street frames their desire for each other as a potentially suspect act to any onlooker not cognizant of the previous experience within the church that occasions the kiss.

Even as Baldwin purges the coming-out dis-closure from his final revision of *Go Tell It*, the radical—and potentially explosive—move that he makes in the depiction of John, the hero, and Elisha, his mentor, is to place their love at the heart of African American culture, the church.[60] James Campbell observes about Baldwin's treatment of the homoerotic relation between the boys: "A shifting focus is being kept in play between flesh and spirit, but the language is arrestingly sensual."[61] This "shifting focus" between flesh and spirit, or street and church/home, allows Baldwin to demonstrate the ways in which faith and desire intersect and get played out through conventional spirituality—presenting the sissy not as anathema to the church but instead as a cornerstone of its ceaseless sanctifying mission.

The Black Sissy in Literary Historical Context

Although I distinguish here between church-sissy proper and swishing-sissy improper in order to clarify the role of these two images in African American cultural discourses, I also want to emphasize the ways in which each label turns on the meaning and affect of the other and easily turns into the other. In the right circumstances a circumspect sissy could easily be perceived as a swish, just as a swish, in a particular mood, could easily be perceived or perceive himself as a circumspect sissy. The sissy has deep anxieties over becoming a swish and so clings ever more tightly to his respectability, just as the swish displays his uniqueness and authenticity by self-consciously refusing to be an ordinary boring sissy. In fact, sissy comportment might be materialized as a tightly constricted posture, as though the body is trying too hard not to swish, gesticulate, flourish the hands, or camp up the speech. Haunted by the swish he fears he cannot help but be, the sissy toes an invisible line so habitually that it becomes the sine qua non of his subliminal consciousness and bodily habitus.

In his 1996 memoir, *One More River to Cross*, Keith Boykin paints a familiar portrait of an unwed uncle who captures perfectly the fluidity of these figures in depicting a church sissy who swishes, a man on the line between two discursive labels:

> A popular church organist and gospel musician, Uncle Michael was a flamboyant gay man. Although he had lived in my grandmother's house all his life and often brought men home with him, I never heard anyone say a disparaging word about him.... In fact, I did not even know at the time that he was gay or, for that matter, what it meant to be gay. I only knew that this hair was processed and that he wore tight-fitting colorful pants,

and shirts unbuttoned to his waist. He was shot and killed in his own bedroom by someone he had let inside the house, and the murderer was never apprehended.[62]

Uncle Michael reminds us of how intrinsically indwelling is the presence of not just the circumspect sissy but also the swish within the black church. Futile outbursts of preachers rhetorically aimed at purging the church and society of the sissy, like those of Adam Clayton Powell Sr. and Jr. during their pastorship of Abyssinian Baptist Church in Harlem from the 1920s through the 1960s, only spotlight how prominent sissies have been within the church.[63] Whether Uncle Michael has desired his tricking or has settled for it under conditions beyond his control, the danger of letting strange men into the house is juxtaposed with Uncle Michael's insider comforts within the grandmother's home and his sanctified role in the church.

As I have elsewhere observed in a discussion of Claude Brown's characterization of a swish in his autobiography, *Manchild in the Promised Land* (1965), the community's attitude toward the swish is paradoxical, at once expressing an embracing ridicule and appreciative abuse.[64] Such men were deemed "funny," a word once commonly used among southern blacks to mean "queer." "Funny," however, is a gentler, less accusatory label than "queer," and accordingly the swish is not ostracized just for who he is, though he may seem on the verge of being ostracized for what he might do.[65] Elders in the community are more likely to say, "That boy can't help the way he is," or, as Hughes writes, "God, Nature, / or somebody / made them that way."[66] The swish is clever at defusing this ridicule by going on the offensive, making fun of himself in such a way that he both asserts his desire positively and discounts the threat of that desire to his community. When Baldwin creates John Grimes of *Go Tell It on the Mountain*, Leo Proudhammer and Black Christopher Hall of *Tell Me How Long the Train's Been Gone*, and Arthur Montana and Jimmy of *Just above My Head*, he drew his characters from men like Boykins's Uncle Michael. Baldwin, though, is not writing in a literary historical vacuum when he fashions these queer fictional characters. The queer black male character has a long pedigree going at least as far back as the first decades of the twentieth century, in literary depiction as well as in the musical expressions of the sissy-man blues.[67] By exploring one little-noted major influence on Baldwin's representation of the sissy, Langston Hughes, we can begin to understand the literary historical significance of the shift that Baldwin makes when he figures John Grimes's ambivalent relation to the homo-swish's lease on the ghetto street. Hughes depicts this figure in his only novel, *Not without Laughter* (1930). Hughes explores in the novel his semiautobiographical protagonist's process of manly maturation expedited by his experience of the Great Migration when

Sandy, the protagonist, is sent for by his mother to leave rural Kansas and join her in Chicago. Of the dangers that Sandy must undergo—including leaving school to get a job as an elevator operator—the most threatening are represented as the temptations lurking on the ghetto street itself. These dangers are embodied most seductively—and at the same time most repulsively—in the body of a lascivious homo-swish. On his first night after arriving in the city, as Sandy is taking his very first walk in his new neighborhood, the very first voice he hears comes from this homo-swish:

> Somebody stopped beside him.
> "Nice evening?" said a small yellow man with a womanish kind of voice, smiling at Sandy.
> "Yes," said the boy, starting across the street, but the stranger followed him, offering Pall Malls. He smelled of perfume, and his face looked as though it had been powdered with white talcum as he lit a tiny pocket-lighter.[68]

More graphically portrayed than any such in Baldwin, Hughes's street swish nonetheless anticipates the imaging of the street as an ominous risk for the sissy-boy, in both cases due to the sissy protagonist's having been reared in relatively guarded home/church environments. Like Wright's "round, yellow" Shorty of *Black Boy*, Hughes's swish is first identified by size—little rather than "fat"—and light skin color. In both Wright and Hughes, lightening the skin tone further alienates the queer from the black familial and gender familiarity—a pattern we will see repeated in LeRoi Jones's novel, *The System of Dante's Hell*, discussed in the next chapter. Hughes structures the narrative so that we are sure to sense the imminent danger before Sandy does by piling up unmistakable cues of the swishing signature: the small stature, the womanish voice, the smile, the predatory insistence, the gift-giving, the perfume, the powdered face, and the "tiny" pocket-lighter—all in the space of a few sentences. It is not this man who is a stranger to the street, but Sandy himself, a fresh peach just ripe enough for picking. Sandy's estrangement from the street is also his alienation from this new black terrain, the culture he must make fully his own without becoming pathologized by its many risks. A surface reading of this encounter would stop here, recognizing a familiar script of the homosexual predator scouring the black urban street for unsuspecting boyish prey.

A subtler reading of this episode would be to highlight Sandy's own sissy temperament. Throughout the novel, we come to see him as a too-good boy, close to his grandmother, quietly insecure in his boyhood, and existing in his own dreamy otherworld. Hughes does not detail exactly what attracts the homo-swish to the boy, but we might speculate that the swish reads something quietly detectable and delectable only to another sissy on the street: perhaps an insecure crimp in his gait, perhaps an unconscious look of yearning in the eyes, perhaps a too-erect posture. Finding out that Sandy comes from Kansas, the street swish tries to engage him in a conversation about the effrontery of the girls out west, always "raring to go," "like wild horses," "so passionate, aren't they." Testing the waters before he dips, the swish talks about the kind of effrontery that he is about to enact in his "softly persistent voice."

> "Say, kid," it whispered smoothly, touching the boy's arm, "listen, I got some swell French pictures up in my room—naked women and everything! Want to come up and see them?"
>
> "No," said Sandy, quickening his pace. "I got to go somewhere."
>
> "But I room right around the corner," the voice insisted. "Come on by. You're a nice kid, you know it? Listen, don't walk so fast. Stop, let me talk to you."
>
> But Sandy was beginning to understand. A warm sweat broke out on his neck and forehead. Sometimes, at the pool hall in Stanton, he had heard the men talk about queer fellows who stopped boys in the streets and tried to coax them to their rooms.[69]

Sandy's own precocious capacity for observing the minutiae in his Kansas hometown helps to protect him from this danger—in this case, his close attention to the men in his hometown pool hall when they discuss swishes. In referring to the swish's voice as "it," a neutering that seems to transfer to the swish himself, Hughes casts the figure as unthinkable and yet familiar for Sandy, at least in terms of the manly banter he has picked up in his down-home pool hall.

This semiautobiographical narrative use of the swish constitutes Hughes's own mode of self-policing, enforcing Sandy's gender conformity and sexual circumspection as a way of propagating the author's own public image as a circumspect voice of the black folk imagination. In bringing the novel to closure through this spotting of the homo-swish, Hughes unintentionally reaffirms the always present figure of the sissy, whose liminality (hidden in the open) is central to the constitution and structure of the African American social body. Sandy's aversion to this public queerness, however, helps to set the limits on the kinds of desire that can be explicitly exhibited in Hughes's text. Ironically, Hughes is able to have it both ways, exhibiting the queer for all to see and keeping him in the shadows, an alternative not pursued, a detour not taken, in Sandy's own mind. Sandy's aversion is not such that he cannot be curious about this man's predilections: "'He thinks I'm dumb,' thought Sandy, 'but I'm wise to him!' Yet he wondered what such men did with the boys who accompanied them. Curious, he'd like to find out—but he was afraid; so at the next corner he turned and started rapidly towards State Street, but the queer fellow kept close beside him, begging." Alarmed by the queer's persistence, Sandy begins to run until he discovers himself in the light of

State Street, a main thoroughfare of the Bronzeville commercial district. "Sandy could see the fellow's anxious face quite clearly now." Running into the safety of the crowded street, Sandy experiences an intense sissy panic after the fact: "The whining voice made him sick inside—and, almost without knowing it, his legs began swerving swiftly between the crowds along the curb."[70] Both "inflamed" and so quickly becoming "a source of fire and temptation" for others on the street, to borrow Baldwin's language, Sandy must flee from the natural curiosity he feels in the midst of his alarming sissy-panic. Even as Hughes fashions the stereotyped recruiting homosexual in order to prove the hero's manhood rites, he leaves that doubt of curiosity dangling in the novel. Like his poem "Café: 3 a.m.," Hughes's novel participates in a tradition along with other Harlem Renaissance texts exploring the complex implications of policing queer desire.[71]

Although Baldwin's argument with Richard Wright over the author's authority and identity is more visible as a public skirmish, his controversy with Langston Hughes is more visceral, inhabiting, as it does, a convergent course of desire that makes Hughes and Baldwin look like opposed circumspect sissy (Hughes) and homo-swish (Baldwin) within African American men's literary tradition. In his instructive chapter on Hughes, Boyd highlights the contested intimacy that characterized his mentoring relationship with Baldwin. "In this state of mixed feelings," Boyd writes, "Baldwin idolized Hughes yet also possibly sought to replace him—to 'slay him.'"[72] Writing rival reviews of each other's work, Hughes and Baldwin emphasize their differences, each to the detriment of the other. In his celebrated biography, *The Life of Langston Hughes*, Arnold Rampersad explains how Hughes links Baldwin's sexually explicit fiction with integration, and integration with the loss of traditional black masculine values: "Privately to Arna Bontemps, he described Baldwin as aiming for a best-seller.... In the same letter, Langston linked what he saw as Baldwin's excesses to the trend of integration sapping the strength of black youth."[73] We should note here the resonance of Hughes's use of the progressive verb "sapping" with Du Bois's phrase "sapping the manhood of the race" to attack Washington's sycophantic, housekeeping politics. Both connote a threat to the virility of the race, a threat to conventional masculine character and conduct. Hughes's dismay over Baldwin and his generation of sexually exposing integrationist writers helps us to understand the changing racial and sexual identifications involved in what it means to communicate images of the race's manhood to the book-buying public on the cusp of desegregation.

On the publication of Baldwin's first novel, Hughes expresses his reservations, evidently picking up on some strain within the novel that touches a nerve. In a letter to Arna Bontemps, Hughes gives his appraisal of *Go Tell It*: "Baldwin over-writes and over-poeticizes in images way over the heads of the folks supposedly thinking them—often beautiful writing in itself—but frequently out of character—although it might be as the people <u>would</u> think if they <u>could</u> think that way. Which makes it seem like an 'art' book about folks who aren't 'art' folks.... It's a low-down story in a velvet bag—and a Knopf binding. Willard Motley–like writing without his heart-breaking characters fitting the poetry Motley weaves around them. As Motley's does, but Baldwin's don't. Has a feeling of writing-for-writing's-sake quality."[74] As the final jab at his former publisher, Knopf, indicates, Hughes's reaction to the rising young writer contains a note of envy. Hughes expresses his discontent with Baldwin's writing as a tendency toward excess: "over-writes," "over-poeticizes," "over the heads"—a characterization of the author that is reprised in the 1963 *Time* magazine cover story on Baldwin. I would suggest that Hughes's ascription of these kinds of writerly excess to the novel approximates attributing excessive swishing to a man's hips. How ironic that a poet decries another author's writing by calling it "poetic," affiliated here with "pretty," an effeminate style, which, unlike Hughes's virile jazz poetics, flaunts its sissy eloquence extravagantly instead of curbing it respectably. Baldwin's materials may be authentic enough, but his techniques are derivative of either white writers ("a la Lillian Smith") or an African American writer like Motley, whose first two novels, *Knock on Any Door* and *We Fished All Night*, have already established his reputation as someone apparently more interested in non-black-cast proletarian fiction than in African American culture.

Hughes's obvious discomfort with this integrationist trend, emblematized through what he sees as dirty-laundry-airing interracial sex, actually hinges on a less obvious discomfort with the same-sexuality that also tends to bubble up in novels by Baldwin, Motley, Chester Himes, and other black male authors of the time. Hughes labels Himes's fifth novel, *The Primitive*, "a really sickening interracial passion tale" and asks rhetorically, "Do they reckon our literrati [*sic*] are now out to ruin the Race????????"[75] Hughes's language of intense disgust—"sickening," "horrifically," "putrid"—reveals his unease with Himes's exposure of deviant desire, not only in his erasing the line separating private from public conduct but also in his tendency to exhibit a black man's stereotypeable behavior in an "interracial passion tale." Moreover, although Hughes does not mention it, he could not have overlooked Himes's portrayal of black homo-swishes who live in the same apartment building with the protagonist—a portrayal that in its structure reminds us of Hughes's own treatment of the aggressive street swish in *Not without Laughter*.

This contest over who rightfully and authentically owns the literary right to depict the race appears on the surface as a skirmish over violent interracial sex, but just beneath the surface this contest is being waged on the liminal body of the homo-swish. In his comment, referred to in Rampersad's quote above, concerning Baldwin's third novel, *Another Country*, Hughes makes the connection between Baldwin's sexually explicit literature and the negative impact of integration on the race: "Seems he is trying to out-Henry Henry Miller in the use of bad BAD *bad* words, or run *The Carpetbaggers* one better on sex in bed and out, left and right, plus a description of a latrine with all the little-boy words reproduced in the telling. (Opinion seems to be, he's aiming for a best-seller).... Cullud is doing everything white folks are doing these days!.... (Integration is going to ruin Negro business....)."[76] Hughes signals his own circumspection in these matters by not continuing the drift that he starts in serializing the novel's sexual promiscuity. Bontemps, however, would be able to read between the lines and know that in addition to "sex in bed and out, left and right," the novel explores cross-racial sex between men and women, "straight" and "gay." Having been criticized himself for failing to man the front against racial disrespect, Hughes must experience some ambivalence, sincerely appalled by what "our" literati are up to and yet reminded of the censorious response to some of his own blues-inspired earthy verse. "The initial negative reaction to *The Weary Blues* objected as much to Hughes's using jazz and blues as literary material as to the flexible sexual morality of the cabarets," James de Jongh reminds us. "Hughes recalled being interrupted, during a reading of these poems in an Atlantic City church, by a note from the pastor demanding that he not read 'any more blues in my pulpit.'"[77] But Hughes's deployment of blues and jazz lyricism in a pulpit may seem rather tame next to Baldwin's and Himes's explosion of "bad" words and sexual excesses, both of which Hughes identifies with best-selling white authors.

Perhaps this masculinist panic over Baldwin's high sissy visibility should not be surprising. In Hughes's case, however, we would have to characterize this conduct as sissy panic, for Baldwin's relatively more "swishing" approach to racialized sexuality could be seen as either shadowing or unmasking (or both at once) Hughes's own more circumspect sissy character. Writing during the emergence of a "sexual revolution" that will bring homosexuality out of the shadows in mass media as well as on the streets, Baldwin's historical context asks of him a different sociosexual stance from what Hughes must have felt compelled to take, whatever his sexual disposition.

Sissies and Swishes in Baldwin's Fiction

A major objective of Baldwin's fiction is to provide a cultural context for articulating black men as erotic subjects without falling into what Darieck Scott labels "the relentless, repetitive sexualization of black bodies" so inescapable in U.S. and indeed global cultures.[78] When Rufus Scott, the protagonist of *Another Country*, mercilessly berates, beats, and rapes his southern white girlfriend, Leona, readers cannot help but associate this behavior with the myth of black men's predation, particularly in relation to white femininity. Having attacked Wright for constructing a character like Bigger Thomas seemingly through the vector of unrelieved racial violence, Baldwin works hard in *Another Country* to de-Biggerize Rufus. Although conventionally masculine in his conduct, Rufus falls into an intimate relationship with Eric, a white male southerner, a bond that sheds light on and complicates his embattled relationship with Leona. Although Rufus's relationship with Eric places the protagonist in a situation not imaginable for Bigger, Rufus's end is no less violent. In a fit of depression, frustration, and self-loathing, Rufus returns to Harlem and jumps off the George Washington Bridge. It is almost as if Baldwin cannot bear to complete Rufus's story for fear of his protagonist's replicating Bigger's fate.[79]

When Baldwin tries to complicate and diversify the possibilities for black manhood, he can easily be seen by and within the black community as overstepping the line that observes what Jeffrey Q. McCune Jr. calls "sexual discretion."[80] Although Baldwin's project is at work in every single novel and play he writes, it is most obvious in his third, fourth, and final novels: *Another Country* (1962), *Tell Me How Long the Train's Been Gone* (1968), and *Just above My Head* (1979). In *Tell Me How Long* especially, with its bisexual, ambitious black actor-hero, Leo Proudhammer, whose desire goes in so many directions at once and who is capable of playing so many different roles, Baldwin seems to be pushing his reluctant audience toward some acknowledgment of the vast and complicated range of desire within the social reality of black manhood character and conduct. *Just above My Head*, Baldwin's sixth and final novel, returns to the material of his first, giving us the church sissy as hero, this time as a gospel singer, but refusing the more timid circumspection of desire contained by *Go Tell It*. It is also in this final novel that Baldwin provides his most sustained image of the black man desired and desiring in relation to another black man.

In *Go Tell It*, however, Baldwin prefigures this black-on-black male love motif in the understated, yearning, ethereal relationship between Elisha and John. In this scene, we as readers meet the older teen through John's eyes:

> When he was young, John had paid no attention in Sunday school, and always forgot the golden text, which earned him the wrath of his father. Around the time of his fourteenth birthday, with all the pressures of church and home uniting to drive him to the altar, he strove to appear more serious and therefore less conspicuous. But he was distracted by his new teacher, Elisha, who was the pastor's nephew and who had but lately arrived from Georgia. He was not much older than John, only seventeen, and he was already saved and was a preacher. John stared at Elisha all during the lesson,

admiring the timbre of Elisha's voice, much deeper and manlier than his own, admiring the leanness, and grace, and strength, and darkness of Elisha in his Sunday suit, wondering if he would ever be holy as Elisha was holy. But he did not follow the lesson, and when, sometimes, Elisha paused to ask John a question, John was ashamed and confused, feeling the palms of his hands become wet and his heart pound like a hammer. Elisha would smile and reprimand him gently, and the lesson would go on.[81]

This passage is characteristic of the novel's treatment of gender nonconformity and sexual desire. John is never explicitly labeled a sissy or homosexual, but Baldwin provides a lattice of physical, attitudinal, and psychological details that, taken together, speak quite loudly to John's gender-sexual predicament. John's fear of being perceived as "conspicuous"—"the pressures of church and home"— could be interpreted in a variety of ways, including that he is worried about being naughty during Sunday school. We know, however, that it is not John who is a "bad boy," since he is tied to the habitus of the home/church, but instead John's younger half brother, Royal (Roy), who, much to the father's pride and dismay, is too much of a mannish boy to avoid the dangers of the street. Roy is the spitting image of Gabriel himself in his youth, before the elder Grimes found a brokered and contested salvation as a preacher. Whereas Roy's conventional gender conduct makes the church an undesirable place that seeks to constrain and curtail the boyish ambitions and desires that the street abets, John's sissiness—his self-conscious desire to be authoritatively restrained in order to belong—makes him especially suitable for the church's vocations.

In fact, John suffers Reid's "best little boy in the world" syndrome discussed in chapter 1, and even more tellingly, he embodies the dreamy predisposition affiliated with sissiness. Rather than listening to Elisha's lesson, he falls into a reverie about how he used to get distracted. John's admiration itself exemplifies his worrying over being distracted by inappropriate objects. He starts by admiring the boy's deeper voice, then moves to Elisha's attractive body, a body on the verge of manhood. From the body, John's attention flows naturally to a desire for Elisha's holiness, as though the lean, graceful, strong body can release the secret to being "holy"—that is, being not only religiously upright but also socially normative. No doubt, John expects the kind of harsh putdown that his father gives him to interrupt his dreaminess, but instead Elisha "would smile and reprimand him gently." What a dilemma for poor John! Even Elisha's reprimand becomes erotically alluring.

That the common culture here is materialized in the black church is paramount, as perhaps no other institution has so palpably shaped for so long the common vocabulary of blackness in the United States. As explained in some excellent recent work on Baldwin's theology by Kornegay, Marlon Rachquel Moore, and Josiah Ulysses Young III, Baldwin queers the church and black theology itself, placing his homo-sissy characters within a religious tradition that struggles with its own inherent queerness.[82] Indeed, what Baldwin illustrates through the novel is how every member of the family necessarily has a queer relation to the church, at least sexually, as each has a convoluted relationship with the patriarchy in which the church is anchored.[83] Gabriel, John's (step)father, finds it difficult to channel his masculine ambition, heterosexual lust, and profligate procreativity into a church orthodoxy whose ministry is dominated by bossy church mothers under the aegis of a sweet, celibate Christ birthed from a virgin mother. If not too sacrilegious, it might be accurate to say that Christ and his church are far too sissified for Gabriel, whose resentment toward Elizabeth's bastard son is partly fueled by Gabriel's sense that the church actually fits the sissy-boy's sensitive intelligence better than it fits his own brutish ambition, lust, and procreativity.

Florence, Gabriel's sister, five years older than he, is consumed with bitterness against men that stems in large part from the way her younger brother is doted on by their mother simply because he is male. Deeply aware of her brother's sexual hypocrisies, Florence sporadically attends his church, in effect waiting to see him trip up and fall into disgrace for his myriad sexual sins. On returning from the Saturday night church service, she exclaims to Gabriel, "'Of all the men I *ever* knew, you's the man who ought to be hoping the Bible's all a lie—'cause if that trumpet ever sounds, you going to spend eternity talking.'"[84] She expresses sympathy for those whom Gabriel takes pride in judging—John especially—and she clings to the church queerly out of a gender animus that doubtfully looks to the final judgment as a vengeance on the very patriarchs whom the patriarchal God supposedly has named as his overseers on earth. Elizabeth, John's mother, struggles to resolve her secret fear and suffering at the hands of her husband with her love and respect for his calling as a man of God. The daughter of a pimp, Elizabeth has lost her true love, a sensitive romantic man, Richard, who commits suicide after being psychically wrecked by unjust imprisonment. Impregnated with Richard's son, Elizabeth out of economic and spiritual desperation accepts Gabriel's bargain to become his wife and take John for his son. Like the ex-colored man's mother, Elizabeth nurtures the sissiness within her son as a conduit to a romantic, forbidden past that she refuses to regret or deny, no matter how taboo. John himself cannot know the backstories of his adult family members, and thus cannot know how much they share with him a gender-queer relation to the church.

As observed above, sissy liminality spurs a chain of speculation, rumor, and suspicion. While speculation can be theoretically productive in understanding how sissiness is gendered and racialized, we should note that it is nearly impossible to segregate its operation from more sinister modes of scrutiny moving from relatively harmless rumor to modes of suspicion that can frequently result in punitive violence. In other words, speculation abets its own dangers not only to the exposed sissy-boy but also to any associate. Elisha's persistently gentle mentoring of John should thus be recognized as a self-conscious risk. Elisha is called to the altar by his own uncle, who is head pastor, to account for his relationship with one of the female church members. The uncle predictably presumes not only Elisha's weakness in being alone with a girl (a theologically correct interpretation of original sin) but also his heteronormativity. In other words, punitive suspicion is not reserved for the sin of homosexuality; it looks for any sign of heterosexual transgression as well.

Despite his uprightness, Elisha himself is prone to get distracted. When John goes to help Elisha prepare the church for evening prayer service, we see the special relation between the two boys. Except for the few men who hold positions of power in the church, it is a place of women and their influence. Baldwin emphasizes this point when he has the nosy Sisters McCandless and Price interrupt the boys' playful preparatory work: "They wore the black cloth coats that they wore all week and they had old felt hats on their heads. John felt a chill as they passed him, and he closed the door."[85] The chill comes from the weather let in, of course, but also from these ascetically clad mothers of the church. Before the chilling women enter, the boys have been cleaning the thrashing floor, the space before the altar where sinners come to wrestle with the Lord in a battle for control of the soul's flesh. This serious work is temporarily displaced onto another kind of work of the spirit, a test of strength between Elisha and John. Significantly, it is Elisha who initiates the match:

> Elisha let fall the stiff gray mop and rushed at John, catching him off balance and lifting him from the floor.... With all the strength that was in him he fought against Elisha, and he was filled with a strength that was almost hatred.... And so they turned, battling in the narrow room, and the odor of Elisha's sweat was heavy in John's nostrils. He saw the veins rise on Elisha's forehead and in his neck; his breath became jagged and harsh, and the grimace on his face became more cruel; and John, watching these manifestations of his power, was filled with a wild delight. They stumbled against the folding-chairs, and Elisha's foot slipped and his hold broke. They stared at each other, half grinning. John slumped to the floor, holding his head between his hands.
>
> "I didn't hurt you none, did I?" Elisha asked. (53)

Baldwin makes it clear that this is not an unusual encounter between the two boys ("usually such a battle ...") (53). This wrestling ritual must be placed alongside the scene between David and Joey in *Giovanni's Room*, a match that becomes explicitly sexual only to turn David against Joey and against his own authentic desire. We might say that the conventional boyish ritual of the wrestling match ironically guides John toward the articulation of the queerness not only within his own desire but also adhering to all desire, secular and spiritual. Baldwin emphasizes the correlation and conflation of this "secular" wrestling match with the "sacred" match that occurs toward the end of the novel. As John "gets religion" on the thrashing floor, again we find him and Elisha locked in a fleshly embrace, Elisha struggling with all his physical might to bring the sinner through to the other side of Jordan, John struggling both to come over and to make his coming over a coming into self-consciousness that will be true to his "natural" course of desire. As Baldwin himself indicates and reenacts in autobiographical texts like *The Fire Next Time*, the sissy-boy's bearing within the church guides his bearing as a man on the stage of the world.[86] Even as Baldwin leaves behind many of the doctrinal tenets of the church, he retains the structure, form, vocabulary, and tenor of his religious upbringing. As Hardy has astutely pointed out: "But even as Baldwin relied on Christian rhetoric in his quest for social justice, his work, as a whole, suggests that while black evangelicalism embodies a posture of resistance against a hostile white world, its redemptive value ultimately fails to overcome the extent to which Christianity has contributed to African disfigurement."[87] We could also say that while the church nurtures Baldwin's (and John's) circumspect sissiness, it also so disfigures his desire that he must leave the institution behind. Still, it continues to shape Baldwin's mode of sissy insurgency as a secular writer and activist.

Baldwin emphasizes how these institutions are formed not merely through the repression of so-called deviant desire but also, more fundamentally, through the impression such desire necessarily makes on and in these crucial institutions, from both within and without. In other words, deviant desire is already within the heart of the church, helping to define its modes and means of being. Like the "two-spirit" tradition among some Native American societies, the nonconforming gender behavior is taken as evidence for the child's special divine gift.[88] If Baldwin aborts John's trajectory on the threshold of his being on his way to an unknown future, in his last novel, *Just above My Head*, he amplifies this trajectory through a church-sissy protagonist, Arthur Montana, who could be seen as completing the story begun with John Grimes. Arthur and his lover, Jimmy, have a relation to neither the gay ghetto experience nor the recognizable narratives of dominant gay identity-formation. Their world is their African American community, their church, and their family. Most crucially, sexual orientation is not the definitive or even a major aspect of their identity, as it becomes for those who occupy the gay ghetto—in line with Baldwin's critique of "gay" identity in the 1984 Goldstein interview. Arthur and Jimmy's same-gender desire definitely shapes their consciousness, but much more imperceptibly than in white gay novels from this "clone" era of the late 1960s to the early 1980s.[89] Jimmy is the closest Baldwin comes to depicting a swish in his fiction. Significantly, as others have noted, Jimmy is the name Baldwin himself is known by among his dearest associates. Arthur, however, is also Baldwin, as suggested by the fact of Baldwin's middle name. Like a swish, Jimmy refuses to play hide-and-seek, the sort of "closet" games expected of homo-sissies in dominant culture, especially in the '50s and '60s, the time frame of the novel. But unlike with the swish, Jimmy's conspicuousness is strikingly unselfconscious. Jimmy is conspicuous because he is so honest with himself, not because of any defensiveness about what others expect from him. Narrated from the perspective of Arthur's elder brother, Hall, we are invited to eye the two lovers from a heterosexual man's empathetic point of view—and ironically, his perspective resists heteronormative assumptions and judgments. As Hall watches the two lovers, he notes how they manage their desire in public: "Neither Arthur nor Jimmy could ever really hide anything, nor did they ever, it must be said, when the chips were down, try; but Arthur was far more veiled, especially, of course, in his relation to Jimmy, around me. I thought Arthur was very funny—downright, as the old folks would say, 'cute.'"[90] Baldwin puns wickedly on the vernacular meanings of "funny" when he has Hall use this adjective to describe his younger brother's temperament and demeanor. As mentioned earlier, E. Patrick Johnson observes that "funny" is a folk synonym for "queer." Baldwin uses this vernacular expression in exactly this way when John Grimes observes a strangeness in his baby photograph on the mantlepiece as distinct from those of his siblings: "None of the other children was naked; no, Roy lay in his crib in a white gown and grinned toothlessly into the camera, and Sarah, somber at the age of six months, wore a white bonnet, and Ruth was held in her mother's arms. When people looked at these photographs and laughed, their laughter differed from the laughter with which they greeted the naked John. For this reason, when visitors tried to make advances to John he was sullen, and they, feeling that for some reason he disliked them, retaliated by deciding that he was a 'funny' child."[91] Interpreting the different mood of laughter that greets the photo of baby John, he assumes that it is his nakedness that distinguishes the visitors' response, given that the sissy-boy fears the difference he intuits within is somehow being physically communicated to others. His "sullen" response to their different laughter, however, indicates that the strangeness that they observe in the photo and in the boy's reaction to their advances is deeper than exposed skin, and John himself provides the apt epithet "funny" to capture this mutual estrangement. Laughter itself seems to straddle a line between the normative and queer as it veers away from an instinctive physiological reaction to the cute children's pictures toward something unfamiliar, strange, uncanny, disorienting, discomfiting—no word in English captures it except perhaps "queer." Hall transposes the old-time reference to the word "cute," while equating it with "funny," disarming the slight sting that bites in adjudging the sissy-boy in such estranging terms.

Perhaps what Hall finds "funny" is his brother's "veiled" manner. We might gloss this adjective through Du Bois's use of it in relation to double consciousness and the caul. For Du Bois, the veil has multiple racial significations, ranging from the metonymic black skin that shades the Negro from white society to the literal Jim Crow curtain that separates whites from being pressed by blacks on public transportation to the metaphorical membrane of psychological ambivalence that splits white unconsciousness from black self-consciousness and conscience. Old folks called the membrane that sometimes covers a newborn's head a "veil," and said that any child so born was endowed with the gift of prescience. Hall's reference to Arthur as "veiled" captures the young man's endearing awkwardness, his hugging the body to itself—the good sissy's fear of letting the body swish into eruptions of exposed desire. More "veiled" than Jimmy, more circumspect, less nonchalant about what others think, Arthur tries to muffle his lover's exposed desire.

Jimmy refuses others' image of his love and thus allows Arthur to find a safe place for exploring the full range of his desire, as Hall instructs us to see: "I mean that Jimmy's presence in Arthur's life, Jimmy's love, altered Arthur's estimate of himself, gave him a joy and a freedom he had never known before, invested him with a kind of incandescent wonder, and he carried this light on stage with him, he moved his body differently since he knew that he was loved, loved, and, therefore, knew himself to be both bound and free, and this miracle, the unending wonder of this unending new day, filled his voice with multitudes, summoned, from catacombs unnameable, whosoever will."[92] Critics often have cited passages like this one in Baldwin's later fiction as evoking a kind of embarrassment, similar to the embarrassment expressed by Hughes in complaining about Baldwin's overwriting in *Go Tell It*. Left naked in the open, the reader tends to feel exposed, to feel embarrassed, by the flaunting of such a network of intimacy, which envelops not just Arthur and Jimmy's bond but also its deep familial—indeed, almost erotic—entanglement with Ruth and Hall. Aware of the risk of exposure, given the habit of projecting perversion onto African American relationships in the American imaginary, Baldwin provides Hall, an involved narrator, as an ordinary countermeasure but one whose heterosexuality is so informed and inspired by Arthur and Jimmy that it proudly fails the test of heteronormativity.

Indeed, although Hall Montana is largely heterosexual, he is far from heteronormative—a fact that shapes our relationship to him as interested narrator of his younger brother's story. Midway through the novel, Hall reveals in very vivid terms his own homosexual experiences while he is abroad during the Korean War:

> And I had fucked everything I could get my hands on overseas, including two of my drinking buddies. I had been revolted—but this was after, not before, the act. Before the act, when I realized from their eyes what was happening, I had adored being the adored male, and stretched out on it, all boyish muscle and throbbing cock, telling myself, What the hell, it beats jerking off. And I had loved it—the adoration, the warm mouth, the tight ass, the fact that nothing at all was demanded of me except that I shoot my load, which I was very, very happy to do. (309)

This passage, which continues for half a page, is far more sexually graphic than any of the depictions of Arthur's sex scenes with Crunch, his first lover; Jimmy; or Guy, the French man with whom he has an intense affair in Paris just before his fatal heart attack in the restroom of a London pub. This self-confession arrives in the midst of a triangulated relationship between Hall, his Harlem drinking buddy, Sidney, and the sometime girlfriend, Martha, whom Sidney eventually weds. Unsure of his own romantic ambivalence toward Martha, Hall clearly uses his service overseas as an excuse to end the relationship without explicitly doing so. When he returns to find her in a relationship with Sidney, he is at once relieved that he need not feel as guilty for having behaved like such a cad to her, but at the same time jealous, seemingly more at losing his best friend, Sidney, than losing his girlfriend to him. The palpable erotic undertow between Hall and Sidney emphasizes one of the novel's most challenging themes: that the erotic flows, sometimes imperceptibly but always erratically, within and across factitious categories socially and discursively segregated by blood kin, friend, stranger, and sexual partner. By deliberately framing Arthur's gay sexual life with greater circumspection than the homosexual trysts of the protagonist's "straight" narrator-brother, Baldwin disrupts not only the line between homosexual and heterosexual but also, more fundamentally, the normative narrative that would position the black queer as a natural outsider in relation to the straight brother's experience. Seeming to answer forcefully the quipping criticisms of respectability-seeking reviewers like Hughes, Baldwin ups the ante in his final novel, appearing to flaunt queer sexuality not just as a shield but as a weapon whose aim is sure.

Because we do not have time here to attend to the novel's myriad stunning complexities exploring human relationality, one extraordinary passage will have to exemplify Baldwin's deployment of sissiness to nuance the entangled cross-identifications that express the insufficiencies of familial, racial, gender, and sexual identities. Toward the beginning of the novel, after Arthur's smashing debut as a gospel performer at the age of thirteen, Hall, seven years older, narrates the mixture of happiness and uneasiness that he feels for his little brother at that moment. His first response to the occasion, however, focuses on a very specific detail that seems to crystallize Hall's attention as both adoring and uneasy:

> I told my brother that the way he wore his hair made him look like a sissy, and that may be the first time I ever really looked at my brother. He cracked up, and started doing imitations of all the most broken-down queens we knew, and he kept saying, just before each imitation, "But I *am* a sissy." He scared me—I hadn't known he was so sharp, that he saw so much—so much despair, so clearly. But he made me laugh until tears rolled down my face, and I ended up on the floor, both arms wrapped around my belly.
>
> Perhaps then we really began to be friends. (29)

It is Arthur's sissy hairstyle that makes Hall *see* him for the first time. Obviously, Hall has been seeing his little brother for thirteen years, but he has never really *seen* him for who he is, or who he might become. Is Hall's pointing out the sissy hairstyle a lame attempt to police his brother's sissiness? Is it a cautious attempt to nudge Arthur to confess what Hall has only now observed, his brother's sissy propensity? Is it both at once? In any case, ironically, Arthur's familiarity, his familial intimacy, has prevented Hall from seeing him clearly—or Hall's own embedded sissiphobia has prevented it. Arthur's response is just as ambiguous and ambivalent. He scandalizes Hall by performing "the most broken-down queens we knew," amplifying Hall's observation of his sissiness by swishing it up—claiming extravagantly what Hall has more tentatively articulated. It is Hall's first sight of Arthur's gospel stage performance that gives incentive to this private stage performance of the swish for Hall's eyes only. In fact, Arthur's gospel performance creates the adoring sensation in the audience exactly because it is limned by an implicit sissy sensorium. Sissiness is among the male gospel singer's greatest resources, as the capacity both to communicate the soul's innermost un/rest and to vocally capture that wrestling match between the church and the street. In this sense, Arthur's private performance for Hall is at once a continuation of the gospel stage performance and a signifying (in queer black lingo, a *reading*) on it. That Arthur prefaces each swish imitation with "But I *am* a sissy" is intended to confess, deny, and disarm simultaneously, as though the swish performance both exposes and masks the observed sissy conduct and character. As is the case with sissiness, the small detail of the hair's style causes Hall's speculation, and Arthur's response both teases, confuses, and confirms the speculation. That mocking laughter—ridicule of the swishes that they both know—should be the basis for a cross-generational fraternal friendship only complicates further how sissiness becomes the frame that clarifies their capacity to see, and to know, each other more deeply. As with John Grimes's estranging sense of himself as "funny" in the naked baby picture, as with the estranging laughter elicited by family and friends at seeing the picture, the shared laughter between the brothers is both an embrace of sissiness and a distancing from it. This represents the beginning of Hall's deepening self-discovery even more than the start of Arthur's sexual awakening, given that Arthur indeed has already, long before Hall's observation, perspicaciously scrutinized "the broken-down queens we knew" as an object lesson to model, discipline, and distance his own sissy conduct and character.

Long underrated and overlooked, *Just above My Head* is, in my judgment, Baldwin's magnum opus, alongside his first novel, *Go Tell It*. Although only now beginning to receive its due, the novel anticipates the intellectual work of race and queer theory, which still lags behind the insights that it forecasts. All the more astonishing, the novel serves as an indirect critique not only of the respectability-craving Hughes crowd but also of the (white) gay homonormalizing social identity that has emerged into mass public view in the decade of the novel's publication. Writing *Just above My Head* in the moment when "gay" has emerged as a more polite, progressive way of identifying homosexuality and when white gay ghettos have become highly visible in the national and televisual imaginary,[93] Baldwin resolutely refuses to set his man-loving-man narrative within this readily available venue. By fashioning and conducting themselves within and against the images tailored by available cultural knowledge, characters like John Grimes, Leo Proudhammer, Arthur Montana, and Jimmy Miller embody how homo-sissies shape that culture not just from its outer edges but also from its most sacred heart.

Baldwin and the Cold War Sissy

If Baldwin in his last novel so self-consciously refuses to gay-ghettoize his black gay characters at the height of the social formation of the white gay ghetto, and instead composes men-loving-men characters who occupy the broad zone of homo-sissy respectability and circumspection within the churchified black community, he nonetheless autobiographically represents his own sissified person as a public target of white male lust—all the more scandalously enacted by a powerful white southerner who *should* embody the Cold War state's front line against the "soft" menace of the sissified male. In Baldwin's 1972 autobiographical polemic, *No Name in the Street*, Baldwin presents us with a shocking sexual anecdote that at once exposes the Cold War hypocrisies of a "law and order" purged of queer desire and connects these "law-and-order" hypocrisies to Jim Crow's ostensible protection of white purity from black rapaciousness: "I have never, for example, written about my unbelieving shock when I realized that I was being groped by one of the most powerful men in one of the states I visited. He had got himself sweating drunk in order to arrive at this despairing titillation. With his wet eyes staring up at my face, and his wet hands groping for my cock, we were both, abruptly, in history's ass-pocket."[94] We could, in the manner of Kathryn Stockton's book *Beautiful Bottom*, interpret this as a parable of alluring shame in which intragender, cross-racial attraction is characteristically affiliated with the penetrated asshole, by spotlighting what Leo Bersani so aptly calls a "malignant aversion" to the specter of anal penetration.[95] To be associated with the asshole is not only to be beset by uncontrollable wastage; it is, more to the point, to be bereft of phallic subjectivity and agency.[96] In this anecdote, it is the white bossman who expresses out-of-control rapacious desire for a black man whose reputation as a public sissy is circumscribed by social and sexual respectability: "It was very frightening—*not the gesture itself*, but the abjectness of it, and the assumption of a swift and grim complicity: as my identity was defined by his power, so was my humanity to be placed at the service of his fantasies." In case we might confuse shame over "the gesture itself" with shock at the violent significance of the gesture as an act of racist political disempowerment, Baldwin proceeds for several pages with his analysis: "This man, with a phone call, could prevent or provoke a lynching."[97] Rather than an act of liberation, the mere gesture here of a white man reaching for a black man's cock shades over into the lynching ritual, in which white men also reach for black men's genitals but as an overt act of castrating violation. Thus, the white southerner's seemingly erotic gesture cannot be separated from the white male supremacist power he holds.[98] "When the man grabbed my cock," Baldwin continues, "I didn't think of him as a faggot, which, indeed, if having a wife and children, house, cars, and a respectable and powerful standing in the community, mean anything, he wasn't." Baldwin is making a crucial distinction here. One's identity as a faggot is not merely a question of whom one desires erotically; it is more fundamentally a matter of one's access to and manipulation of established power in pursuit of gratifying a desire necessarily warped by that abusive power. For Baldwin, those invested with such power necessarily, "fatally, touch the wrong person, not merely because they have gone blind, or have lost the sense of touch, but because they no longer have any way of knowing that any loveless touch is a violation, whether one is touching a woman or a man."[99] This groping southerner should more appropriately be grouped, then, with historical figures like Roy Cohn, legal advisor to Senator Joseph McCarthy, and J. Edgar Hoover, director of the Federal Bureau of Investigation (FBI) over the long course of the Red Scare and antihomosexual purges of the Cold War, both of whom, despite closely held private homosexual relationships, are still able to manipulate the reins of power against marginalized and stigmatized others like African American protestors, gays and lesbians, and political leftists. Hoover's white masculine power, like the groping southerner's, actually protects him from the treatment that ordinary faggots experience every day under the regimes administered nationally by him and locally by groping white southern men. Part of the social historical tragedy (or is it a travesty?) of the white southerner's interaction, then, derives from how his potentially affirming gesture of reaching out to touch another person must necessarily take the form of a coercive grope that seeks instead to reaffirm his upper hand in the racial-sexual hierarchy.[100]

Figuring the southerner who has the law at his beck and call as a local metonym for Hoover's Cold War machinery not only serves to connect Cold War gender conformity to Jim Crow racial violence; it also serves to emphasize how Baldwin must maneuver both regimes at the same time that he negotiates sissiphobic charges of race treachery from young black nationalists like Amiri Baraka. The campaign to name and purge homosexuals from federal and local governments, universities, the military, and other venues of sociopolitical influence is accompanied by stepped-up police enforcement of obscenity and antisodomy laws, focusing especially on exposing and prosecuting men in the possession of homosexual pornography, those seeking clandestine sex in tearooms, and those congregating in bars secretly catering to homosexuals.[101] Protecting the public from homosexuals paradoxically requires the public naming of them in print media that shames any "known homosexuals" who are arrested through the state's multiplying apparatuses of exposure, entrapment, and enforcement, even before their indictment and conviction.[102] As Robert Corber suggests, the upshot of these policing phenomena is the virtual disappearance of homosexuality from respectable public discourse. "Virtually the only way in which homosexuality could become a topic of debate in the political public sphere," Corber writes, "was as a form of psychopathology that threatened national security."[103] Although Corber's statement holds true for the political sphere, as well as for mass visual culture like film and television, it overlooks the flurry of novels about homosexuality between the late 1940s and the early 1960s, due to the Supreme Court's expanding protection of printed texts under the First Amendment "freedom of speech" clause for works of "redeeming social value"—a protection not extended to film, whose corporate self-censorship continued to prohibit the imaging of homosexuality until Jack Valenti's reform of the Motion Picture Association of America's Production Code in 1968. Furthermore, Corber's astute analysis of national security as a justification for homosexual purges nonetheless overlooks the historical likelihood that the *decrease* in official public discourse on homosexuality was accompanied by a spectacular *increase* in the visibility of actual homosexually identified people on America's city streets, as John D'Emilio, K. A. Cuordileone, and others have suggested. "The real or imagined presence of increasing numbers of homosexuals in American life was felt by many anxious heterosexual observers," Cuordileone writes, "whose visceral response was often inflated, brittle, hyper-allegiance to the traditional heterosexual family."[104] In other words, it was the increasing visibility of homosexuals in ordinary American life, especially in the urban centers where African Americans had already migrated, that fueled the sociopolitical demand not only for purging them from official venues of power but also for excising their graphic representation in mass visual culture.

More to our point, although Corber's argument helps us to understand the anxiety over the representation of homosexuality during the height of the Cold War, his conflation of effeminacy with homosexuality downplays the extent to which the sissy—the public perception of a gender-misplaced male—begins to stand in for the homosexual.[105] Indeed, the practice in queer theory of rushing to equate sissy impersonation with homosexual subjectivity ironically could be seen to stem in part from the countercultural Cold War discourse of hinting at homosexuality through a display of sissy attributes, getting around the state's hysterical policing operation by cleverly portraying the hysterics of the sissified, and usually swishing, male. With the intensifying prohibitions against the visual representation of the homosexual, the rare appearance of a public sissy becomes all the more spectacular, embedding in the reception to such display the audience's gender anxiety, especially masculine panic, as well as sexual titillation. Craig M. Loftin has described the dilemma presented by the tendency to equate "effeminate mannerisms" with homosexuality in Metro-Goldwyn-Mayer's production of Robert Anderson's theatrical hit *Tea and Sympathy* in the mid-1950s. The play's homosexual character is "transformed from a suspected homosexual into a neutered 'sissy.'" Loftin notes an increasing "pernicious hostility that many gender-conformist gay men directed toward visibly effeminate male homosexuals. Such hostility was hardly new in gay culture, but it became significantly more pronounced in the 1950s compared to previous decades."[106] This is the historical backstory to Sedgwick's theoretical observation that the "advance [in recent gay-lesbian discourse] may leave the effeminate boy once more in the position of the haunting abject—this time the haunting abject of gay thought itself."[107]

More than just a threat to the family, religion, public morals, or the state, the sissy display in this era nonetheless engendered disturbing intimations of subversion, sedition, and, given the specter of the atom bomb as the final solution to Cold War antinomies, the ultimate fatality of civilization itself. The "soft" man, like Bersani's rectum that betokens the grave, became a sign of catastrophic social death. As Daniel Bell suggested in a 1955 essay, the division of the world into "free" and "Communist" produced within the United States a concomitant binary of "hard" versus "soft," with those labeled as "soft on Communism" as the ultimate representation of political evil.[108] As Cuordileone has pointed out, this hard/soft binary redounds to a political establishment obsessed with distinguishing between a hard and soft manliness, whereby the sissified man, imputing homosexuality, exemplifies the extreme manifestation of softness as menace. The twisted Cold War logic embeds a double jeopardy for gender-nonconforming men. On the one hand, the sissy display embodies the extremity of the threat of subversive softness; on the other hand, the homosexual who can hide his softness becomes a hidden subversive threat lurking in every corner of elite power. The perversity of this logic is amplified by the ironic fact that the nation's manly hardness was being protected by straight men who were reputedly homosexual—J. Edgar Hoover, Roy Cohn, and Whittaker Chambers, to name only a few of the most notoriously powerful. Their vendetta in prosecuting and purging the soft sissies of communist infiltration only serves to vindicate Baldwin's point that homosexually inclined men, when manipulating the levers of American imperial power, cannot be considered faggots.

As we saw with Arthur Montana's mocking imitation of the swish, camping it up for another person, whether straight or homosexual, poses curious ambiguities. Although sissy minstrelsy could be seen as inherently subversive, or at least resistant, in the way it potentially pokes fun at mass hysteria over homosexuality, the very theatricality of such sissified antics could trivialize the act of swishing and thus diminish the threat that was being so obsessively hyped in the corridors of official power.[109] As much as sissy softness was projected as a dire threat to national security, its prurient exposure in the new televisual media seemed to solicit erotic titillation from an ostensibly sexually conformist public. Those exercising state power by weeding out soft men seemed to take as much pleasure in the spectacle of exposing and humiliating this sexual menace as the public who constituted their audience did. Black nationalists charged that civil rights intermediaries like Baldwin were race traitors *because* of the pleasure they took in being sexually exploited by white men in power. One reason this type of scapegoating worked so effectively, however, is that Cold War spectacles had repeatedly staged the public humiliation not only of homo-sissies but also of those gender-conforming men stigmatized as sissy fellow travelers for being "soft" on communism. With so much political explosiveness loaded ironically onto the "soft" unmanly shoulders of the sissy as the harbinger of homosexual subversion, it should not be surprising that sissified impersonation emerged within a celebrity-driven commodity culture in the 1950s as a lucrative career, at least for a few white sissy elites.

In the figure of Truman Capote, the most fitting instance of this development, we find the perfect foil to Baldwin's black sissy insurgency. Capote burst onto the scene in 1948 at the age of twenty-three with the publication of his best-selling novel *Other Voices, Other Rooms*. Although repeatedly characterized as a homosexual novel, like Baldwin's first novel (which appeared five years later), Capote's is best described as a sissy bildungsroman that repeatedly hints at a homosexual predilection through its overwrought symbolism of gender inversion and failure, bodily mutilation and freakishness, and general air of fatally corrupt but seductive perversion. Written in a hyperbolically aestheticized style, the narrative itself is mirrored by the scandalous jacket photograph of the young sissy author, seductively lounging like a girl with his right hand caressing, not quite groping, his crotch (figure 4.1).[110] Having carefully posed himself for this photograph—and many others like it—Capote, like his close friend, Andy Warhol, became the epitome of the mass culture sissy, whose cultural production somehow achieved a notoriety seeming at once to approximate elite cultural status and to expose, if only softly and impishly, the nasty underbelly—we might say the asshole—of the ugly commodification undergirding pretensions to cultural high-mindedness.

Gerald Clarke points out how in interviewing Kansas farmers in 1959 for his book *In Cold Blood*, Capote noted the seductive, hypnotic power of television on his interviewees: "They would sit there talking—and never look at us! They would go on looking straight at the TV screen, even if there was just a station break or an advertisement. If the television wasn't on, if the light wasn't flickering, they began to get the shakes. I guess television has become an extension of

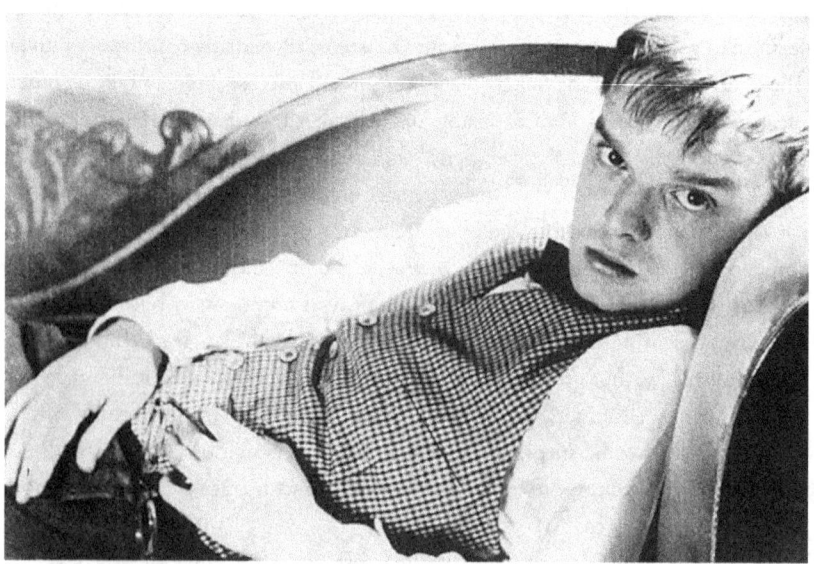

4.1 Front dust-jacket photograph of Truman Capote by Harold Halma from Capote's *Other Voices, Other Rooms*.

people's nervous systems."¹¹¹ In the midst of government propaganda about the "soft" menace and intensified law enforcement against homosexuals, the nonintimidating little screen could bring a mincing celebrity like Capote into American living rooms while allowing viewers to suspend the familiar rush to turn a swish into a homosexual threat. Clarke records a 1959 appearance of Capote, along with Norman Mailer and Dorothy Parker, on David Suskind's show *Open End*: "The Beat Generation came under review. Mailer defended it; Truman attacked it. 'None of these people have anything interesting to say,' Truman declared, 'and none of them can write, not even Mr [Jack] Kerouac. . . . [It] isn't writing at all—it's typing.' The phrase was to be attached to poor Kerouac for the rest of his life. No one recalled Mailer's response. Instinctively, Truman had realized that what television audiences remember is not an argument, but the amusing and pithy phrase they can repeat to their friends the next morning."¹¹² Perhaps it is more than instinct at work here in the televisual reception to a swish figure like Capote versus a conventionally gendered, if not hypermasculine, figure like Mailer. While Mailer's deeply familiar masculine posturing fades into the background, Capote's fey blondness captures the audience's attention. If miniaturized and made intimate in one's living room, the swish's excesses, deserving abuse if encountered on the street, become curiously disarming and titillatingly captivating. Although swish in his manners and gestures, perhaps Capote was televisable exactly because he was circumspect and conventional in his views about social etiquette, morality, and sexuality. Against the abstract, anonymous "soft" threat that peered from every corner of the country, Capote embodied a sharp, sissy tongue in a cute, strange frame. As a much-sought-after guest on such shows, Capote's fame derived as much from this histrionic televisual celebrity as from the scandal-mongering books that he wrote.

Capote's self-parodic antics seem to pale into high cultural annoyance when placed next to Baldwin's polemically saturated and politically targeted sissy insurgency. In many ways Capote and Baldwin mirror each other as homosexually suspect authors whose reputations are made not only through first novels that present problematically sissified protagonists but also through publicity images that seem to insinuate their own sissiness (figures 4.2 and 4.3). In a 1963 *Time* magazine article, Baldwin's cigarette smoking is linked with his "effeminate manner": "He is a nervous, slight, almost fragile figure, filled with frets and fears. He is effeminate in manner, drinks considerably, smokes cigarettes in chains, and he often loses his audience with overblown arguments."¹¹³ Like a limp handshake or George Washington Carver's lapel flower or Arthur Montana's hairstyle, which expose the sissy hidden within the boy, so during the Cold War era the hand holding the cigarette becomes an intensely saturated body part that signifies a man's phallic virility, or lack thereof—the lapel flower, limp wrist, or overly styled hair as a sure signal of masculine failure. In the photo in figure 4.3, Capote's delicate fingers flare out from his wrist as he holds a cigarette decorously between his pointer and middle finger—a posture associated with female smoking. Similarly, Baldwin's cigarette becomes like an exclamation point extending his limp wrist (figure 4.2). However, as a mirror replicates an image by reversing it, so the sissified mass-media images of Baldwin and Capote are also studies in reversal. Whereas Baldwin lent his sissy persona to the soberest cause of his time, racial justice, Capote used his powers of sensitive observation to engage in constant self-conscious pop psychologizing and depoliticizing of racial, class, and sexual matters in books like the career-making *In Cold Blood* (1965) and the posthumous *Answered Prayers* (1986): the former turned literal murderers into seductively monstrous celebrities; the latter turned highbrow celebrities into archly unattractive metaphorical monsters.

4.2 News photograph of Baldwin sitting smoking a cigarette, c. 1963. Getty Images, Bettmann Collection.

4.3 News photograph of Capote smoking a cigarette, c. 1940. Getty Images, Bettmann Collection.

As I suggested earlier, often respectable sissies in African American communities were extra breadwinners with no family of their own: adoptive uncles who took and helped to finance the education of needy nephews and nieces; and respectable (if circumspect enough) teachers, choir ministers, nurses, and secretaries.[114] If Capote's effete white sissy impersonation is the cultural inverse of Baldwin's politically obligated black sissy persona, then the converse of Baldwin is Little Richard (figure 4.4), who burst onto the international scene in 1955, two years after Baldwin's sissy first novel, with his gender-bending, pop-history-making first hit, "Tutti Frutti." Meticulously but brashly blending what he had learned in church, the street, the honky-tonk, the carnival, the revival meeting, and vaudeville, Little Richard takes the persona of the all-out swishing, unapologetic, fierce sissy who fights with his hands as good as his mouth onto the world stage with a song that the suburban white teens could innocently mistake for being about the innocuous pleasures of a newly marketed ice cream flavor. "Tutti Frutti," in its original version, celebrates the pleasures of anal intercourse, ambiguously figured as male-male and/or male-female, as the unexplained exclamation of the androgynous name "Rudi" at the heart of the refrain indicates.[115] In helping to usher in crossover rock and roll as a countercultural menace bubbling up from the nasty nigger bottoms of hysterically policed Cold War society, Little Richard appears to do for pop culture, in a more disastrously disruptive way, what Capote and Warhol do for elite, effete high society. Like Baldwin's clipped and lisping eloquence as a spokesman for the race, Little Richard's snarling, popping, screeching erotic noise announces the arrival of the black sissy not exactly as a credit to the race, but as a flaunting presence whose racialized homoeroticism cannot be totally shamed or purged. In Little Richard, we find the Cold War state coming face to face with a swish performance that announces, or even enacts, the hidden script of homosexuality that sissy impersonation more commonly is thought to imply or insinuate. In the publicity head shot in figure 4.4, Little Richard's marcelled hairstyle goes a couple of steps beyond the style as worn by black men of the time. The ring of curls sits atop his head like a crown, and his carefully groomed eyebrows and moustache emphasize his self-presentation as a pretty, sissified man, one not afraid to broadcast it to the world.

For Little Richard and Little Jimmy, sissiness ironically enhances the consequence of their black cultural expressiveness as artists, hyping a blackness that can be intelligibly read through their sissy performances and at the same time mystifying and blocking the full "legibility" of their black inheritance—to borrow again from Mark Anthony Neal's formulation—by signifying on it, shading it with a fierce sissy posture. If the bloody history of lynching castration haunts the confrontational theatrics of their sissy impersonations, turning the "soft" ass of the sissy into a hard-assed defiance of straight white hegemony, it is also true that they are playing a dangerous Cold War game. Despite an international fame as great as, or greater than, that of the African American artists who undertake cultural ambassador missions to the Third World during the 1950s and '60s, Little Richard and Little Jimmy were unacceptable as black cultural ambassadors of the state, as Baldwin's hefty FBI files attest.[116] The racial implication of Little Richard and Little Jimmy's sissy insurgency makes all the more visible the ways in which a white sissy like Capote accrues his cultural capital as high culture nuisance through the spectral invisibility of his whiteness, and both Capote and Warhol heighten this spectral whitening by emphasizing what José Esteban Muñoz aptly labels (in reference to Warhol) "overwhelming whiteness,"[117] a hyperblondness in their bodily aesthetic that seems to ironize their disgraceful puncturing of the white male privilege on which their celebrity rides (figure 4.5).

4.4 Michael Ochs publicity photograph of Richard Penniman, aka Little Richard, 1952. Getty Images.

If coupling Little Richard and Little Jimmy seems surprising, it may seem even more odd to pair Baldwin with another black homo-swish who achieved unprecedented fame later in the Cold War era, Sylvester James. What Little Jimmy, Little Richard, and Sylvester all have in common, however, is the black cultural experience of being cultivated as church sissies, and then transfiguring that churchified way of being circumspect, and the expressive talents it cultivates, into cultural capital as homo-sissies on the world stage. As David Kirby observes, Little Richard's career begins in the church.[118] Sylvester learns his showmanship beginning at the age of three in his mother's Pentecostal church in Los Angeles. As Joshua Gamson documents, Palm Lane Church of God in Christ also introduced Sylvester to "the life" when the eleven-year-old sissy-boy begins to have sex with various key members of the church, including the choir minister. Refusing the idea that he was sexually abused, Sylvester said about the choir leader, according to Gamson, "'He did a real number on me . . . but it never made me crazy. I was a queen even back then, so it didn't bother me. I rather liked it.'"[119] When he left

BALDWIN'S SISSY HEROICS · 215

4.5 News photograph of Capote with Andy Warhol at Studio 54, 1979. Getty Images, Bettmann Collection.

the church and home at thirteen, it was, he says, due to the hypocrisy of church members who were more concerned about the sexual scandal than for the sissy-boy. Sylvester's career as a disco diva has deep cultural-historical resonances with Baldwin's as a writer and activist and with his semiautobiographical characters of this period, especially the gospel career of Baldwin's last hero, Arthur Montana, who toward the end of his life shifts from sacred to secular singing.

Thinking of Sylvester as the real-life correlate of Arthur brings attention to how the novel that Baldwin was writing over the course of the 1970s is very much in sync with changing conditions for the homo-swish. The vocal, musical, and theatrical skills that fueled Sylvester's disco career were honed in church choirs, as was the case for the reigning divas of disco, including Patti LaBelle, Chaka Khan, Donna Summer, Gloria Gaynor, and Martha Wash (who started as a backup singer for Sylvester).[120] Considered a disco diva himself, Sylvester, who was close friends with many of these women, fashioned an unprecedented crossover career as a black cross-dressing homosexual whose falsetto voice was higher than that of his two female backup singers. Just as Hall sees Arthur's sexuality and relationship with Jimmy as crucial to his gospel career, so Sylvester's sexuality could not be separated or diminished as a disco performer. When his record company attempted to prevent him from wearing what they perceived as women's clothes, Sylvester refused, as he also refused to hide his sexuality and relationships with men. Unlike Arthur, whose romantic life centers around other black men despite a brief relationship with the Frenchman Guy, Sylvester's strongest base was the emerging white gay ghettos, his love interests were white men, and he became known as the queen of Castro Street, then celebrated as the gay mecca of American urban neighborhoods.[121] Sylvester's rise to fame must thus be understood as intricately linked to the post-Stonewall gay movement, and also to the ways in which token black gay men were feted and fetishized in those communities. As explained in Charles Nero's "Why Are Gay Ghettos White?" and visually documented in Marlon Riggs's film *Tongues Untied* (1989), black gay men were tolerated in these new gay ghettos only when they submitted themselves to unrelenting stereotypes adapted from those in dominant American culture: on the one hand, the big-dicked black buck as a fetishized object of perverse desire; on the other hand, the fat dark-skinned drag queen hailing the black mammy. Sylvester smartly parlays and resists the latter stereotype by presenting himself as a fashion-conscious, trend-making gender-bender, tall, dark, and soulful, the converse of an Aunt Jemima. He yields to the gay ghetto stereotype, however, by very self-consciously selecting two heavy-set black women as backup singers. In case the point was not made visually on stage, he named his pair of singers "Two Tons of Fun." In other words, Sylvester negotiates the virulent racism and sissiphobia of the white gay ghettos by both distancing himself from and associating himself with that racist sissiphobia.[122] If Sylvester represents a clear sign of the end of the Cold War's capacity to banish the homo-swish from the nation's mass media in the wake of a self-confident (white) gay rights movement, he also represents the emergence of a post–civil rights, post-Stonewall negotiation of black homo-swish passive aggression.

Punking James Baldwin

Little Richard and Sylvester achieve mass popularity as swishers far from the activist politics and high literary stakes that defined Baldwin's career. Given how any such career of the time depended on the negotiation of racial respectability and manly authority, Baldwin's self-dramatizing appeal to a sissified subjectivity in *No Name in the Street* seems especially curious in light of the verbal bashings perpetrated upon the figure of the black sissy and homosexual in black nationalist writing of the period. In this discourse, any black man who allows contact—much less sexual congress—with a white man is immediately not only suspect but also branded both a faggot and a race traitor. The treatment of the homo-sissy in this discourse helps us to understand the import of Baldwin's decision to respond by amplifying the idea of his own propensity for being taken as the object of a white man's dominating desire. In LeRoi Jones's influential poem "Black Art," published in the volume *Black Fire* in 1968, Jones allegorizes an anonymous civil rights leader not as a proper race man but as a hustling punk volunteering a blowjob for a sheriff: "Another negroleader / on the steps of the white house one / kneeling between the sheriff's thighs / negotiating coolly for his people."[123] Jones chooses the figure of the sheriff as the person often responsible for manhandling nonviolent civil rights campaigners in the interest of segregation and thus as the figurehead of the white man's frontline attack. Baldwin's image of being groped by the powerful southerner seems to confirm Jones's scenario of homosexual racial treachery in the figure of the "negroleader" kneeling between the sheriff's thighs. This sissiphobic charge is also at work when Malcolm X addresses the 1963 Children's Crusade in Birmingham, Alabama, by attacking Martin Luther King Jr. in loaded gender terms, saying, "Real men don't put their children on the firing line."[124] Most infamously, Eldridge Cleaver manages a backhanded attack on Baldwin, even as he puts "the case of James Baldwin aside for a moment," by suggesting that "the intellectual sycophant" desires anal intercourse as a perverse wish to be impregnated by a white man.[125] Deploying sissiphobic imagery, Cleaver speaks of "the cover and camouflage of the perfumed smoke screen of his prose" (98). Even as he rhetorically sets the case of Baldwin aside, Cleaver attacks his fictional characters, especially *Another Country*'s Rufus Scott, as alter egos of the elder author: "Rufus Scott, a pathetic wretch who indulged in the white man's pastime of committing suicide, who let a white bisexual homosexual fuck him in his ass... was the epitome of a black eunuch who has completely submitted to the white man" (104). As a stand-in for Baldwin, Rufus becomes the spectacular proof that exposes the self-hating homosexual black bottom hiding behind the smokescreen of the sissified author. Without ever *directly* accusing Baldwin of homosexual congress with white rulers, Cleaver can simply exploit the sissy as the link that equates the author's "decisive quirk" with his character's *in flagrante* twisted interracial "bisexual homosexual" conduct (102). Cleaver cements this slippery equation by claiming, inaccurately, that Richard Wright promoted "the practice of Negro youths of going 'punk-hunting.'"[126] Whereas on the street the ambiguous marker of a sissy demeanor would be enough to warrant ridicule and dismissal or panic and bashing, in these texts the cross-racial homosexual must be depicted as being caught in the act, must be graphically exhibited for our open scorn.

Perhaps the most instructive instance of such sissiphobic discourse, Reginald Lockett's poem "Die Black Pervert" (also published in *Black Fire*), opens with a direct address to the sissy race traitor:

> You sit there, sissified,
> and brag about the
>   T
>   R
>   I
>   P
>   TO
>   E
>   U
>   R
>   O
>   P
>   E
> You are to take this summer
>   To   t
>   S u
>   d
>   y
> Beethoven,
>   and Chopin
>   mozart.

In Lockett's poem, the race traitor starts out merely "sissified," one who busies himself with prissy, unmanly high-culture pursuits but necessarily ends up an unadulterated FAGGOT, a man who gets his nut off on white men's culture, which is equated with getting his nut off with white men, splattering himself with white sperm.

And become a conditioned—

              FAGGOT—

Carrying on Chuck's tradition
          and
getting an everlasting nut,
Splat, Splat, Splaaaaat[127]

While Lockett's poem scapegoats the sissy transfigured into the caught-in-the-act faggot, it also exposes what Darieck Scott calls the "power-as-pleasure" operating within such images. Scott illustrates how such moments of racialized homosexual penetration are deeply ambivalent: "The vulnerability to penetration are also moments of either power or pleasure, or power-as-pleasure."[128] In this sense, the scapegoating of the black swish as a racial switcher, or double-crossing crossover sexual pervert, necessarily exposes the scapegoater himself to the jeopardy of being someone a bit too familiar with both gender swishing and racial switching. It does sometimes take one to know one.

Rather than following that well-developed line of thought in the scholarship, we can instead focus here on how Baldwin himself ingeniously turns the tables on these homosexual scenes of gender swishery and racial switchery. Rolland Murray is certainly correct in suggesting that *No Name in the Street* is written in direct response to this sort of black nationalist invective.[129] Allowing us to catch him red-handed, so to speak, in exhibiting himself as the passive sexual object of the white southerner's rapacious desire, Baldwin's anecdote seems to answer the black nationalists' somewhat figurative accusations with a literalist confirmation. Baldwin's response is, then, a flagrant exhibition of the scene that such discourse is intended to prohibit. Even as Baldwin seeks to segregate the erotic pleasure of faggotry from the power play of the southerner's groping as a way of countering the black nationalist attack, the scene itself paradoxically seems to reinstate the question of the black switcher's erotic pleasure. Darieck Scott's analysis reminds us that even as Baldwin tries to separate the groping southerner's humiliating act of sexual predation from ordinary faggotry, with its implication of erotic volition and consent, we must contend not only with the probability that the southerner is taking homoerotic pleasure in exploiting his white supremacist claim over Baldwin's black body but also with the possibility that Baldwin could take some involuntary pleasure from having his cock groped in such a context. In other words, when Baldwin eliminates "faggotry" from the southerner's sexual action to foreground the *political* implication of this act as motivated by a white supremacist psyche, he is also seeking to erase from view the prospect of homoerotic pleasure elicited, or more precisely coerced, by being touched in such a way, however involuntary that pleasure may be. The potential of pleasure—the groping southerner's and Baldwin's—deeply troubles Baldwin's political allegorization of this scene. It is exactly the accusation of pleasure that makes the black nationalists' scapegoating of the homo-sissy so powerful as an attack. Cleaver raises the specter of racial self-abasement as masochistic pleasure when he references Baldwin's "embodying in his art the self-flagellating policy of Martin Luther King."[130] Although an instance of ingenious sissy counterattack through subtle passive aggression, Baldwin's scene nonetheless cannot fully evacuate the trace of coerced pleasure from a confession of being sexually victimized by a white man at the helm of Jim Crow law enforcement. Baldwin has the last word, however, as he links this sissified subjectivity to both the white man's intended emasculation and abjection of ordinary southern black men and ordinary black men's heroic resistance, figured in the minute detail of the way they walk the humiliating Jim Crow streets.

The Artistic Tutelage of a Black Sissy-Boy

Like Little Richard and Sylvester, Baldwin is able to retain a sissy demeanor while also offering a contravening defiance of the soft weakness, cowardice, and national insecurity usually projected onto the sissy in dominant U.S. discourse, and he can do so partly thanks to the notion of the sissy as a resourceful liminal figure within African American communities: a boy who is, on the one hand, willing to take it up the ass, but on the other, just as likely to kick ass if manhandled inappropriately, as Little Richard himself was widely known to do on the mean streets of his hometown. Thus, the paradox of the groping incident from *No Name in the Street* is that Baldwin insists on the heroism, however ambivalent and revisionary, of his impassive stance in relation to the white male groper. Imagine how differently the incident would read if the white southerner had groped Baldwin's ass rather than his cock. An ass-groping would place Baldwin more accurately in the position of Cleaver's and Jones's black faggot double-crosser eager to be penetrated by the white ruler. By having the white supremacist reach for the author's cock rather than his ass, Baldwin retains the literal gesture of same-gender attraction while resisting the implication of the sissy's subordination to an empty erotic hole waiting to be filled with the white man's semen. In other words, he retains his power to speak as a sissy, a man whose mannerism attracts sexual attention from another man, without reducing his own mouth to the black nationalist's eager asshole. By necessity, a sissy is a man out of place in the house of white male supremacy. To have an eccentric relation to male supremacy is to be robbed of the power that flows from that status. The problem is how to achieve power without its accompanying logic of supremacy. Baldwin's ambivalent passive aggression enacts the struggle to claim the power without also laying claim to the supremacy that anchors maleness, whiteness, masculinism, and straightness as arbiters of that power.

According to masculinist logic, Baldwin certainly should have responded to the southerner's groping by manfully punching him. In intentionally signaling a sissy response to a white man's queer assault, a response that can be correlated with the "passive resistance" of nonviolent civil rights protest, Baldwin boldly occupies the sissy's frame of reference in order to stand not so much outside as on the threshold separating black from white, manliness from femininity, straightness from faggotry, violation from pleasure, and power from supremacy.[131] From the perspective of this passive-aggressive stance, Baldwin rehearses his rearing as a sissy-boy in the opening paragraphs of *No Name in the Street* by highlighting the liminality of the boy's relation to the mother's skirts: "I may think I was five because I remember tugging at my mother's skirts once and watching her face while she was telling someone else that she was twenty-seven." Then again in the next sentence: "This meant, for me, that she was virtually in the grave already, and I tugged a little harder at her skirts."[132] This position, tugging at the mother's skirts, is perhaps the most definitive early marker of sissiness, and portends from dominant society the incipience or threat of a homosexual disposition. Baldwin intensifies this sissy frame by expounding on his love of caretaking for his newborn siblings over several pages. Relishing the gender-inappropriate role of nursemaid to the newborn, Baldwin emphasizes the pleasure he took as a young man in occupying this status, as he heroicizes the deep knowledge of baby-rearing usually reserved for womanly intuition and maternal instinct: "You know the sound—the meaning—of one cry from another; without knowing that you know it. You know when it's hungry—that's one sound. You know when it's wet—that's another sound. You know when it's angry. You know when it's bored. You know when it's frightened. You know when it's suffering. You come or you go or you sit still according to the sound the baby makes. And you watch over it where I was born, even in your sleep, because rats love the odor of newborn babies and are much, much bigger."[133] Such passages strongly identify the young Jimmy as a mama's boy, one who glories in his maternal intuition. To be a mama's boy, however, is not necessarily a wholly bad affair, for mama's boys more frequently survive the killing streets and backways of America than those real-boy boys, as we see when in *Go Tell It* John's younger brother, Roy, is almost killed from his adventures on the avenue. John immediately assumes that his stepfather "would be at his worst tonight" on getting the news that Roy has been stabbed, but instead he witnesses Gabriel's tenderness as he and Elizabeth wash the blood from Roy's forehead. In a mixture of pride for Roy's mannishness and alarm at the son's physical endangerment, Gabriel shows his favoritism for the bad boy over the too-good one: "And John knew, in the moment his father's eyes swept over him, that he hated John because John was not lying on the sofa where Roy lay," causing John momentarily to wish his brother dead "to bring his father low."[134] Sissy-boys may be relatively safer than their brothers as long as they hug their mothers' apron strings, but sissy-boys, whether in the church or not, face a different kind of danger not only on the street but also, on occasion, from their own father's wrath.

In fashioning John Grimes's strangeness from Baldwin's own sense of being a strange child, Baldwin explores the liminality involved when a boy sees the world over the mother's shoulder, from a sissy-boy's frame of reference. In an interview with Fern Marja Eckman, Baldwin's mother remarks about her eldest son: "'He was my right arm,' says Mrs. Baldwin, gentle but indomitable. 'He took care of them [his siblings] all. Of course, he wasn't a girl, but he was very dependable. . . . I can't say he really was sickly, but he was on the delicate side. He never had the vitality most boys have in growing up. He never got into trouble with other boys—he was too shy.'"[135] Mrs. Baldwin casts her son's sissy conduct through predicates of negation, including delicate, lacking boyish vitality, not trouble-making, too shy—a compendium of sissy conduct and character. She does *not* see these characteristics as an unmanly deficit, however. She directly connects the boy's non-trouble-making conduct with his reading: "He was very easy to raise. He lived in books."[136] We see here the mother's prescient sense of the respectable sissy-boy's penchant for studious housekeeping in the manner of a dutiful daughter. As the son becomes the mother's helper, he risks alienation from the true gender habitat of the adventurous outdoors—or, for the urban black boy, the dangerous streets. In *No Name in the Street* Baldwin relinquishes the prerogative that normally accrues to the eldest son under the assumptions of primogeniture. Obsessed with this patriarchal practice, Baldwin's stepfather wanted to endow a symbolic inheritance on Royal, his eldest son, though "illegitimate," from a previous relationship, rather than on his "illegitimate" sissy stepson. Even though little Jimmy is the one who instead inherits the stepfather's legacy of preaching, the sissy boy more passionately inherits his mother's inheritance, as he becomes the nursemaid to the legion of younger siblings, his stepfather's biological offspring. In *No Name in the Street*, Baldwin emphasizes this by cataloguing his status as the head of a long line issuing from his parents' loins: "I, James, in August. George, in January. Barbara, in August. Wilmer, in October, David, in December. Gloria, Ruth, Elizabeth, and (when we thought it was over!) Paula Maria, named by me, born on the day our father died, all in the summertime."[137] His privilege of naming the youngest derives, no doubt, from an honor bestowed on him for his caretaking role across his youth, even though when Paula Maria is born, Baldwin has already escaped the household and is haunted with a deep guilt for having done so.

This long passage on how to take care of a newborn, rather than being a thoughtless tangent, actually helps to anchor the book-length essay in Baldwin's respectable sissy frame of reference. How odd that an essay devoted to the civil rights struggle and Black Power's armed self-defense should find its bearings by beginning with the male author's intimate and loving knowledge of nursing newborns. Once we understand his strategy of sissy insurgency, however, this beginning is no longer mystifying and instead makes sense. We see how Baldwin's civil rights and Black Power advocacy, if we read carefully, is merely an extension of the sissy caretaking role that he assumed as the eldest son in a large, impoverished, but proud family. He thus displays this effeminate conduct as a "shield" rather than a weapon against the kinds of attack made by nationalists like Cleaver, who were eager to foster guilt by association in linking Baldwin's sissy weakness, cowardice, and racial treachery to "Martin Luther King–type self-effacing love for his oppressors."[138]

Mrs. Baldwin's portrait of little Jimmy and his own self-portrait as a sissy caretaker correlate with his portrait of John Grimes. As the mother's "right-hand man," as Elizabeth calls him, John becomes responsible for sweeping and dusting—reminding us of Booker T. Washington's obsessive cleanliness. Because of the early awareness that something in him is perceived as dirty, John becomes overly sensitive to the dirt around him.[139] This horror of the filth that he cannot refuse to see in every corner indexes the horror of filth that shames his inner life. He instinctively links this sense of delirium that filth personifies to his mother's "dark, hard lines running downward from her eyes, and the deep, perpetual scowl in her forehead"[140]—not only the sympathetic knowledge that a housewife's work battling dirt is never done but also from an empathetic sense that she shares with him a deep feeling of shame. He does not know, though he intuits, that her own shame is directly linked with how she brought him into the world a bastard. Melvin Dixon draws attention to the irony of the bastard son's last name: "Grimes signifies dirt, not only the dirt and grime of human life that can be washed clean through baptism or conversion, but also the moral pollution that clings as tenaciously to the Grimes household as the endless dust John is required to clean."[141] As with Booker T. Washington's iconic cleaning of the schoolroom to gain entrance to Hampton Institute, John's totem becomes the broom. Comparing his fate to that of Sisyphus, John sweeps the Oriental-style carpet, "for the dust rose, clogging his nose and sticking to his sweaty skin, and he felt that should he sweep it forever, the clouds of dust would not diminish, the rug would not be clean."[142] The sissy-boy's fear that the dirt within will cling to his skin—that his strange gender disorder will expose him as a swish—drives his circumspection. Yet despite his attempt to circumscribe his body, language, and mind for a more acceptable public reception, his physiology and temperament seem to expose him. "John is as unsure about religion as he is about his sexuality," Dixon observes. And as Dixon further points out, "John's effeminacy is also hinted at by the taunts of children in his neighborhood,"[143] as well as by Roy, his rough and lawless younger brother, who is the apple of their father's eye. Roy mimics what he takes to be John's sissy manner of speaking:

> John looked at him. Roy was not in a good mood.
> "Oh, I *beg* your pardon," said Roy, in a shrill, little-girl tone he knew John hated.
> "What's the *matter* with you today?" John asked, angry and trying at the same time to lend his voice as husky a pitch as possible.[144]

John, with his best-little-boy ways, can never compete with Roy in their father's house, just as his huskied-up his sissy voice can never compete with Roy's conventionally boyish way of speaking.

Although the sissy's liminal temperament—always on the edge of things watching himself being watched—derives from the nature of the sexual danger that surrounds him, one must learn to see oneself as a sissy object in others' eyes just as one must learn to make a sissy the target of sexual assault. Baldwin, too, had to learn how to become the sissy that others insisted on seeing in him. We can get a glimpse of how he nurtures this nascent sissy self-awareness into a mature sissy insurgency by briefly considering his relation to the person whom he calls his "principal witness," the avant-garde artist Beauford Delaney. Although Baldwin certainly had sissy tutors previously to Delaney—such as, for instance, the Negro Renaissance poet Countee Cullen, who was his schoolteacher—it is Delaney whom Baldwin singles out as "principal witness."[145] When Baldwin was fourteen, he went to Delaney's house and introduced himself. Not long after, Delaney, falling in love with the young Baldwin, who at the time was at the height of his career as a boy preacher, painted a startling portrait of the youth (figure 4.6). Delaney was himself a sissified man twenty years older than the fourteen-year-old Baldwin; he had against the odds settled in segregated Greenwich Village before it had settled on its own identity as a bohemian enclave, and certainly before it became a hotbed of homosexuality. As Baldwin describes his own stint in the neighborhood later, Delaney was constantly targeted both as a sissy and as a "nigger" and was beaten more than once by straight white boys out to make a point.[146] Usually barred from painting nudes in the places where he studied drawing because he could not be allowed to observe white women's bodies, Delaney rarely painted nudes, male or female, so it is particularly stunning and revealing that for his first

4.6 Beauford Delaney, *Dark Rapture (James Baldwin)*, 1941. Courtesy of Michael Rosenfeld Gallery. Copyright Estate of Beauford Delaney by permission of Derek L. Spratley, Esquire, Court Appointed Administrator.

portrait of Baldwin, *Dark Rapture*, he chooses a nude. There is so much to be said about this painting, but what I want to emphasize is that Delaney was teaching Baldwin how to see himself as a sissy, beautiful, black, and mysteriously but resistingly seductive—against the stepfather's insistence on the boy's ugliness. Baldwin claims that Delaney taught him how to see as an artist by urging him to look at a dirty pool of water while out on a walk together. It is only on the second and third looks that Baldwin begins to see a grease stain lining the face of the filthy pool, and within the stain a sensuous reflection of color and then eventually a dazzling reflection of the urban landscape. Here we see how the sissy-boy whose Sisyphean cleaning induced by a sense of inexpungible sexual shame as his mother's right-hand man is transformed into a sissy artist who finds beauty in the filthy pools of everyday reality.

Similarly, Delaney, the black sissy-man looking at the black sissy-boy, trained Baldwin's eyes to see himself with a second, third, fourth, look ad infinitum—to find the beauty in the soil of his own dark skin. In *Dark Rapture* Delaney pays tribute to the boy Baldwin by having him look back on us as our view of him is coterminously coerced and blocked. His genitalia virtually blotted out by the shadows (no crude visual grope is this!), Baldwin's sinewy body splashed with sinuous color raises up from the torso and to the face, where the light makes clear the oversized eyes focused on us watching him being beautifully rendered in oil. Placed on exhibit in one of Delaney's first gallery shows, the viewing of this portrait circulated among the artistic communities in New York, including the many white and black bohemians and avant-garde artists who visited Delaney's studio. As if to model his lesson in revisionary artistic looking, Delaney repainted Baldwin's portrait more than a dozen times between 1944 and the artist's death in 1979. Given Delaney's visual influence on Baldwin's vision, it should not be surprising that the photographic images of Delaney and Baldwin are uncannily similar in profile and posture, as represented in photographs of the two smoking (figures 4.7 and 4.8). It might take the argument too far to suggest that Baldwin literally mimicked Delaney's sissy pose—not in a mocking way like Arthur Montana's imitation of the "broken-down queens," but in a loving embrace of his mentor. It is not unreasonable, though, to understand the young boy as having emulated his admiring and admired elder—down to the sissified gesture of holding a cigarette. In this sense, we could say that Delaney was not only Baldwin's "principal witness"; he was also his principal simulacrum.

Through such intimate and yet public tutelage Baldwin learned how to see himself artistically as a sissy. Of course, by the 1950s, Baldwin had become the sissified object of so many different public media, usually of his own choosing. In myriad publicity photographs, Baldwin the sissy faces us unabashedly, his Bette Davis eyes insisting on his right to be viewed as an artistic subject rather than merely a sexually racialized target of faggotry. While nothing specific in such photographs structurally alerts us to the sissified subjectivity, by the mid-1950s Baldwin was already becoming famous for the publicness of his face as the emerging face of the sensitive, intense black artist peering into the heart of racial power from its sexual margins. Most of the photographs foreground the sissy-boy as studious, hardworking, legitimate artist, but they also boldly figure him in sissy poses. In one publicity shot, we eye him in a girlish pose, with his legs up in the air, no less effeminate but certainly more respectable than Capote's book cover (figure 4.9). Unlike Capote, who fronts the camera in the conventional

4.7 Photograph of Beauford Delaney by Emil Cadoo, c. 1970. Image courtesy of Michael Rosenfeld Gallery. Copyright Janos Gat Gallery.

4.8 Ralph Gatti photograph of Baldwin at home in Saint-Paul-de-Vence, France, in 1979. AFP via Getty Images.

female pose of the nude, with a coyly seductive look on his face, his hand delicately holding his crotch as an invitation to penetrability, Baldwin stares out at us from a prone position indicating studiousness, looking curiously at us rather than downward toward the writing pad that symbolically engages his artist's attention. Such images of Baldwin do the dual work of making the sissy into an artist while insisting that the artist sees so presciently because of his sissified insight. Compared with Capote's book cover photo, Baldwin, desexualized, still occupies the position of the too-good sissy-boy respectably circumspect in his pursuit of high literacy.

Through verbal and visual figurations, this black sissy's liminal subject-position—in the black father's household but not of it, in the white southerner's Cold War Jim Crow nation-state but not of it—affords him an unusual vantage point of sensitive observation. In a brilliant reading of the FBI files on Baldwin,

4.9 Ralph Gatti publicity photograph, "James Baldwin Gets Comfortable to Write" (1963), picturing the author resting on a bed, legs lifted in the air. Getty Images, Bettmann Collection.

BALDWIN'S SISSY HEROICS · 229

Maurice Wallace has remarked on how Baldwin—the object of Cold War FBI and mass-media surveillance—resisted this objectification of his person by unflinchingly gazing back at the camera. Those oversized eyes in a waifish dark body—a look that in "The Devil Finds Work" he identifies with the blond matinee idol Bette Davis—were clearly a source of embarrassment for Baldwin, but at the same time, because "I have my mother's eyes,"[147] his frog eyes embody for him the same comfort zone as that sissified attachment to his mother's skirts. As Wallace points out, however, those oversized eyes staring back at the camera constitute an ideological and material resistance to the Cold War regime of racist, homophobic surveillance that followed him around within and beyond the American borders.[148]

I want to tweak Wallace's reading a bit by suggesting that Baldwin's gazing back also frames the potential gender embarrassment of out-of-placeness as a daring act of sissified insurgence. Returning to the groping passage of *No Name in the Street*, we can see this sissified insurgency at work. After exposing the true scandal of the white southerner's groping gesture, Baldwin turns his (and our) gaze away from the white patriarch and onto the black castigated sons: "It was something like this that I began to see, watching black men in the South and watching white men watching them."[149] On the liminal circumference of that battle between the white man and the black, Baldwin stands watching the black men, and watching the white men watching the black men. In a society where it is a crime against nature for a man to let his eyes linger too long on another man—a crime punishable with legal arrest for solicitation or an extralegal fag-bashing—Baldwin flagrantly images himself with those malingering eyes watching men watching men across the embattled color line. This trope is axiomatic of Baldwin's work, as in the 1961 essay on his testy relation with Norman Mailer, "The Black Boy Looks at the White Boy."[150] We might say that as an act of passive aggression Baldwin fights with his eyes, and at first this may seem like a totally inappropriate kind of warfare for a man to be waging with another man. If we remember that sizing up is an important strategy in manly sports like boxing, to look your opponent squarely in the eye before pummeling him, then we can recognize how Baldwin turns sissy alarm and passivity into a mode of passive-aggressive, un/manly insurgency that—all at once—appropriates, admires, models, mocks, and subverts the heteronorm as it is anchored in racist patriarchal violation.

Although this eye-to-eye pattern of resistant observation marks Baldwin's own genius as a form of sissy heroism, Baldwin attributes a similar mode of heroism to the ordinary mass of black men who refused to be crushed by Jim Crow. Aware of the Jim Crow protocol that a black man should never look a white man straight in the eye, Baldwin, in *No Name in the Street*, records black men who, in the face of this emasculating protocol, developed an insistent way of being men that necessarily caught the wary eye of white men. Baldwin writes, "For that marvelously mocking, salty authority with which black men walked was dictated by the tacit and shared realization of the price each had paid to be able to walk at all."[151] In *Go Tell It* John's sissy walk had been mocked by girls sitting on Harlem stoops. Here southern black men's "salty walk" upends the stereotype of the Jim Crowed man as a stooping, fetching, slouching, dragging Uncle Tom. Aware that Jim Crow displaces them from the heteronormative, these men, in Baldwin's observation, forge their own self-estranged manliness in a heroic manner. "So many of the black men I talked to in the South in those years," Baldwin writes, "were—I can find no other word for them—heroic.... Their heroism was to be found less in large things than in small ones, less in public than in private.... What impressed me was how they went about their daily tasks, in the teeth of the Southern terror."[152] Baldwin knowingly places these black men harassed, sexually and otherwise, by Jim Crow within the province of the conventionally domesticated effeminate: lives charged with tending to "small things" "in private." Analogous to the sissy-boy's clinging to his mother's apron strings or the World War I soldiers forced to drill with broomsticks rather than rifles, such men, nonetheless, perfectly occupy the heroic for Baldwin. In forging this sissified image of the heroic, Baldwin directly counters the black nationalists' performance of armed warriors at the racial front lines as the only appropriate enactment of courageous black manhood. We should not forget that Baldwin's person, his unadorned body, and his persona, the way he staged that body for public consumption, exposed him as a sissy in every public venue. Aware, furthermore, that this sissy facade always brought with it a rush to an assumption of homosexuality and its stigmatizing formulas, Baldwin stared back as the sissy that he had become, letting the stigma stick without allowing it to work its sting. This is why, when Dwight McBride, in his important essay "Can the Queen Speak?," takes Baldwin to task for verbally assuming the position of a heterosexual man in order to speak on behalf of the race in his television interviews, we might contextualize this by remembering that the body itself speaks, and sometimes says something quite different from what the mouth intones.[153] If Baldwin sometimes voiced a heterosexual script—raging against the emasculation of black men by the Jim Crow regime—he as frequently, and as trenchantly as anyone I've ever encountered, also proffered the most devastating critique of the racist heteronorm in a wide range of genres. And he did this not only through his voice but also by allowing his sissified intelligence to be staged for the public eye through the exhibition of his out-of-gender person.

5

Sissy but Not Gay

An Anatomy of the Post–Civil Rights Straight Black Sissy

> Most white people in America project their own inner sexual anxieties onto the Negro to such an extent that they, especially Southerners, imagine black men have large, grotesque genitals that stand in perpetual erection. One Southerner related to me how shocked he was when he came to New York and saw black homosexuals flirting up and down 42nd Street. "I'd have never believed a Negro could be a faggot," he said.
> —CALVIN HERNTON, *Sex and Racism in America*

How do you spot a sissy when he's a straight black man? This may seem like a trickster's rhetorical question, given how the word "sissy" so often implies incipient homosexuality. It may also seem like a trick question because black men—of whatever sexual appetite—have never had the luxury of full "straightness," of heteronormative status, in U.S. culture, even as they have been stereotyped as violently hypermasculine and rapaciously heterosexual. Let me here exhibit one recent version of the sissified straight black man:

> The kitchen had the first floor I ever mopped, the first dishes I washed and dried; it began my full acquaintance with trash removal. It was also the kitchen in which I learned, from setting to clearing, how to mount holiday feasts and elaborate dinners for club meetings.... I know a lot about this, about working side by side with a grandmother, a mother, or a housekeeper, doing the most domestic of chores, taking pride in the work,

sharing standards, agreeing with a wink on what is a good corner to cut; glad for the company. But of course, I've never been able to say of this, "glad to be a woman like Mama."[1]

This passage, drawn from Robert Stepto's 1998 memoir, *Blue as the Lake*, represents the late twentieth-century phenomenon of black male autobiographers who construct their boyhood identity through a sissified demeanor. If Washington's compulsive self-disciplining through housekeeping marks a potentially embarrassing gender compromise of the early Jim Crow era, and Baldwin's commitment to black empowerment is ironically framed through a defiant sissiness in the face of black nationalist gender assaults, what do we make of Robert Stepto's kitchen confession more than twenty-five years later? Standing as they do at opposite poles of the twentieth century, Booker T. Washington's and Stepto's housekeeping passages could serve as bookends exemplifying the changing but persistent figurations of the sissy figure in the spotlight of American public discourse.

This chapter examines the cultural politics of sissy self-representation in the post–civil rights era, the 1960s through the 1990s, taking Baldwin as a pivot. Much scholarly attention has been riveted on heterosexism, homophobic scapegoating, and masculinist posturing of black nationalist discourse. Another crucial dimension of this discourse has often been overlooked: the ways in which the most virulently homophobic anti-Baldwin ranters, like Amiri Baraka and Eldridge Cleaver, are so eager to distance themselves from his sissy exhibition exactly because their authorial voices and expressive forms are so indebted to Baldwin's sissy performance. We here focus especially on how Baraka, as a straight-identified author and activist, struggles to negotiate Baldwin's sissy influence—initially modeling his own early work on that of the great sissy spokesman, and then convulsively refashioning an antisissy persona as a black nationalist at the height of the Cold War. Baraka cannot fully extirpate the Baldwinean influence, however. Furthermore, disturbing any notion of Black Power as a unanimous antisissy fortress, the Oakland Black Panthers charge black cultural nationalists like Baraka with a homophobia fueled by their own masculine insecurity, as the Panthers make the case for a productive coalition among black, women's, and gay liberation movements. Black Panther modes of address emphasize instead brotherliness as a revolutionary value while retaining a commitment to conventional masculine characteristics identified with the battlefield warrior. This emphasis on brotherliness serves as a repository tapped by the following generation, both the homo-sissies who forge a black gay "brother to brother" movement and the straight black sissy public intellectuals like Stepto who come to the fore in the 1990s. Thus, despite the sissiphobic attacks on Baldwin, his sissy insurgency remained impactful through Black Power and into the 1990s.

As we shall probe further in the next chapter, however, publicizing one's own sissiness is no easy matter. This is why there is a tendency for sissiness to be expressed materially in the extreme by visualizing the self as a swish—the exaggerated gestures of a limp wrist, a high-pitched voice that goes up at the end of sentences, the sashaying behind, the penchant for unmanly loud colors in attire. The sissy who rejects this extreme seems always to be bartering on a fluid line, a gender liminality that haunts, sequesters, and prevaricates. The challenge of claiming a sissy identity without becoming the flaunting swish can be observed in Baldwin's own distancing act that occurs at a pivotal moment toward the end of *No Name in the Street*. Despite his overall strategy of sissy insurgency, as discussed in the previous chapter, Baldwin temporarily suspends that strategy when he attempts to address the sissiphobic rantings of Eldridge's Cleaver's "Notes on a Native Son." Seeking to prevent his own irrelevance as a prophetic critic of American racism, seeking a bridge to the new generation of militants—represented in the closure of the text through his alliance with the Black Panthers—Baldwin apologizes for Cleaver's sissiphobia when he writes: "I felt that he used my public reputation against me both naïvely and unjustly, and I also felt that I was confused in his mind with the unutterable debasement of the male—with all those faggots, punks, and sissies the sight and sound of whom, in prison, must have made him vomit more than once. I certainly hope I know more about myself, and the intention of my work than that, but I *am* an odd quantity."[2] Even as he scapegoats the prison sissy as beyond the pale of maleness, he still claims his oddness, his queerness—an ambivalence that betrays the essay's persistent sissy tenor. Such a betrayal from a thinker so committed otherwise to the resistance of scapegoating as a form of collective amnesia indicates the challenge posed by any man who publicly embraces a sissy persona through modern mass media, especially in claiming a sissiness that stays clear of the swishing "extreme." As we shall see, in this period while black nationalist invective against the homo-sissy magnifies the battleground on which real men are ostensibly separated from sissies, a countermovement nevertheless emerges, whereby some public intellectuals don the mantle of the respectable sissy, however cagily, to claim their progressive gender credentials as part of the armory of their race leadership. Thus, the post–civil rights era writers discussed in this chapter are dancing on a fine line when they try to position themselves as sissies who are neither flaunting swishes nor attracted to the same gender. This chapter argues that the public representation of the black sissy undergoes a peculiar transformation during the era of institutional desegregation, a period when black male intellectuals are pressed on one side by a demand to man up by taking black nationalist vigor into historically white venues and on the other side by a demand for these men to display sensitivity to the critiques of the black womanist movement and the appeals of an emerging black gay brother-to-brother discourse. The sissy becomes a highly visible flashpoint during an era in which Afrocentrist psychologists and educators set off alarms about black male genocide, citing black homosexuality as one of the greatest dangers and calling for a return to traditional gender roles in the black family, and at the same time womanists and black gay men attack just such gender traditions as psychologically repressive and socially oppressive.

Expunging the Sissy to Expose the Black Nationalist Warrior

At the outset of his essay collection *Long Black Song* (1972), Houston A. Baker Jr. narrates how he was pressured by a variety of constituencies to stop focusing his research and teaching in the field of his doctoral training, British Victorian literature, and to labor instead in the emerging field of black studies.

> Bobby Seale and the Black Panther party were on-campus realities; black studies ... was being born in New Haven; black cultural nationalism was front-page news in "arts and leisure" sections of newspapers throughout the country....
>
> By the time the request came from the Yale Faculty Wives to deliver lectures on "Black Literature," I, at least, knew what the term signified because I had been solicited by a group of activist students to teach a black literature course in the 1969–1970 academic year.[3]

This incident establishes the racial terms that conspired to make Baker, among the first generation of black scholars to desegregate America's elite universities, into a black studies scholar and a public black intellectual. The gender terms operating in Baker's pivot are less apparent. To commit oneself to studying Victorian aesthetes—"the aesthetic movement in nineteenth-century England"[4]—at a time when the race's leading public intellectuals are lambasting the white aesthetic as a decadent, faggotty enemy of Black Arts is also to endanger the sense of one's proper black manliness. If "Bobby Seale and the Black Panther party were on-campus realities," they necessarily were so largely metonymically, for despite Yale's location surrounded by a black ghetto in which the Black Panther movement was gaining ground, to be ensconced in its ivy-clad neo-Gothic buildings is still to be harbored in the aestheticized Victorianism of an elite academic environment, the very opposite of the mean streets of Oakland where Newton and Seale were hailing the "brothers on the block" to form a radical organization based in armed self-defense.

Just as Baker can rescue his academic vocation by figuratively attaching his Yale conversion to the Black Panthers, so an attribute of the strategy of black nationalist sissiphobic invective is that it can operate powerfully through such metonymy. Any black male figure whose politics can be charged as Tomming can become a sissiphobic target. We see this sissiphobic invective at work in Baraka's simply titled "Civil Rights Poem" from his volume *Black Magic* (1969):

> Roywilkins is an eternal faggot
> His spirit is a faggot
> his projection
> and image, this is
> to say, that if i ever see roywilkins
> on the sidewalks
> imonna
> stick half my sandal
> up his
> ass[5]

As executive secretary of the NAACP, Wilkins stands in for any black male leader who dares to be an intermediating voice for civil rights integrationism. Closing the poem with "ass" accentuates how such a man's behind is anyone's for the taking.[6] This form of guilt by association would be especially effective, given that Wilkins led one of the organizations that collaborated on the 1963 March on Washington, which congressional leaders and the FBI attempted to undermine by putting it in the public record that the organizational mastermind of this protest was none other than a man arrested for public sex with another man and one suspected of communist leanings, Bayard Rustin. Baraka pointed his poison pen not only at targets whom he knew to be straight but also at those, like Baldwin and Rustin, whose known homo-sissiness seemed to verify the nefarious link between faggotry, civil rights advocacy, and Tomming. In "The Dance of the Toms," he is more precise in his aim when he makes Rustin an exemplary case of the Tom by referring to him as "bayard rusty switchin like a fag."[7] This image of the swishing fag is notable, for it delivers a double punch condemning Rustin for both his same-sexuality and his effeminacy. It seems somewhat ironic that Baraka exploits what is presumably self-evidently observable—his "switchin"—in order to accuse him of what is not transparent: his faggotry. The further irony here is that, like Baldwin, Rustin was far from being a swisher, and instead adhered to a rather circumspect and respectable sissiness. In the end, Baraka's attack is intentionally imprecise because Rustin is certainly known to be a faggot but one who scrupulously avoids behaving as a swisher. For Baraka's purposes, however, metonymic imprecision itself is the point, for if one is a faggot, one ostensibly cannot help but switch *like* one, figuratively if not literally. Baraka's pun on the word "swish"—emphasized by favoring the rarer "-itch" spelling of the word over the more common "-ish"—capitalizes on the sloppy logic that a man who betrays his manhood by allowing himself to be penetrated by another man must also be prone to switch his allegiance from a natural black brotherhood to a nefarious submission to white male penetration. As observed in the previous chapter, this is exactly the logic of Cold War anti-"soft" hysteria that equated homosexuals to Reds as national security risks. Given the public profile of this sissiphobic invective into the 1970s, and given the strong influence of the Black Arts Movement on 1990s gangsta rap, it is not surprising that a national discourse projecting greater homophobia to black men solidified by the 1990s.[8]

The over-the-top invective against homosexuals, sissies, punks, and swishes deployed by the likes of Cleaver, Lockett, and Baraka is self-evident. As Baraka acknowledges in his autobiographical and fictional work, switchers were very much in the mix in his hometown neighborhood. To pretend as though switchers cannot be among the brothers on the block is to purge a familiar black presence from the social reality that he is claiming to voice. The question is not so much "Can you conduct a war with swishes on the frontline?" as "Can you ever be sure that the warrior next to you isn't a nonswishing sissy?" Ironically, in Baraka's early work, he repeatedly asks such a question as he turns his gaze on his own gender insecurity, in a Baldwinesque manner, as a material enactment of his own racial self-estrangement.

Can a sissy make a good race warrior? For Huey Newton and Bobby Seale, founders of the Black Panther Party, the answer is an unequivocal maybe. Consider the implications of the refrain that structurally and rhetorically organizes Bobby Seale's 1970 memoir, *Seize the Time: The Story of the Black Panther Party and Huey P. Newton*: "the brothers on the block." Written in the self-confident street lingo of "the brothers on the block," the memoir's audience is repeatedly, explicitly named as those same brothers. The memoir enacts what it teaches: we see modeled in the writing of the memoir the proper relation between two black brothers, Seale and Newton. According to Seale, "Huey P. Newton knew that once you organize the brothers he ran with, he fought with, he fought against, who he fought harder than they fought him, once you organize those brothers, you get niggers, you get black men, you get revolutionaries who are too much."[9] This image of a brother on the block eager to fight and thus ready to shift from fighting each other to fighting the white pig cops might at first seem naturally to exempt swishing faggots. There is no such explicit exemption in Seale or Newton, though the brotherly image is certainly heteronormatively loaded. As we saw in the previous chapter, one of the traditional figures defining the dangers of the black street is the tough-assed swishing faggot, one who is as good with his fists or a blade as any other brother on the block. By refusing explicitly to resort to the kind of sissiphobic invective so illiberally employed by black nationalists like

Baraka, the Oakland Black Panthers were making a subtle but loud statement about the nature of their exclusion, focusing their ire at any brother who refuses to fight, rather than on whether a brother swishes or not while marching to the frontline. Newton and Seale thus leave an opening for the straight and gay black public intellectuals who are ready to claim their sissiness in the 1990s.

Whereas the greatest internal threat for Baraka and other black nationalists is the penetrable sissy, for the Black Panther Party in Seale's narrative this ultimate internal threat is represented, instead, as the "black cultural nationalists" like Baraka himself: "This is where the shit boils down to—to what the people want and not what some intellectual personally wants or some cultural nationalists, like LeRoi Jones, want, or some jive-ass underground RAM motherfucker wants, or what some jive motherfucker in some college studying bullshit says, talking esoteric shit about the basic social-economic structure, and the adverse conditions that we're subjected to so that no black man even understands. Huey was talking about some full employment, some decent housing, some education, about stopping those pigs from brutalizing us and murdering us."[10] Like Washington's sly claim to intellectual authority through housekeeping hygiene, Seale endows Newton with the greatest intellectual heft by immersing him more deeply among "the brothers on the street," in the language of the brothers on the street, by distancing him from any tincture of white men's institutions. That Newton was in fact a college student himself easily gets lost in this narrative. Rather than LeRoi Jones's own favorite negative epithets of "faggot" and "sissy," Seale favors "motherfucker" and "pig" to establish Newton's, and his own, masculine street cred. When he attacks Jones (later known as Amiri Baraka) and the cultural nationalists for engaging in jive-ass bullshit, he is subtly misgendering without resorting to Baraka's faggot epithets.

Seale's mode of attack achieves its manly effect and affect more powerfully because it lacks the aura of insecure and overcompensating masculinity that would easily be read, and mocked, on the streets of Oakland. As Newton himself argues in his 1970 address "The Women's Liberation and Gay Liberation Movements," where he attacks brothers who engage in misogynist and homophobic labeling: "We should be willing to discuss the insecurities that many people have about homosexuality. When I say 'insecurities,' I mean the fear that they are some kind of threat to our manhood. I can understand this fear." Newton moves toward his conclusion by stating: "We should be careful about using those terms that might turn our friends off. The terms 'faggot' and 'punk' should be deleted from our vocabulary, and especially we should not attach names normally designed for homosexuals to men who are enemies of the people, such as Nixon or Mitchell. Homosexuals are not enemies of the people."[11] It is not surprising that Seale adheres to this protocol in attacking the manhood of the black cultural nationalists in his narrative. When Seale wants vividly to capture the revolutionary insufficiency of these men, he does so by berating their lack of knowledge about both the gun laws and the handling of guns. Rather than labeling black cultural nationalists "faggots" or "sissies," he calls them "Paper Panthers." This signifies, of course, that they are merely Panthers on paper, not on the street, but it also connotes their tendency to talk bullshit like fake intellectuals rather than to take action like real revolutionaries.[12] In so deliberately abstaining from the common tactic of sissy-shaming as a way of propping up a masculinist brotherhood, the Black Panthers shift attention to pragmatic issues like housing, food, imprisonment, education, and self-defense against hostile police, as opposed to divisive skirmishes over who is or is not gender-normal enough to join the band of brothers. In fact, the *Black Panther* newspaper showcased its defense captains in domesticating roles that would seem to contradict the dominant media image of an armed body most concerned with battling the police. The Panther principle of service to the people included caretaking activities like teaching children and taking part in the party's free breakfast program, as highlighted in a *Black Panther* weekly newspaper photograph of Warren Heart, defense captain of the

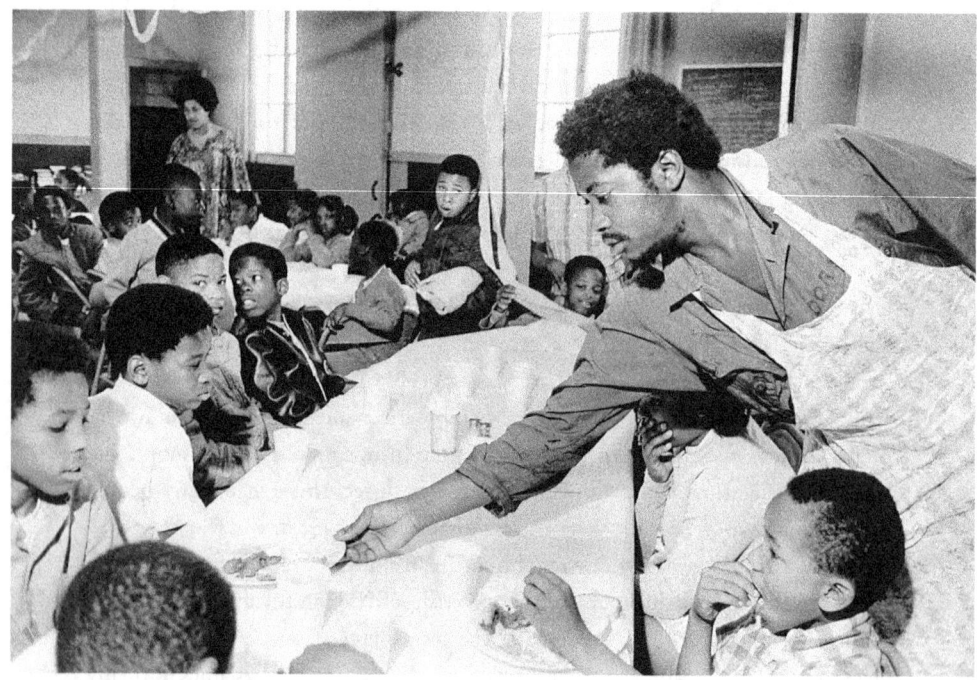

5.1 *Black Panther* newspaper (June 21, 1969) photograph of Baltimore Panther Warren Heart serving free breakfast.

Baltimore chapter, serving food to children (figure 5.1).[13] As Tracye A. Matthews has observed, the gender politics of the Panthers were hotly contested, and the roles taken by men and women in the organization did not always conform neatly to conventional gender norms of the time.[14]

This is not to overlook the tension at work between the Panthers and their rivals the "Paper Panthers," a phrase that stings based in a gender logic that separates actual men of action from those who merely dabble in revolution with pen and paper. When Baker labels himself a recent convert to cultural nationalism in 1972, he is ironically classifying himself with those phony intellectuals whom the real Black Panthers—part of the on-campus reality at Yale in the early 1970s— have condemned as "Paper Panthers." Even in the heated atmosphere of hyperbolic macho that Michele Wallace defines as characteristic of the 1970s, there was more than one way to discredit a male opponent by insinuating that he is misgendered.[15] That Seale and Newton barred use of the all-too-familiar sissiphobic and homophobic terms does not mean that they abandoned the notion of suspect manhood as the basis of their strategy of brotherly consolidation for racial warfare, but it does mean that they helped to subtly shift the field of contest to include sissies and homosexuals as what Newton calls "potential allies" and "friends." One could even go so far as to say that Seale and Newton, in agreeing not to insult queer men as potential allies and friends in the fight against white male supremacy, provide an opening for the critique of sissiphobia and homophobia as inappropriate dimensions of black liberation. This critique also serves as a narrow bridge to the succeeding generation of black sissies, whether straight or gay.

Baraka's Sissy Ambivalence

As important as Seale, Newton, Cleaver, George Jackson, and other male Black Panthers are for understanding the changing relationship to homo-sissiness during the Black Power era, the crown of "most influential black male public intellectual of the period" must be placed on the head of cultural nationalist LeRoi Jones / Amiri Baraka. That Seale names "LeRoi Jones" specifically when he calls out the Paper Panthers indicates this. At first sight, in focusing on his black nationalist poetry, Baraka's sissiphobia seems simple and conclusive. When we shift to his autobiography and fiction, however, we get a more complex portrait. We discover, in fact, that Baraka's treatments of sissiness and homosexuality also serve as a bridge to the following generation of sissies, straight and gay. Indeed, Baraka's semiconfessional fiction strongly identifies him as a sissy, one whose multifarious affiliation with white postwar homosexual enclaves seems to create a sense of self-doubt, as well as others' speculation, about his own sexual orientation. We can thus understand the sociopolitical cultures that spawn the 1990s pro-sissy confessionals by investigating the backstory that feeds it through the influence of Baraka's straight sissy odyssey, which itself is strongly influenced by Baldwin's mass-media public image as an articulate, powerful spokesman for the race. Even as he weds himself strongly to heteronormative patriarchy, Baraka cannot easily or fully divorce himself from the homo-sissy that haunts all of his writing, whether as ambivalent subject or targeted object.[16]

When Baraka maps his artistic trek to downtown Manhattan as a passage to racial self-alienation hinging on gender self-estrangement, he is referencing the path carved by sissy Baldwin and Baldwin's sissy mentor, Beauford Delaney, as well as by the bisexual protagonist manqué of Baldwin's third novel, Rufus Scott of *Another Country* (1962). In *Autobiography of LeRoi Jones* (1984), Baraka describes the phase of his life when he first begins to imagine himself a writer. His sojourn in Greenwich Village begins with a public exhibition of sensitivity when he picks up a copy of the *New Yorker*.

> I had been reading one of the carefully put together exercises *The New Yorker* publishes constantly as high poetic art, and gradually I could feel my eyes fill up with tears, and my cheeks were wet and I was crying, quietly, softly but like it was the end of the world. I had been moved by the writer's words, but in another, very personal way. A way that should have taught me even more than it did. Perhaps it would have saved me many more painful scenes and conflicts. But I was crying because I realized that I could never write like that writer.[17]

The aspiring young writer is brought to tears over his alienation from the "lawns and trees and dew and birds and some subtlety of feeling amid the jingling rhymes"—in other words, the banal comforts of the white middle-class world that enable a white poet to write this kind of verse. The erring young Baraka is, nonetheless, intuitively "chilled" by the *New Yorker* and its poetry, for "the *inside*, of that life" that so "repelled" him "was impenetrable" (168; emphasis in original). It is that sensitive young poet yearning for the "rich elegance and savoir faire" of the *New Yorker* magazine, and it is that "*crying*" sissy self, disarmed and disarming, whom he later desires to purge from every black man's soul.

Significantly, in his early bohemian phase, Baraka responded very differently to Baldwin and his work. Rather than tears, he bursts with pride that comes from a sense of shared ambition and achievement stemming from seeing Baldwin as a model to be emulated. He speaks of looking at Baldwin's photograph on the cover of *Notes of a Native Son* and "admiring the cool black face that stared back at me."

Those are the days when Baldwin represented "the last great black arts figure who related to Europe as center," even before Baldwin begins "to travel back and forth and was no longer the classic black exile in Europe" (191). Later, Baldwin comes to represent for Baraka this cursed ambivalence of desiring white Europe, with its civilizing promises, and at the same time black solidarity. In rejecting bohemia in the end, Baraka is also rejecting expatriation of the more distancing sort, the Wright-like flight to Europe. In *Autobiography of LeRoi Jones*, he writes perceptively: "There was a whole section of that generation that came just after Wright, Jimmy Baldwin's generation, perhaps, who took up residence in Europe, or who came back and forth. Some finally deciding it was better to be formally foreign in a foreign land" (186). Rather than seeing this expatriation as an engagement of anticolonialism, Baraka aligns it with a colonial mentality: "The intellectual worship of Europe is in one sense only the remnants of colonialism, still pushed by the rulers through their 'English Departments' and concert halls!" (187). Baraka will come to see his own stint in Greenwich Village as just such a colonial expatriation. He recognizes that the Baldwinean ambivalence—going back and forth between Europe and the black cause in America—makes for a seductive ideology of estranging intermediacy, a prophetic capacity to stand on the line between two warring camps and rain down ugly truths on the heads of both from a position of transgressive firsthand experience.

Baraka's own authorial identity is haunted by a similar racial intermediacy, and as with Baldwin, this intermediacy is framed through what Baldwin calls in *Another Country* Greenwich Village's "erotic confusion."[18] Baraka's earlier work especially is suffused with "erotic confusion," including, most significantly, that associated with the anxiety and panic related to a self whose conduct could easily be associated with homo-sissiness. The *Autobiography* sketches Baraka's past as an aborted trajectory toward out-Baldwining Baldwin. It is a narrative of self-correcting error, in which Baraka constantly repeats the act of "finding himself" in a changed situation without recognizing it or knowing how he has gotten there. He finds success in the downtown "Beat" scene of Manhattan around 1957 to 1963. Surpassing the *New Yorker*, Baraka becomes the hip center of cutting-edge literariness as the founder and coeditor of *Zazen* (*Yugen*), the literary magazine that helps to shape Beat underground culture into a national identity. But one day this new leader of the in-crowd looks at the poets in *Zazen*, with its trend-setting black cover, and suddenly notices his own racial exceptionality. Like Baldwin's, Baraka's downtown identity is fashioned through both openness and outsiderness, each feeding the other. Throughout the autobiography, Baraka defines himself as "*an outsider*" in explicit reference to Wright's novel.[19] In other words, Wright's *Outsider* protagonist, Cross Damon, maps another aborted trajectory for the young Baraka, a plot that the maturing Baraka will overcome in eventually rejecting a self-defeating embroilment in self-alienating existentialism in favor of radicalized blackness.

This process of finding himself through continual self-correction and conversion defines Baraka's self-narration through a process of self-revision that is anchored in overcoming a misgendered temperament, explicitly articulated through his association with white homo-sissies in the *Autobiography*, and semifictionalized in the erotically confused sissy character Roi, an alter ego of the author, in his novel *The System of Dante's Hell* (1965). In line with our previous discussions of the role that color plays in the gendering of black manhood, the young Baraka is self-conscious of how his "brownness" may be perceived as a form of racial and masculine dilution—or so he imagines, at least. Like Baldwin's portrait of his own liminal sissy-boyhood semifictionally rendered through John Grimes in *Go Tell It*, Baraka portrays himself as a boy growing up in Newark always in between, neither white nor black, but "brown": the lower-middle-class kid striving hard for solid middle-class respectability; not yet good enough for the high yellows, not bad enough for the common street blacks. This class/color position he associates with both mediation and sensitivity.[20] This "brown" intermediacy haunts him into college, where he goes to please his family, but that ends with his willful flunking out. It follows him into the air force, the ultimate gesture of patriotic conformity, but ends with his dishonorable discharge. It follows him to Greenwich Village, where he finds himself straddling black and white, outside and inside, conformity and rebellion, low and high, heterosexual violence and homosexual attraction, but ends with his rejection of the bohemian life as a false alternative, a submerged tributary ultimately flowing from and within the white American mainstream. More disconcerting, once he becomes the poster boy for Beat sensibility, he finds himself first a racial token, the currency through which moneyed whites could rediscover their hip value as being vicariously down with blacks at the nonconforming bottom. And then he finds that he has tokenized himself. He finds himself justifying all the white poets published in *Zazen* by saying, "We were looking for quality literature and that is what we got."[21]

This Baldwin-like "brown" intermediacy not only links Baraka's work to Mailer, Jack Kerouac, Allen Ginsberg, and all the other white hipsters who think they have defected into a cool downbeat, thus escaping the square establishment and approximating hip blackness. It also links him to the work of the previous generation of black writers, whose 1950s project of the integrationist imaginary—a fascination with composing novels with predominantly white characters, like Baldwin's 1956 novel *Giovanni's Room*—reaches an apex at the very moment that Baraka is experimenting with becoming the exceptional black man at the helm of white alternative culture.[22] Baraka's turning against this integrationist fantasy maps another self-correcting motif, as retrospectively formulated in the *Autobiography*. Hidden within Baraka's texts, therefore, are always these inverse integrationist fantasies turned into nightmares of whitewashed sensibility: "So obviously my social focus had gotten much whiter."[23] Hand in hand with this whitewashing nightmare is another inverting motif of the temptations of white bourgeois sexual deviance, Baldwin's "erotic confusion." When the white woman he has been casually seeing gets pregnant, he pops the question. Again before he knows what he's doing, not only is he married with biracial children; he is also seeing other white women, cudgeling an Asian man with whom his wife takes up, and generally slipping mindlessly into the sexual deviations of white middle-class decadence.

And where decadence goes, homosexuality cannot be far behind. In fact, it must be leading the way. Baraka finds himself becoming intimate with Allen Ginsberg and Frank O'Hara, white middle-class homosexuals who not coincidentally are two leading lights of Beat poetry through the inspiration of Walt Whitman and his songs of the open road, his veiled homosexual tributes to the robust love of comrades. Like virtually all of the male writers of integrationist fantasy, Baraka finds himself investigating the psychology of the queer white mind. Unlike the black male writers of the previous generation, however, the young experimental Baraka has direct access to a wholly new phenomenon: the emerging enclaves of more or less "out" homosexuals who were flocking to downtown Manhattan, Chicago, Los Angeles, and San Francisco after World War II. Across the 1950s, homosexuals in America's largest cities founded homophilic organizations, which were often based in a civil rights paradigm of gaining greater tolerance through gender-conforming respectability politics. This flurry of homosexual rights activity, though militant for its time, was also conducted in the utmost secrecy. As Toby Marotta notes: "Homosexual behavior was a felony punishable in New York state by as much as twenty years in jail.... The memory of the antihomosexual furor fueled by Senator Joseph McCarthy in the early 1950s was fresh. The danger of being exposed, fired from one's job, or blackmailed because of one's homosexuality was real."[24] Settling in Greenwich Village in 1957 in the midst of this flurry of underground homosexual activity, Baraka enters into a Beat enclave that is inextricably mixed with this emerging homosexual ghetto identity. In fact, the sense of high risk, nonconformity, and social rebellion evident in Beat culture is feeding as much on the real dangers of associating with homosexuals as on the vicarious endangerment of admiring life in the black ghettos from a distance.

From his white homosexual colleagues, Baraka becomes intimately acquainted with the complicated status dissonance and conflicted meanings of being a white middle-class homosexual man in U.S. culture in the 1950s and early '60s. Unlike the black swishes with whom Baraka is already familiar from his neighborhood in Newark, white urbane homosexuality skirts that odd space between a respectable high society and the disrespectable margins of forbidden, self-destructive street criminality.[25] Among white male homosexuals, Baraka discovers a kind of convoluted social logic of dominant white culture, in which the homosexual is a sign both of advancing European-focused high culture, with its most sophisticated elite civilizing impulses, and of the most degraded, decadent, abhorrent descent into legally punishable impulses of pathological self-destruction. In his 1965 essay "American Sexual Reference: Black Male," Baraka hits on this convoluted logic with stunning clarity: "Most American white men are trained to be fags," he writes.[26] Baraka is speaking both metaphorically and literally, for dominant culture itself cannot decide whether homosexuality is a rare psychological perversion suffered at the extremes of society by immediately identifiable, hopelessly maimed individuals or whether it is a contagious physical-moral disorder spread by the sly recruitment of an invisible menace.

Baraka borrows this hegemonic logic to deconstruct white male supremacy, turning the Nordic standard of robust pioneer manhood into that other aesthetic of Western culture: the beautiful but entirely useless high-art piece: "For this reason it is no wonder their faces are weak and blank, left without the hurt that reality makes—anytime. That red flush, those silk blue faggot eyes." He pictures for us the beautiful, young, blond, blue-eyed boy celebrated in white homosexual pornography before the advent of the macho, bearded Castro Street Clone, and, of course, this boy is an androgynous double for the ideal aesthetic object of high Western culture, the white female nude or the still life—which one doesn't matter. "So white women become men-things," he writes, "a weird combination, sucking the male juices to build a navel orange, which is themselves."[27] Alienated from productive work, the beautiful blond lady, the beautiful blond homosexual, the high-art artifact without use all become reflections of one another: "The nonrealistic, the nonphysical. Think now, the goal of white society is luxury. Work is done by unfortunates. The purer white, the more estranged from, say, actual physical work."[28] This is the anxiety of William Hollingsworth Whyte's "organization man," of Herbert Marcuse's "one-dimensional man," of Mailer's "white Negro" brought to its ultimate resting place. Baraka's critique of the blond aesthetic that binds white civilization to luxury by subordinating all productive labor to "the unfortunates" reminds us as well of the parodic white mass-media sissies from the previous chapter, Warhol and Capote. In fact, Capote lounging like a female nude in the scandalous *Other Voices, Other Rooms* dust-jacket photo could be the poster boy for Baraka's portrait of the nude blond as the white aesthetic's "nonrealistic, the nonphysical." Through his encounter with white homosexuality, then, Baraka stumbles onto the perfect symbol of the "exotic" ensconced within elite culture, the terrifying threat within white men's master narrative of progressive, productive self-control.

In *Autobiography*, he describes himself slipping unawares into this queer bordering space between the high and the forbidden: "I found myself going to the ballet, to cocktail parties, 'coming over for drinks,' to multiple gallery openings with Frank O'Hara and his shy but likable 'roommate.'"[29] The homosexuals are privileged boys with the luxury of grown-up play, and unselfconscious in the privilege of their whiteness, which seems to protect them, however precariously, from the black dirty bottoms. Like those who create a daring homosexual rights movement in the midst of anticommunist "hysteria," these exotic others take for granted their right to belong as middle-class white men even as they are hounded and attacked with both legal and extralegal, verbal and physical systematic violence to purge them as a socially agreed-upon menace to the welfare of the white middle-class norm.

As with Washington and Johnson, I am not interested here in reading Baraka's engagement with sissiness as autobiographical confession, though this certainly can be done, as shown by Ron Simmons.[30] Although Baraka's later homophobic rants have been read by scholars like Simmons and Jerry Gafio Watts as his attempt to suppress his own history of homosexual encounters as semiautobiographically recorded in *The System of Dante's Hell*, I am less interested in the potential confessional dimension of the novel, and more concerned with how a straight-identified black male author-activist after the literary success of Baldwin, who anchored so much of his fiction in homosexual themes, spins his own engagement with the figure of the homo-sissy in the era of emerging Black Power and gay liberation.[31] In the novel he converts the fleshly reality of deadly sins, hellish ghosts, and hectoring demons, all fully alive in Dante's medieval frame of reference, into a modern psychodrama of descending into his mind's own deepest pit.[32] Among the demons that Baraka's first-person narrator encounters in his journey down into the core of his mind is the vice of homosexuality. Scholars have differed on how they read the sexuality of Roi, the protagonist; many assume he is heterosexual despite his homosexual experiences. In one of the most compelling early readings of the novel, Melvin Dixon quite flatly considers Roi "a homosexual" who "probes the depths of same-sex lust as an ironic metaphor for his evasion of self-love," and he proposes that the novel is "overlooked because of its experimental form or perhaps because the protagonist" is homosexual.[33] Influenced by Dixon, Darieck Scott, in a recent riveting interpretation, views the homosexual theme as symbolic, as he observes: "In the novel, sexuality is the means by which or the medium in which blackness is lost and betrayed, and by which it is regained and secured."[34] Thinking through Baraka's semiautobiographical representation of Roi's sexual conduct as a form of homo-sissy panic, we might arrive at a more ambivalent rendering of this protagonist's racial-sexual liminality.

Scott captures the doubleness (betrayal and rescue) of Baraka's relation to the homo-sissy, who here marks both the distinctive *inside* of black culture, as identified in the *Autobiography*, and simultaneously the threshold of foreignness, the queer as a white European phenomenon:

> In Chicago I kept making the queer scene. Under the "El" with a preacher. And later, in the rotogravure, his slick (this other, larger, man, like my father) hair, murrays grease probably. He had a grey suit with gold and blue threads and he held my head under the quilt. The first guy (he spoke to me grinning and I said my name was Stephen Dedalus. And I read Proust and mathematics and loved Eliot for his tears. Towers, like Yeats (I didn't know him then, or only a little because of the Second Coming & Leda). But Africans lived there and czechs. One more guy and it was over. On the train, I wrote all this down. A journal now sitting in a tray on top the closet, where I placed it today. The journal says "Am I like that?"[35]

The disjunction between the narrator's firsthand, first-person experience of anonymous homosexual encounters and his self-estrangement within these encounters is captured through literary references to modernist fiction that would be unfamiliar to many men with whom he engages on the street. Connecting his own experience with that of Stephen Dedalus, James Joyce's protagonist in the *künstlerroman A Portrait of an Artist as a Young Man* (1916), the secrecy of public homosexual sex is abstracted through the obscurantist modernist style adopted from the experimental stream-of-consciousness of Joyce, Marcel Proust, and T. S. Eliot. Notably, Baldwin's first novel, which also thematizes the urban street as a place of un/familiar risk to the self's gender and racial identity, adapts a similar stream-of-consciousness style to capture John Grimes's struggle to repress the tempting (homo)sexualized flesh as a route toward an unfamiliar life beyond the safety of racial belonging within the household and the church. While Baldwin's style still remains comparatively accessible to the ordinary reader—pace Hughes's criticism discussed in the previous chapter—the passage in *System* is obscured through literary references emblematizing the schism between, on the one hand, Roi's high aspirations as a modernist artist, the temptations of sissy literacy that Baraka has observed among his homosexual Beat friends, and, on the other, his desire for immersion in racial belonging within the black bottom. The narrator's question—"Am *I* like *that*?" (emphasis added)—disorients, for it challenges any stable sense of his own sexual identity even as it reconfirms his racial location, in the dark underbelly of Southside Chicago's black bottom. Just as when Baraka racially misrecognizes himself on the cover of the avant-garde little magazine he founds, his relation to the self is one of racial *and gender* alienation here, comparable to Baldwin's and John Grimes's sense of being strange to others and thus to themselves. "Homosexuality figures prominently as a representation of this perversion of one's relation to oneself," Scott astutely observes; "Baraka appears to make it the mark of inauthenticity."[36] I would slightly revise this insight to emphasize how queer sexuality in this passage paradoxically marks both deep self-familiarity—the familial, even—and also deep estrangement. The passage is framed with the black preacher as a familial presence, as the preacher's "grey" pin-striped suit and pomaded hair remind Roi of his own father. The passage closes with the familiarity of the train and the closet. The fusion of the familial and the strange—the queer preacher turning into his father, the weird experience transmuted into a journal written down on the train and hidden in the closet— makes it difficult to distinguish his own authentic firsthand experience from a dreamscape in which he fantasizes a role alien to the self.

As Brown notes, Dedalus also refers to a particular kind of unfathering of one's cultural (racial) roots in order to claim artistic self-generation.[37] This modernist literary method, with its proliferation of obscure allusions, is exactly the sort of "esoteric bullshit" that "some motherfucker in college wants to study," according to Bobby Seale. If LeRoi Jones is to transform into Amiri Baraka, these arch literary habits are exactly the ones he'll need not just to abandon but to eviscerate. Even in seeking to destroy these high literary tendencies that he himself identifies so strongly with the useless white aesthetic of the blond homosexual, however, he finds himself still on the wrong side of the Black Panthers' street cred, as his own brand of cultural nationalism still places him in the camp of the faux-intellectual Paper Panthers. As I have discussed elsewhere, this tension between the self-alienating Beat sensitivity and the black bottom comes to a climax in a scene where Roi is "raped" by a prostitute, Peaches, in the black bottom of Shreveport, Louisiana.[38] As Scott has pointed out, there are multiple significations operating here in the notion of the bottom. Literally, it refers to the topographic locales where African Americans are forced to live in cities—in this case, Shreveport— often called the Black Bottom, but it also refers to the penetrated black anus of homosexual intercourse.[39] Roi's nightmare is not only that Bottom reality of inherited African American abjection, but also the nightmarish awakening itself, the inability to get out of the cave of Eurocentric bohemianism. Even the art of oblique allusion so crucial to modernist craft works against his desire for the real, and as Baraka shifts from sissified Beat modernism to sissiphobic invective, one of the ways in which he signals this shift is to attempt to purge such elitist allusions. In actuality, however, he simply replaces one set of allusions with another. Baraka is resigned to the reality of words themselves, the reality that words constitute themselves purely through allusion.[40]

I place the verb "raped" in quotation marks above to indicate the way in which Roi's identity itself is split between the sissified self and the self that desires to prove its gender normativity, as Peaches forces herself on him while urging him to perform sexually through the same kind of sissiphobic invective that Baraka is beginning to use in his poetry: "Her arms around my hips pulled down hard and legs locked me and she started yelling. Faggot. Faggot. Sissy Motherfucker. And I pumped myself. Straining."[41] By calling out (labeling) the sissy faggot within him, Peaches coerces him to call out (exorcise) the sissy faggot within himself. It is through violent heterosexual intercourse—minus the physical attraction that is supposed to motivate such intercourse—that Roi claims his heteronormative blackness. The role that sissiphobia plays in Roi's reclamation promises to heal the split within the self, but the ostensibly purged sissy faggot, with its violated wounding, continues to haunt the newly found straight black man.

This ambiguous near-rape with Peaches should be contrasted with an earlier, more clear-cut near-rape in Circle 9: Bolgia 1 ("Treachery to Kindred"), titled simply "The Rape." In this episode a gang of "brown" or middle-class boys attempting to prove their street toughness sets out to rape "some dumb whore," who is stumbling drunkenly on the street. Significantly, as Theodore Hudson points out, the narrator himself is head of this gang of five, but his leadership is a ruse, for in order to prove it, he has to mask his compassion for her.[42] Taking her into a car, the boys attempt to commit this gang rape against a woman so drunk she is almost oblivious to their actions. She comes up with a strategy to save herself and to save their manhood, or at least what they take as their manhood, as each is egging the other on but nervously afraid to commit the deed. She says: "I'm sick ... and you boys ketch what I got you'll never have no kids. Nobody'll marry you. That's why I'ma drunk whore fallin in the streets." As they toss her out of the car onto the pavement, the narrator is still ambivalent, feeling both relieved and like a failure: "The plan was still fixed in my mind. But the physical world rushed thru like dirty thundering water thru a dam." He sees her on the pavement: "The smoke had blown away. I saw her body like on a white porcelain table dead with eyes rolled back. I had to get her."[43] The T. S. Eliot–influenced image of the slumped body on the table captures the doubleness of this awful experience for the narrator, caught between his street posturing self-image of what it means to be a black street-gang leader and the intellectual posturing of what it means to be a self-alienated vulnerable, compassionate self. The degraded black woman's body is actually on black pavement, not on white porcelain, so even the image exudes its own fraudulence. Does he want "to get her" to carry through with his rape, or to rescue her out of shame for the damage that they have done to her? The brutality of her fall is made clear: "She smashed against the pavement and wobbled on her stomach hard against the curb." Placing the two fragments together, we see the more disturbing implications of each against the other. The narrator has reaffirmed his leadership status among the gang members without having to commit the sexual crime of gang rape. As they leave the woman in the street, they voice their nervous glee, "screaming in the car, some insane allegiance to me."[44]

These multiple coercions, the gang members' coercion of each other, the boys' coercion of the woman, the woman's successful escape through a verbal trick—all indicate the falseness of the narrator's empty, masking stance as macho hero of the gang. This "treachery to kindred" is not only the boys' treachery against the black woman but also their more subtle treachery to one another masked in gang camaraderie. What Baraka portrays is a mutual self-destructive hatred among these middle-class *brown* boys, whose hatred of their whiteness is really as much hatred of their blackness. They have chosen randomly, after all, a black woman on whom to practice their rape.[45] If the failed gang rape leaves the narrator empty, feeling fraudulent, how is it that the heterosexual coercion with Peaches makes him, at least briefly, feel redeemed? Aren't they both based on the same compulsion to act heterosexually out of the fear of being perceived by others as a sissified half-black half-man?[46] Scott punctuates this idea thus: "It is not only that indoctrination by the dominant culture is like a rape but that rape, literal and metaphorical, material and psychological, is the very mode by which black men become black in the terms of white supremacy."[47]

In *Autobiography of LeRoi Jones*, this sense of being out of control—of being the outside norm to other's allusive otherness—in a delusional world of nonproductive whiteness hits Baraka hard when he realizes that two white males, Andrew Goodman and Michael Schwerner, have put their lives on the line along with a slain young black man, James Chaney. When he finds himself dismissing these two men, killed by the Mississippi Klan, as "white boys" who "were only seeking to assuage their own leaking consciences," he has to check himself: "And in this last outrageous diatribe I was confusing Schwerner and Goodman with the young white poseur-liberals who sashayed safely through the streets of Greenwich Village, the behind-the-lines bleeding hearts. When, on the real side, if I could have stood some hard truth, Schwerner and Goodman were out there on the front lines doing more than I was! But Chaney had been beaten beyond recognition; he had so received the fury of those maniacs but all these people wanted to talk about was the white youths' deaths."[48] Baraka finds himself brought up short by others who have put their lives on the line. The powerful image of "sashaying" here stands in for any concrete evidence of homosexual conduct *in flagrante delicto*—a sort of ad hominem by innuendo, rumor, and suspicion. Note how Baraka exploits the image of "sashaying" to discriminate between the useless blond faggots among whom he himself was metaphorically sashaying while these two young "white boys" were manning, according to Baraka's own logic, the "front lines" of the race war against the Mississippi Klan. His use of "sashay" here shifts the connotation of homo-swish conduct and character from the merely decorative, degenerate nonprocreativity to the sissy as inveterate coward. The front-line self-sacrifice of Schwerner and Goodman makes even Baraka's belligerent poetry look like cowardly sashaying. That these two civil rights martyrs are white, in fact Jewish (like so many of his Beat friends), only intensifies the sense that his own radical blackness may be merely theoretical, academic, or rhetorical, after all—or, as Seale would say, the "esoteric bullshit" of a Paper Panther. Ironically, the fictionalized sexual violence represented in *System* could be interpreted as a psychosocial deflection from the actual racial violence being experienced by civil rights movement protestors, black and white, in the very moment when the novel is written and published. Anchored in the figure of the sissy faggot, the racial-sexual ambivalence labeled "fraudulence" in the novel will later be more brutally and unambiguously categorized as racial-sexual treachery in the black nationalist discourse of the succeeding years.

The fictional narrative of *System of Dante's Hell* and the autobiographical one of *Autobiography of LeRoi Jones* both move him relentlessly toward collective immersion in black solidarity as black nationalism, even though the former's movement is depicted in the form of a hazy dreamscape. In both narratives, ineffectual sissification is the logical outcome of flirting with bohemian pseudo-rebellion, whereby the young black author loses his way amid "the young white poseur-liberals who sashayed safely through the streets of Greenwich Village, the behind-the-lines bleeding hearts." Thus, Baraka necessarily also employs integrationist fantasy in order to turn that protest anger inward in the effort of seeking out and purging the furtive enemy sashaying within the self, that white-identified desire to be unmanned by the unprocreative pleasures of queer bourgeois decadence. "The puritanical excesses of the White Eyes who call the procreative act (or thought of it as) 'evil' are only compensation for their lack of couth in handling the world's business," Baraka writes in "American Sexual Reference: Black Male."[49]

In Baraka's philosophy of race castration and race rape, detailed in "American Sexual Reference," it is white men who are ultimately the ones castrated, having turned themselves into metaphorical/literal homosexuals. The violence that they have committed has so cut them off from vitality that they no longer can see the procreative joy of sex: "I mean for one thousand years the White Eye has killed people for his luxury; as the killing increased, and the cover stories grew more fixed, and the possibility of reform ... lessened, the withdrawal from sex as *creation* grew more extreme. Sex was *dirty*." Baraka has tweaked here Baldwin's lessons in *The Fire Next Time* and *Giovanni's Room*, in which the white American puritanical dread of sex as dirty is interlinked with the binarization of race, whereby a falsely "innocent" whiteness protects itself by projecting onto blacks the sordidness of the black bottom, sexually alluring in its befouling abjection. We should understand Baraka's coarse attack on Baldwin that begins to occur in work like the 1963 essay "Brief Reflections on Two Hot Shots" in connection with his symbolic uses of homo-sissiness in *System*, published two years later. Although it has rarely been recognized in the scholarship, *System* is strongly indebted to Baldwin's first three novels, but especially to his third, *Another Country* (1962), in which the protagonist, Rufus Scott, finds himself sinking into a morass of "erotic confusion" in Greenwich Village, where he has gone to seek success as a jazz musician. Rufus's self-embattled stint downtown resonates with Baraka's autobiographical self-representation as a self-tokenized "brown" man tempted by same-sexuality, cross-racial intercourse, and hip white liberalism at the prospect of an artistic breakthrough administered through access to white liberal insiders. Like Rufus, Jones (the young Baraka) turns to violence spurred by a relationship with a white woman. Like Rufus, Jones attracts, is attracted to, and flirts with the white homo-swishes flocking to Greenwich Village after World War II. Baraka's autobiographical narrative of the trek downtown into white self-estrangement dovetails uncannily with Baldwin's. If Baraka is "saved" by black nationalism in a way that Rufus cannot be, as Baldwin aborts his story in medias res, Baraka's *System* concludes ambiguously with a dream of black collectivity trumped by a white sexual nightmare. Although we do not have space to analyze in depth these resonances between Baldwin/Baraka and Rufus/Roi, the striking ways in which Baraka's autobiographical and fictional narratives emulate this motif of racial estrangement through sexual self-estrangement help to clarify the often overlooked influence that Baraka experiences in the shadow of Baldwin's popularity and achievement as a sissified author and public intellectual in the 1960s, especially after the popular success of *Another Country* and the critical acclaim of *The Fire Next Time*.

If Baldwin is the sissy object lesson and then the foil on and against whom male black nationalist poets fashion their offensive poetics, Malcolm X is their heteronormative model of militant black manliness. Malcolm had perfected the performance of belligerent attack even as his audiences became whiter and whiter, often composed of students at white elite universities. Because he was impeccably dressed in the uniform of the Nation of Islam, there was no mistaking Malcolm's straight masculinity, even if, as Manning Marable and Bruce Perry have suggested, the Black Power hero had earlier been engaged in homosexual activity as a hustler.[50] Having been reared in an aspiring middle-class family, Baraka may have played on the hard streets of Newark, but his childhood was an idyll compared with Malcolm's childhood and youth. Ironically, while Malcolm moves from his Detroit Red zoot-suit attire to the middle-class business suits of the Fruit of Islam, Baraka moves in the contrary direction, having to dress down and play down his own roots in the black middle class.[51] As middle-classness itself becomes suspect with the rise of the Black Panther model of Black Power, Baraka's posture, manner, and speech had to emphasize his facility with the hard streets.

When performing poems for hip black audiences, Baraka refuses the protocols of poetry recitation with which he would have been deeply coached not only through the visual and audio recordings of the previous generation of poets like Langston Hughes but also through his tutelage in proper poetry recitation in the church Baraka attended in his youth.[52] This tension between the church and its repressions and the street and its alluring dangers reminds us of Baldwin's church/street dialectic in *Go Tell It* and other texts. In *Autobiography* Baraka describes his childhood experience in the "yellow" Bethany Baptist Church, where his maternal grandfather, Tom Russ, was a trustee: "The trustees, after those collections, would rise up and file into the back. It was a kind of dignified swagger. It was as important as any position in our world, it was at least as heavy as a civil service job. And I could go through there and see them counting that money, the respected elder gents of the church. And a preacher white as God himself."[53] Despite the admiration that Baraka clearly has for his grandfather's "dignified swagger," his attitude toward the church was negative, because it was a dicty church, one that tried to squeeze out any hint of the African and southern roots of black religion.[54] While for Baraka the grandfather's "swagger" stands in for the church's upright masculinity, the church's yellowness produces a racial ambivalence that, for Baraka, insinuates the potential of sissiness—or, more precisely, church-sissiness. Unlike for Baldwin and his characters (John Grimes, Arthur Montana), Little Richard, and Sylvester James, Baraka's childhood church distances him from the mass racial body in a sea of yellow uppityness that threatens to turn him into a too-good, too-proper church sissy.[55] This idea of the black church as a racially estranging venue seems especially odd, given how the church has historically been an anchor of black culture since emancipation. However, if we consider how Baldwin parallels the church and the avenue as kindred sources of racial and sexual familiarity and estrangement at once, Baraka's narrative can be seen to echo this dynamic, though it may draw a sharper line between the church's estranging uppityness and the street's promise of racial brotherliness. Baraka's insinuation that the church renders a threat of sissification in contrast to the rough code of the boisterous street should also be placed in the context of the black church as a zone of hyperfeminine influence, as discussed in the previous chapter. Baraka's narrative, however, avoids any concomitant insinuation of the kind of sexual seduction that Baldwin suggests in his own autobiography or even, more obliquely, in the fictional John's seduction by the elder boy-saint Elisha. Indeed, if we follow the logic that makes sissiness a prefiguration of queer sexuality, always shadowing the narrative of church sissification is the more disturbing one of the church as a scene of (homo)sexual seduction, if not abuse, as discussed in relation to the pop singer Sylvester James in the previous chapter.[56] Just as John's brother foil, Roi, in Baldwin's *Go Tell It* courts danger on the street as a confirmation of his mannishness, so young LeRoi of the *Autobiography* chooses the raucous street over the too-proper church—a contrast sharpened by the upwardly aspiring social status of Baraka's church versus the lower social status of the storefront Pentecostal. In such a church, clipped, clean, proper speech would have been compulsively encouraged, and proper modes of oratory and recitation were modeled on the Queen's English.

> The brown was like a reserve, an exit or quick passage to somewhere else. You look up you could be getting a scholarship somewhere or shaking Joe Louis's and Sandy Saddler's hand or being introduced by Willie Bryant as a bright Negro child, or reciting the Gettysburg Address in a boy scout suit down at the Old First Church, where George Washington was and most black people wasn't.
>
> But I ran the streets and walked the streets everyday hooked up to black life.[57]

The yellow church with its clipped English stands against the black streets, with its vulgar tongue games of the Dirty Dozens, which name-calls queer sexualities as a combative verbal resource. As he strives to expunge his own church-sissy yellowness or "brownness," Baraka's black nationalist poetry becomes all street swagger minus the grandfather's upwardly aspiring dignity.

We can observe this in his performance of "It's Nation Time" at the 1970 Afrikan People's Congress in Atlanta and of "Kutoa Umoja" at the 1972 National Black Political Convention in Gary, Indiana. His words become bullets fired from a high-capacity rifle. Or they become an African chant, where the words are ritualistically half-sung and bleed into each other in a rapid-fire manner. Profane in substance and delivery, the poem pretends to cease to be a poem, instead becoming, as he writes in "Black Art," "poems that kill. / Assassin poems, Poems that shoot / guns. . . . Setting fire and death to / whities ass."[58] The practice of poetry as weapon has the double benefit of purging the yellow church with its proper patterns of speech and the homo-sissy aesthetic that lured him into the castle of the white homosexual Beats. A useful contrast could be made with the recitation style of a poet like Robert Hayden (1913–1980), who himself would make a remarkable study of the development of a straight sissy-boy and who during the 1960s and '70s was the African American male poet most lauded by the dominant literary establishment. While Hayden recites in the conventional academic style of equanimous, wistful elocution in a high and yet plainspeaking tradition of bardic modernism, Baraka sounds like a street-smart revolutionary warrior, with a delivery sourced from sacred incantation but diction borrowed from the Dozens.[59] Nonetheless, next to Seale's image of the genuine Black Panther revolutionary, Baraka's delivery still harbors that tincture of sissy brownness. Despite his rants against Negro leaders as faggots in his black nationalist poetry, Baraka could not totally shake off the aura of sissiness that haunted him, an aura emanating both from his Baldwinean influence and his past bohemian contacts and works and from the suspect nature of poetry itself as an effete occupation implicated in European civilization, homosexual decadence, and the white aesthetic. For the next generation of black male literati, like the twenty-six-year-old Houston Baker Jr., just beginning his first academic post at Yale in 1969, at the height of Baraka's black nationalist fame, his voice represented not only a brash vernacular intellectual to be envied but also a cautionary case for disidentification.[60]

Black Gay Men Learning to Speak Their Queerness

The touchstone text that brought the post–Black Power phenomenon of the black straight sissy into focus was Don Belton's anthology *Speak My Name: Black Men on Masculinity and the American Dream* (1995), which enlisted a who's who of eminent African American intellectuals reflecting on their own black maleness as an identity both alienating and brothering.[61] Significantly, Belton himself was a black gay man, but in editing this collection he put the emphasis, whether intentionally or not, on black *straight* men addressing their gender and sexual truths.[62] In creating a forum for this conversation, Belton seems to be serving silently as an intermediary between black gay men and their straight counterparts. In fact, the volume itself seems to answer a call made in the preceding two decades for straight men to hold themselves accountable to black women and to black gay men. In doing so, the volume participates in the call-and-response pattern characteristic of the identity-formation anthology as a genre: *Speak My Name*'s identity self-recognition is made possible by black gay anthologies like Joseph Beam's 1986 *In the Life* and Essex Hemphill's 1991 *Brother to Brother*. These black gay male anthologies were in turn called into being by the spate of black feminist anthologies that came out in the 1970s and early '80s, particularly Barbara Smith's *Home Girls* (1983).[63] This is the same domino pattern that pressures masculinity studies out of feminism and whiteness studies out of African American and ethnic studies. Discursively, straight black maleness as an articulated identity category hails itself belatedly through black male gayness, which has previously hailed itself into being through black lesbian feminist critique. In this sense, regardless of their individual gender normalcy or sexual orientation, the *Speak My Name* contributors are already collectively queered—sexually triangulated and obliquely effeminized—by the black gay sissies of *In the Life* and *Brother to Brother*.

Pressured on one side by these affirmative discourses promoting gender and sexual equality and inclusion within the black community and challenging racial assumptions about the sociopolitical priority and authority of heteronormative masculinity, the 1990s straight black sissy memoirists are simultaneously pressured on the other side by highly inflammatory figurations of out-of-control black sexuality, figured in and projected onto the "down-low brother" and gangsta rapper. The public panic over the so-called down-low, the label given to "straight" black men who secretly bed other men, was brought to mass public attention in the remarkable fiction of E. Lynn Harris, whose first novel, *Invisible Life*, focused its readers on the secret double lives of presumably straight black men. According to the "down-low" panic fostered by the post–civil rights logic of racial profiling, any straight-up black man who approaches you on the street could secretly be sexing other men and thus spreading disease and death in his wake, just as rapping gangsters embodied black male identity as sexual threat and social endangerment.[64] The straight sissy contributors to *Speak My Name* have been coached to conduct themselves as black straight men in a particular way that expresses a responsible character in line with womanist and homophilic values. After these womanist and black gay affirmative movements and anthologies, the assumption of racial authority based in the unspoken prerogatives of straight maleness becomes contested to the point of being discredited among the intellectual elite, unless black straight men are willing to foreground their own gender and sexual privilege and complicity as factors of the larger oppression of others previously silenced by them. Indeed, part of the strategy of the womanist and black gay identity anthologies includes a demand for not only accountability from black straight men but also responsiveness to the grievances and appeals made by black women and gay men. The black feminist texts that initiate this series of call-and-response identity volumes are thus anchored in a strong commitment to coalition politics, and as such they encourage an ongoing conversation with others in other intersecting identity groups. This is evident in one of the signal essays of this genre, Barbara Smith's "Toward a Black Feminist Criticism."[65] Smith vents her rage in words that recognize the psychic vulnerability done to black women and lesbians by white sympathizers (patrons, actually) and black men. Accordingly, identifying how this damage makes her feel also becomes an accusation of wrongdoing to be corrected. Once the multiply oppressed find room to assert their voices, much time is spent in identifying errors perpetuated by those who have been speaking presumably on their behalf.

A necessary negative critique names accusingly without scapegoating or name-calling, distancing womanism from black nationalist invective while retaining its commitment to the autonomy and authenticity of blackness as a unifying force. This *pseudo*-alliance that some black male critics enter into with white men—an act of homoraciality—draws attention to what a genuine alliance should be. Smith notes, on the one hand, that black male critics must willfully overlook their own intimate knowledge of black women's everyday lives, and, on the other hand, that their betrayal indicates a true ignorance when it comes to women's identity experience *as women*. She cites and quotes white critics, male and female, and black male critics who have omitted, misread, or misapplied black women's literature in an effort to shore up their sexual and/or racial privilege.

In these identity-formation volumes, this becomes a critical mode in itself, the rehearsal of a catalogue of complaints outlining the wrongs committed in the past, but this plaintive mode serves the larger purpose of forging coalitions with those who are named for their previous errors. After setting forth some first principles for a black feminist critical theory and practice, Smith returns to the impossibility of establishing discrete, definitive boundaries. Her essay ends with an invitation that indicates how the corrective or negative critique makes space for coalitional openings: "I want to encourage in white women, as a first step, a sane accountability to all the women who write and live on this soil. I want most of all for Black women and Black lesbians somehow not to be so alone. This last will require the most expansive of revolutions as well as many new words to tell us how to make this revolution real."[66] Joseph Beam responds to such openings made by Smith and other black feminists with the anthology *In the Life*, the first volume devoted to writings by and about gay-identified men of African descent. Beam's powerful, heart-wrenching essay "Brother to Brother: Words from the Heart" (first published in 1984 and reprinted in his anthology) becomes a rallying cry for "gay Blacks," generating the "brother-to-brother" movement, where African American same-gender-loving men are encouraged to articulate explicitly what was often taken as a tacit form of knowledge.[67] Beam and his colleagues demand also that white gays be called out for their racism and black straight men for their covert or overt valuing of hetero-masculinity over homo-sissiness. The idea was to foster a network of gay men committed to sexual liberation—in coalition with feminists, and gay/lesbian rights and AIDS activists—within the context of African American traditions, history, community, and identity.[68] Speaking in and through the tradition of African American rhetoric, Beam begins the essay as a response to a call, as an "Amen" to what black lesbians have already testified: "I, too, know anger. My body contains as much anger as water. It is the material from which I have built my house: blood red bricks that cry in the rain. . . . It is sometimes the way I show affection. I am angry because of the treatment I am afforded as a Black man. That fiery anger is stoked additionally with the fuels of contempt and despisal shown me by my community because I am gay. I cannot go home as who I am."[69] More specifically, Beam is responding to Audre Lorde, whose statement he quotes at the beginning of his essay: "I know the anger that lies inside me like I know the beat of my heart." Beam takes up her call by modulating his own voice in harmony with hers, without losing the pitch of his own particular pain and anger. The first words of his essay are not his own but a sister's, the sister of *The Cancer Journals* (1980): "What is most important to me must be spoken, made verbal and shared, even at the risk of having it bruised or misunderstood." Unattributed to any speaker except through a footnote, Lorde's words work as an incantation, passed from mouth to mouth, from pain to pain, from heart to heart. The essay moves from the first quote, which looks like Beam's own words until we realize they float above or into the text as an epigraph; from epigraphic words to an indented quotation from Lorde's *Sister/Outsider* (1984); and then to Beam's own words: "I, too, know anger." These also are not Beam's "own" words, but anyone's, those of anyone who has felt that anger articulated for us by the previous articulations.

How different this anger is from that mobilized in Baraka's black nationalist polemics! Of course, it is also a modulation of that earlier movement's articulation of militant, militarized rage. Lorde's anger—and Beam's, and our own—is coupled with pain, "even at the risk of having it bruised or misunderstood." The foregrounding of pain as a revolutionary force would seem odd in the Black Power discourse even of Black Panthers like Seale and Newton, who self-consciously refrain from sissiphobic invective, for the pain of emasculation, of being cut, wounded, penetrated without recourse, is what that movement seeks to turn around, turn over, and turn against the white male supremacist perpetrators. Indeed, using words as weapons—whether as metaphorical rape or sissiphobic assault—had by the 1980s become so strongly associated with black nationalist discourse that pain itself is taken to be the province of women, sissies, and fags, not militant black men. To recognize the pain of being bruised—almost to celebrate the bruise as a badge of unbearable oppression borne—is to invite its sharing, even at the risk of being bruised again. Like Baldwin, Beam is tapping into the wounding that marks sissy vulnerability as a resource: he is wielding it as a passive-aggressive shield rather than resorting to the conventional verbal weapons exploited by the most aggressive modes of the black male as sissiphobic warrior.

Beam and his gay brotherhood of writers virtually idolized Baldwin, as had the young LeRoi Jones (Baraka) and Eldridge Cleaver, but the elder writer's public sissy persona necessarily amplified and intensified Beam's regard instead of creating the kind of gender/racial dissonance overly protested by Baraka and Cleaver. A direct response to Barbara Smith's call, Beam's "Brother to Brother" (and the *In the Life* volume more generally) showcases the hurt he experiences, not from the white man in power but from another ordinary black man on the street, similar to Baldwin's linking of his own homo-sissiness to the "salty swagger" of ordinary black men he sights in the Jim Crow South. Although the regional setting has shifted, the desire for bridging the male gender divide remains consistent: "Almost every morning I have coffee at the same donut shop. Almost every morning

I encounter the same Black man who used to acknowledge me from across the counter. I can only surmise that it is my earrings and earcuffs that have tipped him off that I am gay. He no longer speaks, instead looks disdainfully through me as if I were glass."[70] Subtly in this scenario Beam has not only self-identified as "gay"—presumably inadvertently—to the black cashier and thus to us as his audience; he has also, more subtly, self-identified as a respectable sissy, one who could otherwise pass for straight if he so desired. This tip-off in which the protagonist's sissiness is suddenly exposed through a minute detail of the earrings and cuffs reminds us of Hall Montana's shock at seeing his little brother for the first time in observing his sissy hairstyle during Arthur's debut performance as a gospel singer. Unlike Hall's tentative response, however, the black brother/stranger in the café takes the expected, even routine, approach of rushing from such an ostensibly sissifying detail to known homosexuality. It must also be noted, however, that Beam, as the object of the other's gaze, can only speculate that his own homosexuality is the reason that the other has refused to acknowledge him. In the street culture of urban African American men, small cues of acknowledgment—such as a slight head-nod or a gentle tap of the fist to the heart—carry great symbolic weight as signs of brotherly affection and solidarity against the grain of dominant society's exclusion, degradation, stereotyping, and physical brutality. Making himself the gazed-upon object in his own self-narrative—just as Baldwin makes his protagonist, Arthur, the gazed-upon object in Hall's narrative about him—Beam heightens and intensifies the sense in which the black sissy is estranged within his own territory, is alienated from the other brothers on the block, is, in Baldwin's words, "a stranger in the village," and thus "cannot go home as who I am."[71]

Using the cliché of being looked through like glass, Beam is very much aware that it is an image saturated with allusiveness to one of Baldwin's favorite metaphors: the eye of the other as both empathetic insight and estranging endangerment. "But glass reflects," he continues, "so I am not even that. He sees no part of himself in me—not my Blackness nor my maleness." Just in case we might miss the Baldwinean allusion, Beam caps it with a direct quotation from Baldwin: "'There's nothing in me that is not in everyone else, and nothing in everyone else that is not in me.'"[72] Beam thus names Baldwin as a signal antecedent, one whose own Cold War–era sissy intelligence frames and molds the younger writer's post-Stonewall, post–Black Power gay self-affirmation. Like Baraka's, but from a different angle, Baldwin's influence itself wounds even as it inspires. As Kevin J. Mumford observes in his superb chapter on Beam in *Not Straight, Not White*, Beam hung a portrait of Baldwin in his studio, but he possessed "a kind of ambivalence—even a resentful attachment to the iconic figure"; he was disappointed in both Baldwin and Rustin for not quite living up to his own ambitions for a black gay brotherhood alliance. After hearing Baldwin give a lecture, Beam "criticized Baldwin on a number of levels—as 'speaking to white people,' as tired, and as too closeted—clearly angered by Baldwin's refusal to be more out or clearly identified with black gay life."[73] How ironic that the elder author is, on the one hand, publicly castigated for being too sissified by some black nationalists of the previous generation, and, on the other, privately chastised for not being public enough in his gayness by black gay men of the post-Stonewall generation.

The disappointment that Mumford portrays in Beam results in part from the changed audience of Beam's agenda, from Baldwin's crossover audience invested still in a civil rights frame of reference to Beam's own decision to solely address other black men in an attempt to heal the rift between straight and gay, a rift seemingly widening in the post-Stonewall, post–black nationalist moment. As Mumford writes, "Though Beam found inspiration and support from black lesbians, his political work necessarily focused on addressing the immediate barriers confronting black gay men." Then, quoting Beam's "Brother to Brother," Mumford identifies the other source of ambivalent inspiration for his essay: "Its revolutionary nature stemmed from its conflicted relationship to '60s revolutionaries such as Bobby Seale, Huey Newton, and Eldridge Cleaver [who] dare not speak our name.'"[74] Though not quite accurate, given that Newton had indeed explicitly addressed gay men, if not specifically *black* gay men, Beam understands that the Black Panthers, like Baldwin, represent a bridge to the sort of revolutionary brotherliness that he advocates in the volume. Mumford points out that Beam became involved in organizations devoted to both "the reform of masculinity" and the "prisoner's rights movement."[75] Accordingly, Beam deploys his correspondence with a prisoner whom he identifies as "Ombaka" to embody the idealized rapprochement between straight and gay black men. The epistolary friendship with Ombaka is based in their common interest in becoming writers, a bond that ironically brings the sissy-boy's strength—literateness—to the rescue of the black prisoner, who in turn brings his own manhood credibility to the rescue of the sissy-boy. That Ombaka is a convict in the tradition of Malcolm X, George Jackson, and other inmate-authors in the Black Power pantheon only intensifies the sense of healing that can come from consummating the coalition between straight and gay dreamed of by Newton, but even more decidedly through the shared identity of black brotherliness. In other words, Beam is exploring the ways in which those black straight men most stereotyped as incorrigibly and irredeemably "hypermasculine" actually constitute the best opportunity for brother-to-brother revolutionary love. This is a different strategy of sissy-inclusiveness from that practiced by the straight black sissy public intellectuals of the 1990s, who emphasize their sissy temperament as straight men to build the bridge to their gay brothers and feminist colleagues. Beam is not asking Ombaka—representing all straight black men in the essay—to sissify himself in order to forge this intimate bond, for the bond itself is living proof that black manliness need not be accessed, experienced, or expressed through the conventional vectors of sexism and sissiphobia. As an addressee within "Brother to Brother," Ombaka is not portrayed beyond the minimalist label of straightness, so we have no strong sense of his degree of gender-sexual conformity. Beam is aware, however, that he need not emphasize Ombaka's black manliness beyond the epithet of straightness, for his status as incarcerated and as one who has changed his name in the manner of Malcolm X can stand as metonyms for his unquestionable black straightness, as manifesting a writerly ambition in the Black Panther mold presumably untroubled by the kind of racialized sissy panic so evident in the work of black nationalists like Baraka and Cleaver.

The demand here being made on black straight men by writers like Barbara Smith and Beam is in part an appeal for these men to make themselves vulnerable not only to critique by those previously silenced but also to self-critique as persons possessing attributes that could too easily make them complicit with the gender and sexual hegemony of white men. That owning one's own pain necessarily means making oneself emotionally penetrable as a man is exactly the point. It puts black straight men on the line. Either you acknowledge your own vulnerability in empathizing with ours, or in refusing to do so you perpetuate black male complicity with white patriarchal supremacy. This demand from black women and black gay men comprises one crucial factor that occasions the phenomenon of some black male intellectuals' coming out as straight sissies in the 1990s.

Sissy-Flirtation and 1990s Black Straight Intellectuals

The formation of this straight sissy identity constitutes a revealing moment in the cultural history of autobiography, as it exposes some oversights not only in autobiographical theory but also in race, gender, and queer theory. Nurtured or coerced into constructing themselves as a coherent gender group across the fissures of their erotic attractions and gender dispositions, these black male contributors find themselves having to address each other publicly not just as a brotherhood of race men, *brother to brother*, but instead as diversely gendered men called out as black *straight* or black *gay*, as swinging hipster or flaunting swisher, as player or punk—and once called out, they must respond in kind. If black gay men have already uncloseted themselves in their own identity volumes, co-opting brotherhood as a black gay imperative as they serve as mentors to call out their straight brethren, what can straight men logically uncloset about themselves in response? To cement this newly articulated shared gender agenda, the straight contributors of *Speak My Name* could simply confess their own homophobia, but this is hardly a motivation for deepened male introspection, nor does it necessarily bridge the straight/gay divide that haunts their mutual brothering across the sexual line and across a largely unarticulated gender history. More empathetically, straight contributors use their identity anthologies to confess their own gender insecurity, to embarrass their own manhood retrospectively, and in doing so to assert their kinship with gay black men and indirectly with black women through a shared gender dissonance: "I, too, am a sissy, though not one exactly like you." In other words, they coyly flirt with sissiness—a phenomenon I label "sissy-flirtation"—even as they aggressively assert their heterosexual orientation. Key to this flirtation is the way in which their sissy temperament is represented as transitive, as a sensitizing, temporizing conduct of their boyhood that is shed as they progress to manly leadership but that shapes their character, their capacity to empathize with and embrace the progressive gender/sexuality movements that define the occasion of their entry into prominence as stellar academics, journalists, lawyers, and so on. Dissimilar from the radical theory of constitutive transitivity conceptualized by C. Riley Snorton as discussed in chapter 1, these memoirists seek to limit gender transitivity to a particular stage of boyhood while also valuing its lifelong affect into heterosexual manhood.

The sissy-flirtation in these straight reminiscences—however temporalized and temporized as the transitional phase of boyhood—subliminally retains its original nineteenth-century usage, the affectionate diminutive "little sis." Gay black men have in their identity anthologies preemptively taken away from straight-up black men the affectionate term "brother" (with all its loaded connotations of racial fraternity, social equality, communitarian politics, blood ties, and blood spilled together in battle). It is no coincidence that "brother" is the term used among black male communists in the 1920s and '30s (the African Blood Brotherhood, for instance) and that its usage is amplified by the Black Panthers and other Black Power radicals during the heyday of black liberation in the 1960s and '70s. The power of brothering resides in the homosocial exclusion of women and the repression of homosexuality—as evident in its dominant masculinizing usage in labor unions, secret fraternal organizations, college fraternities, and military platoons, the "band of brothers." In opting to brother each other, black gay anthologists were wresting this powerful name from heteronormative institutions and practices to sissify it, but ironically, in doing so they also supplanted the affectionate usage of "sister" or "girl" as a colloquial, private practice among black faggots. In other words, to legitimize their identity as black men who happen to be gay, they sacrifice, at least publicly, the affectionate usage of "sister" already embedded in the epithet "sissy." Although not all of the brother-to-brother authors presented themselves as respectably masculine (viz the case of Beam), the "brother" epithet itself tends to image not the flaunting swish but the more gender-conforming sissy. Furthermore, because gay black men's use of "brother" is self-consciously analogized from the radicalization of "sister" among black lesbian feminists, "brother" unwittingly silences the sisterhood (woman-to-woman talk as the focus of public attention) at the same time that it silences the sistering potential of reclaiming "sissy" as an affectionate epithet. Just as the Jim Crow infrastructure shaping Washington's *Up from Slavery* dictated his menial relation to feminine labor, so the particular cultural infrastructure shaping the logic of black gay anthologies like *In the Life* and *Brother to Brother* makes improbable such a public reclamation of "sissy" as a term of endearment among black gay men. Imagine the book or essay title "Sissy to Sissy"—brilliant, but perhaps before its time. The same historical currents pressuring black gay men to opt for "brother" over "sissy" in their public rechristening of their identity also pressure black straight men to "speak their names" through the emplotment of sissified reminiscence. Thus, in Belton's *Speak My Name* volume we find prominent public intellectuals like Robin D. G. Kelley, Henry Louis Gates Jr., Houston Baker Jr., Clarence Major, and others, identifying either explicitly or implicitly with the otherwise stigmatized gender condition of the sissy-boy.

Robin Kelley's lead essay in the volume is characteristic of this trend. He meditates on how the physical attributes of his person set up a particular gender dynamic in relation both to African Americans and to whites. Describing himself as a boy whom everyone liked, he assesses the pluses and minuses of this.

> Sure, I was cool, but nobody feared me. That I'm relatively short with dimples and curly hair, speak softly in a rather medium to high-pitched voice, and have a "girl's name" doesn't help matters. And everyone knows that light skin is less threatening to white people than blue-black or midnight brown. Besides, growing up with a soft-spoken, uncharacteristically passive West Indian mother deep into East Indian religions, a mother who sometimes walked barefoot in the streets of Harlem, a mother who insisted on proper diction and never, ever, ever used a swear word, screwed me up royally. I could never curse right.[76]

Kelley observes how slight changes in his look, such as shaving his head, can disrupt this tendency to be liked—that is, to be perceived as a "nice Negro" in the eyes of whites—but in the end he embraces his own niceness as a way to resist the stereotype of the hypermasculine black man prone to violence. "Whatever the source of my ineffable lovability," he writes, "I've learned that it's not entirely a bad thing. In fact, if the rest of the world could look a little deeper, beyond the hardcore exterior—the wide bodies, the carefully constructed grimaces, the performance of terror—they would find many, many brothas much nicer and smarter than myself."[77] Kelley's aim, however, is not just to take down the gangsta stereotype that has gone wild by the early 1990s but also to uproot the larger dynamic that prohibits "niceness" in any man as unmanly: "If our society, for example, could dispense with rigid, archaic notions of appropriate masculine and feminine behavior, perhaps we might create a world that nurtures, encourages, and even rewards nice guys."[78] Like James Weldon Johnson's exploitation of the gentle manliness in the interwar period, Kelley appeals to niceness as a code that can at once safeguard black manliness from white predation while ameliorating its representation as beastly hypermasculinity in dominant discourses. The tension in Kelley's transitive sissy self-representation—a tension that characterizes the other straight sissy memoirs as well—can be glimpsed in his use of the orthographic alternative "brotha" to signal his authentic black manliness. This vernacular spelling intensifies the more general usage of the word "brother" to specify the weight that it carries as a term of manly affection among black men as a collective, and even more specifically nonelite, nonassimilated black men identified with the street, and in the 1990s with the "gangsta" culture of hip-hop. As an exclamatory inflection of "brother," *brotha* seems to reassert Kelley's masculine street cred as a straight-up black man even as he claims a progressive kinship with black women and gay men. If Beam could not effectively title his "Brother to Brother" essay "Sissy to Sissy," it would be just as unworkable to call it "Brotha to Brotha." As a homo-sissy, Beam is not asserting his sameness with Ombaka as a straight black prisoner, nor is he laying claim to the masculine prerogative that "brotha" seeks to communicate. To the extent that Kelley's use of "brotha" marks his temporal distance from the sissy-boy that he was, it also jeopardizes the bridge he seeks to build to gender inclusion with black women and nonstraight black men.

While Kelley's essay pictures a soft boy whose sensitivity saves him from the violence that has become defining for the black male boyhood narratives, Houston Baker's essay for the volume begins with an image of such violence, ignited by the eleven-year-old boy's high-pitched voice: "Then I am suddenly flattened against a limestone wall, bolts of lightning and bright stars flashing in my head. I have been hard and viciously slapped in the mouth as a thunderous voice shouts, 'Damnit! Houston, Jr.! Stop acting like a sissy!' . . . Having heard my falsetto chant, my father turned from the furnace with the quick instinct of an exorcist. He had hit me with the fury of a man seeing a ghost."[79] Baker's essay is a meditation on how his father, "Sr.," came to enact such violence on his son, and how that violence shapes his own manhood in a contrary direction from his namesake. Ironically for Baker, his father's ideal of masculine uprightness is Booker T. Washington: "Washington's manly singleness of purpose and institutional achievements were taught to my father."[80] That this "manly" version of Washington could have had such an influence on the middle-class aspiring southern men of Sr.'s generation indicates how, with time, history can normalize even a leader like Washington, who was attacked in his own time for his lack of "manly singleness of purpose." If Kelley's essay confirms the tendency of the straight sissy narrative to pivot on the influence of a mother's strong apron strings, Baker's meditation helps us to see how it can as easily pivot on the violence of a conventionally masculine father. The logical structure of both versions of paternal causation, however, leads inevitably toward the same happy closure. Despite the paternal violence, or perhaps because of it, Baker cannot "imagine 'Jr.' without a strong woman's touch." The father's hard masculinity becomes tragic: "He could never, for example, have given approving voice to the informal definition of a 'sissy' that is sisterhood. Tragically, he never envisioned a successful man's life as one measured and defined by its intimate, if always incomplete, understanding and sharing of a woman's joys, dangers, voice, and solacing touch—shaped definitively, that is to say, by sisterhood."[81] It is this tragedy of Sr. that enables the gender fulfillment of Jr.: "I am now the middle-aged father of a quite remarkable son. And at this moment I imagine that with God's grace I shall be able to live up to the standard of distinction the concluding marks of my name are meant to signify."[82]

The conventional narrative of black boy endangerment, which can be traced at least as far back as Wright's *Native Son*, invariably hinges on either an absent black father (the trope of Wright's *Black Boy* as well as *Native Son*) or a black father whose presence is violently disciplinary (Baldwin's autobiographical essays and *Go Tell It*). Just as the super-masculine killing violence of Wright's Bigger Thomas can be traced to the legacy of a father lynched in Mississippi before the family's migration to Chicago, so the sissy passive-aggression of Baldwin's John Grimes can be traced to a double legacy: the suicide of the unknown and absent biological father due to false imprisonment and torture and the violent discipline of the all-too-present stepfather. If Kelley constructs a sissy past through his body's phenotypical softness, a softness that can be hardened by changing the body's look, so Baker Jr. constructs a sissy past through a son's shielding action to his father's masculine harshness, a harshness that can be overcome by altered manhood conduct. In Baker's memoir, the black father embodies a source of jeopardy that must be surmounted by the sissy son's assumption of fatherhood itself. Unlike for the homo-sissy narrative of self-affirmation, in which the lack of procreativity marks the narrative as a sissiness that is not merely a stage of development, for the transitive sissy the capacity to procreate signals the natural fulfillment of heteronormativity. Even as Jr.'s gentle fathering signals the ongoing influence of the sissiness that has been outgrown, the status of biological father also marks the achievement of heteronormativity, however modified by a less draconian method of fathering.

It should also be noted how Baker's self-narrative emulates that of black womanists, but with a difference. In "In Search of Our Mothers' Gardens" and other works, black feminists like Alice Walker promote a maternal lineage of cross-generational womanly nurturance as an artistic legacy for recovering black women's voices and histories.[83] Baker's narrative of sissy transitivity focuses not so much on an affirming maternal lineage as on a harmful paternal lineage, against which boyhood sissiness becomes a resource for a gender breakthrough, as the sissy son matures into the heterosexual father. This narrative approach complements that of Robert Stepto's, which we examined at the start of this chapter, whereby the sissy son must learn to negotiate the emulation of his mother as a resource even though he has "never been able to say of this, 'glad to be a woman like Mama.'" While brothering homo-sissies like Beam emphasize their kinship with black feminists' maternal lineage, straight black sissies, when they appropriate that narrative, must carefully mark their unlikeness so as not to conflate a temporary boyhood conduct with an indelible effeminate character.

Other straight sissy narratives in the volume are more subtle in their approach than Baker's. Like Beam, Baker borrows the womanist confession of pain as an expression of gender trouble, but unlike Beam, he does so to illustrate the development of a confident but gentle procreative paternal legacy. The traumatic break from Sr., the hard father, also aligns Baker's narrative with black feminist stories, like Walker's *The Color Purple*, in which violent patriarchal fathers impede healthful black family and community relations. Paternal trauma, however, need not necessarily rationalize the adoption of a transitive sissy-boy conduct. Clarence Major's poignant story about his mother's tentative courting of an older white man, for instance, narrates by showing rather than explaining. We witness a sensitive, gentle relationship between a brave, lonely mother and a quiet, respectful son—a narrative whose fresh take lies in its insistent ordinariness. The kitchen-table talks between mother and son remind us—without any sense of gender or racial protest or violation—how there are millions of such gentle, nontraumatic relationships that have largely gone unrecorded in the annals of African American literature and history. What is so pleasing about the story relates to both the black boy's unremarkable softness and the black mother's unremarkable tentativeness: "I learned for the first time that she did not always know what she was doing. It struck me that she was as helpless as I sometimes felt when confronted with a math or science problem or a problem about sex and girls and growing up and life in general."[84] Like the subject of the mother-son dyad itself, the narrative approach is unapologetically tender. Its soft sensibility is designed to make us forget how black men's narratives about growing up have been manically overdetermined, at least since Richard Wright's *Native Son* and *Black Boy*, by sensational acts of emasculation, rape, trauma, and violence, including trauma resulting from harsh punishment that the black mother might inflict on the black son to, on the one hand, force his manning up and, on the other, remind him to be wary of the killing streets awaiting any black boy in America. While these examples do not exhaust the strategies used for self-narrating transitive sissiness, they do represent the range of narrative approaches at work in such memoirs.

As if the pressure from black gay men were not enough, wannabe sensitive black straight men desiring to narrate their sensitivity also had to contend with a strong, visible, prolific, influential tradition of black women's autobiography. Historically, African American autobiography was dominated by exceptional male narratives, especially the triumvirate of Frederick Douglass, Washington, and Wright, whose works generally muscled out the others. With the publication of *The Autobiography of Malcolm X* in 1965, a memoir that inspired a whole new generation of black autobiographers, especially from ex-convicts, the masculinization of the form seemed unassailable. However, especially with the rise of modern black feminism in the 1960s, African American women had established an enviable presence both as autobiographers and as autobiographical theorists—a presence that inevitably brought vexing results within a publishing economy racially rigged to create a sense of rivalry between black men and women. Black men felt pressured to distinguish their experience against women autobiographers who placed racialized gender identity front and foremost in their own narratives: from Zora Neale Hurston's *Dust Tracks on a Road* (1942), Anne Moody's *Coming of Age in Mississippi* (1968), Maya Angelou's *I Know Why the Caged Bird Sings* (1969), Nikki Giovanni's *Gemini* (1971), Gwendolyn Brooks's *Report from Part One* (1972) and *Report from Part Two* (1996), Angela Davis's *Autobiography* (1974), and Audre Lorde's *Zami* (1982) to Assata Shakur's *Assata* (1987), Deborah McDowell's *Leaving Pipe Shop* (1996), Anita Hill's *Speaking Truth to Power* (1997), and Toi Derricotte's *The Black Notebooks* (1997), in addition to numerous autobiographical essays by figures like Barbara Smith, Alice Walker, Michele Wallace, June Jordan, bell hooks, and Patricia Williams—to name only some of the most prominent writers.[85] How were straight black men to acknowledge what they were learning from their black female and lesbian sisters without reducing their own identity self-reflections to stories of apologetic embarrassment? The gender-bending strategies of the straight sissy narratives above exemplify how some black intellectuals responded to this pressure from the emergence of the black women's renaissance.

Other contemporaneous pressures call the straight black sissy into relief: the sensitive man movement, the Afrocentric agenda, the popularity of gangsta rap, and the rise of queer theory and masculinity studies in the academy. Mainstream pro-men's groups proliferated in the Reagan '80s, often fueled by an antifeminist, heteronormative agenda, including men's recovery groups, Robert Bly's mythopoetic movement, fathers' rights groups, men's rights groups, right-wing Christian groups like the Promise Keepers, and, most notoriously, the myriad statewide militias that nursed their rage and honed their guerrilla skills in the deserts, woods, prairies, and swamps all across the country. As a complement to President Reagan's own hard-crusted cowboy persona, the sensitive man proved that men could stand up to the challenges of new gender configurations while still remaining good old boys—or, more precisely, good old *white* boys. Whether manifested in the entertainment or news media, the men's movements, the new militias, or the changing usages of everyday speech, the sensitive man was assumed to be white and middle class. For, as Sally Robinson has pointed out, it was ultimately white middle-class men who were seen as most deeply wounded by the black, gay, and women's liberation movements, and accordingly it was the heteronormative white man who needed to vent against the proliferation of identity groups seeming to pin him as the villainous top dog in a narrative of others' wrongful victimization.[86]

Where was the straight black male middle-class intellectual to be placed in this volatile mix? He could, and did in some instances, claim the right to sensitive masculinity, as witnessed by the popularity of *The Cosby Show* (1984–1992) and by a spate of post–civil rights memoirs, such as Stephen L. Carter's *Reflections of an Affirmative Action Baby* (1991) and Nathan McCall's national bestseller *Makes Me Wanna Holler* (1994). Unlike sensitive white men, sensitive black men did not have the luxury of manly ambivalence, displaying sensitivity to their own victimization while simultaneously venting against the victims of their own domination. Instead, the image of black men's conduct and character was thoroughly bifurcated through mass culture: on the one side, gentle middle-class black intermediaries, rare exceptions within the race, and on the other side, barbaric poor black youth, frighteningly seductive in the violent extremity of their masculine aggression. In a sense, this is the main theme of McCall's memoir. He starts out as a sensitive boy intimidated and captivated by the other middle school boys "in the slick in-crowd": "When they were standing around in there, they constantly cuffed their crotches, as if they were clutching organs so heavy they might bust through their pants. They often fought in school and cut classes.... I learned a lot by watching them." We might consider the crotch cuffing as signaling masculine posture contrary to Beam's earrings and earcuffs or, perhaps less deliberately, Arthur Montana's sissy hairstyle. Bringing attention to the phallus, however, is an exhibitionist gesture that approximates a belligerent pose of bravado. In some contexts, a boy who does not broadcast through such a gesture might be considered "soft," inviting real boys' verbal or physical violence. McCall pictures himself as being seduced by these boys as he begins to understand that if he does not follow this script, he will remain one of the "solitary lames." "I was captivated by these guys. They seemed to have all the self-confidence I lacked. I was into honor rolls and spelling bees.... I looked all neat and boring, like my mama dressed me for school. They looked—exciting."[87] McCall's narrative traces his development away from sissy literacy—"honor rolls and spelling bees"—into the gang mentality, even though internally, emotionally, his heart rages against what he is becoming. During his first gang street fight, one in which his opponent interrupts his attempt to call a truce by punching him, McCall is alarmed by the violence in which he is engaging: "I wanted to scream, as much in fear as in pain. But I held back. *Only punks cry out. Men take their lumps*" (70; italics in original). We can see here how the confession of pain marks one as not quite man enough, and thus how in the 1990s straight sissy memoirs, making such a confession embraces a sissy disposition. Likewise, when Beam emulates black womanist practice by publicly confessing his pain, he is, in a way, simply confirming what crotch-cupping men already surmise: that he is "soft," potentially penetrable and thus cowardly, and ultimately flirting with faggotry. Despite the idea that his "frail body could never take another beating like that" (71), the fear of being labeled a punk drives the young McCall further into the violence: "It was a cardinal rule on the block that a brother couldn't let himself be beaten by three groups of people: gays, girls, and white boys" (61). Although he does not label himself a feminist or a sissy, McCall's narrative follows the pattern of the other 1990s straight black sissy memoirs in constructing his gender development from "frail" sissiness to raping gangsta to a man coming to reject the macho way, regretting the rapes against black women he has committed and, after a stint in prison, embracing the sensitive boy that he had rejected at age twelve. The 1990s narrative pattern of embracing the sissy within while retaining the claim to masculine heteronormalcy must be understood in the context of the longer black male rape narrative as treated within the tradition of African American men's narratives dating back to Wright's *Native Son*. McCall, in this sense, is responding not only to Wright and the other authors of black protest but also to black nationalists like Baraka and especially Cleaver, whose celebration of the strategy of raping black women as practice for raping white men's daughters seems particularly dissonant in relation to McCall's reclamation of manly sensitivity. Against the black nationalist tenet that black men's greatest strength as warriors is an unequivocal hardening, McCall sees this "hardening" as his greatest error: "I knew my heart was hardening. In fact, I *wanted* it to harden so I wouldn't get scared or feel weird inside when we did crazy things like that. I didn't want anybody to see me equivocate. I think some of the other guys felt the same way, but no one said anything. No one wanted to be called a chump" (62; italics in original). As he rises from convict to *Washington Post* reporter, McCall must, in effect, embrace the sissy within if he is to make it in the white mainstream. His book ultimately makes this case not only for himself but also for other black men who risk being seduced by the gangster life. He learns to use "piercing eye contact with other guys" in prison: "That helped me see my homies and the other toughs at Southampton as they were (and as I had been): streetwise, pseudo baad-asses who were really frightened boys, bluffing, trying to mask their fear of the world behind muscular frames" (207).[88] Whether or not this is a direct reference to Baldwin's *No Name in the Street*, which uses the image of eyeing other black men not as an act of rivalrous jousting but instead as a brotherly embrace (as discussed in the previous chapter), McCall's sense of a reformed manliness self-confident enough to embrace sensitivity captures perfectly the strong influence of Baldwin on the 1990s straight black sissy trend, while also reminding us of James Weldon Johnson's early twentieth-century narratives of black gentle manliness as a resource against rampant racial violence. Significantly, however, for McCall the emphasis has shifted from white supremacist violence to the notion of "black-on-black" violence, a term that emerged in the 1980s to justify the punishing violence of the mass incarceration state.

Like McCall, during the Reagan period Afrocentrists, black nationalists, Nation of Islam Muslims, and increasingly members of the respectable black middle class expressed alarm not so much over the hard-edged pose of warring manhood as over its violently destructive racial effects in word, image, and deed. In a muted dialogue with the predominantly white men's movements, these black movements promised an all-black cure in the return to traditional uber-Africanized manhood rites—male role modeling, initiation ceremonies, black boys' clubs, sex-segregated schooling, competitive sports, and job interview training, as if there were any jobs to be had. In other words, for many African Americans, the answer was not to embrace the sissy within but instead to shore up and discipline the macho man within as a natural resource. The straight sissy intellectuals, rejecting the idea that masculine armature can serve progressive sociopolitical ends, aim to counter this celebration of traditional manhood rituals as a solution to what the Afrocentrists label the threat of black male genocide.

As Mark Anthony Neal has argued, the 1990s exposed a growing fissure between what Du Bois had labeled "the Talented Tenth" and the so-called hip-hop thug. Neal identifies "a crisis of black masculinity" occurring in the decade, "not only in the scapegoated, so-called hip-hop generation, but in the legions of well-adjusted, middle-classed, educated, heterosexual black men."[89] The decade's straight black sissy intellectuals, among whom Neal himself could be included, rather than upping their "investment in a powerful American-style patriarchy ... and its offspring in homophobia, sexism, and misogyny," instead exploit their self-styled straight sissiness to negotiate that crisis and to disrupt that patriarchy.[90] Rather than representing themselves as dangerous boys prone to wilding and in need of the heavy hand of *external* discipline, the straight sissies narrate stories of gentle boys, if anything compulsively *self*-disciplined in their erotic and social relations. While we must keep foremost in our minds the resonance between Washington's compulsive menial labor and the compulsive self-disciplining evident in these sissified postfeminist, postgay, post–civil rights narratives, we must also attend to the specific affects of gender self-embarrassment at work in these latter-day narratives as parables of integrated manhood sensibility. At the heart of the straight black sissy's tutelage is not only an adoring intimacy with the black feminine but also an ambivalent intimacy with white culture at all of its levels, for these men constitute the first generation to come of age under affirmative action's mandate to desegregate these historically white, elite institutions. Whether journalists, lawyers, or academics, they have had to negotiate a way to the top through whiteness itself.

Destined to become the tokens and spokesmen allegorizing the success of racial integration—that is, destined to become, in the anachronistic language of the Bookerite era, "the manhood of the race"—these straight black sissies instead find themselves invariably called on to *mis*represent black manhood. As journalists, they are the ones called on to write articles for predominantly white newspaper audiences on the deadly dangers of ordinary black maleness.[91] As lawyers, they are called on to defend or to prosecute young black "offenders" whose presumed numerous out-of-control bodies are seen as jamming the gears of colorblind justice. As academics, they are called on to represent an exceptional voice of civilized reason against the hollering insensitivities of the ravenous sexism, raw homophobia, and crass commercialism projected onto their hip-hop foster sons. If they are not to be overwhelmed by that mass of black male predators hovering around the gates of their lily-white institutions, they must prove that they can sympathize with the outrageousness of queer activism, that they can master the racially coy sophistications of queer theory, that they can shadowbox with the proponents of whiteness studies (without psychically harming their already wounded white male colleagues), and that they can fraternize with the sensitive white men leading masculinity studies.

Because both queer theory and masculinity studies early on had some difficulty figuring out how to integrate black manhood into their inquiries, these black male intellectuals, especially in academe, have been asked to stand in for the black male mass, explaining and thus moderating the putatively primitive sexism and homophobia of the average straight black man. In Harry Brod's groundbreaking men's studies anthology *The Making of Masculinities* (1987), for instance, the token essay addressing black manhood is provided by Clyde W. Franklin's sociological study titled, aptly, "Surviving the Institutional Decimation of Black Males." As important as Franklin's work is, its token inclusion has the highly ironic effect of reducing black masculinity studies itself to "institutional decimation."[92] Similarly, in the groundbreaking anthology of literary masculinity studies, Joseph Boone and Michael Cadden's *Engendering Men* (1990), black masculinity is represented by Marcellus Blount's essay "Caged Birds: Race and

Gender in the Sonnet," a crucial intervention but nonetheless encaging a singular black male voice in the midst of a new field of study as whitened as the ancient European sonnet.[93] Early queer theory has been even more curious in its unconscious policing of race in relation to queerness. Diana Fuss's foundational anthology *Inside/Out: Lesbian Theories, Gay Theories* (1991) leaves little room for race theory to intervene on that slash marking the dis/juncture of inside and out, marking the coalition between (white) lesbian and (white) gay theories.[94] Michael Warner's important anthology *Fear of a Queer Planet* (1993), for instance, doubles our racial pleasure in a revealing way: we have the queer Phil Harper writing fiercely on the relations among black gay silence, straight black homophobia, and the sexual policing mechanism of a racialized dominant media; next to him, literally, as Harper's essay succeeds Gates's in the volume, we have straight man Gates sensitively writing, in an essay tellingly titled "The Black Man's Burden," on the queer film *Looking for Langston*.[95] Gates, the sensitive black man, is here already occupying structurally the place of the straight black sissy—intimate enough with black homosexuality to call its name for (white) queer theory but still laboring under the burden of prototypical (that is, non-gay) black manhood. Thus, these early masculinity and queer studies anthologies not only "decimated" black men's diverse socioeconomic realities; they also, ironically, thinned black men's gender diversity to the point that even the straight/gay binary becomes exotically rarefied.

Gates plays a pivotal role as the most prominent public face of the straight black sissy: his presence across several of these volumes places him as perhaps the leading figure of this phenomenon. As though there were no articulate black gay sissies to speak for themselves, he becomes in such volumes a metonymic spokesman, one whose gentle manliness gives him authority to speak on behalf of homo-sissies whose verbal "sashaying" may not be respectable enough to include them within these public-facing academic venues. The formal and structural attributes of the straight sissy narrative can be examined further through a focus on his memoir *Colored People* (1994). It should come as no surprise that the sissy-boy discovers his gender dissonance through his relation to the black feminine, particularly the black mother, in the domestic spaces of household duties and homey feelings. We have already seen this with Stepto's eulogy for the now-long-gone kitchen where he labored side by side with the women, as well in Clarence Major's touching reminiscence of the kitchen-table talks he had with his mother. Unlike Washington's unqualified affirmation of his fitness for women's domestic labor, for the late twentieth-century straight sissy this intimacy is paradoxically mediated through distinct gender self-alienation. For Stepto, this comes in the wistful final sentence: "But of course, I've never been able to say of this, 'glad to be a woman like Mama.'" The "but of course" that serves as preamble to the utterance of spoiled likeness comes too forcefully to explain the difference between the mother and her sissy son. Why can't a son—straight, sissy, gay, or otherwise—be "like" Mama? The answer is fatefully tautological: because the mother is a woman. Even if the sissy-boy is a dead likeness of his mother—in looks, manner, or behavior—he cannot be a woman, equated here with the kitchen and its domestic chores, even if he is already too much like one. As examined in earlier figures—for instance, Washington's relationship to his slave mother and his Yankee schoolmarms and wives, James Weldon Johnson's to his mother and white mammy, the ex-colored man's to his passing mother, Baldwin's to his mother and the woman pastor, and John Grimes's to his mother and the white principal—the mother-son dyad is frequently thought to structure the feeling, temperament, posture, and manner of the sissy-boy. As Susan Fraiman points out about Gates's treatment of the boy protagonist in *Colored People*, "Countering stereotypes of the hypermasculine and pathological black male, Gates understandably finds an effective antidote in the type of the studious and approval-seeking mama's boy."[96] I certainly agree, but I would suggest that Gates's self-representation goes even further, forging an intentionally self-embarrassing gender identity that turns the mama's boy into a full-fledged sissy, even to the extent of flirting with the flaunting figure of the swish, whose embarrassing embodiment is kept carefully at bay. Even as these straight sissies flirt with being at home in the kitchen, they are cautious not to go as far as Baldwin at the outset of *No Name in the Street*, where, as we saw in the previous chapter, he binds his own status and role in the family to being a second mother, a nursemaid to his younger siblings.

Even so, there is a sense in which the sissy-boy displaces the dutiful black daughter in these straight sissy narratives, as young Stepto or young Major makes himself at home in that kitchen, identified by black feminists as a quintessential womanist space.[97] Gates achieves the same effect of feminine intimacy framed by gender dissonance when he writes, "I never knew what the women said about the men, but I know they said a lot. I was always disappointed when the women, talking and laughing in the kitchen, would stop when I came within earshot and shift to safer subjects."[98] As the putative object of their talk, Gates can at best eavesdrop on women's kitchen gossip. Even so, this proximity defines not so much a limit as a threshold specially beckoning for him. "Yet Mama's friends, the colored ladies," Gates writes, "seemed to like my company, and I loved theirs."[99] He sites himself in that liminal position of the sissy-boy, not only between feminine and masculine but also occupying a marginal space within the masculine, as he, a male, becomes an unwilling object of the talk and laughter that he overhears. His disidentification is marked by his desire to be among them even as he is objectified by them due to his anatomy.

Ordinarily, we think of the sissy's identity as being marked on or in the body, in the manner, the speech, the bearing, a certain unboyish reserve trapped in a boy's body, a reserve that simplistically tends to be equated with effeminacy. This presumption fits neatly our tendency to conflate the sissy with an incipient homoerotic passion buried within a too-tender male anatomy. The straight male autobiographer, however, must undo this conflation, emphasizing the boy's out-of-place body over the boy's out-of-gender person. For Gates, his sissiness is *not* something erratic within his body, but instead that his body gravitates to improper gender spaces. Like the incipiently homosexual sissy, the straight sissy's body is a site of poignant self-discipline as overcompensation for a perceived masculine lack, often related to sports and to a poignant self-conscious awkwardness in relation to courting, and bedding, girls. The very existence of the *straight* sissy reminds us that what the sissy represses within his body is not merely the swish, his converse, but also the girl that he is and is not. Although the straight sissy would never dream of becoming a swish, his dreams of girlishness barred, deferred, interrupted, distempered, haunt his every move.

One formal device of these narratives entails a sexual blockage related to a boy's awkwardness with girls—a figuration of black boyhood aimed at demythologizing the familiar image of the cool black boy who naturally knows how to sex girls. The sissy is slow at sex because he is fast at books. As mentioned in previous chapters, the sissy's studiousness almost seems to cause his sexual timidity, just as his precocious verbal mastery seems to be brought about as a compensating corrective to a lack of masculine physical dexterity. As his fondness for words affiliates him with girlishness in dominant white culture, paradoxically it more ambiguously identifies him, on the one hand, with the mannishness of fast-talking boys, who are often admired in African American culture (as in the Dozens and rapping), and, on the other hand, with the verbal repartee of witticism-snapping swishing faggots, whose oratorical smarts have traditionally been also admired in African American communities, if with a bit of social embarrassment. "From the first day of first grade," Gates says, "I was marked out to excel. . . . I was quiet, I was smart, I had a good memory, I already knew how to read and write, and I was blessed with the belief that I could learn anything."[100] The sissy-boy's sexual timidity is not a bodily malady, as it is for the respectable church sissy, who must contort his body to block desire for inappropriately male objects. Rather, it is an intellectual kink, as if his girlish thoughts cannot keep pace with his boy's mannish body. "Don't get me wrong: I had my passions and flings of the imagination early on," Gates writes.[101] This unease with seducing actual girls, as opposed to imaginary ones, could easily be mistaken for a homosexual inclination, and Gates, like the other straight black sissies, must risk this charge, must make himself vulnerable to it in order to reap the benefits of black male sensitivity. As discussed in chapter 1, imaginativeness itself, when seemingly hyperbolic or directed at the wrong pursuits, can spark suspicion about a boy's gender conformity, or lack thereof.

In Michael Awkward's poignant 1999 memoir *Scenes of Instruction*, for example, he develops this theme of sexual belatedness: "Because I didn't fully understand the ritual of courting, didn't have the right psychic tools or a sufficient sense of self-confidence to insert myself successfully in the game, I was developmentally behind my siblings, all of whom were involved in relationships. On occasion, I'd listen, with more than a little self-protective amusement, to their contributions to inane conversations with people with whom they were involved or in whom they were interested."[102] This sexual hesitation can easily be mistaken for incipient homosexuality in onlookers, especially when there are other clues of sissiness at stake. It is, significantly, the narrator's older sister who insists, against the evidence of his own internal desire, that he must be gay to behave in such a manner.

> My older sister grabbed a pencil and a piece of paper, smiled, and wrote something that she hid from me with her left forearm. When she was finished, she stared at me intently, a slightly worried and embarrassed look on her face, and told me she'd written a question for which she wanted an answer. In neat swirls, she'd asked, "Michael, are you a homosexual?"
>
> I was stunned by the question and unsure of its motivation. Did I look, act, sound, walk gay? Did she think I desired boys or was unduly attracted to feminine accoutrements and behaviors? Certainly, I wasn't like my male classmate who talked and walked like a girl, or the tough transvestite from Thirteenth Street who wore tighter pants and more makeup than any of the girls in the school. Or Bobby, the swishy white man whom my mother's friend Aunt Naomi had married.[103]

Michael's response to his sister's simple yes/no binary question indicates just how complicated the relationship between gender conduct and sexual orientation is. The question spawns a catalogue of speculative behaviors and known cases against which he identifies, from the local "tough transvestite" to the "swishy white man" married to his mother's friend. For Michael, the answer could be a definitive, categorical no, but instead he engages his sister in a catechism of questions to eliminate the above speculations and cases. In response to the question "'Cause I don't have a girlfriend?'" he finally gets a "Yeah." From the range of potential behaviors—from "Because I don't go around holding my dick" to "'Cause my voice ain't quite changed yet"—that could have led Carol to speculate on her brother's sexuality, the lack of a girlfriend seems both the most logical and yet the least compelling. That is, one could behave in every other way in accord with masculine protocols and still be suspect if one has not yet begun to date. So little evidence could lead to so much suspicion. Even after Michael insists that he is not gay, pointing out that he has discussed with Carol some girls that he's attracted to, Carol is still unsure: "'Michael, you sure you're not a faggot? I'd still love you and all.'" The conversation ends with Michael getting up from the table and going into his bedroom, slamming the door behind him. What is it that places the boy Michael on the sissy line of demarcation? From the inside, it is difficult for Michael to know. Rather than causing an expected panic in Michael, the conversation sends him to his mother's *True Romance* magazines. Ironically, one of the behaviors that might have unconsciously alerted Carol to her brother's sissiness—his introspective studiousness—also guides his response. From the magazines, he comes to a conclusion: "There were two kinds of men in these formulaic stories: those who beat, raped, and loved and left, and were in other ways downright nasty to women, and those who rode in on the equivalent of white horses after the women had been mistreated." Michael understands, though, that his sister's suspicions are fueled by what he calls "my just-my-imagination posture." "My closed-door dreaming had to be replaced or at the very least supplemented by real-life, flesh-and-bones drama."[104] Imagination, dreaminess, and being introspective are themselves cause for speculation. As long as his character or conduct seems not to fit the gender norms, however subtly, the only proof that he is not "fronting," as his sister calls his talk about girls, will be to begin having sex with girls. And for many straight sissy-boys, even the actual act of heterosexual sex may not be enough to dispel the cycle of innuendo, suspicion, rumor, and scandal that we see swirling around gender-nonconforming men—a cycle only intensified in the age of social media, as the general populace has become more scrutinizing of gender behavior in the post–gay rights era.

Just as heterosexual sex may not be enough proof for a gender-nonconforming boy, so same-gender intimacy of an erotic kind should not be enough to pivot the straight sissy into homosexuality. In *Colored People* Gates speaks unflinchingly of boyish rubbing with a male peer. "We didn't go in for kissing, but rubbing felt pretty good," Gates writes.[105] When the other boy stops playing this game with "no explanation," Gates also aborts *our* interest in his same-gender erotic play, with no explanation. This is a matter of backgrounding the queer to create the straight sissy, rather than the more familiar practice of repressing the queer out of shame to construct the hypermasculine straight male. Just as the straight sissy is so self-disciplined that he can defer sexual contact with girls without panicking over an incipient homosexuality, so he is so intimately engaged with his own erotic imagination that he can come in contact with queerness without exploding into violence. This clearly marks him off not only from the mass-media image of ranting homophobic hip-hoppers in the contemporaneous moment but also from the prototypical black man of the Jim Crow era, whose identity is overdetermined by an undisciplined raping appetite in dominant culture but is hedged in by a timid fearfulness within Gates's and other straight sissy-boy narratives. The straight sissy's clumsiness at seduction, hardly a flattering self-portrait, is ironically more than compensated for by an impossibility of masculine sexual violence, whether against females, other sissies, or faggots.

This anatomy of the straight sissy in 1990s black male autobiography goes only so far if we do not recognize the more profound *racial* work being done *historically* by a claim to gentle masculinity. Gates does not represent himself as racially nonviolent in the memoir. The narrative thrusts toward his leadership of a small coterie of teenagers who manfully invade the meanest "hillbilly" hangout with the intention of integrating it by force or shutting it down.[106] Likewise, Gates pictures his own aggression against a disrespectful racist elder, when his father and his friends hold their tongues in fear.[107] These memoirists are exploiting the sissy demeanor with an ambidextrous effect, for it does double duty in many ways, only two of which I'll mention here. The sissy demeanor is a shield that the integrationist boy takes with him into brutal white institutions intent on his failure. As he crosses the color line, he does so gingerly yet firmly, being so attuned to interracial erotic imaginings that he can, in Gates's case, become the first black boy to openly date a white girl in his hometown. This gentle demeanor enables his intermediating role as deft, sensitive integrationist without disabling the fulfillment of an obligation to manfully represent the heterosexual cream of the race. Like Washington in *Up from Slavery* assuring the white male rulers that he can be trusted with their women, so the straight black sissy at the end of the century can be trusted around the white women who are entering these elite institutions in significant numbers along with him. As Washington at the outset of the century fashioned a hygienic manliness to shore up Jim Crow social separation even as he worked intimately with the white establishment, so these 1990s straight black sissies revise black manhood for the peculiar circumstances they face as the first generation of affirmative action desegregation.

In this regard, the post–civil rights straight sissy demeanor enables a particular kind of racial retrospect across the historical divide between Jim Crow and integration. That gentle, sissified boy embodies the autobiographer's nostalgic relation to a different, gentler era, *before* the advent of rapping gangstas dominated the mainstream media, before womanists were so decisive in their demands, before the church sissy who sexes other men behind closet doors became the black gay brother demanding to be heard. The sissy-boy communicates the tenderness of colored community in that previous era, a patina so gentle that it has the power to dissipate the harshest brutalities, racial and sexual, of Jim Crow everyday life. We can see in the cover designs of these books how the figure of the manchild intermediates between the readers' post–civil rights present and a gentle past threatened with psychic extinction. Like the intentionally archaic title itself, *Colored People*, the cover for the 1995 Vintage paperback edition nostalgically references that time ostensibly now gone—a time of segregated schools, colored baseball teams, Sunday school in simple wooden churches built during Reconstruction, and ordinary Negroes making exceptional gains with few resources (figure 5.2). Like an old photograph that almost disintegrates when touched, the sissy-boy also communicates the ephemerality of that past moment, soon to be desegregated out of existence, just as the sissy inevitably must pass on to a sensitively mature heterosexual manhood as a black male leader within elite white institutions.

If the sissy's person performs this gentle intermediating role marking the violent rupture between Jim Crow and post–civil rights integration, how can we understand the self-representation of the sissy-boy's material body in these

5.2 Front cover of 1995 Vintage paperback edition of Henry Louis Gates Jr.'s *Colored People: A Memoir*. Cover design by Susan Mitchell. Cover photograph (silhouette) by Jerry Bauer. Image courtesy of Random House Books.

narratives? I have suggested that unlike the swish, whose identity is flaunted visually across the body as an out-of-gender conduct, the sissy compulsively polices his body's girlish awkwardness into a compensating verbal mastery. It makes sense, then, that the straight sissy-boy would emphasize narrative emplotment as a nostalgic retrospect captured in the freeze-frame of a boyhood idyll. In a photograph on the cover of Awkward's *Scenes of Instruction*, however, the material representation of the sissy's person haunts the narrative of verbal overcompensation (figure 5.3).

The photograph, embedded on the cover of the book, provides visual markers for beginning to materialize the straight sissy anatomy at the same time that it enables us to theorize the straight sissy's embarrassment in relation to the church sissy's shame and swish's flaunting defiance. The little black boy, who has just won the George Washington medal for scoring the highest in his class on a standardized test, sits crying uncontrollably as two of his white male classmates frame him literally and symbolically. This pivotal incident of integrationist success, the

5.3 Front dust jacket of Michael Awkward's *Scenes of Instruction: A Memoir.*

winning of the medal, hinges on various forms of gender embarrassment, signaled visually by Michael's sissy tears, and indicated in the text by inappropriate shouts of pride uttered by Michael's drunken mother when the winner of the award is announced. This embodied embarrassment—not only toward the mother but also toward the boy's own person as he calls himself a "bitch" for weeping so—reminds us to what extent, despite the efforts of feminist autobiographical theorists, both gender studies and queer theory have yet to probe the material infrastructure that shapes self-narrations of compromised gender conduct and character.[108] The camera does fleetingly what the autobiographer can never do: observe himself empirically so that he can mesh the way he feels "inside" with the way he conjectures that others view him from the "outside." The dilemma of sissy embarrassment is especially revealing for this theoretical problem, for the sissy's tears might signal to onlookers a male out of his proper gender place, but for the weeping male subject, the tears express not only a radical disjuncture from his own body but also a disoriented subjectivity whose narration can be plotted coherently only once there is a vehicle—in this case, the vehicle of the sissy-boy—that can rejoin subjectivity back to the body's experience. Because the straight sissy comes to understand himself as such only in narrative retrospect as he takes a measure of comfort in his gentle manliness, his emotional register as a boy is one of embarrassment, a desire to hide within his imagination or in a book. As we saw with Baldwin and his semiautobiographical character John Grimes, the church sissy is plagued with a shame he cannot name. He intuits that his gender performance estranges him from authorities, his peers, his religion, and the world at large, and his response is to constrict his person, his conduct, and his personality, to repress any hint of excess that might expose him further to mockery or violence. If he is lucky to discover ways to sublimate that intense sensitivity into socially productive talents on behalf of the family, the church, and the race, as he often does, this does not necessarily eliminate the shame, but at least it somewhat compensates for the profundity of his estrangement. He can use his sensitivity, caretaking, studiousness, and imagination as insurgent resources to garner a respectability that befits the intensity of his inner life. Whether gay or straight, or swish and churchified, the sissy cannot help but command attention, but it is how he manages that estranging regard—and the material and social resources available to him in any particular historical moment—that determines where on the spectrum of gender nonconformity he will find himself.

In dominant early twenty-first-century culture, the sissy is normally connected with the stigma of gender dysfunction and with the prescience of an improper sexual attraction. We see something quite different at work in the straight black sissy minitrend of the later 1990s, where sissified introspection and retrospection emerge as an empowering vehicle for reclaiming masculine respectability through intentional self-embarrassment—a strategy clearly resonant with Baldwin's sissy persona in *No Name in the Street*. Ironically, for these straight black men, the sissy temperament serves as a cultural resource for interracial intermediation and cross-gender accommodation in relation to white institutions while also intensifying the historical bonds of racial community across gender, sexual, and generational differences. Although the straight sissy narrative enacts a specific cultural dynamic in the 1990s, historically the sissified temperament has been a traditional resource for black straight men for generations, and most especially as a technique of autobiography. It is only in the 1990s, however, with its post–civil rights, postfeminist, post–gay liberation profiling panic, that the straight sissy proclaims himself as such. How do you spot a sissy when he's a straight black man? The point is, you cannot, unless he names himself and, in doing so, attempts to punk the demons that menace black male identity as at once endangered and endangering for us all.

6

Gay but Not Sissy

Race and the Queering of the Professional Athlete

> Homosexuality in this setting is considered such a taboo the coaches and players not only feel free but obligated to joke about it. To be homosexual is to be effeminate, like a girl. . . . On one level they would insist on the complete absence of homosexuality among them. On another they are confirming its presence—in their minds, at least—by endless banter and jokes about it.
> —DAVID KOPAY WITH PERRY DEANE YOUNG, *The David Kopay Story: An Extraordinary Self-Revelation*

> The reflexive connection between homophobia and athletics had been hard-wired into me since I stepped onto the football field at the age of eight.
> —GLENN BURKE WITH ERIK SHERMAN, *Out at Home: The Glenn Burke Story*

The straight black sissy-flirtation trend that emerged among a handful of black public intellectuals during the 1990s indicates one attempt to reform not only the construct of black leadership but also the construct of black manliness more generally in the wake of Black Power, the feminist movement, the gay rights movement, and gangsta rap. While high-profile black academics hailing largely from historically white institutions certainly captured a slice of the public imagination, by no means could we say that the idea of a straight black sissy dominated public discourse during the 1990s and 2000s. Beyond black American intellectuals, however, there was a commensurate discourse forming to describe an ostensibly new gender conduct signaling a breakdown between straight masculinity and homosexuality as sissiness incarnate. One year before Don Belton's *Speak My Name* volume, which sparked the straight black sissy discourse, British journalist Mark Simpson coined the term "metrosexual" in a 1994 essay to describe a phenomenon that we might understand to be analogous to the straight black sissy trend. In "Here Come the Mirror Men" and other essays, Simpson observed that some middle-class heterosexual men in international metropolitan centers were deliberately blurring the line between sexual straightness and the homosexual "lifestyle." Willing to adopt social behaviors, especially those related to fashion and gender self-presentation, these heterosexual men eagerly consume attire, cosmetics, and artistic tastes long identified with gay men. Seemingly no longer feeling that their normative sexuality is jeopardized by a public association with queerness, these men, according to Simpson, cultivate an air of avant-garde sophistication, even going so far as to embrace their own attractiveness to gay men. In a 2002 *Salon* essay titled "Meet the Metrosexual," Simpson opens with a description of the British footballer David Beckham, who "posed for a glossy gay magazine" just before the World Cup:

> You see, "Becks" is almost as famous for wearing sarongs and pink nail polish and panties belonging to his wife . . . , having a different, tricky haircut every week and posing naked and oiled up on the cover of *Esquire*, as he is for his impressive ball skills. He may or may not be the best footballer in the world, but he's definitely an international-standard narcissist, what would once have been called, in the Anglo world at least, "a sissy." Hence in that World Cup game against Brazil that kicked England out of the tournament, Becks was the only English player not to be upstaged aesthetically as well as athletically by the Latins.[1]

Alluding to the long-standing identification of male homosexuality with narcissism (discussed below) and collapsing sissiness and homosexuality, Simpson's treatment of Beckham addresses the seeming contradiction between straightness and sissiness, citing an interview in which Beckham confirms his heterosexuality while also admitting that "he's quite happy to be a gay icon" because "he likes to be admired . . . , and doesn't care whether the admiring is done by women or by men."[2] While Beckham's boast unwittingly mirrors Hall Montana's response to the drinking buddies with whom he has sex while in Korea, the affect and effect are quite different. Hall's heterosexual self-regard becomes increasingly introspective and transformed by his relationship with his queer brother. Being a "gay icon"—that is, an idealized idol of masculine attractiveness for gay men—installs a sturdy window between gay and straight even as it celebrates gay men's desire to gaze at the idol through that segregating window. Simpson at the same time addresses the paradox of so skillful an athlete posing as an aesthete, as though a concern with fashion and physical appearance intrinsically contradicts fit athleticism. Although in some ways comparable to the straight black sissy trend, Simpson's notion of the metrosexual, which proliferated across global media during the 1990s and 2000s and got reductively televised in the Bravo series *Queer Eye for the Straight Guy* (2003–2007), was figured through the racial presumptions of white maleness. This is evident in the various exemplars of metrosexuality referenced in Simpson's *Salon* article, including, most revealingly, his inclusion of the rapper Eminem, who hates "'faggot' boy bands" but nonetheless, "like Beckham[,] can't resist a big fat shiny lens." In other words, Eminem, "who loves to pose half-naked (and drag it up in his videos), and also wears his children as accessories, is clearly and alarmingly metrosexual himself."[3] Detaching the global popularity of rap music from its roots in black American and Afro-Caribbean cultures, Simpson takes Eminem as the epitome of rap style, influenced by queer "narcissism," whitewashing not only rap but also the metrosexual when he writes: "We're all looking at him and he's meeting our gaze with his pretty, hooded baby-blue eyes."[4] That Simpson excludes men of African descent from this global metrosexuality is not surprising, given the racial bias in public discourse of the 1990s and 2000s, wherein gay male identity itself is equated with white male affluence and influence. No doubt ignorant of how African diasporic men have long been associated with fashion forwardness, as Monica L. Miller has brilliantly documented in *Slaves to Fashion*, Simpson cannot see the curious interrelationship between hip-hop style, racialized masculinity, queer fashion, and athletic prowess. Despite these comparable trends whereby straight men publicly identify with sissiness, another more visible and longer-lasting phenomenon emerged in this period: the attempt to segregate gay identity from the stigmatizing stereotypes of sissiness, including effeminacy, weakness, cowardliness, narcissism, and unproductivity, and the role that race plays in this distancing effort. Ironically, as Simpson sought to figure a breakdown between the straight and the homo-sissy through the athletic icon of David Beckham, openly gay athletes were seeking to establish the legitimacy of their own professional sportsmanship through a double move of, on the one hand, piggybacking on the racial desegregation movement while, on the other, distancing themselves (and their open homosexuality) from the sissy.

 The TV show mentioned above, *Queer Eye for the Straight Guy*, is especially instructive for how race, queerness, sport, and fashion concatenate in this period. The cable TV show, like Simpson, erases the oversized role that African American culture plays in determining what is hip, cool, and fashionable through a cast of five white gay men, each focusing on a different aspect of fashion, as they give ostensibly straight men fashion makeovers.[5] Notably, although the cast is all white, some of the men they refashion are African American, disregarding the ways in which black men have a long history of fashion-forwardness that does not conform to white heteronormative, or indeed white gay, assumptions about what is gender-appropriate. The show is a shining example of the period's notion that open gayness equates with a particular display of middle-class metropolitan whiteness. The erasure of black hipness from the show is doubly ironic, given that the crew is self-dubbed the "Fab Five," appropriating the name given to the five black recruits on the 1991 University of Michigan basketball team—thus ghettoizing black male fabulousness within sport in order to claim fashion fabulousness as the exclusive preserve of white queer men. It should also be noted that the original Fab Five basketballers were seen as "bad boys"—sometimes characterized as thuggish—for their "urban" (that is, black cultural) style of play and attire, on and off the court. During this period, big sports franchises like the National Basketball Association (NBA) and National Football League (NFL) performed public hand-wringing over how professional athletes dress, fostering new rules aimed at seeking to distance their athletes, on and off the field, from the highly coveted fashion choices being fomented by African American male "gangsta" rappers. Typecast as overly or thuggishly masculine, these styles, heavily influenced by the growing popularity among young black men for the dress of mass-incarcerated black men, were seen to represent an assault against good sportsmanship, as both the NBA and NFL implied that what these men wore off the court or field of play would encourage thuggishness within the games themselves. Michigan's Fab Five embodied the epitome of this hand-wringing, as sports commentators and fans excoriated their "urban" or "ghetto" style of play even as these young men from cities like Detroit were hailed as some of the most talented ballers to set foot on a college court.

Thus, *Queer Eye*'s blatant appropriation of the "Fab Five" name illustrates the crass way in which dominant media insisted on a polar gender dynamic in which black men should be stigmatized as straightly "hypermasculine" as black bucks while white maleness is granted a more adaptable, and thus progressive, image in response to white gay men's demands for homonormalizing inclusion into dominant white media and thus the white supremacist status quo. This false polarization of rough black athleticism versus a sophisticated, and thus sissified, white male fashion aesthetic has the effect of erasing not only black men's disproportionate impact on fashion but also the inextricability between black men's sportsmanship and their close attention to sophisticated fashion, going a century back to the dapper attire of heavyweight champ Jack Johnson. As Geoffrey C. Ward observes, quoting a contemporaneous newspaper report, Johnson was obsessive about his attire: "One newspaper would report, Johnson had twenty-one 'tasty' suits in his hotel-room closet, and changed clothes twice a day with the help of a maid whose only duty was to keep his clothes at all times 'ready for occupancy.' When it came to fashion, the paper continued, 'Beau Brummel might have been a preliminary but Jack Johnson is a main event.'"[6] This idea of fashion-forwardness as integral to black sportsmen continues with Muhammad Ali at midcentury, to today's black sportsmen who, like successful rappers, have made booming sideline retail businesses from selling fashionable attire, including Michael Jordan (one of the pioneers in the field), Dwyane Wade, Stephen Curry, LeBron James, Lonzo Ball, Russell Westbrook, and David Beckham.[7]

That Simpson spotlights a white English football star and a white American rapper as two of the most prominent exemplars of metrosexuality confirms the ways in which racialized masculinity in the mass-media era has been arbitrated by two poles of the entertainment industry, team sports and mass-market music. For Simpson, Beckham as global athlete manifests (white) masculinity gone awry by being embroiled in a metrosexual aesthetic, given how the uniform of white masculinism has for so long been equated with a violent rejection of the "flaming" attires and manners seen as flowing from a narcissistic sissy obsession with physical appearance. As gangsta rap begins to dominate musical tastes at the turn into the twenty-first century, the association of black music with misogyny and homophobia counters its long history of queer practices, from the sissy-man and bulldagger blues of the early twentieth century to disco in the late twentieth—a history that rap music itself cannot fully escape. Against Simpson's figuring of Eminem as a metrosexual, the reigning image of the musical artist seems to harden in the 1990s—a notion that seems to undercut the advocacy of straight sissiness among some prominent black male intellectuals. Eminem's self-professed contempt for "'faggot' boy bands" was certainly not a singular or exceptional attitude among the most popular rappers of the era, even if, as Mark Anthony Neal has suggested, this generalization of hip-hop covers over a number of complexities.[8] As we shall see, the usage of the epithet "faggot" itself in this period is also shifting to index any man who is "soft" or a "punk" rather than merely or solely one who is attracted to the same gender. If straight black sissy discourse emerges, in part, in response to the masculinist bravura of gangsta rap in an attempt to provide a respectable public image of black men responsive and accountable to the concerns of black feminists and black gay brothers, it is also the case that hip-hop culture itself must be seen as both influenced by and a reaction against the 1970s disco culture, in which black gay men and their beloved black female divas played a signal role.[9] It is easy to forget, as Simpson does, the ways in which black men, straight and otherwise, for generations have sported fashions that in dominant white supremacist culture would be seen as queer—whether the zoot suits of the 1940s, the gender-bending of 1950s rock-and-roll performers like Little Richard, the loudly colored attire of male soul and funk music groups, or the heavy jewelry of hip-hoppers. In his account of becoming a part of the "down-low subculture" of hip-hop, Terrance Dean captures the ways in which this musical culture's entanglement with homosexuality is coded through overcompensatory macho: "So when rappers rhyme about killing the faggot, or treating a man like a bitch, or calling one another faggot-ass niggas, it's an insult to a man's ego. It's a threat to his masculinity. No man wants to be seen as soft, a punk, or a sissy."[10] He further reveals to what extent the vaunted sissiphobia of hip-hop culture deliberately covers its total dependence on homo-sissies: "I began to see how gay men were in all capacities of the entertainment game. If an artist needed to start their own clothing line, we were in the mix. If they wanted to get in television and films, we made it happen. If a singer needed songs, we wrote them. If an artist needed beats, we produced them. If an artist needed a publishing deal, we made it happen."[11] Perhaps the overidentification of gangsta rap with misogyny and homophobia constitutes not only a certain defensiveness familiar in masculinist performance as indicated by Kelley, Collins, and Cheney but also, more particularly, a self-awareness about how the musical idiom is impossibly entangled in the gender and sexual queerness of blackness itself in relation to the ideal of white heteronormative patriarchy.

Just as the opposition between gangsta rap and sissiness is more porous than is usually assumed, so the divide between athleticism and fashion consciousness may not be as sharp for African American pro athletes, even when the sociopolitical demand for masculine respectability is intensified due to these athletes' unusual obligation of racial leadership and the accompanying exorbitant media scrutiny of their gender and sexual conduct. From the successes of Jesse Owens and Joe Louis in the 1930s, to Jackie Robinson and Satchel Paige in the 1940s and '50s, to Muhammad Ali, Bill Russell, and Jim Brown in the 1960s, to Arthur Ashe and Kareem Abdul-Jabbar in the 1970s, to Earvin "Magic" Johnson in the 1980s and '90s, to Colin Kaepernick and LeBron James in the 2000s and beyond, the black professional athlete has come to embody not only extraordinary sportsmanship in the ring and on the court or field but also the public face of fit black manhood outside these sports venues. Building on a long tradition of sports activism, these professional jocks have experienced an extraordinary burden of playing while black and at the same time acting as racial leaders and spokesmen even while retaining an air of masculine respectability against dominant stereotypes of black male incompetence, depravity, bestiality, and criminality. Under heightened media scrutiny eagerly awaiting the slightest misstep in sexual conduct, it would seem that black pro athletes could not as comfortably afford the kind of embrace of sissiness witnessed by some of the most prominent black public intellectuals of the 1990s—a notion that this chapter challenges. As we shall see, in a gay-affirmation movement among professional athletes that emerges in the

1980s and peaks in the 1990s and 2000s, a movement in which black men play a disproportionate role, we find a gender difference between how white and black gay athletes image their relationship to sissiness.

A trickle of pro athletes begin to lobby for policies and practices of inclusion for openly gay men in sport through the penning of memoirs detailing their own traumatic experiences as closeted homosexuals playing sports. Appealing to the sympathy of readers and sports fans, these memoirists base their worthiness to be included as fit athletes based in the racial desegregation model that emphasized not only athletic prowess but also masculine fitness and respectability as barometers of athletic merit. In promoting their fitness as sportsmen, these first openly gay pro jocks emphasize their conformity to masculine conduct as an intrinsic behavior, and in doing so they tend to distance themselves from, and sometimes even scapegoat, the sissy as a figure intrinsically unsuited for sport. Unlike the straight sissy intellectuals, who invent narratives of sissy affiliation to buffer the hard edges of a suspect heterosexuality, these gay sportsmen, to different degrees based partly on race, tend to harden their manliness by casting suspicion on the sissy figure. Because the pro athlete provides one of the most prominent public arbiters of fit manliness across U.S. history, and because in African American culture the pro athlete has come to embody not only the masculine cream of the race but also a leading edge of warring manhood against white supremacist exclusions, an analysis of how these openly gay jocks manage their sexual disclosure through gender and racial posturing can help us understand the changing discourse among racial identification, gender comportment, and sissy stigma at the turn into the twenty-first century. Thus, this chapter focuses on this new form that emerges in the final decades of the twentieth century, which I label *the sports disclosure memoir*, which advocates on behalf of the gay male athlete in a landscape in which same-gender love is gaining public tolerance. By examining the racialization of the pro gay athlete, and how this racialization hinges as much on the changing perception of the homosexual as on sissy suspicion, we can get a sense to what degree increasing tolerance for male homosexuality necessarily portends a concomitant increase in tolerance for the sissy.

In the middle decades of the twentieth century, African Americans had faith that once the military and sports were desegregated, black maleness would no longer be stigmatized as unworthy. This turned out not to be the case. Another line was redrawn, separating the exceptional athletes and soldiers from all the rest. A similar dynamic is currently at work with the attempt to open rough contact sports to openly gay men, but that line was already there to be exploited: the exceptional gay, who is manly enough, versus the rest of them—the sissies, swishers, queens, punks, femmes, cocksuckers, cunts, and pussies. The most popular American contact sports are committed to a mode of hypersurveillance, in which managers, coaches, athletes, and fans are constantly on the lookout for any perceived sign of sissy conduct. They are constantly imagining the sissy infiltration that needs to be guarded against. The sissy lives on that line drawn at the boundary of the field where his exclusion must repeatedly be seen to be enacted. The field, the sport, and the manly virtue of sportsmanship itself must be protected against the fainting weakness, wincing cowardice, and mincing softness that are fantasized as the essence of sissy temperament. Despite the sport's performance of hypersurveillance, a determined sissy-boy can fashion a "straight" outer shell that protects him from prying eyes. But it is exactly that outer shell of masculine conformity that causes him, self-consciously, anxiously, to overcompensate, whether in the classroom or on the field. If a boy wishes to purge his inner sissy, what better way than to prove himself in rough team sports? Ironically, the overcompensatory conduct that marks a circumspect sissy temperament is easily confused, by onlookers, with the manly self-confidence expected of a fit athlete. In this sense, the sissy is both a liminal presence and a subliminal object of fantasy in sports like football, as David Kopay and Perry Deane Young observe in the epigraph to this chapter. I would suggest that sportsmanship itself is constituted through the explicit exclusion of the sissy, for the sissy is the contrary, the foil, of fit manliness. It is exactly this explicit exclusion, however, that makes the sissy a liminal and subliminal figure haunting the sport's definition of itself.[12] Most assuredly sissies play football, but they do not and cannot play the sport *as sissies*.

Sportsmanship as Sissy Panic

As discussed in chapter 2, disability studies has alerted us to the ways in which the notion of physical fitness intersects powerfully with race and gender in both obvious and subtle ways. In U.S. culture, upright masculinity is closely tied to assumptions about and expectations of a "fit" body, where fitness correlates with certain notions of what a male's body should look like and how it should perform in athletic competition as a gauge for how it should look and behave beyond sports.[13] This idea of fitness is not necessarily static, as we can easily observe from changing standards of what constitutes even an ideal male body.[14] But despite changes in various details, masculinity has remained governed by the idea that there is a uniform look of fitness in the first place. There are more ways to fail in achieving the fit masculine body suitable for rough contact sports than there are ways to succeed.

The intense anxiety, and even trauma, that many boys experience in not possessing such a body—whether due to genetics, accident, or habit—is deeply related to sissiphobia, the panic of being perceived as or becoming a sissy as a result of inadequacy in playing sports. Conversely, the best way to avoid the jeopardy of suspect sissiness is athletic achievement. In *Colored People*, one of the black straight sissy memoirs examined in the previous chapter, Henry Louis Gates Jr. communicates the kind of disappointment that adheres to such a failure not only for the boy but also for intimate others, especially fathers. Gates describes the bond between his father and brother that was impossible for him to replicate, given his lack of athleticism: "But sports created a bond between Rocky and my father that excluded me, and, though my father had no known athletic talent himself, my own unathletic bearing compounded my problems. For not only was I overweight; I had been born with flat feet and wore 'corrective shoes.'"[15] For the young Gates, there is no way out. Much as adolescent girls tend to be obsessed with their body image, boys also tend to be obsessed with theirs, if in a different way toward a different end. Any boy's body that does not conform to the athletic mold is at risk of being sissified by others, regardless of the boy's conforming character and conduct in all other regards. The coercion to at least try out for sports can be overwhelming. For Gates, it was in hardball that he sought his masculine redemption and paternal approval: "Everyone my age did Little League, after all. They made me a Giant, decided I was a catcher because I was 'stout, like Roy Campanella,' dressed me in a chest protector and a mask, and squatted me behind a batter." Gates ends the anecdote by referencing a telltale sign of sissiness that the uniform—or in this case a baseball glove—could not overcome: "It's hard to catch a baseball with your eyes closed."[16] The hope is always that the armature of contact sports can compensate for whatever else is lacking in a boy whose body is deemed less than perfectly fit for play. Athletic skill, however, is hardly enhanced by body armor. Learning to keep your eyes open when a hardball is flying toward your face should seem instinctive, second nature, but it is certainly not the case for everyone, if for anyone. A father's own lack of athleticism, as Gates observes, frequently does not diminish the importance of such in a son. In fact, there is a good reason that sports movies so frequently employ the plot cliché of a father who has experienced mediocrity in sports overcompensating by wish-fulfilling athletic ambitions in his son. Sports failure, as common as it is, remains haunted by the sissy, even among the majority of men who themselves never succeed at sports even at the lowest levels of competition. "Daddy and Rocky would make heavy-handed jokes about queers and sissies," Gates writes. "I wasn't their direct target, but I guess it was another form of masculine camaraderie that marked me as less manly than my brother."[17] Men who do not succeed can still participate through, on the one hand, vicarious sports spectatorship, and, on the other, sissiphobic discourse maligning other men who are not sports-spectator savvy. To those males who feel unfit even to participate in this vicarious ritual, this masculine camaraderie centered on sports spectatorship can itself feel like a closed loop, shutting them not just out of sports but more fundamentally out of manhood itself.

Not being good at sports can induce a sort of sissy panic not only in a boy himself but also in others. I would suggest that such panic defines what it means to be a good sportsman, the ethics and ethos of sportsmanship. What are taken as *universal* values of the masculine actually operate as evaluative exclusions, serving to separate those who are properly gendered from those who are not. Certainly, one can be a good man without being a star athlete, but such good manliness is still measured by those values governing athletic prowess. And the most celebrated pro athletes cannot afford to let down their guard for a second. Sportsmanship is never really achieved; at best, it is always in process of being proven. Thus, attaining the ideal of masculine fitness is a ceaseless project based in a con/test of gender performance, assumed as the essence of habitual conduct, on and off the court, and thus the truest measure of a man's character.

We can see this in practice in an anecdote told by one of pro sports' greatest athletes of all time, Wilt Chamberlain. This anecdote is especially instructive given that Chamberlain is considered one of the most aggressively masculine of men, one who claimed in his 1991 autobiography, *A View from Above*, to have slept with twenty thousand women. A physically towering physique at seven feet and one inch tall with 275 pounds of muscle, why such a man would need to prove so aggressively his masculine credentials is especially puzzling, and yet it is so familiar as to be wholly expected. An episode of Malcolm Gladwell's *Revisionist History* podcast, "The Big Man Can't Shoot," focuses on the illogical resistance of Wilt Chamberlain and other basketball players to using the underhand free-throw shot.[18] In a 1962 game, the Philadelphia Warriors against the New York Nets, Chamberlain used the underhand shot to score a record-bashing one hundred points in a single game, a record that remains unmatched (figure 6.1). Despite this phenomenal achievement—one that corrected his only weak spot as a player—Chamberlain never used the underhand shot again. Gladwell interviews the white basketball player Rick Barry, a contemporary of Chamberlain's, who perfected the underhand shot. Barry's father had advised Barry to experiment with the shot when his son was a junior in high school, but Barry resisted from fear of being ridiculed. When he does first use it, just as he had feared, a man in the stands yells out, "Hey, Barry, you big sissy, shootin' like that." The guy next to him responds, "What are you makin' fun of him for? He doesn't miss." This gave Barry the confidence to continue using the shot as he moves into college and then pro basketball. Barry becomes a promoter of the underhand shot.

Chamberlain discusses his disdain for the "granny shot" in his first autobiography, *Wilt* (1973), where he makes it clear that he stopped using the effective shot only because it would make others perceive him as a sissy: "But I felt silly—like

6.1 Wilt Chamberlain using the much-mocked "granny shot"—more appropriately labeled the "sissy shot"—in 1968 Philadelphia 76ers vs. Boston Celtics game at the Boston Garden. Copyright 1968 NBAE. Photo by Dick Raphael / NBAE via Getty Images.

a sissy—shooting underhanded. I know I was wrong. I know some of the best foul shooters in history shot that way. Even now, the best one in the NBA, Rick Barry, shoots underhanded. But I just couldn't do it."[19] In the later memoir *A View from Above*, as Chamberlain repeats much of his explanation of why he was a poor free-throw shooter, curiously he totally erases the line about fearing being perceived as a sissy: "When I shot free throws, I used to have this deep, deep knee bend. But after the knee injury, I had to change my style of shooting. When I started to miss from the line—using this new style—I changed to a third style. The more I kept missing, the more I kept messing around with different methods and techniques.... But the whole thing became a major psychological hang-up."[20] What stands out here is how his initial success in using the underhand shot has totally disappeared from his narrative. Because Chamberlain might be seen as trying to closet any suspicion of homosexuality, rather than to disclose such, we might consider Chamberlain's two memoirs as foils to the gay disclosure memoir that emerges in 1977 with David Kopay. However, what Chamberlain's sports memoirs share with that genre is an intense sissy-avoidance resulting from sissy-panic. The altered self-narrative from 1973 to 1992 seems like a highly calculated disappearance of the specter of the sissy. It is far less shameful for an athlete to say that his one failure in the sport derives from an injury than to say, as he did in the earlier 1973 autobiography, that it was from fear of being perceived as a sissy.

By the time of his retirement, when he writes the second autobiography, Chamberlain is being dogged by whispered rumors of homosexuality because he never married. The twenty thousand women he claimed to have bedded and his high-minded justification for not marrying both seem calculated, like the altered story about the free shot, to expunge the specter of the homo-sissy from the public memory of his sports life.[21]

In the "Big Man Can't Shoot" interview, Barry explains that his own initial resistance to the granny shot had been exactly the same as Chamberlain's more honest initial response: Barry had told his father, "Dad, they're gonna make fun of me. That's the way the girls shoot. I can't do that."[22] Not only whether one can handle a ball, but also exactly how one does so, is one of the key determinants of fit athleticism. It is not a matter of skill, given that shooting underhanded requires no less skill, objectively, than shooting overhanded. What makes the underhanded shot girlish in the first place? As Gladwell's podcast points out, female basketball players shun the shot as thoroughly as male ones do. Of course, they would. Not even female athletes want to play "like girls." Dubbed the "granny shot," the underhand free throw is stigmatized for one reason alone—the perception that it's handling the ball "like a girl," as the saying goes. The unrelenting and ongoing stigma against the granny shot—which we might appropriately label the "sissy shot"—indicates the depth and intensity of the sissy as the most important oppositional figure defining masculine fitness in sports—even for female athletes!

Like Chamberlain, the great player Kareem Abdul-Jabbar, whose foul-shot percentage was just as miserable as Chamberlain's, expressly refused to try it, although Barry lobbied him to do so. Given the close affiliation of Barry, his father, and son with the sissy shot, one must speculate whether the sissy shot also gets racially profiled as too white for the best black players, especially given the racial stereotype of basketball skill summed up in the phrase "White men can't jump."[23] Abdul-Jabbar's public image stands in contrast with Chamberlain's, though. The former is known for being one of sports' most thoughtful gentlemen—in fact, a very self-aware gentle man who reads voraciously, writes elegantly, speaks softly, and practiced meditation long before it was popularized.[24] Whereas Chamberlain was a political conservative who supported Nixon, Abdul-Jabbar has been very politically engaged as a progressive Democrat, and he has all the "soft" connotations associated with Democrats in the post–civil rights period: he is articulate, well-read, an excellent writer, a practitioner of yoga and meditation. Unlike Chamberlain, Abdul-Jabbar has never had a hint of scandal or braggadocio. Abdul-Jabbar comes in the generation after Chamberlain, so one would expect some progress on the thorny question of the underhand shot. This is not the case, however, as we enter the NBA's pro–gay rights era.

In the generation after Abdul-Jabbar, Shaquille O'Neal also has a thoughtful image, dubbing himself "the Big Aristotle." Unlike Abdul-Jabbar, "Shaq," who aspired to become a rap artist, has occasionally stirred up minor scandals for his trash talk, such as when he ripped the Sacramento Kings by calling them "the Queens." Somewhere between Chamberlain and Abdul-Jabbar in terms of his macho posture, O'Neal nonetheless has exactly the same response to the sissy shot, resolutely refusing to try it despite his less-than-stellar foul-shot average. We can understand why, in 1962, a Wilt Chamberlain might be hesitant, but in 2017, after the national adoption of marriage equality and policies allowing gays to serve openly in the military, and after the NBA's pursuit of an openly gay Jackie Robinson to break the sexual-orientation taboo, the sissy shot remains one of basketball's greatest on-court taboos.

If Wilt Chamberlain's anecdote provides a real-life instance of the kind of panic elicited by the perception of a sissy on the court of play, Richard Wright's last published novel, *The Long Dream*, provides a revealing fictional case. This fictional episode also reminds us of how black male literary writers have often built their public image as properly gendered authors by fashioning a relationship to sports. Two of Wright's first published articles, for instance, were journalistic reports on the boxing matches of Joe Louis and black fans' response to them.[25] Through a quick glance at *Long Dream*'s sissy-bashing episode, we can see how sissy avoidance defines the essence of sportsmanship. Against the background of a lynching committed against a black youth, Chris, for his consensual liaison with a white woman, Wright inserts a scene that depicts the violence of compulsory masculinity. While the protagonist, Fish (also known as "Fishbelly"), and his pals (Zeke, Sam, and Tony) are innocently playing baseball, their routine form of pastoral escape from the realities of Jim Crow, an intruder disturbs this pastoral: "Tony motioned his thumb to the right and Fishbelly turned and saw plump, short, black Aggie West, a glove under his arm, coming mincingly toward him. Fishbelly frowned. Aggie West showed a wide, sweet smile."[26] Like the autobiographical narrator's more subtle sissy characterization of Shorty in *Black Boy*, discussed in chapter 1, the boys mark Aggie's sissiness through three adjectives and one adverb: "plump," "short," "black," and "mincingly." Any one of the adjectives alone would not capture the boy's gender discordance, but the adverb climaxes the insinuation, and the fourth adjective, "sweet," caps the sissy suspicion as a factual matter.[27] The precision and propriety of Aggie's speech signal this as much as his mincing plumpness, little stature, and sweet smile do. The boys stop him at that invisible line that demarcates the boundary of the baseball field, which they are sworn to protect from sweet Aggie's sissy trespass.

Aggie's sissiness is immediately equated with the particular sexual disposition of faggotry. They move from calling him "sissy," "pansy," and "fruit" to labeling him "fairy" and "homo." The panoply of epithets at once communicates the myriad ways to stigmatize a presumed sissy temperament as well as an intrinsic uncertainty concerning the exact nature of that gender disorder. When the boys try to hold the gender front at first by exploiting verbal violence, Aggie persistently refuses to accept the logic of this line. "'I love to play the piano and I also love to play ball,' Aggie explained."[28] Like James Weldon Johnson's ex-colored man, or Little Richard's memory of being ostracized as a sissy in his youth for learning to play the piano, Aggie's love of the piano here represents gender discordance.[29] Beyond the piano as an instrument that can sissify a boy, to "*love*" playing anything with this histrionic emphasis is in itself a symptom of Aggie's gender crime: "'Play the piano, you fairy,' Tony has said to him. 'That's all you fit for!'"[30] Logically, Aggie asserts his facility for crossing their imaginary line separating the sissy from real boys, just as his gender character itself is a cross between male anatomy and effeminate mannerisms. And Aggie's assertion makes sense. It would seem that the same skills of hand-eye coordination and ambidexterity required to play the piano well could translate to playing baseball well.[31] Such a correspondence, however, threatens to erase that invisible line that the boys are trying to guard and that Aggie insists does not exist. Aggie keeps returning to the scene of the crime because he knows that that rigged, imaginary baseball diamond belongs to him as much as to the other boys. They, too, know this intuitively; otherwise they would feel no compunctions about their assault. Against Cleaver's notion that the boys go punk-hunting, instead it is Aggie who trespasses on their terrain of competitive team sport. Though they see him as out of his place, he nonetheless insists that the baseball diamond belongs to him, as a community asset for boys' play, as much as to them.

Once the boys have run Aggie off by brutally assaulting him, they immediately feel pangs of remorse. In the frenzy of their hatred and violence, and as Aggie's blood stains his normally clean clothes, the boys necessarily confuse their hatred of queers with their hatred of themselves as subjugated black males marginalized from dominant masculinity. Set in 1940s Mississippi, the narrative obliquely references the racial battleground that defined baseball as America's pastime in that decade, as Jackie Robinson finally breaks the color barrier in 1947. The boys' gender violence against Aggie mirrors the racial violence against Robinson when he first took the field, reminding us of how the fans' attack on Robinson's racial identity was also necessarily an assault on his fit manliness as a sportsman: "'Move on, queer nigger!' Zeke screamed."[32] Aggie is a "queer nigger" not only because he is both black and sissy but also because a nigger is necessarily queer. "Much of the violence . . . is motivated by the boys' fear of what they do not understand," Maggie McKinley observes, "a somewhat stereotypical urge to lash out at the strange, unfamiliar, frightening or embarrassing."[33] To some extent, this may be true, but in a deeper sense, as Baraka observes about the familial presence of the swishes in his New Jersey neighborhood as discussed in chapter 5, Aggie is all too familiar to the boys, as someone who has an ordinary presence in the community. Wright underscores that the boys understand exactly the inexcusable violation that they've committed through their self-reflection directly following the event. McKinley's next point hits closer to home: "Wright invests Fish with an almost subliminal understanding that his own violence is enacted against something other, and more abstract, than the immediate threat with which he is faced."[34] Not satisfied to leave this insight of the boys' racial-sexual inversion a subtle subtext edifying the racial violence that surrounds it, Wright instead engages the victorious boys in their own dialogue over their culpability:

> "We treat 'im like the white folks treat us," Zeke mumbled with a self-accusative laugh.
> "Never thought of that," Sam admitted, frowning.
> "Why you reckon he acts like a girl?" Fishbelly asked.
> "Beats me," Tony said. "They say he can't help it."
> "He could if he really *tried*," Zeke said.
> "Mebbe he can't. . . . Mebbe it's like being black," Sam said.
> "Aw naw! It ain't the same thing," Zeke said.
> "But he ought to stay 'way from us," Fishbelly said.
> "That's just what the white folks say about us," Sam told him.[35]

By tying sissy panic to lynching hysteria, Wright captures the high cost of social unity figured as gender uniformity. In contrast with the scenes in *Black Boy* discussed in chapter 1, where sissiphobia is intended to shore up Richard's capacity to man up against Jim Crow emasculation, through this scene we come to know that the highest gender norm constitutes the deepest pathology of masculine desire, its need to violate a subordinated other so as to maintain a facade of masculine order under threat by white supremacy's violation of black manhood. As observed below in the discussion of Dave Pallone's sports disclosure memoir, etiology plays a large role in debates over "girlish" or effeminate comportment in boys. Zeke's notion that Aggie *could* comport himself otherwise, "if he really *tried*," accords with Pallone's diatribe against flagrantly sissified mannerism not as natural *behavior* (a matter of intrinsic character), which would be justifiable as innate, but instead as a *habit* (merely learned conduct) that swishes learn from imitating other swishes. As these sports disclosure memoirs invariably insist on the notion that homosexuality is inborn, they sometimes tend to denaturalize swishing as inexcusable because it should be seen as histrionically contrived gender performance. To defend gay character against moral opprobrium as an unnatural "lifestyle" or practice, these memoirists are occasionally eager to cast sissiness itself as an artificial habit deserving such.

Wright's Aggie West episode reminds us how the much celebrated ethic and ethos of sportsmanship, commonly called "fair play," historically has been silently tethered to unfair advantage—that is, to violent acts of racial and gender exclusion. Obviously, blocking anatomical or cisgender females from competing with men has been so entrenched that until relatively recently, women were forbidden from even competing in sport among themselves.[36] Less visible, however, is another gender barrier, one blocking the sissy from the field of play, where the sissy here is the manifest threat of a male who does not ostentatiously conform to masculine gender norms. This is not a question of changing the written rules of the game; it is instead a matter of the unwritten rules that prohibit a boy who tosses (his ass or a baseball) like a girl from participating in sport, no matter how closely he follows the written rules or how expertly he plays otherwise. Good sportsmanship, in other words, is not so much a matter of what we blandly call "fair play" as a false claim to universal ethics; it is more crucially a matter of *man-play*, a phrase I use to mean the promotion of athletic games designed to display all the attributes identified with fit manliness while also being able to engage males in intimate contact with other males as though that intimacy has no erotic implications. We already have language for this behavior in the term "horseplay," which describes the roughhousing of two boys or men in a raucous homosocial contest that ironically also affirms their intimate companionship, ostensibly with no hint of the erotic. The persistent confusion between being gay and being sissy serves the express purpose of protecting the field of play from those who cannot or will not conform to masculine norms even more than sexual ones.

The Sissy as Liminal Foil in the Sports Disclosure Memoir

Society's historical refusal to distinguish between the sissy and the homosexual becomes, after World War II, a major flashpoint in the gay rights movement. In fact, especially by the 1970s, middle-class white homosexual men begin to demand their right to be included, and indeed openly embraced, within the most sacred preserves of American masculine empowerment—institutional politics, the military, and contact team sports—by seeking to segregate the sissy from the homosexual. For a brief moment around the 1969 Stonewall Rebellion, which is taken as the turning point in histories of the LGBTQ movement, there is a robust gay liberation movement which demands not so much inclusion of queers in the status quo as the radical abolition of that status quo in accord with racial, gender, and sexual liberation. As the country makes a swift and sharp turn rightward, largely in reaction against these radical cultural movements, the idea of gay liberation is sidelined in favor of what Dennis Altman calls the "Americanization of the homosexual"; what Urvashi Vaid, the former head of the Lesbian Gay Task Force, has called the "mainstreaming" of the LGBTQ agenda; what Michael Warner calls "the normalized movement"; and what recent queer theorists have dubbed homonormativity.[37] The late 1970s and early '80s are thus a watershed moment for the consolidation of this mainstreaming strategy, one tactic of which, I would argue, concerns the fight to divorce the sissy epithet from straight-appearing homosexual boys and men.

Perhaps the most blatant manifestation of this phenomenon of gay-affirmative sissiphobia can be glimpsed in the rise of the Castro Street Clone.[38] Named for the gay neighborhood in San Francisco where this "look" was perfected, the Clone uses dress, posture, physique, gait, grooming, and pose to claim a right to gender normativity through the performance of masculine fitness. The Castro Clone aesthetic favored clothes still identified with manual laborers—jeans, plaid shirts, "wife-beaters," and brogans, which function as a manly uniform no less than the politician's suit, the soldier's regimentals, or the athlete's pads do. Although most were securely middle-class office workers, they sported their gym-perfected musculature with the same theatrical confidence as their laborers' attire, and against the 1960s preference for long hair, they fashioned their hair military-style but with well-trimmed mustaches and occasionally beards—facial hair as a showcase of virility. They also sought to emulate a deportment, swagger, and stance that marked their gender-straightness. Just as African Americans, to affirm the right to belong as citizens, distanced themselves visually from any sign of the stereotyped nigger that served to justify their exclusion, so homosexuals and lesbians distanced themselves from fruity and dykey stereotypes as far back as the country's first gay-affirmative organizations, the Mattachine Society (New York, 1950) and the Daughters of Bilitis (San Francisco 1955), whose mission statement, printed in *The Ladder*, included as one of its objectives to win acceptance "by advocating a mode of behavior and dress acceptable to society."[39] The Castro Clone, however, intensified this strategy as an exclusionary way of life within a "gay ghetto," which at the time modeled itself on the fraternal and sports clubs from which so many of these men had been excluded in larger society.

As others have noted, the Castro Clone's uniformity was not just about a physical and sartorial claim to straight masculinity as the highest value of gay men's object of desire; it was as much about the act of excluding those who seemed not to conform to this macho ideal of white male supremacy: most prominently prohibited from this scene were effeminate men, cross-dressers, "out-of-shape" bodies, older "queens," and nonwhites. The Clone's uniform whiteness tacitly marked him as fit for American ruling-class manhood. As the Clone was promenading up and down San Francisco's Castro Street to show off his straight white masculinity, so in the nation's legislative halls, military quarters, football fields, and judicial courts "straight"-appearing openly white gay men were making their case for integration into the country's most cherished fraternal fortresses of manly fitness. In the masculine preserve of the military, the first successful legal test case was mounted in 1975. Air Force Technical Sergeant Leonard Matlovich (1943–1988), after twelve years of distinguished service in which he was awarded the Bronze Star and the Purple Heart, disclosed his homosexuality and eventually won his right to an honorable discharge from the military.[40] In the same year, David Kopay, a ten-year running back in the NFL, became the first professional athlete to make a public disclosure of his homosexuality. His *New York Times* best-selling memoir, *The David Kopay Story*, coauthored with Perry Deane Young, appeared two years later. In 1983, Jerry Studds, a Democratic representative from Massachusetts, became the first federally elected official to proclaim publicly his homosexuality, in the midst of a scandal that revealed his sexual liaison with a male Capitol page. Each of these men makes his case for gay-affirmative inclusion based on the notion that he is an ordinary male, of high moral character and normative gender conduct, whose only distinction happens to be that he erotically desires other men.

Although David Kopay (b. 1942) was the first pro athlete to out himself, he still stands with only one other *white* pro athlete in North American contact sports of boxing, baseball, football, basketball, or ice hockey to have done so.[41] In football, Roy Simmons (1956–2014), a four-year veteran guard nicknamed "Sugar Bear," came out in 1992 on the *Phil Donahue Show* and wrote a sports disclosure memoir, *Out of Bounds: Coming Out of Sexual Abuse, Addiction, and My Life of Lies in the NFL Closet* in 2006. Esera Tuaolo (b. 1968), a Samoan American nine-year defensive tackle, outed himself in an interview on *Real Sports with Bryant Gumbel* in 2002 and published a sports disclosure memoir, *Alone in the Trenches: My Life as a Gay Man in the NFL*, in 2006. Wade Davis (b. 1977), a four-year cornerback, announced his sexuality in 2012 and has since been a vocal spokesman on behalf of gay rights in sports. Kwame Harris (b. 1982), a ten-year offensive tackle, was outed as a result of a domestic violence lawsuit made by his former male lover, and affirmed his gayness in an interview with CNN in 2013. In 2019 African American free agent Ryan Russell came out as bisexual to ESPN.[42] The only footballer to announce his gayness before a professional career started rather than after it was over is Michael Sam (b. 1990), an African American defensive end from the University of Missouri who made the disclosure just before the 2014 NFL draft.[43] American football may be the most important sport among the four examined here, given its prominence in cementing the image of fit masculinity as well as its highly racialized dynamic as America's most popular sport.[44]

Only two basketballers have outed themselves. John Amaechi (b. 1970), a nine-year power forward and center in the NBA, announced his sexuality on ESPN's *Outside the Lines* in 2007 in tandem with his memoir, *Man in the Middle*, notably published by ESPN books. In 2013 Jason Collins (b. 1978), who had played center for thirteen years in the NBA, became the first pro athlete to disclose his homosexuality during his active career through a *Sports Illustrated* article that he authored. In 1982 Glenn Burke (1952–1995) became the first baseball player to out himself, in the magazine *Inside Sports*; he published *Out at Home: The True Story of Glenn Burke* in 1995. Billy Bean, the other openly gay white pro athlete among these most popular sports, followed in 1999, and his *Going the Other Way: Lessons from a Life in and out of Major League Baseball* appeared in 2003. In 1990, former baseball umpire Dave Pallone published a memoir, coauthored with Alan Steinberg, titled *Behind the Mask: My Double Life in Baseball*. I include Pallone's narrative here even though he is not an athlete because umpiring and refereeing historically have also been white male preserves, and ones whose aura of masculine prerogative has been surveilled as religiously as the sport itself.

The last rough contact sport discussed here, boxing, has four openly gay athletes. The first is Emile Griffith (1938–2013), world-champion boxer from 1959 to 1977, who confirmed his homosexuality in 1995 in a *Sports Illustrated* article; rumors had been spreading since 1992, when he was severely beaten on exiting a gay bar. Griffith interests me because of the legend that his fatal knockout of Benny Paret in 1962 was fueled by Paret's tapping his ass and calling him a *maricón* during the weigh-in.[45] The only boxer to have come out while still taking to the ring, Orlando Cruz (b. 1981), is a Puerto Rican feather- and lightweight who has been boxing since 2000. Identifying himself as both a proud Puerto Rican and a proud gay man, he has won seven of his ten bouts since coming out and is ranked as one of the top boxers in his class. Yusaf Mack (b. 1980) is a middleweight boxer who was in the ring from 2000 to 2014. Having made a gay pornographic film titled *Holiday Hump'n* with two black male porn stars in 2015, he at first denied and then confirmed his homosexuality.

I have chosen these four male contact sports because each represents the most popular sport in the U.S. in different eras across the twentieth century, and each also has played a pivotal role both in the history of racial desegregation in sport as well as in the coming-out narrative of sports.[46] Other individual, noncontact sports—most notably swimming, ice skating, tennis, golf, soccer, and track and field—have seen the emergence of openly gay and lesbian athletes, some of whom have written sports coming-out narratives.[47] Although no longer sacrosanct precincts of white male exclusion, even within those sports with the greatest percentage of black players—football and basketball—race continues to frame their ideology of sportsmanship.[48] Likewise, these most masculine of American sports remain preserves of sissiphobia, even as a trickle of gay men have created headlines by coming out or being outed, in virtually every case *after* their sports careers have ended. In wading into the waters of gender and sexual stigma that have surrounded and still surround these sports, gay players have looked to the watershed experience of Jackie Robinson as the script that can best help them through the waves, and Robinson's sports memoir, *I Never Had It Made* (1972), published five years before Kopay's disclosure narrative, created the narrative template for gay sports memoirs. Despite the tendency to want to make Robinson a puppet in the hands of the white general manager of the Brooklyn Dodgers (Branch Rickey, who is credited with hiring Robinson in 1945), Robinson was already a battle-tested lieutenant in the racial war on the homefront.[49] His barrier-breaking could easily be turned into American myth: here is a man who, due to his meritorious sportsmanship, moral probity, and docile obedience to his white manager, reaffirms manly sport as "fair play." As we shall see, however, the failed race to discover a gay Jackie Robinson helps to shatter the myth that sportsmanship (athletic skill and ethics) alone could overcome the gender barriers set up to protect white sportsmen's false narrative that sport proves their white male heterosexual supremacy.

With the success of Kopay's *New York Times* best-selling autobiography in 1977, later pro players have used his book as a secondary model, after Robinson's, for telling their own stories, invariably referencing Kopay's narrative as an inspiring source at a particular moment in their own story—collectively producing a minor subgenre that I call the *sports disclosure memoir*. As we shall see by contrasting Kopay's memoir with Roy Simmons's *Out of Bounds*, published three decades later, the substance of this subgenre remains remarkably consistent, even as its shape is resignified through subtly changed historical contexts of athletic heroism, gay affirmation, and, most importantly for us, the complex dynamics stemming from the subject's racialized gender identification. Just as race haunts each of these narratives in suggestive and puzzling ways, so male gender differentiation, projected onto the liminal figure of the sissy, also haunts each narrative to an extent that spectacular sportsmanship as fit manliness is figured as much through gender uniformity, enforced through sissiphobic discourse, as through racial identification.

The visual archive of Kopay's memoir showcases the same look being sported by the Castro Street Clone. The memoir's photography is insistent in taking what becomes the Clone aesthetic as a resource for framing Kopay as an ordinary guy, masculine to the bone. Kopay includes a photograph of himself with his frat brothers

6.2 University of Washington Rose Bowl starting team (1964), Kopay standing far left. From David Kopay's *The David Kopay Story*.

to signal his gender normalcy, at least as far as everyday appearance is concerned. That Kopay's fraternity photo would be coterminous with the Clone aesthetic should not be so surprising, as the photo of the 1964 University of Washington Rose Bowl starting lineup is also commensurate with this look (figure 6.2). The sole black player centers the photograph in a way that at once exposes and obscures the uneasy place that racial difference occupied even in desegregated college football of that era. Of course, we are so used to seeing images of uniform rows of white men ostensibly unaware of both their whiteness and their gender posturing that our vision must be defamiliarized to understand the strangeness of such racialized gender uniformity. But more revealing than the memoir's photographic showcase is Kopay's insistent ekphrastic references to this white-boy-next-door visual frame. The blond, blue-eyed, muscular athlete defines not only his own identity but also that of his object of desire, so much so that its insistent repetition throughout the story provides a stabilizing structure in a narrative awash with the travails of unfulfilled desire.

In ninth grade Kopay decides to enroll in a Catholic boys' junior seminary, a decision that comports with his desire for fraternal environments. He emphasizes how the seminary sought to discourage any semblance of intimacy between boys: "Even with every kind of sex forbidden, the brothers and priests were still visibly concerned about appearances and masculine manners. The best student in the grade ahead of mine was also one of the most serious and devout postulants, but he was never allowed to become a novitiate. The reason had to be his effeminate manners."[50] As we know from the history of predatory priests in the Catholic Church, we should note the similarity between what this young postulant is facing at the junior seminary and what the young Sylvester James faced as a church sissy in his mother's Pentecostal church, as discussed in chapter 4. Both institutions harbor men in leading positions able to prey on young boys, and as an overcompensating act, both seek to purge the offending sissy not to protect the boy but to protect the institution itself. In this case, however, there is no evidence that the postulant is a homosexual; the basis of the purge is simply that he is gender nonconforming. As a gender-conforming athlete, Kopay can look on in panic fearing that he might be called out if he is not hypervigilant, which in turn can only ramp up his gender panic to be distanced from the stigmatized sissy-boy. Given that there is no theological or scriptural basis for banning sissies from religious institutions, just as there are no laws dedicated to this project, the only rationale for such purges can be that a sissy, whatever his sexual conduct, cannot help but turn into someone who partakes in same-gender sex and thus encourages "innocent" others to do so as well.

Even as Kopay himself pens this gay-affirmative outing memoir, he shapes the narrative through the same logic that the Catholic Church promotes, excising any trace of a sissy gesture by showcasing a fraternal bonding totally defined by athletic performance and masculine hardness. Immediately following his discussion of the effeminate postulant, he writes:

> In spite of the rules it seemed that everybody was paired off with a special friend.... I never felt I had a best friend, but I did have two special relationships—one with a boy who was by far the best athlete in the school, the other with Father Ernest Hyman, the head prefect.
>
> The athlete was two years older and a captain of the basketball team. He had blond hair, blue eyes, sharp features and stood six feet three. He moved with a real swagger.... We competed so hard we would fight over the least infraction, and Father Hyman and the other students would often have to pull us apart. And yet, somewhere within all this outward violence there was a deep feeling between us. (41–42)

This template of the blond, blue-eyed swaggering athlete is the racialized gender iconography of the white-boy-next-door that protects Kopay from being conflated with the effeminate postulant who has been purged from the school, as well as from the narrative itself, only to appear later, symbolically, as an overweight queer predator who seduces Kopay into a sexual relationship in exchange for monetary support. Kopay's white-boy-next-door template is repeated throughout the memoir in the series of athletic men whom the narrator fantasizes about, desires, and occasionally hooks up with sexually. His first romantic relationship was with his college teammate who is given the fictional name "Ted Robinson" in the memoir. "He was blond, had a long V-shaped face with a deep dimple in his chin," Kopay writes. "His shoulders were narrow and his upper body slender, but his hips and legs were those of a well-trained athlete."[51]

While avoiding one prevailing stereotype of queer maleness, the contagious sissy whose contagion is all the more dangerous because it is not self-evident on the body, the narrative ironically plunges unwittingly into another prevailing stereotype of unfit maleness: narcissism. Since at least the late nineteenth century, alongside the sexological theory of the homosexual as a gender invert, was the psychoanalytic theory of the homosexual as perversely narcissistic, most famously theorized in Freud's 1914 essay "On Narcissism."[52] A man who desires another man really desires a replica of himself, it was believed, and this narcissistic desire signals the pathological nature of homosexuality resulting from a stunted oedipal development. One could argue that the Castro Clone aesthetic feeds on this cultural stereotype of youthful manly narcissism as a militant badge of gay white male community-making, disavowing the much greater stigma of sissiness for the lesser stigma of a narcissistic display hinging on a carnivalesque cornucopia of magic mirrors reflecting hyperwhite hypermasculinity. College fraternities and sports teams before desegregation, after all, could also be charged with such narcissism, given the superficial similarity in physical looks of such groups. Sissy-disavowal is also embedded in the very structure of Kopay's narration. The manic pace of sports narration diminishes those occasional moments of sexual self-reflection in which the narrative pauses to remind us of how unequivocally Kopay's queer desires are seen as butting headfirst against the strictures of football decorum, even though homosexuality is repeatedly observed as much more common in the sport than outsiders could imagine. This narrative pace and style might be called "swagger," an approximation in language of the masculine gait that a male must perform if he is not to fall into a swishing sissy walk. Just as the young LeRoi Jones admires his grandfather's swagger to the point of envy, despite the yellowness of the institution within which the elder displays it, so Kopay fantasizes (with some envy) a fellow jock as an idealized version of a wholly masculinized self, even though the dominant society regards their sexual relationship as a contradiction of the very masculinity that he projects. Contrary to Baldwin, who exploits as a sissy resource John Grimes's suspect walk and "that marvelously mocking, salty authority with which black men walked" under the grip of Jim Crow, Kopay's narrative appropriates swagger to signal his attraction to and identity with normative masculine conduct despite the homosexual nature of his character.

This performance of "swagger," as the signal for toughness, becomes a self-conscious motif within the story, as gender normalcy is necessarily triangulated not only in relation to a properly gendered cisgender female but also through another male whose masculine fitness is often idealized as an objective point for measuring one's own. Kopay, for instance, tells of a time at a frat party when, in an effort to impress his older brother, Tony, "I decided to play Mister Tough with some guys there we thought were party crashers." After describing the fight, he writes: "I, the hero of the night who hadn't landed a punch, joined in the buddy-buddy talk after the fight but for days after felt guilty. I knew Tony almost got his eye gouged out in a fight I had started to get attention, to make myself look tough in my buddies' eyes—and in my brother's eyes too."[53] This desire to be included in the homosocial network of hegemonic white masculinity in Kopay's narrative pivots on the narrator's desire for and desire to embody that white male supremacist ideal. We can see this narcissistic impulse in the narration through its representation of Kopay as both desirable subject and desired object of his own sexual predilections. In one paperback reprint version of the 1977 memoir, we are presented with Kopay suited up and holding the football in a freeze-frame running directly toward the camera. He is, without a doubt, the tough, normal athlete indiscernible from any rugged straight man. Kopay, moreover, markets himself unashamedly as the narcissistic subject and object of the Castro Clone's "straight-appearing" desire when he agrees to be pictured on the cover of the gay porn magazine *Mandate* (figure 6.3). Obviously a brilliant marketing ploy to sell more of his books, the cover photo frames him not as a football player but as a porn fantasy, nude down to his crotch in a slightly innocent boy-next-door pose with an inviting smile, not the usual pornographic sneer, with hands placed confidently on his hips.

Kopay's memoir, thus, has a twofold structure for sissy-avoidance. On the one hand, it seeks to purge the sissy from its purview thematically and formally. Without having to say explicitly "I am *not* a sissy," the narrative says it through its tacit endorsement of the Catholic boys' school's purging of the sissy postulant. On the other hand, this sissiphobia operates not only through expulsion but also through active affirmation of conventionally bullying violent behavior, more identified with the victims of sissiphobia and with deeply closeted homosexuals than with openly gay men. When he pictures himself as going out of his way to initiate a fistfight with his frat brothers, his motive is to impress his blood brother, no doubt out of a sense that his elder brother would not approve of his homosexuality—a fear confirmed later in the narrative. As with the underhand foul shot, it is not enough to conduct oneself in aggressive ways that conform to the masculine ideal of a fit athlete; one must also be hypervigilant about *not* appearing to collude with sissiness in any form.

We can see Kopay's strategy at work in other sports disclosure memoirs too. Dave Pallone's 1990 memoir, *Behind the Mask*, reminds us that normative masculinity

6.3 David Kopay appears on the cover of gay porn magazine *Mandate*, May 1977, the same year that his gay disclosure memoir is published.

determines not only who is fit to play but also who is fit to coach, manage, own, and referee the masculine preserve of contact team sports. Umpires usually start out as jocks in the sports they referee. Although they can be seen as failed jocks, they nonetheless are understood to be essential to the proper gender functioning of the sport.[54] In picking up a young Puerto Rican for a sexual tryst while umping winter ball in Puerto Rico, Pallone bases their mutual attraction on their manliness.[55] Umping "takes balls." Likewise, as Pallone asserts, "what really took a lot of balls were the chances I took *off* the field."[56] Thus Pallone equates the ballsiness of playing the sport well with the ballsiness of the gay sportsman who dares to experiment with homosexuality (however secretly) despite its great stigma within sports. Pallone is here referencing his first sexual encounter with a pro baseball player in 1984. The structure of Pallone's desire is shaped by the same narcissistic yearning for the idealized fit young white athlete that characterized Kopay's.[57] This conflation between desiring the butch jock sexually and desiring to *be* the butch jock is exactly what fuels the fear that the intimacy of teammates will be confused with the narcissistic intimacy of homosexuals. Pallone takes his sissiphobia a step further, however. It is not merely that he wants to look good to others but also,

GAY BUT NOT SISSY · 307

conversely, that he doesn't want to disgust them: "It would have bothered me for another reason: I believe gays are born gay, but I don't believe we're born effeminate. If I'm with a friend today and I see a gay man who's extremely effeminate, I'll remark, 'I think he goes home and practices.' Effeminate behavior doesn't offend me; it confuses me. I think everybody should be what they really are and what they really feel, so I don't believe it's wrong for a man to be effeminate. I just think some gays take it too far."[58] By expressing ostensible tolerance for effeminate men, on the one hand, but confusion, on the other, Pallone distances himself from the swishing sissy to such an extent that he cannot comprehend such behavior. His issue is not so much with effeminate men but instead with gay men who "take it too far," where "too far" is, of course, so subjective as to be purely a matter of his own judgment. Consistent with the way in which sissiness itself always constitutes a liminal phenomenon, Pallone's "confusion" exposes how these disclosure memoirs tend to fashion homosexuality into a fixed identity deserving of social inclusion while rendering sissiness as a suspect transitive practice to be policed as a social threat. Pallone thus naturalizes homosexuality while othering swishing sissiness. The gay man is born that way, but the effeminate man is not. It is the swish who is responsible for the ridicule and hatred aimed erroneously at men like himself who just happen to be attracted to other men. One could even go so far as to say that Pallone is devoted to pro baseball because he is devoted to the masculine type that he imagines all pro baseball players embody. This line of unreasoning hinges on the assumption that the sissy is totally absent from baseball—at least, any sissy who takes swishing so far as to be detected as such.

Although white baseballer Billy Bean's approach is not quite as aggressively violent as Kopay's or morally accusatory as Pallone's, the subtleties of his sissy avoidance are just as revealing. Bean begins *Going My Own Way* by disidentifying with an assumption of sissy behavior, the tendency toward daydreaming fantasy, but he does so by turning it toward a wholly macho end: "Even as a kid, I lived to wear a uniform. But my first choice might have been a little ambitious. At my fourth birthday party, I'm tearing open a present from Mom, a full-body Superman outfit."[59] We should contrast Bean's Superman fantasy with Rod Ferguson's cross-racial/gender identification with Wonder Woman discussed in chapter 1. The difference between cross-identifying with a heroic female and cross-identifying with the ultimate male superhero indexes the difference between flagrant sissification versus sissy-avoidance and repression. Similarly, as a child Bean adopts the sissy characteristic of becoming an avid reader, but the narrator enacts sissy-disavowal in emphasizing what the boy reads—very boyish comic books: "Mom says I taught myself to read before my fourth birthday by devouring those dog-eared comic books.... Even though I was just a pint-sized kid, I always managed to kill the intruder, foil the bad guys, and save Mom from danger" (4). By thematizing the Superman fantasy as an inspirational source for his baseball prowess, Bean is able to acknowledge, however cagily, a repressed sissy propensity ironically through the overcompensatory gender identification with America's most beloved superhero.

Two factors seem to drive Bean's implicit sense of not being a normal boy: his small size and his lack of a father. The latter deficiency is used to explain the most blatant evidence of sissy conduct as a compensatory behavior: "I developed some unusual habits to compensate. When I was in third grade, Mom noticed that I'd started laying out my clothing in neat piles, picking out just the right combination of colors for the next school day. . . . Before long, I was giving Mom fashion tips" (6). Notice that Bean labels this conduct simply "unusual"—reminiscent of Baldwin's more sophisticated interrogation of estrangement as a gender-nonconforming structure of feeling and social posture. Given that Bean would assuredly know that the conduct fits so clearly a network of stereotypes signaling a sissy character, it is especially significant that Bean avoids the "sissy" label with a more euphemistically acceptable adjective. The young Bean's "unusual" attachment to his mother, however, is fully understandable through the eyes of the narrator, empathizing with the father-deficient boy: "Being the son of a single mother *did* have its advantages. Mom and I developed an intense attachment. I slept in her bed in our one-bedroom apartment until I was five. The men Mom dated, jealous of our bond, accused her of coddling me. The implication was clear: there was something wrong with loving your firstborn too much" (6; emphasis in original). Bean is highlighting one trajectory, the incipient homosexual boy, by subtly distancing and displacing the more transparent one, the effeminate sissy-boy. He puts the accusation in the mouth of one of his mother's many lovers: "'The boy will never grow up to be a *man*,' I remember one insisting" (6; emphasis in original). Against this image of the effeminate boy, however, Bean represents himself as thoroughly boyish in every other way. When his mother decides against his playing team sports "for the safety of her undersized boy and holding a low opinion of organized sports," the little Bean slyly solves the problem by asking his friend's father to intercede: "A few nights later during dinner, we heard a knock on the front door. It was Tommy's dad. I feigned surprise as best an eight-year-old could" (8–9). Despite the "unusual" attachment to his mom, the little boy values sports over that intimacy. When push comes to shove, he knows that any man will be able to claim to know what's best for the boy better than the mother the boy is so close to.

Like Kopay, Bean also finds a way of straightening out his gender conduct off the field as well. Rather than becoming the bully himself, however, he more cautiously creates a partnership with the biggest bully in his school, trading protection for doing the bully's homework—reminiscent of Johnson's ex-colored boy's relationship with Red, as discussed in chapter 3. When the school authorities discover that the second-grader is doing the homework of the third-grade bully, Billy is "placed in a new class for advanced kids" (11)—an outcome that maneuvers to boast a sissy precociousness accidentally resulting from a schoolboyish pact. Both Kopay's and Bean's compact with bullying—in both cases abetting others toward such "bad" behavior while keeping themselves out of harm's way—tacitly depends on their whiteness. As white boys, especially as jocks, their behavior is tacitly approved, while any black boy in the same circumstance would find himself punished, suspended from school, and/or arrested. Unaware of how gay self-affirmation here is plotted through society's approval of white male aggression, these gay uplift narratives reveal how sissiphobia relies indirectly on the double standard that gives white boys greater leeway for "bad" behavior. Whereas a rough athlete's propensity for "badness" is condoned when he is white, it is always a source of criminal jeopardy when he is black, even when he is an athlete.

Concerning the other deficient factor often attributed to sissies, small size, Bean asserts that to become a credible athlete, he must overcome this deficiency through sheer will: "My body may have looked like Jimmy Olsen's, but I was determined to sculpt it into Superman's."[60] Like skin color, size factors into the perception of sissiness in different ways for white boys versus boys of color. Because U.S. society tends to image and imagine black males as being larger than their actual size and thus to project onto them the criminal danger of being oversized, black sissiness may be more easily overlooked in a smaller-sized black boy than a smaller white boy. Whereas mass media provides Bean with a white Superman ideal on which to model his body and thus to distance himself from sissy suspicion due to his smallness, black boys cannot have the same relation to the Superman ideal. Mass media images of large black men are prone to conflate that size with predatory character, even when such men are fit athletes. The effect that this has on the racial imaginary of black boys is most certainly complicated, but it is not difficult to understand how black boys, rather than being able to take pure delight in their size or musculature, would possess double consciousness in learning to fear how nonblack people might respond apprehensively to their size. And, as we shall see through the cases of Samoan footballer Esera Tuaolo and biracial British basketballer John Amaechi, darker versus lighter skin also plays a complex role in the perception of a sissy disposition and thus of fitness for athletic play.

What we discover in Kopay's, Pallone's, and Bean's sports disclosure narratives is how what I earlier termed the "circumspect sissy" shapes the character and conduct of the sissy-boy athlete in a similar way to the church sissy. Both the sissy athlete and the church sissy obsess on respectable self-presentation, in terms not only of gestural manner and speaking voice but also of the physical size and fitness of a boy's body. Anxiously fearful that a homosexual propensity will be exposed as masculine deficit, circumspect sissies surveil and constrict their bodies to ensure the perception of conventional masculinity. Like Washington's sissy hygiene, such compulsive attention and self-awareness ironically belie the repeated claims of an innate masculinity threatened only by society's false stereotyping of the homosexual as inveterate sissy. Like the ex-colored man's color consciousness, which precipitates a crisis of masculinity, these athletes' narrations of homosexual disclosure cannot help but also address a concomitant gender crisis that they'd prefer to repress. Whether or not they, as boys, were perfectly "normal" when it comes to the character of their gender experience and expression, they unwittingly must contend with the inescapable assumption that male same-gender attraction will bear some tincture of sissification. Like the church sissy's oratorical and musical talents, however, the all-consuming intensity of their circumspection seems to drive their sports talents and ambitions—securing an obeisance not only to masculine norms but also to the ideals of sportsmanship as manifested in the practice of man-play.

These three sports disclosure memoirs written by white athletes display an uncannily similar approach to sissy-avoidance and disavowal. Mostly unaware of how their racial assignation exposes, buffers, or masks their homosexuality, and how it accordingly exposes, buffers, or masks their potential for being perceived as sissies, the narratives largely ignore how whiteness, in its various material manifestations, intersects with sexuality and gender impersonation. In turning to sports disclosure memoirs penned by athletes of color, this dynamic of sissy-avoidance becomes even more complicated by how the narrators relate their gender nonconformity as in/commensurate with their racial identities. In former pro defensive lineman Esera Tuaolo's *Alone in the Trenches*, for instance, the superhero fantasy reappears, but in a quite different way from Bean's Superman fantasy. As he grows up in Hawaii in an immigrant Samoan family, Tuaolo's physical size also defines his relationship to both his sexuality and his gender character, as well as to his racial identification, but in terms of being oversized rather than undersized. The notion of the big sissy or the fat sissy complements the stereotype of the little sissy-boy, for conventional masculinity regulates body size from both directions. A boy who is deemed too small for sports has to prove himself with extra gusto; one who is deemed oversized is often seen as someone who *should* be involved in rugged sport, particularly when the boy is racially othered, both to replace soft fat with hard muscle and to prove that his "extra" flesh is not the result of a weak sissy nature. Underlying this mandate to corral the big nonwhite boy into rough team sports is the racial assumption that without sports participation, the boy will surely become a criminal, predatory threat to white society—more specifically, to white ladyhood. Tuaolo identifies at first not with Superman but instead with Wonder Woman, like Rod Ferguson. Tuaolo writes, "I preferred make-believe to the pain in my life. I turned myself into Wonder Woman and deflected negative feelings with my bracelets."[61] Unlike Kopay, Pallone, and Bean, however, Tuaolo forthrightly confesses his early sissy predisposition. This initial identification as a sissy-boy constitutes a common feature of sports disclosure memoirs by men of color. Tuaolo's self-identification as a sissy-boy, moreover, is directly related to his Samoan lineage as a direct response to first learning what the word *mahu* means:

> When I was five years old, I heard a friend call another friend *mahu*. I asked him what that meant. "Faggot," he told me in Samoan. *Oooh, he likes boys,* I thought, *that's bad.*
>
> Then I thought, *Uh-oh.*
>
> I never liked playing with stuff other boys wanted to play with. I played with Ken and Barbie dolls. I wanted an Easy-Bake oven. I was fascinated by the way my sisters dressed. I tried on their jewelry when they weren't looking. I remember watching GI Joe on TV and thinking he was cute. I had a crush on a buddy at a young age.

This revelation of the boy Tuaolo's sexual orientation comes through its familiar connection with gender-nonconforming conduct. The boy's response is rational. He immediately changes his conduct to eradicate every sign of gender nonconformity: "*Oh shit*, I thought. *Mahu. That might be me.* I started playing with things other boys played with. I asked for a cowboy gun. I started being tougher. I ended up calling other kids *mahu*."[62] The young Tuaolo hopes that by changing his sissy conduct, he can change his homosexual character. Tuaolo's narrative, however, is framed through an ethnic difference that places his experience in a slightly different light from that of the white gay sports narrators. He identifies homophobia with the arrival of missionaries to Samoa. Implicitly, Tuaolo is suggesting that if the island nation had never been Christianized, his struggles with gender identity would have been minimized. Raised in a Pentecostal church, he hears the Christian message that homosexuality is an abomination. Remaining a devout Christian as he learns to embrace his homosexuality, this sinful view of homosexuality leads to attempts at repression and heterosexual courting, then a double life, and finally a rejection not of Christianity altogether but of that particular belief held by most evangelicals and fundamentalists.[63]

Tuaolo's memoir gives some glimmers of how same-sexuality is framed differently in different national and ethnic communities. His strong identity as a Samoan Hawaiian shapes in self-conflicted ways his gender and sexual conduct. When Tuaolo's older brother, Tua, a homosexual and ceremonial chief, dies of AIDS, Tuaolo responds not only with expected grief but also with some anger. When Tua saw his little brother at gay gatherings, he did not acknowledge him. The elder brother urged Tuaolo not to come out of the closet. He did not otherwise talk to Tuaolo concerning their shared sexuality. Rather than a mentor, Tua almost served to block the younger brother's embrace of homosexuality. Given Tua's position in the community, his funeral becomes a mass gathering in tribute to his contributions, but his sexuality and the fact that he died of AIDS are scrupulously expunged from public view.[64] This creates a double grief on Tuaolo's part. It is in the report on the funeral that Tuaolo interrupts the narrative to provide a different pre-Christian view of gender fluidity: "In Polynesian culture, it's okay to be a *faafafine*, an effeminate and affected gay man who dresses and acts like a woman. That's what people expected of gay men. People still teased or beat up the *faafafines*—they weren't completely accepted—but they were able to hold responsible positions as witch doctors and the like."[65] Tuaolo's description of a "third" gender tolerated and even in some ways venerated in Polynesian culture accords with work on this topic done by gender studies scholars in the social sciences.[66] Notably, however, Tuaolo understandably conflates Western contemporary vocabulary—"gay men"—with language from Polynesian culture—"faafafine"—even as he attempts to distinguish between the two. Tuaolo perceptively does have a sense that there is a difference between gender identity and sexual orientation, and this is driven home to him in how Tua did not fit the cultural configuration of the faafafine in that he was not an effeminate, cross-dressing man, but instead a very masculine one:

> Tua was a man's man. To be masculine *and* gay was not okay. We Samoans were supposed to be feared throughout the Pacific as powerful warriors. For someone like Tua or me to be gay undermined that warrior image because being gay meant someone was weak. Our being gay threatened the Samoan cultural ideal.
>
> It's similar with the stereotypes for various sports. No one seems surprised if a figure skater or a gymnast is gay—those athletes are stereotyped as more feminine, probably because their sports require such grace and finesse. Football players, on the other hand, are supposed to be warriors. Being gay—which is equated with being weak—threatens that tough image.[67]

Despite its self-evident conflations between homosexuality and effeminate conduct, this is one of the most precise articulations in these sports disclosure memoirs of the way nonconforming gender identity interacts with the perception of homosexuality as it relates to different sports. It also reminds us of how the warrior is so strongly defined against the sissy as the embodiment of cowardice and homosexuality as the prototype of the sissy, as discussed in previous chapters. Nonetheless, even in making this rather clear-eyed assessment, Tuaolo ironically practices a version of sissy-avoidance that more aggressively characterizes the white-authored sports disclosure form. Although he has earlier described in some detail his own sissy-boy disposition, here he classes himself with his brother as "a man's man." Even as he calls out the flawed logic whereby weakness is equated with sissiness, which in turn is equated with homosexuality, he recodifies that illogic by insisting that, because he and Tua were not weak, were warriors, they were exceptional in being gay men who were not faafafine. As with racial exceptionality, so these sports disclosure memoirists appeal to their exceptional status as gay men who should not be tainted with the weakness, cowardice, and softness bound to the sissy's person. In other words, despite its racial complications, to rescue male homosexuality from sissiness, his memoir rehearses the notion of "straight" gay men's gender exceptionality—the normalizing capacity to be gay but not sissy.

By the time that Tuaolo moves toward closure, after he comes out on national television on the show *Real Sports with Bryant Gumbel*, he fully adopts the idea that he is the opposite of a sissy: "Some people expect me to be different now that I'm out, to talk in a higher voice or act like a woman. That's just not me. I grew up in a straight way. Even now that I'm out, I'm too straight for the gay community, but I'm too gay for the straight community.... I never felt the need to be a Nellie. My perception of being gay is me."[68] This assertion contradicts the image of the sissy-boy that initiates the narrative. He is now so "straight" that he is "too straight" for the gay community. Straightness here clearly refers to gender conduct, not sexual attraction. Ironically, his field cred as a football player has helped him to purge the sissy-boy that he earlier confessed to being. In his confusions—gender, racial, and sexual—Tuaolo helps to clarify what is at stake in the out gay pro athlete's unrelenting adoption of a public gender-straightness, even as he simultaneously wants to make a clear distinction between dominant (white) America's hang-ups about gender nonconformity versus his own culture's more fluid understanding of sexual behavior in relation to gender-nonconforming character. One wonders, however, to what extent this intensifying sissy-avoidance is not only a dynamic of man-play parading as sportsmanship but also a matter of the amped-up media scrutiny afforded by the pseudo-intimacy of televisual fame. If we could argue that Baldwin self-consciously sustained his sissy conduct, however respectably proper in manner, as he became a televisual spokesman for the race, we might accordingly speculate that Tuaolo felt compelled to butch up for the television cameras, and metonymically for the memoir hawked on television—a conventionalizing gender conduct before the camera already habituated by the straight warrior conduct required to be a lineman in the NFL, itself a creature fashioned by fixated televisual gender expectations. To be an NFL lineman is to be *not* a sissy, and to face the TV cameras as an openly gay lineman intensifies the need to distance the athlete from the sissy stigma.

Although no doubt Tuaolo would have penned this narrative based in the same structure of sissiphobia and sissy-avoidance even without the precedent of Kopay's highly influential memoir, that he has the model of Kopay surely helps to orient this narrative strategy.[69] The repetition of this strategy in memoir after memoir from the 1970s to today reaffirms the gender ideology whereby the sissy becomes a liminal vehicle through which homosexuality can be compatible with fit athleticism while exorcising sissiness as the epitome of unfit sportsmanship. We can see this sissy-avoidance still at work in the most recent gay male sports disclosure narrative, John Amaechi's *Man in the Middle*, published in 2007. Identifying as biracial, "brown," British (raised in Manchester by a white mother), fat, and not that interested in sports as a boy, Amaechi nonetheless scripts his narrative strictly according to the sissy-avoidance codes of the earlier autobiographies. As with Tuaolo, Amaechi's ethnic difference and big size are crucial to his early identity as not quite an ordinary boy: "At any rate, my self-consciousness about my body made me want to avoid sports of any kind. I just said no to rope-climb, vaulting, track, even cricket, where players wore uniforms whiter than the snow in Russia. I wanted to wipe the entire subject out of my life."[70] Like previous memoirists, Amaechi identifies fantasy escapism as crucial to his sense of himself. Like a good sissy-boy, he becomes an avid reader: "It's no surprise my taste ran to the escapist. There were no social pressures or demands, no put-downs directed at me, and it was always others who felt the sting of hurtful words" (17). If for Bean being undersized puts him in jeopardy of being assumed a sissy, Amaechi's size, like Tuaolo's, serves to shield him from suspicion: "I heard the occasional reference to 'poofs,' usually from sixth formers, the oldest students. . . . But the insults were never directed at me. No one ever dared accuse the biggest guy in the room of being a fag" (24). Like previous sports disclosure narratives, Amaechi assumes that straight-appearing is a justification for sports-worthiness. As long as he conducts himself in accordance with hegemonic masculinity, his homosexuality should be embraceable by coaches, colleagues, and fans. Reflecting on his basketball career toward the end of the narrative, he asserts: "Homosexuality is an obsession among ballplayers, trailing only wealth and women. They just didn't like 'fags'—or so they insisted over and over and over again. It soon became clear they didn't understand fags enough to truly loathe them. Most were convinced, even as they sat next to me on the bus or plane or threw me the ball in the post, that they had never met one" (268). Riffing on the idea contained in the title of the memoir's second chapter, "Invisible Giant," just as his big brownness makes him ironically invisible—his peers not knowing how to categorize a big brown boy—so his homosexuality is an invisible attribute to his presumably straight peer athletes. This invisibility functions silently as his claim to gender normativity. Because he is not a sissy, or more precisely a swish, he can become a reasonably successful pro basketballer. It also stands to reason that if his teammates could truly come to know fags—that is, exceptional "straight" homosexuals like himself—their obsession with faggots as a threat to fit athleticism would dissipate. As a big man in the middle of the basketball court—one not suspected of being a big faggot—Amaechi can claim Ralph Ellison's status as the "invisible man" only by eradicating the true invisible man, the big sissy, from this sports narrative of gay self-acceptance.

It must also be considered that even as Amaechi represents himself as ordinarily gendered, despite his childhood sissy tendencies, his narrative resolve also depends on his being exceptionally racialized. His biraciality makes him stand out in his native Manchester. He imagines what it might have been like to grow up in Boston, where his mother lived for a brief period, if he had grown up in a black American community. His disidentification from blackness is highly ironic, given that when people on the street spot this big "brown" man, they naturally assume that he must be athletic, because his brownness is casually perceived simply as blackness. Even as he insists on a liminal identity between white and black, his size contributes to others' perception of his blackness at the same time that it most likely serves to mask any hint of gender nonconformity. In this twenty-first-century memoir, a male's color and size remain factors of masculine fitness, just as at the beginning of the twentieth, James Weldon Johnson could pen a faux-memoir based on the very notion that a man's skin color and size could determine not only his masculine but also his racial fitness, whether for the Caucasian or the Negro race. Amaechi's treatment of race accords with another crucial feature of the sports disclosure memoir: the tendency to use man-play not only to distance the gay from the sissy but also to claim sportsmanship's capacity to supersede the black/white racial binary. Amaechi justifies adopting two white teenagers based on his own experience as a "brown" boy raised by a white mother: "Interracial parenting felt not just ordinary but natural." Race is an issue only for others, even though so much of the narrative is structured through an obsession with racial disidentification, no less than Johnson's *Autobiography of an Ex-Coloured Man* or Baraka's *System of Dante's Hell*: "Anyway, we were enjoying the experience far too much to worry about what others thought. To me it wasn't important that other people understood" (227). While Amaechi makes invisible the matter of a single homosexual adopting two teenage boys, he foregrounds the racial issue even as he claims its irrelevance. The bond between the brown father and the white boys—"one part redneck and one part skinhead" (227)—transcends race due to their devotion to sports. We might say that a deeper invisible bond that facilitates this familial arrangement is Amaechi's gender straightness. Just as his basketball career is possible because he is overread as black, which contributes to his being *not* read as a sissy, so his adoption of the white boys, budding athletes, is also this (self-)perception of a gender normalcy that is coded through his athletic blackness. Just as in American sport one cannot arrive at fit athleticism without going through racial assumptions, so one cannot arrive at unfit athleticism without an articulated aversion to the sissy figure.

A Gay Jackie Robinson? Queer Sports in Black, White, and Color

Once we begin to examine the relatively short history of life narratives written by and about openly gay pro athletes, we find that race invariably plays a signal role in structuring these narratives, including those of white gay athletes. The disproportionate number of black men among these openly gay pro jocks might partly explain this. A more apt explanation, though, must consider African Americans' acculturation into collective obligations of social protest. Even as sportsmanship is tethered to a historical notion of white male supremacy while claiming to be a racially neutral barometer of athletic fitness, fit athleticism in the United States inescapably revolves around blackness. Harry Edwards in his classic *Revolt of the Black Athlete* and John Hoberman in *Darwin's Athletes* have documented the illogically shifting rationales that at first posit an inferior black physicality that is unfit for sportsmanship and then reverse into the idea of a genetically wired black physicality that overdetermines black men's athletic prowess.[71] Refusing to acknowledge how every sport requires mental as well as physical skill, it has been preferable to reduce the toughest sports to native (biological) physical skill than to admit the fallacy of white male supremacy. The out gay athlete as prototypically black threatens to topple the national narrative that plots black athletic supremacy through the racial caricature of the hypermasculine and hyperheterosexual black jock. Ironically, in the white disclosure memoir the straight black athlete becomes a touchstone, helping to masculinize the white gay jock by intimate association and also helping to organize these coming-out stories through a racial framework based in black athletes' brave battles against the Jim Crow color barrier.

If white male uniformity to the point of narcissism anchors Kopay's and Pallone's bid to a fit manliness through overly competent athleticism, paradoxically racial analogy structures the mooring of white disclosure narratives as social protest. One way in which these memoirs exploit intimacy with blackness to promote gay sportsmanship is by referencing the Jackie Robinson breakthrough as a precedent. Although a common lament in these sports disclosure narratives concerns how homophobia has prevented an athlete from reaching his full potential, the irony is that players like Jackie Robinson were able to excel at the highest level in the face of open hostility and violence due to white supremacy. "I wish I had come out while I was still playing. I think it could have made an impact on the level of Jackie Robinson breaking the color barrier," Tuaolo writes. "It would have helped the game of football and society at large. But, living in the fear that I was, it's hard for me to imagine myself doing that."[72] Even though Robinson's own sports memoir about breaking the color line, *I Never Had It Made*, is released only five years before Kopay's, Kopay and his coauthor, Perry Deane Young, cannot risk a comparison that would make Kopay's burden, however lamentable, pale in comparison with Robinson's. To match Robinson's racial heroism, Kopay would have had to brave the field with his gayness flaring in his fans' faces, instead of masking his sexuality behind a straight facade. Because there were no laws or policies analogous to Jim Crow forbidding Kopay from playing as a homosexual (however venomous the stigma of sports homophobia), the analogy begins to break down once we begin to seriously consider the different conditions of racial versus heterosexist oppression.

Toward the end of Billy Bean's *Going the Other Way*, he too draws the tentative comparison to Jackie Robinson:

> There's precedent for social change in baseball. After my incidental outing, fans and sportswriters rush to anoint me the gay Jackie Robinson. Let me make one thing perfectly clear: I'm no Jackie Robinson.
>
> Like other early black major leaguers, Robinson overcame enormous obstacles that I can grasp only from reading history books. He was subjected to barbaric racism. He received death threats.... By turning the other cheek and focusing on the game, he survived with dignity.[73]

He goes on to summarize the heroic history of Robinson's desegregation of the Dodgers, one of Bean's own pro teams, while emphasizing his own failure to live up to that standard: "Faced with similar hostility, I had retreated, lied, and hid. Even though it took a tremendous toll on me, not to mention everyone around me, I could pretend to be something I wasn't—I ducked the kind of conflict Robinson and Rickey confronted."[74] Of course, Bean also has the precedent of African American baseballer Glenn Burke, whose experience of being drummed out of baseball due to homophobia is occasionally mentioned in the narrative.[75] Diverting attention away from his own Jackie Robinson potential, even as he acknowledges how the "fans and sportswriters rush" to grant him that heroic role, Bean instead emphasizes the need for a player both extraordinarily skilled and extraordinarily brave, as well as emphasizing that such a player will need supporters in and outside of baseball to come to his aid the way Branch Rickey and some white players did for Robinson.

Black pro athletes can claim with greater confidence this Robinson lineage and legacy even while recognizing the particular divergences between racism and heterosexism. When Glenn Burke pens his sports disclosure memoir, *Out at Home*, in 1995, he overtly claims the lineage of Jackie Robinson to bolster the historic significance of his gay-affirmative sportsmanship. That Burke refused to deny his sexuality by ruses such as getting married to please the Dodgers management also gives him greater authority to lay claim to Robinson's lineage. In Billy Bean's generous foreword to Burke's memoir, he makes this point: "Glenn was much braver than I. He refused to let homophobia change him. He didn't hide from his truth.... Glenn had his loving family, and a hometown group of friends around him for support."[76] By penning the foreword to Burke's disclosure memoir, Bean possesses the authority of firstness, the first MLB player to have come out of the closet. As the self-humbling tone of the foreword indicates, however, Bean understands how Burke might be seen to deserve greater credit, and thus greater authority, as the first gay pro baseballer. Shadowing Bean's sense of humility in regard to Burke is the latter's implicit sense that Burke is more deserving of the Jackie Robinson lineage, explicitly because Burke was less closeted and implicitly because of Burke's racial affiliation with Robinson. Note how Bean emphasizes the phalanx of family and friends who provided a support network for Burke's resistance to the heteronorm. Bean recognizes explicitly that this support network is based in the legacy of civil rights protest movements. He also projects, though, a greater tolerance for homosexuality among African Americans—the racial structure also evident in Kopay's memoir. In this foreword, Bean hints at the sense, perhaps even some envy, that it must have been easier for Burke to be so self-confident in his sexuality, a confidence that the white athlete is denied in part due to his hegemonic white maleness and its expectations. It is certainly ironic that what is usually conceived as a double burden—being black and gay—can be turned into a perceived advantage. Knowing how to maneuver racist oppression, the logic goes, gives Burke some know-how in how to maneuver homophobic oppression. Also at stake here, however unstated, is an assumption that Burke, as an African American player, also has the benefit of black athletic superiority, which can compensate for any perceived lack of fitness due to homosexual orientation. In drawing a more secure line between Burke and the Jackie Robinson legacy, Bean displays his own racial insecurity in making any comparison with the black athlete. His resistance to such a comparison acknowledges Burke's greater (native) athletic skill, as well as his greater braveness as a queer man, thus implying that the ousting of Burke from baseball was a greater loss for the game than would've been the case if he himself had been more open, resulting in a foreshortened career due to such an ouster.

In the introduction to *Out at Home*, Burke's coauthor, Erik Sherman, gives a slightly different take on Burke's homosexual openness, claiming that "Burke remained in the closet primarily because of his love of baseball."[77] Sherman also recasts Bean's sense that Burke's self-confidence was bolstered largely by the African American community to connect Burke more closely with the predominantly white Castro.[78] Although Sherman's take on Burke's degree of disclosure differs from Bean's, and to some extent from that of the narrative itself, Sherman is eager to seal the tie with the Jackie Robinson narrative. He begins the introduction with that story.[79] In making the analogy with Robinson, Sherman also points to a contrast between the eventual victory of African Americans as pro athletes versus the ongoing stigma against homosexuality that prevents Burke from achieving his rightful glory as the progeny of Robinson: "Nearly thirty years after Robinson broke baseball's color barrier, another black Dodger rookie, this one out of Oakland, California, came to understand another prejudice. This prejudice had nothing to do with the color of his skin. It was, instead, about his sexual preference."[80] Neatly separating color prejudice from homophobia, Burke's coauthor discounts what becomes apparent within the narrative itself: that just as Burke's athleticism could not be divorced from the Robinson legacy, so his response to homophobia could not be divorced from the racial identification that binds him to Robinson as a sportsman and as a citizen.[81]

Published twenty years after *The David Kopay Story*, though, Burke's *Out at Home* also pays homage to Kopay as the first pro athlete to out himself in a sports memoir. Burke's professional career started the year Kopay outs himself, so rightly Burke's narrative has a double inheritance, blending Robinson's most celebrated feat with Kopay's lesser-known but no less significant political action. That Burke takes a risk by exposing his homosexuality is evident from the outset of the narrative. He begins with the episode in which Tommy Lasorda, manager of the Dodgers, inexplicably blows up at him in 1977: "I couldn't help but think his malice toward me had gone deeper than my wanting a chance to play or my practical jokes. Maybe it had to do with my getting along with the other player a bit too well. Or maybe he knew about my close relationship with his gay son, Spunky. Or worse, maybe he knew that I was gay, too."[82] Lasorda's rabid homophobia leads him later to cut Burke from the team. No doubt, the deepest source of Lasorda's fury derived from his disappointment with Spunky, Lasorda's son, as the manager/father scapegoats Burke as displaced punishment against his own son's more flaunting homosexuality. Burke's association with Spunky, who "was a transvestite some of the time, but not all the time" and who was "extremely flamboyant," indicates an open defiance of the taboo on both homosexuality and sissiness within sport. To hang with such a person necessarily would lead to guilt by association and speculation about Burke's own sexuality: "The Dodgers always had suspicions that there was a sexual relationship between us. I've never responded to that suspicion. That's my business" (24). Burke proceeds to speculate that "a good portion of the team knew about my homosexuality," but "because I hadn't admitted to it, much less even been questioned about it," it is left an open secret. "It helped that I acted like the 'King Kong' tag that had been placed on me instead of the prototypical 'sissy' label that most straights recognize homosexuals as" (25). Burke's relation to Spunky and to the sissy label represents a kinder, more embracing attitude toward non-gender-conforming men than Pallone's, Kopay's, Bean's, or even Tuaolo's and Amaechi's. Even though speculation about Burke's too-close association with sissiness may have been the cause of his being ousted from baseball, he does not scapegoat the sissy figure, in this case his friend Spunky, to exonerate himself. A pretty clear example of how speculation operates endemically in the perception of sissiness, Burke nonetheless refuses the predictable act of sissy dissociation evident in the nonblack disclosure narratives.

If Burke does not follow the established pattern of the sexual double life, his narrative subtly scripts another kind of double life: that of a black man who maintains deep roots in the African American community while also venturing out into the white gay mecca of the Castro, seeking to integrate and transcend across race, if in a different way from the biracial Amaechi. Rather than working overtime to separate his worlds—gay and straight, black and white, jock and nonjock—Burke is extraordinary in how he takes risks, confiding in his closest teammates, staying close with his family and "homeboys" in Oakland, forging a tight friendship with other jockish black gay men, socializing in the Castro, and soon after his retirement developing a long-term relationship with a white man who is very politically active in gay rights. He invites two of his friends to the World Series at Yankee Stadium: "The three of us had a lot in common. We were all gay black men who loved sports and really worked hard at staying in shape together" (31). Sport as a bond among men is, without a doubt, one of the most telling signifiers of gender normalcy. Working hard at staying in shape, however, could as easily mark the homeboys as exemplars of the new Castro gay aesthetic as it could mark them as fit athletes. Burke's bond with his black gay brothers, however, accrues an extra measure of bonding power due to their shared racial identification as a reflection of their shared sexual identification as a reflection of their love of sports, implicitly *despite* that shared sexuality. There is no such representation of bonded identification through gayness in the white-authored disclosure memoirs. Indeed, Burke's narrative seems to confirm Bean's right to envy a seemingly easier path for the black gay athlete because he is black. Even the title of Burke's memoir, *Out at Home*, riffs on the idea that the black pro jock *can* be more comfortable in his own gay skin not only at home base, as a metaphor for the sport as a whole, but also at home, in his familial household and in his neighborhood, among his family, friends, and acquaintances. If the world of sport wants to stigmatize him for his relatively out stance, he always has recourse to the support provided by his literal home.

Similarly, Burke's narrative more felicitously intersects his defiance of homophobia with his everyday experience of defying racism. Like Robinson's *Never Had It Made*, Burke's memoir emphasizes his intolerance of everyday racism, as indicated by an incident he describes during his stint in the minors. Burke hangs tight with two black teammates, Cleo Smith and Marvin Webb, all three from Oakland. While in Utah, the three are accosted by Mormons who, when the athletes refuse to buy a copy of the Mormon newspaper, charge, "Well, you blacks are the cause of all the problems in the world." Cleo and Marvin hold Burke back from kicking "that boy's ass all over the street" (39). Unlike Kopay's egging his frat brothers on to fight in a display of bullying or Bean's hanging out with a bully to enhance his own small size, Burke's recounting of his desire to kick some ass seems less gratuitous as a performance of sissy-avoidance. The incident emphasizes, again, how masculine camaraderie might come, ironically, in his friends' holding him back from a fight, even when warranted, rather than egging him on as some proof of macho credibility. Of course, his black male friends have no doubt that, if Burke were to kick the Mormons' ass, his semi-pro status would not save him from the law's vendetta against black men. Unlike white athletes, Burke cannot afford the normative conduct of fighting to defend himself against an attack. This is one in a series of racially charged incidents, as the narrative does not discriminate between such everyday experiences of racism and the homophobia he suffers at the hands of the Dodgers and A's baseball management. It is in the tight networks of family, straight buddies, and gay intimates that he finds comfort and understanding. When his black straight friend Marvin sees Burke associating with homo-swishes, Marvin treats them with respect rather than shunning them, as might be expected of a straight jock in the 1970s. When Marvin realizes that Burke is sexually involved with Burke's former junior high school teacher, Mr. Mendler, Marvin says to him, "I don't care what you are or what you did with Mr. Mendler, you're still my friend" (48).

Rather than a tale of a boy who struggles to repress his sissiness, Burke's is instead one of a boy who belatedly comes to understand why he was never attracted to girls around the age of twenty-three (similar to Bean's sexual awakening around the same age). After his first experience, with Mr. Mendler, he describes sexual epiphany in very romantic terms: "So when I found that 'loving' feeling, it was very emotional. I wasn't a hound. I was very sensitive back then. And the fact that Mr. Mendler was older helped me out a lot too" (47). In the well-worn tradition of black sportsmen like Paul Robeson and Joe Louis who aggressively counter the myth of the oversexed black buck by emphasizing instead the conventional romance plot, Burke images himself as a love-struck innocent, the very opposite of the "hound." Not attracted to the boy-next-door jock like Pallone or Kopay, Burke seems to seek out as romantic partners older white men who are highly educated and not paradigmatically masculine. Although Burke observes that he himself was always masculine, he does not engage in overcompensatory claims or actions to prove it—a notable contrast with the memoirs of Kopay, Pallone, Tuaolo, Amaechi, and Bean. This cool attitude toward his own masculinity is particularly poignant relative to his friendship with Tommy Lasorda's son, Spunky. "Spunky and I were different in the sense that I was very masculine and he was very feminine," he writes. "His flamboyancy was probably a reaction to his father" (25). Burke is comfortable associating with swishing sissies because his own masculinity is rather matter-of-fact. The closest Burke comes to sissy-avoidance is when he celebrates his natural muscularity and stature, which he sees as the basis of his extraordinary skill at basketball as well as baseball. "I grew to about five-ten, 180 pounds by age fifteen," he writes. "I was easily the strongest kid in the Colt League. My crowning moment was hitting a ball measured at five hundred feet" (75).

Unlike most other sports disclosure memoirs, Burke's does not describe a boyhood tortured by the perception of being either an undersized or oversized sissy. He records a very ordinary experience on the streets and fields around Oakland, a loving family, and an easeful path toward sexual self-acceptance, with the clear exception of his being dumped from the majors because of his refusal to play the paranoid game of hiding his sexuality. He labels himself a protector of kids and those not capable of fending for themselves, quite different from the bullying posture depicted by Pallone, Kopay, and Bean. Rejecting the hatefulness of evangelical Christianity without rejecting Christianity, the narrative insists on judging people by their conduct, reserving the label "Christian" for those who accord themselves with the nonjudging, justice-seeking tenets of Christ depicted in the Gospels. His is an ethic of doing onto others, regardless of race, sexuality, or gender performance—an ethic that draws attention to the hypocrisy of the sports establishment's claim to being a meritocracy: "The Lord was my best friend growing up. I mean it. I had a lot of friends, but He was the most important to me" (79). His passion for the church he attended in youth, "Ebenezer Church off Ashley Street," is epitomized through his participation in senior and junior choir. Reminiscent of Baldwin's characters, Baldwin himself, Little Richard, and Sylvester James, the image of the church choir sissy is as close as he comes to the notion of his own sissiness, but his singing is characterized as a warm nostalgic memory from a happy childhood, not as some sort of dissonant, estranging, unusual, or agonizing gender confusion and contention within the church. His almost-utopian strain subtly binds race problems to matters of gender and sexual difference: "Maybe if more people followed Christ's Word, we could have a kind of heaven on earth" (80).

This does not mean that the only trouble in *Out at Home* emanates from baseball's homophobia. The memoir records, as mentioned earlier, everyday incidents of racism and homophobia with an even, easygoing hand, even as such random acts can occasionally enrage him. Burke's attraction to nonathletic, higher-educated, older white men also gestures toward a certain degree of racial ambivalence insofar as the narrative very vividly records the racial trouble that can accompany gay cross-racial relationships. Burke's idyllic portrait of his times in the Castro is severely undercut by the tribulations of his long-term relationship with Michael J. Smith, the editor of *Black Men / White Men: A Gay Anthology* (1983) and founder of Black and White Men Together (BWMT), a gay men's racial justice organization, but one whose history is tarnished by a perception of also being an interracial hookup club.[83] In the memoir, Burke details the emotional and psychological abuse he suffers from Smith's controlling attitude toward him. Often belittling Burke's intellect and mocking him in front of both Smith's and Burke's friends, and exploiting Burke's fame to line his own pockets, Smith sees Burke as his own personal sexual object to be handled and mishandled as he pleases—not an unusual mentality among some white men who engage in sexual relations only with black men. Smith becomes upset that Burke refuses to give up his Oakland homeboys and other "low-class" friends: "Really, he didn't even want me to have Castro friends either. Just his friends."[84] Although the memoir tries hard to transcend racial and sexual differences as incidental to Burke's own embrace of diversity as a Christian ethic, the angry exposure of an abusive interracial relationship at the center of the narrative fractures its easeful, cool narration of racial-sexual harmoniousness.

After the relationship finally ends (the two men having broken up and gotten back together several times), Smith publishes an essay, "The Double Life of a Gay Dodger," in *Black Men / White Men*, without Burke's permission or even knowledge. Burke describes the outing essay that Smith publishes by cataloguing the venal motives driving the published essay as well as the factual inaccuracies about Burke's life that Smith fabricated to sensationalize the baseball player's experience. Culminating the list of inaccuracies is a statement that Smith attributes to Burke: "And the last major problem I had with the article was Michael quoting me as saying, 'I didn't know if I could be gay without being a sissy.'"[85] Burke saves this inaccuracy for last because it is the one that enrages him most. Burke seeks to debunk this notion first by reasserting his secure and undeniable masculinity, then by reemphasizing his ethic of the nonjudgmental embrace of diverse persons, regardless of gender conduct: "He had to be kidding with that one. I had seventeen-inch biceps and loved the fact I was built like a fucking tank.

I couldn't be a sissy if I wanted to. Not even in my wildest dreams. I knew that from the first moment I came out. Homosexuals come in all shapes and sizes. I've always accepted that fact."[86] Skirting a line between sissy-avoidance and sissy-embrace, Burke, unlike the white sports disclosure narrators, is careful to couple his own self-confident masculinity with his unwavering embrace of gender-nonconforming sissies and swishes.

Burke's apparent ease with and embrace of swishing sissies, drag queens, and effeminate men is captured in his hanging out in gay bars and in the Castro. Burke paints a picture of the Castro as a home away from home, one transcending racial identification and gender conduct. Michael Smith's behavior in relation to other black sex partners contradicts this raceless idyll, as it captures the kind of racism that was rampant in the Castro during the 1970s and '80s: "In fact, Michael only dated black men. But those relationships never lasted more than one or two weeks. He was a user. A destroyer. He had at least a one-nighter with almost every black guy who hung out at the Pendulum. He thought this would make me jealous. And angry. Instead, I would get somewhat depressed over the whole thing. But at the same time, I was flattered by his obsession with me. Must have been that Ivy League look of his!"[87] As other black gay authors from this period, like Joseph Beam and Marlon Riggs, have documented, black men were frequently stereotyped, exoticized, and met with demands for multiple identification cards to discourage their entrance into the bars and clubs of newly formed white gay ghettos.[88] Smith's carousing and cruising the Pendulum, one of the clubs that did cater to African Americans, signals his exclusive preference for black men. The fear of bar owners was that any place that was too accepting of black men would turn into a "black" bar, effectively a segregated space, one that whites would hesitate to visit once a certain tipping point of blacks was evident. This is exactly what happens at the Pendulum, as Burke himself records: "But then in the late eighties the Pendulum became a dark, loud, and boisterous all-black bar. It can actually be pretty dangerous in there at times. Plus, I got burned out there. Every time I was on the street, someone would ask, 'What time are you headed for the Pendulum?'"[89] Burke's attitude toward blackness—"dark, loud, and boisterous" and "pretty dangerous"—echoes the dominant white gay discourse about places frequented by blacks, and it exposes Burke's own degree of discomfort within his own skin. In fact, once Burke himself is HIV-infected and homeless, he hangs out on the streets of the Castro panhandling to the same men who had ostensibly befriended him when he was Michael J. Smith's lover. It is not his erstwhile white Castro friends who come to rescue him in his final days but his sister, who saves him from the street, takes him home with her, and nurses him until his death. The tragic end to Burke's Castro idyll reveals the precarious status of many black gay men seeking solace in white gay ghettos in this period. In the end, Burke's onetime celebrity as a professional jock could not compensate for his disregard of the sexual rules governing sportsmanship as man-play, nor could it overcome the racism underpinning the superficial cross-racial camaraderie of his beloved Castro.

If the ragged edges of race cannot fully be softened in Burke's memoir through his gentler approach to gender queers and the emerging white queer hegemony of the time, similarly David Kopay is not able fully to create his hoped-for complementarity between blackness and white homosexuality as a way of authenticating the minority status of white gay men. Chapter 4 of *The David Kopay Story* references the sports color line as an analogy for his sexual orientation in these terms: "Recently I've come to the conclusion that a lot of my extra drive came from the same forces that brought black athletes out of the ghettos to the forefront of professional sports. They were out to prove—among other things—that they were not inferior because of their race. I was out to prove that I was in no way less a man because I was homosexual."[90] In addition to referencing obliquely the heroic narrative of Jackie Robinson, Kopay builds audience sympathy by creating mutual empathy between his situation and that of African Americans—using his intimate relationship with gay-tolerant straight black players to masculinize himself as a gay athlete. When he moves to Washington, DC, to play for the Redskins, he attributes the city's gay-friendly environment in part to "the fact that a majority of the population and almost the entire city government is composed of black people, who generally tend to look on another minority with compassion because of their own history of being oppressed" (132). Later, Kopay provides a catalogue of black Redskin players who knew that he was gay but accepted him unconditionally: "It seemed to make for a kind of unspoken bond between us. I knew they had been harassed just because of the color of their skin, and they knew that my difference was also something to be accepted for what it was—not what other people might think it is" (173). Black athletes' greater tolerance for Kopay's hidden homosexuality authenticates his call for the larger public to accept gayness as a legitimate social identity deserving equal treatment on the field and in U.S. law. It is, in fact, difficult to imagine Kopay's narrative of sexual disclosure without its reliance on the racial frame of black athleticism as an authenticating force.

This use of blackness to prop up (white) homosexual inclusion does not, however, diminish the narrative's tendency to exploit blackness also as a nonnormative foil. If Kopay borrows masculine cred from black athleticism, it is also the case that, in a crucial instance, the figure of the black swishing sissy represents a moment for white heteronormative bonding. After their Las Vegas wedding ceremony, Kopay and his new wife go with another couple to see Little Richard perform in the hotel theater: "Everybody was laughing about his costumes and even I was joining in the jokes about being gay" (172). The irony here is that Little Richard, as discussed in chapter 4, was probably the first swishing sissy, along with Liberace, to garner a mass crossover audience in America. On the one hand, Kopay legitimates his athleticism, and thus his fit masculinity, through his sympathetic cross-racial bond with his presumably straight black teammates. On the other hand, he turns to a black sissy to manifest his aversion to, and distance from, the swishing homosexual. Little Richard's greater bravery, performing rock and roll as his swish self, gets repudiated and erased through narration that wants to claim Kopay's own bravery for making it in pro football as a closeted homosexual.

Similarly, Bean's *Going the Other Way* frames his sexual disclosure with episodes of cross-racial intimacy, analogizing his own victimization as a gay white man in sports to that of black players who have suffered discrimination due to their race: "Before long, I connected with the half-dozen or so black players on the Tigers. Palacios told me I played ball like a 'brother,' one of the best compliments I'd ever received. My style came from growing up in a public-school district in which white kids were the minority. . . . We made no distinctions along racial and ethnic lines, only on whether a guy could play ball."[91] Bean continues this fantasy of virtual blackness when he goes to an all-black party with his teammates, dances, and receives their approval. "'Beaner parties like a brother,'" one of his black teammates announces to the white players "with a huge grin."[92] Like Burke's idyll of a raceless Castro, Bean's notion that sports is the embodiment of true American racial equality, a democracy based in hard work and merit, sets up the case he makes at the end of the memoir for treating gay athletes like black ones—judging them solely on their sports skill, hard work, moral character, and social conduct, rather than on their sexual orientation.[93]

If white gay disclosure memoirs rely on racial cross-identification to authenticate their narratives of gay oppression in sports, black gay disclosure memoirs necessarily cast slightly different relations among race, homosexuality, sissiness, and sport, even though sissy-avoidance remains operable, if to a lesser degree. Published thirty years after Kopay's memoir and two years before Bean's, Roy Simmons's *Out of Bounds* ultimately registers a more inclusive tenor, like Burke's *Out at Home*, in relation to queer gender conduct. Whereas Kopay's ethical universe is one in which an ideal of white-boy-next-door romance shapes his self-outing, Simmons inhabits a universe in which his own introduction to sex begins at age eleven when he is anally raped by his forty-year-old next-door neighbor, who "stood straight and tall, a towering man at 6'3"—muscular, handsome, and broad-shouldered."[94] If Kopay's narrative is unselfconsciously framed by his family's ascent into white middle-class conventionality, a respectability threatened only by Kopay's public announcement of his homosexuality, Simmons's, like

Burke's, is shaped by the particularities of black poverty and marginalization. As a result, there is a desperation in Simmons's story not so evident in Kopay's, Pallone's, or Bean's.

At the very outset of the narrative, Simmons places himself in the classic position of the sissy, a boy raised with females. "The truth of the matter is, I grew up in the company of women," he writes. "I found out that I could fit into a girl's world as easily as I fit into the world of boys. I'd go from playing touch football on the dirt road outside our house to playing Suzie Homemaker Oven with the neighborhood girls.... Boys or girls. One way was just as good as the other to me."[95] Like Wright's Aggie West, the boy Simmons refuses to recognize the line separating conventional girlishness from appropriate boyish games. Simmons continues down this sissy path by admitting, as we also saw in Tuaolo's and Amaechi's memoirs, that he was not a natural athlete. Only his size funnels him into sport, but "my size and strength didn't translate well at first to football. Even though nobody could tackle me, I guess my spirit was more like a floppy old puppy dog instead of the killer bear that the coaches seemed to want me to be."[96] Perhaps this "softness" explains Simmons's football nickname, "Sugar Bear," an endearing moniker that suggestively enfolds the African American vernacular for sissiness, a sweet man or "sugar in the blood."[97] Later in high school, Simmons became, much to the chagrin of his teammates, "a proud member of FHA, Future Homemakers of America, which meant that while the rest of the football team was making bird houses in wood shop, I took Home Economics and made cookies."[98] This sissy potential is deliberately short-circuited by the narrative with a claim to athletic toughness. When some of his teammates begin to hassle him, insisting that "only fags take Home Ec," Simmons shuts the bullying down by telling them that such comments will not be tolerated: "Back then I was bigger and faster than anyone else on the team. I was team captain, too, which meant that I could deal out laps around the field if I felt one of my players was underperforming or simply in need of a good ass-whooping."[99] Even though he loves home ec, which classes him as a sissy, he is not a sissy in the sense of being a "pussy" or coward. Waffling between his embrace of the African American folk figure of the fierce sissy and his desire to distance gender queerness from unmanly weakness, Simmons's narrative confirms the ambivalent attitude toward the "sweet man" that historically characterizes black folk culture.

Given the different racial frames of these memoirs, even experiences that on the surface seem very similar begin to feel quite different when we dig deeper. One tension within the sports disclosure memoir is its bifurcation between the claim to superior athletic discipline and aggression, on the one hand, and a plea for the sympathetic understanding of the victimized condition resulting from the stigma of homosexuality, on the other. The victim status of the coming-out narrative's author threatens to toss these jocks back into a sissy frame of reference, one based in pitiable vulnerability rather than muscular agency. Once Simmons's football career is over, for example, he has few resources to draw on, and his drug addiction ruins any chance that he can recover financially from the myriad acts of generosity to family and friends that deplete his bank account while he is playing. He ends up prostituting himself on the streets of San Francisco. (We can only surmise whether Burke's panhandling had at any point turned into sexual hustling while he was homeless in the Castro, for his narrative is more tempered and idealized than Simmons's.) Although Kopay is never at risk of street hustling, he conducts his own sexual hustle in order to support himself one summer: he is introduced to a wealthy married businessman, an ardent football fan, who becomes Kopay's "Sugar Daddy," an arrangement that he insists was a common practice for football players in the off-season. However, rather than representing himself as a hustler who exploits the man's closeted homosexual desire, Kopay images himself as the victim of an unattractive old queen who made the young footballer feel dirty every time he engaged in sexual intercourse with him. Ironically, as Simmons understands, to be too clean is itself a signal of a sissy temperament. Unlike Simmons, whose life takes him into the gutter as he engages street prostitution, theft, homelessness, and cross-dressing after the end of his football career, Kopay's narration is, in some ways, akin to Washington's *Up from Slavery* in that Kopay's acceptance by American society relies on his presentation of a supercleanliness that obsessively demands his boy-next-door worthiness. In Kopay's case, however, supercleanliness is intended to bolster his claim to the right to white normativity. To cleanse homosexuality in making it ready for entry into manly sports and thus into the American white middle class, he preserves the stain that justifies the sissy's exclusion from that norm.

Shameless Sissy Jocks: Emile Griffith and Dennis Rodman

Given the ways in which the sports disclosure narrative is so intrepidly defined by sissiphobia, can we imagine a time when a swishing sissy can claim the mantle of sportsmanship? In the African American vernacular, the figure of the tough-assed street swisher—like Little Richard, Sylvester, or Aggie West—unravels and upends the categorical dichotomy that demands that the sissy be the inimical foil to fit manliness as superior athleticism. Given how America's cultural imagination is so captured by unsubtle binary oppositions—white and black, straight and gay, masculine and feminine, macho and effeminate—it is difficult to imagine a disruption of this ironclad dichotomy between the fainting sissy and the brutal athlete. I'd like to provide a brief glimpse at two pro jocks who come very close to disrupting this oppositional logic. Emile Griffith and Dennis Rodman are the best exemplars thus far of shameless sissies in contact professional sports like boxing and basketball, respectively.

One would expect a boxing champ to be among the most sissiphobic of athletes, given the infamous brutality of the sport. The first openly gay boxing champ, however, is anything but, as his authorized biographer and film documentary represent him. Like Burke and Simmons, Emile Griffith participates in a much gentler mode of sissy-avoidance, though it might be suggested that the death of his most infamous opponent, Cuban boxer Benny Paret, from injuries sustained in their 1962 bout underscores how an attempt to intimidate a homo-sissy athlete through trash talk might not be the wisest strategy when the opposing boxer is so talented. Griffith's sports disclosure narrative, *Nine . . . Ten . . . and Out: The Two Worlds of Emile Griffith* (2008), authored by Ron Ross based on extensive interviews with the boxer, is an immigrant story, like Amaechi's, but one structured through the particular lens of a West Indian boy who migrates young to Harlem from St. Thomas, Virgin Islands. Griffith is born in 1938 into a large, tight, poor family. Emile evidently was the spitting image of his father, a policeman "whom nature endowed with an Adonis-like physique." According to his biographer, "At the age of eight it was already apparent that he was not just a chip off the old block—he was a scaled down model." If young Emile was cast in the physical image of his muscular father, he was devoted to his mother: "Around the house she never had to ask him twice to help out. He took the job as Mother's Little Helper very seriously, just as he did as Big Brother to his siblings."[100] Like Baldwin and his character John Grimes, Emile assumed the role of his mother's trusted helper. When Griffith migrates to Harlem at the age of fourteen, he seems to have been a targetable sissy-boy, one who learned to protect himself on Harlem's tough streets. He describes how he was not a rough, tough kid, so he would choose running away rather than trying to fight when his opponents were too numerous. As teacher's pet and tenor choirboy who refused to join a gang, Griffith, the full-fledged church sissy, was a fresh target on the Harlem streets. He carried a switchblade but never used it.[101] This growing-up narrative reads more like Sylvester's than like that of a future boxing champ. If not quite the fierce swish that Little Richard conducted himself as in his youth, Griffith nonetheless, in carrying a never-used knife, avails himself of that hard-assed swish potential.

In addition to singing, Griffith loved fashion design. He secures a job boxing hats and becomes fascinated with becoming a designer of women's hats. In other words, unlike Bean's, his sissiness is not described as a childhood phase but instead as essential to his character. When Howard Albert, the owner of the hat factory and a failed boxer himself, first spots Griffith, he immediately tries to interest him in prizefighting. Griffith is so clueless that when Albert asks him if he's done any boxing, the boy responds, "I've been doing it for almost one year now. Catherine and Mabel bring the hats in to me and I box and place them on the proper shelves" (4). Griffith seems to display no embarrassment over his sissy interests. Like Burke and Simmons, Griffith flagrantly defies the sportsman's code, refusing to dissociate from gender queers. Throughout his career, "Emile was at home and interacted with other gay men, cross-dressers, transvestites, male impersonators" (35). When he buys a big house for his mother and other family members with his boxing earnings, he moves in with his lover and they sleep in the same bed. At the height of his career, sportswriters, instead of quoting the usual trash talk from Griffith, would report on his fashion sense. Decades before Mark Simpson's hailing of the (white) metrosexual, Griffith was synthesizing a sissy interest in fashion with extraordinary athleticism, not just in any sport, but in the toughest sport of boxing. He is quoted before his key match against the great Mexican boxer Gaspar Ortega in 1961: "The Jackie Kennedy pillbox will remain in vogue; she's done a great job of 'selling' for the millinery world. But hats will come in a greater variety of shape and materials than ever this year" (46). It could not have been that Griffith was oblivious to the macho role that he supposedly needed to perform in order to be considered a serious contender. Clearly, he was not naive about the punishing cruelty that the world meted out to sissy-boys. In addition to his own scrapes in Harlem, he had seen firsthand gay-bashings in San Juan when he spent time there with his half brother, a baseball player. It was during his time in San Juan that he had learned the meaning of that fateful word *maricón* (25). The only explanation for his insistent sissy conduct has to be that he knowingly refused to repress this behavior even in face of the stigma that it assured.

If the boxing clubs were whispering about Griffith's taboo sexual and gender conduct, he seemed to shake it off and remain true to his own designs. When Benny Paret openly ridicules him during a weigh-in before the 1961 bout, however, Griffith takes notice, and it seems to shake him, perhaps so much so that it may have contributed to his loss of the championship to Paret. Griffith overhears Paret doing "an exaggerated imitation of his high-pitched voice. He winced as he watched him do a limp wrist parody with a flourish, swishing his hips and pointedly glanced over at him" (50). This scene should be contrasted with that in Baldwin's *Just above My Head*, where Arthur imitates tired queens for the entertainment and education of his elder brother. Whereas Arthur's swish performance is intended to confess a homosexual disposition ironically by mocking the mode of conduct that so many respectable sissies and homosexuals sought to avoid, Paret's "exaggerated imitation" lacks such ambivalence, and instead intends trash-talk by brandishing sissy stigma against his rather openly gay opponent. The stakes are raised at the weigh-in before his second bout with Paret. Griffith describes it in his own words: "There was Paret almost right up against me making these stupid, suggestive motions with his body. I looked down at him from the scale, still not sure of what he was doing. He grinned at me in a spiteful, disrespectful way pointed his finger. 'Hey, maricon, I'm going to get you and your husband'" (58). Griffith describes his embarrassment, humiliation, and rage—so intense that his managers have to hold him back and remind him to save it for the ring. We cannot be sure that this sissy-baiting exchange is directly responsible for the deadly punishment Paret experienced at the hands of Griffith in that grueling match. It is difficult not to speculate, however, that Paret's demise stemmed from Griffith's desire for vengeance. It reminds us, in any case, how powerful the use of sissy shaming is, even when it is aimed at a man so self-evidently secure in his queer gender conduct and sexual orientation as Griffith was. It is the height of irony that many years after Griffith's retirement, his gender queerness is exposed to an international audience again when, in 1992, he is bashed on leaving a gay bar. The ritualized, officially sanctioned violence of the boxing ring, including the violence of sissy shaming, cannot help but spill out into the sporadic, tacitly sanctioned violence against homo-sissies on the street.

Accordingly, Griffith's story reminds us how the sissy is, and always has been, at the center of sport's most physically aggressive venue, the boxing ring, figuratively and literally. While Griffith's career confirms this fact, Paret's "exaggerated imitation" confirms it metonymically in a more oblique way. In performing sissy antics with such acumen, Paret unintentionally exhibits his own capacity for swish conduct. He no doubt imagined himself the perfect straight boxer, but his bullying through sissy impersonation literally imaged him as the sissy boxer he wanted to despise.

If Griffith managed to balance sissy conduct with fierce pugilism, Dennis Rodman fashioned a public image as a swish pro basketballer. Published in 1996 at the height of the controversy over the Clinton administration's "Don't Ask, Don't Tell" policy, Rodman's *Bad as I Wanna Be* narrates his development as what I call a sartorial queer, a straight-appearing, straight-acting man who loves to cross-dress. In his brilliant essay on Rodman, "Black Men in the Mix," Lindon Barrett captures the baller's exceptional gender and racial status in national U.S. culture.

Barrett observes that, unlike the famous drag impresario RuPaul, who is not considered a "man" in the conventional sense, Rodman, "by virtue of being a highly competitive and successful professional athlete, does present himself and is perceived as a 'man.'"[102] Barrett goes on to deconstruct Rodman's character as paradoxically based in the most mythic of American myths, the self-fashioned individual. This individuality, however, expresses both the splintering and "the convergence of blackness, masculinity, and the market with a moral imaginary for which each of the three, to greater or lesser degrees, may form a crisis."[103] We might classify Rodman as a straight sissy, as his rise to fame as a straight cross-dresser is coterminous with the 1990s straight sissy phenomenon discussed in the previous chapter. If Mark Simpson were not so blinkered by racial ignorance, he could've found the fittest exemplar of the metrosexual not in Beckham or Eminem but rather in the bad-boy basketballer Dennis Rodman.

Promoting his sports disclosure memoir in full drag in a white wedding gown, with his bride's party a group of women dressed in tuxedos, Rodman lambastes the hypocrisies of a sports industry obsessed with the beauty of men's bodies and body parts while pretending to take offense at men who love men or men who love to look like beautiful women. Unlike Griffith, whose quiet, unprotesting sissy character could perhaps have passed among strangers, Rodman's tough cross-dressing sissy persona is calculated for mass-media effect. Whether he is doing it to gain the spotlight or because he has a sexual agenda to push, his sartorial queerness is so outlandish that many simply attributed it to plain eccentricity. Nonetheless, Rodman's memoir carries a serious message about queer inclusiveness and self-reflection. He confesses that he wanted to be white when he was a kid, and also to being a sissy: "I grew up among women, and as a kid I would sometimes dress up as a girl. You play house, you play doctor—everybody does that, but some people like it more than others."[104] As with Bean, Burke, and Simmons, his sissiness is associated with a female-dominated household. Using a football simile to link up cross-dressing as a natural part of his makeup, Rodman, like Aggie West and Emile Griffith, refuses to subscribe to the binarism that locks out the sissy as the anathema of sportsmanship: "I'm becoming the all-purpose person. I'm like the running back that can break one to the outside and also go over the middle to catch a pass" (178). Seesawing between muscular braggadocio and sentimental confession, Rodman's self-reflection on gender and sexuality comes across equally as defiant as insecure.

In addition to embracing a swishing gender presentation as a cross-dresser, Rodman also takes a wholly sissy-affirmative stance, one unusual at that time even for gay athletes, much less a straight one. Because of his devotion to girlish things, he confesses to confusion about his own sexual orientation growing up in the projects (see 105). As he himself observes, if he were gay, he'd have no reason to hide it, given how he exposes his own swishing nature. He makes an unrelenting attack on the hypocrisy of the sports world where gender and sexuality are concerned.

> Man hugs man. Man pats man on ass. Man whispers in man's ear and kisses him on the cheek. This is classic homosexual or bisexual behavior. It's in the gay bible. You tell people this and they're like, "Oh, no it's not. It's just a man's thing."
>
> And I say, "You're damned right. IT IS A MAN'S THING."
>
> I'm not saying you have to be gay to do these things, but you have to accept that it falls in the large confines of homosexual behavior. (169)

Rodman clearly likes to mind-fuck his audience, almost as if he disdains the small-minded hypocrisies of his teammates and fans. When *Sports Illustrated* speculates that he may be bisexual, he responds by wearing an "I'm not gay but my boyfriend is" T-shirt in West Hollywood (the gay district of LA) "since it fits into my idea of keeping people guessing" (169). It must be noted, however, that in the following chapter, titled "Madonna: An Old-Fashioned Tale of Romance," Rodman details his sexual relationship with the pop music star, confirming his sexual straightness. Nonetheless, in insisting on the naturalness of queer desire, Rodman refuses outright the kind of gender-shaming conduct expected of athletes. He calls out the false sense of disgust required of any straight man when faced with the prospect of a homosexual liaison: "If you ask a man if he's ever thought about being with another guy, he'll probably say, 'Oh, no. That's disgusting. I could never be with another guy.'" For him, this response is itself unnatural and dishonest. "To that I say, 'Yeah, you have. . . . If you had never thought about it, you'd have to think about it before you gave me an answer'" (170). Whereas the gay disclosure memoirs tend to assume the naturalness of a straight man's disgust at sissiness, Rodman calls it into question in the most straightforward manner.[105] Refusing to segregate sissy conduct from homosexual desire, Rodman effectively exposes the sissy insecurity constituting the masculine norm, and does so without equating gayness and sissiness by making himself, a straight sissy, the object-lesson of his own tale.

Unlike Kopay's best-selling memoir, or Burke's now much-lauded autobiography, Rodman's has not been hailed as a prophetic gay-affirmative text, despite the book's best-selling status when it was first published, and despite a minor scholarly industry devoted to studying it. Kopay, Bean, Amaechi, Tuaolo, Jason Collins, Kwame Harris, and other out athletes have become highly vocal spokesman on behalf of gay rights in sports. Burke has been recognized as a pioneer by the baseball establishment. Not taken seriously because he did not come out as gay in any conventional sense, and because his cross-dressing was seen as nothing more than confused attention-grabbing from a psychologically disturbed, socially maladjusted sexual freak, Rodman has been treated like lesser-known flamboyant sissies, ridiculed, chastised, and sidelined as irrelevant.

The Mass-Media Pomo Gay Jock

Given the significant breakthroughs accomplished in the waning years of the twentieth century and especially during the eight years of President Barack Obama's administration in the twenty-first century—with the legalization of marriage equality, the defeat of "Don't Ask, Don't Tell," and the administration's advocacy on behalf of trans people—one would expect that great strides would be made relative to gender nonconformity in sports. The sissy-embracing stories of Rodman and Griffith betoken the potential for a shake-up that has yet to arrive, however. Around the edges and at the lower levels of athletic play, we can begin to see some fraying, as girls are sometimes welcomed into play alongside boys in the prepuberty youth leagues. At the same time, the controversy enflamed over a flurry of state laws seeking to prohibit trans girls from competing in sports with cis girls reveals that whatever progress has been made along these lines is at best sporadic and fragile.[106] Rather than trickling down from the professional leagues, it just may be that changing attitudes will bubble up from the bottom gradually. Two of the most recent representations of gay breakthrough in sport, though, indicate just how far America has yet to go before the sissy no longer serves as the natural foil to the jock and as an anathema figure for sportsmanship. The real-life story of Michael Sam and the fictional one of Spencer Porter show, respectively, how hard it is to deploy the racial discourse of the Jackie Robinson legacy to represent the gay breakthrough and how hard it is to defeat the sissy stereotype as the foil to the all-American (white) jock.

At first glance, it would appear that Michael Sam would've been the perfect scenario for a gay Jackie Robinson moment in football. He was a beloved All-American defensive end on the University of Missouri football team, one who had bravely come out to his teammates and the whole university without backlash. Conventionally good-looking, masculine, and well-spoken, he was seen as making the play that enabled Missouri to win its 2013 bowl game in his senior year. Despite a difficult family situation, he had succeeded at school as well as on the field, and thus embodied a favored mass-media figure of the exceptional (and token) African American who excels despite familial dysfunction. The rush to position Sam as the gay Jackie Robinson occurred immediately after Sam publicized his sexuality in anticipation of the NFL draft. While some commentators predicted that he'd be an early pick, others, watching his predraft performance, questioned his suitability as a pro defensive player, given his size and speed. Using the draft to stage the historic moment, Sam and his followers gathered to watch the draft, and unfortunately for them, they had a long wait, for he was not selected until the seventh round, the very bottom of the draft. Sam and his backers were quick to charge homophobia as the cause. After he was cut from the Rams during preseason play, and then from the Cowboys, Sam and his fans kept up the drumbeat accusing the sport of homophobia.

Sam's outing and entry into the pro league make a critical misstep when compared with Jackie Robinson's in 1947 and Joe Louis's entry into heavyweight boxing in 1935. Rightly contextualizing Sam's "failure" through the theory of homonormative visibility, Jeffrey Q. McCune frames it this way: "If the dominant LGBT narrative has become largely preoccupied with coming out and visibility, then Sam is a case study of the way that blackness recalibrates the guarantees of outness and offers much less in terms of career success. In this way, Sam's iconography—though momentary—is one that dissipates as he performs queerness in the public. In other words, his heightened visibility subjected him to greater publicity and the stakes of his recruitment became higher for the teams of interest, while his performance on the field was then also subjected to a heightened level of review and consideration."[107] Hitting the ball out of the park, McCune observes how Sam's racial identification mediates and interrupts the preordained success narrative from being a "gay" first. I would further point out that this aborted spectacle was also a failure of the narrative of the black first. Both Robinson and Louis had been carefully tested and vetted *as athletes* as well as groomed behind the scenes to appeal to a crossover racial audience on their debuts. These athletes and their handlers had meticulously followed the civil rights playbook: those representing the race had to not just be decent at what they did but extraordinary, not just *as* good but *twice* as good. It seems as though Sam had availed himself of the mass-media stage for a breakthrough but did not have the mental, emotional, and physical framework invoked by that long African American historical legacy. Louis, Robinson, and other black sports pioneers made it seem easier than it was exactly because they entered the fray with such skill, finesse, self-confidence, and equanimity in the midst of blatant racism. Because Sam did *not* face such roaring mobs of homophobes, but instead found a generally positive response primed by the NFL's open promotion of a gay Jackie Robinson moment, the breakthrough suit may have seemed even more tailor-made. Indeed, at times it appeared that Sam and his backers got it backward: they assumed that finding the poster boy for a breakthrough would make the athlete great, when instead finding the great athlete as the poster boy is what makes the breakthrough possible. When Sam signed up as eagerly for a projected reality TV show that would document his postdraft experience for Oprah Winfrey's OWN network as he did for the draft, the confusion between the spectacle of sport and the spectacle of poster-boy gay athleticism became apparent. In a sense, the new technologies of mass media—twenty-four-hour sports networks on cable television, the internet, and social media—gave Sam instant legitimacy as a breakthrough sportsman, intensifying the confusion between the breakthrough as staged spectacle and sportsmanship as skilled spectacle.

This trust in mass-media spectacularity to serve as the rationale for a breakthrough was most visible in the staged kiss that occasioned Sam's finally being selected in the draft. Despite the delayed gratification of the moment, when the kiss between Sam and his white boyfriend of three months, Vito Cammisano, a former swimmer for Missouri, went viral, it seemed as though it could compensate for being chosen so low in the draft (figure 6.4). Calculated for televisual and social media effect, the kiss might be compared to the publicity photos that Louis's managers had placed in newspapers to promote a wholesome image of the good black boy ensconced in domestic bliss to achieve a crossover appeal (figure 6.5). Such images were intended to communicate that Louis would not be defying Jim Crow protocol, particularly by wooing white women as the one previous black heavyweight champ, Jack Johnson, had done. While Sam's cross-racial kiss seemed to piggyback postracial progress on top of gay sports inclusiveness, it backfired in making race, previously beneath the surface, a contested topic, as many commentators on social media wondered why so many black gay celebrities chose white mates.[108] One could say that although Sam had learned the lessons of the sports disclosure memoirs in hewing to form as a conventionally masculine jock, he had failed to understand the extent to which race can so easily trip up narratives of idyllic sexual progress.

Exploring occasions when professional athletes in a moment of heightened excitement on the court have been perceived by fans as overstepping the unwritten codes protecting sport from visible homoeroticism, Phillip Brian Harper has analyzed a kiss on the lips between Earvin "Magic" Johnson and Isiah Thomas during

6.4 Draftee Michael Sam and his lover, Vito Cammisano, seal the draft selection moment with a symbolic kiss intended to stage the full acceptance of gay rights in sports based on the mass kiss-ins that had been staged to protest marriage inequality in the preceding decade. ESPN.

6.5 Publicity photograph of Joe Louis kissing his fiancée, Marva Trotter (1940s). Wide World Photos Inc.

the 1988 NBA finals and the uproar that it created.[109] Beyond the panic over the prospect that a kiss between men must signal homosexuality, the greater panic emerges from the sense that except for the kiss, the two athletes in every way comport with the dictates of normative masculinity—indeed, their athletic prowess is supposed to be their most telling proof of that fit masculinity. If Sam's cross-racial kiss is designed to mark the arrival of the gay professional jock as a Jackie Robinson moment, in effect to indoctrinate homosexuality as wholesomely acceptable within the domestic sphere where professional sports is most commonly viewed, its controversial outcome may suggest that the idea of the gay Jackie Robinson breakthrough is itself misbegotten. It is sports history attempting to repeat itself only to discover that if the first breakthrough is the stuff of racial superheroism, the belated gay rehearsal is the stuff of homosexual melodrama.

If it is admittedly impossible to stage an athletic breakthrough using mass-media spectacle to substitute for extraordinary sportsmanship, it is also the case that fictionalizing gay athleticism as the breakthrough of millennial postmodernity is no less tricky. The arc of fictional character Spencer Porter (played by Marshall Williams) indicates how the sissy remains the bugbear whose very presence both signals and limits the victorious narrative of gay inclusiveness in contact sport. The popular Fox network TV series *Glee*, which ran from 2009 to 2015, won accolades for its postmodern multicultural inclusiveness, as it featured a cast that included not only black, white, Asian, Hispanic, and Native American characters but also biracial, differently abled, differently sized, gay, lesbian, bi, and trans characters finding themselves through competitive choral singing and dance performance. Although the fictional glee club is supposed to embody a motley crew of marginalized outsiders, the pathetic victims of and foils to the football heroes, the narrative places the club structurally in the position of the little sports team with a big, strong heart.

Central to the series is the arc of a swishing homo-sissy named Kurt Elizabeth Hummel (played by out gay actor Chris Colfer), who becomes the biggest target of bullying when a hulking football player, David Karofsky (played by heterosexual actor Max Adler), relentlessly seeks him out for punishment. While the show appears to defeat racial, sexual, and gender stereotypes through its intrepid multicultural cast, its plots repeatedly rehearse and reaffirm those gender and racial stereotypes. For instance, while Kurt plays a key role in the glee club as one of its most sympathetic characters, he is still typecast as a swishing sissy (a fey pale blond after the fashion of Capote and Warhol). A lovable high-culture swish more than a tough one, he is best friend to the Jewish American female star of the series, Rachel Berry (who has two gay fathers), and the glue who holds glee club together through his sardonic wit, refusal to give up, and undying loyalty to performance as high art. As his foil, Karofsky is stereotyped as the dark, oversized, thoughtless hulk of a football lineman, so fearful of his own homosexuality that he scapegoats the only openly gay student in the school. In the final season, after a tear-jerking apology to Kurt, Karofksy is converted into a sensitive but still masculine bear cub, an identity that acknowledges the postmodern diversification of gay male identities but is noticeably marginalized as fringe and not desirable relative to the romance between swishing Kurt and his preppy-queer boyfriend Blaine.[110]

Also in the final season, a new football character is introduced, Spencer Porter, a no-nonsense receiver but aspiring quarterback who sports a severe blond crewcut and is in every way the epitome of the macho jock except that he is unabashedly attracted to men (a reprisal of the Castro Clone). In this sense, Porter is the direct progeny of the white sports disclosure memoirists, for he eschews everything stereotypically gay, sissy, or effeminate except his incidental and irrelevant sexual desire for other males. In the first episode of season 6, his character is introduced with the line "Could you stop being such a whiny Hummel and get back in there," spoken to another (black) football player, overheard by Rachel, who is scandalized by his open use of "Hummel" (Kurt's last name), as a homonym for "homo," as a homophobic epithet. When Rachel protests to Spencer, another character says it's OK because he's "totally gay." Porter himself then replies, "Kind of a postmodern gay teen. You see, positive representations of gays in the mass media has [sic] given me the confidence I need to be myself, which, turns out, is kind of an arrogant jerk."[111] Like the white sports disclosure narrators, Porter is represented as a bully himself to seal his macho cred, and in a later episode, he merely watches as the footballers bully the glee members. It is no accident that the first person to approach Porter about joining glee is Kurt. Porter expresses appropriate disgust as a masculine gay boy for the idea of queer performance—a rebuff of the assumption that because Kurt is openly gay, he would be the best intermediary to convince openly gay Porter. It is only after falling head-over-heels for a long-haired blond artsy music geek, Alistair, that Porter softens his image and, in order to impress Alistair, begins to let his guard down. Porter is the one who eventually persuades Alistair to join glee, kissing him when Alistair agrees, and singing a schmaltzy duet to close the sequence. Porter's romance with Alistair is crucial to maintaining his masculine pose, much as Michael Sam's fit jockish muscularity is maintained even as he kisses another boy thanks to the contrast between the big, bulky-muscled black football player and his wispier lover, a white man with a swimmer's build.

It is notable how the *Glee* writers, as they eventually showcase a sissiphobic gay footballer, seem incapable of dealing with the predominant blackness of football as a sport, or with the fact that most out gay football players have been black, not white. Occasional black players are given shadowy cameo roles (like the unnamed black football player who is the object of Porter's Hummel/homo quip) to authenticate the social realism that would otherwise be lacking if blacks were totally absent from the team. The scripts, though, keep the spotlight on white football players, whether as crossover glee club members or as bullies.[112] Given that black sportsmen frequently seek or even achieve some fame as singers, it is especially revealing that the show cannot imagine a black football player as the bridge between jockish athleticism and artsy glee sissiness. Despite an emphasis on main characters who cross over from football to glee as especially important role models of postmodern progressive inclusiveness, such progressiveness is typed aggressively as white, whitewashing not only sport and glee but also the idea that gender crossover between them is an exclusive privilege of white maleness.

The story of American sport has often been told through the lens of race, and well it should be.[113] It is hard to imagine our nation's most popular contact sports without the black male as a lightning rod of controversy or a standard-bearer of extraordinary achievement beyond the odds. If racial fitness in both mass media and academic scholarship has been an undeniable frame without which U.S. sports would not be legible, so gender fitness has been an equally detectable frame, but one that has received much less attention in academe or beyond.[114] In recent years, media stories about professional sportsmen coming out as gay have sporadically gained the spotlight, but more as temporary spectacle than through any sort of sustained analysis and critique. And even though so many of the first professional players from rough contact team sports to out themselves or to be outed as gay have invariably been men of color, most frequently black, very little notice has been given to the intricate intersection linking the racial complexion of our most popular professional sports to the gender assumptions that operate to structure what constitutes athletic fitness. Society seems still to need the sissy as the most visible foil to fit manliness, and it erects sports' highest barriers to keep such gender-treacherous men off the court. The biggest threat to sports' masculine preserve is not the gay man who can jump and shoot but the swishing sissy who can pitch, toss, and catch.

POSTSCRIPT

Whatever Happened or Will Happen to the Sissy-Boy?

As I was putting the finishing touches on this manuscript, news of another pro gay athlete surfaced, a blond, slender soccer player named Collin Martin, who plays for Minnesota United. Not only was he at the time the only openly gay professional sportsman in all of global football or soccer; he was also the only openly gay athlete in all professional male team sports. His uneventful coming out manifests the double life of queer sexuality in the first decades of the twenty-first century. The increasing inclusion of some queer subjects, those identified as "gay" and "lesbian," does not guarantee a radically transformed politics in regard to such categories as race, class, transness, nationality, or citizenship status. In "Left of Queer," David L. Eng and Jasbir K. Puar pointedly critique the intensification of homonormativity as "pinkwashing": "As homonormative and homonationalist subjects continue to be interpellated into the logics of queer liberalism and pinkwashing today, these precarious groups are further pathologized and abandoned. These inclusions and exclusions speak to the morphing capacities of queerness, demonstrating that LGBTQ alignments with nationalist and racist ideologies are in fact not aberrations but, rather, constitutive of a normative queer liberal rights project itself."[1] An apt neologism, "pinkwashing," accords with Eve Kosofsky Sedgwick's observation that as the gay achieves normative subject status, "there is a danger . . . that that advance may leave the effeminate boy once more in the position of the haunting abject—this time the haunting abject of gay thought itself."[2] Perhaps even the theoretical term "homonormative" is too timid a moniker for the ideological change occurring as white middle-class gays and lesbians are incorporated into the nation's ruling establishment. It took very little for the most virulently, openly racist and misogynist presidential candidate in modern U.S. history to gain the support of white gay Republicans, some of whom had previously pivoted to vote for Barack Obama, the most gay-affirmative candidate to date.[3] Estimates of the gay/lesbian vote for Trump range from 14 to 20 percent—far short of the 52 percent of white women, but far above the percentage of African Americans swayed by Trump's ostensibly populist charisma.[4] Even as Trump assured gays and lesbians during the campaign that he would make friendly with them, he exploited anxieties over gender-nonconforming subjects so as to draw a line between sexual orientation as acceptable and gender nonconformity—signaled especially by attacks on trans persons—as still unacceptable.

Sissiphobia hovered over Donald Trump's presidency, as he proved the sociopolitical effectiveness of the big white male bully, especially when that figure is embodied through a righteously aggrieved white masculinity. That the previous occupant of that office and his spouse—President and First Lady Obama—campaigned vigorously against bullying as a grave social sin can appear to be the utmost historical irony. As Jackson Katz observes, "As a black male leader who was un-afraid to talk about 'empathy' and the need to have dialogue with America's enemies, he [Obama] represented a potential new masculine presidential archetype."[5] If the Obamas and their politically correct allies were intent on employing empathy to make the nation safe for sissies, "shemales," "illegals," victims of police brutality, and various and sundry other un-American undesirables, the Trumpers understood that gun-toting vulgar belligerence can outmuscle the moral high ground in the "real" America. "By the halfway point of Obama's first term," Katz suggests, "liberals and progressives . . . had taken to chastising the president for his 'spineless' inability to 'stand up' to Republican bullies."[6] We should not overlook, as well, the extent to which an image of black power—the Obamas—coming to the defense of bullied sissies ricocheted against both black people and those gender-nonconforming subjects that the Obamas sought to include and raise up. The full-throated answer to the Obamas' antibullying campaign, quite naturally, was a bully president: not one who speaks softly and carries a big stick, but one who spouts loud, absurd boasts and has a small member, mocked metonymically through ridicule of his little hands.

The Trump campaign thus sheds a light on how considerable progress on sexual orientation politics collides with a retrenchment of white hegemonic masculinity. Trump capitalized on a bloc of voters weary of gender politeness and yearning for a day when men behaved like men and women like women. If the 2016 presidential campaign hailed the victorious reign of the white male bully, as the verbal brawl between Trump and Florida's Cuban American senator Marco Rubio attests, we might dub the unspoken target of this trouncing the "uppity sissy"—any man, especially any white man, who dared to break ranks and side with the soft enemy within. After Trump labeled Rubio "Little Marco" during the Republican primary campaign, Rubio retorted by remarking on Trump's "little hands." Trump's response spelled out what was already obvious—that this "debate" was a matter of whose penis is bigger: "And he referred to my hands—if they're small, something else must be small. I guarantee you there's no problem. I guarantee you."[7] If Trump made soft punks of his white male Republican rivals while aggrandizing his own oversized virility, it is not because he possessed an unassailable upright masculinity. Citing "decades of research into school bullying," Katz writes: "Far from the stereotype of bullies as socially awkward loners, they are often popular and successful kids."[8] Trump's charisma resulted exactly from his politically incorrect deployment of a bullying masculinity that even sissies hate to admit they admire as much as they fear. If Trump's attempts to bully Hillary Clinton with predictable sexist jibes throughout the campaign rightly elicited outrage on the left, the treatment of his bullying tactics against Rubio and other male rivals elicited mainly amusement, as though Trump's behavior, and Rubio's reaction, constituted little more than expected schoolyard hijinks between two incorrigible white male teenagers. Coming after Obama's effort to reform this belligerent paradigm of presidential politics, Trump's literalization of the "bully pulpit" seemed especially gender-reactionary in its sissiphobia.

As I was trying to finish the book, another small-scale social media scandal erupted related to Dak Prescott, the highly regarded—as sportsman and man—black quarterback for the Dallas Cowboys. Prescott had given an interview in which he confessed to being depressed at the onset of the COVID-19 pandemic, in response to his brother's suicide in the wake of their mother's death. Seeming to emulate the Trump modus operandi of casting suspicion on male vulnerability as masculine softness, the infamous white sports critic Skip Bayless attacked Prescott on the Fox Sports 1 TV show *Undisputed* on 10 September 2020 by suggesting that in confessing his experience of situational depression, Prescott had unwittingly opened himself and his team to a justifiable takedown by any team worthy of exploiting this weakness in leadership.[9] Seeing this confession as a big crack in the fortress of hard, iron leadership that a quarterback must display, no matter the personal injury being experienced internally, Bayless pontificated for a solid ten minutes on Prescott's confession as an error in judgment that would lead to the team's unraveling on the field of play. Roundly attacked, with calls for his being fired, Bayless eventually issued a clarification, if not an apology, insisting that he had full sympathy for anyone experiencing "clinical depression" and implying that because Prescott's depression was not clinically diagnosed, Prescott had still made a fatal error—of strategic leadership if not of sports ethics—by displaying his emotional vulnerability to his rival teams. Bayless might just as well have called Prescott a sissy, for everything he uttered on the 10 September show and afterward in his nonapology throws the epithet at the black quarterback through the usual sissiphobic mode of sowing suspicion through innuendo. Effectively insisting that Prescott man up, Bayless's authority derives from nothing less than his overconfident white maleness, given that he is notably one of the few major sports commentators who has no experience playing either college or pro sports—having made a career by writing about sports since he was in high school. Given the racial politics in which black quarterbacks are treated more skeptically by the white pro football establishment—a minority club among overwhelmingly black players—Bayless's hyperbolic attack could easily be seen as harboring racial implications. It may be that Bayless's attack was so long-winded and convoluted exactly because he could not more directly call Prescott a sissy, which would have been more honest, nor could he appear to be suggesting that Prescott, as a *black* quarterback, had not yet mastered the intelligence and discipline required of the most lauded position in the American sports pantheon.

As the vernacular usage of a word like "sissy" has changed, so has the social perception of the referent, or those persons to whom such labels are applied. With the increasing inclusion of same-gender-loving people into U.S. law and society, the word "gay" itself has bifurcated in curious ways that were not predictable in the 1960s and '70s. The legacy of this bifurcation is still evident as late as the 2000s in a small scandal that occurred with the singing of "The Good Old Song" as a battle cry at University of Virginia sporting events. Composed in the 1890s, before "gay" referenced homosexuality in the common vernacular, the lyrics include these lines: "We come from Old Vir-Gin-I-A, / Where all is bright and gay." In order both to retrieve the archaic meaning of the word and to eliminate any double entendre that would implicate the song with homosexuality, as early as the 1970s some fans started altering the lyric by shouting "NOT GAY" immediately following the phrase "bright and gay." In 2003, when the controversy erupted, the Supreme Court was in the midst of hearing the case of *Lawrence v. Texas*, and in June of that year it struck down by a 6–3 majority the Texas same-sex sodomy law. Perhaps influenced by the court hearings and the broader public discussion in which it was clear that LGBTQIA rights were progressing swiftly, a smattering of fans chanting "NOT GAY" had turned into a landslide, and a much more influential queer movement, both nationally and on the University of Virginia campus, would not allow this insult to continue. After the circulation of a petition and the intervention of the university's officials, the chant was abandoned, and eventually the fight song was totally revamped.[10]

I would suggest that as a group achieves greater social inclusion, and as the epithet once used to stigmatize it becomes neutralized, authorized, and affirmatory, other negative usages can pop up to restigmatize either that group or other groups seen as intimately proximate. The usage of "swish" might be atrophying as other terms like "femme," referencing more an obvious gender-role identity than a bodily action, replaces it. While "faggot" has achieved censorious social opprobrium similar to "nigger," other epithets begin to acquire a largely affirming signification, as in the case of "queer." Under the radar, other usages continue to subside, swell, or fester. This is the case with the phrase "That's so gay," which emerged in the vernacular, especially on social media, among teenage youth in the 2000s.[11] On the one hand, that middle and high schoolers would be speaking so openly about what is gay and what is not indicates the growing familiarity and acceptability of queer identities in the post–civil rights era. On the other, as "gay" references a generally acceptable *sexual* orientation—that is, becomes homonormalized—the use of "gay" as a negative epithet for the *gender* temperament of sissiness acquires a new life. When kids say, "That's so gay," they take it as a cute, innocuous way of indicating their hip understanding of sexuality, even as they continue to ascribe stereotypical gender characteristics and conduct long associated with sissiness: softness, effeminacy, cowardice, histrionic speech, emotionality, and Capote-like cultural campness and triviality. Is the "That's so gay" epithet a sign of sexual-orientation progress but retrograde reaction in relation to gender-inclusiveness? Perhaps the popularity of the phrase is itself a sign of the intensified panic over a changing gender surveillance whose outcome is yet to be determined. As the phrase "That's so gay" fades in popularity, as surely it will, will another sissiphobic epithet simply take its place, or will the act of sissy stigmatizing itself become socially inappropriate?

To read sissies as insurgents may seem utterly counterintuitive to the way we usually conceive of such boys and men. The sissy is still considered opposite to all of the leading figures of masculine competence. To insist that the sissy is a necessary presence in all of the man-making venues discussed in this study—sports, military, the church, politics, governance, academe, activism—is not to suggest that he is a gender subversive, toppling masculinity from the margins or undoing it at its core. Nonetheless, the sissy figure can occasionally erupt into consciousness in such a way that his presence temporarily disrupts the smooth, racially conditioned operation of masculine empowerment in hegemonic institutions, spaces, activities, and affects. At the same time, the increasing awareness of trans identity puts pressure on sissiness from another direction. Whereas once noticeably effeminate men would produce the knee-jerk reaction of mockery or violence aimed at the offensive faggot, now when such a man is spotted, he might easily be assumed to be in some transitional state toward trans womanhood. With the rise of nonbinary sexualities and genders, the acceptance of concepts like the gender spectrum, and even a trickle of parents who hold off on naming the gender of their newborns until the child can decide the gender at an appropriate age, perhaps we are entering a time when the sissy as such will become archaic, even obsolete.[12] Will the word "sissy" survive if American culture does progress beyond the traditional gender binary? Or will it mutate to stigmatize some other experience of gender? Only time—and the tireless efforts of those committed to gender equality for all—will tell. If, in the long arc of time, we do lose the sissy as an emblematic figure of masculine failure, we should never forgot the history of gender nonconformity and insurgency that the sissy has embodied and represented against a brutally strict gender hierarchy that sought to subordinate and marginalize not only all women and African American men but also any man who refused to submit to the masculinist protocols of conventional conduct and character taken as the essence of manhood.

NOTES

Chapter 1. Can the Sissy Be Insurgent?

1. John Reid, *The Best Little Boy in the World* (1973; repr., New York: Ballantine Books), 1977. Reid's bildungsroman about the challenges of coming out as a gay youth in Nixonian America has even inspired investigations of "best little boy" syndrome in social psychology. See, for instance, John E. Pachankis and Mark L. Hatzenbuehler, "The Social Development of Contingent Self-Worth in Sexual Minority Young Men: An Empirical Investigation of the 'Best Little Boy in the World' Hypothesis," *Basic and Applied Social Psychology* 35, no. 2 (March 2013): 176–190.
2. Charles I. Nero, "Reading Will Make You Queer: Gender Inversion and Racial Leadership in Claude McKay's Home to Harlem," *Palimpsest: A Journal on Women, Gender, and the Black International* 2, no. 1 (2013): 74–86. Nero's article is especially helpful because he uncovers a long historical connection in African American literature between boys who read (too much) and the perception of incipient homosexuality. As we shall see, this is a trope that is not limited to African American culture, but is also evident in larger U.S. culture. Nero cites the study by Signithia Fordham, *Blacked Out: Dilemmas of Race, Identity, and Success at Capital High* (Chicago: University of Chicago Press, 1996), in which a connection is made by African American school children between a boy's academic success and queerness in Washington, DC, of the 1980s. Due to a facile equation between sissiness and homosexuality, figured especially through vernacular uses of terms like "gay" and "faggot," such studies often lack the linguistic subtlety and historical contextualization fully to understand the implications of contemporary black lingo seeming to link educational achievement with queerness in some subsets of the African American population.
3. Roderick Ferguson, "Sissies at the Picnic: The Subjugated Knowledges of a Black Rural Queer," in *Feminist Waves, Feminist Generations: Life Stories from the Academy*, ed. Hokulani K. Aikau, Karla A. Erickson, and Jennifer L. Pierce (Minneapolis: University of Minnesota Press, 2007), 191.
4. Ferguson, "Sissies at the Picnic," 191.
5. Vershawn Ashanti Young, *Your Average Nigga: Performing Race, Literacy and Masculinity* (Detroit: Wayne State University Press, 2007), xv.
6. Judith Butler has, of course, become strongly identified as the formative theorist of performativity in books like *Gender Trouble: Feminism and the Subversion of Identity* (New York: Routledge, 1990), esp. 134–141. For an argument in favor of performance over performativity as a way to theorize identity, see E. Patrick Johnson's *Appropriating*

Blackness: Performance and the Politics of Authenticity (Durham, NC: Duke University Press, 2004), which theorizes the import of performance as grounding us in "material ways of knowing" (6–12). Johnson clarifies what's at stake in preferring performance over performativity: "Racial performativity informs the process by which we invest bodies with social meaning. Yet I must reemphasize . . . that to read blackness merely as 'playful' is to fall into a willful denial of what it means to live 'black.' Indeed, blackness offers a way to rethink performance theory by forcing it to ground itself in praxis, especially within the context of a white supremacist, patriarchal, capitalist, homophobic society" (9). Although my study is rooted in a theory of conduct more than performance theory, it takes seriously this critique of performativity and pursues Johnson's insistence on praxis as crucial to understanding how "the 'living of blackness' becomes a material way of knowing" that "supersedes or explodes performance" (8).

7 Ahmed writes, "Phenomenology helps us to explore how bodies are shaped by histories, which they perform in their comportment, their posture, and their gestures." She continues: "We could say that history 'happens' in the very repetition of gestures, which is what gives bodies their tendencies." See Sara Ahmed, *Queer Phenomenology: Orientations, Objects, and Others* (Durham, NC: Duke University Press, 2006), 56.

8 E. Patrick Johnson, *Appropriating Blackness*, 6–12.

9 Houston A. Baker Jr., "Critical Memory and Black Public Sphere," in *The Black Public Sphere,* ed. Black Public Sphere Collective (Chicago: University of Chicago Press, 1995), 8.

10 Booker T. Washington, *Up from Slavery* (1901; repr., New York: Penguin Books, 1986).

11 Kenneth Mostern, *Autobiography and Black Identity Politics: Racialization in Twentieth-Century America* (Cambridge: Cambridge University Press, 1999), 42.

12 Margaret Walker, *Richard Wright, Daemonic Genius: A Portrait of the Man, a Critical Look at His Work* (New York: Warner Books, 1988), 88.

13 Walker and Wright had a rather rough falling-out. In addition, she seems overly concerned with Wright's lack of romantic interest in black women in general, and perhaps in her in particular; see Margaret Walker, *Richard Wright, Daemonic Genius*, 88–89.

14 The word "speculation" is loaded with negative connotations, but as Harper suggests, speculation may be the most apt tool when trying to unpack "structures of feeling," the phrase coined by the English cultural theorist Raymond Williams. Harper writes: "The account that I offer will necessarily be speculative, my being no more able than any 'outside' party to apprehend fully the various affective elements in these exchanges, owing to their being not somehow 'unconscious' but, as Williams insists, *embryonic* with respect to discernible and articulate forms"; see Phillip Brian Harper, *Private Affairs: Critical Ventures in the Culture of Social Relations* (New York: New York University Press, 1999), 136. Also see Phillip Brian Harper, "The Evidence of Felt Intuition: Minority Experience, Everyday Life, and Critical Speculative Knowledge," in *Black Queer Studies: A Critical Anthology*, ed. E. Patrick Johnson and Mae G. Henderson (Durham, NC: Duke University Press, 2005), 106–123. On the theory of the structure of feeling, Harper cites Raymond Williams, "Structures of Feeling," in *Marxism and Literature* (Oxford: Oxford University Press, 1977), 132; the concept can also be found

in Williams's earlier book, *The Country and the City* (New York: Oxford University Press, 1973), 26–27 and 35–45. Neal makes a point similar to Harper's when he, at the outset of *Looking for Leroy*, reflects back on his youthful speculation about the sexuality of the fictional character Leroy, the black male dance student from the TV drama *Fame*. Against the grain of encrusted stereotypes of black male bodies, Neal observes, those manifestations of black maleness that do not fit the stereotypes tend to become "illegible," unless they can be pigeonholed into another stereotype of queerness; see Mark Anthony Neal, *Looking for Leroy: Illegible Black Masculinities* (New York: New York University Press, 2013), 1–4.

15 See, for instance, Kwame Holmes, "What's the Tea? Gossip and the Social Production of Black Gay History," *Radical History Review* 122 (May 2015): 64–66; C. Riley Snorton, "Rumor Has It," in *Nobody Is Supposed to Know: Black Sexuality on the Down-Low* (Minneapolis: University of Minnesota Press, 2014), 121–146; and Darius Bost, *Evidence of Being: The Black Gay Cultural Renaissance and the Politics of Violence* (Chicago: University of Chicago Press, 2019), 29.

16 See Adrienne Rich, "Compulsory Heterosexuality and Lesbian Existence," in *Powers of Desire: The Politics of Sexuality*, ed. Ann Snitow, Christine Stansell, and Sharon Thompson (New York: Monthly Review Press, 1983), 177–205.

17 Richard Wright, *Black Boy (American Hunger)*, the restored text established by the Library of America, 1945 (New York: HarperPerennial, 1993), 227.

18 Wright, *Black Boy*, 229.

19 For a more extensive reading of this scene in relation to what I have called "race rape," the equation of racially emasculating practices with metaphorical white-male on black-male rape, see Marlon B. Ross, "Race, Rape, Castration: Feminist Theories of Sexual Violence and Masculine Strategies of Black Protest," in *Masculinity Studies and Feminist Theory: New Directions*, ed. Judith Kegan Gardiner (New York: Columbia University Press, 2002), 318–323.

20 It is worth noting that Black Aesthetic theorists and nationalists viewed Wright as one of their greatest progenitors, based especially in his construction of the "bad Negro" character Bigger Thomas. See, for instance, Addison Gayle's laudatory chapter on Wright, "The Black Rebel," in *Way of the New World: The Black Novel in America* (Garden City, NY: Anchor/Doubleday, 1975), 167–202, and his biography, *Richard Wright: Ordeal of a Native Son* (Gloucester, MA: Peter Smith, 1983); Larry Neal, "And Shine Swam On: An Afterword," in *Black Fire: Anthology of Afro-American Writing*, ed. Amiri Baraka and Larry Neal (New York: William Morrow and Company, 1968), 645–652; and Eldridge Cleaver, *Soul on Ice* (1968; repr., New York: Laurel/Dell, 1992), 103–107.

21 Wright, *Black Boy*, 285.

22 Wright, *Black Boy*, 285–286.

23 Wright, *Black Boy*, 33.

24 See James Baldwin, *Notes of a Native Son* (1955; repr., Boston: Beacon, 1990), 13–23.

25 Cleaver, *Soul on Ice*, 103.

26 Cleaver, *Soul on Ice*, 103.

27 Cleaver, *Soul on Ice*, 103–104.

28 Cleaver, *Soul on Ice*, 104 (phrase "[Italics added.]" in original).

29 Rogin instructively compares blackface minstrelsy to sexual cross-dressing; see Michael Rogin, *Blackface, White Noise: Jewish Immigrants in the Hollywood Melting Pot* (Berkeley: University of California Press, 1996), 30–35.

30 The representation of Jim Crow's large hips might likely allude to the display of Sarah Baartman's buttocks in circus shows in Great Britain and in graphic representations of her hips in cartoon and scientific literature in the early 1800s. On the history and lasting impact of Baartman's exploitation, see the essays in Natasha Gordon-Chipembere, ed., *Representation and Black Womanhood: The Legacy of Sarah Baartman* (New York: Palgrave Macmillan, 2011).

31 John W. Roberts historicizes the oral legend of the bad man in early twentieth-century black culture in *From Trickster to Badman: The Black Folk Hero in Slavery and Freedom* (Philadelphia: University of Pennsylvania Press, 1989), 171–220, documenting how the notion of badness acquires a dual meaning in African American culture that, on the one hand, perceives the bad man as dangerously amoral in his violence, but, on the other, takes him as a battling hero who puts white men and their superior weaponry to shame. According to Clarence Major, the use of "bad" to mean "positive to the extreme" or "the very best" comes across the Atlantic with the enslaved Africans, and accrues its inverted meaning as "a simple reversal of the white standard" in the process; see Major, *Juba to Jive: A Dictionary of African-American Slang* (New York: Penguin Books, 1994), 15.

32 According to Hazel Rowley, Wright started working on *The Long Dream* in 1957 and published it in 1958; see Rowley, *The Life and Times of Richard Wright* (Chicago: University of Chicago Press, 2001), 484; and Michel Fabre, *The Unfinished Quest of Richard Wright*, 2nd ed., trans. Isabel Barzun (1973; repr., Urbana: University of Illinois Press, 1993), 450–454. In 1950 Baldwin begins work on *Crying Holy*, the manuscript published as *Go Tell It* in 1953. See David Leeming, *James Baldwin: A Biography* (New York: Knopf, 1994), 75–78.

33 William Blake, *Poetry and Prose of William Blake*, ed. David V. Erdman (Garden City, NJ: Doubleday and Company, 1970), 36, 37.

34 C. Riley Snorton, *Black on Both Sides: A Racial History of Trans Identity* (Minnesota: University of Minneapolis Press, 2017), esp. 5–11.

35 Eve Kosofsky Sedgwick, in *Tendencies* (Durham, NC: Duke University Press, 1993), 157.

36 Because I take "effeminacy" to be one important vector signaling sissiness but only one angle among many from which the sissy-boy recognizes himself and is recognized by others, I prefer "sissiphobia" to Sedgwick's term. I want to challenge the assumption that nonconforming boyish conduct necessarily falls into girlish conduct even while acknowledging Sedgwick's point that our discourse is riddled with binary gender thinking. Tim Bergling has coined a similar term in his journalistic book *Sissyphobia: Gay Men and Effeminate Behavior* (New York: Haworth / Harrington Park, 2001), to describe, wholly from a white middle-class perspective, the animosity against effeminate gay men within white gay communities.

37 Sedgwick, *Tendencies*, 157.

38 Jack Halberstam, *Female Masculinity* (Durham, NC: Duke University Press, 1998), 275.

39 Halberstam, *Female Masculinity*, 276.
40 And with the far-too-gradual acceptance of trans personhood in the twenty-first century, that which is speculated as sissy behavior can be projected onto trans identity as well. Clearly, however, not all sissy-boys can predict or predicate trans character just as not all sissy-boys prognosticate a homosexual in waiting. The term "gender fluid" has become a progressive way to signal any person who feels discomfort ascribing to either pole of the gender or sex binary.
41 Some prominent examples of scholarship on the differing cultural configurations of same-gender sexuality include Evelyn Blackwood, ed., *Anthropology and Homosexual Behavior*, Research on Homosexuality no. 12 (New York: Haworth, 1986); Rudi C. Bleys, *The Geography of Perversion: Male-to-Male Sexual Behavior outside the West and the Ethnographic Imagination, 1750–1918* (New York: New York University Press, 1995); Joseph Carrier, *De Los Otros: Intimacy and Homosexuality among Mexican Men* (New York: Columbia University Press, 1995); Roger N. Lancaster, *Life Is Hard: Machismo, Danger, and the Intimacy of Power in Nicaragua* (Berkeley: University of California Press, 1992); Juana María Rodríguez, *Queer Latinidad: Identity Practices, Discursive Spaces* (New York: New York University Press, 2003); José Quiroga, *Tropics of Desire: Interventions from Queer Latin America* (New York: New York University Press, 2000); Gayatri Gopinath, *Impossible Desires: Queer Diasporas and South Asian Public Cultures* (Durham, NC: Duke University Press, 2005); Jarrod Hayes, *Queer Nations: Marginal Sexualities in the Maghreb* (Chicago: University of Chicago Press, 2000); Gilbert Herdt, *Same Sex, Different Cultures: Exploring Gay and Lesbian Lives* (Boulder, CO: Westview, 1997); and Walter L. Williams, *The Spirit and the Flesh: Sexual Diversity in American Indian Culture* (Boston: Beacon, 1986).
42 Marlon B. Ross, "Some Glances at the Black Fag: Race, Same-Sex Desire, and Cultural Belonging," in "Reading the Signs," ed. Anne Herrmann and Ross Chambers, special issue, *Canadian Review of Comparative Literature / Revue Canadienne de Littérature Comparée* 21 (1994): 193–219.
43 Ferguson, "Sissies at the Picnic," 193.
44 Ferguson, "Sissies at the Picnic," 188.
45 Amiri Baraka (aka LeRoi Jones), *The Autobiography of Leroi Jones* (Chicago: Lawrence Hill Books, 1984).
46 Mark Anthony Neal, *Looking for Leroy*, 8.
47 Mark Anthony Neal, *Looking for Leroy*, 8.
48 W. E. B. Du Bois, *Black Reconstruction in America, 1860–1880* (1935; repr., New York: Free Press, 1998), 56.
49 Booker T. Washington, *The Story of the Negro* (1909; repr., Philadelphia: University of Pennsylvania Press, 2005), 1:332.
50 Theodore Roosevelt, *The Rough Riders* (New York: Charles Scribner's Sons, 1899), 144–145.
51 Christopher B. Booker, *"I Will Wear No Chain!": A Social History of African American Males* (Westport, CT: Praeger, 2000), 128.
52 Booker, *"I Will Wear No Chain!,"* 125.
53 Roosevelt, *Rough Riders*, 143–144.

54 John Richards, "Some Experiences with Colored Soldiers," in *World War I at Home: Readings on American Life, 1914–1920*, ed. David F. Trask (New York: John Wiley and Sons, 1970), 143.
55 John Richards, "Some Experiences with Colored Soldiers," 142.
56 Neil A. Wynn, *The Afro-American and the Second World War*, rev. ed. (New York: Holmes and Meier, 1993), 10.
57 Phyllis R. Klotman, "Military Rites and Wrongs: African Americans in the U.S. Armed Forces," in *Struggles for Representation: African American Documentary Film and Video*, ed. Klotman and Janet K. Cutler (Bloomington: Indiana University Press, 1999), 42.
58 W. E. B. Du Bois, "Returning Soldiers," *The Crisis* 18 (May 1919): 13. On Du Bois's support of black participation in World War I as a way to counter Jim Crow, see Shane A. Smith, "'The Crisis' in the Great War: W. E. B. Du Bois and His Perception of African-American Participation in World War I," *The Historian* 70, no. 2 (July 2008): 239–262; and Mark Ellis, "W. E. B. Du Bois and the Formation of Black Opinion in World War I: A Commentary on 'The Damnable Dilemma,'" *Journal of American History* 81, no. 4 (1995): 1584–1590.
59 Some of the first histories written by black men focused on African American participation in U.S. wars in an uplift agenda that assumes soldierly value as proof for the manhood rights of citizenship. See, for instance, George Washington Williams's *A History of the Negro Troops in the War of the Rebellion* (New York: Harper and Brothers, 1887); and his earlier book, *The History of the Negro Race in America from 1619 to 1880* (New York: G. P. Putnam Sons, 1882); and Joseph Thomas Wilson's *The Black Phalanx: A History of the Negro Soldiers of the United States in the War of Independence, the War of 1812, and the Civil War* (1887; repr., New York: Da Capo, 1994).
60 Calvin C. Hernton, "Dynamite Growing out of Their Skulls," in *Black Fire: An Anthology of Afro-American Writing*, ed. LeRoi Jones and Larry Neal (New York: William Morrow and Company, 1968), 92.
61 Martin Luther King Jr., *Why We Can't Wait* (New York: Penguin/Mentor, 1963), 37.
62 King, *Why We Can't Wait*, 38.
63 King, *Why We Can't Wait*, 38–39.
64 *Oxford English Dictionary* (hereafter OED), June 2017, s.v. "sissy, n.," www.oed.com/view/Entry/180429.
65 See Peter Stallybrass and Allon White, *Politics and Poetics of Transgression* (Ithaca, NY: Cornell University Press, 1986), 26. Of course, the same linguistic blockage plagues sexological terminology, as "invert" indicates a person whose sexual attraction turns normal gender conduct on its head. The extreme binarism assumed in the language of sexology can be proved only by observing the bodily conduct of actual persons.
66 OED, June 2017, s.v. "butch, n.," www.oed.com/view/Entry/25321. The 1928 novel *The Well of Loneliness*, with commentary by Havelock Ellis (London: Jonathan Cape, 1928), by the English writer Radclyffe Hall provides an early semiautobiographical portrait of a "butch"/femme lesbian dyad, but the word "butch" is never used in the narrative itself. The protagonist takes on a male name, Stephen, and dresses and behaves according to masculine protocols. In line with discourse of the time, Hall represents Stephen as a tragic figure, based in sexological discourse as an invert, a man trapped in a woman's

anatomy. This might be understood as an early twentieth-century exploration of transgender identity, though the novel has traditionally been read as a lesbian text.

67 The idea of "panic" as a normal manly response to a gender-disordered male came to mass public attention in the case of Jonathan Schmitz, who murdered Scott Amerdure after the latter confessed his attraction to the former on the *Jenny Jones Show* in 1995. Schmitz's lawyers exploited the "gay panic defense" in attempting to reduce the degree of the conviction. In *Between Men: English Literature and Male Homosocial Desire* (New York: Columbia University Press, 1985), Eve Sedgwick has theorized homosexual panic as an affect necessary to homosociality, the attempt to subordinate women and femininity in part by excluding homosexuality from rituals of male bonding: "For a man to be a man's man is separated only by an invisible, carefully blurred, always-already-crossed line from being 'interested in men,'" Sedgwick writes. "Those terms, those congruences are by now endemic and perhaps ineradicable in our culture" (89–90).

68 *OED*, June 2017, s.v. "punk, n.1 and adj.2," www.oed.com/view/Entry/154685. "Punk" has a complicated etymology with slightly different histories in England and the United States. The *OED* records the first usages around 1757 in England to signify a prostitute, but as early as 1698 to indicate "a boy or young man kept by an older man as a (typically passive) sexual partner." The dictionary records the word appearing as U.S. slang around 1893 to mean "a person of no account" or "a petty criminal, a hoodlum, a thug." By 1907, the word had already accrued the meaning of "a young male companion of a tramp, *esp.* one who is kept for sexual purposes." By the early 1930s, the word is being used to mean a homosexual man, "chiefly in African American usage," at the same period when it connotes "a coward, a weakling" in dominant culture. Clarence Major includes two entries on "punk" in *Juba to Jive*. The first indicates "derogatory term for male homosexual; a homosexual's companion," while the second is not defined solely through same-sex attraction: "male pejorative term for any male without similar interest; a weak man; any male who gives in to anally intercourse in prison; same as 'sissy'" (367).

69 I want to emphasize again the difficulty, if not impossibility, of using law as a weapon against sissy conduct. Sumptuary laws in the West made it illegal for men to dress as women or vice versa, and cross-dressing, although not uniformly stringently enforced, was a clearly enforceable legal offense. It is certainly easier to focus on gender inappropriate clothing than on gender inappropriate conduct, unless that conduct veers off into the realm of a sexual act. A man properly dressed as such can still comport himself in an unmasculine way, as we will see in the case of George Washington Carver, but defining in law exactly what constitutes improper masculine bodily conduct is another matter.

70 In a now-classic essay, "Is the Rectum a Grave?," in *AIDS: Cultural Analysis, Cultural Activism*, ed. Douglas Crimp (Cambridge, MA: MIT Press, 1988), 197–222, Leo Bersani theorizes the male penetrated anus as the site of the greatest stigma and thus as the site of queer liberation.

71 An exception might be the Radical Faerie movement, which emerged in the 1970s, but this movement constitutes more a subset of homosexuals who celebrate various forms of effeminacy as a mode of political resistance to the straitjacket of masculinity.

72 Much excellent scholarship has been written on the role of domestic sensibility in Stowe. See, for instance, Ann Douglas, *The Feminization of American Culture* (New York: Doubleday, 1977), 244–256; Jane Tompkins, *Sensational Designs: The Cultural Work of American Fiction, 1790–1860* (New York: Oxford University Press, 1985), 131–153; Richard H. Brodhead, *Cultures of Letters: Scenes of Reading and Writing in Nineteenth-Century America* (Chicago: University of Chicago Press, 1993), 42–47; Julie Ellison, *Cato's Tears and the Making of Anglo-American Emotion* (Chicago: University of Chicago Press, 1999); Faye Halpern's *Sentimental Readers: The Rise, Fall, and Revival of a Disparaged Rhetoric* (Iowa City: University of Iowa Press, 2013), 54–63; and Joseph Fichtelberg's *Critical Fictions: Sentiment and the American Market, 1780–1870* (Athens: University of Georgia Press, 2013), 3.
73 Harriet Beecher Stowe, *Uncle Tom's Cabin, or Life among the Lowly* (Boston: John P. Jewitt, 1852), 56.
74 Addison Gayle Jr., *The Black Situation* (New York: Horizon Press, 1970), 52.
75 As has often been observed of Stowe's novel, although the dark-skinned Uncle Tom may be its hero, it is the light-skinned intelligent mulatto, George Harris, who is allowed to escape to freedom in Canada and, in a future beyond the narrative, perhaps to Africa.
76 Riché Richardson, *Black Masculinity and the U.S. South: From Uncle Tom to Gangsta Rap* (Athens: University of Georgia Press, 2007), 168, 169.
77 Mark Anthony Neal, *New Black Man* (New York: Routledge, 2005), 15.
78 See John Henrik Clarke, ed., *William Styron's Nat Turner: Ten Black Writers Respond* (Boston: Beacon, 1968).
79 On the history of the molly, see Rictor Norton's *Mother Clap's Molly House: The Gay Subculture of England, 1700–1830* (London: GMP Publishing, 1992).
80 Obviously, this sentence was written before Donald Trump occupied the White House with such unembarrassed appeals to a boastful, blustery, bullying masculinity as the essence of self-unaware incompetent white male leadership.

Chapter 2. Sissy Housekeeping

1 Booker, "I Will Wear No Chain!," 134.
2 Kevin P. Murphy, *Political Manhood: Red Bloods, Mollycoddles, and the Politics of Progressive Era Reform* (New York: Columbia University Press, 2008), 12.
3 Kevin P. Murphy, *Political Manhood*, 14.
4 Alan Trachtenberg, *The Incorporation of America: Culture and Society in the Gilded Age* (New York: Hill and Wang, 1982), 163.
5 Booker, "I Will Wear No Chain!," 14.
6 W. E. B. Du Bois, *The Souls of Black Folk*, introduction by Donald B. Gibson, notes by Monica M. Elbert (1903; repr., New York: Penguin Books, 1989), 5–6.
7 Hazel Carby, *Race Men* (Cambridge, MA: Harvard University Press, 1998), 10.
8 See OED Online, entry "sycophant," http://www.oed.com.proxy01.its.virginia.edu/view/Entry/196102?rskey=IEONR6&result=1&isAdvanced=false#eid.

9 Marcus H. Boulware, *The Oratory of Negro Leaders, 1900–1968* (Westport, CT: Negro Universities Press, 1969), 48.
10 Booker T. Washington, *Up from Slavery* (1901; repr., New York: Penguin Books, 1986), 221.
11 *OED*, September 2020, s.v. "emancipate, v.," https://www-oed-com.proxy01.its.virginia.edu/view/Entry/60718?rskey=c3mT8T&result=2. We cannot overlook here that, of course, women had no access to suffrage, to office-holding, to the most crucial components of emancipated citizenship.
12 Washington, *Up from Slavery*, 220.
13 William Dean Howells, introduction to *Lyrics of Lowly Life*, in Paul Laurence Dunbar, *The Life and Works of Paul Laurence Dunbar* (Nashville: Winston-Derek, 1992), 14.
14 Howells, introduction to Dunbar, *Lyrics of Lowly Life*, 15–16.
15 See Park, *Race and Culture*, 280. For a fuller analysis of Park's phrase, see Davarian L. Baldwin, "Black Belts and Ivory Towers: The Place of Race in U.S. Social Thought, 1892–1948," *Critical Sociology* 30, no. 2 (March 2004): 408–418; and Marlon B. Ross, *Manning the Race: Reforming Black Men in the Jim Crow Era* (New York: New York University Press, 2004), 243–247.
16 Booker T. Washington, "The Better Part," Thanksgiving Peace Jubilee Exercises, Chicago, Illinois, 16 October 1898, in *The Booker T. Washington Papers, 1895–1898*, vol. 4, ed. Louis R. Harlan (Urbana: University of Illinois Press, 1975), 492.
17 Washington, "The Better Part," 492.
18 Louis R. Harlan, *Booker T. Washington: Making of a Black Leader* (London: Oxford University Press, 1972), 236. On Du Bois's brief mention of this oratorical misstep, see *Souls*, 38.
19 Quoted in Sheldon Avery, *Up from Washington: William Pickens and the Negro Struggle for Equality, 1900–1954* (Newark: University of Delaware Press, 1989), 16.
20 I employ the slightly pejorative phrase "Bookerite" to indicate both Washington's exaggerated image and its distribution and controversy in his time and after.
21 On Pickens's masculine self-representation in *Bursting Bonds*, see Ross, *Manning the Race*, 94–105.
22 On Trotter's "assertive masculinity" as a political tactic, see Booker, *"I Will Wear No Chain!,"* 132–134. For a concise contrast between Washington and Trotter and how this feud was triangulated through Du Bois, see Stephen R. Fox, *The Guardian of Boston: William Monroe Trotter* (New York: Atheneum, 1970), 32–41.
23 Quoted in Avery, *Up from Washington*, 17, 16.
24 On Miller's biography see Butler A. Jones, "The Tradition of Sociology Teaching in Black Colleges: The Unheralded Professionals," in *Black Sociologists: Historical and Contemporary Perspectives*, ed. James E. Blackwell and Morris Janowitz (Chicago: University of Chicago Press, 1974), 146–148.
25 On the history of the American Negro Academy, and Miller's role in it, see Alfred A. Moss Jr.'s *The American Negro Academy*, 30–33, 63–64, 92–96, 190–194.
26 Kelly Miller, *Race Adjustment: Essays on the Negro in America* (New York: Neale, 1908), 14.

27 Kelly Miller, *Race Adjustment*, 25.
28 Kelly Miller, *Race Adjustment*, 14.
29 Kelly Miller, *Race Adjustment*, 15.
30 On the protest violence that Trotter cagily promoted against Washington, see Stephen R. Fox, *Guardian of Boston*, 49–58.
31 Jackson Katz, *Man Enough? Donald Trump, Hillary Clinton, and the Politics of Presidential Masculinity* (Northampton, MA: Interlink Books, 2016).
32 See Ida B. Wells-Barnett, *Crusade for Justice: The Autobiography of Ida B. Wells*, ed. Alfreda M. Duster (Chicago: University of Chicago Press, 1970), 264.
33 Wells-Barnett, *Crusade for Justice*, 281.
34 Patricia A. Schechter, *Ida B. Wells-Barnett and American Reform, 1880–1930* (Chapel Hill: University of North Carolina Press, 2001), 130, 131.
35 Jacqueline Goldsby, *A Spectacular Secret: Lynching in American Life and Literature* (Chicago: University of Chicago Press, 2006), 64.
36 Schechter, *Ida B. Wells-Barnett*, 145.
37 Schechter, *Ida B. Wells-Barnett*, 131.
38 Erica R. Edwards, *Charisma and the Fictions of Black Leadership* (Minneapolis: University of Minnesota Press, 2012), 21.
39 Washington entered Hampton in October 1872 at the age of sixteen.
40 Washington, *Up from Slavery*, 52.
41 Washington, *Up from Slavery*, 54.
42 *OED*, September 2020, s.v., "sissy, n. and adj.," https://www-oed-com.proxy01.its.virginia.edu/view/Entry/180429?redirectedFrom=sissy.
43 Du Bois makes the claim in reference to his assistant at the *Crisis*, Augustus Granville Dill, who was arrested for sodomy in 1927. See *Autobiography of W. E. B. Du Bois: A Soliloquy on Viewing My Life from the Last Decade of Its First Century* (New York: International Publishers, 1968), 282; David Levering Lewis, *W. E. B. Du Bois: Biography of a Race, 1868–1919* (New York: Henry Holt, 1993), 204–205; and Ross, *Manning the Race*, 254–255.
44 Jacqueline Jones, *Labor of Love, Labor of Sorrow: Black Women, Work and the Family, from Slavery to the Present* (1985; repr., New York: Vintage, 1995), 36.
45 José Esteban Muñoz defines "disidentification" thus: "Disidentification is the third mode of dealing with dominant ideology, one that neither opts to assimilate within such a structure nor strictly opposes it; rather, disidentification is a strategy that works on and against dominant ideology"; see *Disidentifications: Queers of Color and the Performance of Politics* (Minneapolis: University of Minnesota Press, 1999), 11.
46 Washington, *Up from Slavery*, 17–18.
47 Harlan, *Making of a Black Leader*, 5, 15.
48 See Eugene D. Genovese, *Roll, Jordan, Roll: The World the Slaves Made* (New York: Vintage Books, 1976), 505.
49 Sara Ahmed, *The Cultural Politics of Emotion*, 2nd ed. (New York: Routledge, 2015), 103. Recent queer theory has begun instructively to deconstruct the role of shame in the discourses and experiences of nonconforming gender and sexuality. See, for instance, Michael Warner, *Trouble with Normal: Sex, Politics, and the Ethics of Queer*

Life (Cambridge, MA: Harvard University Press, 1999), 33–40; Sedgwick, *Touching Feeling: Affect, Performativity, Pedagogy* (Durham, NC: Duke University Press, 2003), 35–65; and Heather Love, *Feeling Backward: Loss and the Politics of Queer History* (Cambridge, MA: Harvard University Press, 2007).

50 On Washington's use of the phrase "school of American slavery," see *Up from Slavery*, 16.

51 Sterling D. Spero and Abram L. Harris, *The Black Worker: The Negro and the Labor Movement* (New York: Columbia University Press, 1931), 170, 31–35; William H. Harris, *The Harder We Run: Black Workers since the Civil War* (New York: Oxford University Press, 1982), esp. 42–50; Philip S. Foner, *Organized Labor and the Black Worker, 1619–1973* (New York: International Publishers, 1974), 74–81, 104–107; and Herbert Hill, *Black Labor and the American Legal System: Race, Work, and the Law* (Madison: University of Wisconsin Press, 1985), 1–34.

52 *Webster's Deluxe Unabridged Dictionary*, 2nd ed. (1983), s.v. "menial."

53 See Du Bois, *Dusk of Dawn: An Essay toward an Autobiography of a Race Concept* (1940; repr., New Brunswick, NJ: Transaction, 1984), 89.

54 Du Bois, *Dusk of Dawn*, 15.

55 Du Bois, *Dusk of Dawn*, 34.

56 Du Bois, *Dusk of Dawn*, 35.

57 Houston A. Baker Jr., *Turning South Again: Re-thinking Modernism / Re-reading Booker T.* (Durham, NC: Duke University Press, 2001), 50. Baker ignores the extent to which Douglas wants to de-emphasize "the actual relation of the sexes" as an explanation for the cultural operation of purity and taboo; see Mary Douglas, *Purity and Danger: An Analysis of the Concepts of Pollution and Taboo* (London: Routledge, 1966), 4.

58 See Ross, *Manning the Race*, 24, 42–48. Jacqueline Goldsby theorizes "the extent to which the market motives of mob violence were determined by the nation's turn to corporate capitalism as much as by southern agribusiness's racist political economy" (*Spectacular Secret*, 29).

59 Baker also takes the next step in seeing homoeroticism in Washington's relations with his white male mentors—resorting again to the binary trap that insists on heterosexual hypermasculinity versus (homo)sexualized emasculation when black male identity is at stake.

60 Anne McClintock, *Imperial Leather: Race, Gender and Sexuality in the Colonial Contest* (New York: Routledge, 1995), 184.

61 "The gospel of the toothbrush, as General Armstrong used to call it, is a part of our creed at Tuskegee" (*Up from Slavery*, 174–175). Of course, the hygiene and eugenics movements were both at their height in the North and West during Washington's adulthood, even though they were slower to be adopted in the white South. On the belated rise of eugenics in the South, see Edward J. Larson, *Sex, Race, and Science: Eugenics in the Deep South* (Baltimore: Johns Hopkins University Press, 1995), esp. 40–62.

62 On the articulation of home economics as a way for women to remain within the domestic sphere while claiming a right to professionalization, see Leslie Kanes Weisman,

"The Home as Metaphor for Society," in *Discrimination by Design: A Feminist Critique of the Man-Made Environment* (Urbana: University of Illinois Press, 1992), 87–99.

63 Eugene D. Genovese's explanations of attitudes toward clothing and cleanliness among the captives and their masters help to provide a historical context for Washington's obsession with these matters (*Roll, Jordan, Roll*, 550–561).

64 See Stallybrass and White, *Politics and Poetics of Transgression*, 125–148; and Sigmund Freud, *Civilization and Its Discontents*, trans. and ed. James Strachey (1930; repr., New York: W. W. Norton, 1961), 40. McClintock also pursues the class, gender, racial, and colonialist logic of marketing cleanliness in chapter 5 of *Imperial Leather*.

65 Stuart M. Blumin, *The Emergence of the Middle Class: Social Experience in the American City, 1760–1900* (New York: Cambridge University Press, 1989), 127.

66 Blumin mentions African Americans once in parentheses, an odd omission in a book on the emergence of the middle class in America during the nineteenth century; see *The Emergence of the Middle Class*, 253.

67 See Daniel T. Rodgers, *The Work Ethic in Industrial America, 1850–1920* (Chicago: University of Chicago Press, 1974), 14, 31–34. On the problem of free labor as a racial dilemma in postbellum politics, I have also consulted Eric Foner's *Short History of Reconstruction, 1863–1877* (New York: Harper and Row, 1990), 55–81; Du Bois's *Black Reconstruction in America, 1860–1880*, esp. 17–31, 58–83; David R. Roediger, *The Wages of Whiteness: Race and the Making of the American Working Class* (London: Verso, 1991), 65–87; and Nell Irvin Painter's *Standing at Armageddon: The United States, 1877–1919* (New York: Norton, 1987), 1–15, 21–22.

68 Rodgers, *Work Ethic in Industrial America*, 94–124. Significantly, once Washington achieves his exceptional status as an elite black leader admired by most of white America, neurasthenia helps to signal this ascent and his right to belong; see Harlan, *Making of a Black Leader*, 238; and Harlan, *Booker T. Washington: The Wizard of Tuskegee, 1901–1915* (London: Oxford University Press, 1983), 282.

69 Commenting on the British explorers, Patrick Brantlinger writes: "Their racist view of Africans as a natural laboring class, suited only for the dirty work of civilization, expresses a nostalgia for lost authority and for a pliable, completely subordinate proletariat that is one of the central fantasies of imperialism"; see *Rule of Darkness: British Literature and Imperialism, 1830–1914* (Ithaca, NY: Cornell University Press, 1988), 183. McClintock makes a similar point in *Imperial Leather*, 212.

70 In Query XIV, Jefferson writes: "Besides those of colour, figure, and hair, there are other physical distinctions proving a difference of race. They have less on the face and body. They secrete less by the kidneys, and more by the glands of the skin, which gives them a very strong and disagreeable odour." See Thomas Jefferson, *Notes on the State of Virginia*, ed. William Peden (1785; repr., University of North Carolina Press, 1996), 138–139.

71 Robert E. Park, *Race and Culture: Essays in the Sociology of Contemporary Man* (Glencoe, NY: Free Press, 1950), 239.

72 See Charles S. Johnson, *The Negro in Chicago: A Study of Race Relations and a Race Riot* (Chicago: University of Chicago Press, 1922), 304, 317–319.

73 One representative instance of such a reading can be found in David Howard-Pitney's discussion of Washington in *The Afro-American Jeremiad: Appeals for Justice in America* (Philadelphia: Temple University Press, 1990), 53–72. On the influence of the masculinist self-made man narrative on African American autobiography, see Valerie Smith, *Self-Discovery and Authority in Afro-American Narrative* (Cambridge, MA: Harvard University Press, 1987), esp. 27–34. In *Long Black Song: Essays in Black American Literature and Culture* (1972; repr., Charlottesville: University Press of Virginia, 1990), Houston A. Baker Jr. puts an interesting twist on this view of Washington by pointing out how the autobiography constructs him as an "organization man" (94).

74 In *The Feminization of American Culture*, Ann Douglas sees middle-class white women's feminization of U.S. culture as a hollow victory, reducing culture to effete theology, vacuously sentimental ethics and reading habits, passive mass consumption, and unrigorous modes of pedagogy in educational institutions. Other critics, including Jane Tompkins, contrarily argue that feminization was indeed a real, if mixed, victory for women's political, moral, and cultural empowerment; see *Sensational Designs: The Cultural Work of American Fiction, 1790–1860* (New York: Oxford University Press, 1985), 162, 217n3. In *The Bonds of Womanhood: "Woman's Sphere" in New England, 1780–1835* (New Haven, CT: Yale University Press, 1977), Nancy F. Cott examines the emerging split between what she calls the "canons of domesticity" and "feminism," but she judges the cult of domesticity to be as historically enabling for women as it was constraining (see esp. 197–206). Astutely, Cott points out that despite the rhetoric of sharply divided gender spheres, "it was the paradox of domesticity to make women's work roles imitate men's; despite the intent to stress how they differed, domestic occupations began to mean for women what worldly occupations meant for men" (72–73). In *The Incorporation of America*, Alan Trachtenberg discusses the complicated exploitation of "feminization" by men who desired to refine the national culture, to soften unruly feelings between the classes, and to provide an antidote to the drudgery and competition of mechanized labor and market forces (140–153). For a similar argument, see Michael Kimmel, *Manhood in America: A Cultural History* (New York: Free Press, 1996), esp. 157–188.

75 According to Jacqueline Jones, during slavery "fathers shared the obligations of family life with their wives. In denying slaves the right to own property, make a living for themselves, participate in public life, or protect their children, the institution of bondage deprived black men of access to the patriarchy in the larger economic and political sense." Nonetheless, she observes the specific ways that "men and women worked together to support the father's role as provider and protector"; see Jones, *Labor of Love, Labor of Sorrow*, 36.

76 See Tera W. Hunter, *Bound in Wedlock: Slave and Free Marriage in the Nineteenth Century* (Cambridge, MA: Harvard University Press, 2017), 196–232.

77 In *My Father's Shadow: Intergenerational Conflict in African American Men's Autobiography* (Philadelphia: University of Pennsylvania Press, 1991), David L. Dudley has pointed out the absence of sexual and marital relations in black men's autobiography up to the 1950s (31–32). In his essay "Chapter One of Booker T. Washington's *Up from Slavery* and the Feminization of the African American Male," in *Representing Black*

Men, ed. Marcellus Blount and George P. Cunningham (New York: Routledge, 1996), Donald Gibson also makes this point lucidly (103, 110n24).

78 Both Ann duCille's *The Coupling Convention: Sex, Text, and Tradition in Black Women's Fiction* (New York: Oxford University Press, 1993) and Claudia Tate's *Domestic Allegories of Political Desire: The Black Heroine's Text at the Turn of the Century* (New York: Oxford University Press, 1992) focus on the great import of the relation between cultural formations of marriage for African Americans and the racial-political implications of taking vows in African American women's fiction. Though often subordinated in men's autobiographies, this plot still silently undergirds the prerogatives of masculine fitness.

79 Edith Armstrong Talbot, *Samuel Chapman Armstrong: A Biographical Study* (New York: Doubleday and Page Company, 1904), 175.

80 Washington, *Up from Slavery*, 147.

81 Tate, *Domestic Allegories of Political Desire*, 129–130.

82 Washington, *Up from Slavery*, 39.

83 Talbot, *Samuel Chapman Armstrong*, 175.

84 Washington, *Up from Slavery*, 40.

85 Harlan, *Making of a Black Leader*, 86–87.

86 Washington, *Up from Slavery*, 154.

87 On Washington's defensive strategy for warding off the real potential for violent retaliation resulting from the visible success of Tuskegee, see Kenrick Ian Grandison, "Landscapes of Terror: A Reading of Tuskegee's Historic Campus, 1881–1915," in *The Geography of Identity*, ed. Patricia Yaeger, vol. 5 of *Ratio*, produced by the University of Michigan Institute for the Humanities (Ann Arbor: University of Michigan Press, 1996), 334–367.

88 Washington, *Up from Slavery*, 147.

89 Harlan, *Making of a Black Leader*, 138.

90 See Washington, *Up from Slavery*, 124–125.

91 Washington, *Up from Slavery*, 125.

92 Washington, *Up from Slavery*, 125.

93 Harlan, *Making of a Black Leader*, 126.

94 Washington, *Up from Slavery*, 267.

95 Washington, *Up from Slavery*, 269–270.

96 Washington, *Up from Slavery*, 75.

97 Tera W. Hunter, *To 'Joy My Freedom: Southern Black Women's Lives and Labors after the Civil War* (Cambridge, MA: Harvard University Press, 1997), 17.

98 Hortense Spillers, "Mama's Baby, Papa's Maybe: An American Grammar Book," in *Black, White, and in Color: Essays on American Literature and Culture* (Chicago: University of Chicago Press, 2003), 203–229.

99 Talbot, *Samuel Chapman Armstrong*, 105.

100 Talbot, *Samuel Chapman Armstrong*, 104–105.

101 Armstrong, quoted in Talbot, *Samuel Chapman Armstrong*, 105.

102 In *Living In, Living Out: African American Domestics and the Great Migration* (New York: Kodansha International, 1994), Elizabeth Clark-Lewis charts the history of domestic labor as performed primarily by black women from slavery to the period of the

Great Migration (see esp. 43). Jacqueline Jones points out that after emancipation, a relatively small percentage of women in the sharecropper class went to work as domestics (4.1 percent in 1880, 9 percent in 1900), but with the migration, domestic labor became a dominant breadwinning vocation; see Jones, *Labor of Love, Labor of Sorrow*, 90, 112, 127–134, 154.

103 Clark-Lewis, *Living In, Living Out*, 25.
104 Washington, *Up from Slavery*, 17–18.
105 Harlan, *Making of a Black Leader*, 15.
106 Washington, *Up from Slavery*, 43.
107 Quoted in Harlan, *Making of a Black Leader*, 42.
108 Washington, *Up from Slavery*, 43.
109 On the controversy surrounding Douglass's second wife, see Rayford W. Logan's introduction to *Life and Times of Frederick Douglass, Written by Himself* (1892; repr., New York: Collier/Macmillan, 1962), 20, as well as Douglass's own comments in his *Life and Times of Frederick Douglass*, where he says, "No man, perhaps, had ever more offended popular prejudice than I had then lately done" (534).
110 Washington, *Up from Slavery*, 26–27.
111 It is interesting, though, that Washington retains the connection between the white mistress and learning to read the Bible when he credits Nathalie Lord, a Yankee teacher at Hampton, with instilling in him the practice of reading from the Bible before beginning the business of the day (see Washington, *Up from Slavery*, 67).
112 Harlan, *Making of a Black Leader*, 13.
113 Washington, *Up from Slavery*, 14.
114 Washington, *Up from Slavery*, 29.
115 Maurice Wallace points out that Washington's autobiography contains ambivalences in relation to outdoors work (as field hand) and indoors work (as houseservant); see Wallace, *Constructing the Black Masculine: Identity and Ideality in African American Men's Literature and Culture, 1775–1995* (Durham, NC: Duke University Press, 2002), 258.
116 Washington, *Up from Slavery*, 38.
117 On the reform movement in the Progressive era, see Painter, *Standing at Armageddon*, 253–282; Trachtenberg, *The Incorporation of America*, 161–181; Robert H. Wiebe, *The Search for Order, 1877–1920* (New York: Hill and Wang, 1967), 164–195; and Howard Mumford Jones, *The Age of Energy: Varieties of American Experience, 1865–1915* (New York: Viking, 1971), 155–178.
118 Washington, *Up from Slavery*, 97.
119 See Washington, *Up from Slavery*, 98. Washington's articles on the Native American experiment appear from September 1880 to May 1881 and are reprinted in Louis R. Harlan, ed., *The Booker T. Washington Papers, 1860–89*, vol. 2 (Urbana: University of Illinois Press, 1972), 78–132.
120 Harlan, *Washington Papers*, 2:82.
121 Harlan, *Washington Papers*, 2:83.
122 On Washington's mixed report to the government concerning his colonial charges at Tuskegee, see Harlan, *Making of a Black Leader*, 283–284.

123 Washington, *Up from Slavery*, 54–56.
124 Armstrong letter included in Talbot, *Samuel Chapman Armstrong*, 49.
125 For an alternative, compelling reading of Washington's use of the word "contact" in *Up from Slavery* (and Douglass's use as well), see Maurice Wallace, *Constructing the Black Masculine*, 264–265. On the theory of homoraciality, see Ross, *Manning the Race*, 11–12, 25.
126 Washington, *Up from Slavery*, 57.
127 Washington, *Up from Slavery*, 57.
128 Harlan makes this point: "The Spartan regiment of Hampton resembled that of an army camp, whose distinguishing feature is not battle readiness but close order drill" (*Making of a Black Leader*, 61).
129 Homi K. Bhabha, *The Location of Culture* (London: Routledge, 1994), 112–115.
130 McClintock, *Imperial Leather*, 64. For a similar elaboration of Bhabha, see Rey Chow, *Writing Diaspora: Tactics of Intervention in Contemporary Cultural Studies* (Bloomington: Indiana University Press, 1993), 51.
131 Armstrong, quoted in Talbot, *Samuel Chapman Armstrong*, 149.
132 Armstrong, quoted in Talbot, *Samuel Chapman Armstrong*, 277.
133 Bhabha prefers to distinguish between mimicry and identification (*Location of Culture*, 61).
134 Talbot, *Samuel Chapman Armstrong*, 191.
135 Harlan, *Making of a Black Leader*, 201.
136 Houston A. Baker Jr., *Modernism and the Harlem Renaissance* (Chicago: University of Chicago Press, 1987), 15–36.
137 On the role of race in relation to disability, see Christopher M. Bell's introduction to *Blackness and Disability: Critical Examinations and Cultural Interventions* (East Lansing: Michigan State University Press, 2011), 1–7; Dea H. Boster, *African American Slavery and Disability: Bodies, Property, and Power in the Antebellum South, 1800–1860* (New York: Routledge, 2013), 20–28; Dennis Tyler Jr., "Losing Limbs in the Republic: Disability, Dismemberment, and Mutilation in Charles Chesnutt's Conjure Stories," *Journal of Literary and Cultural Disability Studies* 11, no. 1 (2017): 36–39; and Rosemarie Garland-Thomson, *Extraordinary Bodies: Figuring Physical Disability in American Culture and Literature* (New York: Columbia University Press, 1997), 7–15, 60–78.
138 Washington, *Up from Slavery*, 56.
139 This scene strikes me as analogous to the famous closure of Charlotte Brontë's novel *Jane Eyre* (London: Smith, Elder and Company, 1847). In Jessie Redmon Fauset's *There Is Confusion* (New York: Boni and Liveright, 1924), a similar closure is effected. In all of these cases, the wounding serves a leveling purpose in terms of gender, class, and, in Washington's case, race.
140 Washington, *Up from Slavery*, 294.
141 Maurice Wallace, *Constructing the Black Masculine*, 265.
142 As with my own situation as a closeted sissy-boy whose gender anomalies were perhaps illegible to peers in a desegregating South beset by racial assumptions and confusions about how to interpret overly literate black boys, as observed in chapter 1, it

may be that those white male rulers who engaged with Carver in close quarters—like Henry Ford and Andrew Carnegie—were incapable of reading his gender nonconformities because their assumptions about his racial exceptionalism overshadowed their sissiphobic suspicion.

143 Nina Sun Eidsheim suggests the tradition of black male falsetto can actually be coded as "hypermasculine": "By enlisting falsetto, a vocal technique and recognizable timbral shift, male performers can utilize larger portions of their voices while maintaining an image of masculinity. Indeed, the most recognized and recognizable African American male vocalists of the 1960s . . . made liberal use of falsetto technique as timbral mediation. Applying this particular technique and timbre to a high vocal range signaled hypermasculinity." See Eidsheim, *The Race Sound: Listening, Timbre, and Vocality in African American Music* (Durham, NC: Duke University Press, 2019), 107. For a longer, brief history of the falsetto voice in American popular music, see Simon Ravens, *The Supernatural Voice: A History of High Male Singing* (Suffolk: Boydell and Brewer, 2014), 201–205. See also Mark Anthony Neal, *Songs in the Key of Black Life: A Rhythm and Blues Nation* (London: Routledge / Taylor and Francis Group, 2013), 46–48.

144 Holt (1899–1963), whose legal name was Margaret Van Vechten Saunders Holt, wrote under the pen name "Rackham." See Rackham Holt, *George Washington Carver: An American Biography* (Garden City: Doubleday, Doran, and Company, 1943), 6.

145 Holt, *George Washington Carver*, 38.

146 Holt, *George Washington Carver*, 38.

147 Holt, *George Washington Carver*, 202.

148 Washington repeatedly rails against any sign of luxury among the former slaves who become the primary clientele of Tuskegee, seeing such objects as pianos, organs, sewing machines, and French grammar books as impractical extravagances not suited for the Negro's economic stage of development. See Washington, *Up from Slavery*, esp. 110–117.

149 Monica L. Miller, *Slaves to Fashion: Black Dandyism and the Styling of Black Diasporic Identity* (Durham, NC: Duke University Press, 2009), 5.

150 Monica L. Miller, *Slaves to Fashion*, 8, 10–11.

151 See Holt, *George Washington Carver*, 194.

152 Linda O. McMurry, *George Washington Carver: Scientist and Symbol* (New York: Oxford University Press, 1981), vii–viii. McMurry documents a letter that Carver wrote seeking advice about a potential wife in 1905. McMurry speculates about the reasons this potential proposal never materialized, including the couple's incompatible goals, Carver's being a natural loner, his dedication to work and religion, and finally "the remote possibility of a physical disability." McMurry concludes, "At any rate, despite numerous match-making efforts by his friends, Carver never seriously considered marriage again" (*George Washington Carver*, 48).

153 McMurry, *George Washington Carver*, 13, 14.

154 McMurry, *George Washington Carver*, 110.

155 See McMurry, *George Washington Carver*, 30–31.

156 See McMurry, *George Washington Carver*, 22–23. As Clark-Lewis notes about this occupation in DC, "the laundress was like a private contractor with regular clients—someone

to respect and emulate (*Living In, Living Out*, 143). See also Tera Hunter, *To 'Joy My Freedom,* 57–58, 62–65. Against the grain of Washington's celebration of self-help entrepreneurism, *Up from Slavery* rails against the DC black laundresses for their profligate ways, as he suggests that they erroneously provide for their daughters "six or eight years of book education [which] had weaned them away from the occupation of their mothers" (90–91).

157 Quoted in McMurry, *George Washington Carver*, 60.
158 See Kenrick Ian Grandison, "Negotiated Space: The Black College Campus as a Cultural Record of Postbellum America," *American Quarterly* 51, no. 3 (1999): 529–579.
159 In *Wrestling Angels into Song: The Fictions of Ernest J. Gaines and James Alan McPherson* (Philadelphia: University of Pennsylvania Press, 1995), Herman Beavers observes how self-made manhood is associated with the figure of the inventor as scientific tinkerer, a figure of democratizing manliness that he suggests appears in works by black male writers such as Ralph Ellison (11–14).

Chapter 3. Un/fit Manliness

1 James Weldon Johnson, *Black Manhattan* (1930; repr., New York: Da Capo, 1991), 128.
2 Robert F. Reid-Pharr has demonstrated how after gradual emancipation in the northern states, free people of color realized that they could never experience genuine freedom until slavery was abolished for all, regardless of color. See *Conjugal Union: The Body, the House, and the Black American* (New York: Oxford University Press, 1999). By codifying the black/white racial binary, the *Plessy* decision blocked any notion of an interstitial colored group, forcing all U.S. people of African descent into a singular racial family and political ship, to sink or sail forward together.
3 Goldsby, *Spectacular Secret*, 167.
4 On Johnson's Bookerite tendencies at the turn of the century, see Eugene Levy, *James Weldon Johnson: Black Leader, Black Voice* (Chicago: University of Chicago Press, 1973), 63–68, 100–107.
5 Levy also points out how well Johnson was able to work closely with a wide range of individuals in the NAACP—including both Walter White, whom Johnson was responsible for hiring, and Du Bois—without incurring personal animosities (*James Weldon Johnson*, 225–227).
6 "In Spite of the Handicap" is the title of James D. Corrothers's 1916 autobiography, in which he details his personal uplift despite the crutch of racism; see Corrothers, *In Spite of the Handicap: An Autobiography* (New York: George H. Doran Company, 1916).
7 James Weldon Johnson, *Negro Americans, What Now?* (New York: Viking, 1935), 103.
8 Skerrett writes, "Johnson's withdrawals are strategic: they are undertaken as much to strengthen and refresh his sense of purpose as to escape the difficulty at hand"; see Joseph T. Skerrett Jr., "Irony and Symbolic Action in James Weldon Johnson's *The Autobiography of an Ex-Coloured Man*," *American Quarterly* 32 (1980): 547.
9 James Weldon Johnson, *Along This Way: The Autobiography of James Weldon Johnson* (1933; repr., New York: Da Capo, 2000), 391.

10 Johnson, *Along This Way*, 411.
11 On Du Bois's shifting politics and resignation during the early Depression, see David Levering Lewis, *W. E. B. Du Bois*, 305–311, 336–348.
12 Johnson, *Along This Way*, 411.
13 Johnson, *Along This Way*, 393.
14 Although we do not have space to analyze this theme, Johnson's autobiography makes a significant shift away from the strategy of diminishing the role of the wife in the narrative that we saw in Washington. Grace Nail Johnson is important to Johnson's image of himself as a man of the world.
15 Johnson, *Along This Way*, 6–7.
16 Johnson, *Along This Way*, 9.
17 See Mary White Ovington, *The Walls Came Tumbling Down: The Autobiography of Mary White Ovington* (New York: Harcourt Brace, 1947), 6–7.
18 Johnson, *Along This Way*, 10. In his most popular poem, "The Creation," Johnson had also revised and inverted the stigmatized mammy figure when he describes God as molding man by stooping down in the dust "like a mammy bending over her baby"; see "The Creation," in James Weldon Johnson, ed., *The Book of American Negro Poetry*, rev. ed. (1922; repr., San Diego: Harcourt Brace and Company, 1950), 120.
19 Johnson, *Along This Way*, 13–14.
20 Valerie Smith, *Self-Discovery and Authority*, 50.
21 Johnson, *Along This Way*, 18, 17.
22 Johnson's highly successful career as a popular songwriter constitutes another dimension of his gentle character that could be analyzed more deeply here. Shana L. Redmond, for instance, documents the ways in which his being known as the composer of "Lift Every Voice and Sing" and other songs and poems familiar to black folk plays a crucial role in Johnson's success in garnering membership for the NAACP across the South; see Redmond, *Anthem: Social Movements and the Sound of Solidarity in the African Diaspora* (New York: New York University Press, 2014), 63–81.
23 Johnson, *Along This Way*, 22.
24 Johnson, *Along This Way*, 31.
25 Eugene Levy notes that Stanton School, which Johnson attended and later made into a high school as its principal, had the same curriculum as public schools across the nation because Bookerite industrial training was not adopted there until 1887; see Levy, *James Weldon Johnson*, 13.
26 See, for instance, Johnson, *Along This Way*, 45.
27 Johnson, *Along This Way*, 64.
28 On the narrative of Jim Crow train car confrontation, see Ross, *Manning the Race*, 5–6, 372–376, 116–117.
29 Johnson, *Along This Way*, 65.
30 Levy, *James Weldon Johnson*, 21.
31 Monica L. Miller, *Slaves to Fashion*, 192.
32 Johnson, *Along This Way*, 93.
33 Johnson, *Along This Way*, 47–48.
34 See Johnson, *Along This Way*, 152.

35 Johnson, *Along This Way*, 237.
36 Roosevelt clearly is a model American for Johnson. When agreeing to write a column for the *New York Age*, he says he arranged to have what he wrote "appear under my name as contributing editor, a title I copied from Theodore Roosevelt"; see Johnson, *Along This Way*, 303. Also Johnson proudly notes how, after he consults Roosevelt concerning his trip to Haiti, Roosevelt "slapped me on the shoulder and wished me luck" (Johnson, *Along This Way*, 345).
37 Johnson, *Along This Way*, 289.
38 See Johnson's attempt at making a distinction between his support of the Nicaraguan policy while attacking the Haitian policy (*Along This Way*, 344–345); and Levy, *James Weldon Johnson*, 202–203.
39 Brian Russell Roberts, *Artistic Ambassadors: Literary and International Representation of the New Negro Era* (Charlottesville: University of Virginia Press, 2013), 42–43, 46–47.
40 Johnson, *Along This Way*, 258–259.
41 Johnson, *Along This Way*, 286.
42 James Weldon Johnson, "Self-Determining Haiti," *The Nation* 111 (1920): 345.
43 Johnson, "Self-Determining Haiti," 346.
44 Johnson, "Self-Determining Haiti," 265–266.
45 Johnson, "Self-Determining Haiti," 347.
46 Johnson, *Along This* Way, 347. Although the implication in *Along This Way* is that U.S. blacks have much to learn from Haiti about avoiding colorism, it would be surprising if Johnson did not understand that color politics played a negative role in Haiti's history of civil warfare. See Rayford W. Logan, "James Weldon Johnson and Haiti," *Phylon* 32, no. 4 (1960): 397.
47 Johnson, *Along This Way*, 412.
48 On Johnson's ambivalence about assimilation, see Levy, *James Weldon Johnson*, 67–68, 93–94, 111–112. Charles Chesnutt had in 1900 advocated "amalgamation" (the biological mixing of all races to create one race) in a series of articles entitled "The Future American" appearing in the *Boston Evening Transcript* in 1900, reprinted in *Charles W. Chesnutt: Essays and Speeches*, ed. Joseph R. McElrath Jr., Robert C. Leitz III, and Jesse S. Crisler (Stanford, CA: Stanford University Press, 1999), 121–136. Also see Arlene A. Elder, "'The Future American Race': Charles W. Chesnutt's Utopian Vision," *MELUS* 15, no. 3 (Autumn 1988): 121–129.
49 Johnson, *Along This Way*, 411–412.
50 Carl Van Vechten, "Introduction to Mr. Knopf's New Edition," in *The Autobiography of an Ex-Coloured Man* (1927; repr., New York: Vintage / Random House, 1989), xxxiii–xxxiv (italics in original).
51 Johnson, *Along This Way*, 239.
52 Scott Herring, *Queering the Underworld: Slumming, Literature, and the Undoing of Lesbian and Gay History* (Chicago: University of Chicago Press, 2007), 115.
53 Herring, *Queering the Underworld*, 115.
54 Houston A. Baker Jr. has noted the influence of *Souls of Black Folk* on *Autobiography*, calling it a "fictional rendering" of Du Bois's book; see Baker, "A Forgotten Prototype: *The Autobiography of an Ex-Coloured Man* and *The Invisible Man*," *Virginia*

Quarterly Review 49, no. 3 (1973): 435–436. Other critics have similarly noted the Du Boisian tenor of the narrator's consciousness, including Valerie Smith, *Self-Discovery and Authority*, 57–58; Kimberly W. Benston, "Facing Tradition: Revisionary Scenes in African American Literature," *PMLA* 105, no. 1 (1990): 102; and Eric J. Sundquist, *The Hammers of Creation: Folk Culture in African American Fiction* (Athens: University of Georgia Press, 1992), 37–39. Robert Stepto provides a thorough analysis of Johnson's revisions of both Washington's *Up from Slavery* and Du Bois's *Souls of Black Folk* in *From behind the Veil: A Study of Afro-American Narrative*, 2nd ed. (1979; repr., Urbana: University of Illinois Press, 1991), 106–121.

55 Valerie Smith, *Self-Discovery and Authority*, 54.
56 Gayle Wald, "The Satire of Race: James Weldon Johnson's *Autobiography of an Ex-Coloured Man*," in *Cross-Addressing: Resistance Literature and Cultural Borders*, ed. John C. Hawley (Albany: State University of New York Press, 1996), 144.
57 James Weldon Johnson, *The Autobiography of an Ex-Coloured Man* (1927; repr., New York: Vintage / Random House, 1989), 32–33.
58 Johnson, *Autobiography of an Ex-Coloured Man*, 6.
59 Baker, "Forgotten Prototype," 436; see also Valerie Smith, *Self-Discovery and Authority*, 52; Gayle Wald, "The Satire of Race," 145.
60 Marvin P. Garrett, "Early Recollections and Structural Irony in *The Autobiography of an Ex-Colored Man*," *Critique: Studies in Contemporary Fiction* 13, no. 2 (2013): 13.
61 Johnson, *Autobiography of an Ex-Coloured Man*, 38, 43.
62 Johnson, *Autobiography of an Ex-Coloured Man*, 6–7.
63 Johnson, *Autobiography of an Ex-Coloured Man*, 23.
64 Benston, "Facing Tradition," 102. Garrett puts a similar observation in moral rather than psychoanalytic terms ("Early Recollections," 9). Phillip Brian Harper points out that the narcissism also positions the narrator in a conventionally feminine identity, one which makes him available to perform the domesticated woman's role in his relationship with the wealthy benefactor later in the novel; see *Are We Not Men? Masculine Anxiety and the Problem of African-American Identity* (New York: Oxford University Press, 1986), 109–111. J. Lee Greene associates the mirror scene with the feminine constructions of beauty in fairy tales like Snow White, indicating how whiteness itself can be read as feminizing in this situation and how the narrator's look is implicitly tied to "fictive portraits of southern belles, white and black—Beauty incarnate"; see Greene, *Blacks in Eden: The African American Novel's First Century* (Charlottesville: University Press of Virginia, 1996), 91.
65 Michael Warner has offered a trenchant critique of this association between narcissism and homoeroticism as codified in psychoanalysis, and has pointed out how this association depends on an assumed difference between girls as natural objects of desire and boys as natural subjects; see "Homo-Narcissism; or, Heterosexuality," in *Engendering Men: The Question of Male Feminist Criticism*, ed. Joseph A. Boone and Michel Cadden (New York: Routledge, 1990), esp. 190–192.
66 Johnson, *Autobiography of an Ex-Coloured Man*, 18.
67 Johnson, *Autobiography of an Ex-Coloured Man*, 17.
68 Johnson, *Autobiography of an Ex-Coloured Man*, 26.

69 See Johnson, *Autobiography of an Ex-Coloured Man*, 27.
70 As we will see in chapter 6, Richard Wright uses piano-playing as a sign of sissiness in the midst of Jim Crow lynching as well in his last novel.
71 In *The Queen's Throat: Opera, Homosexuality, and the Mystery of Desire* (New York: Poseidon, 1993), Wayne Koestenbaum brilliantly draws the connection between the opera diva and sexual queerness. This opera house scene also riffs on Du Bois's short story "The Coming of John" in *Souls of Black Folk*, where the titular hero is humiliated by a white childhood friend, who, not recognizing him, has him removed from the opera house.
72 See Johnson, *Along This Way*, 36–39.
73 Johnson, *Along This Way*, 38.
74 Johnson, *Autobiography of an Ex-Coloured Man*, 27.
75 Johnson, *Autobiography of an Ex-Coloured Man*, 46, 47.
76 Johnson, *Autobiography of an Ex-Coloured Man*, 56.
77 Nella Larsen will amplify the gender dynamics of this sort of revulsion for southern Negro folk in her 1928 novella, *Quicksand*, which is clearly deeply influenced by Johnson's *Autobiography of an Ex-Coloured Man*. Both Larsen and Johnson can be seen as offering a critique of Bookerite condescension toward the folk.
78 Johnson, *Autobiography of an Ex-Coloured Man*, 88.
79 Johnson, *Autobiography of an Ex-Coloured Man*, 94.
80 Kevin Mumford, *Interzones: Black/White Sex Districts in Chicago and New York in the Early Twentieth Century* (New York: Columbia University Press, 1997), 116.
81 Johnson, *Autobiography of an Ex-Coloured Man*, 107.
82 Johnson, *Autobiography of an Ex-Coloured Man*, 108.
83 On the sweetback in New Negro Renaissance literature, see Ross, *Manning the Race*, 134–140.
84 Johnson, *Autobiography of an Ex-Coloured Man*, 109.
85 Van Vechten reworks this bar shoot-out scene in the conclusion of *Nigger Heaven* (1926; repr., New York: Avon, 1951), turning it into a tragic satire on the impossibility of New Negro male ambitions toward high culture.
86 Johnson, *Autobiography of an Ex-Coloured Man*, 114.
87 Johnson, *Autobiography of an Ex-Coloured Man*, 75.
88 Johnson, *Autobiography of an Ex-Coloured Man*, 116.
89 Henry Louis Gates Jr., introduction to *Autobiography of an Ex-Coloured Man* (1927; repr., New York: Vintage / Random House, 1989), xx.
90 Johnson, *Autobiography of an Ex-Coloured Man*, 116.
91 Johnson, *Autobiography of an Ex-Coloured Man*, 121.
92 Michael G. Cooke, *Afro-American Literature in the Twentieth Century* (New Haven, CT: Yale University Press, 1984), 47. Phillip Brian Harper makes a similar point in psychoanalytic terms; see Harper, *Are We Not Men?*, 111.
93 Johnson, *Autobiography of an Ex-Coloured Man*, 123, 121.
94 Cooke, *Afro-American Literature in the Twentieth Century*, 47. Some critics have suggested that the millionaire patron is in fact a passing colored man; see, for instance, Maurice J. O'Sullivan Jr., "Of Souls and Pottage: James Weldon Johnson's *The Autobiography*

of an Ex-Coloured Man," CLA Journal 23, no. 1 (Fall 1979): 64. Cheryl Clarke has provided the most extensive reading of the patron as a homosexual; see Clarke, "Race, Homosocial Desire, and 'Mammon' in *Autobiography of an Ex-Coloured Man*," in *Professions of Desire: Lesbian and Gay Studies in Literature*, ed. George E. Haggerty and Bonnie Zimmerman (New York: MLA, 1995), esp. 87–91.

95 Johnson, *Autobiography of an Ex-Coloured Man*, 121.
96 Johnson, *Autobiography of an Ex-Coloured Man*, 120.
97 See Levy, *James Weldon Johnson*, 134. Skerrett reads the millionaire bachelor as, in fact, the evil alter ego of the idealized bond with Dr. Summers ("Irony and Symbolic Action," 553).
98 Johnson, *Autobiography of an Ex-Coloured Man*, 121.
99 Johnson, *Autobiography of an Ex-Coloured Man*, 124.
100 Harper, *Are We Not Men?*, 110.
101 Johnson, *Autobiography of an Ex-Coloured Man*, 143.
102 Johnson, *Autobiography of an Ex-Coloured Man*, 130.
103 Cheryl Clarke, "Race, Homosocial Desire, and 'Mammon,'" 90.
104 Johnson, *Autobiography of an Ex-Coloured Man*, 141.
105 Johnson, *Autobiography of an Ex-Coloured Man*, 187–188.
106 Eugenia Collier, "The Endless Journey of the Ex-Coloured Man," *Phylon* 32, no. 4 (1971): 372; see also Trudier Harris, *Exorcising Blackness: Historical and Literary Lynching and Burning Rituals* (Bloomington: Indiana University Press, 1984), 72–73.
107 Goldsby, *Spectacular Secret*, 199.
108 Johnson, *Autobiography of an Ex-Coloured Man*, 197.
109 See Johnson, *Autobiography of an Ex-Coloured Man*, 202, 209–210.
110 Johnson, *Autobiography of an Ex-Coloured Man*, 211.
111 Kathleen Pfeiffer argues that *Autobiography* rejects the black/white binary by enabling the narrator to refuse "the caste status of a black man" by rejecting "the rule of color division"; see Pfeiffer, "Individualism, Success, and American Identity in *The Autobiography of an Ex-Colored Man*," *African American Review* 30, no. 3 (1996): 405. The narrator's passing for white can be celebrated as subversive only if Johnson's politics—and the politics of race—are ignored or discounted. For another reading that follows Pfeiffer's line of thought but with more nuance and attention to racial politics, see Wald, "The Satire of Race," 141; and Samira Kawash, *Dislocating the Color Line: Identity, Hybridity, and Singularity in African-American Narrative* (Stanford, CA: Stanford University Press, 1997), 135–155.
112 Johnson, *Autobiography of an Ex-Coloured Man*, 210.
113 Johnson, *Autobiography of an Ex-Coloured Man*, 3.
114 Johnson, *Along This Way*, 154.
115 Johnson, *Along This Way*, 155.
116 As Shawn Christian has observed, the authors of the Harlem Renaissance were very heavily involved in shaping the secondary school curriculum as teachers as well as editors of literary textbooks. That so many, including Johnson, committed themselves to this teacherly project indicates not only the kinds of restraints placed on the careers open to them but also their devotion to school teaching and curricular

development as important vectors of black uplift and cultural formation. See Christian, *Harlem Renaissance and the Idea of a New Negro Reader* (Amherst: University of Massachusetts Press, 2016).

117 Johnson, *Along This Way*, 156.

Chapter 4. Baldwin's Sissy Heroics

A portion of chapter 4 was previously published in *African American Review* 46, no. 4 (Winter 2013): 633–651.

1 W. J. Weatherby, *James Baldwin: Artist on Fire* (New York: Donald I. Fine, 1989), 109.
2 Barbara Ann Kipfer and Robert L. Chapman, eds., *Dictionary of American Slang* (New York: Collins, 2007), 506.
3 Tom Dalzell, *The Routledge Dictionary of Modern American Slang and Unconventional English*, 2nd ed. (London: Taylor and Francis, 2017), 775, https://www-taylorfrancis-com.proxy01.its.virginia.edu/books/mono/10.4324/9781315195827/routledge-dictionary-modern-american-slang-unconventional-english-tom-dalzell.
4 Sedgwick, "How to Bring Your Kids Up Gay," 157.
5 Major, *Juba to Jive*, 461. Perhaps the term "swish" emerges among homosexuals, black and/or white, but it experiences broader usage within the black vernacular in the period indicated by Majors. It is not surprising that Dalzell indicates a 1990s American usage in the prison population through the term "swish tank," which means "a holding cell in a jail where homosexual suspects and prisoners are kept" (*Routledge Dictionary of Modern American Slang and Unconventional English*, 775).
6 The pulp fiction of Iceberg Slim, the pen name of Robert Beck, vividly portrays the prominence of the street swish in Southside Chicago working-class culture in novels like *Trick Baby: The Story of the White Negro* (Los Angeles: Holloway House, 1967), *Pimp: The Story of My Life* (Los Angeles: Holloway House, 1969), and *Mama Black Widow* (Los Angeles: Holloway House, 1969).
7 Vershawn Ashanti Young, *Your Average Nigga*, 53–71. Mark Anthony Neal glosses the recent vernacular usage of "faggot" similarly in his analysis of the "quintessential 'homo-thug'" character Omar from the HBO television series *The Wire*. Neal points out how "faggot" has come to be distinguished from "gay" to connote a particular kind of nonmasculine gender impersonation (*Looking for Leroy*, 92–93).
8 The dip-and-bounce gait has come to epitomize an array of stereotyped characteristics defining black "ghetto" "hypermasculinity." Cataloguing the attributes of black masculinity, Vershawn Ashanti Young mentions first the walk: "The men I observed walked with that lanky dip I wish I could perfect" (*Your Average Nigga*, xl). In *Race Rebels: Culture, Politics, and the Black Working Class* (New York: Free Press, 1994), Robin D. G. Kelley captures well the zoot-suit culture of black and brown men who forge a distinct way of talking, dressing, and walking in Harlem and Los Angeles during and after World War II (see 161–181). More recently, in *Slaves to Fashion* Monica Miller traces the backstory of this black masculine urban culture, focusing on black men's embodiment, attire, and promenade.

9 In *Queer Pollen: White Seduction, Black Male Homosexuality, and the Cinematic* (Urbana: University of Illinois Press, 2011), David A. Gerstner examines the key influence of cinema on Baldwin's social perspective and aesthetic form, noting that "the cinema and its distinctive properties are where Baldwin's queerness of queer subjectivity moves between the gradations of black and white, the light and the dark" (73).
10 James Baldwin, *The Fire Next Time* (1963; repr., New York: Vintage / Random House, 1993), 16.
11 Baldwin, *Fire Next Time*, 20.
12 Trudier Harris, *Black Women in the Fiction of James Baldwin* (Knoxville: University of Tennessee Press, 1985), 25.
13 Stephen C. Finley, "Homoeroticism and the African-American Heterosexual Male: Quest for Meaning in the Black Church," *Black Theology* 5, no. 3 (2007): 321. Also Jawanza Kunjufu, *Adam! Where Are You? Why Most Black Men Don't Go to Church* (Chicago: African American Images, 1997). Recent queer theology has focused attention on homoerotic themes historically repressed in traditional Judeo-Christian hermeneutics. For instance, see Marlon Rachquel Moore, *In the Life and in the Spirit: Homoerotic Spirituality in African American Literature* (Albany: State University of New York Press, 2014); Stephen D. Moore, *God's Beauty Parlor: And Other Queer Spaces in and around the Bible* (Stanford, CA: Stanford University Press, 2001); Theodore W. Jennings Jr., *The Man Jesus Loved: Homoerotic Narratives from the New Testament* (Cleveland: Pilgrim, 2001) and *Jacob's Wound: Homoerotic Narrative in the Literature of Ancient Israel* (New York: Continuum, 2005).
14 Finley, "Homoeroticism and the African-American Heterosexual Male," 308.
15 Clarence E. Hardy III, *James Baldwin's God: Sex, Hope, and Crisis in Black Holiness Culture* (Knoxville: University of Tennessee Press, 2003), 5.
16 Ashon T. Crawley, "'Let's Get It On!': Performance Theory and Black Pentecostalism," *Black Theology* 6, no. 3 (September 2008): 319.
17 As Richard N. Pitt observes, "Pentecostal and Holiness churches were on the leading edges of the trend toward ordaining women primarily because of their experimental nature and the value they place on the prophetic preaching voice." See Pitt, *Divine Callings: Understanding the Call to Ministry in Black Pentecostalism* (New York: New York University Press, 2012), 186. See also Davarian L. Baldwin, *Chicago's New Negroes: Modernity, the Great Migration, and Black Urban Life* (Chapel Hill: University of North Carolina Press, 2007), 167–170, 183–186.
18 Crawley, "'Let's Get It On!,'" 326, 325.
19 James R. Goff Jr., *Fields White unto Harvest: Charles F. Parham and the Missionary Origins of Pentecostalism* (Fayetteville: University of Arkansas Press, 1988), 97.
20 For a vivid description of the ambivalence in regard to women's role in the church, see Melvin D. Williams's *Community in a Black Pentecostal Church: An Anthropological Study* (Pittsburgh: University of Pittsburgh Press, 1974), 31–32, 44. In his history *The Azusa Street Mission and Revival: The Birth of a Global Pentecostal Movement* (Nashville: Thomas Nelson, 2006), Cecil M. Robeck Jr. observes about the early white male leadership of the Pentecostal movement, Charles F. Parham and Warren Faye Carothers: "It must be noted that they were both of their time, and they were both

white men ministering in the South." He continues, "Both men viewed white, Anglo-Saxon Protestants as in some way especially blessed by God, a superior people, and this inevitably placed American Americans and other people of color at a distinct disadvantage" (48). However, as Robeck and other scholars document, African Americans were eventually able to overcome this disadvantage, especially as the movement moved westward from Houston to Los Angeles.

21. Arthur E. Paris, *Black Pentecostalism: Southern Religion in an Urban World* (Amherst: University of Massachusetts Press, 1982), 27. See also Melvin D. Williams, *Community in a Black Pentecostal Church*, 167–172, for an ethnographic description of the interactive "subcultures" of the Pentecostal storefront church and the "hustler" subculture of the street and street corner.

22. See Arlene Sánchez-Walsh, "Re-scripting Pentecostal Saints: Curious Life of Mother Rosa Horn," *Pantheos*, 26 July 2014, https://www.patheos.com/blogs/amsanchezwalsh/2014/07/re-scripting-pentecostal-saints-curious-life-of-mother-rosa-horn/.

23. Goff, *Fields White unto Harvest*, 138.

24. Davarian L. Baldwin, *Chicago's New Negroes*, 188.

25. See Jill Watts, *God, Harlem U.S.A.: The Father Divine Story* (Berkeley: University of California Press, 1992), esp. 32–44, 72–97.

26. Baldwin, *Fire Next Time*, 28.

27. Jeffrey Q. McCune Jr., "Transformance: Reading the Gospel in Drag," *Journal of Homosexuality* 46, nos. 3–4 (2004): 160.

28. Baldwin, *Fire Next Time*, 25.

29. James Baldwin, *The Price of the Ticket: Collected Nonfiction, 1948–1985* (New York: St. Martin's, 1985), 560–561.

30. Baldwin, *Fire Next Time*, 38.

31. Baldwin, *Fire Next Time*, 29.

32. Baldwin, *Fire Next Time*, 47.

33. See Major, *Juba to Jive*, 451. The import of "the street" as an African American idiom emerging around World War II is perfectly captured by Ann Petry's 1946 novel of that title.

34. Lillian Harris, dubbed "Pig Foot Mary," was a Harlem street vendor who got her start selling pig feet, chitterlings, corn, and other delicacies familiar to migrants from the South, enabling her to become a wealthy real estate magnate in the 1920s. See David Levering Lewis, *When Harlem Was in Vogue* (New York: Oxford University Press, 1981), 109–110.

35. Baldwin, *Price of the Ticket*, 678 (italics in original).

36. Baldwin, *Price of the Ticket*, 678.

37. Baldwin, *Price of the Ticket*, 685.

38. Baldwin, *Go Tell It*, 20–21.

39. Baldwin, *Go Tell It*, 20. This "white" figure may be modeled on Gertrude E. Ayer, who greatly influenced Baldwin and who was the first black principal in the New York Public Schools. Herb Boyd describes her as "a sprightly, very attractive light-skinned woman"; see Boyd, *Baldwin's Harlem: A Biography of James Baldwin* (New York: Atria Books, 2008), 13.

40 Baldwin, *Go Tell It*, 36.
41 Michael Cobb, *God Hates Fags: The Rhetoric of Religious Violence* (New York: New York University Press, 2006), 55.
42 In the plot of *Go Tell It*, Gabriel, the man whom John knows as a father but is really his stepfather, fathers a son, Royal, out of wedlock during a brief affair with a "loose" woman who is a domestic at the white household where he does chores. Because of his refusal to acknowledge Royal as his son, the boy grows up on the streets and ends up violently killed in Chicago, where Royal's mother has fled after Gabriel has secretly stolen money from his wife to provide some aid, actually to rid her from the town. When Gabriel goes north to Harlem, he meets Elizabeth, who already has a baby son, John. Out of apparent grace but more sinisterly a sense of atoning for his own guilt in relation to his own bastard son, Gabriel marries Elizabeth and informally adopts John as his own. Gabriel and Elizabeth then procreate Roy, John's younger half brother, ironically the mirror image of Royal in that both avoid churchiness and enjoy instead the dangers of the street. That John, rather than Roy, becomes the churchified son stokes Gabriel's fury, as it seems to stymie his own redemption through a biological son who can carry on his lineage as a preacher, even though Gabriel also takes pride in the street mannishness of Roy in contrast with John's sissiness.
43 Wright struggles hard to wrest manly weaponry out of his sensitive sissy relation to the world in *Black Boy*. Ironically, the only incident of a real weapon fired against whites narrated in the autobiography focuses on a grieving woman, the rumor of whom "renders him sleepless for nights" (73), as Richard mentally cross-dresses in the character of the avenging female in fantasizing racial revenge. In "Blueprint for Negro Writing," Wright celebrates the Dirty Dozens as one of the vernacular resources on which black writers can mold a social realistic artistry: "the swapping of sex experiences on street corners from boy to boy in the deepest vernacular." See Richard Wright, "Blueprint for Negro Writing," *New Challenge* 2, no. 2 (Fall 1937): 56.
44 Baldwin, *Price of the Ticket*, 690.
45 Richard Goldstein, "'Go the Way Your Blood Beats': An Interview with James Baldwin," in *James Baldwin: The Legacy*, ed. Quincy Troupe (New York: Simon and Schuster, 1989), 180.
46 Baldwin, "Here Be Dragons," in *Price of the Ticket*, 684.
47 Baldwin, *Price of the Ticket*, 681.
48 Boyd, *Baldwin's Harlem*, 6.
49 Baldwin, *Price of the Ticket*, 681.
50 Baldwin, *Price of the Ticket*, 681. The idea that Baldwin had no one to show his poetry to is not tenable, given who his teachers were, including Countee Cullen in junior high, and his work on his high school's literary magazine, *Magpie*; see Boyd, *Baldwin's Harlem*, 23–37, 49–52.
51 Baldwin, *Go Tell It*, 215.
52 E. L. Kornegay Jr., *A Queering of Black Theology: James Baldwin's Blues Project and Gospel Prose* (Basingstoke, UK: Palgrave Macmillan, 2013), 102.
53 Cobb, *God Hates Fags*, 54. Melvin Dixon goes even further, suggesting that John is "converted *out* of religion; he is delivered out of the moral authority of the church

and of his preacher stepfather"; see Dixon, *Ride Out the Wilderness: Geography and Identity in Afro-American Literature* (Urbana: University of Illinois Press, 1987), 125.

54   Baldwin, *Go Tell It*, 216.
55   Baldwin, *Go Tell It*, 219.
56   Baldwin, *Go Tell It*, 221.
57   See Phillip Brian Harper's brilliant gender history of the kiss as a figure of heteronormativity put at risk at any moment when two men kiss in public, even in the context of doing so as pro black male athletes televised on the basketball court. See Harper, *Private Affairs*, 1–29.
58   Baldwin, *Go Tell It*, 220, 221.
59   See Baldwin, *Go Tell It*, 216–217.
60   "The homosexual theme in Baldwin's first novel has gone mostly unremarked," James Campbell observed in *Talking at the Gates: A Life of James Baldwin* (New York: Penguin Books, 1991), 78. Since then, much work exploring gender, homoeroticism, and homosexuality in Baldwin's fiction has appeared. Trudier Harris's *Black Women in the Fiction of James Baldwin* (1985) began this process. Dwight McBride, ed., *James Baldwin Now* (New York: New York University Press, 1999), created a watershed, followed up by works like Keith Clark's *Black Manhood in James Baldwin, Ernest J. Gaines, and August Wilson* (Urbana: University of Illinois Press, 2002) and Matt Brim's *James Baldwin and the Queer Imagination* (Ann Arbor: University of Michigan Press, 2014), among others.
61   Campbell, *Talking at the Gates*, 78.
62   Keith Boykin, *One More River to Cross: Black and Gay in America* (New York: Anchor Books / Doubleday, 1996), 7–8. José Esteban Muñoz composes another vivid portrait of a black swish in his tribute to the celebrated New York drag queen Kevin Aviance, whose mastery of the vogue technique is legendary; Muñoz, *Cruising Utopia: The Then and There of Queer Futurity* (New York: New York University Press, 2009), 80.
63   On the father-and-son antihomosexual crusade at Abyssinian, see Powell Sr.'s autobiography *Against the Tide* (New York: Richard R. Smith, 1938), 209–220; and Angelique Harris, "Review: Homosexuality and the Black Church," *Journal of African American History* 93, no. 2 (2008): 262–270.
64   Marlon B. Ross, "Some Glances at the Black Fag: Race, Same-Sex Desire, and Cultural Belonging," in "Reading the Signs," ed. Anne Herrmann and Ross Chambers, special issue, *Canadian Review of Comparative Literature / Revue Canadienne de Littérature Comparée* 21 (1994): 193–219.
65   For an excellent discussion of how "queer" and "funny" tend to be used in black vernacular, see E. Patrick Johnson's "'Quare' Studies, or (Almost Everything I Know about Queer Studies I Learned from my Grandmother)," in *Black Queer Studies: A Critical Anthology*, ed. Johnson and Mae G. Henderson (Durham, NC: Duke University Press, 2005), 124–157.
66   Langston Hughes, "Café: 3 a.m.," in *Collected Poems of Langston Hughes*, ed. Arnold Rampersad and David Roessel (New York: Alfred A. Knopf, 1994), 406. For an excellent approach to textual traces of Hughes's homosexuality and reading of his poem

"Cafe, 3 a.m.," see Shane Vogel, *Scene of Harlem Cabaret: Race, Sexuality, Performance* (Chicago: University of Chicago Press, 2009), 104–131.

67 On the "sissy-man blues," see Tyina Steptoe, "Big Mama Thornton, Little Richard, and the Queer Roots of Rock 'n' Roll," *American Quarterly* 70, no. 1 (March 2018): esp. 57–65; Kortney Ziegler, "Black Sissy Masculinity and the Politics of Dis-respectability," in *No Tea, No Shade: New Writings in Black Queer Studies*, ed. E. Patrick Johnson (Durham, NC: Duke University Press, 2016), 196–215; and Kevin J. Mumford, "Homosex Changes: Race, Cultural Geography, and the Emergence of the Gay," *American Quarterly* 48, no. 3 (September 1996): 406–408.

68 Langston Hughes, *Not without Laughter* (1930; repr., New York: Collier Books / Macmillan, 1969), 284.

69 Hughes, *Not without Laughter*, 285.

70 Hughes, *Not without Laughter*, 285–286.

71 On the representation of gender-nonconforming men in McKay's *Home to Harlem* (1928), Fisher's *Walls of Jericho* (1928), and Thurman's *Blacker the Berry* (1929) and *Infants of the Spring* (1932), see Ross, *Manning the Race*, 309–354, 379–394. Also see Thomas H. Wirth, introduction to *Gay Rebel of the Harlem Renaissance: Selections from the Work of Richard Bruce Nugent* (Durham, NC: Duke University Press, 2002), 1–61, which instructively places the life and work of Richard Bruce Nugent in the context of a homophilic subculture of the Harlem Renaissance; and Anna Pochmara, *The Making of the New Negro: Black Authorship, Masculinity, and Sexuality in the Harlem Renaissance* (Amsterdam: Amsterdam University Press, 2011), esp. 62–82, 141–178.

72 Boyd, *Baldwin's Harlem*, 34.

73 Arnold Rampersad, *The Life of Langston Hughes*, 2 vols. (New York: Oxford University Press, 1986–1988), 2:335. Rampersad has come under attack for his treatment of Hughes's sexuality in the two-volume biography. I have addressed this in "White Fantasies of Desire: Baldwin and the Racial Identities of Sexuality," in McBride, *James Baldwin Now*, 13–55. See also Charles I. Nero's "Re/Membering Langston: Homophobic Textuality and Arnold Rampersad's *Life of Langston Hughes*," in *Queer Representations: Reading Lives, Reading Cultures*, ed. Martin Duberman (New York: New York University Press, 1997), 188–196.

74 Hughes to Bontemps, 18 February 1953, in *Arna Bontemps–Langston Hughes Letters, 1925–1967*, sel. and ed. Charles H. Nichols (New York: Paragon House, 1990) (hereafter cited as Nichols, *Bontemps-Hughes Letters*), 302–303. On this letter, see also Rampersad, *Life of Langston Hughes*, vol. 2 (335); Weatherby, *James Baldwin* (112–117); Leeming, *James Baldwin* (157–160); and Ross, "White Fantasies of Desire."

75 Hughes to Bontemps, 24 October 1956, in Nichols, *Bontemps-Hughes Letters*, 350.

76 Hughes to Bontemps, 28 May 1962, in Nichols, *Bontemps-Hughes Letters*, 447–448 (italics and capitals in original).

77 James de Jongh, *Vicious Modernism: Black Harlem and the Literary Imagination* (Cambridge: Cambridge University Press, 1990), 24.

78 Darieck Scott, *Extravagant Abjection: Blackness, Power, and Sexuality in the African American Literary Imagination* (New York: New York University Press, 2010), 7.

79 In "Notes on a Native Son," Eldridge Cleaver anchors his opposition between Wright and Baldwin on Bigger's conventional masculinity, however self-annihilating, with Rufus Scott: "a pathetic wretch who indulged in the white man's pastime of committing suicide, who let a white bisexual homosexual fuck him in his ass, and who took a Southern Jezebel for his woman, with all that these tortured relationships imply, [he] was the epitome of a black eunuch who has completed submitted to the white man." When Cleaver writes that Baldwin despised "not Wright, but his masculinity," he is partly correct insofar as Baldwin is through the narrative framing a sharp critique of conventional masculinity and all of its violations. See *Soul on Ice*, 104, 106.

80 Jeffrey Q. McCune Jr., *Sexual Discretion: Black Masculinity and the Politics of Passing* (Chicago: University of Chicago Press, 2014), 6–23.

81 Baldwin, *Go Tell It*, 13.

82 See Kornegay, *Queering of Black Theology*, which aptly labels Baldwin's style "gospel prose" (3); Marlon Rachquel Moore, *In the Life and in the Spirit*, 39–61; and Josiah Ulysses Young III, *James Baldwin's Understanding of God: Overwhelming Desire and Joy* (New York: Palgrave Macmillan, 2014), especially 24–33.

83 For a helpful reading of Baldwin's critique of patriarchy through the gendered characterizations of Gabriel, Elizabeth, and Florence, see David Ikard, *Breaking the Silence: Toward a Black Male Feminist Criticism* (Baton Rouge: Louisiana State University Press, 2007), 49–79.

84 Baldwin, *Go Tell It*, 214–215.

85 Baldwin, *Go Tell It*, 56.

86 Marlon Rachquel Moore provides a helpful sketch of Baldwin's autobiographical take on his religious upbringing in relation to his use of Christian narratives in his fiction in *In the Life and in the Spirit*, 39–42.

87 Hardy, *James Baldwin's God*, xi.

88 On the two-spirit or "berdache" tradition, see Walter L. Williams, *The Spirit and the Flesh: Sexual Diversity in American Indian Culture* (Boston: Beacon, 1986).

89 For instance, see John Rechy, *City of Night* (1963), *Numbers* (1967), and *Rushes* (1979); Andrew Holleran (pen name of Eric Garber), *Dancer from the Dance* (1978), and *Nights in Aruba* (1983); Edmund White, *Nocturnes for the King of Naples* (1978) and *A Boy's Own Story* (1982); Larry Kramer, *Faggots* (1977); Armistead Maupin, *Tales of the City* series (1978, 1982); George Whitmore, *The Confessions of Danny Slocum* (1980); David Leavitt, *Family Dancing* (1984) and *The Lost Language of Cranes* (1986); James Robert Baker, *Adrenaline* (1985); and Robert Ferro, *The Family of Max Desir* (1983) and *Second Son* (1988). Many of these writers belonged to the gay-male writing club the Violet Quill, aimed at fostering a queer (white male) literary renaissance; on the history of this literary group, see David Bergman's *The Violet Hour: The Violet Quill and the Making of Gay Culture* (New York: Columbia University Press, 2004).

90 Baldwin, *Just above My Head* (New York: Dell, 1979), 536.

91 Baldwin, *Go Tell It*, 29.

92 Baldwin, *Just above My Head*, 538.

93 Several 1980s books help to document this change in social consciousness about the gay ghetto's emergence int he 1970s. Frances FitzGerald's *Cities on a Hill: A Journey through Contemporary American Cultures* (New York: Simon and Schuster, 1986) includes a vivid portrait of the Castro as a new frontier for gay men (25–110); Dennis Altman's *The Homosexualization of America, the Americanization of the Homosexual* (New York: St. Martin's, 1982) presciently captures how deeply the new gay culture had become imbibed by American society; Edmund White's gay travelogue, *States of Desire: Travels in Gay America* (London: André Deutsch, 1980), illustrates how homosexuality had become much more openly visible and integrated, if still ambivalently, into every corner of American geography; as well as John D'Emilio's scholarly history, *Sexual Politics, Sexual Communities: The Making of a Homosexual Minority in the United States, 1940–1970* (Chicago: University of Chicago Press, 1983).
94 James Baldwin, *No Name in the Street* (New York: Laurel/Dell, 1972), 61.
95 Kathryn Stockton, *Beautiful Bottom, Beautiful Shame: Where "Black" Meets "Queer"* (Durham, NC: Duke University Press, 2006), 149–176; Leo Bersani, "Is the Rectum a Grave?," in *AIDS: Cultural Analysis, Cultural Activism*, ed. Douglas Crimp (Cambridge, MA: MIT Press, 1988), 199.
96 The extent to which the asshole as an erotic subject has remained taboo can be glimpsed from how long it took to outlaw state sodomy laws within the United States despite increasing tolerance toward gay, lesbian, and transgender minorities. See David A. J. Richards's *The Sodomy Cases: Bowers v. Hardwick and Lawrence v. Texas* (Lawrence: University Press of Kansas, 2009), 108–121; and chapter 1 of David L. Eng's *The Feeling of Kinship: Queer Liberalism and the Racialization of Intimacy* (Durham, NC: Duke University Press, 2010), 23–57.
97 Baldwin, *No Name*, 61 (italics added), 62.
98 For a brilliant discussion of Baldwin's complex critique of cross-racial same-gender sex in relation to liberating desire, see Robert Reid-Pharr's "Dinge," in *Black Gay Man: Essays* (New York: New York University Press, 2001), esp. 91–98.
99 Baldwin, *No Name*, 63.
100 For my fuller analysis of this passage from *No Name in the Street*, see Ross, "Baldwin's Sissy Heroics," *African American Review* 46, no. 4 (Winter 2013): 633–651.
101 Bayard Rustin becomes embroiled in this homophobic surveillance when he is arrested on charges of lewd vagrancy in Pasadena, California, in 1953. See John D'Emilio, *Lost Prophet: The Life and Times of Bayard Rustin* (Chicago: University of Chicago Press, 2003), 191–192. For a vivid portrayal of the tactics and effects of the homosexual Red scare on one enclave of elite white gay men, see Barry Werth's biography, *The Scarlet Professor: Newton Arvin: A Literary Life Shattered by Scandal* (New York: Nan A. Talese / Doubleday, 2001).
102 On Hollywood's response to the antihomosexual campaign, see Vito Russo's *The Celluloid Closet: Homosexuality in the Movies* (New York: Harper and Row, 1991).
103 Robert J. Corber, *Homosexuality in Cold War America: Resistance and the Crisis of Masculinity* (Durham, NC: Duke University Press, 1997), 85. See also Craig M. Loftin's excellent history *Masked Voices: Gay Men and Lesbians in Cold War America* (Albany: State University of New York Press, 2012), esp. 203–222.

104 K. A. Cuordileone, *Manhood and American Political Culture in the Cold War* (London: Routledge, 2005), 71; D'Emilio, *Sexual Politics, Sexual Communities*, 40–53.

105 Another instance of this conflation of the sissy and homosexual as a Cold War representation can be found in Richard Dyer, *The Matter of Images: Essays on Representations* (New York: Routledge, 1993).

106 Loftin, *Masked Voices*, 203–204.

107 Sedgwick, "How to Bring Your Kids Up Gay," 157.

108 Daniel Bell, "Interpretation of American Politics," in *The Political Right* (1955; repr., New York: Anchor Books, 1964), 67–70.

109 There is an ongoing debate over whether this swishing style—often identified with camp—reifies or subverts the status quo. For a trenchant discussion of this debate, see David Bergman's *Gaiety Transfigured: Gay Self-Representation in American Literature* (Madison: University of Wisconsin Press, 1991), in which he tends to take the side of subversion (105).

110 On the scandal created by the dust-jacket photo, see Gerald Clarke, *Capote: A Biography* (New York: Simon Schuster, 1988), 158–161.

111 Gerald Clarke, *Capote*, 322–323.

112 Gerald Clarke, *Capote*, 315.

113 "At the root of the Negro problem is the necessity of the white man to find a way of living with the Negro in order to live with himself" (*Time*, 17 May 1963, 26). At the height of his fame, Baldwin graces the cover of this issue of *Time* with a title captioned "Birmingham and Beyond: The Negro's Push for Equality." For further analysis of the *Time* cover and article, see Ross, "Baldwin's Sissy Heroics," 634–635; and Lee Edelman, *Homographesis: Essays in Gay Literary and Cultural Theory* (New York: Routledge, 1994), 43–44.

114 Baldwin himself comments on his early perception of the obligation that he would shoulder in "The Devil Finds Work" (*Price of the Ticket*, 561). In fact, as he becomes economically successful, he does fulfill the social role of the circumspect sissy in helping to provide and nurture siblings, nephews, nieces, cousins, and, indeed, complete strangers in trouble with law enforcement.

115 On rewriting the song for a crossover market, see Charles White, *The Life and Times of Little Richard, the Quasor of Rock* (New York: Harmony Books, 1984), 50–52, 55. David Kirby documents the explicitly queer content and audience for the original performances of the song; see *Little Richard: The Birth of Rock 'n' Roll* (New York: Continuum, 2010), 117. The exclamation at the heart of the refrain marks an ambiguous referent, which could be a personal pronoun, male or female, or an adjective like "roody." Just as the explicitly queer sexual lyrics of the sissy-man and bulldagger blues become deliberately euphemistic as such music crosses over with artists like Ma Rainey, Betsy Smith, and Billie Holiday, so Little Richard's deliciously raunchy lyrics are sanitized as he garners crossover rock 'n' roll success.

116 On black cultural ambassadorship during the Cold War, see Penny von Eschen, *Satchmo Blows Up the World: Jazz Ambassadors Play the Cold War* (Cambridge, MA: Harvard University Press, 2004).

117 José Esteban Muñoz, *Disidentifications: Queers of Color and the Performance of Politics* (Minneapolis: University of Minnesota Press, 1999),

118 Kirby, *Little Richard*, 34.

119 Joshua Gamson, *The Fabulous Sylvester: The Legend, the Music, the Seventies in San Francisco* (New York: Henry Holt and Company, 2005), 23.

120 On the shaping of disco from black urban and gay culture, see Judy Kutulas, "'You Probably Think This Song Is about You': Women's Music from Carole King to the Disco Divas," in *Disco Divas: Women and Popular Culture in the 1970s*, ed. Sherrie A. Inniss (Philadelphia: University of Pennsylvania Press, 2003), 186–192.

121 The gay clone, and its relation to race and gender conformity, will be discussed further in chapter 6.

122 For an excellent discussion of the gendering of 1970s black soul music contrasting the "sentimental masculinity" of Luther Vandross with the "overly 'feminine'" performances of Sylvester, see Mark Anthony Neal's *Looking for Leroy*, esp. 156.

123 Amiri Baraka and Larry Neal, eds., *Black Fire: An Anthology of Afro-American Writing* (New York: William Morrow and Company, 1968), 303.

124 Quoted in M. S. Handler, "Malcolm X Terms Dr. King's Tactics Futile," *New York Times*, 11 May 1963, 9, ProQuest Historical Newspapers, https://digitalgallery.bgsu.edu/student/files/original/ded70ab64d7d2c5d5b556034476a13a4.pdf.

125 Cleaver, *Soul on Ice*, 100–101.

126 Cleaver, *Soul on Ice*, 103. Cleaver is most likely referencing the Aggie West episode of Wright's last-published novel, *The Long Dream*—discussed in chapter 6 of this study. Cleaver gets it right when he observes that punk-hunting "seems to me to be not unrelated . . . to the ritualistic lynchings and castrations inflicted on Southern blacks by Southern whites," but gets it wrong in suggesting that this was "one of Wright's few comments on the subject of homosexuality." As we shall see, the episode is also *not* one of punk-hunting, as the sissy character insists on playing ball with the other characters, rather than on their going in search of a sissy to pummel.

127 Lockett, *Black Fire*, 354–355.

128 Darieck Scott, *Extravagant Abjection*, 175–176. The notion of the black homosexual as doubly racially suspicious has been grippingly fictionalized in Scott's best-selling novel *Traitor to the Race*, which updates Melvin Dixon's *Vanishing Rooms*, which is itself a riff on Baldwin's *Giovanni's Room*. In addition to Scott, see Michele Wallace, *Black Macho and the Myth of the Superwoman* (1978; repr., London: Verso, 1990), 34–69; Cheryl Clarke, "The Failure to Transform: Homophobia in the Black Community," in *Home Girls: A Black Feminist Anthology*, ed. Barbara Smith (New York: Kitchen Table / Women of Color Press, 1983), 197–208; Stefanie K. Dunning, *Queer in Black and White: Interraciality, Same Sex Desire, and Contemporary African American Culture* (Bloomington: Indiana University Press, 2009), 47–52; Gershun Avilez, *Radical Aesthetics and Modern Black Nationalism* (Urbana: University of Illinois Press, 2016), 133–165; and E. Patrick Johnson, *Appropriating Blackness*, 52–57.

129 Murray, *Our Living Manhood: Literature, Black Power, and Masculine Ideology* (Philadelphia: University of Pennsylvania Press, 2007), 27–35.

130 Cleaver, *Soul on Ice*, 105.
131 As discussed in chapter 1, understanding the gender liability attached to the word "passive," Martin Luther King Jr. seeks to wrest nonviolence from gender stigma by calling it instead "nonviolent direct action" in direct response to the sissiphobic snipes of Malcolm X and other black nationalists. See King, *Why We Can't Wait* (New York: Penguin/Mentor, 1963), 24–25, 36–40.
132 Baldwin, *No Name*, 3.
133 Baldwin, *No Name*, 6–7.
134 Baldwin, *Go Tell It*, 42–43.
135 Fern Marja Eckman, *The Furious Passage of James Baldwin* (New York: M. Evans and Company, 1966), 41.
136 Eckman, *Furious Passage*, 41.
137 Baldwin, *No Name*, 7.
138 Cleaver, *Soul on Ice*, 104.
139 Baldwin, *Go Tell It*, 31, 21–22.
140 Baldwin, *Go Tell It*, 22.
141 Dixon, *Ride Out the Wilderness*, 128.
142 Baldwin, *Go Tell It*, 26.
143 Dixon, *Ride Out the Wilderness*, 127.
144 Baldwin, *Go Tell It*, 23 (italics in original).
145 On Cullen's tutelage of Baldwin as a schoolboy, see Boyd, *Baldwin's Harlem*, 23–32. See also Eckman, *Furious Passage*, 49–50.
146 On Delaney's early years in Greenwich Village, see David Leeming, *Amazing Grace: A Life of Beauford Delaney* (New York: Oxford University Press, 1998), 71.
147 Baldwin, *Price of the Ticket*, 559.
148 See Maurice Wallace, *Constructing the Black Masculine*, 133–146.
149 Baldwin, *No Name*, 64.
150 Baldwin, *Nobody Knows My Name: More Notes of a Native Son* (New York: Dell, 1961), 168–190.
151 Baldwin, *No Name*, 64.
152 Baldwin, *No Name*, 66.
153 Dwight McBride, "Can the Queen Speak? Racial Essentialism, Sexuality, and the Problem of Authority," in *Black Men on Race, Gender and Sexuality: A Reader*, ed. Devon W. Carbado (New York: New York University Press, 1999), 253–275.

Chapter 5. Sissy but Not Gay

A portion of chapter 5 was previously published in the 2017 special issue of *FORECAAST* (Forum for European Contributions in African American Studies) titled "Blackness and Sexualities," edited by Michelle M. Wright and Antje Schuhmann.

1 Robert B. Stepto, *Blue as the Lake: A Personal Geography* (Boston: Beacon, 1998), 67–68.
2 Baldwin, *No Name*, 171–172 (italics in original).
3 Baker, *Long Black Song*, xii.

4 Baker, *Long Black Song*, xi.
5 Amiri Baraka, *Black Magic: Collected Poetry 1961–1967* (Indianapolis: Bobbs-Merrill, 1969), 140. "Faggot" is one of Baraka's favorite words in the poetry of this period.
6 As previously discussed, Darieck Scott's insight that such evocations of black bottoming in black nationalist discourse reflects back on the attacker's taking pleasure in what he is attacking; see Scott, *Extravagant Abjection*, esp. 28–31, 153–171. The speaker's seemingly violent desire to stick half his sandal up Wilkins's ass could so easily be read as a displaced homosexual fantasy of a desire for anal sex.
7 Amiri Baraka, *Selected Poetry of Amiri Baraka / LeRoi Jones* (New York: William Morrow and Company, 1979), 146.
8 In his introduction to *Dangerous Liaisons: Blacks, Gays and the Struggle for Equality* (New York: New Press, 1999), a volume of essays devoted to the idea of healing an assumed conflict between blacks and gays, Eric Brandt addresses the commonly held notion of the 1990s that blacks are more homophobic than whites, citing one survey that seems to confirm this notion and another that seems to contradict it (8–9). Some of the other essays in the volume also tend to assume this conflict between gays and blacks. For example, despite attempting to historicize the emergence of homophobia specifically in the black nationalist movement, Henry Louis Gates Jr. nevertheless totalizes the idea of the black community's homophobia: "That the black community is homophobic and rabidly heterosexual is a reflection of the black movement's failure to 'transform' its proponents with regard to the boundless potential of human sexuality"; see "Blacklash?," in Brandt, *Dangerous Liaisons*, 34. For another instance of the discourse that associates blackness with homophobia, see the essay collection *The Greatest Taboo: Homosexuality in Black Communities* (Los Angeles: Alyson, 2001), edited by Deloy Constantine-Simms, with a foreword by Gates. As we shall see, in the 1990s and 2000s Gates becomes a prominent spokesman on behalf of black gays and lesbians, a role cemented through his autobiographical posture as a straight black sissy.
9 Bobby Seale, *Seize the Time: The Story of the Black Panther Party and Huey P. Newton* (1970; repr., Baltimore: Black Classic Press, 1991), 64.
10 Seale, *Seize the Time*, 63–64.
11 Huey P. Newton, *To Die for the People: The Writings of Huey P. Newton*, ed. Toni Morrison (1972; repr., New York: Writers and Readers, 1995), 154.
12 See Seale, *Seize the Time*, 113–132.
13 "Free Breakfast in Baltimore," *Black Panther* 3, no. 9 (21 June 1969): 15, in Marxists Internet Archive, https://www.marxists.org/history//usa/pubs/black-panther/03n09-jun%2021%201969.pdf, accessed 30 October 2020.
14 Tracye A. Matthews, "'No One Ever Asks What a Man's Role in the Revolution Is': Gender Politics and Leadership in the Black Panther Party, 1966–71," in *Sisters in the Struggle: African American Women in the Civil Rights-Black Power Movement*, ed. Bettye Collier-Thomas and V. P. Franklin (New York: New York University Press, 2001), 230–256.
15 For a brilliant reading of Newton's iconography that illustrates its sexually seductive complexities in relation to consumed images of African savagery, see Robert Reid-Pharr's *Once You Go Black: Choice, Desire, and the Black American Intellectual* (New

York: New York University Press, 2007), 133–137. On the history of the use of sexism and homophobia in some discourses of the Black Power movement, see Michele Wallace, *Black Macho and the Myth of the Superwoman*, esp. 34–69; Paula J. Giddings, *When and Where I Enter: The Impact of Black Women on Race and Sex in America* (New York: Bantam Books, 1984), 299–324; Joyce Hope Scott, "From Foreground to Margin: Female Configurations and Masculine Self-Representation in Black Nationalist Fiction," in *Nationalisms and Sexualities*, ed. Andrew Parker et al. (New York: Routledge, 1992), 296–312; bell hooks, *Black Looks: Race and Representation* (Toronto: Between the Lines, 1992), 96–113; Madhu Dubey, *Black Women Novelists and the Nationalist Aesthetic* (Bloomington: Indiana University Press, 1994), 16–29; Cheryl Clarke, "Failure to Transform," 201–203; and Lee Edelman, *Homographesis: Essays in Gay Literary and Cultural Theory* (New York: Routledge, 1994), 53–59.

16 Against the idea that the Black Arts Movement and black nationalism can be cordoned off to the 1960s and '70s, scholars have recently begun to reassess their ongoing influence. See especially Margot Crawford, *Black Post-Blackness: The Black Arts Movement and Twenty-First-Century Aesthetics* (Urbana: University of Illinois Press, 2017); and Avilez, *Radical Aesthetics and Modern Black Nationalism*.

17 Amiri Baraka, *The Autobiography of LeRoi Jones* (Chicago: Lawrence Hill Books, 1984), 168.

18 James Baldwin, *Another Country* (1962; repr. New York: Vintage / Random House, 1993), 10.

19 Baraka, *Autobiography*, 230–231.

20 Baraka, *Autobiography*, 55.

21 Baraka, *Autobiography*, 231.

22 Critics have observed that in the mid-twentieth century African American writers turned to what has been misguidedly labeled "raceless" fiction by the critic Robert Bone; see Bone, *Negro Novel in America* (1958; repr., New Haven, CT: Yale University Press, 1965), 178–185. Ralph Ellison points to this trend in his *New Masses* article "Recent Negro Fiction," where he praises William Attaway's first novel, *Let Me Breathe Thunder*; see *New Masses* 40, no. 6 (5 August 1941): 22–26. Ulysses Lee first uses the term "white life" as a label for white-cast novels in an *Opportunity* magazine review of Attaway's novel. For Lee, the white-cast novel is a "pitfall" for most black writers, but one that Attaway avoids; in "On the Road," review of *Let Me Breathe Thunder* by William Attaway, *Opportunity* 17, no. 9 (September 1939): 283. Although Ellison viewed Attaway's white-themed novel as a curious byway, in the late 1940s and early 1950s this approach became a major trend for African American writers. See Lawrence Jackson, *The Indignant Generation: A Narrative History of African American Writers and Critics, 1934–1960* (Princeton, NJ: Princeton University Press, 2011), 233–236; see also Gene Andrew Jarrett's collection, especially his "Introduction: 'Not Necessarily Race Matter,'" in *African American Literature beyond Race: An Alternative Reader*, ed. Jarrett (New York: New York University Press, 2006), 1–22; and John Christopher Charles, "Talking like White Folks: The Rise of the Post World War II African American White-Life Novel" (PhD diss., University of Virginia, 2007).

23 Baraka, *Autobiography*, 231.

24 Toby Marotta, *Politics of Homosexuality* (Boston: Houghton, Mifflin, 1981), 15; and D'Emilio, *Sexual Politics, Sexual Communities*, 40–53.
25 In *Against Nature: Essays on History, Sexuality and Identity* (London: Rivers Oram Press, 1991), Jeffrey Weeks describes homosexuality in the nineteenth century as characterized (and linked) in these polar extremes: "Perhaps the only people who lived wholly in the subculture were the relatively few 'professionals,' the chief links between the world of aristocratic homosexuality and the metropolitan subculture of Molly houses, pubs, fields, walks, squares, and lavatories" (54).
26 Amiri Baraka, *Home: Social Essays* (1966; repr., Hopewell, NJ: Ecco Press, 1998), 216.
27 Baraka, *Home*, 216.
28 Baraka, *Home*, 217.
29 Baraka, *Autobiography*, 235.
30 In "Some Thoughts on the Challenges Facing Black Gay Intellectuals," in *Brother to Brother: New Writings by Black Gay Men*, ed. Essex Hemphill (Boston: Alyson, 1991), 211–228, Simmons interprets *The System of Dante's Hell* autobiographically and suggests that Baraka's homophobic statements derive from internalized homophobia in reaction to his own homosexual tendencies. Theodore R. Hudson more conservatively cautions against reading especially *The System of Dante's Hell* as "literal incidents or states in Jones' life adapted to the mechanics and conventions of fiction." At the same time, Hudson acknowledges that the novel "contains bits of ascertainable factual autobiography"; see Hudson, *From LeRoi Jones to Amiri Baraka: The Literary Works* (Durham, NC: Duke University Press, 1973), 111; see also E. Patrick Johnson, *Appropriating Blackness*, 57–60.
31 On Watts's instructive assessment of Baraka's homosexual experiences, see Jerry Gafio Watts, *Amiri Baraka: The Politics and Art of a Black Intellectual* (New York: New York University Press, 2001), 335–336. Fred Moten makes a similar point concerning Baraka's downtown bohemian-era drama *The Toilet*: "This is the fantasy Baraka engages and cannot abide, distorts and records in *The Toilet*, letting us know, in spite of himself, that the space of the black avant-garde is a sexual underground. Therein he attempts to redraw the distinction between eros and the sexual act, homosociality and homosexuality"; see Moten, *In the Break: The Aesthetics of the Black Radical Tradition* (Minneapolis: University of Minnesota Press, 2003), 163.
32 For a detailed reading of *The System* in light of Dante's *Inferno*, see Kimberly Benston, *Baraka: The Renegade and the Mask* (New Haven, CT: Yale University Press, 1976), 10–30. Hudson argues instead that the "framework of the book is not patterned closely after Dante's *Inferno*, as the title and frontispiece would lead one to believe" and proceeds to mark the differences; see Hudson, *From LeRoi Jones to Amiri Baraka*, 112. Lloyd W. Brown identifies the social realism within this psychodrama when he says, "In effect, Baraka has transformed the Christian's mythic image of hell into the everyday realities of social, racial, and moral divisiveness"; see Lloyd W. Brown, *Amiri Baraka* (Boston: Twayne, 1980), 66.
33 Dixon, *Ride Out the Wilderness*, 79.
34 Darieck Scott, *Extravagant Abjection*, 187.
35 Amiri Baraka, *The System of Dante's Hell* (New York: Grove, 1965), 57–58.

36　Darieck Scott, *Extravagant Abjection*, 187.

37　Lloyd W. Brown, *Amiri Baraka*, 75.

38　For a full discussion of the prostitute passage, see Marlon B. Ross, "Camping the Dirty Dozens: The Queer Resources of Black Nationalist Invective," in "Plum Nelly: New Essays in Black Queer Studies," ed. Dwight McBride and Jennifer Devere Brody, special issue, *Callaloo* 23, no. 1 (Winter 2000): 290–312.

39　In addition to Darieck Scott's *Extravagant Abjection*, 198, see K. Ian Grandison's explanation of the historical and economic function of the Bottom as a racialized landscape in "Negotiated Space: The Black College Campus as a Cultural Record of Postbellum America," *American Quarterly* 51, no. 3 (1999): 529–579.

40　In *Native Sons: A Critical Study of Twentieth-Century Black American Authors* (Philadelphia: J. B. Lippincott, 1968), Edward Margolies writes: "One suspects . . . that from the beginning Jones has mistrusted poetry, possibly hated it (as an expression of white civilization), and that he has devoted his career to purging himself of his poetic sensibilities" (194). Although I don't think that Baraka associates poetry totally with "white civilization," the enactment of this struggle *within* his poetry is one of its most compelling characteristics. Benston aptly describes this aspect of Baraka's work (*Baraka*, 14).

41　Baraka, *System*, 140.

42　Hudson, *From LeRoi Jones to Amiri Baraka*, 114–115.

43　Baraka, *System*, 116–117 (ellipses in original).

44　Baraka, *System*, 117.

45　This scene could be read as an anticipatory critique of Cleaver, who infamously claims in *Soul on Ice* to learn how to rape white men's daughters by first practicing on black women in his neighborhood (26–27).

46　Ikenna Dieke summarizes the sexuality in *System* as possessing "two antipodal dimensions": "The first, sexual villainy, assumes the manifest forms of homosexuality and rape. . . . In contrast, the book's second Sadean dimension, sexuality as a symbolic process, represents an involvement with, as well as an affirmation of, reality. Baraka insists that both elements be viewed as a complex dialectic"; see Dieke, "Sadeanism: Baraka, Sexuality, and the Perverse Imagination in *The System of Dante's Hell*," *Black American Literature Forum* 19, no. 4 (1985): 163. Despite the claim of a complex dialectic, reality becomes simply equated with heterosexuality in Dieke's analysis, and it is not clear how so, but Dieke argues that a synthesis is reached by the end of the novel; see Dieke, "Sadeanism," 166.

47　Darieck Scott, *Extravagant Abjection*, 193. Baraka spells out his own theory of what I have labeled race rape in *Home: Social Essays* (1966; repr., Hopewell, NJ: Ecco Press, 1998), 227–232, discussed further below. For a fuller discussion of my theory of race rape, see Marlon B. Ross, "Race, Rape, Castration: Feminist Theories of Sexual Violence and Masculine Strategies of Black Protest," in *Masculinity Studies and Feminist Theory: New Directions*, ed. Judith Kegan Gardiner (New York: Columbia University Press, 2002), 305–318. On the use of sexual coercion, see also Farah Jasmine Griffin, *"Who Set You Flowin'?": The African-American Migration Narrative* (New York: Oxford University Press, 1995), 167.

48　Baraka, *Autobiography*, 285.

49 Baraka, *Home*, 228.
50 Manning Marable, *Malcolm X: A Life of Reinvention* (New York: Viking, 2011), 64–69; Bruce Perry, *Malcolm: The Life of a Man Who Changed Black America* (Barrytown, NY: Station Hill, 1991), 77–79, 82–83.
51 On the symbolism of Malcolm's zoot suit, see Robin D. G. Kelley's "The Riddle of the Zoot: Malcolm Little and Black Cultural Politics during World War II," in *Race Rebels*, 161–181. On Baraka's middle-class upbringing, see Jerry Gafio Watts, *Amiri Baraka*, 21–84.
52 A glimpse of Baraka's recitation style can be seen in "Ain't Gonna Shuffle No More (1964–1972)," episode 11 of the documentary series *Eyes on the Prize* (Blackside Media and PBS, 1990). As Jerry Watts points out, Baraka's famous poem was itself based on a popular rallying cry, "It's nation time," heard in protests across the country during the late 1960s (*Amiri Baraka*, 234–235).
53 Baraka, *Autobiography*, 19.
54 Baraka, *Autobiography*, 57–58. A slang term popular in the early decades of the twentieth century, "dicty" has a strong connotation of black people trying too hard to assert an elite status, which invariably mimics upper-class white conduct. See Clarence Major's entry on the word in *Juba to Jive*, 135.
55 For a similar description of Bethany Baptist, see Amiri Baraka, *Blues People: Negro Music in White America* (New York: William Morrow and Company, 1963), 58.
56 While Baldwin toys with the implication of the church as a scene of homoerotic seduction in *Go Tell It* when describing the relationship between John and Elisha, and even more overtly in his own autobiographically retrospective essays, in *Just above My Head* he depicts the incestuous rape of a good church daughter by her own zealous father—seemingly revealing an eagerness to expose the heterosexual scandal at the heart of the church while simultaneously depicting Arthur's sexual relationships not only as consensual but also as relatively chaste, based in reciprocal love, rather than in a sexually perverse power play.
57 Baraka, *Autobiography*, 56.
58 Amiri Baraka, *The LeRoi Jones / Amiri Baraka Reader*, ed. William J. Harris in collaboration with Baraka (New York: Thunder's Mouth, 1991), 219.
59 Hayden grew up very poor in a chaotic family situation in Detroit. Severely nearsighted and rather sickly, he was teased by his peers for his lack of boyishness and athleticism. He became an avid reader as a child, pursued higher education enthusiastically, and took the opportunity to study with the great gay modernist poet W. H. Auden while at the University of Michigan during the 1940s. To hear Hayden reciting the poem "Those Winter Sundays," a boyhood memory of his father's preparation for work on a Sunday morning, see Poetry Reading Live channel, YouTube, posted 15 December 2013, https://www.youtube.com/watch?v=XmJYs6PQKVc.
60 Baraka's vituperous work and conduct gained him great influence as a spokesman on behalf of black nationalism, but it was a great risk for his career in academe, a needed resource of income for even the most successful poets, then and now.
61 Similar anthologies come out around the same time, with similar effect, but lacking the intensity of reminiscence and introspection. See, for instance, Thelma Golden,

ed., *Black Male: Representations of Masculinity in Contemporary American Art* (New York: Whitney Museum of Modern Art, 1994); Marcellus Blount and George P. Cunningham, eds., *Representing Black Men* (New York: Routledge, 1996); and Devon W. Carbado, ed., *Black Men on Race, Gender, and Sexuality* (New York: New York University Press, 1999). It would be productive to compare these 1990s anthologies with their precursor text, *William Styron's Nat Turner: Ten Black Writers Respond*, ed. John Henrik Clarke (Boston: Beacon, 1968). The ten black male writers are reacting to what they see as a major crisis in historical black heroism precipitated by Styron's novel on Turner, who is characterized as both sexually entangled with a white woman and homosexually entangled with one of his followers.

62 The other gay author among the contributors is Randall Kenan, and Belton conducts a conversation with two gay icons: Essex Hemphill and Isaac Julien.

63 Barbara Smith, ed., *Homegirls: A Black Feminist Anthology* (New York: Kitchen Table / Women of Color Press, 1983). Other noteworthy anthologies include Toni Cade Bambara, ed., *The Black Woman: An Anthology* (New York: New American Library, 1970); La Frances Rodgers-Rose, ed., *The Black Woman* (Beverly Hills, CA: Sage, 1980); Gloria Hull, Patricia Bell Scott, and Barbara Smith, eds., *All the Women Are White, All the Blacks Are Men, but Some of Us Are Brave: Black Women's Studies* (New York: Feminist Press, 1982); and Cherríe Moraga and Gloria Anzaldúa, eds., *This Bridge Called My Back: Writings by Radical Women of Color* (New York: Kitchen Table / Women of Color Press, 1983).

64 E. Lynn Harris, *Invisible Life* (1991; repr., New York: Doubleday/Anchor, 1994). For an excellent theoretical analysis of the down-low discourse, see C. Riley Snorton, *Nobody Is Supposed to Know: Black Sexuality on the Down-Low* (Minneapolis: University of Minnesota Press, 2014); Jeffrey Q. McCune Jr.'s instructive ethnographic study, *Sexual Discretion*; and Keith Boykin, *Beyond the Down Low: Sex, Lies, and Denial in Black America* (New York: Carroll and Graf, 2005). On Harris's "double life" fiction and its influence on African American culture, see my essay "'What's Love but a Second-Hand Emotion?': Man-on-Man Passion in the Contemporary Black Gay Romance Novel," *Callaloo* 36, no. 3 (Summer 2013): 669–687.

65 Barbara Smith's essay was first published in Hull, Scott, and Smith, *All the Women Are White, All the Blacks Are Men, but Some of Us Are Brave*, 157–175.

66 Barbara Smith, "Toward a Black Feminist Criticism," 173.

67 Joseph Beam, "Brother to Brother: Words from the Heart," in *In the Life: A Black Gay Anthology*, ed. Joseph Beam (Boston: Alyson, 1986), 230–242.

68 In "By the Year 2000," Max Smith makes the distinction between "gay Blacks," who are black same-gender-loving men who identify first with blackness and tend to socialize within African American communities, and "Black gays," who are black same-gender-loving men whose social orientation is toward the white gay ghettos; see Beam, *In the Life*, 226.

69 Beam, "Brother to Brother," 230–231.

70 Beam, "Brother to Brother," 231.

71 "Stranger in the Village" is the title of Baldwin's last essay in his collection *Notes of a Native Son* (1955; repr. Boston: Beacon, 1990), 159–175.

72 Beam, "Brother to Brother," 231. Baldwin culminates the plot of his second novel, *Giovanni's Room*, with the white, homosexually repressed protagonist looking out a window only to see his own disturbing reflection "fading away before my eyes," and seeking to escape what he sees, finding himself before a mirror, which makes him not only "terribly aware" of his own inauthentic self but also, because of that inauthenticity, treacherous to the ones he loves most, his male and female beloveds; see *Giovanni's Room* (New York: Dell, 1956), 220–221.

73 Kevin J. Mumford, *Not Straight, Not White: Black Gay Men from the March on Washington to the AIDS Crisis* (Chapel Hill: University of North Carolina Press, 2016), 141.

74 Mumford, *Not Straight, Not White*, 138.

75 Mumford, *Not Straight, Not White*, 134, 133.

76 Robin D. G. Kelley, "Confessions of a Nice Negro, or Why I Shaved My Head," in *Speak My Name: Black Men on Masculinity and the American Dream*, ed. Don Belton (Boston: Beacon, 1995), 14.

77 Kelley, "Confessions of a Nice Negro," 20.

78 Kelley, "Confessions of a Nice Negro," 21.

79 Baker, "On the Distinction of 'Jr.,'" in Belton, *Speak My Name*, 78.

80 Baker, "On the Distinction of 'Jr.,'" 81.

81 Baker, "On the Distinction of 'Jr.,'" 82.

82 Baker, "On the Distinction of 'Jr.,'" 82.

83 See Alice Walker, "In Search of Our Mothers' Gardens," in *In Search of Our Mothers' Gardens: Womanist Prose* (San Diego: Harcourt Brace Jovanovich, 1983), 231–243.

84 Clarence Major, "My Mother and Mitch," in Belton, *Speak My Name*, 136.

85 The 1980s and '90s represent a renaissance of scholarly work on the topic of black women's self-narratives. Some of the notable critical/theoretical work includes Claudia Tate, *Black Women Writers at Work* (New York: Continuum, 1983); Valerie Smith, *Self-Discovery and Authority in Afro-American Narrative* (Cambridge, MA: Harvard University Press, 1987); Mary Helen Washington, *Invented Lives: Narratives of Black Women, 1860–1960* (New York: Anchor, 1987); JoAnn Braxton, *Black Women Writing Autobiography: A Tradition within a Tradition* (Philadelphia: Temple University Press, 1989); Françoise Lionnet, *Autobiographical Voices: Race, Gender, Self-Portraiture* (Ithaca, NY: Cornell University Press, 1989); Frances Smith Foster, *Written by Herself: Literary Production by African American Women, 1746–1892* (Bloomington: Indiana University Press, 1993); Barbara Omolade, *The Rising Song of African American Women* (New York: Routledge, 1994); Katherine Clay Bassard, *Spiritual Interrogations: Culture, Gender, and Community in Early African American Women's Writing* (Princeton, NJ: Princeton University Press, 1999); and Sandra Pouchet Paquet, *Caribbean Autobiography: Cultural Identity and Self-Representation* (Madison: University of Wisconsin Press, 2002).

86 Sally Robinson, *Marked Men: White Masculinity in Crisis* (New York: Columbia University Press, 2000), 52–86.

87 Nathan McCall, *Makes Me Wanna Holler: A Young Black Man in America* (New York: Vintage, 1995), 27.

88 The irregular spelling of "baad," like crotch-cupping, indicates a vernacular intonation of the word that marks a masculine conduct that refuses white America's institutional emasculation of black men. This spelling is popularized by Melvin Van Peebles's classic *Sweet Sweeback's Baadasssss Song* (Detroit: Cinemation Industries, 1971) and its blacksploitation progeny. John W. Roberts traces the history of this usage in *From Trickster to Badman* (see chapter 1, note 31). Clarence Major includes twenty-two entries in which "bad" is used as an intensifying adjective qualifying a thing or action as ambivalently positive, if not positively good (*Juba to Jive*, 15–18).

89 Mark Anthony Neal, *New Black Man*, 3.

90 Mark Anthony Neal, *New Black Man*, 3.

91 As a journalist, McCall's memoir captures the dilemmas of being a black reporter working for white establishment papers during the Reagan counter-revolution of the 1980s; *Makes Me Wanna Holler*, esp. 322–341.

92 Franklin, "Surviving the Institutional Decimation of Black Males: Causes, Consequences, Intervention," in *The Making of Masculinities: The New Men's Studies*, ed. Harry Brod (Boston: Unwin and Hyman, 1987), 155–169.

93 Marcellus Blount, "Caged Birds: Race and Gender in the Sonnet," in *Engendering Men: The Question of Male Feminist Criticism*, ed. Joseph A. Boone and Michael Cadden (New York: Routledge, 1990), 225–238. Blount's own anthology, *Representing Black Men*, coedited with G. P. Cunningham (New York: Routledge, 1996), embodies the response to *Engendering Men*'s racial call, and Phillip Harper's *Are We Not Men?*, published in the same year, made apparent what was tokenized in Boone and Cadden, *Engendering Men*.

94 Diana Fuss, ed., *Inside/Out: Lesbian Theories, Gay Theories* (New York: Routledge, 1991).

95 Phillip Brian Harper, "Eloquence and Epitaph: Black Nationalism and the Homophobic Impulse in Responses to the Death of Max Robinson," in *Fear of a Queer Planet: Queer Politics and Social Theory*, ed. Michael Warner (Minneapolis: University of Minnesota Press, 1993), 239–263; and Henry Louis Gates Jr., "The Black Man's Burden," also in Warner, *Fear of a Queer Planet*, 230–238.

96 Fraiman, *Cool Men and the Second Sex* (New York: Columbia University Press, 2003), 87.

97 When Barbara Smith, in consultation with Audre Lorde, founds their publishing house devoted to publishing work by and for feminist women of color in 1980, she calls it Kitchen-Table Women of Color Press. In Alice Walker's *The Color Purple* (New York: Harcourt, Brace, Jovanovich, 1982), we see how Celie, the protagonist, starts out burdened by kitchen duties. The kitchen seems to be the site of her gender oppression, but as the novel progresses, it is transformed into the site of her empowerment. On this idea of the domestic as a site of transformative power, see Barbara Smith's introduction to *Home Girls*, xix–xxvi; and bell hooks's "Homeplace: A Site of Resistance," in *Yearning: Race, Gender, and Cultural Politics* (Boston: South End Press, 1990), 41–49.

98 Henry Louis Gates Jr., *Colored People: A Memoir* (1994; repr., New York: Vintage Books, 1995), 13.

99 Gates, *Colored People*, 103.

100 Gates, *Colored People*, 93–94.
101 Gates, *Colored People*, 106.
102 Michael Awkward, *Scenes of Instruction: A Memoir* (Durham, NC: Duke University Press, 1999), 60.
103 Awkward, *Scenes of Instruction*, 61.
104 Awkward, *Scenes of Instruction*, 62.
105 Gates, *Colored People*, 105.
106 Gates, *Colored People*, 191–201.
107 Gates, *Colored People*, 85.
108 This approach builds on queer affect theory related to shame in various works, including Sedgwick, *Tendencies*, 182; Eve Kosofsky Sedgwick, ed., *Novel Gazing: Queer Readings in Fiction* (Durham, NC: Duke University Press, 1997), esp. 9–25; Eve Kosofsky Sedgwick, *Touching Feeling: Affect, Performativity, Pedagogy* (Durham, NC: Duke University Press, 2003); Heather Love, *Feeling Backward: Loss and the Politics of Queer History* (Cambridge, MA: Harvard University Press, 2007); and Sara Ahmed, *The Cultural Politics of Emotion*, 2nd ed. (New York: Routledge, 2015).

Chapter 6. Gay but Not Sissy

1 Mark Simpson, "Meet the Metrosexual: He's Well Dressed, Narcissistic and Obsessed with Butts, but Don't Call Him Gay," *Salon*, 22 July 2002, https://www.salon.com/2002/07/22/metrosexual/.
2 Simpson, "Meet the Metrosexual."
3 Simpson, "Meet the Metrosexual."
4 Simpson, "Meet the Metrosexual."
5 I consider the cast all-white even though one of the crew, Jai Rodriquez, is of Puerto Rican and Italian descent and thus is televised as, and could easily be read as, a "white Hispanic."
6 Geoffrey C. Ward, *Unforgivable Blackness: The Rise and Fall of Jack Johnson* (New York: Knopf, 2004), 58.
7 Mallory Chin, "These 15 Athletes Own Clothing Lines (and You Probably Had No Idea)," *TheThings.com*, https://www.thethings.com/athletes-with-clothing-lines/, accessed 3 November 2020. On the interest Jack Johnson, who was quite the dandy, took in interior design, for instance, see *The Autobiography of Jack Johnson: In the Ring and Out* (New York: Citadel/Carol, 1992), 66–68.
8 For a discussion of how hip-hop culture has been "scapegoated" not only in dominant media but also among African American elites, see Mark Anthony Neal, *New Black Man*, esp. 3–16. The discourse on misogyny and homophobia in rap music is, of course, prolific. See, for instance, Kelley, *Race Rebels*, 214–223; Patricia Hill Collins, *Black Sexual Politics: African Americans, Gender, and the New Racism* (New York: Routledge, 2004), esp. 75–85, 91–92; Charise Cheney, *Brothers Gonna Work It Out: Sexual Politics in the Golden Age of Rap Nationalism* (New York: New York University Press, 2005), 63–96; and Terrance Dean's memoir, *Hiding in Hip Hop: On the Down Low in the Entertainment Industry—from Music to Hollywood* (New York: Atria, 2008).

9   On the complex relationship between hip-hop and disco, see Nelson George, *Hip Hop America* (New York: Penguin, 1998), 1–21; and Denise Sullivan, *Keep on Pushing: Black Power Music from Blues to Hip Hop* (Chicago: Lawrence Hill Books, 2011), 145–174.
10 Terrance Dean, *Hiding in Hip Hop*, 206.
11 Terrance Dean, *Hiding in Hip Hop*, 225.
12 There are few attempts at a systematic study of sportsmanship, most notably Robert L. Simon, *Fair Play: The Ethics of Sport* (Boulder, CO: Westview/Perseus, 2004), esp. 41–68; and James W. Keating, "Sportsmanship as a Moral Category," *Ethics* 75, no. 1 (1 October 1964): 25–35. Such studies tend to rely on ostensibly race- and gender-blind understandings of the logic of sportsmanship through metaphysics.
13 For a discussion of this way of thinking, see the poignant personal essay by Tobin Siebers, "My Withered Limb," in "Disability, Art, and Culture (Part One)," special issue, *Michigan Quarterly Review* 37, no. 2 (Spring 1998), http://hdl.handle.net/2027/spo.act2080.0037.202, which discusses how his "crippled" leg shapes others' and his own perception of his fitness as a man.
14 On the history of physical culture and changing ideals of the fit body in England and America, see Michael Anton Budd, *The Sculpture Machine: Physical Culture and Body Politics in the Age of Empire* (New York: New York University Press, 1997), esp. 70–80.
15 Gates, *Colored People*, 80.
16 Gates, *Colored People*, 81.
17 Gates, *Colored People*, 83.
18 Thanks to my primary physician, Dr. William E. Fox, for bringing my attention to Gladwell's "Big Man Can't Shoot" episode, *Revisionary History* podcast, season 1, episode 3, 30 July 2017, http://revisionisthistory.com/episodes/03-the-big-man-cant-shoot/.
19 Wilt Chamberlain and David Shaw, *Wilt: Just like Any Other 7-Foot Black Millionaire Who Lives Next Door. An Autobiography* (New York: Macmillan, 1973), 126. Chamberlain goes on to catalogue potential reasons for his poor free-shot record (see 127). Significantly, such explanations emphasize masculine aspects of Chamberlain's physique: size, strength, hand size. None of these, however, would explain why he stopped using the granny shot.
20 Wilt Chamberlain, *A View from Above: The Life of a Legend in His Own Words* (New York: Signet, 1992), 62–63.
21 Chamberlain, *View from Above*, 258–262, 266–267.
22 Quoted in Gladwell, "Big Man Can't Shoot."
23 A common plot line of basketball-themed movies inverts this stereotype, whereby a scrawny white male magically outperforms fit black men on the court—clearly a fantasy stemming from white male envy. The epitome of this fantasy is the 1992 film *White Men Can't Jump*.
24 Abdul-Jabbar has published many books, including autobiographies, as well as books on the history of sport, the racial history of the military, the Harlem Renaissance, Native American experience, and race relations. See, for instance, Kareem Abdul-Jabbar

with Anthony Walton, *Brothers in Arms: The Epic Story of the 761st Tank Battalion, World War II's Forgotten Heroes* (New York: Broadway Books, 2004); Kareem Abdul-Jabbar, *On the Shoulders of Giants: My Journey through the Harlem Renaissance* (New York: Simon and Schuster, 2007); Kareem Abdul-Jabbar with Stephen Singular, *A Season on the Reservation: My Sojourn with the White Mountain Apache* (New York: William Morrow and Company, 2000); Kareem Abdul-Jabbar with Raymond Obstfeldand, *Writings on the Wall: Searching for a New Equality beyond Black and White* (New York: Liberty Street / Time, 2016).

25 See Richard Wright's two essays on Louis: "Joe Louis Discovers Dynamite," *New Masses* 17, no. 2 (8 October 1935): 18–19; and "High Tide in Harlem: Joe Louis as a Symbol of Freedom," *New Masses* 28, no. 2 (5 July 1938): 18–20.

26 Richard Wright, *The Long Dream* (1958; repr., New York: Harper and Row, 1987), 35.

27 "Mincing" is one of those words that readily indexes a sissy suspicion and is often listed as a synonym for "sissy" and "swish" in dictionaries. "Sweet" in African American folk expression, when applied to a man, has an interesting double capacity in that it can imply (hetero)sexual prowess, as in the epithet "sweetback," as well as sissy insinuation, as in "sweet man."

28 Wright, *Long Dream*, 35.

29 In an interview with Tom Snyder, Little Richard rehearses this notion that in his youth, he was ridiculed for learning to play piano even though he ran with the boys doing boy things as well. See Snyder interview with Little Richard, *The Late Late Show with Tom Snyder*, broadcast 14 January 1997, posted to YouTube on 16 August 2014, https://www.youtube.com/watch?v=4mB3u2jGGXY.

30 Wright, *Long Dream*, 35.

31 I remember being coached when I first went out for baseball as a middle schooler that throwing a hardball overhanded was "all in the wrist." I wonder now if my miserable failure at this skill was because unconsciously the wrist itself was a node of anxiety for me, considering how a limp wrist is among the most vicious signs of a sissy propensity.

32 Wright, *Long Dream*, 36.

33 Maggie McKinley, *Masculinity and the Paradox of Violence in American Fiction, 1950–75* (New York: Bloomsbury, 2015), 56.

34 McKinley, *Masculinity and the Paradox of Violence*, 56.

35 Wright, *Long Dream*, 37 (italics in original).

36 On the gender ideology that excluded women from sport, see Allen Guttmann, *A Whole New Ball Game: An Interpretation of American Sports* (Chapel Hill: University of North Carolina Press, 1988), 139–158. Women are very, very slowly beginning to break down the gender barrier barring them from contact team sports. Women who have played pro football have been on special teams, usually as placekickers. In 2019 Toni Harris became the first woman to receive a college football scholarship "at a skill position." See Emily Caron, "Female Football Player Makes History with Full Scholarship Offer," *Sports Illustrated*, 27 February 2019, https://www.si.com/college-football/2019/02/27/female-football-player-toni-harris-makes-history-college-scholarship-offer. The rash of state laws being passed to prohibit trans girls from competing with cis girls in sports during the first decades of the twenty-first century indicates how

invested society is in protecting the gender line that separates male from female sport, a line that also operates to cast sissiness as anathema to good sportsmanship. The idea that a trans girl has a natural physiological and genetic advantage over cis girls is, at heart, an argument against gender-fluid sportsmanship aimed ultimately at protecting male play as a higher form of sportsmanship than female games.

37 Altman, *The Homosexualization of America*; Urvashi Vaid, *Virtual Equality: The Mainstreaming of Gay and Lesbian Liberation* (New York: Anchor/Doubleday, 1995); Michael Warner, *The Trouble with Normal: Sex, Politics, and the Ethics of Queer Life* (Cambridge, MA: Harvard University Press, 1999), esp. 61–80; on the theory of homonormality, see Lisa Duggan, "The New Homonormativity: The Sexual Politics of Neoliberalism," in *Materializing Democracy: Toward a Revitalized Cultural Politics*, ed. Russ Castronovo and Dana Nelson (Durham, NC: Duke University Press, 2002), 175–194; Roderick Ferguson, "Race-ing Homonormativity: Citizenship, Sociology, and Gay Identity," in *Black Queer Studies*, ed. E. Patrick Johnson (Durham, NC: Duke University Press, 2005), 52–67, and *Aberrations in Black: Towards a Queer of Color Critique* (Minneapolis: University of Minnesota Press, 2003), 138–148; and Jasbir K. Puar, *Terrorist Assemblages: Homonationalism in Queer Times* (Durham, NC: Duke University Press, 2007), 38–39.

38 Still the best treatment of the rise of the Castro Clone is Altman's *Homosexualization of America*, 1–35; see also Edmund White, *States of Desire*, 33–56.

39 On the emergence of these organizations in the 1950s, see Barry D. Adam, *The Rise of a Gay and Lesbian Movement* (Boston: Twayne / G. K. Hall, 1987), 60–68; Michael Bronski, *A Queer History of the United States* (Boston: Beacon, 2011), 176–204; and D'Emilio, *Sexual Politics, Sexual Communities*, 75–125.

40 See Randy Shilts, *Conduct Unbecoming: Lesbians and Gays in the U.S. Military* (New York: St. Martin's, 1993); and Mike Hippler, *Matlovich, the Good Soldier* (Boston: Alyson, 1989). Matlovich appeared on the cover of *Time* magazine for 8 September 1975, and a made-for-TV movie depicted his fight for military justice on NBC in 1978. On the fight for lesbian and gay inclusion in the military, see Allan Bérubé, *Coming Out under Fire: The History of Gay Men and Women in World War II* (New York: Free Press, 1990).

41 In June 2018 the first American male professional soccer player, Minnesota United team member Collin Martin, came out as gay, adding another white pro male player to the roster in an increasingly popular U.S. sport. See Andy Towle, "'Minnesota United' Pro Soccer Player Collin Martin Comes Out as Gay," *Towleroad Gay News*, 29 June 2018, http://www.towleroad.com/2018/06/collin-martin/. The first openly gay male pro soccer player was Afro-British Justin Fashanu, whose life has been depicted in both a 2017 biography by Jim Read and a film, *Forbidden Games: The Justin Fashanu Story* (London: Fulwell 73 Productions and Black Sun Media, 2017), directed by Jon Carey and Adam Darke.

42 See Ryan Russell, as told to Kevin Arnovitz, "No Distractions: An NFL Veteran Opens Up on His Sexuality," ESPN.com, 29 August 2019, https://www.espn.com/nfl/story/_/id/27484719/no-distractions-nfl-veteran-opens-sexuality. See also Neil

Vigdor, "Ryan Russell, N.F.L. Free Agent, Comes Out as Bisexual," *New York Times*, 30 August 2019, https://www.nytimes.com/2019/08/30/us/ryan-russell-nfl-bisexual.html; and Jason Duaine Hahn, "Get to Know NFL Player Ryan Russell's Dancer Boyfriend, Corey O'Brien," *People*, 26 November 2019, https://people.com/sports/who-is-ryan-russell-boyfriend-corey-obrien/.

43 I have included in this roster of gay pro players only those who have "self-confessed" as such. Obviously, there is plenty of social media speculation spinning around various other players, such as, most notably, basketballer Dwight Howard. See Will Leitch, "The Weird Dwight Howard Saga Shows the NBA Still Has a Problem with the Closet," *Intelligencer*, 17 November 2018, http://nymag.com/intelligencer/2018/11/the-dwight-howard-saga-and-the-nbas-problem-with-the-closet.html.

44 For excellent analyses of football's racial dynamic, see the essays in David J. Leonard, Kimberly B. George, and Wade Davis, eds., *Football, Culture and Power* (Abingdon, UK: Routledge / Taylor and Francis Group, 2017).

45 See Ron Ross's *Nine . . . Ten . . . and Out! The Two Worlds of Emile Griffith* (New York: Dibella Entertainment, 2008); and the film directed by Dan Klorer and Ron Berger, *Ring of Fire: The Emile Griffith Story* (Los Angeles: Hole in the Fence Productions, 2005). Griffith's life story also served as the basis of a contemporary jazz opera, *Champion*, which debuted in St. Louis in 2013, with music composed by Terence Blanchard and libretto by Michael Cristofer.

46 Professional wrestling probably has had the largest number of openly gay competitors, but often viewed as "straight" camp, it represents a virtual send-up of man-play as sportsmanship. Wrestling management has been unusually receptive to secretly or openly gay competitors. In the early era of wrestling, Pat Patterson (1941–2020) was relatively open about his sexuality and his lover, another wrestler, but the WWE left it an open secret until 2014. See his disclosure memoir, Pat Patterson with Bertrand Hébert, *Accepted: How the First Gay Superstar Changed WWE* (Toronto: ECW Press, 2016). In 2013, African American Darren Young (b. 1983, aka Fredrick Rosser) became the first wrestler to come out publicly while still active. Following him was independent black wrestler "Money" Matt Cage (b. 1988), who came out in 2015. Five previous wrestlers had open secrets or came out as gay or bisexual after retirement. On Young, see Thomas Barrabi, "Darren Young Gay: WWE Wrestler 'Deeply in Love' with Boyfriend 'Nick,' Sources Say," *International Business Times*, 16 August 2013, http://www.ibtimes.com/darren-young-gay-wwe-wrestler-deeply-love-boyfriend-nick-sources-say-photo-1388459. On Cage, see Doyle Murphy, "'Money' Matt Cage Comes Out as Gay," *New York Daily News*, 25 June 2015, http://www.nydailynews.com/news/national/pro-wrestler-money-matt-cage-gay-article-1.2270187. See also C. T. Summers, "Wrestler Orlando Jordan: Bi and Proud," *Edge Media Network*, 15 September 2006, https://boston.edgemedianetwork.com/printstory.php?ch=&sc=&sc3=&id=39541; Greg Oliver, "Terry Garvin: A Career Overshadowed," *Slam! Wrestling*, 2 January 2006, http://slam.canoe.com/Slam/Wrestling/2005/12/22/1365103.html; Curtis M. Wong, "WWE Legend Pat Patterson Comes Out as Gay," *Huffington Post*, 13 June 2014, updated 2 February 2016, https://www.huffingtonpost.com/2014/06/13/pat-patterson-comes

-out_n_5492726.html; and Mike Mooneyham, "Barnett 'an Unforgettable Figure,'" *Wrestling Gospel*, 26 September 2004, http://www.mikemooneyham.com/2004/09/26/barnett-an-unforgettable-figure/.

47 Other notable male athletes who have availed themselves of this form include swimmer Mark Tewsbury, *Inside Out: Straight Talk from a Gay Jock* (Mississauga, ON: Wiley, 2006); and Greg Louganis, *Breaking the Surface* (1995; repr., Naperville, IL: Sourcebooks, 2006).

48 For analysis of the racial dynamics of basketball, see the essays in Todd Boyd and Kenneth L. Shropshire, eds., *Basketball Jones: America above the Rim* (New York: New York University Press, 2000). Gerald Early's essay, "Why Baseball *Was* the Black National Pastime," is especially insightful on the racial psychology of baseball as a nostalgic sport of both Jim Crow and desegregation versus "the black dominance in basketball as the conjunction of both social and material success and sociopathology" in the late decades; see "Why Baseball *Was* the Black National Pastime," in Boyd and Shropshire, *Basketball Jones*, 31. In "Gladiators, Gazelles, and Groupies," Julianne Malveaux explores the psychic ambivalence elicited by the gender and racial dynamics of baseball from the perspective of a gender-exclusionary spectacle that exploits some of the worst stereotypes of black manliness; in Boyd and Shropshire, *Basketball Jones*, 51–58.

49 See Jackie Robinson (as told to Alfred Duckett), *I Never Had It Made* (New York: G. P. Putnam's Sons, 1972), 30–35.

50 David Kopay with Perry Deane Young, *The David Kopay Story, an Extraordinary Self-Revelation* (1977; repr., New York: Donald I. Fine / Primus, 1988), 41.

51 Kopay, *David Kopay Story*, 78.

52 Freud, "On Narcissism: An Introduction," in *The Freud Reader*, ed. Peter Gay (New York: W. W. Norton, 1989), 545–562. For an exemplary case of how queer theorists have used and critiqued this idea of homosexual narcissism, see David Bergman's discussion of it in U.S. literature in *Gaiety Transfigured*, esp. 44–63; and Tim Dean's *Beyond Sexuality* (Chicago: University of Chicago Press, 2000), 200.

53 Kopay, *David Kopay Story*, 75, 76.

54 In 2015, Sarah Thomas became the NFL's first female referee. See Ashley Fox, "Meet Sarah Thomas, NFL's First Female Official," ESPN.com, 17 April 2015, http://www.espn.com/nfl/story/_/id/12669370/meet-sarah-thomas-first-female-nfl-official-referee.

55 Dave Pallone, *Behind the Mask: My Double Life in Baseball* (New York: Signet/Penguin, 1990), 102.

56 Pallone, *Behind the Mask*, 238 (italics in original).

57 See Pallone, *Behind the Mask*, 238.

58 Pallone, *Behind the Mask*, 238–239.

59 Billy Bean with Chris Bull, *Going the Other Way: Lessons from a Life in and out of Major League Baseball* (New York: Marlowe and Company, 2003), 3.

60 See Bean, *Going the Other Way*, 18.

61 Esera Tuaolo with John Rosengren, *Alone in the Trenches: My Life as a Gay Man in the NFL* (Naperville: Sourcebooks, Inc., 2006), 12.

62 Tuaolo, *Alone in the Trenches*, 12 (italics in original).

63 See, for instance, Tuaolo, *Alone in the Trenches*, 13–14.
64 On the complex relation between homosexuality and AIDS in minority communities, see Cathy J. Cohen, *Boundaries of Blackness: AIDS and the Breakdown of Black Politics* (Chicago: University of Chicago Press, 1999); Phillip Brian Harper, "Eloquence and Epitaph: Black Nationalism and the Homophobic Impulse in Responses to the Death of Max Robinson," in *Fear of a Queer Planet*, ed. Michael Warner (Minneapolis: University of Minnesota Press, 1993), 239–263; and Dagmawi Woubshet, *The Calendar of Loss: Race, Sexuality, and Mourning in the Early Era of AIDS* (Baltimore: Johns Hopkins University Press, 2015).
65 Tuaolo, *Alone in the Trenches*, 131 (italics in original).
66 See, for instance, the articles in Evelyn Blackwood, ed., *Anthropology and Homosexual Behavior*, Research on Homosexuality no. 12 (New York: Haworth, 1986), rpt. from the *Journal of Homosexuality* 11, nos. 3–4 (Summer 1985), particularly Serena Nanda, "The Hijras of India: Cultural and Individual Dimensions of an Institutional Third Gender Role," 35–54; J. Patrick Gray, "Growing Yams and Men: An Interpretation of Kimam Male Ritualized Homosexual Behavior," 55–68; and David F. Greenberg, "Why Was the Berdache Ridiculed?," 179–190. See also Lee Wallace, "Fa'afafine, Queens of Samoa and Sexual Elision," in *Sexual Encounters: Pacific Texts, Modern Sexualities* (Ithaca, NY: Cornell University Press, 2003), 138–158. Much of the current research on fa'afafine is being done by sociobiological psychologists Doug VanderLaan, Paul Vasey, and their associates. See, for instance, VanderLaan and Vasey, "Male Sexual Orientation in Independent Samoa: Evidence for Fraternal Birth Order and Maternal Fecundity Effects," *Archives of Sexual Behavior* 40, no. 3 (June 2011): 495–503, which seeks to unearth sociobiological causes for the prevalence of "third gender" persons in Samoan society; and Vasey and VanderLaan, "Materteral and Avuncular Tendencies in Samoa," *Human Nature* 20, no. 3 (September 2009): 269–281.
67 Tuaolo, *Alone in the Trenches*, 131 (italics in original).
68 Tuaolo, *Alone in the Trenches*, 274.
69 Tuaolo credits Kopay for inspiring him to come out and write such a narrative, as he explains that Kopay's book "gave me hope," "gave me courage"; see Tuaolo, *Alone in the Trenches*, 168. With a new edition of *The David Kopay Story* in 1988, Kopay takes the opportunity to reflect and denounce his earlier treatment of gay effeminate men. Rather than disrupting the shape of the original narrative, however, the revision comes as a belated appendix, titled "A Decade Later," demonstrating his growth as an LGBTQ activist, one who is called to represent the whole community—a community that, by 1988, has begun to add at least two more initials to LGB; see *David Kopay Story*, 253.
70 John Amaechi with Chris Bull, *Man in the Middle* (New York: ESPN Books, 2007), 16.
71 Harry Edwards, *The Revolt of the Black Athlete* (New York: Macmillan, 1969); John Hoberman, *Darwin's Athletes: How Sport Has Damaged Black America and Preserved the Myth of Race* (Boston: Houghton Mifflin, 1997).
72 Tuaolo, *Alone in the Trenches*, 276.
73 Bean, *Going the Other Way*, 233.
74 Bean, *Going the Other Way*, 234.

75 See Bean, *Going the Other Way*, esp. 114–115.
76 Bean, foreword to Glenn Burke with Erik Sherman, *Out at Home: The Glenn Burke Story* (New York: Excel, 1995), xi.
77 Sherman, introduction to Burke, *Out at Home*, 2.
78 Sherman, introduction to Burke, *Out at Home*, 3.
79 Sherman, introduction to Burke, *Out at Home*, 1–2.
80 Sherman, introduction to Burke, *Out at Home*, 2.
81 For the afterword he wrote for the 2015 reissue of *Out at Home*, Sherman makes a more affirmative claim to Burke's openness (164). In that edition, he also caps the foreword by again asserting Burke's lineage with Robinson. See Burke, *Out at Home*, 164, 179.
82 Burke, *Out at Home*, 23.
83 Michael J. Smith's sexual agenda driving the social justice message is embarrassingly self-evident in *Black Men / White Men: A Gay Anthology* (San Francisco: Gay Sunshine, 1983). Even without Burke's exposé of Smith, the volume's exploitative display of exoticized black men would reveal the sexual motives behind Smith's dubious racial politics.
84 Burke, *Out at Home*, 108.
85 Smith quoted in Burke, *Out at Home*, 93–94.
86 Burke, *Out at Home*, 94.
87 Burke, *Out at Home*, 110–111.
88 See, for instance, Beam, "Brother to Brother"; and Riggs, "Tongues Untied," in *Brother to Brother: New Writings by Black Gay Men*, ed. Essex Hemphill (Boston: Alyson, 1991), 200–205; and also Riggs's film *Tongues Untied* (San Francisco: Frameline California Newsreel, 1989).
89 Burke, *Out at Home*, 101.
90 Kopay, *David Kopay Story*, 11.
91 Bean, *Going the Other Way*, 56.
92 Bean, *Going the Other Way*, 57.
93 In the memoir's postscript, Bean provides another episode of cross-racial intimacy. He describes a black boy who comes up to him after a speech at New York's Harvey Milk High School for GLBT Youth (see 247–248). When the kid walks away in tears, Bean recognizes "the purpose of the book, and the importance of its message"; see Bean, *Going the Other Way*, 247–248.
94 Simmons, with Damon Dimarco, *Out of Bounds: Coming Out of Sexual Abuse, Addiction, and My Life of Lies in the NFL Closet* (New York: Carroll and Graf, 2006), 13.
95 Simmons, *Out of Bounds*, 15.
96 Simmons, *Out of Bounds*, 48.
97 E. Patrick Johnson traces the historical usage of this term, alongside "tea," as a euphemism for same-gender-loving people in *Sweet Tea: Black Gay Men of the South. An Oral History* (Chapel Hill: University of North Carolina Press, 2008), 17–19.
98 Simmons, *Out of Bounds*, 52.
99 Simmons, *Out of Bounds*, 53.
100 Ron Ross, *Nine . . . Ten . . . and Out*, 8.

101 Ron Ross, *Nine . . . Ten . . . and Out*, 28.
102 Lindon Barrett, "Men in the Mix: Badboys, Heroes, Sequins, and Dennis Rodman," *Callaloo* 20, no. 1 (Winter 1997): 106.
103 Barrett, "Men in the Mix," 108.
104 Dennis Rodman with Tim Keown, *Bad as I Wanna Be* (New York: Delacorte, 1996), 138, 178.
105 Rodman's memoir is as confused about racial identity as it is clearsighted about gender queerness, taking to an extreme the notion of sports as a raceless venue. See especially Rodman, *Bad as I Wanna Be*, 134–135.
106 On this controversy, see Wyatt Ronan, "Breaking: 2021 Becomes Record Year for Anti-transgender Legislation," Human Rights Campaign, 13 March 2021, https://www.hrc.org/press-releases/breaking-2021-becomes-record-year-for-anti-transgender-legislation.
107 Jeffrey Q. McCune Jr., "Michael Sam and the Sport of Queer Failure," in *Football, Culture and Power*, ed. David J. Leonard, Kimberly B. George, and Wade Davis (Abingdon: Routledge / Taylor and Francis Group, 2017), 204.
108 See, for example, Jameson Cherilus, "When I Saw Michael Sam Kiss His White Boyfriend, I Didn't Know What to Think," Thought Catalog, 16 May 2014, https://thoughtcatalog.com/jameson-cherilus/2014/05/when-i-saw-michael-sam-kiss-his-white-boyfriend-i-didnt-know-what-to-think/.
109 Phillip Brian Harper, *Private Affairs: Critical Ventures in the Culture of Social Relations* (New York: New York University Press, 1999), 23–27. Ironically, both "Magic" Johnson and Isiah Thomas have openly gay sons, and both men have been very public in supporting them.
110 We discover the bear cub's fringe undesirability when Blaine, Kurt's true love and eventual husband, briefly hooks up with Karofsky while Blaine and Kurt are on a relationship hiatus. Karofsky's aesthetic unsuitability for a conventionally cute boy like Blaine is communicated as a disgusting reaction shared between Kurt and Rachel.
111 *Glee*, season 6, episode 1, "Loser like Me," dir. Bradley Buecker, produced by Kenneth Silverstein, script by Ryan Murphy, Brad Falchuck, and Ian Brennan (Fox Television, aired on 9 January 2015).
112 No doubt, the writers feared appearing politically incorrect by focusing on black football players as bullies of the geeky glee club members. Anytime the show gestures toward the outsized role of blacks in music or sport, it reasserts the centrality of white performers like Rachel, Kurt, and his lover, Blaine. Neither of the biracial (black and Jewish) footballers who are glee members—Noah "Puck" Puckerman (portrayed by Mark Stalling) and Jacob "Jake" Puckerman (portrayed by Jacob Artist)—is strongly identified with blackness as it is visualized throughout the series.
113 See, for instance, Shaun Powell, *Souled Out? How Blacks Are Winning and Losing in Sports* (Champaign: Human Kinetics, 2008); Kenneth L. Shropshire, *In Black and White: Race and Sports in America* (New York: New York University Press, 1996); Charles K. Ross, ed., *Race and Sport: The Struggle for Equality on and off the Field* (Jackson: University of Mississippi Press, 2004); Hoberman, *Darwin's Athletes*; Amy

Bass, ed., *In the Game: Race, Identity, and Sports in the Twentieth Century* (New York: Palgrave Macmillan, 2005); Harry Edwards, *Revolt of the Black Athlete*.

114 Perhaps the best book on the topic is Michael A. Messner's *Power at Play: Sports and the Problem of Masculinity* (Boston: Beacon, 1992), in which he interviews thirty former male athletes about a range of personal questions related to how sports has shaped their values, personalities, and lives, including race, gender, sexuality, and class.

Postscript

1 David L. Eng and Jasbir K. Puar, "Introduction: Left of Queer," *Social Text* 38, no. 3 (December 2020): 1.
2 Sedgwick, *Tendencies*, 157.
3 See Juju Chang and Marjorie McAfee, "Gay Republicans Explain Why They Are Proudly Supporting Donald Trump," ABC News, 23 October 2016, https://abcnews.go.com/Politics/gay-republicans-explain-proudly-supporting-donald-trump/story?id=42977880.
4 Matthew Tharrett, "How Many LGBT People Voted for Donald Trump? Are the Numbers Surprising?," Logo, 9 November 2016, http://www.newnownext.com/lgbt-vote-donald-trump/11/2016/; and Mary Emily O'Hara, "Meet the LGBTQ Voters Who Backed Trump," NBC News, 15 November 2016, https://www.nbcnews.com/feature/nbc-out/meet-lgbtq-voters-who-backed-trump-n684181.
5 Jackson Katz, *Man Enough? Donald Trump, Hillary Clinton, and the Politics of Presidential Masculinity* (Northampton, MA: Interlink Books, 2016), 205.
6 Katz, *Man Enough?*, 205.
7 See Danielle Kurtzleben, "Male Democratic Candidates Will Have to Answer Gender Role Questions in 2020 Race," *All Things Considered*, National Public Radio, 27 March 2019, https://www.npr.org/2019/03/27/707358130/male-democratic-candidates-will-have-to-answer-gender-role-questions-in-2020-rac.
8 Katz, *Man Enough?*, 235.
9 Skip Bayless and Shannon Sharpe, "Dak Opens Up," *Skip and Shannon: Undisputed*, Fox Sports, YouTube, 10 September 2020, https://www.youtube.com/watch?v=5B3_9oRXXfI. See also David Hookstead, "Skip Bayless Criticizes Dak Prescott for Admitting He Battled Depression," *Daily Caller*, 11 September 2020, https://dailycaller.com/2020/09/11/skip-bayless-dak-prescott-suicide-depression/; and Jorge Alonso, "Skip Bayless Criticizes Dak Prescott for Showing 'Weakness' after Revealing He Suffered from Depression over Brother's Suicide," Brobible, 10 September 2020, https://brobible.com/sports/article/skip-bayless-criticizes-dak-prescott-depression/.
10 Eventually, the word "gay" was omitted altogether when the song was refashioned to avoid continuing controversy. On the controversy over the chant, see Cyd Zeigler, "'Not Gay' at UVA: University of Virginia Students Chant Has Included 'Not Gay' since the 1970s," *OutSports*, 1 January 2003, https://www.outsports.com/2013/2/20/4011054/not-gay-at-uva; "University of Virginia Students Blast 'Not Gay' Unofficial Fight Song Chant with Resolution," *Queer Voices*, *Huffington Post*, 28 September 2012,

updated 2 February 2016, https://www.huffpost.com/entry/university-of-virginia-not-gay-fight-song-chant-resolution-_n_1923041; and Karen Van Neste Owen, "'The Good Old Song': Is It Beloved by All?," *University of Virginia Magazine*, Fall 2013, http://uvamagazine.org/articles/the_good_old_song_is_it_beloved_by_all.

11 See "'That's So Gay' Phrase Has Lasting Impact for LGBT Youth, Study Finds," *Queer Voices*, *Huffington Post*, 28 August 2012, updated 2 February 2016, https://www.huffingtonpost.com/2012/08/28/thats-so-gay-phrase-impact-lgbt-youth_n_1837330.html.

12 It must be noted, however, that there is a new social ritual much more widespread than those parents who suspend gender assignment until a child can name their own gender identity: the gender reveal party, a celebration in which parents open an envelope to announce to themselves, as well as invited friends and family, the "sex" of the not-yet-born child, a ritual made possible by advances in prenatal detection technology.

BIBLIOGRAPHY

Abdul-Jabbar, Kareem. *On the Shoulders of Giants: My Journey through the Harlem Renaissance*. New York: Simon and Schuster, 2007.
Abdul-Jabbar, Kareem, with Mignon McCarthy. *Kareem*. New York: Random House, 1990.
Abdul-Jabbar, Kareem, with Raymond Obstfeld. *Writings on the Wall: Searching for a New Equality beyond Black and White*. New York: Liberty Street / Time, 2016.
Abdul-Jabbar, Kareem, with Stephen Singular. *A Season on the Reservation: My Sojourn with the White Mountain Apache*. New York: William Morrow and Company, 2000.
Abdul-Jabbar, Kareem, with Anthony Walton. *Brothers in Arms: The Epic Story of the 761st Tank Battalion, World War II's Forgotten Heroes*. New York: Broadway Books, 2004.
Adam, Barry D. *The Rise of a Gay and Lesbian Movement*. Boston: Twayne / G. K. Hall, 1987.
Ahmed, Sara. *The Cultural Politics of Emotion*. 2nd ed. New York: Routledge, 2015.
Ahmed, Sara. *Queer Phenomenology: Orientations, Objects, Others*. Durham, NC: Duke University Press, 2006.
Almáguer, Tomás. "Chicano Men: A Cartography of Homosexual Identity and Behavior." *differences* 3, no. 2 (1991): 75–100.
Alonso, Jorge. "Skip Bayless Criticizes Dak Prescott for Showing 'Weakness' after Revealing He Suffered from Depression over Brother's Suicide." Brobible, 10 September 2020. https://brobible.com/sports/article/skip-bayless-criticizes-dak-prescott-depression/.
Altman, Dennis. *The Homosexualization of America, the Americanization of the Homosexual*. New York: St. Martin's, 1982.
Amaechi, John, with Chris Bull. *Man in the Middle*. New York: ESPN Books, 2007.
Angelou, Maya. *I Know Why the Caged Bird Sings*. New York: Bantam / Random House, 1970.
Attaway, William. *Let Me Breathe Thunder*. 1939. Repr., Chatham, NJ: Chatham Booksellers, 1969.
"At the Root of the Negro Problem Is the Necessity of the White Man to Find a Way of Living with the Negro in Order to Live with Himself." *Time*, 17 May 1963, 26–27.
Avery, Sheldon. *Up from Washington: William Pickens and the Negro Struggle for Equality, 1900–1954*. Newark: University of Delaware Press, 1989.
Avilez, Gershun. *Radical Aesthetics and Modern Black Nationalism*. Urbana: University of Illinois Press, 2016.

Awkward, Michael. *Scenes of Instruction: A Memoir*. Durham, NC: Duke University Press, 1999.

Baker, Houston A., Jr. "Critical Memory and the Black Public Sphere." In *The Black Public Sphere*, edited by the Black Public Sphere Collective, 7–37. Chicago: University of Chicago Press, 1995.

Baker, Houston A., Jr. "A Forgotten Prototype: *The Autobiography of an Ex-Coloured Man* and *The Invisible Man*." *Virginia Quarterly Review* 49, no. 3 (1973): 433–449.

Baker, Houston A., Jr. *Long Black Song: Essays in Black American Literature and Culture*. 1972. Repr., Charlottesville: University Press of Virginia, 1990.

Baker, Houston A., Jr. *Modernism and the Harlem Renaissance*. Chicago: University of Chicago Press, 1987.

Baker, Houston A., Jr. "On the Distinction of 'Jr.'" In Belton, *Speak My Name*, 78–82.

Baker, Houston A., Jr. *Turning South Again: Re-thinking Modernism / Re-reading Booker T*. Durham, NC: Duke University Press, 2001.

Baker, James Robert. *Adrenaline*. New York: Signet, 1985.

Baldwin, Davarian L. "Black Belts and Ivory Towers: The Place of Race in U.S. Social Thought, 1892–1948." *Critical Sociology* 30, no. 2 (March 2004): 397–450.

Baldwin, Davarian L. *Chicago's New Negroes: Modernity, the Great Migration, and Black Urban Life*. Chapel Hill: University of North Carolina Press, 2007.

Baldwin, James. *Another Country*. 1962. Repr., New York: Vintage / Random House, 1993.

Baldwin, James. *The Devil Finds Work*. New York: Dell, 1976.

Baldwin, James. *The Fire Next Time*. 1963. Repr., New York: Vintage / Random House, 1993.

Baldwin, James. "Gide as Husband and Homosexual." *New Leader* (13 December 1954): 18–20.

Baldwin, James. *Giovanni's Room*. New York: Dell, 1956.

Baldwin, James. *Go Tell It on the Mountain*. 1953. Repr., New York: Dell, 1980.

Baldwin, James. *If Beale Street Could Talk*. New York: Dell, 1974.

Baldwin, James. *Just above My Head*. New York: Dell, 1979.

Baldwin, James. *Nobody Knows My Name: More Notes of a Native Son*. New York: Dell, 1961.

Baldwin, James. *No Name in the Street*. New York: Laurel/Dell, 1972.

Baldwin, James. *Notes of a Native Son*. 1955. Repr., Boston: Beacon, 1990.

Baldwin, James. *The Price of the Ticket: Collected Nonfiction, 1948–1985*. New York: St. Martin's, 1985.

Baldwin, James. *Tell Me How Long the Train's Been Gone*. New York: Dell, 1968.

Bambara, Tony Cade, ed. *The Black Woman: An Anthology*. New York: New American Library, 1970.

Baraka, Amiri (aka LeRoi Jones). *The Autobiography of LeRoi Jones*. Chicago: Lawrence Hill Books, 1984.

Baraka, Amiri (aka LeRoi Jones). *The Baptism and the Toilet*. New York: Grove, 1966.

Baraka, Amiri (aka LeRoi Jones). *Black Magic: Collected Poetry 1961–1967*. Indianapolis: Bobbs-Merrill Company, 1969.

Baraka, Amiri (aka LeRoi Jones). *Blues People: Negro Music in White America*. New York: William Morrow and Company, 1963.

Baraka, Amiri (aka LeRoi Jones). *Home: Social Essays*. 1966. Repr., Hopewell, NJ: Ecco Press, 1998.

Baraka, Amiri (aka LeRoi Jones). *The LeRoi Jones / Amiri Baraka Reader*. Edited by William J. Harris in collaboration with Baraka. New York: Thunder's Mouth Press, 1991.

Baraka, Amiri (aka LeRoi Jones). *Preface to a Twenty-Volume Suicide Note*. New York: Totem Press in association with Corinth Books, 1961.

Baraka, Amiri (aka LeRoi Jones). *Selected Poetry of Amiri Baraka / LeRoi Jones*. New York: William Morrow and Company, 1979.

Baraka, Amiri (aka LeRoi Jones). *The System of Dante's Hell*. New York: Grove, 1965.

Baraka, Amiri (aka LeRoi Jones), and Larry Neal, eds. *Black Fire: An Anthology of Afro-American Writing*. New York: William Morrow and Company, 1968.

Barrabi, Thomas. "Darren Young Gay: WWE Wrestler 'Deeply in Love' with Boyfriend 'Nick,' Sources Say." *International Business Times*, 16 August 2013. http://www.ibtimes.com/darren-young-gay-wwe-wrestler-deeply-love-boyfriend-nick-sources-say-photo-1388459.

Barrett, Lindon. "Men in the Mix: Badboys, Heroes, Sequins, and Dennis Rodman." *Callaloo* 20, no. 1 (Winter 1997): 106–126.

Bass, Amy, ed. *In the Game: Race, Identity, and Sports in the Twentieth Century*. New York: Palgrave Macmillan, 2005.

Bassard, Katherine Clay. *Spiritual Interrogations: Culture, Gender, and Community in Early African American Women's Writing*. Princeton, NJ: Princeton University Press, 1999.

Bayless, Skip, and Shannon Sharpe. "Dak Opens Up." *Skip and Shannon: Undisputed*, Fox Sports, YouTube, 10 September 2020. https://www.youtube.com/watch?v=5B3_90RXXfI.

Beam, Joseph. "Brother to Brother: Words from the Heart." In *In the Life: A Black Gay Anthology*, edited by Joseph Beam, 230–242. Boston: Alyson, 1986.

Beam, Joseph, ed. *In the Life: A Black Gay Anthology*. Boston: Alyson, 1986.

Bean, Billy, with Chris Bull. *Going the Other Way: Lessons from a Life in and out of Major League Baseball*. New York: Marlowe and Company, 2003.

Beavers, Herman. *Wrestling Angels into Song: The Fictions of Ernest J. Gaines and James Alan McPherson*. Philadelphia: University of Pennsylvania Press, 1995.

Beck, Robert (aka Iceberg Slim). *Mama Black Widow*. Los Angeles: Holloway House, 1969.

Beck, Robert (aka Iceberg Slim). *Pimp: The Story of My Life*. Los Angeles: Holloway House, 1969.

Beck, Robert (aka Iceberg Slim). *Trick Baby: The Story of the White Negro*. Los Angeles: Holloway House, 1967.

Bell, Christopher M. *Blackness and Disability: Critical Examinations and Cultural Interventions*. East Lansing: Michigan State University Press, 2011.

Bell, Daniel. "Interpretation of American Politics." In *The Political Right*. 1955. Repr., New York: Anchor Books, 1964.

Belton, Don, ed. *Speak My Name: Black Men on Masculinity and the American Dream*. Boston: Beacon, 1995.

Benston, Kimberly W. *Baraka: The Renegade and the Mask*. New Haven, CT: Yale University Press, 1976.

Benston, Kimberly W. "Facing Tradition: Revisionary Scenes in African American Literature." *PMLA* 105, no. 1 (1990): 98–109.

Bergling, Tim. *Sissyphobia: Gay Men and Effeminate Behavior*. New York: Haworth / Harrington Park, 2001.

Bergman, David. *Gaiety Transfigured: Gay Self-Representation in American Literature*. Madison: University of Wisconsin Press, 1991.

Bergman, David. *The Violet Hour: The Violet Quill and the Making of Gay Culture*. New York: Columbia University Press, 2004.

Bersani, Leo. "Is the Rectum a Grave?" In *AIDS: Cultural Analysis, Cultural Activism*, edited by Douglas Crimp, 197–222. Cambridge, MA: MIT Press, 1988.

Bérubé, Allan. *Coming Out under Fire: The History of Gay Men and Women in World War II*. New York: Free Press, 1990.

Bhabha, Homi K. *The Location of Culture*. London: Routledge, 1994.

Blackwood, Evelyn, ed. *Anthropology and Homosexual Behavior*. Research on Homosexuality no. 12. New York: Haworth, 1986. Originally published in *Journal of Homosexuality* 11, nos. 3–4 (Summer 1985).

Blake, William. *Poetry and Prose of William Blake*. Edited by David V. Erdman. Garden City, NY: Doubleday and Company, 1970.

Bleys, Rudi C. *The Geography of Perversion: Male-to-Male Sexual Behavior outside the West and the Ethnographic Imagination, 1750–1918*. New York: New York University Press, 1995.

Blount, Marcellus. "Caged Birds: Race and Gender in the Sonnet." In *Engendering Men: The Question of Male Feminist Criticism*, edited by Joseph A. Boone and Michael Cadden, 225–238. New York: Routledge, 1990.

Blount, Marcellus, and G. P. Cunningham, eds. *Representing Black Men*. New York: Routledge, 1996.

Blumin, Stuart M. *The Emergence of the Middle Class: Social Experience in the American City, 1760–1900*. New York: Cambridge University Press, 1989.

Bone, Robert. *The Negro Novel in America*. 1958. Repr., New Haven, CT: Yale University Press, 1965.

Booker, Christopher B. *"I Will Wear No Chain!": A Social History of African American Males*. Westport, CT: Praeger, 2000.

Boone, Joseph A., and Michael Cadden, eds. *Engendering Men: The Question of Male Feminist Criticism*. New York: Routledge, 1990.

Bost, Darius. *Evidence of Being: The Black Gay Cultural Renaissance and the Politics of Violence*. Chicago: University of Chicago Press, 2019.

Boster, Dea H. *African American Slavery and Disability: Bodies, Property, and Power in the Antebellum South, 1800–1860*. New York: Routledge, 2013.

Boulware, Marcus H. *The Oratory of Negro Leaders, 1900–1968*. Westport, CT: Negro Universities Press, 1969.

Boyd, Herb. *Baldwin's Harlem: A Biography of James Baldwin*. New York: Atria Books, 2008.

Boyd, Todd, and Kenneth L. Shropshire, eds. *Basketball Jones: America above the Rim*. New York: New York University Press, 2000.

Boykin, Keith. *Beyond the Down Low: Sex, Lies, and Denial in Black America*. New York: Carroll and Graf, 2005.

Boykin, Keith. *One More River to Cross: Black and Gay in America*. New York: Anchor/Doubleday, 1996.

Brandt, Eric, ed. *Dangerous Liaisons: Blacks, Gays and the Struggle for Equality*. New York: New Press, 1999.

Brantlinger, Patrick. *Rule of Darkness: British Literature and Imperialism, 1830–1914*. Ithaca, NY: Cornell University Press, 1988.

Braxton, Joanne M. *Black Women Writing Autobiography: A Tradition within a Tradition*. Philadelphia: Temple University Press, 1989.

Brim, Matt. *James Baldwin and the Queer Imagination*. Ann Arbor: University of Michigan Press, 2014.

Brod, Harry, ed. *The Making of Masculinities: The New Men's Studies*. Boston: Unwin Hyman, 1987.

Brodhead, Richard H. *Cultures of Letters: Scenes of Reading and Writing in Nineteenth-Century America*. Chicago: University of Chicago Press, 1993.

Bronski, Michael. *A Queer History of the United States*. Boston: Beacon, 2011.

Brontë, Charlotte. *Jane Eyre*. London: Smith, Elder and Company, 1847.

Brooks, Gwendolyn. *Report from Part One*. Detroit: Broadside, 1972.

Brooks, Gwendolyn. *Report from Part Two*. Chicago: Third World Press, 1995.

Brown, Claude. *Manchild in the Promised Land*. New York: Signet / New American Library, 1965.

Brown, Lloyd W. *Amiri Baraka*. Boston: Twayne, 1980.

Budd, Michael Anton. *The Sculpture Machine: Physical Culture and Body Politics in the Age of Empire*. New York: New York University Press, 1997.

Burke, Glenn, with Erik Sherman. *Out at Home: The Glenn Burke Story*. New York: Excel, 1995.

Butler, Judith. *Gender Trouble: Feminism and the Subversion of Identity*. New York: Routledge, 1990.

Campbell, James. *Talking at the Gates: A Life of James Baldwin*. New York: Penguin Books, 1991.

Capote, Truman. *Answered Prayers: The Unfinished Novel*. New York: Random House, 1986.

Capote, Truman. *In Cold Blood: A True Account of a Multiple Murder and Its Consequences*. New York: Random House, 1965.

Capote, Truman. *Other Voices, Other Rooms*. New York: Random House, 1948.

Carbado, Devon W., ed. *Black Men on Race, Gender, and Sexuality*. New York: New York University Press, 1999.

Carby, Hazel. *Race Men*. Cambridge, MA: Harvard University Press, 1998.

Carey, Jon, and Adam Darke, dirs. *Forbidden Games: The Justin Fashanu Story*. London: Fulwell 75 Productions and Black Sun Media, 2017.

Caron, Emily. "Female Football Player Makes History with Full College Scholarship Offer." *Sports Illustrated*, 27 February 2019. https://www.si.com/college-football/2019/02/27/female-football-player-toni-harris-makes-history-college-scholarship-offer.

Carrier, Joseph. *De Los Otros: Intimacy and Homosexuality among Mexican Men*. New York: Columbia University Press, 1995.

Carter, Stephen L. *Reflections of an Affirmative Action Baby*. New York: Basic Books, 1991.

Chamberlain, Wilt. *A View from Above: The Life of a Legend in His Own Words*. New York: Signet, 1992.

Chamberlain, Wilt, and David Shaw. *Wilt: Just like Any Other 7-Foot Black Millionaire Who Lives Next Door. An Autobiography*. New York: Macmillan, 1973.

Chang, Juju, and Marjorie McAfee. "Gay Republicans Explain Why They Are Proudly Supporting Donald Trump." ABC News, 23 October 2016. https://abcnews.go.com/Politics/gay-republicans-explain-proudly-supporting-donald-trump/story?id=42977880.

Charles, John Christopher. "Talking like White Folks: The Rise of the Post World War II African American White-Life Novel." PhD diss., University of Virginia, 2007.

Cheney, Charise L. *Brothers Gonna Work It Out: Sexual Politics in the Golden Age of Rap Nationalism*. New York: New York University Press, 2005.

Cherilus, Jameson. "When I Saw Michael Sam Kiss His White Boyfriend, I Didn't Know What to Think." Thought Catalog, 16 May 2014. https://thoughtcatalog.com/jameson-cherilus/2014/05/when-i-saw-michael-sam-kiss-his-white-boyfriend-i-didnt-know-what-to-think/.

Chesnutt, Charles W. "The Future American." In *Charles W. Chesnutt: Essays and Speeches*, edited by Joseph R. McElrath Jr., Robert C. Leitz III, and Jesse S. Crisler, 121–136. Stanford, CA: Stanford University Press, 1999.

Chesnutt, Charles. "Her Virginia Mammy." In *The Wife of His Youth and Other Stories of the Color Line*, 25–59. 1899. Repr., Ann Arbor: University of Michigan Press, 1968.

Chin, Mallory. "These 15 Athletes Own Clothing Lines (And You Probably Had No Idea)." *TheThings.com*. https://www.thethings.com/athletes-with-clothing-lines/, accessed 3 November 2020.

Chow, Rey. *Writing Diaspora: Tactics of Intervention in Contemporary Cultural Studies*. Bloomington: Indiana University Press, 1993.

Christian, Shawn. *The Harlem Renaissance and the Idea of a New Negro Reader*. Amherst: University of Massachusetts Press, 2016.

Clark, Keith. *Black Manhood in James Baldwin, Ernest J. Gaines, and August Wilson*. Urbana: University of Illinois Press, 2002.

Clarke, Cheryl. "The Failure to Transform: Homophobia in the Black Community." In *Home Girls: A Black Feminist Anthology*, edited by Barbara Smith, 197–208. New York: Kitchen Table / Women of Color Press, 1983.

Clarke, Cheryl. "Race, Homosocial Desire, and 'Mammon' in *Autobiography of an Ex-Coloured Man*." In *Professions of Desire: Lesbian and Gay Studies in Literature*, edited by George E. Haggerty and Bonnie Zimmerman, 84–97. New York: MLA, 1995.

Clarke, Gerald. *Capote: A Biography*. New York: Simon and Schuster, 1988.

Clarke, John Henrik, ed. *William Styron's Nat Turner: Ten Black Writers Respond*. Boston: Beacon, 1968.

Clark-Lewis, Elizabeth. *Living In, Living Out: African American Domestics and the Great Migration*. New York: Kodansha International, 1994.

Cleaver, Eldridge. *Soul on Ice*. 1968. Repr., New York: Laurel/Dell, 1992.

Cobb, Michael. *God Hates Fags: The Rhetoric of Religious Violence*. New York: New York University Press, 2006.

Cohen, Cathy J. *The Boundaries of Blackness: AIDS and the Breakdown of Black Politics*. Chicago: University of Chicago Press, 1999.

Collier, Eugenia. "The Endless Journey of the Ex-Coloured Man." *Phylon* 32, no. 4 (1971): 365–373.

Collins, Patricia Hill. *Black Sexual Politics: African Americans, Gender, and the New Racism*. New York: Routledge, 2004.

Constantine-Simms, Deloy, ed. *The Greatest Taboo: Homosexuality in Black Communities*. Los Angeles: Alyson, 2001.

Cooke, Michael G. *Afro-American Literature in the Twentieth Century: The Achievement of Intimacy*. New Haven, CT: Yale University Press, 1984.

Cooper, Wayne F. *Rebel Sojourner in the Harlem Renaissance*. New York: Schocken, 1987.

Corber, Robert J. *Homosexuality in Cold War America: Resistance and the Crisis of Masculinity*. Durham, NC: Duke University Press, 1997.

Corrothers, James D. *In Spite of the Handicap: An Autobiography*. New York: George H. Doran Company, 1916.

Cott, Nancy F. *The Bonds of Womanhood: "Woman's Sphere" in New England, 1780–1835*. New Haven, CT: Yale University Press, 1977.

Crawford, Margo. *Black Post-Blackness: The Black Arts Movement and Twenty-First-Century Aesthetics*. Urbana: University of Illinois Press, 2017.

Crawley, Ashon T. "'Let's Get It On': Performance Theory and Black Pentecostalism." *Black Theology* 6, no. 3 (September 2008): 308–329.

Crimp, Douglas, ed. *AIDS: Cultural Analysis, Cultural Activism*. Cambridge, MA: MIT Press, 1988.

Cuordileone, K. A. *Manhood and American Political Culture in the Cold War*. London: Routledge, 2005.

Dalzell, Tom. *The Routledge Dictionary of Modern American Slang and Unconventional English*. 2nd ed. London: Taylor and Francis, 2017.

Davis, Angela. *An Autobiography*. New York: Random House, 1974.

Dean, Terrance. *Hiding in Hip Hop: On the Down Low in the Entertainment Industry—from Music to Hollywood*. New York: Atria, 2008.

Dean, Tim. *Beyond Sexuality*. Chicago: University of Chicago Press, 2000.

De Jongh, James. *Vicious Modernism: Black Harlem and the Literary Imagination*. Cambridge: Cambridge University Press, 1990.

D'Emilio, John. *Lost Prophet: The Life and Times of Bayard Rustin*. Chicago: University of Chicago Press, 2003.

D'Emilio, John. *Sexual Politics, Sexual Communities: The Making of a Homosexual Minority in the United States, 1940–1970*. Chicago: University of Chicago Press, 1983.

Derricotte, Toi. *The Black Notebooks: An Interior Journey*. New York: W. W. Norton, 1997.

Dieke, Ikenna. "Sadeanism: Baraka, Sexuality, and the Perverse Imagination in *The System of Dante's Hell*." *Black American Literature Forum* 19, no. 4 (1985): 163–166.

Dixon, Melvin. "'I'll Be Somewhere Listening for My Name." In *A Melvin Dixon Critical Reader*, edited by Justin A. Joyce and Dwight A. McBride, 147–152. Jackson: University Press of Mississippi, 2006.

Dixon, Melvin. *Ride Out the Wilderness: Geography and Identity in Afro-American Literature*. Urbana: University of Illinois Press, 1987.

Dixon, Melvin. *Vanishing Rooms*. New York: Plume, 1991.

Douglas, Ann. *The Feminization of American Culture*. New York: Doubleday, 1977.

Douglas, Mary. *Purity and Danger: An Analysis of the Concepts of Pollution and Taboo*. London: Routledge, 1966.

Douglass, Frederick. *Life and Times of Frederick Douglass, Written by Himself*. 1892. Repr., New York: Collier/Macmillan, 1962.

Douglass, Frederick. *Narrative of the Life of Frederick Douglass, an American Slave, Written by Himself*, edited by Houston A. Baker Jr. 1845. Repr., New York: Penguin Books, 1986.

Dubey, Madhu. *Black Women Novelists and the Nationalist Aesthetic*. Bloomington: Indiana University Press, 1994.

Du Bois, W. E. B. *The Autobiography of W. E. B. Du Bois: A Soliloquy on Viewing My Life from the Last Decade of Its First Century*. New York: International, 1968.

Du Bois, W. E. B. *Black Reconstruction in America, 1860–1880*. 1935. Repr., New York: Free Press, 1998.

Du Bois, W. E. B. *Dusk of Dawn: An Essay toward an Autobiography of a Race Concept*. 1940. Repr., New Brunswick, NJ: Transaction, 1984.

Du Bois, W. E. B. "Returning Soldiers." *Crisis* 18 (May 1919): 13.

Du Bois, W. E. B. *The Souls of Black Folk*. 1903. Repr., New York: Penguin Books, 1989.

duCille, Ann. *The Coupling Convention: Sex, Text, and Tradition in Black Women's Fiction*. New York: Oxford University Press, 1993.

Dudley, David L. *My Father's Shadow: Intergenerational Conflict in African American Men's Autobiography*. Philadelphia: University of Pennsylvania Press, 1991.

Duggan, Lisa. "The New Homonormativity: The Sexual Politics of Neo-liberalism." In *Materializing Democracy: Toward a Revitalized Cultural Politics*, edited by Russ Castronovo and Dana Nelson, 175–194. Durham, NC: Duke University Press, 2002.

Dunning, Stephanie K. *Queer in Black and White: Interraciality, Same Sex Desire, and Contemporary African American Culture*. Bloomington: Indiana University Press, 2009.

Dyer, Richard. *The Matter of Images: Essays on Representations*. New York: Routledge, 1993.

Early, Gerald. "Why Baseball *Was* the Black National Pastime." In *Basketball Jones: America above the Rim*, edited by Todd Boyd and Kenneth L. Shropshire, 27–50. New York: New York University Press, 2000.

Eckman, Fern Marja. *The Furious Passage of James Baldwin*. New York: M. Evans and Co., 1966.

Edelman, Lee. *Homographesis: Essays in Gay Literary and Cultural Theory*. New York: Routledge, 1994.

Edwards, Erica R. *Charisma and the Fictions of Black Leadership*. Minneapolis: University of Minnesota Press, 2012.

Edwards, Harry. *The Revolt of the Black Athlete*. New York: Macmillan, 1969.

Eidshem, Nina Sun. *The Race Sound: Listening, Timbre, and Vocality in African American Music*. Durham, NC: Duke University Press, 2919.

Elder, Arlene A. "'The Future American Race': Charles W. Chesnutt's Utopian Vision." *MELUS* 15, no. 3 (Autumn 1988): 121–129.

Ellis, Mark. "W. E. B. Du Bois and the Formation of Black Opinion in World War I: A Commentary on 'The Damnable Dilemma.'" *Journal of American History* 81, no. 4 (1995): 1584–1590.

Ellison, Julie. *Cato's Tears and the Making of Anglo-American Emotion*. Chicago: University of Chicago Press, 1999.

Ellison, Ralph. *Invisible Man*. 1952. Repr., New York: Vintage / Random House, 1972.

Ellison, Ralph. "Recent Negro Fiction." *New Masses* 40, no. 6 (5 August 1941): 22–26.

Eng, David L. *The Feeling of Kinship: Queer Liberalism and the Racialization of Intimacy*. Durham, NC: Duke University Press, 2010.

Eng, David L., and Jasbir K. Puar. "Introduction: Left of Queer." *Social Text* 38, no. 3 (December 2020): 1–24.

Eyes on the Prize. Episode 11, "Ain't Gonna Shuffle No More." Blackside Media and PBS, 1990.

Fabre, Michel. *The Unfinished Quest of Richard Wright*. 2nd ed. Translated by Isabel Barzun. 1973. Repr., Urbana: University of Illinois Press, 1993.

Fauset, Jessie Redmon. *There Is Confusion*. New York: Boni and Liveright, 1924.

Ferguson, Roderick. *Aberrations in Black: Toward a Queer of Color Critique*. Minneapolis: University of Minnesota Press, 2003.

Ferguson, Roderick. "Race-ing Homonormativity: Citizenship, Sociology, and Gay Identity." In Johnson and Henderson, *Black Queer Studies*, 52–67.

Ferguson, Roderick. "Sissies at the Picnic: The Subjugated Knowledges of a Black Rural Queer." In *Feminist Waves, Feminist Generations: Life Stories from the Academy*, edited by Hokulani K. Aikau, Karla A. Erickson, and Jennifer L. Pierce, 188–196. Minneapolis: University of Minnesota Press, 2007.

Ferro, Robert. *The Family of Max Desir*. New York: Dutton, 1983.

Ferro, Robert. *Second Son*. New York: Crown, 1988.

Fichtelberg, Joseph. *Critical Fictions: Sentiment and the American Market, 1780–1870*. Athens: University of Georgia Press, 2013.

Finley, Stephen C. "Homoeroticism and the African-American Heterosexual Male: Quest for Meaning in the Black Church." *Black Theology* 5, no. 3 (2007): 305–326.

Fisher, Rudolph. *The Walls of Jericho*. 1928. Repr., Ann Arbor: University of Michigan Press, 1994.

FitzGerald, Frances. *Cities on a Hill: A Journey through Contemporary American Cultures*. New York: Simon and Schuster, 1986.

Foner, Philip S. *Organized Labor and the Black Worker, 1619–1973*. New York: International, 1974.

Foner, Philip S. *A Short History of Reconstruction, 1863–1877*. New York: Harper and Row, 1990.

Fordham, Signithia. *Blacked Out: Dilemmas of Race, Identity, and Success at Capital High*. Chicago: University of Chicago Press, 1996.

Foster, Frances Smith. *Written by Herself: Literary Production by African American Women, 1746–1892*. Bloomington: Indiana University Press, 1993.

Fox, Ashley. "Meet Sarah Thomas, NFL's First Female Official." ESPN.com, 17 April 2015. http://www.espn.com/nfl/story/_/id/12669370/meet-sarah-thomas-first-female-nfl-official-referee.

Fox, Stephen R. *The Guardian of Boston: William Monroe Trotter*. New York: Atheneum, 1970.

Fraiman, Susan. *Cool Men and the Second Sex*. New York: Columbia University Press, 2003.

Franklin, Clyde W., II. "Surviving the Institutional Decimation of Black Males: Causes, Consequences, Intervention." In *The Making of Masculinities: The New Men's Studies*, edited by Harry Brod, 155–169. Boston: Unwin and Hyman, 1987.

"Free Breakfast in Baltimore." *Black Panther* 3, no. 9 (21 June 1969): 15. In Marxists Internet Archive, https://www.marxists.org/history//usa/pubs/black-panther/03n09-jun%2021%201969.pdf, accessed 30 October 2020.

Freud, Sigmund. *Civilization and Its Discontents*. Translated and edited by James Strachey. 1930. Repr., New York: W. W. Norton, 1961.

Freud, Sigmund. "On Narcissism: An Introduction." In *The Freud Reader*, edited by Peter Gay, 545–562. New York: W. W. Norton, 1989.

Fuss, Diana, ed. *Inside/Out: Lesbian Theories, Gay Theories*. New York: Routledge, 1991.

Gamson, Joshua. *The Fabulous Sylvester: The Legend, the Music, the Seventies in San Francisco*. New York: Henry Holt and Company, 2005.

Garland-Thomson, Rosemarie. *Extraordinary Bodies: Figuring Physical Disability in American Culture and Literature*. New York: Columbia University Press, 1997.

Garrett, Marvin P. "Early Recollections and Structural Irony in *The Autobiography of an Ex-Colored Man*." *Critique: Studies in Contemporary Fiction* 13:2 (2013): 5–14.

Gates, Henry Louis, Jr. "Blacklash?" *New Yorker*, 17 May 1993, 42–44. Repr. in Brandt, *Dangerous Liaisons*, 25–44. New York: New Press, 1999.

Gates, Henry Louis, Jr. "The Black Man's Burden." In *Fear of a Queer Planet*, edited by Michael Warner, 230–238. Minneapolis: University of Minnesota Press, 1993.

Gates, Henry Louis, Jr. *Colored People: A Memoir*. 1994. Repr., New York: Vintage Books, 1995.

Gates, Henry Louis, Jr. Introduction to James Weldon Johnson, *The Autobiography of an Ex-Coloured Man*, v–xxiii. 1927. Repr., New York: Vintage / Random House, 1989.

Gayle, Addison, Jr. *Richard Wright: Ordeal of a Native Son*. Gloucester, MA: Peter Smith, 1983.

Gayle, Addison, Jr. *The Way of the New World: The Black Novel in America*. Garden City, NY: Anchor/Doubleday, 1975.

Genovese, Eugene D. *Roll, Jordan, Roll: The World the Slaves Made*. New York: Vintage Books, 1976.

George, Nelson. *Hip Hop America*. New York: Penguin, 1998.

Gerstner, David A. *Queer Pollen: White Seduction, Black Male Homosexuality, and the Cinematic*. Urbana: University of Illinois Press, 2011.

Gibson, Donald. "Chapter One of Booker T. Washington's *Up from Slavery* and the Feminization of the African American Male." In *Representing Black Men*, edited by Marcellus Blount and George P. Cunningham, 95–110. New York: Routledge, 1996.

Giddings, Paula J. *When and Where I Enter: The Impact of Black Women on Race and Sex in America*. New York: Bantam Books, 1984.

Giovanni, Nikki. *Gemini: An Extended Autobiographical Statement on My First Twenty-Five Years of Being a Black Poet*. Indianapolis: Bobbs-Merrill, 1971.

Gladwell, Malcolm. "The Big Man Can't Shoot." *Revisionist History* (podcast), season 1, episode 3, 30 July 2017. http://revisionisthistory.com/episodes/03-the-big-man-cant-shoot/.

Glee. Ryan Murphy, creator and executive producer. Fox Television Network. Hollywood, CA: Twentieth Century Fox Television, 2009–2015.

Goff, James R., Jr. *Fields White unto Harvest: Charles F. Parham and the Missionary Origins of Pentecostalism*. Fayetteville: University of Arkansas Press, 1988.

Golden, Thelma, ed. *Black Male: Representations of Masculinity in Contemporary American Art*. New York: Whitney Museum of Modern Art, 1994.

Goldsby, Jacqueline. *Spectacular Secret: Lynching in American Life and Literature*. Chicago: University of Chicago Press, 2006.

Goldstein, Richard. "'Go the Way Your Blood Beats': An Interview with James Baldwin." In *James Baldwin: The Legacy*, edited by Quincy Troupe, 173–185. New York: Simon and Schuster, 1989.

Gopinath, Gayatri. *Impossible Desires: Queer Diasporas and South Asian Public Cultures*. Durham, NC: Duke University Press, 2005.

Gordon-Chipembere, Natasha, ed. *Representation and Black Womanhood: The Legacy of Sarah Baartman*. New York: Palgrave Macmillan, 2011.

Grandison, Kenrick Ian. "Landscapes of Terror: A Reading of Tuskegee's Historic Campus, 1881–1915." In *The Geography of Identity*, edited by Patricia Yaeger, 334–367. Vol. 5 of *Ratio*, produced by the University of Michigan Institute for the Humanities. Ann Arbor: University of Michigan Press, 1996.

Grandison, Kenrick Ian. "Negotiated Space: The Black College Campus as a Cultural Record of Postbellum America." *American Quarterly* 51, no. 3 (1999): 529–579.

Gray, J. Patrick. "Growing Yams and Men: An Interpretation of Kimam Male Ritualized Homosexual Behavior." In Blackwood, *Anthropology and Homosexual Behavior*, 55–68.

Greenberg, David F. "Why Was the Berdache Ridiculed?" In Blackwood, *Anthropology and Homosexual Behavior*, 179–190.

Greene, J. Lee. *Blacks in Eden: The African American Novel's First Century*. Charlottesville: University Press of Virginia, 1996.
Griffin, Farah Jasmine. *"Who Set You Flowin'?": The African-American Migration Narrative*. New York: Oxford University Press, 1995.
Guttmann, Allen. *A Whole New Ball Game: An Interpretation of American Sports*. Chapel Hill: University of North Carolina Press, 1988.
Hahn, Jason Duaine. "Get to Know NFL Player Ryan Russell's Dancer Boyfriend, Corey O'Brien." *People*, 26 November 2019. https://people.com/sports/who-is-ryan-russell-boyfriend-corey-obrien/.
Halberstam, Jack. *Female Masculinity*. Durham, NC: Duke University Press, 1998.
Hall, Radclyffe. *The Well of Loneliness*. With commentary by Havelock Ellis. London: Jonathan Cape, 1928.
Halpern, Faye. *Sentimental Readers: The Rise, Fall, and Revival of a Disparaged Rhetoric*. Iowa City: University of Iowa Press, 2013.
Handler, M. S. "Malcolm X Terms Dr. King's Tactics Futile." *New York Times*, 11 May 1963, 9. ProQuest Historical Newspapers. https://digitalgallery.bgsu.edu/student/files/original/ded70ab64d7d2c5d5b556034476a13a4.pdf.
Hardy, Clarence E., III. *James Baldwin's God: Sex, Hope, and Crisis in Black Holiness Culture*. Knoxville: University of Tennessee Press, 2003.
Harlan, Louis R. *Booker T. Washington: The Making of a Black Leader, 1856–1901*. London: Oxford University Press, 1972.
Harlan, Louis R., ed. *The Booker T. Washington Papers, 1860–89*. Vol. 2. Urbana: University of Illinois Press, 1972.
Harlan, Louis R., ed. *The Booker T. Washington Papers, 1895–1898*. Vol 4. Urbana: University of Illinois Press, 1975.
Harlan, Louis R. *Booker T. Washington: The Wizard of Tuskegee, 1901–1915*. London: Oxford University Press, 1983.
Harper, Phillip Brian. *Are We Not Men? Masculine Anxiety and the Problem of African-American Identity*. New York: Oxford University Press, 1986.
Harper, Phillip Brian. "Eloquence and Epitaph: Black Nationalism and the Homophobic Impulse in Responses to the Death of Max Robinson." In *Fear of a Queer Planet*, edited by Michael Warner, 239–263. Minneapolis: University of Minnesota Press, 1993.
Harper, Phillip Brian. "The Evidence of Felt Intuition: Minority Experience, Everyday Life, and Critical Speculative Knowledge." In Johnson and Henderson, *Black Queer Studies*, 106–123.
Harper, Phillip Brian. *Private Affairs: Critical Ventures in the Culture of Social Relations*. New York: New York University Press, 1999.
Harris, Angelique. "Review: Homosexuality and the Black Church." *Journal of African American History* 93, no. 2 (2008): 262–270.
Harris, E. Lynn. *Invisible Life*. 1991. Repr., New York: Doubleday/Anchor, 1994.
Harris, Trudier. *Black Women in the Fiction of James Baldwin*. Knoxville: University of Tennessee Press, 1985.

Harris, Trudier. *Exorcising Blackness: Historical and Literary Lynching and Burning Rituals*. Bloomington: Indiana University Press, 1984.

Harris, William H. *The Harder We Run: Black Workers since the Civil War*. New York: Oxford University Press, 1982.

Hayes, Jarrod. *Queer Nations: Marginal Sexualities in the Maghreb*. Chicago: University of Chicago Press, 2000.

Hemphill, Essex, ed. *Brother to Brother: New Writings by Black Gay Men*. Boston: Alyson, 1991.

Herdt, Gilbert H. *Same Sex, Different Cultures: Exploring Gay and Lesbian Lives*. Boulder, CO: Westview, 1997.

Hernton, Calvin C. "Dynamite Growing out of Their Skulls." In *Black Fire: An Anthology of Afro-American Writing*, edited by LeRoi Jones and Larry Neal, 78–104. New York: William Morrow and Company, 1968.

Hernton, Calvin C. *Sex and Race in America*. New York: Doubleday/Anchor, 1965.

Herring, Scott. *Queering the Underworld: Slumming, Literature, and the Undoing of Lesbian and Gay History*. Chicago: University of Chicago Press, 2007.

Hill, Anita. *Speaking Truth to Power*. New York: Doubleday, 1997.

Hill, Herbert. *Black Labor and the American Legal System: Race, Work, and the Law*. Madison: University of Wisconsin Press, 1985.

Hippler, Mike. *Matlovich, the Good Soldier*. Boston: Alyson, 1989.

Hoberman, John. *Darwin's Athletes: How Sport Has Damaged Black America and Preserved the Myth of Race*. Boston: Houghton Mifflin, 1997.

Holleran, Andrew (Eric Garber). *Dancer from the Dance*. New York: William Morrow and Company, 1978.

Holleran, Andrew (Eric Garber). *Nights in Aruba*. New York: William Morrow and Company, 1983.

Holmes, Kwame. "What's the Tea? Gossip and the Social Production of Black Gay History." *Radical History Review* 122 (May 2015): 55–69.

Holt, Rackham (Margaret Van Vechten Saunders). *George Washington Carver: An American Biography*. Garden City, NY: Doubleday, Doran, and Company, 1943.

hooks, bell (Gloria Watkins). *Black Looks: Race and Representation*. Toronto: Between the Lines, 1992.

hooks, bell (Gloria Watkins). *Yearning: Race, Gender, and Cultural Politics*. Boston: South End Press, 1990.

Hookstead, David. "Skip Bayless Criticizes Dak Prescott for Admitting He Battled Depression." *Daily Caller*, 11 September 2020. https://dailycaller.com/2020/09/11/skip-bayless-dak-prescott-suicide-depression/.

Howard-Pitney, David. *The Afro-American Jeremiad: Appeals for Justice in America*. Philadelphia: Temple University Press, 1990.

Howells, William Dean. Introduction to *Lyrics of Lowly Life*. In Paul Laurence Dunbar, *The Life and Works of Paul Laurence Dunbar*, 13–17. Nashville: Winston-Derek, 1992.

Hudson, Theodore R. *From LeRoi Jones to Amiri Baraka: The Literary Works*. Durham, NC: Duke University Press, 1973.

Hudson, Theodore R. "University of Virginia Students Blast 'Not Gay' Unofficial Fight Song Chant with Resolution." Queer Voices. *Huffington Post*, 28 September 2012, updated 2 February 2016. https://www.huffingtonpost.com/2012/09/28/university-of-virginia-not-gay-fight-song-chant-resolution-_n_1923041.html.

Hughes, Langston. *Arna Bontemps / Langston Hughes Letters, 1925–1967*. Edited by Charles H. Nichols. New York: Paragon House, 1990.

Hughes, Langston. *The Collected Poems of Langston Hughes*, edited by Arnold Rampersad and David Roessel. New York: Alfred A. Knopf, 1994.

Hughes, Langston. *Not without Laughter*. 1930. Repr., New York: Collier Books / Macmillan, 1969.

Hull, Gloria T., Patricia Bell Scott, and Barbara Smith, eds. *All the Women Are White, All the Blacks Are Men, but Some of Us Are Brave: Black Women's Studies*. New York: Feminist Press, 1982.

Hunter, Tera W. *Bound in Wedlock: Slave and Free Marriage in the Nineteenth Century*. Cambridge, MA: Harvard University Press, 2017.

Hunter, Tera W. *To 'Joy My Freedom: Southern Black Women's Lives and Labors after the Civil War*. Cambridge, MA: Harvard University Press, 1997.

Hurston, Zora Neale. *Dust Tracks on a Road: An Autobiography*. 1942. Repr., New York: Harper Perennial, 1991.

Ikard, David. *Breaking the Silence: Toward a Black Male Feminist Criticism*. Baton Rouge: Louisiana State University Press, 2007.

Jackson, Lawrence P. *The Indignant Generation: A Narrative History of African American Writers and Critics, 1934–1960*. Princeton, NJ: Princeton University Press, 2011.

Jarrett, Gene Andrew. "Introduction: 'Not Necessarily Race Matter.'" *African American Literature beyond Race: An Alternative Reader*, edited by Jarrett, 1–22. New York: New York University Press, 2006.

Jefferson, Thomas. *Notes on the State of Virginia*. 1785. Repr. Edited by William Peden. Chapel Hill: University of North Carolina Press, 1996.

Jennings, Theodore W., Jr. *Jacob's Wound: Homoerotic Narrative in the Literature of Ancient Israel*. New York: Continuum, 2005.

Jennings, Theodore W. *The Man Jesus Loved: Homoerotic Narratives from the New Testament*. Cleveland: Pilgrim Press, 2001.

Johnson, Charles S. *The Negro in Chicago: A Study of Race Relations and a Race Riot*. Chicago: University of Chicago Press, 1922.

Johnson, E. Patrick. *Appropriating Blackness: Performance and the Politics of Authenticity*. Durham, NC: Duke University Press, 2004.

Johnson, E. Patrick, ed. *No Tea, No Shade: New Writings in Black Queer Studies*. Durham, NC: Duke University Press, 2016.

Johnson, E. Patrick. "'Quare' Studies, or (Almost) Everything I Know about Queer Studies I Learned from My Grandmother." In Johnson and Henderson, *Black Queer Studies*, 124–157.

Johnson, E. Patrick. *Sweet Tea: Black Gay Men of the South, an Oral History*. Chapel Hill: University of North Carolina Press, 2008.

Johnson, E. Patrick, and Mae G. Henderson, eds. *Black Queer Studies: A Critical Anthology*. Durham, NC: Duke University Press, 2005.

Johnson, Jack. *The Autobiography of Jack Johnson: In the Ring and Out*. New York: Citadel/Carol, 1992.

Johnson, James Weldon. *Along This Way: The Autobiography of James Weldon Johnson*. 1933. Repr., New York: Da Capo, 2000.

Johnson, James Weldon. *The Autobiography of an Ex-Coloured Man*. 1927. Repr., New York: Vintage / Random House, 1989.

Johnson, James Weldon. *Black Manhattan*. 1930 Repr., New York: Da Capo, 1991.

Johnson, James Weldon, ed. *The Book of American Negro Poetry*. Rev. ed. 1922. Repr., San Diego: Harcourt Brace and Company, 1950.

Johnson, James Weldon. *Fifty Years and Other Poems*. Boston: Cornhill, 1921. Electronic edition: Twentieth-Century African American Poetry. Alexandria: Chadwyck-Healey, 1998. http://gateway.proquest.com/openurl/openurl?ctx_ver=Z39.88-2003&xri:pqil:res_ver=0.2&res_id=xri:ilcs-us&rft_id=xri:ilcs:ft:20daap:Z00 0328496:0.

Johnson, James Weldon. *Negro Americans, What Now?* New York: Viking, 1935.

Johnson, James Weldon. "Race Prejudice and the Negro Artist." *Harper's Magazine* 157 (1 June 1928): 769–776.

Johnson, James Weldon. "Self-Determining Haiti." *Nation* 111 (1920): 236–238, 265–267, 295–297, 345–347.

Jones, Butler A. "The Tradition of Sociology Teaching in Black Colleges: The Unheralded Professionals." In *Black Sociologists: Historical and Contemporary Perspectives*, edited by James E. Blackwell and Morris Janowitz, 146–148. Chicago: University of Chicago Press, 1974.

Jones, Howard Mumford. *The Age of Energy: Varieties of American Experience, 1865–1915*. New York: Viking, 1971.

Jones, Jacqueline. *Labor of Love, Labor of Sorrow: Black Women, Work and the Family, from Slavery to the Present*. 1985. Repr., New York: Vintage, 1995.

Jordan, William. "'The Damnable Dilemma': African-American Accommodation and Protest during World War I." *Journal of American History* 81, no. 4 (1995): 1562–1583.

Joyce, James. *A Portrait of the Artist as a Young Man*. 1916. Repr., New York: Modern Library, 1996.

Joyce, James. *Ulysses*. Paris: Shakespeare and Company, 1922.

Kanyon, Chris, with Ryan Clark. *Wrestling Reality: The Life and Mind of Chris Kanyon, Wrestling's Gay Superstar*. Toronto: ECW Press, 2011.

Katz, Jackson. *Man Enough? Donald Trump, Hilary Clinton, and the Politics of Presidential Masculinity*. Northampton, MA: Interlink Books, 2016.

Kawash, Samira. *Dislocating the Color Line: Identity, Hybridity, and Singularity in African-American Narrative*. Stanford, CA: Stanford University Press, 1997.

Keating, James W. "Sportsmanship as a Moral Category." *Ethics* 75, no. 1 (1 October 1964): 25–35.

Kelley, Robin D. G. "Confessions of a Nice Negro, or Why I Shaved My Head." In Belton, *Speak My Name*, 12–22.

Kelley, Robin D. G. "The Riddle of the Zoot: Malcolm Little and Black Cultural Politics during World War II." In *Race Rebels: Culture, Politics, and the Black Working Class*, 161–181. New York: Free Press, 1994.

Kimmel, Michael. *Manhood in America: A Cultural History*. New York: Free Press, 1996.

King, Martin Luther, Jr. *Why We Can't Wait*. New York: Penguin/Mentor, 1963.

Kipfer, Barbara Ann, and Robert L. Chapman, eds. *Dictionary of American Slang*. New York: Collins, 2007.

Kirby, David. *Little Richard: The Birth of Rock 'n' Roll*. New York: Continuum, 2010.

Klorer, Dan, and Ron Berger, dirs. *Ring of Fire: The Emile Griffith Story*. Hole in the Fence Productions, 2005.

Klotman, Phyllis R. "Military Rites and Wrongs: African Americans in the U.S. Armed Forces." In *Struggles for Representation: African American Documentary Film and Video*, edited by Klotman and Janet K. Cutler, 34–70. Bloomington: Indiana University Press, 1999.

Koestenbaum, Wayne. *The Queen's Throat: Opera, Homosexuality, and the Mystery of Desire*. New York: Poseidon, 1993.

Kopay, David, and Perry Deane Young. *The David Kopay Story: An Extraordinary Self-Revelation*. 1977. Repr., New York: Donald I. Fine / Primus, 1988.

Kornegay, E. L., Jr. *A Queering of Black Theology: James Baldwin's Blues Project and Gospel Prose*. Basingstoke, UK: Palgrave Macmillan, 2013.

Kramer, Larry. *Faggots*. New York: Random House, 1977.

Kunjufu, Jawanza. *Adam! Where Are You? Why Most Black Men Don't Go to Church*. Chicago: African American Images, 1997.

Kurtzleben, Danielle. "Male Democratic Candidates Will Have to Answer Gender Role Questions in 2020 Race." *All Things Considered*, National Public Radio, 27 March 2019. https://www.npr.org/2019/03/27/707358130/male-democratic-candidates-will-have-to-answer-gender-role-questions-in-2020-rac.

Kutulas, Judy. "'You Probably Think This Song Is about You': Women's Music from Carole King to the Disco Divas." In *Disco Divas: Women and Popular Culture in the 1970s*, edited by Sherrie A. Inniss, 173–193. Philadelphia: University of Pennsylvania Press, 2003.

Lancaster, Roger N. *Life Is Hard: Machismo, Danger, and the Intimacy of Power in Nicaragua*. Berkeley: University of California Press, 1992.

Larsen, Nella. *"Quicksand" and "Passing."* New Brunswick, NJ: Rutgers University Press, 1986.

Larson, Edward J. *Sex, Race, and Science: Eugenics in the Deep South*. Baltimore: Johns Hopkins University Press, 1995.

Leavitt, David. *Family Dancing*. New York: Warner Books, 1984.

Leavitt, David. *The Lost Language of Cranes*. New York: Alfred A. Knopf, 1986.

Lee, Ulysses. "On the Road." Review of *Let Me Breathe Thunder*, by William Attaway. *Opportunity* 17, no. 9 (September 1939): 283–284.

Leeming, David. *Amazing Grace: A Life of Beauford Delaney*. New York: Oxford University Press, 1998.
Leeming, David. *James Baldwin: A Biography*. New York, Knopf, 1994.
Leitch, Will. "The Weird Dwight Howard Saga Shows the NBA Still Has a Problem with the Closet." *Intelligencer*, 17 November 2018. http://nymag.com/intelligencer/2018/11/the-dwight-howard-saga-and-the-nbas-problem-with-the-closet.html.
Leonard, David J., Kimberly B. George, and Wade Davis, eds. *Football, Culture and Power*. Abingdon, UK: Routledge / Taylor and Francis Group, 2017.
Levy, Eugene. *James Weldon Johnson: Black Leader, Black Voice*. Chicago: University of Chicago Press, 1973.
Lewis, David Levering. *W. E. B. Du Bois: Biography of a Race, 1868–1919*. New York: Henry Holt, 1993.
Lewis, David Levering. *When Harlem Was in Vogue*. New York: Oxford University Press, 1979.
Lionnet, Francoise. *Autobiographical Voices: Race, Gender, Self-Portraiture*. Ithaca, NY: Cornell University Press, 1989.
Loftin, Craig M. *Masked Voices: Gay Men and Lesbians in Cold War America*. Albany: State University of New York Press, 2012.
Logan, Rayford W. Introduction to *Life and Times of Frederick Douglass, Written by Himself*, 15–24. New York: Macmillan, 1962.
Logan, Rayford W. "James Weldon Johnson and Haiti." *Phylon* 32, no. 4 (1960): 396–402.
Lorde, Audre. *Sister/Outsider: Essays and Speeches*. Freedom, CA: Crossing Press, 1984.
Lorde, Audre. *Zami: A New Spelling of My Name: A Biomythography*. Freedom, CA: Crossing Press, 1982.
Louganis, Greg, with Eric Marcus. *Breaking the Surface*. 1995. Repr., Naperville: Sourcebooks, 2006.
Love, Heather. *Feeling Backward: Loss and the Politics of Queer History*. Cambridge, MA: Harvard University Press, 2007.
Major, Clarence. *Juba to Jive: A Dictionary of African-American Slang*. New York: Penguin, 1994.
Major, Clarence. "My Mother and Mitch." In Belton, *Speak My Name*, 127–136.
Malveaux, Julianne. "Gladiators, Gazelles, and Groupies: Basketball Love and Loathing." In *Basketball Jones: America above the Rim*, edited by Todd Boyd and Kenneth L. Shropshire, 51–58. New York: New York University Press, 2000.
Marable, Manning. *Malcolm X: A Life of Reinvention*. New York: Viking, 2011.
Marcuse, Herbert. *One-Dimensional Man: Studies in the Ideology of Advanced Industrial Society*. Boston: Beacon, 1964.
Margolies, Edward. *Native Sons: A Critical Study of Twentieth-Century Black American Authors*. Philadelphia: J. B. Lippincott, 1968.
Marotta, Toby. *The Politics of Homosexuality*. Boston: Houghton Mifflin, 1981.
Matthews, Tracye A. "'No One Ever Asks What a Man's Role in the Revolution Is': Gender Politics and Leadership in the Black Panther Party, 1966–71." In *Sisters in the Struggle: African American Women in the Civil Rights–Black Power Movement*,

edited by Bettye Collier-Thomas and V. P. Franklin, 230–256. New York: New York University Press, 2001.

Maupin, Armistead. *More Tales of the City*. New York: Harper and Row, 1982.

Maupin, Armistead. *Tales of the City*. New York: Harper and Row, 1978.

McBride, Dwight. "Can the Queen Speak? Racial Essentialism, Sexuality, and the Problem of Authority." In *Black Men on Race, Gender and Sexuality: A Reader*, edited by Devon W. Carbado, 253–275. New York: New York University Press, 1999.

McBride, Dwight, ed. *James Baldwin Now*. New York: New York University Press, 1999.

McBride, Dwight. "Straight Black Studies: On African American Studies, James Baldwin, and Black Queer Studies." In Johnson and Henderson, *Black Queer Studies*, 68–89.

McCall, Nathan. *Makes Me Wanna Holler: A Young Black Man in America*. New York: Vintage, 1995.

McClintock, Anne. *Imperial Leather: Race, Gender and Sexuality in the Colonial Contest*. New York: Routledge, 1995.

McCune, Jeffrey Q., Jr. "Michael Sam and the Sport of Queer Failure." In *Football, Culture and Power*, edited by David J. Leonard, Kimberly B. George, and Wade Davis, 203–211. Abingdon, UK: Routledge / Taylor and Francis Group, 2017.

McCune, Jeffrey Q., Jr. *Sexual Discretion: Black Masculinity and the Politics of Passing*. Chicago: University of Chicago Press, 2014.

McCune, Jeffrey Q., Jr. "Transformance: Reading the Gospel in Drag." *Journal of Homosexuality* 46, nos. 3–4 (2004): 151–167.

McDowell, Deborah E. *Leaving Pipe Shop: Memories of Kin*. New York: W. W. Norton, 1996.

McKay, Claude. *Home to Harlem*. 1928. Repr., Boston: Northeastern University Press, 1987.

McKay, Claude. *A Long Way from Home: An Autobiography*. 1937. Repr., San Diego: Harcourt Brace Jovanovich, 1970.

McKinley, Maggie. *Masculinity and the Paradox of Violence in American Fiction, 1950–75*. New York: Bloomsbury, 2015.

McMurray, Linda O. *George Washington Carver: Scientist and Symbol*. New York: Oxford University Press, 1981.

Mead, Chris. *Champion Joe Louis: Black Hero in White America*. New York: Charles Scribner's Sons, 1985.

Messner, Michael A. *Power at Play: Sports and the Problem of Masculinity*. Boston: Beacon, 1992.

Miller, Kelly. *Race Adjustment: Essays on the Negro in America*. New York: Neale, 1908.

Miller, Monica L. *Slaves to Fashion: Black Dandyism and the Styling of Black Diasporic Identity*. Durham, NC: Duke University Press, 2009.

Moody, Anne. *Coming of Age in Mississippi*. New York: Dell/Laurel, 1968.

Mooneyham, Mike. "Barnett 'an Unforgettable Figure.'" *Wrestling Gospel*, 26 September 2004. http://www.mikemooneyham.com/2004/09/26/barnett-an-unforgettable-figure/.

Moore, Marlon Rachquel. *In the Life and in the Spirit: Homoerotic Spirituality in African American Literature*. Albany: State University of New York Press, 2014.

Moore, Stephen D. *God's Beauty Parlor: And Other Queer Spaces in and around the Bible*. Stanford, CA: Stanford University Press, 2001.

Moraga, Cherríe, and Gloria Anzaldúa, eds. *This Bridge Called My Back: Writings by Radical Women of Color*. New York: Kitchen Table / Women of Color Press, 1983.

Moss, Alfred A., Jr. *American Negro Academy: Voice of the Talented Tenth*. Baton Rouge: Louisiana State University Press, 1981.

Mostern, Kenneth. *Autobiography and Black Identity Politics: Racialization in Twentieth-Century America*. Cambridge: Cambridge University Press, 1999.

Moten, Fred. *In the Break: The Aesthetics of the Black Radical Tradition*. Minneapolis: University of Minnesota Press, 2003.

Motley, Willard. *Knock on Any Door*. New York: D. Appleton-Century Co., 1947.

Motley, Willard. *We Fished All Night*. New York: Appleton-Century-Crofts, 1951.

Mumford, Kevin J. "Homosex Changes: Race, Cultural Geography, and the Emergence of the Gay." *American Quarterly* 48, no. 3 (September 1996): 395–414.

Mumford, Kevin J. *Interzones: Black/White Sex Districts in Chicago and New York in the Early Twentieth Century*. New York: Columbia University Press, 1997.

Mumford, Kevin J. *Not Straight, Not White: Black Gay Men from the March on Washington to the AIDS Crisis*. Chapel Hill: University of North Carolina Press, 2016.

Muñoz, José Esteban. *Cruising Utopia: The Then and There of Queer Futurity*. New York: New York University Press, 2009.

Muñoz, José Esteban. *Disidentifications: Queers of Color and the Performance of Politics*. Minneapolis: University of Minnesota Press, 1999.

Murphy, Doyle. "'Money' Matt Cage Comes Out as Gay." *New York Daily News*, 25 June 2015. http://www.nydailynews.com/news/national/pro-wrestler-money-matt-cage-gay-article-1.2270187.

Murphy, Kevin P. *Political Manhood: Red Bloods, Mollycoddles, and the Politics of Progressive Era Reform*. New York: Columbia University Press, 2008.

Murray, Rolland. *Our Living Manhood: Literature, Black Power, and Masculine Ideology*. Philadelphia: University of Pennsylvania Press, 2007.

Nanda, Serena. "The Hijras of India: Cultural and Individual Dimensions of an Institutional Third Gender Role." In Blackwood, *Anthropology and Homosexual Behavior*, 35–54.

Neal, Larry. "And Shine Swam On: An Afterword." In *Black Fire: Anthology of Afro-American Writing*, edited by Amiri Baraka and Larry Neal, 638–656. New York: William Morrow and Company, 1968.

Neal, Mark Anthony. *Looking for Leroy: Illegible Black Masculinities*. New York: New York University Press, 2013.

Neal, Mark Anthony. *New Black Man*. New York: Routledge, 2005.

Neal, Mark Anthony. *Songs in the Key of Black Life: A Rhythm and Blues Nation*. London: Routledge / Taylor and Francis Group, 2013.

Nero, Charles I. "Reading Will Make You Queer: Gender Inversion and Racial Leadership in Claude McKay's *Home to Harlem*." *Palimpsest: A Journal on Women, Gender, and the Black International* 2, no. 1 (2013): 74–86.

Nero, Charles I. "Re/membering Langston: Homophobic Textuality and Arnold Rampersad's *Life of Langston Hughes*." In *Queer Representations: Reading Lives, Reading*

Cultures, edited by Martin Duberman, 188–196. New York: New York University Press, 1997.

Nero, Charles I. "Why Are Gay Ghettos White?" In Johnson and Henderson, *Black Queer Studies*, 228–245.

Newton, Huey P. *To Die for the People: The Writings of Huey P. Newton*, edited by Toni Morrison. 1972. Repr., New York: Writers and Readers, 1995.

Norton, Rictor. *Mother Clap's Molly House: The Gay Subculture of England, 1700–1830.* London: GMP, 1992.

O'Hara, Mary Emily. "Meet the LGBTQ Voters Who Backed Trump." NBC News, 15 November 2016. https://www.nbcnews.com/feature/nbc-out/meet-lgbtq-voters-who-backed-trump-n684181.

Oliver, Greg. "Terry Garvin: A Career Overshadowed." *Slam! Wrestling*, 2 January 2006. http://slam.canoe.com/Slam/Wrestling/2005/12/22/1365103.html.

Omolade, Barbara. *The Rising Song of African American Women.* New York: Routledge, 1994.

O'Sullivan, Maurice, J., Jr. "Of Souls and Pottage: James Weldon Johnson's *The Autobiography of an Ex-Coloured Man.*" *CLA Journal* 23, no. 1 (Fall 1979): 60–70.

Ovington, Mary White. *The Walls Came Tumbling Down: The Autobiography of Mary White Ovington.* New York: Harcourt Brace, 1947.

Owen, Karen Van Neste. "'The Good Old Song': Is It Beloved by All?" *University of Virginia Magazine*, Fall 2013. http://uvamagazine.org/articles/the_good_old_song_is_it_beloved_by_all.

Pachankis, John E., and Mark L. Hatzenbuehler. "The Social Development of Contingent Self-Worth in Sexual Minority Young Men: An Empirical Investigation of the 'Best Little Boy in the World' Hypothesis." *Basic and Applied Social Psychology* 35, no. 2 (March 2013): 176–190.

Painter, Nell Irvin. *Standing at Armageddon: The United States, 1877–1919.* New York: Norton, 1987.

Pallone, Dave, with Alan Steinberg. *Behind the Mask: My Double Life in Baseball.* New York: Signet/Penguin, 1990.

Paquet, Sandra Pouchet. *Caribbean Autobiography: Cultural Identity and Self-Representation.* Madison: University of Wisconsin Press, 2002.

Paris, Arthur E. *Black Pentecostalism: Southern Religion in an Urban World.* Amherst: University of Massachusetts Press, 1982.

Park, Robert E. *Race and Culture: Essays in the Sociology of Contemporary Man.* Glencoe, NY: Free Press, 1950.

Patterson, Pat, with Bertrand Hébert. *Accepted: How the First Gay Superstar Changed WWE.* Toronto: ECW Press, 2016.

Perry, Bruce. *Malcolm: The Life of a Man Who Changed Black America.* Barrytown, NY: Station Hill, 1991.

Petry, Ann. *The Street.* 1946. Repr., Boston: Houghton-Mifflin, 1974.

Pfeiffer, Kathleen. "Individualism, Success, and American Identity in *The Autobiography of an Ex-Colored Man.*" *African American Review* 30, no. 3 (1996): 403–419.

Pickens, William. *Bursting Bonds: The Autobiography of a "New Negro."* Edited by William L. Andrews. 1923. Repr., Bloomington: Indiana University Press, 1991.

Pitt, Richard N. *Divine Callings: Understanding the Call to Ministry in Black Pentecostalism*. New York: New York University Press, 2012.

Pochmara, Anna. *The Making of the New Negro: Black Authorship, Masculinity, and Sexuality in the Harlem Renaissance*. Amsterdam: Amsterdam University Press, 2011.

Powell, Adam Clayton, Sr. *Against the Tide: An Autobiography*. New York: Richard R. Smith, 1938.

Powell, Shaun. *Souled Out? How Blacks Are Winning and Losing in Sports*. Champaign: Human Kinetics, 2008.

Puar, Jasbir K. *Terrorist Assemblages: Homonationalism in Queer Times*. Durham, NC: Duke University Press, 2007.

Quiroga, José. *Tropics of Desire: Interventions from Queer Latin America*. New York: New York University Press, 2000.

Rampersad, Arnold. *The Life of Langston Hughes*. 2 vols. New York: Oxford University Press, 1986–1988.

Ravens, Simon. *The Supernatural Voice: A History of High Male Singing*. Suffolk: Boydell and Brewer, 2014.

Read, Jim. *Justin Fashanu: A Biography*. Derby: DB, 2012.

Rechy, John. *City of Night*. New York: Grove, 1963.

Rechy, John. *Numbers*. New York: Grove, 1967.

Rechy, John. *Rushes*. New York: Grove, 1979.

Redmond, Shana L. *Anthem: Social Movements and the Sound of Solidarity in the African Diaspora*. New York: New York University Press, 2014.

Reid, John. *The Best Little Boy in the World*. 1973. Repr., New York: Ballantine Books, 1977.

Reid-Pharr, Robert. *Conjugal Union: The Body, the House, and the Black American*. New York: Oxford University Press, 1999.

Reid-Pharr, Robert. "Dinge." In *Black Gay Man: Essays*, 85–98. New York: New York University Press, 2001.

Reid-Pharr, Robert. *Once You Go Black: Choice, Desire, and the Black American Intellectual*. New York: New York University Press, 2007.

Rich, Adrienne. "Compulsory Heterosexuality and Lesbian Existence." In *Powers of Desire: The Politics of Sexuality*, edited by Ann Snitow, Christine Stansell, and Sharon Thompson, 177–205. New York: Monthly Review Press, 1983.

Richards, David A. J. *The Sodomy Cases:* Bowers v. Hardwick *and* Lawrence v. Texas. Lawrence: University Press of Kansas, 2009.

Richards, John. "Some Experiences with Colored Soldiers." In *World War I at Home: Readings on American Life, 1914–1920*, edited by David F. Trask, 140–144. New York: John Wiley and Sons, 1970.

Richardson, Riché. *Black Masculinity and the U.S. South: From Uncle Tom to Gangsta Rap*. Athens: University of Georgia Press, 2007.

Riggs, Marlon. "Tongues Untied." In Hemphill, *Brother to Brother*, 200–205.

Riggs, Marlon, dir. *Tongues Untied*. San Francisco: Frameline California Newsreel, 1989.

Robeck, Cecil M., Jr. *The Azusa Street Mission and Revival: The Birth of the Global Pentecostal Movement*. Nashville: Thomas Nelson, 2006.

Roberts, Brian Russell. *Artistic Ambassadors: Literary and International Representation of the New Negro Era*. Charlottesville: University of Virginia Press, 2013.

Roberts, John W. *From Trickster to Badman: The Black Folk Hero in Slavery and Freedom*. Philadelphia: University of Pennsylvania Press, 1989.

Robinson, Jackie. *I Never Had It Made*. As told to Alfred Duckett. New York: G. P. Putnam's Sons, 1972.

Robinson, Sally. *Marked Men: White Masculinity in Crisis*. New York: Columbia University Press, 2000.

Rodgers, Daniel T. *The Work Ethic in Industrial America, 1850–1920*. Chicago: University of Chicago Press, 1974.

Rodgers-Rose, La Frances, ed. *The Black Woman*. Beverly Hills, CA: Sage, 1980.

Rodman, Dennis, with Tim Keown. *Bad as I Wanna Be*. New York: Delacorte, 1996.

Rodríguez, Juana María. *Queer Latinidad: Identity Practices, Discursive Spaces*. New York: New York University Press, 2003.

Roediger, David R. *The Wages of Whiteness: Race and the Making of the American Working Class*. London: Verso, 1991.

Rogin, Michael. *Blackface, White Noise: Jewish Immigrants in the Hollywood Melting Pot*. Berkeley: University of California Press, 1996.

Ronan, Wyatt. "Breaking: 2021 Becomes Record Year for Anti-transgender Legislation." Human Rights Campaign, 13 March 2021. https://www.hrc.org/press-releases/breaking-2021-becomes-record-year-for-anti-transgender-legislation.

Roosevelt, Theodore. *The Rough Riders*. New York: Charles Scribner's Sons, 1899. https://babel.hathitrust.org/cgi/pt?id=hvd.32044014506059;view=1up;seq=9.

Ross, Charles K., ed., *Race and Sport: The Struggle for Equality on and off the Field*. Jackson: University of Mississippi Press, 2004.

Ross, Marlon B. "Baldwin's Sissy Heroics." *African American Review* 46, no. 4 (Winter 2013): 633–651.

Ross, Marlon B. "Camping the Dirty Dozens: The Queer Resources of Black Nationalist Invective." In "Plum Nelly: New Essays in Black Queer Studies," edited by Dwight McBride and Jennifer Devere Brody, special issue, *Callaloo* 23, no. 1 (Winter 2000): 290–312.

Ross, Marlon B. *Manning the Race: Reforming Black Men in the Jim Crow Era*. New York: New York University Press, 2004.

Ross, Marlon B. "Race, Rape, Castration: Feminist Theories of Sexual Violence and Masculine Strategies of Black Protest." In *Masculinity Studies and Feminist Theory: New Directions*, edited by Judith Kegan Gardiner, 305–318. New York: Columbia University Press, 2002.

Ross, Marlon B. "Some Glances at the Black Fag: Race, Same-Sex Desire, and Cultural Belonging." In "Reading the Signs," edited by Anne Herrmann and Ross Chambers, special issue, *Canadian Review of Comparative Literature / Revue Canadienne de Littérature Comparée* 21 (1994): 193–219.

Ross, Marlon B. "'What's Love but a Second-Hand Emotion?': Man-on-Man Passion in the Contemporary Black Gay Romance Novel." *Callaloo* 36, no. 3 (Summer 2013): 669–687.

Ross, Marlon B. "White Fantasies of Desire: Baldwin and the Racial Identities of Sexuality." In *James Baldwin Now*, edited by Dwight A. McBride, 13–55. New York: New York University Press, 1999.

Ross, Ron. *Nine . . . Ten . . . and Out! The Two Worlds of Emile Griffith*. New York: Dibella Entertainment, 2008.

Rowley, Hazel. *Richard Wright: The Life and Times*. Chicago: University of Chicago Press, 2001.

Russell, Ryan, as told to Kevin Arnovitz. "No Distractions: An NFL Veteran Opens Up on His Sexuality." ESPN.com, 29 August 2019. https://www.espn.com/nfl/story/_/id/27484719/no-distractions-nfl-veteran-opens-sexuality.

Russo, Vito. *The Celluloid Closet: Homosexuality in the Movies*. New York: Harper and Row, 1991.

Sánchez-Walsh, Arlene. "Re-scripting Pentecostal Saints: Curious Life of Mother Rosa Horn." *Pantheos*, 26 July 2014. https://www.patheos.com/blogs/amsanchezwalsh/2014/07/re-scripting-pentecostal-saints-curious-life-of-mother-rosa-horn/.

Schechter, Patricia A. *Ida B. Wells-Barnett and American Reform, 1880–1930*. Chapel Hill: University of North Carolina Press, 2001.

Schropshire, Kenneth L. *In Black and White: Race and Sports in America*. New York: New York University Press, 1996.

Scott, Darieck. *Extravagant Abjection: Blackness, Power, and Sexuality in the African American Literary Imagination*. New York: New York University Press, 2010.

Scott, Darieck. *Traitor to the Race*. New York: Plume, 1996.

Scott, Joyce Hope. "From Foreground to Margin: Female Configurations and Masculine Self-Representation in Black Nationalist Fiction." In *Nationalisms and Sexualities*, edited by Andrew Parker et al., 296–312. New York: Routledge, 1992.

Seale, Bobby. *Seize the Time: The Story of the Black Panther Party and Huey P. Newton*. New York: Random House, 1970. Repr., Baltimore: Black Classic Press, 1991.

Sedgwick, Eve Kosofsky. *Between Men: English Literature and Male Homosocial Desire*. New York: Columbia University Press, 1985.

Sedgwick, Eve Kosofsky. "How to Bring Your Kids Up Gay: The War on Effeminate Boys." In *Tendencies*, 154–164. Durham, NC: Duke University Press, 1993.

Sedgwick, Eve Kosofsky, ed. *Novel Gazing: Queer Readings in Fiction*. Durham, NC: Duke University Press, 1997.

Sedgwick, Eve Kosofsky. *Tendencies*. Durham, NC: Duke University Press, 1993.

Sedgwick, Eve Kosofsky. *Touching Feeling: Affect, Performativity, Pedagogy*. Durham, NC: Duke University Press, 2003.

Shabazz, Malcolm, with Alex Haley. *The Autobiography of Malcolm X*. 1965. Repr., New York: Ballantine Books, 1973.

Shakur, Assata. *Assata: An Autobiography*. Chicago: Chicago Review Press / Lawrence Hill Books, 1987.

Shilts, Randy. *Conduct Unbecoming: Lesbians and Gays in the U.S. Military*. New York: St. Martin's, 1993.

Siebers, Tobin. "My Withered Limb." In "Disability, Art, and Culture (Part One)," special issue, *Michigan Quarterly Review* 37, no. 2 (Spring 1998). http://hdl.handle.net/2027/spo.act2080.0037.202.

Simmons, Ron. "Some Thoughts on the Challenges Facing Black Gay Intellectuals." In Hemphill, *Brother to Brother*, 211–228.

Simmons, Roy, and Damon Dimarco. *Out of Bounds: Coming Out of Sexual Abuse, Addiction, and My Life of Lies in the NFL Closet*. New York: Carroll and Graf, 2006.

Simon, Robert L. *Fair Play: The Ethics of Sport*. Boulder: Westview/Perseus, 2004.

Simpson, Mark. "Here Come the Mirror Men: Why the Future Is Metrosexual." *The Independent*, 15 November 1994. Repr. in *Metrosexy: A 21st Century Self-Love Story*, 2–4. Seattle: CreateSpace/Amazon, 2013.

Simpson, Mark. "Meet the Metrosexual: He's Well Dressed, Narcissistic and Obsessed with Butts, but Don't Call Him Gay." *Salon*, 22 July 2002. https://www.salon.com/2002/07/22/metrosexual/.

Skerrett, Joseph T., Jr. "Irony and Symbolic Action in James Weldon Johnson's *The Autobiography of an Ex-Coloured Man*." *American Quarterly* 32 (1980): 540–558.

Slim, Iceberg. See Beck, Robert.

Smith, Barbara, ed. *Home Girls: A Black Feminist Anthology*. New York: Kitchen Table / Women of Color Press, 1983.

Smith, Barbara. Introduction to *Home Girls: A Black Feminist Anthology*, xix–lvi. New York: Kitchen Table / Women of Color Press, 1983.

Smith, Barbara. "Toward a Black Feminist Criticism." In *All the Women Are White, All the Blacks Are Men, but Some of Us Are Brave: Black Women's Studies*, edited by Gloria T. Hull et al., 157–175. New York: Feminist Press, 1982.

Smith, Lillian. *Strange Fruit*. 1944. Repr., San Diego: Harcourt, Brace and Co., 1972.

Smith, Max C. "By the Year 2000." In *In the Life: A Black Gay Anthology*, edited by Joseph Beam, 224–229. Boston: Alyson, 1986.

Smith, Michael J., ed. *Black Men / White Men: A Gay Anthology*. San Francisco: Gay Sunshine Press, 1983.

Smith, Shane A. "'The Crisis' in the Great War: W. E. B. Du Bois and His Perception of African-American Participation in World War I." *The Historian* 70, no. 2 (July 2008): 239–262.

Smith, Valerie. *Self-Discovery and Authority in Afro-American Narrative*. Cambridge, MA: Harvard University Press, 1987.

Snorton, C. Riley. *Black on Both Sides: A Racial History of Trans Identity*. Minnesota: University of Minneapolis Press, 2017.

Snorton, C. Riley. *Nobody Is Supposed to Know: Black Sexuality on the Down-Low*. Minneapolis: University of Minnesota Press, 2014.

Snyder, Tom. Interview with Little Richard. *The Late Late Show with Tom Snyder*, 14 January 1997. YouTube, posted 16 August 2014. https://www.youtube.com/watch?v=4mB3u2jGGXY.

Spero, Sterling D., and Abram L. Harris. *The Black Worker: The Negro and the Labor Movement*. New York: Columbia University Press, 1931.

Spillers, Hortense. *Black, White, and in Color: Essays on American Literature and Culture*. Chicago: University of Chicago Press, 2003.

Spurlin, William J. "Culture, Rhetoric, and Queer Identity: James Baldwin and the Identity Politics of Race and Sexuality." In *James Baldwin Now*, edited by Dwight McBride, 103–121. New York: New York University Press, 1999.

Stallybrass, Peter, and Allon White. *The Politics and Poetics of Transgression*. Ithaca, NY: Cornell University Press, 1986.

Stepto, Robert B. *Blue as the Lake: A Personal Geography*. Boston: Beacon, 1998.

Stepto, Robert B. *From behind the Veil: A Study of Afro-American Narrative*. 2nd ed. 1979. Repr., Urbana: University of Illinois Press, 1991.

Steptoe, Tyina. "Big Mama Thornton, Little Richard, and the Queer Roots of Rock 'n' Roll." *American Quarterly* 70, no. 1 (March 2018): 55–77.

Stockton, Kathryn Bond. *Beautiful Bottom, Beautiful Shame: Where "Black" Meets "Queer."* Durham, NC: Duke University Press, 2006.

Stowe, Harriet Beecher. *Uncle Tom's Cabin, or Life among the Lowly*. Boston: John P. Jewitt, 1852. Project Gutenberg Ebooks, 6 June 2017, http://www.gutenberg.org/ebooks/203.

Styron, William. *The Confessions of Nat Turner: A Novel*. New York: Random House, 1967.

Sullivan, Denise. *Keep on Pushing: Black Power Music from Blues to Hip Hop*. Chicago: Lawrence Hill Books, 2011.

Summers, C. T. "Wrestler Orlando Jordan: Bi and Proud." *Edge Media Network*, 15 September 2006. https://boston.edgemedianetwork.com/printstory.php?ch=&sc=&sc3=&id=39541.

Sundquist, Eric J. *The Hammers of Creation: Folk Culture in African American Fiction*. Athens: University of Georgia Press, 1992.

Talbot, Edith Armstrong. *Samuel Chapman Armstrong: A Biographical Study*. New York: Doubleday and Page, 1904.

Tate, Claudia. *Black Women Writers at Work*. New York: Continuum, 1983.

Tate, Claudia. *Domestic Allegories of Political Desire: The Black Heroine's Text at the Turn of the Century*. New York: Oxford University Press, 1992.

Tewksbury, Mark. *Inside Out: Straight Talk from a Gay Jock*. Mississauga, ON: Wiley, 2006.

Tharrett, Matthew. "How Many LGBT People Voted for Donald Trump? Are the Numbers Surprising?" Logo, 9 November 2016. http://www.newnownext.com/lgbt-vote-donald-trump/11/2016/.

"'That's So Gay' Phrase Has Lasting Impact for LGBT Youth, Study Finds." *Queer Voices. Huffington Post*, 28 August 2012, updated 2 February 2016. https://www.huffingtonpost.com/2012/08/28/thats-so-gay-phrase-impact-lgbt-youth_n_1837330.html.

Thurman, Wallace. *The Blacker the Berry*. 1929. Repr., New York: Collier/Macmillan, 1970.

Thurman, Wallace. *Infants of the Spring*. 1932. Repr., Boston: Northeastern University Press, 1992.

Tompkins, Jane. *Sensational Designs: The Cultural Work of American Fiction, 1790–1860*. New York: Oxford University Press, 1985.

Towle, Andy. "'Minnesota United' Pro Soccer Player Collin Martin Comes Out as Gay." *Towleroad Gay News*, 29 June 2018. http://www.towleroad.com/2018/06/collin-martin/.

Trachtenberg, Alan. *The Incorporation of America: Culture and Society in the Gilded Age*. New York: Hill and Wang, 1982.

Troupe, Quincy, ed. *James Baldwin: The Legacy*. New York: Simon and Schuster, 1989.

Tuaolo, Esera, with John Rosengren. *Alone in the Trenches: My Life as a Gay Man in the NFL*. Naperville: Sourcebooks, 2006.

Tyler, Dennis, Jr. "Losing Limbs in the Republic: Disability, Dismemberment, and Mutilation in Charles Chesnutt's Conjure Stories." *Journal of Literary and Cultural Disability Studies* 11, no. 1 (2017): 34–51.

"University of Virginia Students Blast 'Not Gay' Unofficial Fight Song Chant with Resolution." Queer Voices. *Huffington Post*, 28 September 2012, updated 2 February 2016. https://www.huffpost.com/entry/university-of-virginia-not-gay-fight-song-chant-resolution-_n_1923041.

Vaid, Urvashi. *Virtual Equality: The Mainstreaming of Gay and Lesbian Liberation*. New York: Anchor/Doubleday, 1995.

VanderLaan, D. P., and P. L. Vasey. "Male Sexual Orientation in Independent Samoa: Evidence for Fraternal Birth Order and Maternal Fecundity Effects." *Archives of Sexual Behavior* 40, no. 3 (June 2011): 495–503.

Van Peebles, Melvin. *Sweet Sweeback's Baadasssss Song*. Detroit: Cinemation Industries, 1971.

Van Vechten, Carl. "Introduction to Mr. Knopf's New Edition." In *Autobiography of an Ex-Coloured Man*, xxxiii–xxxviii. 1927. Repr., New York: Vintage / Random House, 1989.

Van Vechten, Carl. *Nigger Heaven*. 1926. Repr., New York: Avon, 1951.

Vasey, Paul, and Doug VanderLaan. "Materteral and Avuncular Tendencies in Samoa." *Human Nature* 20, no. 3 (September 2009): 269–281.

Vigdor, Neil. "Ryan Russell, N.F.L. Free Agent, Comes Out as Bisexual: 'It's So Much Better than Hiding.'" *New York Times*, 30 August 2019. https://www.nytimes.com/2019/08/30/us/ryan-russell-nfl-bisexual.html.

Vogel, Shane. *The Scene of Harlem Cabaret: Race, Sexuality, Performance*. Chicago: University of Chicago Press, 2009.

Von Eschen, Penny. *Satchmo Blows Up the World: Jazz Ambassadors Play the Cold War*. Cambridge, MA: Harvard University Press, 2004.

Wald, Gayle. "The Satire of Race: James Weldon Johnson's *Autobiography of an Ex-Coloured Man*." In *Cross-Addressing: Resistance Literature and Cultural Borders*, edited by John C. Hawley, 139–155. Albany: State University of New York Press, 1996.

Walker, Alice. *The Color Purple*. New York: Harcourt, Brace, Jovanovich, 1982.

Walker, Alice. "In Search of Our Mothers' Gardens." In *In Search of Our Mothers' Gardens: Womanist Prose*, 231–243. San Diego: Harcourt Brace Jovanovich, 1983.

Walker, Margaret. *Richard Wright, Daemonic Genius: A Portrait of the Man. A Critical Look at His Work*. New York: Warner Books, 1988.

Wallace, Lee. "Fa'afafine, Queens of Samoa and Sexual Elision." In *Sexual Encounters: Pacific Texts, Modern Sexualities*, 138–158. Ithaca, NY: Cornell University Press, 2003.

Wallace, Maurice. *Constructing the Black Masculine: Identity and Ideality in African American Men's Literature and Culture, 1775–1995*. Durham, NC: Duke University Press, 2002.

Wallace, Maurice. "On Being a Witness: Passion, Pedagogy, and the Legacy of James Baldwin." In Johnson and Henderson, *Black Queer Studies*, 276–286.

Wallace, Michele. *Black Macho and the Myth of the Superwoman*. London: Verso, 1978, 1990.

Ward, Geoffrey C. *Unforgivable Blackness: The Rise and Fall of Jack Johnson*. New York: Knopf, 2004.

Warner, Michael, ed. *Fear of a Queer Planet: Queer Politics and Social Theory*. Minneapolis: University of Minnesota Press, 1993.

Warner, Michael. "Homo-Narcissism; or, Heterosexuality." In *Engendering Men: The Question of Male Feminist Criticism*, edited by Joseph A. Boone and Michel Cadden, 190–206. New York: Routledge, 1990.

Warner, Michael. *The Trouble with Normal: Sex, Politics, and the Ethics of Queer Life*. Cambridge, MA: Harvard University Press, 1999.

Washington, Booker T. "The Better Part." Address to the Thanksgiving Peace Jubilee Exercises, Chicago, 16 October 1898. In Harlan, ed., *The Booker T. Washington Papers, 1895–1898*, vol. 4, 490–492.

Washington, Booker T. *The Story of the Negro*. 1909. Repr., Philadelphia: University of Pennsylvania Press, 2005.

Washington, Booker T. *Up from Slavery*. 1901. Repr., New York: Penguin Books, 1986.

Washington, Mary Helen. *Invented Lives: Narratives of Black Women, 1860–1960*. New York: Anchor, 1987.

Watts, Jerry Gafio. *Amiri Baraka: The Politics and Art of a Black Intellectual*. New York: New York University Press, 2001.

Watts, Jill. *God, Harlem U.S.A.: The Father Divine Story*. Berkeley: University of California Press, 1992.

Weatherby, W. J. *James Baldwin: Artist on Fire*. New York: Donald I. Fine, 1989.

Weeks, Jeffrey. *Against Nature: Essays on History, Sexuality and Identity*. London: Rivers Oram, 1991.

Weisman, Leslie Kanes. "The Home as Metaphor for Society." In *Discrimination by Design: A Feminist Critique of the Man-Made Environment*, 87–99. Urbana: University of Illinois Press, 1992.

Wells-Barnett, Ida B. *Crusade for Justice: The Autobiography of Ida B. Wells*. Edited by Alfreda M. Duster. Chicago: University of Chicago Press, 1970.

Werth, Barry. *The Scarlet Professor: Newton Arvin: A Literary Life Shattered by Scandal*. New York: Nan A. Talese / Doubleday, 2001.

White, Charles. *The Life and Times of Little Richard, the Quasor of Rock*. New York: Harmony Books, 1984.

White, Edmund. *A Boy's Own Story*. New York: E. P. Dutton, 1982.

White, Edmund. *Nocturnes for the King of Naples*. New York: St. Martin's, 1978.

White, Edmund. *States of Desire: Travels in Gay America*. London: André Deutsch, 1980.
Whitmore, George. *The Confessions of Danny Slocum*. New York: St. Martin's, 1980.
Whyte, William Hollingsworth, Jr. *The Organization Man*. New York: Simon and Schuster, 1956.
Wiebe, Robert H. *The Search for Order, 1877–1920*. New York: Hill and Wang, 1967.
Williams, George Washington. *The History of the Negro Race in America from 1619 to 1880*. New York: G. P. Putnam's Sons, 1882.
Williams, George Washington. *A History of the Negro Troops in the War of the Rebellion, 1861–1865: Preceded by a Review of the Military Services of Negroes in Ancient and Modern Times*. New York: Harper and Brothers, 1887.
Williams, Melvin D. *Community in a Black Pentecostal Church: An Anthropological Study*. Pittsburgh: University of Pittsburgh Press, 1974.
Williams, Raymond. *The Country and the City*. New York: Oxford University Press, 1973.
Williams, Raymond. "Structures of Feeling." In *Marxism and Literature*. Oxford: Oxford University Press, 1977.
Williams, Walter L. *The Spirit and the Flesh: Sexual Diversity in American Indian Culture*. Boston: Beacon, 1986.
Wilson, Joseph Thomas. *The Black Phalanx: A History of the Negro Soldiers of the United States in the War of Independence, the War of 1812, and the Civil War*. 1887. Repr., New York: Da Capo, 1994.
Wirth, Thomas H., ed. *Gay Rebel of the Harlem Renaissance: Selections from the Work of Richard Bruce Nugent*. Durham, NC: Duke University Press, 2002.
Wong, Curtis M. "WWE Legend Pat Patterson Comes Out as Gay." *Huffington Post*, 13 June 2014, updated 2 February 2016. https://www.huffingtonpost.com/2014/06/13/pat-patterson-comes-out_n_5492726.html.
Woubshet, Dagmawi. *The Calendar of Loss: Race, Sexuality, and Mourning in the Early Era of AIDS*. Baltimore: Johns Hopkins University Press, 2015.
Wright, Richard. *Black Boy (American Hunger)* [the restored text established by the Library of America]. 1945. Repr., New York: HarperPerennial, 1993.
Wright, Richard. "Blueprint for Negro Writing." *New Challenge* 2, no. 2 (Fall 1937): 53–65.
Wright, Richard. "High Tide in Harlem: Joe Louis as a Symbol of Freedom." *New Masses* 28, no. 2 (5 July 1938): 18–20.
Wright, Richard. "Joe Louis Discovers Dynamite." *New Masses* 17, no. 2 (8 October 1935): 18–19.
Wright, Richard. *The Long Dream*. 1958. Repr., New York: Harper and Row, 1987.
Wright, Richard. *Native Son* [the original 1940 edition]. 1940. Repr., New York: HarperPerennial, 1966.
Wright, Richard. *The Outsider* [the restored text established by the Library of America]. 1953. Repr., New York: HarperPerennial, 1993.
Wright, Richard. *Savage Holiday*. 1954. Repr., Jackson: University of Mississippi Press, 1994.
Wynn, Neil A. *The Afro-American and the Second World War*. Rev. ed. New York: Holmes and Meier, 1993.

Yerby, Frank. *The Foxes of Harrow*. New York: Dial, 1946.

Young, Josiah Ulysses, III. *James Baldwin's Understanding of God: Overwhelming Desire and Joy*. New York: Palgrave Macmillan, 2014.

Young, Vershawn Ashanti. *Your Average Nigga: Performing Race, Literacy and Masculinity*. Detroit: Wayne State University Press, 2007.

Zeigler, Cyd. "'Not Gay' at UVA: University of Virginia Students Chant Has Included 'Not Gay' since the 1970s." *OutSports*, 1 January 2003. https://www.outsports.com/2013/2/20/4011054/not-gay-at-uva.

Ziegler, Kortney. "Black Sissy Masculinity and the Politics of Dis-respectability." In *No Tea, No Shade: New Writings in Black Queer Studies*, edited by E. Patrick Johnson, 196–215. Durham, NC: Duke University Press, 2016.

INDEX

Note: Page numbers followed by *f* refer to figures.

Abdul-Jabbar, Kareem, 288, 294–295, 392n24
African Americans, 63, 78; communism and, 116; cultural formations of marriage for, 362n78; interracial bonds and, 122; Johnson and, 136, 162; labor and, 70, 73, 77; as mediators of U.S. imperialism, 135; middle class and, 360n66; Pentecostalism and, 374n20; as professional athletes, 320; sissy conduct among, 41; social protest and, 317; tolerance for homosexuality of, 319; Trump and, 343; urban spaces and, 171, 208, 249
Ali, Muhammad, 287–288
Along This Way (Johnson), 115–117, 126, 137–141, 143–144, 147–149, 151–154, 159, 162, 165, 368n46
Amaechi, John, 301, 310, 315–316, 321, 323, 328, 330, 334
Armstrong, Samuel Chapman, 69, 77, 79–80, 83–85, 106; biography of, 78, 129; Washington and, 37, 73, 80, 82, 84, 87, 90–98, 134, 154, 359n61
Atlanta University, 119, 127–128, 134, 149–150; women of, 130, 145
Autobiography of an Ex-Coloured Man, The (Johnson), 111, 114, 116, 134, 138, 140–161, 168, 371n111; Larsen and, 370n77; *Souls of Black Folk* (Du Bois), 368n64
Awkward, Michael, 276, 280

Baker, Houston A., Jr., 9–10, 142–143, 236, 241, 256, 264–267; on Johnson, 368n64; on Washington, 72, 87, 96, 359n57, 359n59, 361n73
Baldwin, James, 12–13, 18–22, 30, 34, 36, 46–48, 165–169, 171, 181, 186, 188–189, 211–213, 212f, 228f, 229f, 314, 330, 380nn113–114; *Another Country*, 194–196, 218, 242–243, 253; Ayer and, 374n39; Baraka and, 234, 237, 242–244, 247, 252–254, 259; Beam and, 259–261; black sissy trend and, 271; Burke and, 323; church and, 172–175, 176, 178–179; Cleaver and, 218–219, 221, 224, 234–235, 378n79; Cold War and, 207, 209, 215, 229–230; Cullen and, 375n50, 382n145; Delaney and, 225–227; *The Fire Next Time*, 172, 179, 200, 252–253; gender queerness and, 16; *Giovanni's Room*, 184, 199, 244, 252, 381n128, 389n72; "Here Be Dragons," 180–181, 183–185; Hughes and, 193–194; Jim Crow and, 183, 205, 207, 221, 229–231, 259, 305; *Just above My Head*, 168, 190, 196, 200–203, 205, 217–219, 331, 387n56; menial labor and, 65; straight sissies and, 274; street and, 170, 178, 180; *Tell Me How Long the Train's Been Gone*, 190, 196
Baraka, Amiri, 12–13, 30, 48, 207, 238–239, 241–242, 245–246, 248–251, 262, 385nn31–32; *The Autobiography of Leroi Jones*, 242–244, 247–248, 251–252, 254–255, 297; Baldwin and, 234, 237, 242–244, 247, 252–254, 259; middle-classness of, 253; poetry and, 254, 256, 386n40, 387n52; rape and, 270, 386n47; Rustin and, 237; *The System of Dante's Hell*, 191, 244, 247, 252–253, 316, 385n30, 386n46
Barry, Rick, 292–294
Beam, Joseph, 256, 258–263, 265, 267, 269–270, 325
Bean, Billy, 301, 308–312, 315, 318–323, 327–328, 330, 333–334, 398n93

Beckham, David, 284–285, 287, 333
Belton, Don, 256, 264, 284, 388n62
Benston, Kimberly W., 145, 386n40
Bersani, Leo, 206, 208, 355n70
Bhabha, Homi, 94, 364n130, 364n133
Black Arts Movement, 236, 238, 384n16
Black Belt, 74, 94; Washington and, 113, 120, 122
Black Boy (Wright), 12, 15–18, 123–124, 183, 191, 266–267, 295, 297, 375n43
black leadership, 9, 64, 66, 283
black liberation, 35, 37, 241, 263
black male identity, 68, 71, 257, 282, 359n59
black manhood, 20–21, 34, 37, 52–54, 60, 115, 147–148, 159, 161, 272–273, 297, 354n59; Baldwin and, 196, 231; black professional athletes and, 288; gender roles and, 49; Jim Crow and, 68, 70; marginal man and, 111; progressive, 43; skin color and, 244; straight black sissies and, 48, 272, 278; Uncle Tom and, 46; Washington on, 56
black nationalism, 384n16; Baldwin and, 167; Baraka and, 48, 252–253, 387n60; dark-skinned men and, 44
blackness, 28–30, 72, 76, 317, 332, 350n6; alienation from, 5; in *Along This Way* (Johnson), 148–149, 155, 160; Amaechi's, 316–317; Baraka and, 244, 247, 250–252; Beam and, 260; beauty and, 146; Burke and, 325; church and, 197; disability and, 96; football and, 340; "gay Blacks" and, 388n68; *Glee* and, 399n112; in *Go Tell It on the Mountain* (Baldwin), 182; heteronormative, 250; homophobia and, 383n8; intellectual achievement and, 89; Johnson and, 165; narcissism and, 145; outness and, 336; queerness of, 288; sissiness and, 214; urban masculine, 170; virtual, 327; white homosexuality and, 326; womanism and, 257
Black Power, 18, 35, 44, 263, 283; Baldwin and, 224, 234; Baraka and, 241, 247, 253; discourse of, 259, 384n15
Bontemps, Arna, 193, 195
Boyd, Herb, 185, 193, 374n39
Burke, Glenn, 283, 301, 318–331, 333–334, 398n81, 398n83

Campbell, James, 189, 376n60
Capote, Truman, 29, 31, 47, 209–214, 210f, 213f, 216f, 227, 229, 246, 339
Carver, George Washington, 10–13, 30–31, 46–47, 54, 80, 90, 98–109, 102f, 104f, 105f, 107f, 211, 355n69, 365n142, 365n152
Castro Street Clones, 26, 40, 246, 299, 302
Chamberlain, Wilt, 292–295, 293f, 392n19
Chesnutt, Charles, 139, 161, 368n48
church sissy, 32, 46, 182–183, 189, 215, 278, 310–311; Baldwin and, 168–169, 171, 174, 178–179, 185–186, 188, 196, 200; Baraka and, 254–255; Griffith as, 330; sexual timidity of, 275; shame and, 281; straight sissy and, 280; Sylvester as, 304
Cleaver, Eldridge, 18–20, 238, 241, 259, 261–262, 270; Baldwin and, 218–219, 221, 224, 234–235, 378n79; punk-hunting and, 296, 381n126; *Soul on Ice*, 19, 386n45
Cobb, Michael, 182, 187
Cold War, 208–209, 238, 380n105; Baldwin and, 229–230, 260; Baraka and, 234; black cultural ambassadorship during, 380n116; Capote and, 29, 211; gender conformity and, 207; government purges during, 31, 206; Little Richard and, 214–215; masculinist violence and, 180; Sylvester and, 215, 218
Collins, Jason, 301, 334
communism, 116, 208–209
conduct, 6–8, 11–12, 17, 27, 41, 292, 297, 331, 347, 350n6, 355n69; black manhood, 196, 266, 269; Christian, 173; effeminate, 99, 103, 224, 313; gentle manly, 118, 127, 130, 135, 140, 143; heterosexual codes of, 78; homosexual, 46, 219, 251; hygienic, 85; manly, 11, 15, 19, 44, 48, 112, 128, 137; masculine, 15, 48–49, 161, 175, 187, 193, 289, 305, 390n88; racial, 87, 154, 159; sexual, 14, 175, 288, 304, 312; white, 387n54. *See also* gender conduct; sissy conduct
Crisis, The, 35, 117, 358n43
cross-dressing, 19–20, 352n29, 355n69; Burke and, 334; Carver and, 101, 102f; Rodman and, 332–333; Simmons and, 329; Sylvester and, 217

Delaney, Beauford, 228f; Baldwin and, 23, 225–227, 242, 382n146

Dirty Dozens, 183, 255, 375n43

Dixon, Melvin, 224–225, 247, 375n53, 381n128

double consciousness, 52, 112, 141–142, 202, 310

Douglass, Frederick, 45, 54, 88, 124, 268, 363n109, 364n125

Du Bois, W. E. B., 32, 35, 62–63, 70–71, 80, 83, 108, 129, 271, 358n43; Jim Crow and, 61, 71, 202, 354n58; Johnson and, 113, 115, 117, 120, 122, 126, 135, 366n5; menial labor and, 77, 158; Miller and, 60–61; sissiphobia and, 154; veil and, 202; Washington and, 51–56, 58, 65–66, 68–70, 357n22

Dunbar, Paul Laurence, 57–58, 67

effeminacy, 27, 37, 39, 208, 275, 285, 347, 352n36, 355n71; Carver's, 11; in *Go Tell It on the Mountain* (Baldwin), 225; Rustin's, 237

Eminem, 285, 287, 333

faggotry, 17, 19, 220, 222, 227, 237, 270, 297

fashion, 285–288; Griffith and, 330–331; Johnson and, 133; metrosexuality and, 284; Sylvester and, 217; thug, 44

feminine, the, 39, 52; ecstatic worship and, 173; housekeeping and, 84; sissy conduct and, 25

femininity, 6, 8, 38–39, 109, 146, 222, 355n67; white, 107, 121, 124, 196

feminism, 48, 256, 361n74; black, 268

femme, 40, 170, 289, 346

Ferguson, Roderick, 4–5, 12, 28, 41, 147, 308, 311

Finley, Stephen, 173, 183

gangsta rap, 238, 257, 268, 283, 286–288

Gates, Henry Louis, Jr., 154, 264, 273–275, 277–278, 279f, 291, 383n8

Gayle, Addison, Jr., 45, 351n20

gay rights movement, 180, 218, 283, 298

gender conduct, 7, 9–11, 13, 23, 59, 76, 154, 281, 284, 324; Baldwin's, 166–167, 184; Bean's 309; black men and, 47; Carver's, 98, 103; Castro District and, 325; church doctrine and, 172; effeminacy and, 38; Griffith's, 331–332; Johnson and, 115, 120, 129, 131, 166; language and, 29; masculinity and, 21, 26–27; nonconforming, 4; normative, 300; queer, 327, 332; race and, 142–143, 149; sexual orientation and, 276, 314, 354n65; of sissies, 25; sissiphobia and, 14; sissy-shaming and, 15; skin color and, 112, 114; Washington's, 10, 98, 100, 162

gender identity, 7, 21, 401n12; black men and, 72, 268; Carver's, 105; Gates's, 274; Johnson and, 123, 161; sissiness and, 42; Tuaolo and, 312–313; Washington's, 87; white masculinity and, 29

gender nonconformity, 15, 23, 38, 170, 281, 311, 347; Amaechi and, 316; black men and, 49; Carver's, 54, 101; church and, 183; in *Go Tell It on the Mountain* (Baldwin), 186, 197; Johnson and, 13; male, 14, 38; in sports, 335; Trump and, 344; Tuaolo and, 312, 314; Washington's, 100; Wright and, 18, 21; Young and, 5

gender norms, 30, 240, 277; masculine, 298

gender performance, 10, 42, 174, 323; church sissy and, 281; masculinity and, 292

Glee, 339–340

Goldsby, Jacqueline, 63, 114, 159, 359n58

good Negro, 21; Washington and, 9, 75

gossip, 12, 14–15, 42, 99

Go Tell It on the Mountain (Baldwin), 21, 65, 167–168, 171–172, 181, 183, 189–190, 196–200, 205, 222, 244, 305, 352n32; black fathers and, 266, 375n42; church and, 31, 186, 254, 281, 387n56; Hughes on, 193, 202; sissy walk in, 187, 231; street and, 186, 254

Grandison, K. Ian, 81, 108, 386n39

Great Migration, 179, 190, 363n102

Griffith, Emile, 12, 31, 301, 330–333, 335, 395n45

Halberstam, Jack, 24–25

Hampton Institute, 34, 37, 54, 64, 87, 94, 224

Harlan, Louis, 59, 67, 80–82, 86, 89, 92, 96

Harlem Renaissance, 73, 115–116, 122, 126, 371n116, 377n71; Abdul-Jabbar on, 392n24; Alfred A. Knopf and, 140; Hughes and, 193; Summers as patron of, 134

Harper, Philip Brian, 14, 157, 160, 187, 273, 337, 350–351n14
Harris, E. Lynn, 257, 388n64
Hayden, Robert, 255, 387n59
Hemphill, Essex, 256, 388n62
heteronormativity, 15, 23, 187, 199, 202, 266, 376n57; Washington and, 72; white, 43
Himes, Chester, 194–195
Holt, Rackham, 101, 103, 365n144
homoeroticism, 134, 145, 161, 337; narcissism and, 369n65; racialized, 214; Washington and, 359n59
homonormativity, 184, 299, 343
homophobia, 24, 45, 68, 180, 262, 271; athletics and, 283, 317–320, 322, 324, 335; Baraka's, 385n30; black cultural nationalism and, 30, 234, 383n8; black liberation and, 241; black men and, 238, 272; black music and, 287; Black Power movement and, 384n15; rap music and, 391n8; in Samoa, 312; sissiphobia and, 14; straight black, 273
homosexuality, 14–15, 22, 24, 44, 199, 249, 260, 263, 283, 289, 319, 338, 379n93; AIDS and, 397n64; Baldwin and, 169, 195, 205, 225, 231, 376n60; Baraka and, 241, 245–247, 249, 385n31, 386n46; basketball players and, 315; black, 236, 273; Carver and, 100, 103, 106, 109; Chamberlain and, 293–294; Cold War and, 207–209, 214, 245; "The Good Old Song" and, 346; hip-hop and, 288; Hughes's, 376n66; Johnson and, 148–149, 154, 156; male bonding and, 355n67; military and, 300; narcissism and, 284, 305, 396n52; Newton and, 239; nineteenth-century, 385n25; Parham and, 177; Pentecostalism and, 169, 312; reading as sign of incipient, 4, 349n2; sissiness and, 27–29, 42–43, 67–68, 103, 106, 233, 276, 284–285, 314, 349n2; sports and, 283, 300–301, 305, 307, 315, 320, 329; sports disclosure memoirs and, 297, 308, 311, 313, 327–328; straight sissy and, 277; white, 326; Wright and, 18, 381n26
homo-sissy, 266, 285, 330; Baldwin and, 19, 47, 171, 185, 198, 205; Baraka and, 242, 247–248, 255; Beam and, 265; black nationalism and, 167, 218, 221, 235; Chamberlain and, 294; as race traitor, 17
Howells, William Dean, 57–58, 62, 66–67
Hudson, Theodore R., 250, 385n30, 385n32
Hughes, Langston, 46, 135, 190–195, 202–203, 205, 248, 254; sexuality of, 376n66, 377n73

innuendo, 9, 52, 177, 251, 277, 345; sissy and, 11–12, 15, 42

Jackson, George, 241, 261
James, LeBron, 43, 288
James, Sylvester. *See* Sylvester
Jim Crow, 4, 20f, 21, 48, 55, 64, 98, 278–279, 318, 352n30, 367n28; Baldwin and, 183, 205, 207, 221, 229–231, 259, 305; black athletes and, 317, 396n48; black male leadership and, 47; Carver and, 68, 105, 108; Cold War and, 205, 207, 229; disenfranchisement, 73; Du Bois and, 61, 71, 202, 354n58; Gates and, 277; gender conduct and, 100; gender disidentification and, 67; higher education and, 103; Johnson and, 113–114, 117, 119, 123, 127–130, 133–135, 141; Louis and, 337; lynching, 370n70; maleness and, 34; masculinist violence and, 180; menial labor and, 65, 68–72, 234, 264; mulatto discourse and, 112; one-drop rule and, 24; school and, 27; skin color and, 43; speechifying and, 57; violence of, 23; Washington and, 9, 47, 51–52, 58–59, 61–62, 65, 72, 109, 234, 264, 278; Wright and, 12, 15–17, 18–20, 123, 128, 183, 295, 297
Johnson, E. Patrick, 9, 30, 201, 398n97
Johnson, Earvin "Magic," 288, 337, 399n109
Johnson, Jack, 286–287, 337, 391n7
Johnson, James Weldon, 46–47, 61, 112, 115, 121–125, 126, 131–132, 145–149, 158, 162–164, 165–166, 247, 274, 316, 366n8, 369n54, 370n77, 371n116; assimilation and, 368n48; Atlanta University and, 119, 127–128, 130, 134, 145, 149–150; Bookerite tendencies of, 366n4; Central America and, 37, 47, 125, 136, 138, 162, 164; cleanliness and, 144; consular service and, 31, 37; "The Creation," 367n18; ex-colored man and, 12–13, 43, 141, 150, 161, 167; gentle manliness and, 46, 118–120, 143,

265, 271; Great Depression and, 116–118, 125, 367n11; Haiti and, 136, 138–139, 368n36, 368n38, 368n46; Jim Crow and, 23, 113–114, 117, 119, 123, 127–130, 133–135, 141; Johnson, Grace Nail, and, 116, 121, 367n14; "Lift Every Voice and Sing," 163, 367n22; NAACP and, 366n8; Nicaragua and, 135–137, 368n38; Stanton School and, 367n25; Van Vechten and, 126, 140, 148; Venezuela and, 135, 137, 139
Jones, Jacqueline, 66, 68, 361n75, 363n102
Jones, LeRoi. *See* Baraka, Amiri

Kaepernick, Colin, 43, 288
Katz, Jackson, 62, 344
Kelley, Robin D. G., 264–266, 288, 372n8
King, Martin Luther, Jr., 21, 35–36, 117, 218, 221, 382n131
Kirby, David, 215, 380n115
Kopay, David, 31, 283, 293, 300, 302–310, 303*f*, 307*f*, 312, 315, 317–323, 326–329, 334, 397n69
Kornegay, E. L., Jr., 187, 198

Larsen, Nella, 129, 370n77
literacy, 16, 88–89, 188; Baldwin and, 229; black masculinity and, 5; in *Go Tell It on the Mountain* (Baldwin), 167, 181–182; in "Here Be Dragons" (Baldwin), 183, 186; sissy, 248, 270; sophisticated, 4, 30, 124, 134
Little Richard, 29–30, 47, 213–215, 215*f*, 218, 221, 254, 287, 296, 323, 326–327, 329–330, 380n115, 393n29
Locke, Alain, 46, 114, 126, 135
Lockette, Reginald, 219–220, 238
Lorde, Audre, 258–259, 268, 390n97
Louis, Joe, 288, 295, 322, 335–337, 338*f*, 393n25
lynching, 62, 370n70, 381n126; castration, 30, 206, 214; hysteria, 297; Johnson and, 114, 123, 129, 131, 133, 135, 148, 152–153, 155, 159, 162–163; Washington and, 72, 99, 113

Mailer, Norman, 211, 230, 244, 246
Major, Clarence, 170, 179–180, 264, 267, 273–274, 352n31
Malcolm X, 45, 253, 261–262, 387n51; compulsive heterosexuality and, 15; King and, 35–36; sissiphobia of, 218, 382n131

maleness, 14, 25–26, 29, 39, 41, 222, 235, 260; black, 19–20, 27–28, 48, 256, 272, 289, 351n14; Jim Crow, 34; queer, 168, 305; straight, 257; white, 157, 285–286, 319, 341, 345
manhood, 61–66, 112–113, 127–129, 154, 238, 250, 271, 347; African, 44; American, 36, 300; Black Panther Party and, 239–241; of civil rights leadership, 45; conduct, 266; credibility, 261; emancipated, 57; gentle, 114; heterosexual, 263, 279; patriotism and, 180; pioneer, 246; pro athletes and, 289; rites, 43, 61, 94; self-made, 366n159; sissy-avoidance and, 30; sports spectatorship and, 292; voice and, 8. *See also* black manhood
Martin, Collin, 343, 394n41
masculine, the, 17, 24–27, 31, 39, 41, 274; gender hierarchy within, 33; values of, 292
masculine empowerment, 80, 95, 347; American, 298
masculine respectability, 37, 281, 288
masculinity, 6, 174; black, 5, 28–30, 34, 43, 45, 49, 97, 271–272, 372n8; conventional, 25, 41, 112, 311, 378n79; hegemonic, 25, 31–32, 39–40, 43, 100, 306, 315, 344; heterosexual, 32, 157; normative, 21, 63–64, 143, 160, 306, 338; white, 29, 31, 34, 43, 111–112, 143, 159–160, 287, 300, 306, 344
masculinity studies, 180, 256, 268; black, 30, 272
McClintock, Anne, 74, 94, 360n64, 360n69
McCune, Jeffrey Q., Jr., 178, 196, 335–336, 388n64
metrosexual, 284–285, 287, 331, 333
military, 31–37, 47–48, 85, 137–138, 207, 289, 295, 298, 300, 392n24, 394n40
Miller, Kelly, 60–62, 129, 357nn24–25
Miller, Monica L., 103, 133, 372n8
mimicry, 77, 94–96, 364n133
minstrelsy, 19–20, 33, 96, 163, 352n29; sissy, 209
Moore, Marlon Rachquel, 198, 378n86
mulatto, 43, 111, 127; discourse, 112; marginal, 114, 139, 160
Mumford, Kevin J., 151, 260–261

INDEX · 437

NAACP, 113–114, 117, 122, 163, 166, 170, 237, 366n5, 367n22

narcissism, 145, 284–285, 305, 317, 369nn64–65, 396n52

National Basketball Association (NBA), 286, 293–295, 301, 338

National Football League (NFL), 286, 300, 314, 335

Neal, Mark Anthony, 14, 45, 271, 287, 351n14, 372n7; illegibility and, 27, 30; legibility and, 41, 214

Nero, Charles I., 3–4, 12, 147, 181, 217, 349n2

New Negro, 45, 112, 122, 370n85; Johnson and, 139, 159

New Negro Renaissance: literature, 370n83; patronage, 164; politics, 47

Newton, Huey, 236, 238–241, 259, 261, 383n15

No Name in the Street (Baldwin), 187, 205–206, 218, 220–224, 230–231, 235, 271, 274, 282, 379n100

Obama, Barack, 334, 343–345

Pallone, Dave, 297, 301, 306–308, 310, 312, 317, 321, 323, 328

Paret, Benny, 301, 330–332

Parham, Charles H., 175–177, 373n20

Park, Robert E., 58, 76, 111–112, 114, 130, 139, 144, 150, 160, 357n15

passive aggression, 182, 218; Baldwin and, 221–222, 230; sissy, 22, 266

Pentecostalism, 167–169, 174, 176

performativity, 6, 41–42, 349–350n6; gender, 7

Pickens, William, 52, 59–60, 65, 113, 127, 129, 138, 154; masculine bravado and, 131, 357n21

Plessy v. Ferguson, 112, 127, 366n2

Prescott, Dak, 345–346

professional athletes, 286, 292, 337; black, 30, 43, 288, 319–320; coming-out narratives of, 48; gay, 13, 26, 37, 167, 317; gay affirmation and, 288–289

professional sports, 48, 330, 338, 341, 345; black athletes and, 326; sissy aversion and, 31

Queer Eye for the Straight Guy, 285–286

queerness, 192, 200, 235, 277, 284–285, 333, 336, 343, 349n2, 351n14; Baldwin and, 373n9; gender, 5, 16, 100, 288, 328, 332, 399n105; Pentecostalism and, 176–178, 198; race and, 273; sexual, 288, 370n71

queer sexuality, 177, 203, 249, 254, 343

queer theory, 24, 72, 180, 205, 268, 272–273, 281; black sissy conduct and, 29; shame and, 358n49; sissiness and, 28, 208; straight sissy and, 262

race rape, 252, 351n19, 386n47

racial leadership, 58; African American pro athletes and, 288; Johnson and, 120, 123, 166; mulatto and, 114; sissiness and, 5; Washington and, 8, 10, 55, 86, 166

Rampersad, Arnold, 193–194, 377n73

Reconstruction, 118, 126–127, 130, 279; radical, 113

Red Scare, 167, 206, 379n101

Roberts, John W., 352n31, 390n88

Robinson, Jackie, 288, 295–296, 302, 317–320, 322, 326, 335–336, 398n81

Rodman, Dennis, 30, 329–330, 332–335, 399n105

Rogin, Michael, 19–20, 352n29

Roosevelt, Theodore, 32–33, 52, 121, 136, 368n36

rumor, 14–15, 175–177, 198–199, 251, 277

Rustin, Bayard, 46, 237, 260, 379n101

Sam, Michael, 300, 335–338, 337f, 340

Scott, Darieck, 195, 220, 247–249, 251, 381n128, 383n6

Seale, Bobby, 236, 238–241, 249, 252, 255, 259, 261

Sedgwick, Eve Kosofsky, 24–25, 170, 208, 343, 352n36, 355n67

sexuality, 14, 24–25, 185, 347; American ideal of, 180; black, 98, 257; black men's, 72; Christianity and, 323; human, 383n8; movements, 263; nonconforming, 358n49; nonstandard, 49; normative, 284; queer, 177, 203, 254, 343; racialized, 195; racially segregated, 92; Rodman and, 333; same-gender, 5,

438 · INDEX

28, 46, 158, 194, 237, 253, 312, 353n41; sports and, 400n114; swish and, 169, 211; in *The System of Dante's Hell* (Baraka), 386n46; trans identity and, 23; whiteness and, 311
Simmons, Ron, 247, 385n30
Simmons, Roy, 300, 302, 327–331, 333
Simpson, Mark, 284–285, 287, 331, 333
sissification, 15, 31, 33–34, 49, 67, 69–70, 252, 308, 311; church and, 254; racial, 68
sissiphobia, 13–14, 28–30, 45, 68, 166, 180, 250, 262, 290; Baraka's, 241; *Black Boy* (Wright), 297; Black Panther Party and, 240–241; Cleaver's, 235; in *The David Kopay Story*, 302; gay-affirmative, 299; hip-hop culture and, 288; in *Just above My Head* (Baldwin), 204; sports and, 48, 302; Sylvester and, 217–218
sissy-avoidance, 13, 30, 311, 327; Bean and, 308; Burke and, 322–323, 325; Chamberlain and, 293; Griffith and, 330; Kopay and, 306; Tuaolo and, 313–315
sissy conduct, 11, 25, 28–29, 42, 54, 309; Baldwin's 223, 314; black, 29, 41; Carver's, 98; disciplining of, 15; in *Go Tell It on the Mountain* (Baldwin), 168; Griffith's, 331–332; in *Just above My Head* (Baldwin), 204–205; law and, 355n69; Rodman and, 334; sports and, 290; Tuaolo's, 312; Washington's, 9
sissy-flirtation, 263, 283
sissy-shaming, 15, 240
Skerrett, Joseph T., Jr., 115, 366n8, 371n97
Smith, Barbara, 256–259, 262, 268, 388n65, 390n97
Smith, Michael J., 324–325, 398n83
Smith, Valerie, 125, 141
Snorton, C. Reilly, 23, 48, 162, 178, 263
Souls of Black Folk (Du Bois), 52, 58, 60, 81, 129, 368–369n54, 370n71
sports disclosure memoir, 26, 31, 48, 167, 289, 297, 302, 311–314, 316, 328. *See also* Burke, Glenn; Kopay, David; Pallone, Dave; Rodman, Dennis; Sam, Michael; Tuaolo, Esera
sportsmanship, 6, 290, 292, 298, 315–316, 329, 333, 335–336, 339, 392n12, 394n36; black pro athletes and, 30, 286, 288, 302, 317; gay pro athletes and, 285, 317, 319; man-play as,

311, 314, 326, 395n46; sissy avoidance and, 295, 314
Stallybrass, Peter, 39, 74
Stepto, Robert, 34, 234, 267, 273–274, 369n54
Stonewall Rebellion, 14, 170, 298
Stowe, Harriet Beecher, 18, 356n72; *Uncle Tom's Cabin*, 44–45, 356n75
straight black sissy, 267–268, 270–273, 278, 283–285, 383n8; discourse, 287; memoirists, 5, 32, 257; public intellectuals, 234, 261, 271; trend, 271, 281, 283, 285. *See also* Gates, Henry Louis, Jr.
straight sissy, 257, 262, 271, 275, 277–278, 280–282, 332; black, 256; intellectuals, 289; memoir, 167, 265, 270, 291; narrative, 266–268, 273–274, 278. *See also* Baraka, Amiri; Gates, Henry Louis, Jr.; Rodman, Dennis
Styron, William, 46, 388n61
Summers, T. O., 116, 134–135, 152, 155, 157, 371n97
sweetback, 152–153, 158, 370n83, 393n27
swish, 38, 40, 46, 169–170, 189–190, 201, 204, 209, 211, 225, 235, 263, 274, 280–281, 308, 339, 346, 372n5, 393n27; black, 220, 376n62; comportment, 180; conduct, 332; homo-, 184, 191–194, 215, 217–218, 251; performance, 204, 214, 331; straight sissy and, 275; street, 169, 171, 179, 186, 191–192, 194, 372n6. *See also* Griffith, Emile; Little Richard
sycophancy, 53–55, 58, 60, 62, 71, 137
Sylvester, 29, 47, 215–218, 221, 254, 304, 323, 329–330, 381n122

Talented Tenth, 45, 55, 128, 149, 158, 271
Tomming, 21, 237
too-good boy, 6, 26, 28, 46, 80; in *Along This Way* (Johnson), 144; Baldwin as, 177, 229; in *Black Boy* (Wright), 15; church and, 183; in *Go Tell It on the Mountain* (Baldwin), 21, 223; in *Not without Laughter* (Hughes), 191; soldier as, 37; submission and, 182; Washington as, 9, 75
trans identity, 22–23, 347, 353n40
Trotter, William Monroe, 52, 60–63, 108, 113, 131, 137, 154, 357n22, 358n30

Trump, Donald J., 43, 343–345, 356n80
Tuaolo, Esera, 29, 300, 310–315, 318, 321, 323, 328, 334; Kopay and, 397n69
Turner, Nat, 46, 66, 388n61
Tuskegee Institute, 11, 31, 54, 73, 80–81, 90–92, 97–98, 103, 108, 135

Uncle Tom, 18–21, 25, 30, 44–46, 49, 231. *See also* Tomming
Up from Slavery (Washington), 10, 13, 57, 64, 67, 69–70, 81, 86–87, 92, 278, 366n156; feminine labor and, 264; Johnson and, 154, 369n54; mimicry and, 94; narration of, 329; racial reciprocity in, 166; rhetoric of, 60

Van Vechten, Carl, 126, 140, 148, 370n85

Walker, Alice, 267–268
Walker, Margaret, 14–16, 18–19, 350n13
Wallace, Maurice, 97, 230, 363n115
Wallace, Michele, 241, 268
Warhol, Andy, 47, 210, 214, 216f, 246, 339
Warner, Michael, 273, 299, 369n65
Washington, Booker T., 8–11, 13, 21, 31, 35–37, 45–47, 55, 57, 60, 78, 80–82, 88–89, 91–100, 103, 112–115, 162–163, 268, 278, 357n20, 359n59, 360n68, 363n111; Armstrong and, 37, 73, 80, 82, 84, 87, 90–98, 134, 154, 359n61; black soldiers and, 32, 34; Carver and, 11, 105, 107–109; cleanliness and, 69, 73–77, 79, 83–85, 87, 89–90, 95, 99, 108, 139, 224, 234, 239, 360n63; Du Bois and, 30, 51–54, 56, 61, 66, 68, 70–72, 108, 122, 158, 193; and Hampton Institute, 34, 37, 54, 64, 87, 94, 224; Jim Crow and, 9, 47, 51–52, 58–59, 61–62, 64–65, 72, 109, 234, 264, 278; Johnson and, 119–121, 128, 135–137, 139, 143, 150–151, 165–166; masculine uprightness of, 265–266; menial labor and, 271; Trotter and, 52, 60–63, 108, 357n22, 358n30; Tuskegee Institute and, 73, 80, 90–92, 97–98, 103, 135; Wells and, 62–63
Wells-Barnett, Ida B., 52, 127; Washington and, 62–63, 154
White, Allon, 39, 74
white supremacy, 55, 95, 318; black masculinity and, 21, 29, 34, 49, 72, 77, 113, 297; rape and, 251
World War II, 35, 170, 180, 372n8, 374n33
Wright, Richard, 12, 22, 268, 270, 351n20, 370n70; Baldwin and 18–19, 193, 196; Baraka and, 243; Cleaver and, 18, 219, 378n79; Jim Crow and, 12, 15–17, 18–20, 123, 128, 183, 295, 297; *The Long Dream*, 18, 295–297, 352n32, 381n126; *Native Son*, 266–267, 270; Walker, Margaret, and, 14, 350n13

Young, Perry Deane, 290, 300, 318, 372n8
Young, Vershawn Ashanti, 5, 12, 17, 170, 181

www.ingramcontent.com/pod-product-compliance
Lightning Source LLC
Chambersburg PA
CBHW071824230426
43672CB00013B/2758